SECRETS
OF
THE FORCE

SECRETS

OF

THE FORCE

THE COMPLETE, UNCENSORED, UNAUTHORIZED ORAL HISTORY OF
STAR WARS

EDWARD GROSS
AND MARK A. ALTMAN

ST. MARTIN'S
PRESS
NEW YORK

First published in the United States by St. Martin's Press, an imprint of St. Martin's Publishing Group

www.stmartins.com

Designed by Steven Seighman

Library of Congress Cataloging-in-Publication Data

Names: Altman, Mark A., author. | Gross, Edward (Edward A.), author.
Title: Secrets of the force : the complete, uncensored, unauthorized oral history of Star wars / Mark A. Altman and Edward Gross.
Description: First edition. | New York : St. Martin's Press, 2021.
Identifiers: LCCN 2021006897 | ISBN 9781250236876 (hardcover) | ISBN 9781250236883 (ebook)
Subjects: LCSH: Star Wars films—History and criticism.
Classification: LCC PN1995.9.S695 A456 2021 | DDC 791.43/7509—dc23
LC record available at https://lccn.loc.gov/2021006897

Our books may be purchased in bulk for promotional, educational, or business use. Please contact your local bookseller or the Macmillan Corporate and Premium Sales Department at 1-800-221-7945, extension 5442, or by email at MacmillanSpecialMarkets@macmillan.com.

First Edition: 2021

10 9 8 7 6 5 4 3 2 1

DEDICATIONS

From EDWARD GROSS

To my wife, **Eileen**. Our love story may have begun a long time ago in a galaxy not so far away, but it feels like only yesterday. Thirty-four years on, there's no question the Force will be with us. Always.

To our sons, **Teddy, Dennis,** and **Kevin**, all three Star Warriors in their own right, Teddy and Dennis loving the original trilogy and Kevin the sequel trilogy. They bring balance to the Force with their feelings for the prequel trilogy.

To our daughter-in-law **Lindsay**. Amazingly, *Star Wars* played no small role in making her a part of the family.

To our daughter-in-law **Yumi**, who joyfully embraces all of this pop culture stuff, from *Star Wars* to *Back to the Future* and the Marvel Cinematic Universe. Sorry, you're definitely one of us now!

To our future daughter-in-law **Nicole**, who doesn't know the difference between a Wookiee and Jawa, but we love her anyway.

To **Kevin Oldham**, my fellow Jedi with whom I've seen every *Star Wars* movie since the beginning. It wouldn't have been the same without you.

To **Mark A. Altman**, my cowriter and friend. How incredible that we still get to do this thing we love so much.

To **Everyone**—no, not in the world, but those who have labored to bring *Star Wars* to life in all its incarnations. I may not love it all, but I genuinely appreciate the effort.

From MARK A. ALTMAN

To **Isaac & Ella Altman**, the biggest rebels (and *Star Wars*) fans I know—and the aspiring authors who coined our book's title. May the Force be with you . . . always.

To **Naomi**, my princess.

To my parents, **Gail & Michael**, who first introduced me to a galaxy far, far away (and Farrell's ice cream) in 1977. Which I liked more is still a toss-up.

To **Steven A. Simak**, for your help with this book and your friendship, I will be indebted to you for both forever.

To **Fredrick C. Clarke**, the scruffy-looking nerf herder who started it all. Without *Cinefantastique*, I doubt I'd have gotten so many of the amazing opportunities to visit all the galaxies far, far away from *Wars* to *Trek* . . . and a few not so far away as well.

To **Edward Gross**, I was honored that you would join me.

To **George Lucas**, thank you for sharing your worlds with us. You are a visionary, a genius, a master filmmaker, and, on rare occasions, maclunkey.

DATALOG

PART THREE
THE PREQUELS
1999–2005

PART FOUR
THE SEQUELS AND BEYOND
2012–

THE SAGA

The Skywalker Saga
Star Wars, Episode I: The Phantom Menace (1999)
Star Wars, Episode II: Attack of the Clones (2002)
Star Wars, Episode III: Revenge of the Sith (2005)
Star Wars (later retitled *Episode IV: A New Hope*) (1977)
Star Wars, Episode V: The Empire Strikes Back (1980)
Star Wars, Episode VI: Return of the Jedi (1983)
Star Wars, Episode VII: The Force Awakens (2015)
Star Wars, Episode VIII: The Last Jedi (2017)
Star Wars, Episode IX: Rise of Skywalker (2019)

The Anthology Films
Star Wars: Rogue One (2016)
Star Wars: Solo (2018)
Star Wars: Kenobi (2022)
Star Wars: Rogue Squadron (TBA)

Television
The Star Wars Holiday Special (1978)
Caravan of Courage: The Ewok Adventure (1984)
The Battle for Endor (1985)
Star Wars: Droids (1985)
Star Wars: Ewoks (1985)
Star Wars: Clone Wars (2003)
Star Wars: The Clone Wars (2008)
Star Wars: Rebels (2014)
Star Wars: Resistance (2018)
The Mandalorian (2019)
Star Wars: The Bad Batch (2021)
Star Wars: The Book of Boba Fett (2021)
Star Wars: Ahsoka (2022)

Star Wars: Andor (2022)
Star Wars: Rangers of the New Republic (TBA)
Star Wars: Acolyte (TBA)
Star Wars: Visions (TBA)
Star Wars: Lando (TBA)
Star Wars: Detours (TBA)
Star Wars: Underworld (unproduced)

A NEW HOPE SPRINGS ETERNAL
"You don't need to see his identification."

By Mark A. Altman

You've never heard his name and I have no idea whatever became of him, but in my mind he is as evil as any Sith Lord, vile bounty hunter, or gangrenous gangster Hutt. A Dark Lord whose evil machinations know no bounds. Who am I talking about? Well, in 1980, he was a cherubic young student at Roy H. Mann junior high school and in early May, this unassuming young marshmallow of evil, Lance Schulman, slid the Marvel Super Special adaptation of *The Empire Strikes Back* across my desk in Mr. Rubin's science class and told me to read the panel he had gently placed in front of me. I glanced down at the comic and read the words that would shatter my young mind: "No . . . *I am your father.*" I looked up aghast with burning hate in my eyes. Had I possessed a lightsaber at the time, not realizing yet that anger leads to hate and hate leads to suffering, I would have probably driven it through his hard, cold heart, assuming he had one, but alas I did not. What I actually did and said has been lost to the sands of time, but I do know for certain to this day I still loathe that m@$*#$#r.

But what I do love is *Star Wars*. The first time I ever heard of it was in the pages of *Starlog* magazine, and shortly thereafter, I picked up the paperback novelization at a local Waldenbooks (remember those!). I was a big fan of the Fantastic Four at the time, so the Dr. Doom–like visage of Darth Vader immediately caught my interest, but as a die-hard *Star Trek* fan, I was immediately inclined to patronize anything that had "Star" in the title.

Of course, when *Star Wars* did finally come out, seeing it proved more challenging than I expected. Unlike today, when wide releases play on a plethora of screens in multiplexes across every city, *Star Wars* was harder to find in its initial release. Not to mention, I wanted to see it on the biggest screen possible with the best sound. Even as a ten-year-old, I had impeccable taste. As friends of mine would see it multiple times and the buzz continued to grow, May ticked into June and I still hadn't seen the movie everyone was talking about—even though I had amassed a vast collection of reviews and articles from *The New York Times* to *Rolling Stone* to the New York *Daily News*. It was bad enough my parents hadn't let me see *Jaws* because they considered it too violent for my young, impressionable mind, but now I was missing out on a movie I knew I had already grown obsessed with before even seeing it. I was clipping every article I could from the newspaper including Molly Haskell's review in *The Village Voice*. Then one day, my parents suggested we go on a road trip. I wasn't sure where we were going, but it was a sweltering summer day and I was looking forward to getting out of the house. We drove over the Verrazzano Bridge through Staten Island and on to New Jersey. I didn't know where we were going, but I didn't think it would be so far. As our long journey into night continued, I spotted out of the corner of my eye a movie marquee at the Paramus Park Mall that read "Star Wars & The Other Side of Midnight." I excitedly pointed and jumped up and down as the car continued to cruise past the mall, dejectedly realizing that was not our destination. Instead, we found ourselves at Farrell's, an ice cream parlor, a few miles past the mall. We had a delicious lunch, some amazing ice cream, and then began our long trip back home. It was only then I realized this had all been a calculated and cunning plan from my parents to surprise my brother and me to go see *Star Wars*. This time as we passed the Paramus Park Mall, where the film was playing in 70mm, we turned into the parking lot and found a spot. I could probably tell you forty years later the exact spot where we parked. I was ecstatic. We were finally going to see *Star Wars*. And like so many of you, I can vividly recall the first crawl—no *Episode IV*, no *A New Hope*—as it climbed up the screen, and then one of the most remarkable openings in movie history as the massive Rebel Blockade Runner was chased over Tatooine by an even larger Imperial Star Destroyer.

It's safe to say this movie changed my life. I had always wanted to make movies and television ever since falling in love with Hitchcock films and *Star Trek*, but *Star Wars* cinched it. Its incredible mix of audacity, creativity, inspiration, and acerbic wit absolutely captivated me.

Over the years I've been less enamored with many of the subsequent installments. I remember going to an advance screening of *The Phantom Menace* the night I was leaving for the Cannes Film Festival with my first movie,

Free Enterprise, and I emerged from the theater in a daze. As I walked glassy-eyed past friends who were lined up for the next screening, they asked me how the film was. I replied, shell-shocked, "Awful." They thought I was kidding. I wasn't. I sat on the plane to Cannes for ten hours unable to talk to anyone about losing my religion, and it was another week before the film opened and we could commiserate about everything we loathed about it. (That said, it's one of my son's favorite *Star Wars* movies and he knows more about *Star Wars* than me, so go figure.) But for every *Phantom Menace,* there's still a *Rogue One* to surprise us; or delight at the innovation and heart of *The Clone Wars* and *Rebels* TV series or *The Mandalorian,* which proved this is the way to do *Star Wars* right on any screen. Not to mention it's a joy to hear Lucas talk about how the prequels were his indictment of the Bush/Cheney presidency, which gave me a modicum more appreciation for them over time.

One of the greatest joys of *Star Wars* has been sharing my love of the franchise with my children. In the case of my son, Isaac, the learner really has become the master, having recently programmed during the 2020 COVID quarantine his own ultimate *Star Wars* marathon, which began with the prequels, continued through every episode of *The Clone Wars* and *Rebels,* the original films, *The Mandalorian, Resistance,* and the sequels. He told me he was skipping the Ewok telefilms and *Holiday Special* because they weren't canon. I was quite simply in awe of his devotion to that hokey ancient religion. And the fact that he is the same age now that I was when I first saw *Star Wars* in a theater is not lost on me.

The fact is I will always love *Star Wars* and always hope the next adventure is the greatest one yet. And that's the spirit and audacity of filmmaking that this book celebrates and not the missteps, for as I often say, A New Hope springs eternal. Welcome back to a galaxy, far, far away. We're home.

A GREAT DISTURBANCE IN THE FORCE

"Rebellions are built on hope."

by Edward Gross

Are you one of those people who have significant "movie moments" in your life? You know, key memories that are tied to seeing a particular film. Personally, I've got three that are packed fairly closely together.

The first was in 1971 as an old man of eleven when friends and I went to the Marine Theatre in Brooklyn, New York, to catch a James Bond triple feature consisting of the first three 007 movies (representing the first time I'd seen any of them), *Dr. No, From Russia with Love,* and *Goldfinger.* It was just . . . awesome!

Flash forward to December 1978, when a group of us went to the Patchogue Theatre on Long Island to watch *Superman: The Movie,* which we were so blown away by that when it was over, we stood up, looked at each other, and plopped back down in our seats to watch it a second time. Remember the moment when Superman catches a plummeting Lois Lane and *then* grabs the helicopter that has fallen from the *Daily Planet* rooftop—all accompanied by John Williams's Superman Theme—*with* his cape flapping in the wind? Still gives me chills.

The third was in May 1983 during the week that the third *Star Wars* film, *Return of the Jedi,* was released. It wasn't so much about *Jedi* itself as it was the fact that that same week 20th Century Fox released a double feature of the first two films, *Star Wars* and *The Empire Strikes Back.* What this meant is that my friend Kevin Oldham and I caught the first two films on a Saturday afternoon and immediately after drove to another theater and got on line to buy tickets—*not* "online," but literally standing in line for hours—for the third.

In other words, we didn't need Disney+ or Blu-rays to watch the original *Star Wars* trilogy in a single day. Just an incredible opportunity that somehow managed to surpass the experience of watching the films individually and forever carved out a place in my heart and imagination for George Lucas's saga.

There are two other distinct *Star Wars*–related memories that come to mind. The first was in late 1977 when I was part of *The Colonial Times* newspaper at Wm. Floyd High School. We were out in a portable classroom putting the latest issue together when Kevin and his brother, Rich, came in asking if we wanted to see *Star Wars* for the first time at a theater about an hour away. Needless to say, that probably wasn't the best issue of the newspaper produced (far from it), but somehow we finished, jumped in their VW Bug, and made that one-hour trip in about forty minutes. *So* worth it!

The other was in 1997 and the release of *Star Wars: A New Hope*—The Special Edition. We stood on line for literally five hours, chatting, laughing, sharing our concerns and hopes for the film we were about to see. I also think I invented something that day. As time went on, we were starving and I used the payphone (nope, no cells then) to call a local pizza place to deliver a pie. When he asked for an address, I told him the line at the Cinema 150 in Syosset. He incredulously said, "I can't deliver a pizza to a movie line"—which neither I nor my stomach was having any of. "Why not? I'll be the guy waving you down." Half an hour later he showed up, I did exactly that, and we enjoyed our pizza. So did other members of the crowd when that pizza guy ended up coming back six or seven times. *See* the unexpected ways *Star Wars* impacts the universe?

Now, truth in advertising, I have always been a much bigger fan of *Star Trek* than I was of *Star Wars* (though shows like *Star Trek: Discovery* and *Star Trek: Picard* are doing their best to ruin that). But I've been along for the journey to a galaxy far, far away for the past four decades and am *thrilled* to continue to be taken for the ride, particularly as part of the franchise makes a successful transition to television.

I consider the way that *Star Wars* has impacted on my life and I actually have to look to one of my sons, who was using a dating site and connected with someone in a conversation. They asked each other what they were interested in, and she wondered whether he was into movies. He said he was and listed some of them. List completed, she offered a sigh of disappointment and said, "I was hoping you'd be into *Star Wars*." His response, "Oh my God, I was just afraid I'd come across as a nerd!" After which he sent her a photo of the huge UK poster of the original film that he'd "inherited" from me, and that had been on his wall for years.

They began dating and eventually got married, elements of their wedding (including the homily) being *Star Wars*–themed. Could one argue that this was the Force at work? That's certainly what I'm going with.

Secrets of the Force is a true love letter to *Star Wars*: an opportunity to take a look at the franchise as a whole, presenting the views of a wide variety of people who have either been involved in its making or have been thinking about it for years, and its impact on the world as a whole. Through all the highs and lows that you'll read about over *Star Wars*' journey through the decades, its ongoing power and influence can't be denied.

For me, this was a chance to give something back to an entertainment that has been with me for the vast majority of my life and I hope will be for the rest of it.

Part One

A STAR (WARS) IS BORN

LAUNCH BAY '77

"You came in that thing? You're braver than I thought."

1977. The year that *Damnation Alley* changed cinema forever.

Not quite. But that was the big-budget film starring Jan Michael Vincent and radioactive cockroaches that 20th Century Fox executives had pegged to be their summer blockbuster way back when, along with *The Other Side of Midnight*, based on the bestselling novel. Instead, it was an $11 million space opera that filmmaker George Lucas almost didn't get made that rocketed to the top of the box-office charts and became the number-one-grossing film of all time, which changed the way movies were released and consumed forever.

George Lucas had gone from the commercial failure of the experimental *THX 1138* for Warner Bros., to minting money for Universal Pictures with the massive smash that was *American Graffiti*, only to see the studio ignominiously pass on bankrolling his next film, a fantasy space saga about a boy, a girl, and a universe. So instead, Lucas prevailed on Alan Ladd, Jr., the head of production at 20th Century Fox, to green-light his intergalactic fairy tale. Despite little support among the board of directors at the studio, "Laddie," as he was known to his friends, took a leap of faith on the young filmmaker. But studio execs weren't the only ones dubious of the prospects for the film. Even Lucas's own cadre of close friends and former University of Southern California (USC) cronies, which included filmmakers Brian De Palma (who was auditioning actors for *Carrie* at the same time Lucas was reading talent for *Star Wars*), John Milius (*Conan the Barbarian*), Willard Huyck and Gloria Katz (*Indiana Jones and the Temple of Doom*), and Matthew Robbins and Hal Barwood (*Dragonslayer*), all dismissed the film after screening an early unfinished cut. Only Steven Spielberg and future film critic (and occasional screenwriter) Jay Cocks would suspect there was more to that initial rough cut than met the eye.

It was also the perfect time for escapist fantasy fare in the late seventies as America had recently endured the resignation of a president in the wake of the Watergate scandal, the end of the Vietnam War, the ongoing Cold War with the Soviet Union, and the primetime success of the *Roots* miniseries on ABC, which helped pull back the scab of America's original sin, slavery, in a way that exposed its atrocities to an entirely new generation. There were also early glimmers of a high-tech future that would transform America, such as the incorporation of Apple Computers, the release of the popular Atari 2600 home gaming system, and the maiden voyage (atop a Boeing airplane, at least) of the Space Shuttle *Enterprise*, even as the country experienced the anxiety of blackouts, a serial killer on the loose in New York, soaring crime rates, and a crippling energy crisis.

Among the films that provided an escape for movie fans that year were John Travolta dancing his way to superstardom in *Saturday Night Fever*, the car chase shenanigans of *Smokey and the Bandit*, the return of gentleman secret agent James Bond in the wildly entertaining *The Spy Who Loved Me*, Woody Allen dealing with the vagaries of urban romantic relationships in the even more entertaining (and Oscar-winning) *Annie Hall*, and Steven Spielberg's sci-fi classic *Close Encounters of the Third Kind*. But no film was as transformative, impactful, enduring, and beloved that year as a little space fantasy that was released in the summer of '77 called, simply, *Star Wars*. No *Episode IV*, no *A New Hope*, just . . . *Star Wars*.

And thus, on May 25, 1977, a Rebel Blockade Runner thundered over Tatooine, pursued by an even more massive Imperial Star Destroyer. In the process, it changed cinema forever, spawning numerous sequels, prequels, and spin-off TV ventures; movie cash-ins from *Message from Space* to *Starship Invasions* to *Battle Beyond the Stars* to, some would argue, *Battlestar Galactica* (which Mark Hamill joked to the authors that the cast referred to disparagingly as "Battlestar Copycatica"); an appallingly bad *Holiday Special*; and, of course, countless merchandise from action figures to R2-D2 popcorn makers.

And now, almost five decades later, *Star Wars* continues to dominate the pop culture landscape after Lucasfilm and its assets were acquired in 2012 by the Walt Disney Company, which has produced another trilogy of films, two stand-alone entries (*Rogue One* and *Solo*), and a critically acclaimed television series on the Disney+ streaming service, *The Mandalorian*, paving the way for many more to come, including a Cassian Andor stand-alone series, an Ahsoka Tano series, an Obi-Wan Kenobi miniseries starring Ewan McGregor, and others on the horizon. But it all began in the early 1970s, when a young George Lucas wasn't able to secure the rights to *Flash Gordon* and conceived his own unique space fantasy adventure instead.

GEORGE LUCAS
(executive producer, screenwriter/director, *Star Wars*)

I wanted *Star Wars* to give people a faraway, exotic environment for their imagination to run free. It's a fantasy, much closer to the Brothers Grimm than to *2001*. My main reason for making it was to give young people an honest, wholesome fantasy life—the kind my generation had. We had Westerns, pirate movies, all kinds of great things. *Star Wars* is a movie for the kid in all of us.

HARRISON FORD
(actor, "Han Solo")

What *Star Wars* has accomplished is really not possible. But it has done it, anyway. Nobody rational would have believed that there is still a place for fairy tales. There is no place in our culture for this kind of stuff. But the need is there: the human need to have the human condition expressed in mythical terms.

GARY KURTZ
(producer, *Star Wars, The Empire Strikes Back*)

Star Wars is an homage to all the adventure-action-fantasies, not just in film but also the thirties' pulp magazines, Burroughs, Verne, etc. Nostalgia means re-creating an era that people remember living through, so in that sense, it isn't a nostalgic science fiction film, apart from the fact it's the sort of movie that people remember acting out in their backyards.

BILL CONDON
(director, *Gods & Monsters*)

Star Wars was one of the first science fiction films to have teenage kids as its leads. Lucas brought the teenagers from *American Graffiti* with him into the world of Saturday afternoon sci-fi serials.

RANDY STRADLEY
(editor, Dark Horse Comics)

Star Wars fulfills the role that myths used to play in our lives. It paints a world in broad, easy to understand strokes, sets up big problems for its heroes, and lets us see the heroes overcome their obstacles in a way that allows we, the viewers, to think, "Yeah, that's what I would've done." It's wish fulfillment and morality tale in one.

JEREMY BARLOW
(writer, *Darth Maul: Son of Dathomir, Star Wars:*
Knights of the Old Republic)

Star Wars has endured because it appeals to the best qualities inside of all of us. It's a story of aspiration and redemption—that anyone, no matter how seemingly insignificant, can leave the farm on Tatooine and find their destiny among the stars . . . and that no matter how far a person's fallen into the abyss, love and family can always bring them back toward the light. Those are some pretty powerful and very human themes that resonate with everyone.

RAY MORTON
(senior editor, *Script* magazine)

Whatever else it is, *Star Wars* is a science fiction movie. Early on, science fiction was not a major genre in either U.S. or world cinema. Up until the 1950s, only a handful of sci-fi movies were produced, with the most significant being *Metropolis, Frau im Mond*, and *Things to Come*. Science fiction became more popular in the post–World War II atomic age, but mostly in the low-budget B-movie realm. There were only a few (relatively) big-budget, studio-produced science fiction films made in the 1950s, including *Destination Moon, The Day the Earth Stood Still, The Thing from Another World*, and *Forbidden Planet*, and only a few more in the 1960s—most notably *2001: A Space Odyssey* and *Planet of the Apes*—and 1970s—most notably *The Andromeda Strain, Soylent Green*, and *Logan's Run*. Everything else was B or exploitation fare.

ALAN DEAN FOSTER
(author, *Star Wars* novelization and the sequel, *Splinter of the Mind's Eye*)

People who love science fiction were looking for *Star Wars*—for that kind of film—their whole lives. I forget which chief justice said it, but the comment was, "I may not be able to define pornography, but I know it when I see it." The fact is that *Star Wars* was different and fun and enjoyable at a time when people needed that sort of escape. That's one of the good things about science fiction, as escapism. It just happened to hit at the right time. Why *Star Wars*? There was nothing else like it out there. There simply wasn't.

For decades, science fiction movies had been consumed with the fear of science run amok in films like Frankenstein *and* Island of Lost Souls *along with films about dystopian civilizations like Fritz Lang's seminal* Metropolis *and H. G. Wells's* Things to Come. *The notable exception was the fun and diverting cliffhangers of the movie serials like* Buck Rogers *and* Flash Gordon, *which provided an entertaining diversion—and air-conditioning—for movie fans of the thirties and forties. But as the Cold War settled in, in the fifties, the dangers of science and technology, as well as the ongoing antagonisms between the military and scientists, was front and center in films like* Where Worlds

Collide, The Thing from Another World, War of the Worlds, *and* Invasion of the Body Snatchers, *a metaphor using aliens for the fear of the growing Red Menace. Even* Forbidden Planet, *which paved the way for TV series like* Star Trek, *depicted a world in which a race is wiped from existence for trying to play God. The visual effects of movies like those of George Pal were state-of-the-art for the time, but these films largely remained dismissed by critics as kid stuff.*

That all changed in the 1960s with the beginning of the Apollo program. Space travel began to feel like something truly achievable and it, like the arrival of Star Trek *in 1966, took space exploration seriously and treated science with a degree of verisimilitude while also remaining largely secular in its outlook, unlike the religion-tinged sermons of the fifties sci-fi thrillers. A true game-changer of the genre, however, was 1968's* 2001: A Space Odyssey, *in which auteur Stanley Kubrick attempted to bring a degree of seriousness and authenticity to science fiction. In addition, the visual effects by a young Douglas Trumbull were unlike anything audiences had ever experienced, setting a new bar for cinematic science fiction. Even that year's* Planet of the Apes *treated the satire of Pierre Boulle's* Monkey Planet *with complete seriousness, despite the potentially comedic pitfalls inherent in its premise. This desire for verisimilitude helped make director Franklin Schaffner's* Planet of the Apes *one of the greatest movies of all time and a remarkable achievement in the science fiction genre, spawning numerous sequels, remakes, and merchandise.*

By the early seventies, though, in the wake of Watergate, the social upheavals of the time, and Vietnam, sci-fi became decidedly dour with a series of dystopian dramas ranging from The Omega Man *to* Soylent Green *to* Zardoz *to* Logan's Run. *What had once been fun, escapist fare was a reminder that if the world didn't change the way it was going, things were not going to get better. But for director George Lucas, whose first feature film,* THX 1138, *was one of these very same dystopian films, things were about to change . . . for the better.*

ALAN DEAN FOSTER

In the days before *Star Trek* and *Star Wars*, science fiction was a very small, restricted genre. A subgenre of literature. A lot of the fans and the writers were mostly male and they went to science fiction conventions instead of comic conventions, because the only comic convention, per se, was the San Diego Comic-Con. It was a very small, enclosed area. I think the two things that really sparked interest in it in the modern era before *Star Wars* and *Star Trek* were the moon landings. It inspired people not so much because they suddenly said, "Hey, there's men on the moon. I need to pick up this science fiction book about the moon landing," but because so many people involved with the moon program, when they were being interviewed by Walter

Cronkite or Huntley and Brinkley, would say, "I really got interested in becoming an astronaut because of science fiction." That hit a lot of people.

RAY MORTON

In the early seventies, the Hollywood studios considered science fiction a niche genre—it appealed to a very specific, but very limited audience. This made them reluctant to finance big-budget science fiction films, because they didn't think they could sell enough tickets to make them profitable. *Planet of the Apes* was a big hit that crossed over to mainstream audiences, but was considered an anomaly. It took *2001* five years to earn back its costs and that's what the studios considered the norm. Even when they were good, science fiction films were usually not well regarded by critics, and many filmmakers and studio executives considered the genre a lowly one.

ALAN DEAN FOSTER

2001 really opened people to the possibility of science fiction being something more than bug-eyed monsters and guys in latex suits. Those were the two things that existed in films primarily. But it was certainly a smaller subgenre. [Author] Kevin Anderson and I were talking the other day and I'd sent him a picture of this astronaut in an observation bubble in space, and she's wearing a *Star Trek* T-shirt and giving the Vulcan salute. In the background you can see Earth below her, a Soyuz spacecraft docked on one side and solar panels on the other. It looks like a science fiction painting. I sent it to Kevin and a bunch of people and he wrote back and said, "We're living our future." And that's why more people get interested in science fiction. This was all kind of an explosion that came about before *Star Wars* and *Star Trek*.

RAY MORTON

And *Star Wars* is not just science fiction, it's space opera—a subgenre of science fiction that combines science fiction with fantasy. If straight science fiction movies were scarce, cinematic space opera was practically nonexistent. The only real space opera in the American cinema was the low-budget serials of the 1930s, '40s, and '50s—with the Flash Gordon, Buck Rogers, and Commando Cody series and *The Phantom Empire* being the most significant examples. When it was thought of at all, space opera tended to be dismissed by studios, producers, and critics alike as low-budget kids' stuff and nothing more.

In this context, George Lucas's idea to make an A-budget movie in an extremely marginal and fairly disreputable genre was a really curious one. The idea was definitely quirky, both creatively and commercially risky, and one that was certainly unexpected, especially coming from the writer/director of a recent, mainstream hit. That Lucas was able to persuade Alan Ladd, Jr., to bankroll the development of such a project was nothing short of equally astonishing.

That decision from the then 20th Century Fox studio head ultimately was a result of the death of the Hollywood studio system that had been in place from nearly the beginning, and the rise of the so-called "New Hollywood."

DALE POLLOCK
(author, *Skywalking: The Life and Films of George Lucas*)
The death of the studios came in the form of bloated musicals and special effects extravaganzas in the 1960s as they tried to reclaim an audience that had decisively turned to television. And when those films began to bomb, the studios began to fall apart. I'm talking about films like *Doctor Dolittle*, Julie Andrews's *Star!, Paint Your Wagon*—I mean, these films were not appealing to anybody under the age of fifty, so there was an audience hungry for movies about themselves. But the studios weren't making those films or if they were, they were making them really badly with directors like Otto Preminger, who didn't have a clue with movies like *Skidoo!*, which he did in the late sixties. It's the perfect example of a studio that doesn't have a clue. So the old directors couldn't deliver on this; the studios needed a new group of filmmakers.

ALAN DEAN FOSTER
People in Hollywood no longer knew what would work. They really had no idea, so they started to try different things. In the late 1960s, the whole culture of the country was changing due to Vietnam and there was a lot of experimentation. The problem of doing experimental science fiction is that it's expensive, right? Much easier to put a couple of guys on motorcycles and have them drive around than it was to put a couple of guys on a spaceship and have them fly around.

GEORGE LUCAS
They were making blockbusters ever since *Birth of a Nation*. This whole industry has been built on making blockbusters. *American Graffiti* was a very avant-garde movie that nobody wanted to do, but because *Easy Rider* was a hit, it allowed me to be a hit, because the studio had done *Easy Rider* and it made money.

JONATHAN KIRSHNER
(author, *Hollywood's Last Golden Age: Politics, Society, and the Seventies Film in America*)
In Hollywood, things started to open up around 1967 and it had to do with a confluence of factors. Obviously, you have the shuttering of the Production

Code Authority, and that's in the '66 to '68 period where Jack Valenti [former head of the Motion Picture Association of America] wants to move away from the old Production Code Authority toward the new rating system that he champions. There were some films in '66 that are turning points, like *Who's Afraid of Virginia Woolf?*, but what's going on there is the end of censorship, which opens up a lot of opportunities. But you have changes in the industry. The studios are losing money, they're uncertain, they're often in the hands of big corporations, so they're willing to take some chances on newer, younger talent that was enormously influenced by the kind of art house films of the late fifties and early sixties and the European imports. They wanted to make more personal, more ambitious small films.

JEANINE BASINGER
(film historian, founder and curator of the Cinema Archives of Wesleyan University)

Between 1969 and 1980, the whole filmmaking industry in America changed drastically. Basically, you had two things happen that seem to be incompatible, but merged into a strange kind of filmmaking world. First, the New Hollywood became a world of tycoons who came from a corporate culture. It was the era of large business takeovers of the old studios, so you had what are called "suits" coming into play, which resulted in a whole different world. They were talking about tax shelters and tax credits, presale agreements and advanced exhibit guarantees. It became a business model, not with the old guys who came out of business to be the runners of Hollywood, but business tycoons.

At the same time, you had the new young filmmakers coming in, many of whom had come out of film school. You had Francis Ford Coppola, Martin Scorsese, Stanley Kubrick, Brian De Palma—all of these guys who were very creative, who had studied films historically and aesthetically. And so they were changing the whole content and style of the Hollywood movie, with this strange connection between business, blockbuster business, and filmmaking. The way that movies were planned, produced, and distributed really changed drastically. And that is the New Hollywood.

DALE POLLOCK
There was a whole group of young filmmakers who had gone to film school in the late 1960s; they'd gone to NYU and USC and UCLA, and they were ready. The Francis Ford Coppolas and other people were really just waiting for this opportunity to move in. And so you had this period of incredible flux in the early seventies where the studios are desperate to land a hit, and all of

a sudden *Easy Rider* does hit. They're like, "We're going to make a lot of films like *Easy Rider*," but they didn't know *how* to make films like *Easy Rider*.

GEORGE LUCAS

It was sixty years after the studios started, so all the people that began when they were in their twenties were now retiring and the studios were getting bought up by corporations. And the corporations didn't have any idea how to run a studio, so they were hiring film students. It's really being in the right place at the right time. All of us, this whole group that was a part of it, got ushered into the film business, because the studios didn't know what they were doing and you didn't have to be related to somebody to actually get into the industry.

MICKY DOLENZ
(musician, The Monkees)

What these guys did, with *Easy Rider* being the breakthrough movie, is they essentially deconstructed the Hollywood major film industry. From then on, it was never the same. To some degree, I also think that's what *Head* is about: deconstructing the motion picture industry via The Monkees experience. There's a scene where Mike Nesmith and I are cavalry officers in the Wild West. There are Indians attacking us. Teri Garr is lying there with an arrow through her; the whole movie was pastiches on different Hollywood scenarios. I'm standing there and suddenly get hit with a bunch of special effects arrows. I look down and break them off and I say, "Bob [Rafelson], I've had it. I can't do this anymore." I throw the arrows onto the ground and I turn around and storm off, going right through the backdrop of this awesome Western set. That, to me, is sort of the central conceit of the movie. It was breaking through the old-school barriers of the Hollywood studio system. Then the producers, of course, went off and made *Easy Rider* after that.

DALE POLLOCK

An MGM had no conception of how to try and make a movie like *Easy Rider*, so there was an opportunity for a new generation to come in that understood where cinema was going, understood the impact of Bergman, Fellini, and these other filmmakers, and the French New Wave in the sixties began to percolate into American filmmakers. We had the first graduating classes from real film schools that were plugged in to what was happening in the moment. Not film history, which had been the previous approach at USC. They were not interested in teaching filmmakers, they were training film historians, but all of a sudden they changed and you had this real wave of people just itching to get in there and make their kinds of movies. The collapse of the studio system afforded them that opportunity.

JONATHAN KIRSHNER

The New Hollywood was, I think, special. And why it was special is because the studios were so uncertain, that they were willing to give space to filmmakers that they were unwilling to give them in the same way before or after. But Hollywood studios are the closest thing, I think, we have to pure capitalism. Everybody decries that Hollywood is like this or that, but Hollywood wants to make movies and make money. I don't think that has ever changed. So they're always looking for the way to do that, and that's the yardstick that the industry judges itself by. And this has always been the challenge for filmmakers who view themselves as working in a mass art form. You can't get around that, it is an art form but it's also the most expensive art form, so you have to make compromises.

JEANINE BASINGER

The concern of Hollywood in the Golden Era was always the audience. They cared about the audience. That's why they worried about censorship, they worried about happy or sad endings and clarity of narrative. Their concerns were always linked to audience reaction. They did previews and tried to understand what people wanted. They followed the genres: they knew people liked Westerns, so they made Westerns. They knew people liked musicals, so they made musicals. Their decisions were all audience-connected. But in this new world, they were money-connected, and the artistic filmmakers' movies were self-connected in a way. They were making personal expressions, so you're moving farther away from a direct connection to selling a product that pleased an audience and weren't really concerned with that. And, of course, when you bring in a great many people from a corporate structure, from Gulf & Western and things like that, these are not people who have been interested in storytelling, concerned with storytelling, and know how to make movies.

JONATHAN KIRSHNER

You also have this demographic change in the audience itself. It goes from being the mass medium of the forties to more youthful, more urban, more hip type[s] of audiences, generally speaking. So there's this subculture of this New Hollywood that emerges around 1967 and it's caught up in the tunnel of generational change that's taking place in social change and social contestations and it rides out. It has about ten years. And then society changes, and also the industry catches up with what's going on and the blockbuster model emerges as the successor to the New Hollywood experimentation.

JEANINE BASINGER

Everything shifted and it became a different system, a different product. And the audience began to be more selective. The audience was being molded to go for the event movie of the year: the movie that you *had* to see. If you haven't seen this movie, you're a jerk. If you can't talk about this movie at a cocktail party, you're not going to go home with anybody that night. You have to find the big event movie and have some wiseass opinion about it. So, again, it all shifted, and movies stopped being the important, mysterious, personal escape, a wonderful kind of private and delicious experience for you as an individual. It became more of a talking point for social reasons that everyone just shifted towards.

The New Hollywood had consisted of innovative directors like William Friedkin and Peter Bogdanovich, the force behind, respectively, The French Connection *and* The Exorcist, *and* The Last Picture Show. *But the advent of the movie blockbuster, which really began with Steven Spielberg's 1975 production of* Jaws *and would take root two years later with George Lucas and the first* Star Wars, *spelled the death knell to the studios' new direction.*

DALE POLLOCK

Jaws wasn't necessarily seen as the game-changer, but the feeling was more, "This is what we've been waiting for." They'd been waiting to figure out how they could deliver a mass appeal movie that cuts across every audience segment. You look at a film like Spielberg's *Sugarland Express*—no mass audience was going to that. All of a sudden *Jaws* becomes a personal project for him and becomes an enormous financial hit. Then *Star Wars* makes sense: another personal project that becomes an enormous financial hit.

JEANINE BASINGER

To the credit of directors like Marty and Coppola and everybody, they really loved and still do love movies and wanted to tell movie stories, but they were wanting to move the art form forward, play with cinema and bring new energy, new ideas, new concepts forward into the filmmaking process, while creating personal cinema. So they did care, but their ideas were also influenced by the whole international historical aspect of filmmaking. They became less connected to a straight-forward, clear, maybe even generic product. So for the average person in the audience, they're probably going to stay home, turn on their TV, watch an old-fashioned narrative with people sitting on the couch talking, and then they're going to go out to the blockbuster event movie.

BRIAN JAY JONES
(author, *George Lucas: A Life*)

People forget that *Star Wars* is an independent film for the most part and had that movie not hit, people would have been like, "That was a nice experimental independent film." Because even a movie like *Raiders of the Lost Ark* is kind of an independent film. Lucas and Spielberg were saying, "We're going to pay for this, we're going to raise the money for it, we're going to make it, and then you, Paramount, are going to distribute it," which is very much in the same vein as *Easy Rider*.

JONATHAN KIRSHNER

Jaws as a big summer hit is a harbinger of the blockbuster, but you need *Star Wars* to really nail it.

DALE POLLOCK

Now, were these projects really developed by the studios in the way movies were in the forties, fifties, and sixties? No. They were in essence developed outside of the studio. At the same time, Spielberg had to go to Universal for financing on *Jaws,* but he had total control while developing the script with Carl Gottlieb. So, I think the corporations were trying to reassert themselves in the seventies, though the blockbuster was the greatest thing that ever came along for them.

ALAN DEAN FOSTER

From the first days of film, the industry was financially driven, right from the time when people went to penny arcades and dropped pennies in to look at flickering pictures. It was always about the money, and when something comes along that changes the business financially, artistic interests fall by the wayside.

BRIAN JAY JONES

I think there's irony in the fact that Coppola's the one that wants to do independent small films and Lucas is the one that essentially destroys it, because he comes up with the blockbuster template. Actually, it's probably Spielberg with *Jaws,* and then you have George Lucas coming right behind it. From there for a while, every summer there's a Lucas or Spielberg film, because they kind of wrecked that side of it. But, again, to me, New Hollywood means that you're like, "Oh, good, there's a new Steven Spielberg film coming out." For the most part, unless it was on TV, you didn't really get, "Alfred Hitchcock Presents . . ." until they finally said that on television. You kind of knew it was Hitchcock or John Ford, but nowadays more than anything else, it's creator-driven content, the look, the feel, the style of films that's still very reflective of the New Hollywood mentality.

JEANINE BASINGER

In the wake of the blockbuster, it became harder for a director who wanted to work consistently, or anybody who wanted to work consistently, in the New Hollywood, for the simple reason that they're making fewer films. They suddenly had to be gigantic successes and the audience diminished. A director like John Ford could make a hundred movies and even if half of them failed, they could keep going. They were under contract and there was security in it. It was always a challenge if you were considered unreliable financially, like an Orson Welles, but the truth is, it became harder and harder to have a successful ongoing directorial career. Even somebody like Marty faced a great challenge when his *Last Temptation of Christ* was a failure at the box office. For a lot of reasons, it was very hard for him to get financing. So the whole system became more difficult, more challenging, and it came down to the fact that you needed a big hit.

JONATHAN KIRSHNER

All of the things that brought about the New Hollywood are changing by 1977. Even the cultural things that are going on in society, what the audience is kind of shopping for, is changing. *Star Wars* is a story of a ragtag group of underdog good guys taking on evil and winning, right? That's not *Chinatown*, that's not *Rocky*. At the 1976 Academy Awards, *Rocky* wins Best Picture. What does it beat? *Taxi Driver, Network, All the President's Men,* and even Hal Ashby's Woody Guthrie bio, *Bound for Glory.* There's a cultural shift in what American society is, and in 1980 Reagan is president, right? And *Star Wars* is a turning page on all of that. Certainly, it's not coincidental that once you get into 1977, you're into the Carter presidency and you don't have Dick Nixon to kick around.

JEANINE BASINGER

So fewer films are being made, which means it's harder to get them financed and approved. You're put into a corporate system where your ideas are being reviewed by businessmen who don't have experience in filmmaking. It just gets harder to do anything and everything, and harder to predict what the audience is going to respond to. That's William Goldman's era where he famously says about film, "Nobody knows anything," and nobody does. What they knew in the old days was, "get a product, put a star in a product, make the product generic, and you have a chance." Plus, everybody is going to the movies two or three times a week, so get a product out there, don't spend too much on it. Don't spend heavy amounts of money promoting it, keep it flowing and you'll be enormously successful. Now you have a system where you can't count on people going; they aren't going to the movies anywhere near as often. So everybody gets skittish about what they're going to finance, what they're going to make.

JOHN KENNETH MUIR
(author, *Science Fiction and Fantasy Films of the 1970s*)

Jaws and *Star Wars* proved to Hollywood that people were hungry, not for social commentary or provocative but often downbeat speculation about the future, but for entertaining, well-made, old-fashioned films. Given the context, it's not difficult to see why people were hungering for simple, well-told tales that reinforced traditional values. The audience sought escapism. In particular, they wanted well-made, technological escapism. *Jaws* fit the bill, as it was a scary horror film, dependent on Spielberg's technical acumen to achieve its terror. And *Star Wars* was cutting edge in terms of special effects, showcasing a whole new world while simultaneously reinforcing old myths/fairy tales.

BRIAN JAY JONES

To me, New Hollywood means more about the creative side than the financial side. I know the financial side is hugely important, but to me, it has more to do with the way you start to get projects that are more director-driven. Until the New Hollywood came along, you weren't necessarily like, "Oh, there's a Stanley Donen feature coming out now. Let's all go down and see the new Stanley feature." But once the New Hollywood comes along and you're like, "Oh, okay, we know who Martin Scorsese is. Brian De Palma? We know who that is." You start getting these filmmakers with distinct personalities and you can tell from the style of film, which you still see today.

DALE POLLOCK

Those filmmakers created their own problems by making *Jaws*, making *Star Wars* and transforming the industry into a blockbuster-oriented business where everything began to depend on what your opening weekend was. It's ironic that that generation changed the rules. And that that, in effect, prevented a lot of future films from being made, because they couldn't deliver that big opening weekend of *Star Wars, Close Encounters, Jaws,* and all the other films of the mid-to-late seventies. So in a way, the filmmakers themselves destroyed this little period of innovation, because they introduced the blockbuster. For a time, Spielberg and Lucas were going along the lines of Scorsese and De Palma, and then they splintered off because no one could match the success that they were having. And yet Lucas always felt he was an independent filmmaker. He never saw himself as anything else, because he couldn't stand working for a movie studio with anyone telling him what to do.

GEORGE LUCAS
That little myth got started by a critic who didn't know much about the movie business. It's amazing how the media has sort of picked it up as a fact. There's an ecosystem in the film business. What happens is when Steven and I make our movies and they make billions of dollars, well, half that money goes to theater owners. For every billion we make, a half billion goes to them. What do they do with that money? They make more multiplexes. More multiplexes mean more screens, which means more room for more movies. Thus, room for more non-mainstream films, for art films. We have ruined nothing. Absolutely nothing. In fact, we have helped smaller films flourish. And another thing: the films of the seventies weren't that great. I grew up in that era and it's a complete myth. There were four or five movies that were really interesting and were about something, and most of the others weren't about anything.

JEANINE BASINGER
I think *Jaws* and *Star Wars* were seen as both aberrations and opportunities, but mostly opportunity. If you are in any kind of business, if you're in an ice cream store and the ice cream rival across the street puts in a new flavor, you're going to get that flavor. You can make one movie and make a gazillion instead of having to make fifty movies and make millions? That's what they saw in the old Hollywood. If a movie made $200,000, that was profitable and that was great, but here, you're suddenly making two million and then twenty million and then two hundred million. So it was opportunity. This is a business that looks at patterns that it could never know if you're trying to sell something to the hearts and minds of people. You can't get a grip on the hearts and minds of as many people as live in the world or in the United States or even in Cleveland. So it was an inspiration for business success. And of course, with *Jaws,* it was a fantastic movie. That's the thing that everybody forgets. How many *Jaws* are you going to have in your lifetime?

JOHN KENNETH MUIR

Before he was caught up in the blockbuster machine, Lucas gave the world one of the starkest and most powerful visions of the future in *THX 1138*, and then created another, wholly personal film (though one more relatable) in *American Graffiti*. In short, he was making the films he wanted to make, according to his unique vision, and *Star Wars* fits the bill, too. Spielberg, lest we forget, made *The Sugarland Express* before *Jaws* and, again, was the type of New Hollywood movie brat who in his art, joined his technical understanding of film grammar at the same time that he pursued his own story ideas and vision. Both men are a part of the New Hollywood, not separate from it. But their visions "pivoted" the culture; their interests dovetailed with the public's in a major way, thus spawning the age of the blockbuster. But we should understand that the shift was also about marketing and the way *Jaws* and *Star Wars* were distributed.

DALE POLLOCK

In the aftermath of *Jaws*, we got *Jaws 2* and *Jaws 3*. Then there was *Star Wars*, which was followed by *The Empire Strikes Back* and *Return of the Jedi*, let alone the prequels and sequels. So this idea of continuing blockbuster success that could be spun off into further franchises took root. And right from that point, everyone's looking for a franchise and how they could make every film in a series profitable.

JONATHAN KIRSHNER

Robert Altman was offered a ton of money to make a movie and that movie was called *MASH II*. That's the kind of thing the studios wanted, and Altman, to his credit, instead shuttered his studio and that's when he went into his era of working more in the theater and then doing film versions of some theatrical productions. He emerges ten years later, so in that respect, he's very admirable. But by then, the tolerance for personal, gritty films that are designed for smaller audiences was not the way to go when the studios were looking to find these franchises. *Star Wars* is an easy target here, and justifiably so, because it's a case where the merchandise becomes more important than the movie. Well, for people who care about movies, that's not okay.

DALE POLLOCK

There have certainly been sequels previously in Hollywood, but nothing on the scale considered here where *Star Wars* proved you could spin off an infinite number of stories set in the universe established in the very first film. He's got enough characters and enough storylines in the *Star Wars* universe that you could just keep going forever. Was this change a good thing? Well, I think it certainly geared people towards it. Movies used to open every day during the week and it was only after this era that the Friday night opening became so big, and the opening weekend became big. And clearly the audience was loving it, because they were the ones showing up. That trend continues to this day with the studios looking for franchises, sequels, and remakes. That's the biggest change in Hollywood in the last fifty years, the death of the one-time movie and the rise of the franchise.

JOHN KENNETH MUIR

The George Lucas of the 1970s was a brilliant filmmaker. In a span of about half a decade, he directed three amazing films: *THX 1138, American Graffiti,* and *Star Wars.* Think about how different each of those films are from the others. Imagine what he might have done had he continued to direct projects that interested him, instead of getting into the franchise-building, toy-merchant business. He changed the world with *Star Wars,* but he also gave up, essentially, his career as an artist.

George Walton Lucas was born on May 14, 1944, in Modesto, California, then a small town. His life was filled with dreams of venturing off into the big world and becoming a race car driver, while the societal expectations were that he would follow his father into business at the Lucas Stationery Store. His childhood life was changed forever by the family purchase of a television set that was on a rotating table, which would allow the family to watch programs during dinner. A naturally shy boy, who wasn't particularly gifted at school, the young George Lucas lost himself in the world of comic books, such as Flash Gordon *and Walt Disney's* Scrooge McDuck, *as well as radio series like the supernatural mystery/suspense show* The Whistler. *While seemingly unrelated, these three tales made up the cornerstones of the young Lucas's existence. The thing they all have in common is adventure. Scrooge McDuck, at the time, was almost an Indiana Jones–type, always on the search for adventure and riches, while* The Whistler *and* Flash Gordon *dove into the realms of the fantastic that stretched and challenged Lucas's imagination.*

By 1967, after some flirtations with cinematography and photography in undergraduate programs, Lucas firmly settled upon directing as a field of study, returning to his alma mater of USC as a graduate student in the Film Production Program. While there, he completed several short films, the most important of which to his career being THX 1138 4EB. *This short film won him a scholarship from Warner Bros., which awarded him the opportunity to shadow a feature film production of his choosing. He chose* Finian's Rainbow, *directed by Francis Ford Coppola—which would turn into the most valuable friendship of his career. Classmates at USC such as Walter Murch, John Milius, and Matthew Robbins made up the "Film School Generation," a group of filmmakers who dreamed of dismantling the Hollywood studio system and creating their own decentralized, artist-driven industry.*

GEORGE LUCAS

I grew up in a very small town in central California. There were two movie theaters there and we'd go to the movies every once in a while. I enjoyed the movies, but I didn't become obsessed with them or anything. As I got older, I'd just sort of go to the movies to chase girls; I didn't actually know there was something on the screen. But I'd always been interested in visual art. In the early years I used to listen to these Disney story records where you'd put on the story, turn the page, and you got to see the pictures as you did it. And I listened to a lot of radio. I loved to imagine what was actually happening, filling in the blanks.

We got a television when I was about ten years old, though in the beginning there wasn't that much to watch. There were a lot of Westerns, and most of what I grew up on in the Golden Age of Television was Westerns, so if anything had any influence, it was probably that. But if it hadn't been for seeing *Flash Gordon* and *Perils of Pauline* serials . . . there is a through-line from them to *Star Wars* and certainly *Raiders of the Lost Ark*. But my real interest was art, drawing, photography—those sorts of things. When I was a kid, I drew for companionship. My parents couldn't afford a babysitter, so if they had to go somewhere to play cards with somebody, they'd take me along. And because I started drawing at four or five, obviously that was something I was comfortable with and was interested in. They would give me paper and a pencil and I'd be off and go draw. So in my head, I guess I assumed I wanted to be an artist and then I had an experience . . . you know, you have maybe one or two or three moments where something happens that changes the direction you're going to go in. And it happened to me in third grade in grammar school in Los Angeles.

As he recalls it, Lucas was not interested in what the teacher was saying or the subject. To him, it was just someone standing there talking, so in response, under his desk he would draw things that did interest him to keep his mind occupied during the school day.

GEORGE LUCAS

I wasn't paying attention and the teacher caught me. She decided she was going to humiliate me and put me on the spot. She said, "So, what's going on over there? What's more important than our class? What's under the table?" And I just thought, "I'm screwed; I'm just going to be burned." She said, "Why don't you bring that up?" and so I brought up the picture that I'd been drawing. She said, "Okay, tell us about it," and I said, "Okay, well, here's where the cowboys are and they're chasing Indians over a cliff, and the cowboys are shooting at the Indians. The Indians are bombing the cowboys"—I really enjoyed that. And she did something pretty amazing. She said, "Okay, we're going to put newspaper print paper on the easel and every Wednesday we'll give you fifteen minutes and you come up and draw a story for the class, but then you have to pay attention." I said, "Okay." Now had she gone the other way, considering the shape I was in at that time in my life, I don't know what would have happened.

BRIAN JAY JONES

What got him to the career he chose, and ultimately how he became the kind of filmmaker he was, is solely through the need to control the narrative. It goes through his entire life. The eventual crash of his car was his wake-up call that he needed to get his shit together.

GEORGE LUCAS

I didn't know anything about movies. I didn't know anything but that I liked to build things. When I was very young, I built houses and clubhouses and soapbox derbies and ball houses, chess sets and all those kinds of things. I was a woodworker and I'd love to do that. Then when I got a little older, I started to build cars and work on cars and go racing and doing all that stuff. Then I was in an accident and figured I should change my life.

BRIAN JAY JONES

In everything there is controlling the narrative of his life and being in charge and having absolute control. Film really spoke to him, because it was something he found out that he was great at. What I find interesting about Lucas when you compare him with Spielberg, is that Spielberg was the kind of kid that was filming his trains crashing into each other at eight years old. Lucas isn't doing that. Lucas is the gearhead. He loved cars and he loved motorcycles, and he basically got this career that his father is trying to hand to him on a plate and he's rebelling, because, right there, he's not in control of his destiny if he does that. His father is handing him the destiny. It's Vader and Luke already there. It's like the father's got this destiny that he thinks the son is preordained for, and Lucas was pushing back against that. And then he's a complete fuckup of a student and so on, because it's kind of a youthful rebellion.

DALE POLLOCK

Control was everything for him, and it remained so his entire career. He is the ultimate control freak in Hollywood down to the smallest detail of what a character is wearing. What separates him from the studios is that he is, or was, in control, not millions of shareholders. Just him. I even asked him, "Did you ever consider taking Lucasfilm public?" He looked at me like I was crazy. "Why would I do that?" "Well, you'd raise a lot more money that way," and he said, "Yeah, but I have my own money. Why would I use someone else's?" And he was right.

GEORGE LUCAS

My life is making movies, and I've got a lot of stories that are stored up in my head that I hope to get out before my time is up. It's just a matter of "how can I get through all the stories in the amount of time I have left." I "serendipitied" into starting companies, and building technology, and doing a lot of other things that are related to me getting to make movies that I want to make. I've never had a real plan of, "I want to get from here to there and I've got to do this." The underlying plan to everything is, I've got a bunch of movies to tell, and this is the one I'm going to do next. And then I focus on the one at hand.

BRIAN JAY JONES

The story I love with him is he's like, "I'm watching these movies in my studio here at Skywalker Ranch, and then I go watch the movies in the theaters out there in Modesto and the sound is awful. What's going on?" And they're like, "Well, we don't have the sound system you do and studio sound systems suck." He's like, "Well, every studio, every movie theater, needs to have this sound system," and he actually gets them to pay for it. That's a part of the process he should have no control over. Elvis has left the building! I mean, he has no say over that, but he runs the table on it. That, to me, is astounding. That's the kind of thing I learned about him that just blew me away: his ability to just take absolute control of everything and run the table with it. "You don't have it? Fine. Fuck you. I'll build it myself." He just does this consistently.

GEORGE LUCAS

When I went on my own, first we started at my house with a little screening room and then we put in a sound mixer machine and we slowly built up, because we had a place to mix the movies. We had to have a place to cut the movies. Everything I've done, I've done literally to be in the backwoods by myself creating the capability of making movies. And it was very hard. Then, the equipment was very expensive and the process was very expensive, and that's why I developed a lot of the technology over the years, to make that more simple and much cheaper. A much simpler process. That was really how the company got created.

BRIAN JAY JONES

The whole idea of THX Sound to me was stunning, because he was like, "Yes, I have THX." I always assumed it was the equipment, but it wasn't. It's just the specs. And he's telling these movie theaters, "I have the specs for this and you're going to pay me for the specs so you can retrofit your system. Oh, and do you want to know what film I have that's going to sound great in THX? It's a film called *Return of the Jedi*." In a way, he's using his powers for good so we can make movie theaters sound great, so then not just his film, but other films will sound great in it. So on the one side, you've got the film lover, but he's basically holding *Jedi* over their heads. And he does it again with digital film later: "Everybody needs to have a digital projector. You should retrofit and put all these digital projectors in. I have a movie called *Star Wars Episode I* that's coming out in digital." What a coincidence. And he does this constantly. That's what blows me away about him, and those things in particular, because he should, by all rights, have no say over that, yet he insists on it and they agree. Simply unbelievable.

GEORGE LUCAS

I didn't want anything to do with Hollywood and I've never made a film in Hollywood. As a result, I had to have all my own stuff. I said, "Why should we use the existing equipment when we can make it better?"

MARK HAMILL
(actor, "Luke Skywalker")

I thought he was an incredibly gifted filmmaker. I knew his work from *American Graffiti* and I thought the script for *Star Wars* was fantastic. It said "by George Lucas," and I didn't know that Gloria Katz and Willard Huyck helped him with it. They wrote a lot of the comic dialogue, the banter. But I thought George was an incredibly brilliant filmmaker. He's second to none at doing the kind of thing he does better than anybody else, so I had a deep respect for him.

And Lucas had a deep respect for and friendship with a fellow young wunderkind, writer/director Francis Ford Coppola, his mentor, who would prove key to launching his career. Coppola was born on April 7, 1939, to father Carmine Coppola, a flutist with the Detroit Symphony Orchestra, and mother Italia

Coppola. *The young Francis led an admittedly privileged life, with a bohemian lifestyle, with art and culture as the highlight of his existence. Francis was stricken with polio at an early age. As such, much of Coppola's early life was led in his imagination, as he was bedridden for a good portion of his childhood. But as polio became a treatable disease, the hopes, aspirations, and ambition for a better future came to light. In contrast to his future friend George Lucas, Francis was always encouraged to pursue a career in the arts.*

In the 1960s, Coppola moved to Los Angeles to pursue graduate studies in Cinema from the UCLA Film School. When he won the annual Samuel Gold-wyn Award for the best screenplay written by a UCLA student, Pilma, Pilma, *Seven Arts hired Coppola to adapt the late Carson McCullers's novel* Reflections in a Golden Eye *as a vehicle for Marlon Brando. This led to an assignment on* Patton *(with Edmund H. North), the film for which he won an Academy Award for best adapted screenplay.*

GEORGE LUCAS

Francis is about five years older than I am, but he was the first film student to actually make it into the film industry. He started working for a Canadian company called Seven Arts as a writer, because he'd won the Samuel Gold-wyn writer scholarship at UCLA. And so they hired him, saying, "We just bought this book. Turn it into a screenplay. We want it done in two weeks." And that's basically what he did for a living. Out of that, he talked them into letting him direct a movie and he got to do some writing on some good mov-ies, like *Paris Is Burning* and *Patton*. Of course, then they'd give it to another writer and say, "We've got a script. It's done, but it needs another rewrite." Out of that, though, he got a job to direct *Finian's Rainbow*. But then, one of the quirky realities is that Seven Arts bought Warner Bros.

HOWARD KAZANJIAN
(producer, *Return of the Jedi*)

George and I met each other at USC Cinema, now the School of Cinematic Arts. George was a year behind me, but back in the sixties, there were fewer than seventy-five full-time cinema majors. We knew everyone, had classes together and did things together. I graduated and went into the very first As-sistant Directors Training Program. Eighteen months later George and I met at Warner Bros. Studio where he had won the USC/WB six-month scholar-ship. I was an assistant director on *Finian's Rainbow*. George called me on the set and asked if he could visit and naturally I invited him down. I introduced him to Francis Coppola and the rest is history.

GEORGE LUCAS

I had gotten the Warner Bros. scholarship for the summer, a work scholarship for six months where you go to Warner Bros., they assign you to a department—script, photography, editing—and you spend six months there working with professionals. Well, as it turns out, they'd just closed down. Jack Warner was leaving and there was nothing going on. All the departments had been closed. There was nobody there. In fact, the day I arrived Jack Warner was moving out. I said, "What's going on?," and they said, "We're moving Jack Warner out of his office." It was literally the week that Seven Arts was taking over and they said to me, "We don't know what to do with you, because there are no departments that are open."

The only choice was to place him on the backlot, because there was only one movie in production, which was Finian's Rainbow. *This was where Lucas met Coppola for the first time. One thing that Lucas brought to the table is the fact that he'd previously had another scholarship working for Carl Foreman at Columbia Pictures, where he got to shoot documentaries, which he found enjoyable. But as Lucas was on the set of* Finian's Rainbow, *he found there was nothing for him to do but sit around. After a few days, his mind began to wander.*

GEORGE LUCAS

I'd had a tour and gone over to the animation department, which is where I started in film school, and it was empty. I said, "Well, I'll just skip this and I'm going to go over to the animation department, find some short ends and make a movie." Back then film was really expensive, and when you were doing independent films in those days they would cost you at least $150,000 or $200,000 just to buy the raw stock, have it processed, rent the cameras, and do that stuff. So to make a movie it was just impossible, because people couldn't come up with a few hundred thousand dollars. So everybody would steal short ends—when you finish shooting something, they'd take what's left in the camera and you could get that. It would be like, a hundred feet or fifty feet or whatever. You can splice it all together and you'd use it to make a movie with.

Francis found out about it and he said, "I heard you were in the animation department. What's that all about?" And I said, "Well, I think you're boring. I've done this and I don't want to do Hollywood movies. They have no interest to me at all." Again, this was the sixties and we hated the establishment. All of us in film school hated the establishment in every possible way, and I had no interest in working in a studio. I didn't like the studios, I didn't like the system, I didn't like the movies they made. I said, "I'm going to be a documentary cameraman; I'm going to do more experimental type of films. I do not like character-driven drama. I don't like plots. I'm not into this stuff. Film cinema is pure; it's not photographing a stage play, it's not photographing a book. It's its own medium." Well, he was a stage director and a writer, but between the two of us, we formed a bond, because photography, editing, directing actors, and writing scripts are all tied together when you're making a movie. So we complemented each other well; I was really good at some of the stuff he didn't know that much about, and he was really good at this stuff I didn't know about, because I had no interest in going there. So I became his assistant. But we were both young and everybody else on the crew was like, over sixty and they sort of looked down on us like we were subhuman. Eventually, we finished the movie he was doing, then we went and did a movie all across the United States.

That movie was The Rain People, *released in 1969 and starring Shirley Knight, James Caan, Robert Duvall, and Robert Modica. For it, a crew of eight— including Coppola and Lucas—began in New York and drove across the country. Upon arriving in Nebraska, they decided to rent a small warehouse and turned it into a studio to put the movie together.*

JONATHAN RINZLER
(author, *The Making of Star Wars*)

In some ways, I think that Coppola, Spielberg, and Lucas are like brothers. They love each other, but they're also very competitive. So, while one says, "I'm going to do this," the others say, "Well, I'm going to do it first!" [laughs] They also help each other out in a lot of ways, as brothers do.

GEORGE LUCAS

I was born and raised near San Francisco and I wanted to go back there. I had to go to a conference there and got a chance to meet and talk to John Korty, who was a local filmmaker making independent feature films. I went back and said to Francis, "This is what we've got to do. We're not going back to Hollywood." And we didn't. San Francisco was perfect, kind of bohemian. So we just literally came from Ogallala, Nebraska, and moved right into San Francisco and tried to have a situation independent of the studios. And when we started to go to the studios and beg for money, we didn't want them running anything or coming up or bothering us or anything like that. But we started a little company there and I got a chance to make a movie for a studio.

So I said, "I'll do one that's kind of half an experimental film and half kind of a story film. I'll never get a chance to do this again, and I may never get a chance to make a movie again." As it turned out, I made the movie that is what we now call a "cult classic," but at the time it bankrupted our company and sent us off in other directions. That film was *THX 1138*.

Their company was American Zoetrope and the film was another take on Lucas's acclaimed student film. Cinefantastique *magazine described the plot this way:* "THX 1138 *is a mind-bending look into a future century and into a civilization that exists totally underground, its hairless citizens computer-controlled, euphoric with compulsory drugs and having arrived at the ultimate in human conformity under a robot police force . . . The story is concerned with the efforts of Robert Duvall, who plays* THX 1138 *in a society where a prefix and a number suffice for a name, to escape his drug-induced state, which leads to love, an unknown and even forbidden emotion in his dehumanized surroundings, and finally his attempt to escape completely from the subterranean world itself."*

GEORGE LUCAS

My primary concept in approaching the production of *THX 1138* was to make a kind of cinema verité film of the future—something that would look like a documentary crew had made a film about some character in a time yet to come. However, I wanted it to look like a very slick, studied documentary in terms of technique. I'm very graphics-conscious, and I don't believe that a documentary has to look bad because it follows a cinema verité style. It can look good and still look real. Simply stated, that was my approach to every element of the production—the sets, the actors, the wardrobe, everything. At the same time, I wanted the picture to look slick and professional in terms of cinematic technique. I felt that the realism of the film's content would be enhanced by having the actors and their surroundings look slightly scruffy, even a little bit dirty, as they might well look in the society depicted. They wore no makeup, which helped to keep them from looking too slick and clean. No film ever ends up exactly as you would like it to, but, with minor exceptions, *THX* came out pretty much as I had visualized it, thanks to some excellent assistance—and a whole lot of luck.

Unfortunately, luck wasn't still with the film at the time of its release in 1971. The studio didn't understand it and audiences virtually ignored it in theaters. And for Lucas, the most infuriating aspect of the whole experience was the never-ending interference from executives.

GEORGE LUCAS

THX freaked them out when they saw it and they tried to recut and shorten it. "You can't understand it anyway, why are you trying to shorten it? It's not going to make any more sense." But they said, "We can do it." "You know, I put my heart and soul into this thing and to me it means something. You've just come in here and whacked a few fingers off and think there's nothing to it." So I was really angry about that. Then they did the same thing with *American Graffiti*, because they thought it was a terrible movie. They put it on the shelf and they cut five minutes—the magic number.

ERIC TOWNSEND

(author, *The Making of Star Wars Timeline*)

THX 1138 was released on March 11, 1971. As a result of its failure, Warner Bros. decided to defund American Zoetrope. The studio also requested that Coppola return $300,000 that they had put up for the development of several other films, including *Apocalypse Now* and *The Black Stallion*.

Warner Bros.' demand for a return of that money put Coppola, Lucas, and everyone else in a precarious situation. And through all of this, Lucas actually learned quite a bit from his mentor Coppola, particularly about writing and directing actors. Their careers would veer off in an unexpected way when Coppola was given the opportunity by Robert Evans at Paramount Pictures to direct the adaptation of Mario Puzo's bestseller The Godfather, *which, of course, would go on to win the 1972 Academy Award for Best Picture of the Year (among others), as would its critically acclaimed and Oscar-winning sequel two years later,* The Godfather Part II.

GARY KURTZ

(producer, *American Graffiti, Star Wars*)

Warner Bros. didn't like *THX* when it first came out and it also got trapped in a feud between Warner Bros. and Francis Coppola's organization when they backed out of financing his group of pictures. It was the only picture produced under that program. It was finished just about the time they had a falling-out. They also didn't understand the picture and just didn't really know what to do with it. It did very well in its initial release, but got pulled right away.

GEORGE LUCAS

Writing and directing were very important things, but Francis didn't completely convince me that that was the kind of moviemaking I would be interested in. Oddly enough, after *THX* our company went bankrupt and we had to make some money. I couldn't make any money. I couldn't get arrested, for God's sake. I was still like, a year out of film school. I said, "Francis, you're the director. You're going to have to run and get a job and pay off this loan." He said, "Well, they've offered me this thing. It's a potboiler gangster movie, but it's Italian and I liked the spaghetti scenes and all that kind of stuff, and they're going to pay me a lot of money." I said, "Well, I don't think you have any choice," though he didn't want to make it. He was just hired to direct, but he did a lot more than direct that movie. He worked on the screenplay, he cast it, and he fought with the studio. It was really one of the most horrific experiences I've ever seen a director go through in terms of people trying to get him kicked off the picture all the time, studio executives that were just involved in everything and he had to fight every single day. You know, the studio hated the cast, they hated the music, they hated the story. Everything he did, they hated. There was blood everywhere on that movie, but he did get it made the way he wanted it.

He said to me at the time, "I don't think you should be doing these experimental films, these kind of weird things that don't make sense. You shouldn't be doing science fiction films with robots where it's all kind of artsy-fartsy. I dare you to make a comedy." And I said, "I guess I don't have anything to do. I can write a screenplay." So I started working on *American Graffiti*, which is about how I grew up. I figured at least it would justify all the years I wasted cruising the main street of town. Even though I got offered some jobs from Hollywood with lots of money, I just decided that this is what I wanted to do. And once I committed to that, then I spent a couple of years trying to convince the studios to make it.

JONATHAN RINZLER

That's what makes *Star Wars* so great—it's a mega-franchise, huge phenomenon, but unlike the other ones, this is original material, created by a single person, seen through his highly idiosyncratic mind, who, at his heart, was an independent filmmaker, and had been from his days at USC. I think it's worth mentioning, some of George's oldest friends have said, it's kind of too bad *Star Wars* became such a huge hit. Because it prevented him from making other movies that would've been much weirder and thoughtful and maybe more interesting—like *American Graffiti* and *THX*. They were sort of closer to him in some ways.

ERIC TOWNSEND

In May 1971, George and his wife, Marcia, traveled to Europe, because *THX 1138* was being featured at the Cannes Film Festival. On the way, they spent the week with Francis Ford Coppola, who was shooting *The Godfather* in New York. While there, Lucas arranged a meeting with David Picker, president of United Artists, to discuss his ideas for *American Graffiti*. Then, while at Cannes, he called Picker and met him in his hotel room, where the two of them once again discussed *American Graffiti*. As a result, Lucas was given a development deal with United Artists for $5,000 to write the script, $5,000 when the script was finished, and another $15,000 if the film was produced. The plan would be for a two-film deal, the first to be *American Graffiti* and the second to be a Flash Gordon–esque space fantasy. They must have been seriously considering it, because in August they registered the title *The Star Wars* with the MPAA for Lucas's vague plans of making a space fantasy film.

Although contracts were signed between Lucas—and the recently created Lucasfilm, Ltd.—and United Artists for American Graffiti, *once the studio received the script in early 1972, they passed on the project. After that, Universal read the script and turned it down as well. UA would also officially pass on* The Star Wars *on May 29, 1973.*

ERIC TOWNSEND

Coppola's *The Godfather* was released and became a critical and box office success. Universal reversed its opinion of *American Graffiti* assuming Lucas could get Coppola involved, so he was brought on as a producer. He shot the film between June 26, 1972, and August 4, 1972.

BRIAN JAY JONES

American Graffiti was small enough that Lucas could still control pretty much everything, and he was smart enough at that time to have a good lineman in Gary Kurtz, who was taking care of a lot of the detail work that Lucas probably thought he had taken care of, but Gary Kurtz I'm sure did. Here's another thing I love about *Graffiti* and that I love about Lucas. Coppola is the one who told Lucas, "No one's going to take you seriously as a director unless you can write." *American Graffiti* and everything Lucas has done is an original screenplay, an original story. Even *Raiders of the Lost Ark* is based on his concept and his story. Whereas Coppola is making *The Godfather*, he's making *The Outsiders*—he's the one who likes films based on novels. The irony of that is just beautiful.

So, anyway, *Graffiti* is a script that Lucas wrote and he recognizes his own inability in it and hands it off to Gloria Katz and Willard Huyck to punch it up and gives them points, which he does with *Star Wars* as well. Again, he's a great collaborator in the sense that he knows where his superpowers lie. He's like, "We've got a good story here, it's got some problems, but you guys take care of that." So that project is still small enough that he can keep his fingers in most of the pie, but it's also his first gateway drug in a sense to the way you can make movies and the kind of movies he's going to make. It's the place where he starts to really understand and appreciate the value of great sound, for example. And he's got a great collaborator in Walter Murch, who goes out there and they're like, "We're going to record the music, the rock and roll." First of all, how amazing is it that he gets all the rights to the rock music in that movie? I mean, just amazing. But Murch is the one who says, "We're going to make this sound like it's coming out of the car radios or the PA system of a school." So they do all this weird cool stuff to get the sounds sounding very organic. I love the story about them walking around in the backyard with the speakers swinging off ropes so they can record the sounds like it's coming out of passing cars. They're doing a lot of really innovative hard work that makes Lucas, I think, appreciate the process even more and really value that stuff.

Lucas is one of our really first valuers of the way movies sound, which ultimately the exclamation point of that is THX [the digital sound certification]. He really knew that for film, 50 percent is the way it sounds. This is a gateway drug. It's the place where he's learning some really cool tricks, especially when you don't have a lot of money to make the movie sound the way that he hears it in his head, and to make it look the way he envisions it and to make it cut together.

GEORGE LUCAS

I made the film and we showed it at a preview test screening. The audience absolutely went berserk, but the studio hated it, said it wasn't fit to show an audience, "How dare you?" And they were not going to release it. They said, "We're going to see if maybe the TV department wants to put it on as a movie of the week." We'd bring the film down from San Francisco and instead of showing it in the studio screening room, we booked a five-hundred-seat theater. We would go and say, "Ask all your friends, everybody at the studio, everybody come and see the movie." So these four guys were sitting there in a huge crowd that went berserk. Absolutely berserk. And after about three or four of these screenings, we went through the publicity department and the marketing department and then to the film department, where a high-up executive said no. But the underlings said, "You should really see this movie. It's good." So we did the same thing for them and then they said, "Okay, we'll release it."

BRIAN JAY JONES

One of the stories I love about *American Graffiti* is when he's making that movie and he's got the suits always telling him, "No one's going to understand this. You've got four different characters, four different storylines going on. You're trying to resolve them all by the third act. No one's going to understand what's going on." And I always tell everybody, "That's a *Seinfeld* episode." You know what I mean? Lucas is so far ahead of the curve on this and he's like, "Guys, stop treating your audience like they're stupid. People are going to get it and we're going to put it together and we're going to cut it together right so that they will get it." It may not seem that innovative when we watch it now almost fifty years later, but at the time that had people scratching their heads, which is funny. You go back to it and it's like, "Why did this film have people scratching their head?"

GEORGE LUCAS

They released it in August 1973, which is the worst time to be released, and it wasn't a giant hit. It did okay, making maybe twenty million. Now that's sort of the lower end of having a hit. If it's below twenty, forget it. You're not going to go anywhere. So it made a little over twenty million in its first week, second week maybe twenty-two, third week it made twenty-five and it just kept going for a whole year. It stayed in the theaters for an entire year and it never dropped. So for a $700,000 investment, they made a $100 million return and then suddenly I was very hot. Yet before that, I couldn't get work anywhere.

BRIAN JAY JONES

Lucas learns a lot of good tricks from *American Graffiti* about storytelling and narrative and the filmmaking process. I love the stories of him hanging himself off the outside of a car in the middle of the night so he can get the best shot. And then after he says cut, everyone's milling around later and they're like, "Did anybody cut George loose?" They go and find him and he's sound asleep in the harness hanging off the side of the car. This is just him killing himself. Again, it's funny, because he hates directing. He thinks directing is the absolute most miserable job, but he constantly did it until he finally got to the point where he could hand it over and still control every step of the process. But he made himself physically ill making *Graffiti*, which he does again during the making of *Star Wars*.

His anxiety stemmed from his battles with Universal Pictures, including the seemingly arbitrary decision to edit five minutes out of the film prior to its release. After American Graffiti *became a huge hit, the studio rereleased it with those five minutes (including a sequence with Harrison Ford) restored in the cut. Decades later, Lucas would even revise the opening shot of the diner in the wake of the* Star Wars *Special Editions by changing the skyline for the film's DVD release.*

BRIAN JAY JONES

When you go back and watch *American Graffiti* with those minutes edited back in, it's like, "Okay, this thing with the used car salesman, it does feel like padding," but we write stuff, you write stuff, you're a writer, you know how it feels. Sometimes you're like, "I don't have golden words syndrome, but I put that in there for a reason." To have the suits again telling him to edit, basically because they can, that is a formative moment in his career as a filmmaker, because that's the moment when he says, "Fuck you!" He's not going to let anybody, if he can help it, ever again tell him how to edit his own film. I really do believe that that's the moment when he becomes *George Lucas*.

DALE POLLOCK

When you go back to *THX* and *American Graffiti*, both films were incredibly negative experiences for him. The way he described it to me is that it was as if someone took one of his children and mutilated them. That's how seriously he took what they did to *American Graffiti*. I think *THX* he wrote off to the fact he had been naive. He felt Francis Coppola had screwed him on the deal. I don't think the film came out being what he wanted it to be, but *American Graffiti* was his life. So when they started editing his life, that's what forever turned him against the studio system. He knew that he was going to have to go to a studio to get *Star Wars* made. Fine. He knew he would never be able to raise the money for it and didn't make enough on *American Graffiti* to finance what he thought he would need to do *Star Wars*. At the same time, he also knew that he would only be going to a studio for the first film, and if this film was successful, he was going to own the rest of them. That was his plan from the outset. The way he looked at Ned Tanen at Universal was the way a Jewish concentration camp survivor views Hitler. It really is, and he never got over it. He even said, "I'll get the first *Star Wars* made and that will be the last time I will ever work with a major Hollywood studio."

Part Two

THE ORIGINAL TRILOGY

1977–1983

2

HOPE & GLORY: *STAR WARS*

"Never tell me the odds!"

Director Francis Ford Coppola, of course, followed the one-two punch of *The Godfather* and *The Godfather Part II* with 1979's Vietnam epic *Apocalypse Now* for United Artists, which is a project that—on a much smaller scale—Lucas had actually planned on directing, having cowritten the original script with John Milius. The filmmakers had even talked about filming it in Vietnam with 16mm cameras during the war itself. When that was clearly untenable, another war movie manifested itself. Only this war movie took place in space despite having its roots in the Vietnam conflict itself with Lucas's sympathy being with the Vietnamese, the ill-equipped rebels, fighting against a far superior fighting force, the Americans, the Empire.

JONATHAN RINZLER
(author, *The Making of Star Wars*)

Originally, [*Apocalypse Now*] was George and John Milius's idea. It's very different than the Coppola one. George really wanted to make it, he shopped it around all over Hollywood. You could argue that's the one film Lucas didn't get to make, except Coppola *did* get to make it.

BRIAN JAY JONES
(author, *George Lucas: A Life*)

It's interesting that people are stunned when you tell them that Lucas was actually working on the first draft of *Apocalypse Now,* and that in Lucas's mind that was his film to make. So when he gets done with *American Graffiti,* the film he's kind of got in the queue, he thinks to do next, is *Apocalypse Now.* He wants to make this Vietnam movie and, of course, Francis has it locked up in his deal with Warner when he went in and gave them seven scripts for films, and *Apocalypse* is one of them. Lucas thinks that that's terribly unfair, and it's another nail in Francis Ford Coppola's coffin as far as he's concerned. But I think there was already a rift growing just over the way that Coppola was running American Zoetrope. It was kind of like Coppola's own version of the Beatles with Apple, with all these zealots and hanger-ons using all the money and Coppola's like, "Oh, but we're independent filmmakers," and everyone's taking the money and playing pool and drinking espressos.

JONATHAN RINZLER

There were rumors that there had been a falling-out between Coppola and Lucas regarding *Apocalypse Now*. [I heard] George say no to that. He'd always supported Coppola in the making of it. There might've been competition, but that's it. George wanted to film it in 16mm and do this whole hand-held look [at the Vietnam War] and make it a dark comedy, *Dr. Strangelove*–type version for *Apocalypse Now*. And he ended up using some of those ideas for the Vietnam sequence in *More American Graffiti* with the Toad storyline.

BRIAN JAY JONES

Watching Francis be very careless with his money made Lucas crazy, and created another thing where he was like, "I'm not doing that with my money. If I'm spending my money, it's at least going back into the system," whereas he didn't think Coppola was doing that. So the Zoetrope experience was already dividing them a little bit. Again, the seams are showing, and then once he gets ready to make *Apocalypse Now* and starts expressing interest, Coppola is like, "Well, that film's kind of locked up and I want to make that." Lucas is super pissed at him about that and I know Lucas didn't think that was fair, but that was Coppola's deal to make. I think Lucas would have made a similar deal when he's trying to get his films financed. It's so interesting in that you've got Zoetrope coming in right after *Easy Rider* and you've got that whole independent film cresting moment, and then it's gone in a second. And here's Coppola trying to stand at the front of the line, waving his hand and no one's following him now. It's like the independent film movement was kind of up and then gone immediately. Like in the nineties when Tarantino and Kevin Smith come along with these huge independent films, and it only survives, finally, because they get studio-wise in a way that the studios didn't do back in the late sixties.

JONATHAN RINZLER

Have you ever heard the story of the reporters who asked Lucas and Coppola, midway through their careers, "What would you do if you had a billion dollars?" I don't remember their exact response, but it was something like—Coppola's response was, "I'd spend it all on something gigantic, and then I'd need to borrow another billion dollars!" And Lucas was like, "I'd put half of it in the bank, then I'd very calculatedly figure out how to use the other half as wisely as possible."

GEORGE LUCAS
(executive producer, screenwriter/director, *Star Wars*)

[With *Star Wars*] I had an idea to do this kind of film about psychological motifs that are in mythology, and if they're still accurate today. The great thing about mythology is that it was an oral medium up until we learned how to write. Before that with Homer and everybody, they would just tell the story. They would go to people's houses and tell a story and get a free dinner and that's how they made their living, and then those stories were passed down from father to son who told people what the rules are. It's the same thing as the church and all the things we've got that make us a community that we all believe in. They used to go from a family to a tribe and from a tribe to a city and then to a country. So I asked myself, "I wonder if people still think the way they thought then."

RAY MORTON
(senior editor, *Script* magazine)

Lucas's most significant creative decision in crafting the script for *Star Wars* was to purposefully infuse his narrative with a mythic structure—the classic "hero's journey" plot identified by Joseph Campbell in his book *The Hero with a Thousand Faces* as one that has recurred in the legends, folk tales, and fairy stories of every culture across the globe. Lucas then enhanced this decision by peopling his story with archetypal characters resembling those who have appeared in the narratives of all of the world's storytelling traditions. In my opinion, it was this choice by Lucas to deliberately construct his B-movie narrative around these universal prototypes and archetypes from the collective myth that made it possible for *Star Wars* to connect with so many different people in so many different countries in the deep and meaningful way that it did and continues to do. Audiences in every part of the world could and can watch the film and find something familiar and resonant in it.

GEORGE LUCAS

It was quite a bit of research—it went on for two years. I was writing, and doing research at the same time. It was really studying a lot about mythology and about fairy tales, and general sociology and psychology.

DALE POLLOCK

(author, *Skywalking: The Life and Films of George Lucas*)

He deserves credit for having the ability to take elements within yourself and find the common ground for millions of people across the world who identify with those elements. It's pretty staggering that he was able, in the structural and mythic elements of the first *Star Wars* film, to attract a global audience with people whose lives could not be more different than his or the characters he's conveying.

RAY MORTON

Lucas enhanced *Star Wars*' cultural universality even more by peppering his narrative with numerous elements culled from high-end genre literature, various philosophies and religions, and pop culture vehicles such as movies, TV shows, comic strips, and comic books. He took this process even further when he shot the movie and incorporated many visual references and quotes from movies and otherwise into the picture and utilized filmmaking techniques from every era of cinema from the silent days to the present. All of these familiar references gave viewers additional ways to connect with the film on both conscious and subconscious levels.

GEORGE LUCAS

I think I proved that they were interested, because a psychological motif is the same kind of thing, even though it's not in *Star Wars*. But when you're telling a story that is a boring part and everybody's sleeping, you say, "Well, let's cut that out." And so you do. And then you say, "Wow, this thing where he's puzzled over his mother and wants to kill his father—everybody likes that part." So then you keep that part in. But they didn't really know what they were doing. They were just getting responses from the audience and it wasn't until Freud came along that people realized, "Oh, these are psychological stories." He's been around for a long time and those stories are just as strong today. But it's a lot about good and evil, and a lot about heroes.

RAY MORTON

And it's fun. *Star Wars* is a really entertaining movie: it's exciting, thrilling, funny, imaginative, suspenseful, and sometimes scary. Whatever Lucas's other intentions, he wanted to give audiences a great time and at that he more than succeeded. I'm certainly not the first to make this observation, but after a decade of gritty, realistic, and often quite downbeat films, bringing pure, optimistic entertainment back to the movies was both startling and refreshing and certainly one of the major reasons for *Star Wars*' incredible success.

BRIAN JAY JONES

Lucas has got his hands in a lot of different projects at the time, but he keeps coming back to the *Star Wars* project that he can't really explain to anybody. The mythology on that is that he wanted to do that movie his entire life. When I spoke to Randall Kleiser, his college roommate at USC, he says, "Lucas was upstairs and I always remember he was drawing these little star troopers . . ." Randall Kleiser has recited the story constantly for like, the last forty years. I was tracing that story back and one of the very first times it's told, Lucas immediately knocks it down. Lucas immediately says, "Not at that time. I would probably have been drawing cars." So at one point, Lucas busted his own mythology, whether he meant to or not, because it was like, 1978. It's not one of the things that, if you were going to do this movie, you would have the young George Lucas waking up in his bedroom and the light would be shining in and he would see the ghost of Ben Kenobi standing in the closet saying, "Young George, you will make a movie . . ." You would romanticize this. And Lucas actually doesn't really romanticize his desire to make that movie for a long time. Once he finally decides to make it, he's a dog with a bone and then the narrative does change constantly after that.

GEORGE LUCAS

Originally I wanted to make a Flash Gordon movie with all the trimmings, but I couldn't obtain the rights to the characters. So I began researching and went right back and found where Alex Raymond (who had done the original Flash Gordon comic strips in the newspapers) had gotten his idea from. I discovered that he'd gotten his inspiration from the works of Edgar Rice Burroughs and especially from his *John Carter of Mars* series of books. I read through the series, then found that what had sparked Burroughs off was a science-fantasy called *Gulliver on Mars,* written by Edwin Arnold and published in 1905. That was the first story in this genre that I have been able to trace. Jules Verne had gotten pretty close, I suppose, but he never had a hero battling against space creatures or having adventures on another planet. A whole new genre had developed from that idea.

GARY KURTZ
(producer, *Star Wars, The Empire Strikes Back*)

We wanted to see a space opera, but science fiction had taken this turn of being postapocalyptic, very depressing. There hadn't been a rousing space opera movie since *Forbidden Planet* in 1956.

RAY MORTON

One of Lucas's great innovations was to give his space opera the feel and form of an old-time movie serial—specifically by opening the script and film with a crawl similar to the ones that opened the *Buck Rogers* and *Flash Gordon Conquers the Universe* serials to explain the narrative's backstory and then by structuring his plot so that there was an exciting action sequence (often containing a cliffhanger element) every ten or fifteen minutes, thus giving audiences the feeling that they were binge-watching a bunch of episodes of some long-forgotten chapter-play in quick succession.

GEORGE LUCAS

So *Star Wars* is about good and evil and what makes a hero. What's friendship? What's the idea of sacrificing yourself for something larger? They're all really basic things and a movie about that was very obvious. But it's actually not that obvious to a lot of people unless you have somebody tell you every generation that this is what our country believes in, this is what we believe in. *Star Wars* was taken and put into a form that was very easy for everybody to accept, so it didn't fall into a contemporary mode where you could argue about it. It went everywhere in the world, because they could say, "Oh, the things I believe in are the same as that." Most people in the world believe exactly the same thing and share the same beliefs.

Playing an important part in the genesis of Star Wars *in Lucas's imagination was a seminal conversation he had with his mother when he was eight years old, asking her why, if there was only one God, were there so many religions?*

GEORGE LUCAS

It's a question that has fascinated me ever since. If you really look at it and most people say, "Well, what's the difference between a Shia and a Sunni? What about a Catholic and a Protestant, or we're all believing in a Jewish God? But what about the Jewish god and the gods that came before?" Buddha's a little bit different, but in the end, if you just think of it as one God, everybody may express it differently, but it's still the same ideas: don't kill people, be compassionate and love people. And that's basically all *Star Wars* there.

BRIAN JAY JONES

What I think is very interesting with *Star Wars* is that it's not preordained in the sense that when he gets done with *Graffiti* he wants to do *Apocalypse,* and then when he can't get that, he's like, "Okay, great, I'm doing Flash Gordon."

He's not like, "I'm going to do the science fiction project I've been think-ing about for the last seven years." No, he's like, "I'm going to get the rights to Flash Gordon," and then when he doesn't get those rights, he's sulking around and Coppola is the one who says, "Why don't you write your own damn science fiction piece, George?" It came from the fact that he was sort of hunting around for the next project, which is what we all do.

As a kid growing up in Modesto, California, George Lucas had two loves, cars and movies, so it's not surprising both were on his mind in the wake of his grad-uation from film school. As he began to conceive his epic sci-fi fable, what began as The Star Wars *would gradually evolve into something very different in the years to come as Lucas struggled to produce his homage to the genre movies he grew up with.*

GEORGE LUCAS

I had the *Star Wars* project in mind even before I started shooting *American Graffiti*. On our first vacation after that film, my wife Marcia and I went to Hawaii. That was great except I wrote the whole time I was there. I'd already started thinking about *Star Wars*. A director can leave his work at the studio; a writer can't. There's always a pen and paper available. A writer is thinking about what he's supposed to be doing, whether he's actually doing it or not, every waking hour. He's constantly pondering problems. I always carry a lit-tle notebook around and sit and write in it. It's terrible. I can't get away from it. I began writing *Star Wars* in January 1973—eight hours a day, five days a week, from then until March 1976 when we began shooting. Even then I was busy doing various rewrites in the evenings after the day's work. I wrote four entirely different screenplays for *Star Wars,* searching for just the right ingre-dients, characters, and storylines. It's always been what you might call a good man in search of a story.

DALE POLLOCK

I was struck by the incredible detail of George Lucas's imagination. He could remember things and see what he wanted to do in such tremendous detail. When you talk about the word visionary, someone who can envision their work on the screen, he had that capability. He could envision in his mind ex-actly what *Star Wars* was. It looked like he could even envision exactly what Indiana Jones would look like. He really had this capacity to take detail and turn it into a vision that he could then realize on film forever—despite the frustrations he had. Like Woody Allen says, you're lucky if you get 40 percent of what you want on the screen. Lucas lowered that to about 20 percent and he kept going back in, tinkering with it, to get it closer. Can you imagine a painter who gives his painting to a museum and comes back two years later saying, "I've been thinking about it; I want to re-do it. But give me back the original, we don't want that one out there anymore." What artist has *ever* had the ability to do this? Only the guy who owns his own films has that ability.

GEORGE LUCAS

I wanted to make an action movie—a movie in outer space like Flash Gordon used to be. Ray guns, running around in spaceships, shooting at each other—I knew I wanted to have a big battle in outer space, a dogfight thing. I wanted to make a movie about an old man and a kid. And I knew I wanted the old man to be a real old man, and have a sort of teacher-student relationship with the kid. I wanted the old man also to be like a warrior. I wanted a princess, too, but I didn't want her to be a passive damsel in distress. What finally emerged through the many drafts of the script has obviously been influenced by science fiction and action-adventure I've read and seen. And I've seen a lot of it. I was trying to make a classic sort of genre picture, a classic space fantasy in which all the influences are working together. There are certain traditional aspects of the genre I wanted to keep and help perpetuate in *Star Wars*.

DALE POLLOCK

What emerged from *Star Wars* that was different from science fiction films that preceded it is that it was more than an action film. It was a personal quest; a story of self-discovery. It's a coming-of-age story that works on so many different levels.

RAY MORTON

Star Wars is a wonderful movie. First and foremost, it's a grand and marvelously crafted entertainment. It was also extraordinarily successful at the box office. It became and all these years later remains a pop culture phenomenon. It was highly influential, making science fiction the dominant genre in mainstream American filmmaking and the blockbuster its primary mode. There are some pretty extraordinary accomplishments for a single movie. And it all started with a wonderful screenplay. And in creating that screenplay, George Lucas jumped off from a really unusual place.

ERIC TOWNSEND
(author, *The Making of Star Wars Timeline*)

In January 1973, Lucas began creating lists of names that could be used in his space story. A second list became a list of locations that could be used in the story: Yoshiro and Aquilae are desert planets; Brunhuld and Alderaan are city planets; Anchorhead, Bestine, Starbuck, Lundee, Yavin, Kiseel, and Herald Square. Aquilae is where the Hubble and Beber people live, Yavin becomes a jungle planet, whose natives are eight-foot-tall Wookies, Ophuchi is a gaseous cloud planet where lovely women can be found, Norton II is an ice planet, and a Station Complex is noted among the space cruisers.

Early in 1973 he also met with artist Ralph McQuarrie to talk about his as of yet untitled space fantasy film. Lucas had met McQuarrie through two former classmates from USC, Hal Barwood and Matthew Robbins. The pair, who were attempting to create their own science fiction film, Star Dancing, *hired McQuarrie to create some concept artwork. At the time, McQuarrie had worked mostly for Boeing as a technical illustrator. Lucas had gone with his old USC friends to see some of McQuarrie's paintings for* Star Dancing.

RALPH MCQUARRIE
(production illustrator, concept artist, *Star Wars*)
Hal and Matthew introduced me to George Lucas about two years before he actually approached me to work on *Star Wars*. George mentioned at the time we first met that he wanted to look at some of the slides. He said he was interested in doing a science fiction film—he didn't call it *Star Wars* at that time—with a kind of comic book subject matter.

ERIC TOWNSEND
Lucas also began compiling ideas for his new project in a two-page document entitled "The Journal of the Whills, Part One." Writing eight hours a day, five days a week, he collected an enormous amount of ideas, some of which would eventually make it into the original *Star Wars* trilogy, some that would make it into the prequels and others that would be scrapped. Ultimately, though, it was decided that "The Journal of the Whills" was too complicated and confusing, so Lucas decided to start over—although he did keep certain story details and names in later drafts. On April 17, 1973, he started writing a fourteen-page treatment of the project, now called *The Star Wars*.

JOHN L. FLYNN
(author and film historian)
By May 1973, he had completed a ponderous thirteen-page story treatment, handwritten on notebook paper. It told "the story of Mace Windu, a revered Jedi-bendu of Ophuchi who was related to Usby C.J. Thape, a padawaan leader to the famed Jedi." His agent, Jeff Berg, and attorney, Tom Pollock, didn't

understand a single word, but nonetheless agreed to submit it to United Artists and Universal, both of which turned it down. What's interesting is that although it's somewhat crude and unpolished, the thirteen-page story treatment sketches out most of the action which will follow in the series. The main group's adventures on Aquilae (in the desert and the cantina), Leia's rescue from the prison complex, the dogfight in space, and the medal ceremony all survive to the final draft of *Star Wars*. There's a chase across space and in the asteroid, and the intrigue on the city-planet of Alderaan which form the basis to *The Empire Strikes Back*, and a jungle battle that finds life in *Return of the Jedi*. The characters also remain surprisingly faithful to their first inception, even though certain changes do occur. Leia continues as a princess, while the character of Luke Skywalker is made a teenager; the aging general in the treatment becomes Ben Kenobi, desert rat and aging Jedi Knight. There are two bumbling bureaucrats who are transformed into two bumbling robots; the furry aliens evolve into both Chewbacca and the Ewoks, and the Sovereign becomes the Emperor. The only central character that is missing from this early screen treatment is Darth Vader.

RAY MORTON

Inspired by the plot of Akira Kurosawa's *The Hidden Fortress*, this seminal version of *Star Wars* was set in the thirty-third century. The galaxy is experiencing a civil war between the ruling evil Empire and the members of a growing rebellion. Following a successful rebel attack on the Empire's giant new battle station, the Emperor puts a price on the head of the young rebel Princess Leia. Rebel General Luke Skywalker is tasked with escorting the Princess and her retinue of courtiers to a safe haven on the planet Ophuchi. Traversing the desert planet Aquilae, the band joins forces with a band of young rebel boys. Escaping Imperial forces in a stolen spacecraft, the rebels fly through an asteroid field and land on the planet Yavin, where Skywalker battles aliens as Leia is finally captured by the Empire. In the final act, Skywalker and the boys raid the Imperial prison and rescue the Princess. A massive space dogfight between the rebel and Imperial spacecraft ensues. In the end, the rebels triumph, defeat the Imperial pilots, and finally deliver Leia to Ophuchi and the story ends with a great celebration.

ERIC TOWNSEND

At the end of May or early June of 1973, Lucas presented the new draft of *The Star Wars* to Universal, which had recently financed *American Graffiti* and still had Lucas under contract. Although Lucas was not thrilled with the way Universal had handled *American Graffiti*, by contract he had to give the studio ten days to decide on his next project. After ten days, he hadn't heard anything, so he informed them that their time was up and he was looking into other options.

Just ten days later Lucas met with Fox's Alan Ladd, Jr., who had previously been contacted by Lucas's agent, Jeff Berg, to fill him in on this proposed project, and the exec was genuinely interested in it and its potential. The result was an eight-page deal memo that stated Lucas would receive $150,000 for writing and directing, Gary Kurtz would receive $50,000 to produce, and Lucas's wife, Marcia, and Hollywood veteran Verna Fields would come on as editors with Walter Murch as production supervisor.

RAY MORTON

Lucas then developed his treatment into a rough draft, which he then revised into an official first draft that changed the story considerably and added an important metaphysical element. In these drafts, the protagonist is sixteen-year-old Annikin Starkiller, son of Kane Starkiller. Kane is one of the last of the legendary Jedi Bendu—an order of noble priests/warriors who utilize a mystical energy field called the Force of Others. Most of the rest have been hunted down and killed by the Knights of the Sith, evil agents of the Empire. Seeking to avoid the Sith, Kane—who due to severe injuries is now half-man/half-machine—lives in exile on the remote planet Utapau with Annikin and his youngest son Deak, where he is training Annikin to be a Jedi.

As the story begins, a Sith warrior discovers Kane on Utapau and attacks the Starkiller homestead, killing Deak. After Kane destroys the Sith, he and Annikin travel to the rebel planet Aquilae, one of the last free planets holding out against the Empire. There they meet up with Kane's old friend and fellow Jedi, Aquilaen General Luke Skywalker. Kane tells Skywalker that he is dying and asks him to take Annikin on as his Padawan learner (apprentice Jedi) and complete his training. Skywalker agrees and makes Annikin a captain in his army. When the Empire attacks Aquilae using their giant new battle station, Skywalker and Annikin help Aquilae's young Princess Leia and her two young brothers to escape the destruction. Along the way, they meet up with two stranded Imperial robots—R2-D2 and C-3PO (mechanized versions of the Imperial bureaucrats depicted in the treatment). They then set out to deliver the royal siblings to safety on the neutral Ophuchi system. During their journey, they travel across a vast desert to a grungy spaceport and steal a spaceship, then fly through an asteroid field and crash on a planet populated by fearsome furry giants called Wookies. The rebels join forces with the Wookies to fight off the

Sith, but Leia is captured and taken to the space fortress. Skywalker trains the Wookies to fly space fighters. Annikin sneaks aboard the space fortress to rescue Leia as Skywalker and the Wookies conduct an aerial attack on the fortress. In the course of a titanic battle, Annikin rescues Leia and escapes from the space fortress with her just before Skywalker and his furry pilots blow up the fortress. In the end, Annikin and Leia fall in love and Annikin is named the protector of Aquilae.

In Lucas's next draft, the Princess is reduced to a minor character. Instead, evil Sith Lord and imperial operative Darth Vader captures twenty-five-year-old rebel leader Deak Starkiller at the outset of the story. Vader drains Deak—a Jedi—of his powers, but not before Deak dispatches R2-D2 and C-3PO to find his eighteen-year-old brother Luke on the planet Utupau. After traveling across a desert, the robots find Luke, an archaeology student, and show him a holographic message from Deak instructing Luke to take a mysterious object called the Kyber Crystal to their father, a legendary Jedi Knight and a leader of the rebellion. Jedis use the Kyber Crystal to control the Force of Others, which has two distinct halves—Ashla (the good side) and Bogan (the bad side). After some initial hesitation, Luke accepts the mission. He and the robots travel across the desert to a grungy spaceport, where Luke hires pirate Han Solo to take them to his father on the planet Organa Major. Solo steals a spaceship and the band travels into space. They arrive at Organa Major, only to find it has been destroyed by the Empire's new weapon, a giant battle station called the Death Star with the power to destroy an entire planet. Next they travel to the planet Alderaan, where they find that Deak is being held in an Imperial prison contained within a floating city suspended in the clouds. Luke and Han rescue Deak and use the Kyber Crystal to restore his powers. The group then journeys to the jungle planet of Yavin, where the rebels have their headquarters and where they find Luke and Deak's father, a wizened ancient called The Starkiller. Luke's father trains Luke to be a Jedi, after which Luke leads a squadron of rebel starfighters (piloted by humans, not Wookies) in an aerial attack on the Death Star. Darth Vader leads a squadron of Imperial fighters into a dogfight with the rebels. Ultimately, the rebels prevail and Luke blows up the Death Star.

By the third full draft of the script, the narrative began to resemble the one we're familiar with: young farm boy Luke Starkiller, son of the late, great Jedi Anakin Starkiller, teams up with exiled Jedi Knight Ben Kenobi and space pirate Han Solo to rescue rebel Princess Leia from the clutches of Darth Vader, after which Luke joins the raid on the Death Star and uses the Force (no longer ". . . of Others," no longer controlled by the Kyber Crystal, and now unified into a single entity with both a good and bad side) to destroy the battle station. A fourth draft refined this storyline further and became the production script.

BRIAN JAY JONES

If you read the first drafts—plural—of what finally became *Star Wars,* I'm astounded that anybody green-lit it. I mean, again, thank God he's got Alan Ladd, Jr., from Fox in his corner, because the first *Star Wars* script is, in my opinion, unreadable. It's got too many ideas, there's way too much backstory. Lucas is very into backstory. He's like Jim Henson in the sense of world-building, and you're like, "Get on with it. You've got to get on with it." So the first few drafts of *Star Wars* are really draggy and you can't really tell what it's about. And, again, Lucas's elevator pitch on this is terrible. One of the first times when somebody is asking him, "What are you working on next?," he's like, "Well it's kind of like James Bond with sword and sorcery" and you're like, "What?" First of all, not even close to what it finally became, but you're left asking, "Who approved this?" Thank God somebody did, but it's like a dog walking on its back legs. What's astounding is that it happens at all, and I think that's kind of what *Star Wars* is. I mean, it's amazing it happened at all. It kind of had everything working against it for a long time, until suddenly it didn't. But the element of time was against them and money was against them and the suits were against them, and it kind of seemed like nothing was falling into place. Again, amazing he found someone to believe in him enough to be like, "I can't make heads or tails out of this; I can't tell who the hero is and you're changing it as we're going along, and every single draft is different, but, okay, we have faith in you."

The first draft of The Star Wars *would eventually see the light of day in an adaptation by Jonathan Rinzler in an eight-part comic book series for Dark Horse Comics, published in 2012, that adapts Lucas's earliest version of the film.*

JONATHAN RINZLER

It was so much fun. I felt beyond fortunate to be able to do it. I convinced George to do it—first he didn't want to do it—but with Dark Horse's help, we kind of convinced him. We showed him what it could look like, and then he was excited about it. So I took his rough draft and I put it into a Word document, where I could edit it. First thing I had to do was divide it up into comic book issues. I think it was a question of budget issues with Dark Horse. I think they would've preferred six, but I thought eight would be better. In terms of scenes, it tended to break down very easily into eight divisions. The only thing I added was a scene at the gas station where there was a fight. So I gave the whole thing to George, and I highlighted the things that I added. I added a fair amount of dialogue, because, at certain points, I think he was roughing things in, and he wasn't as concerned about dialogue at that stage. For instance, at the scene where Annikin reunites with his father, they don't even say anything to each other in the script. And George okayed everything; he was fine with it. In retrospect, it was fun, because I really felt by that time I had worked with George on *Star Wars Frames,* and other books, and I really felt like I knew what George wanted in terms of scenes and action and dialogue. And he just approved it. In that case I was lucky, because Randy Stradley was the editor and obviously he has a ton of experience. The first issue went through maybe three or four different drafts. He said, "This is how you do a comic book. You can't do that, you've got to do this, don't ever do that." It was great.

Of course, George though—in between the time he got excited, and the time when we got close to drawing the first issue—he sold the company. I went to his office at Skywalker to show him, and he's like, "Don't show this to me, show this to Kathleen Kennedy, she's running the show now." And that was okay, it made it easier for us. I know a lot of people have said it's a terrible comic, but that was the whole point. Some of it didn't work, and some of it was stupid. But here's what it would look like, here's what it could look like visually, because it would never be a movie.

The rough draft was his blue sky of [filmmaking]. He knew perfectly well he couldn't film that version. He knew it was just a rough draft. And he said to me, even as we were doing [the comic], in typical George, "I'll approve this, but I don't know why you want to do it. There's a reason why I didn't film that draft." I said, "I know it's got flaws, but it's also great. And fans would really like to see it." George just mumbled and I said, "Aren't you interested in how your favorite directors got somewhere? Wouldn't you like to see a book on Kurosawa which showed an early version of *Seven Samurai*?" And George said, "No, I don't want to see that." And I said, "Oh, come on!" This is the guy who saved everything. Why would he save everything if he didn't want people to see it!

GEORGE LUCAS

When I told Alan Ladd about the idea for *Star Wars,* he said, "I don't understand this. Dogs flying spaceships? This is ridiculous and I don't understand what you're talking about, but I think you're talented. So whatever you want to do is fine with me." Now how many times have you heard, "I trust the talent, not the script"? It's just that those were the days . . . there was a little thin thread of rationality that came through the film industry in the seventies. It was amazing. Everybody talks about how it happened, but mostly it was because all the moguls had died off, corporations bought the studios and everything was in chaos. So you had odd people being hired to run things and they didn't know about power yet and all that kind of stuff, because they weren't getting stock options. So it was an amazing little time.

BRIAN JAY JONES

There's a great scene in the TV series *Mad Men* when Harry's talking with the guy who goes out to become the Hare Krishna. He's got the spec script he's written for *Star Trek* and he's like, "You tell Mr. Roddenberry that I will sign anything." That's kind of the way you get when you're pitching something and you want it. You're like, "Whatever, I'll just sign it." Lucas never really was the guy who was like, "Just put it down in front of me and I'll sign that; I want to make this happen."

JEANINE BASINGER

(film historian, founder and curator of the Cinema Archives of Wesleyan University)

George Lucas is one of the most important people in film history, because he understood the changes that had happened in the movie business. He had maintained the desire to tell stories, because he was a movie lover, but he wasn't afraid of change. He embraced things like sci-fi and storytelling and always understood that story was the primary thing. You know, you come along in his career and he makes something like *Red Tails*. That was a wonderfully creative thing to do and it was a very strong story—and it was a story that should be told. It's a story that needed to be told. It didn't catch on with the public, but Lucas was in a position at that time that it didn't matter to him. He didn't need to make a lot of money, but he would have made that story if he'd known about it when he was young and hungry, too.

BRIAN JAY JONES

What's helpful given Ladd's background is Lucas could go into his office, and even if he couldn't explain it, because he and Ladd had sort of a similar filmic language, he could be like, "This is *Captain Blood*." He could just throw stuff out and Ladd would be like, "Oh, okay. I get it."

JEANINE BASINGER

Alan Ladd had a business plan which was sensible: find smart, talented, creative people and back them. That's the business plan at least, because it's tangible. So he was right to believe in George Lucas; he had read the situation correctly and had good instincts. He had grown up in the business and around it, and he wasn't afraid of it.

"Laddie" certainly proved that when Lucas's people came to him with provisions to the deal that would give Lucas unprecedented ownership of sequels to Star Wars *and, later, merchandise.*

GEORGE LUCAS

American Graffiti was a huge success and I had a deal with Fox to write and direct *Star Wars* for $125,000, but it was a deal memo, not a contract. I was the hottest director in Hollywood and they said, "Oh my God, he's going to come in here and ask for a million dollars. No director has ever gotten a million dollars. What are we going to do?" And Fox was sort of on the ropes and I'm talking to them and I said, "Look, I'll take the agreed salary. I'm not going to ask for one million dollars. I signed the deal memo and that's what I believe in. But everything is not mentioned in the deal memo on the re-look at it, and that was sequels," because I'd already written the three movies and I knew I wanted to make them regardless of whether the first one made any money or not. So I was offering if, in fact, the movie would be a turkey, they wouldn't want to make the next one. But they would then say, "We own the rights, you can't do it." And so out of that I got the sequel rights.

ALAN DEAN FOSTER

(author, *Star Wars* novelization and the sequel, *Splinter of the Mind's Eye*)
When I worked on the outline for the *Star Wars* novel *Splinter of the Mind's Eye* with George Lucas, the first film was still in production. George didn't know, nobody knew, that he was creating a social phenomenon. We sat down to consciously design a book which could be filmable on a low budget, but now George no longer had to worry about that. I'm not saying that my book wouldn't make a good film, but I would like to see, for example, a whole fleet of Imperial cruisers instead of just one at a time. I would like to see the Imperial homeworld and the Emperor's palace. I have to say, he was the only filmmaker I ever sat down with who really listened to me. Here was this guy making a movie that no one knew would be a success or failure. I had nothing to do with the film, but since I was writing the book, I had to read the first script. We discussed that script in some detail, and George listened. He certainly didn't have to, he had complete creative control, but he valued another person's viewpoint.

BRIAN JAY JONES

I talk about how his need for control stuns me, but what shocks me is how reckless he can be, and I mean it in a good way, because it's creatively reckless in the series that he goes all in all the time in the name of his own projects. So there he is doing it with *Splinter of the Mind's Eye* and he's like, "I'm taking the rights to the sequel and I'm going to make it regardless of how the first film does; I'm in control."

ERIC TOWNSEND

By September, Lucas began collecting dogfight footage from movies based on World War II and began editing fragments together to try to get a general idea of how his space battles would work in *Star Wars*.

GEORGE LUCAS

I couldn't really explain what I wanted to do with storyboards. They didn't really believe in the storyboards, because storyboards are great if you're doing matte paintings. They're static and you'd say, "Well, this is the shot," and sometimes an animation back in those days was a big procedure. You'd just paint the picture and say, "That's what it is." You didn't have to do extremely complex things. So what I did on *Star Wars* was I took a lot of old documentary films of air battles from World War II and cut them into the sequences of, "This is going to be the trench run, this is going to be the attack on the Death Star" before I even finished the script.

GARY KURTZ

Before the storyboards were done, we recorded on videotape any war movie we could find involving aircraft that came up on television. So we had this massive library of parts of old war films like *The Dam Busters*; *Tora, Tora, Tora*; *The Battle of Britain*; *Jet Pilot*; *The Bridges of Toko-Ri*; *633 Squadron*; and about forty-five others. We went through them and picked out scenes to transfer to film to use as guidelines in the battle. We cut them together into a battle sequence to get an idea of the movement. It was a very bizarre looking film, all black and white, a dirty 16mm dupe. There would be a shot of a pilot saying something, then cut to a long shot of the plane, explosions, crashes. It gave a reasonably accurate idea of what the battle sequence would look like, and more importantly, the feeling of it.

ERIC TOWNSEND

And then, in January 1974, Lucas purchased a one-story Victorian home built in 1869 and began remodeling it to become the Lucasfilm office. The home office would later be known as Park Way, its carriage house becoming editing rooms. Lucas also signed a legal agreement with himself, Lucasfilm legally loaning out "George Lucas, director" to the Star Wars Corporation. Then, in May, he completed a rough draft screenplay.

JOHN L. FLYNN

The first draft screenplay alters and expands much of the original material, but is still very crude and bloated in cinematic terms. Lucas's yearlong effort introduces two villains: a sadistic general named Darth Vader and Prince Valorum, a Black Knight of the Sith. The characters are both interesting, but still at this point in the saga somewhat one-dimensional. By making them into one person who starts out as the embodiment of evil then changes in reaction to another's evil deeds, Lucas has the essence of the space fantasy's tragic figure. Also, he seems to transpose Kane Starkiller's disability (he must remain in protective cybernetic armor to maintain his life systems) onto later conceptions of Vader. Han Solo, who earlier had been a huge green-skinned smuggler, remains somewhat unchanged (except in appearance) by the final draft. The characters of Owen and Beru Lars would eventually become farmers (not anthropologists), and play a much more important role as Luke's uncle and aunt. Of course, the two bumbling bureaucrats are now bumbling robots.

Other sequences, like the group's adventure in the desert and cantina of Aquilae, Leia's rescue from the prison complex, the dogfight in space, and the rewards ceremony, also continue untouched to the final draft. There's an asteroid chase and the use of cloud city that would show up in *The Empire Strikes Back*. And the jungle battle that would eventually form one of the key sequences in *Return of the Jedi* has been fleshed out in much greater detail. The earlier sequences on Utapau and in the capital of Aquilae also provide interesting clues to characterization. For example, Grand Moff Tarkin appears, not as a governor, but as a religious leader; and Kane's decision to leave his son in the hands of a master is similar to that made by Ben Kenobi surrendering Luke to the master Yoda in *Empire*. But there was still much work to be done before the script could be a film. Even a revised draft finished in July only produced a slightly revised version of the first script. Lucas knew the script was still a mess and worked hard to produce another version.

While Lucas was putting his own money in to fund the development of Star Wars, *he was getting increasingly frustrated by the fact that Fox had not produced a contract based on the initial deal memo. While he was able to retain sequel rights (so long as production began on the second film within a two-year period), he was later also able to maintain control over the name* Star Wars *in conjunction with the film's merchandising, which may very well be the dumbest corporate move since Decca Records turned down The Beatles.*

GEORGE LUCAS

The licensing [merchandising], which was the other part of this, just wasn't a big thing. Especially in the movie business; a little bit in television, but not in the movie business, because it takes a year or two to make toys. The movie comes out and is out for six weeks and that's the end of it, and a toy has to be out there for six months or a year. So nobody wanted to do stuff, but I did with my experience from *American Graffiti* where they just threw it out there without much advertising, but the word spread. I wanted to be able to build an audience for this thing. And the one thing there was in licensing was posters and T-shirts and you could make those deals really easily. But I said, "If I get the licensing, I can make a whole bunch of T-shirts and posters and I can send people out to Disneyland and everywhere and can advertise the movie." Obviously everybody thought that was really brilliant, but I was really just protecting myself. And what happened after that was *Star Wars* came out and then we went to a toy company. We helped them build these little action figures, not G.I. Joes, and they became very successful and we ended up making a lot of money. A little bit more on the movie, but mostly movies don't make money.

DAN MADSEN
(owner, the Official Lucasfilm/Star Wars Fan Club, 1987–2001)

Star Wars has always been the merchandising king. *Star Trek*, while it's been popular and has an amazing merchandising background behind it, just couldn't match it. It's always interesting, because as I ran the official fan clubs for both *Star Wars* and *Star Trek*, and most of the time I ran them at the same time, I had them both, so I was able to see from my perspective the kinds of interest in both of these franchises. And *Star Wars* always dwarfed *Star Trek* when it came to licensing.

Star Trek was just never able to reach the general public like *Star Wars* has. *Star Wars* has gone beyond the hardcore fanbase, and appeals to the general public in a way that *Star Trek* has never been able to do. That was the big difference, there was just so much more to get when it came to *Star Wars* than when it came to *Star Trek*. It didn't take long, when the movie became a hit. It's kind of like, "Boom, boom, boom, boom," things just start showing up left and right. I'm buying them in the stacks that my allowance would allow me to.

BRIAN JAY JONES
This deal is insane. We forget, because Lucas did it first and then essentially changed the way people look at films and marketing and merchandising, that it's so normal to us. We forget that up until that time, for the most part, movie merchandise kind of sucked. The big merchandising that had come out of a movie before were action figures based on, I think, *Willy Wonka & the Chocolate Factory*. Something terrible like that. And there was merchandising

around *Doctor Dolittle,* of all stupid things, so people were like, "Nobody wants to buy toys. They're not evergreen on the shelf." So he was lucky that merchandising before *Star Wars* had been a bust.

DALE POLLOCK

It's a big point in my book that Fox had given away the merchandising rights for the toys to Kenner for nothing, and that infuriated Lucas as much as anything. He felt that that decision had cost him hundreds of millions of dollars, which fueled part of his hatred for Fox and, later, his full control of merchandise. And because he had the ability to bring the sequels elsewhere for distribution, he got the sequel rights to stay with Fox for *Empire* and *Jedi.* They would earn 30 to 40 percent, spending nothing on production, just taking a distribution fee. It was incredibly profitable for Fox.

BRIAN JAY JONES

The narrative out there is that Lucas completely fooled them. He didn't. Fox knew there were merchandising rights and they weren't going to give them away for free, but they'd give them to him for next to nothing to use as a negotiation tool. But he gets the rights to that and then does nail down those sequel rights, which, again, is the big one. And it turns out that they're inextricably linked—importantly linked. The merchandising pays for the sequel, ultimately. But when they're negotiating stuff, Fox is like, "All right, we'll concede that you can have your sequel rights," because, again, there's no real franchises. I mean, what were the franchises before *Star Wars*? *Planet of the Apes* maybe, but it wasn't the juggernaut of *Star Wars.*

As November 1974 rolled around, Lucas hired Ralph McQuarrie to bring his artistic expertise to the film and create sketches, and eventually paintings, of key elements from Lucas's material.

RALPH MCQUARRIE

George wanted me to support his script with visuals. George felt that it was the kind of script that people weren't very impressed with. The idea seemed kind of funky; he envisioned the picture as a real visual experience, much more so than a story. It wasn't true science fiction. George called it a science fantasy, and even the fantasy aspect was nontraditional. He had a lot of ideas. He had comic book pages and other source material he wanted me to see. Once I got to work, he liked what I was doing and he would come by every once in a while to check up on things. My ideas seemed to be in line with his. George was very specific about most of the work.

IRVIN KERSHNER
(director, *The Empire Strikes Back*)

Ralph is incredible. He's not just a great technician, he has a very lucid mind. There's simply no waste there. He thinks on two levels at once: the dramatic and the specific.

GEORGE LUCAS

There was a lot of design work that had to be done, but I also deliberately wrote *Star Wars* to be within the state of technology and within the realm of how I could make it at a reasonable price. It's designed for no costume changes. There are a lot of tricks in that movie that are done to cut costs way down. I wrote it with all that stuff in mind. When you really look at it, it takes place in the desert and on a Death Star. That's it.

RALPH MCQUARRIE

I think we had four paintings when we first went into Fox. We used the two robots coming across the desert, the lightsaber duel, the stormtroopers in the hall with drawn lightsabers, and the attack on the Death Star. He liked these paintings and they embodied what he was interested in putting across on the screen. I think it gave him a chance to develop his ideas at his leisure, so to speak, rather than working in the heat of production where you've got a lot of people involved and money's being spent at great rates. Then he would've had to struggle with production designers and all kinds of craftsmen. I don't think that he necessarily felt he had to engage an expensive production designer at this preliminary stage, because he had his own ideas. George could have drawn everything himself, literally. He draws quite well, laboriously and a little bit crudely, but he can draw. But George had very specific ideas and while he was working on the script, Gary Kurtz was trying to find people who could do all these props. Colin Cantwell came in to do the models, and I would go to his studio and photograph his models as they were in progress. I put those into the paintings as well as I could. When they got updated, sometimes I changed the paintings.

On January 28, 1975, Lucas completed a second draft of the film's screenplay, now titled Episode One in the Adventures of the Starkiller. *A third draft was completed on August 1, a fourth on January 6, 1976.*

JOHN L. FLYNN

The new story was set in the Republic Galactica, which was ravaged by civil war, and focused on a quest for the Kyber Crystal, a powerful energy source that controlled the Force of Others. Fans of Alan Dean Foster's *Star Wars* novel *Splinter of the Mind's Eye* will no doubt recognize the reference to the crystal. The roll-up concluded with a prophetic promise: "In times of greatest despair there shall come a savior, and he shall be known as 'the Son of Suns.'" This draft finally brought George Lucas's epic vision into focus. While the story remains consistent with his original synopsis, the action, broken into three distinct locations, was certainly manageable from both an aesthetic and technical point of view. He had pared his story down, blended characters, and discarded material which would eventually comprise the other two films. Lucas had also transformed the two most endearing characters in the saga into their final forms. Darth Vader was now a Dark Lord of the Sith and the chief adversary of Luke and the forces of good. Han Solo is no longer a green-skinned alien (like the bounty hunter Greedo), but a young Corellian pirate. In fact, Solo's character is drawn as a thinly disguised version of George's own mentor, Francis Ford Coppola. And although the Kyber Crystal would ultimately be dropped from the series (as the physical embodiment of the Force), Lucas had found the central impetus upon which the action would turn. Hitchcock often referred to it as a "MacGuffin."

Lucas now also knew that this story was only part of a much greater whole. He sent a synopsis of the screenplay to Alan Ladd, Jr. The Fox executive greeted the draft with much enthusiasm, but questioned him about the other episodes. It seemed strange to everyone—but Lucas—to start a motion picture in the middle of the action.

While writing and revising the various drafts of the screenplay for *Star Wars*, Lucas had kept changing his mind as to the focus of the story. He scribbled out in longhand on specially selected blue-and-green-lined paper various story synopses. Between drafts one and two he wrote a prequel of sorts which dealt with Luke's father and his relationship to Darth Vader and Ben Kenobi. George decided he didn't like it, and wrote a completely different treatment with Luke as the central figure. The plot was not all that different from the second screenplay (or the finished film, for that matter), but featured Han Solo as Luke's older, battle-weary brother. He returns to Tatooine to enlist Luke in the rescue of their father, an old Jedi Knight. At one point Lucas even toyed with the idea of making Luke a young girl who fell in love with Solo. The climactic assault by hundreds of Wookiees [now the final spelling of the species' name] on the Death Star remained unchanged. Several revisions later, he knew he had enough material to make several motion pictures. He determined that the first trilogy would tell the story of a young Jedi named Ben Knovi as well as Luke's father and the betrayal of Darth Vader. The series would be set twenty years before the action in *Star Wars*. The middle trilogy would feature Luke as a young man struggling to learn about the Force, and the final three films would focus on Luke as an adult helping to dismantle the last remnants of the Empire. The whole saga would take place over a sixty-year period, with C-3PO and R2-D2 as the common narrative thread to the whole series.

ERIC TOWNSEND

Lucas wrote a six-page synopsis, entitled "The Adventures of Luke Starkiller—Episode One: The Star Wars," for Alan Ladd, Jr., in May 1975. In some ways, this was a summation of the second draft of the story, with several notable changes. The biggest change is the reintroduction of Princess Leia, as the damsel-in-distress that must be rescued, a familiar storyline in the series and fairy tales that Lucas loved as a child. "The Starkiller" becomes a character of legend that was killed off long before the new story begins. With Leia back in the story, the character of Luke Starkiller also switches back to being a young boy. It was here that the idea of both characters being twins first emerged, since the two of them were essentially developed out of one. Around this time, Lucas also began compiling pages of typed notes that included an early version of Ben Kenobi, then known as the "Old Man."

MARK HAMILL
(actor, "Luke Skywalker")

There was still confusion about Luke's name when we were in production. We had a scene where we actually had to say my name. Leia says, "Aren't you a little short to be a stormtrooper?" and I go, "Huh?" I remove my helmet and go, "I'm Luke Skywalker, I'm here to rescue you." Rather matter of factly, as per the script. But we had shot that scene before we changed my name to Luke Skywalker. So I saw on my call sheet and I said, "Wait a minute, is this scene 38, or whatever?" They said that to my dresser and he said, "Oh, yeah, they've got to do that again." And I said, "Why?" He said, "I don't know. I think they changed the name." I thought, "Well, if they want to change the name, they should just go to an angle over my shoulder and I can dub it." But George wanted that moment where I throw off my helmet in a medium close-up. And I said, "What did they change my name to?" And he said, "I heard the name Luke Skywalker." Mind you, for four or five weeks, whatever it was, from when I read it, to Africa back to England when we were shooting the main scenes, I was another name. I was Luke Starkiller. That seemed, to me, kind of tough. And I liked that. And they said, "We don't like the word kill in your name. It's too negative." And I said, "So what did they change it to? Luke Skywalker?" It sounded like Luke Flyswatter. I was just rankled. It was like getting used to a certain thing and people want to change it. Now it's the other way around. Luke Starkiller sounds wrong.

JOHN L. FLYNN

The third draft of the script was completed on August 1, and it demonstrates Lucas's command and final understanding of his great saga. Even though the dialogue is still somewhat crude, it captures the spirit and imagination that would become the *Star Wars* movie. Now all Lucas had to do was polish some rough edges and rethink his notions about the Force. He would eventually jettison the Kyber Crystal in the fourth screenplay, and convey the Force in metaphysical terms. He would have the fourth draft in March of 1976, which was the one Lucas chose to film. The narrative covers most of the action in the movie, with two important deletions. In the script, Biggs, who is now Luke's older friend, returns to Tatooine to discuss the Space Academy and his decision to join the rebels in their war against the Empire. This scene was actually filmed, but later trimmed during the final editing of the motion picture.

GEORGE LUCAS

Basically, the [Biggs/Luke deleted Tatooine sequence] didn't work. That whole thing came about because I had a lot of friends who read the script and said, "Oh, this isn't going to work. This is terrible. You're just making *THX* all over again. It's all about robots and things. You got to put people in this thing. For the first twenty minutes, there's no people." And, I was, "Uh-huh, okay." So I put Luke in very early, but then we cut it together and it didn't work. So I put it back the way it was originally intended which is for the first twenty minutes it just had the droids in it.

JOHN L. FLYNN

The other sequence cut from the film details Han's negotiations with Jabba the Hutt prior to his liftoff from Tatooine. Again, parts of this sequence were filmed, but later discarded, only to be retrieved and updated digitally for the Special Edition released in 1997. Lucas also changed Luke's surname from Starkiller to Skywalker and took out any references to the Kyber Crystal or Leia's witch-like powers. Additionally, Ben Kenobi was originally going to live, but Lucas decided at the last moment to kill him off. The final product of *Star Wars* is a testament to Lucas's persistence and creative imagination.

ERIC TOWNSEND

It was during the writing of this third draft that Lucas made a conscious effort to steer the story into more of a traditional fantasy/fairy-tale structure. Those elements were always a part of the story, but he began to simplify and focus them into something that an audience would more easily identify with. Scenes were added showing Luke hanging out with friends in the town of Anchorhead, Darth Vader is mentioned as being a one-time disciple of Ben Kenobi, who had stolen one of Kenobi's Kyber Crystals at the battle of Condawn. It also mentions the Clone Wars for the very first time, stating that Kenobi had fought in the battle and kept a diary of the conflict.

The fourth draft, titled The Adventures of Luke Starkiller as Taken from the Journal of the Whills, Saga 1: The Star Wars, *includes additional backstory for Darth Vader including the connection to Ben Kenobi and Luke's father. The backstory between Vader and Kenobi included a duel between the two which ends with Vader falling into a volcanic pit, necessitating the special suit and breathing mask. The additional Sith Lords that were seen in previous drafts were cut from this story, as well as the Kyber Crystals. The parts of the story that took place in the Alderaan prison now take place on the Death Star itself. "The Force of Others" becomes simply "the Force."*

RAY MORTON

As everyone knows, and Lucas himself freely admits, he's not the greatest writer of dialogue, leading to the wonderful Harrison Ford crack: "George, you can type this shit, but you sure can't say it." To help him polish the speeches in his screenplay, Lucas brought in his old friends and cowriters on the Oscar-nominated script for *American Graffiti*: Gloria Katz and Willard Huyck. Katz and Huyck had a great talent for penning clever, witty dialogue, and they were extremely adept at writing both period and genre material with a modern spin. Katz and Huyck polished the dialogue, added a lot of humor, and helped flesh out the characters, most notably that of Princess Leia and making her tougher and more formidable. While they can't be considered cowriters of *Star Wars* on an equal basis with Lucas the way they were on *Graffiti*, their contribution was significant and extremely valuable.

By October 1975, it seemed that preproduction had hit a road bump: the Fox board of directors brought things to a halt, demanding that the budget be lowered to $7.5 million. In response, Lucas began revising the script to cut costs to lower the budget. In order to appease the Powers That Be, Lucas was able to reduce the budget to $7 million.

THOMAS PARRY
(studio executive, United Artists, 1974-77)

When *Star Wars* was in development at Fox, Dennis Stanfill, who was the chairman of Fox, put it into turnaround where the studio decides not to make the picture, but they put money into development, they give it back to the filmmaker. The filmmaker then has a period of time to go out and find somebody else to make it, and if that other studio chooses to make it, the original studio gets paid back for their investment. So, Dennis Stanfill puts *Star Wars* into turnaround, because the budget had climbed from nine million to eleven million dollars. And he thought it's too much of a risk for us. So, George Lucas, who had been Mike Medavoy's client when he was a talent manager, calls up Mike [who was then president] at United Artists and says, "I got this script in turnaround, I'd like to send it over to you." So, it was the end of the day—and I knew nothing about any of this—Mike calls me into his office and throws the script at me and says, "Read this tonight." So, I read *Star Wars*.

What I remember so much about the script was, in the back of the script was about ten to twelve pages of all the production designs. All of the renderings of the sets. I went home, and I read it, and I wrote up a memo: "I think we might want to do this, because it might have the same kind of franchise possibilities that the James Bond franchise had."

By the time Mike and Marcia [Nasatir] read it, Tom Pollock—George's attorney—called up Dennis Stanfill and said, "George can cut two million dollars out of the budget if you'd be willing to make the picture for nine million again. However, the deal we'd make would be different." And Dennis said, "Well, what would that deal be?" And Tom said, "Well, we want all the sequel/remake rights." And, at the time, there were no sequels, there were no remakes. And they wanted all the rights to the characters. All the merchandising rights. So Dennis Stanfill thought, "Wow, what a great deal for us." And I see Dennis every once in a while, and I have yet to actually have this conversation with him—it's probably the single most embarrassing thing to happen to him in his life. Because that two-million-dollar savings, it cost that studio several billion dollars.

BRIAN JAY JONES

The board was like, "What is your boy wonder doing here, Alan? He's going to wreck us all." So at the front end of that, they thought that this film was going to be a failure, and when it wasn't a failure, they were like, "What was our take on that?" And Ladd's like, "Nine percent," or whatever it was, and that's when it hit the fan.

I think Lucas understood that Ladd was the one who had his back, and thank God he did, because Ladd is the one who was willing to stand up to the board. It's almost like when you're sitting in a meeting and you've got this one guy who's looking at his watch going, "Just spoke with him. He's five minutes away, I promise you." And then five minutes later he's like, "No, no, he just texted me, he's three minutes away." Ladd is doing this to the board the whole time during *Star Wars*: "He's got it under control. He's a little over budget, but he's got it under control." Then the next minute he's like, "Again, he's slightly over," but Ladd is holding it together for Lucas. I think Lucas understood and appreciated that.

GEORGE LUCAS

I was twenty-eight when I did *Star Wars*. I was working in England, and I was doing a film that nobody understood, in a genre that nobody liked, in a country where film was fading fast—so it was not an easy experience. Many of the crew didn't like me—I was American, and I was young. Most people thought it was a joke. I had very little money, and a studio on my back all the time. It was very difficult. And I had come off two pictures that had been recut after I finished, so I had this fear that the studio was going to take my movie away and recut it.

ERIC TOWNSEND

The producers were up against a wall, since filming was to begin on March 28, 1976, in the desert. Lucas began trying to cut costs and wherever possible, eliminating or combining scenes, shrinking the size of Ben Kenobi's home, to moving docking bays indoors and completely cutting the cloud city of Alderaan. The budget delays affected production personnel as well. Director of photography Geoffrey Unsworth backed out of the picture and was replaced with Gilbert Taylor. Editor Richard Chew was dropped in favor of local editor John Jympson.

CHRISTIAN GOSSETT
(comic book artist, *Tales of the Jedi*)
Creative limitation. The Death Star was one set. Ask the guys over there, and they'll say, "You know the Death Star was one set? We reused things." The pillars that Luke hangs his grappling hook on were in the Blockade Runner and turned sideways. When you've got to work like that, there's a certain sense that comes to the artist and you get really interesting things. The great films you can predict. That's just one thing, but also classic film is classic film. You never really know or people would make classics every time, but you can watch the great films and they don't date like that. You look at *Casablanca*,

and, sure, it's a forties film, but you could watch it any day and it's amazing. *Star Wars* has that, all three [original] *Star Wars*.

Lucas also turned down an offer to finally make Apocalypse Now *with Francis Ford Coppola. After* The Godfather Part II, *Coppola could afford to finally make his film. Part of Lucas's decision to reject the offer was based on the fan mail he was receiving in regards to* American Graffiti.

JONATHAN RINZLER

At one point he was making *Star Wars,* and Coppola came to him and said, "You can make *Apocalypse Now,* you can get the money to make it." So George had a choice between *Apocalypse Now* and *Star Wars.* George had done two films up to that point, he had done *THX 1138* and *American Graffiti. THX* depressed everyone and no one went to go see it. *American Graffiti* was this huge sleeper-hit, and he was getting hundreds of letters from people saying that movie changed their lives and they had been suicidal and they wanted to go on living, so Lucas decided he didn't want to make a depressing movie about the Vietnam War, he'd rather go on making a fairy tale, because he liked it better. So Coppola went off to make *Apocalypse Now.*

And Lucas's decision to pursue a fairy tale paid off: on December 13, 1975, the 20th Century Fox board of directors officially gave the green light to The Star Wars *and approved the $7 million budget. The film survived nearly entirely through the support of Alan Ladd, Jr., who still believed in the project.*

ERIC TOWNSEND

At the start of 1976, Lucas was still refining the film's screenplay, turning in a fourth draft titled *The Adventures of Luke Starkiller as Taken from the Journal of the Whills, Saga 1: The Star Wars.* This draft features additional backstory for Darth Vader, including a connection to Ben Kenobi and Luke's father. Meanwhile, casting got underway and so did preparations to organize things in England for the shoot. On top of that, the contract between Lucas and Fox was signed only a week prior to the commencement of shooting, driving home the fact that this whole thing could have fallen apart at any time.

As to the casting for the film, many of the actors were selected during a joint casting session for Lucas and Brian De Palma, the latter looking for actors for his adaptation of Stephen King's Carrie *(the first movie made from the author's work).*

BRIAN JAY JONES

Lucas is like Jim Henson in the sense of finding solutions to weird problems hidden in plain sight, so much to the effect that people just take it for granted when they do it this way now. One of the things Jim Henson did was he would actually tape what the camera saw right next to the camera, in what they now call the Media Village, and he would never look through the eyepiece. He would just watch the monitor, so he knew exactly what the camera was seeing, and everybody does that now. And Lucas does this with casting in that he tapes everybody, which makes perfect sense, but wasn't common back then. Now everybody is like, "You want to see how everybody looks thrown together and how they actually look on tape, not just sitting there in a room with them." So that, I think, is one of the cool and weird innovations with him and casting. He's like, "I'm taping them all," and he sits there in a room for months and months running every Hollywood A- and B-lister and C-lister, even, through that room to read.

It's very interesting that he had two different final casts going. He's got the one we know, then he's got the one with Terri Nunn, Christopher Walken, and somebody else as Luke. He even got the two final casts of three to play off of each other, and asked his friends which they felt worked better. People were like, "Christopher Walken is a little too quirky. That other cast is a little more fun than that one. And with Terri Nunn, you're dealing with a minor and will have to stop filming every day for a certain amount of time." But it's interesting to get down to basically two sets of finalists, which—and I hate to admit knowing this, because it's a little bit embarrassing—is the same thing they did with *The Brady Bunch*. There were blonde kids and black hair kids and it was going to depend on who was cast as the parents. A dark-haired Joyce Bulifant could have been Carol Brady. So Lucas essentially has got two different versions of the "Brady Kids" going. He took the advice from his friends seriously. Thinking it through, sometimes you don't know how much of it is apocryphal, like when he talked about casting Glynn Turman as a black Han Solo and a Japanese Princess Leia, and he's like, "I knew I was going to put them together and thought that might be a little much." And I'm like, "Did you really know that at the time you were making the first film?" I don't believe that.

CARRIE FISHER
(actress, "Princess Leia Organa")

George cast an ensemble piece, the three of us together. Apparently, there were another three in case we didn't work, but at no time would it have been mix and match. We didn't get along just like that. We carefully psyched each other out. Harrison used to yell at me for not being able to decide where to eat and Mark and I used to sing TV jingles together, but with suspicion. It took us about a week to decide exactly what George saw in the three of us together.

JOHN L. FLYNN

The inspiration for many of the characters in the *Star Wars* saga comes from many of the sources George consulted while writing the first film. Whereas the characters themselves may have undergone various changes in gender and form, their basic personalities remain firmly rooted in mythic or literary traditions. Lucas studied dozens of ancient legends, including King Arthur; read a variety of fantasy and science fiction stories, including Tolkien's *Lord of the Rings* trilogy; and isolated the most common elements of archetypal characters in an effort to produce a story that is somewhat universal. It's fascinating to view these characters in hindsight, to see how certain premises and personalities were kept intact and how others were transformed or simply abandoned.

DAN MADSEN

When I interviewed [George Lucas]—I must have interviewed him . . . so many times for the Lucasfilm Fan Club—and every time I flew out to Skywalker Ranch, and met him in his office in the main house, we'd sit there for probably forty-five minutes to do the interviews. And he told me one time, that his initial concept for Luke and Leia—and this is in one of his interviews that's in the Lucasfilm Fan Club magazine—he said, one of his original ideas for Luke and Leia, was that they'd be Little People. But he said, "I never could find actors that I thought could do the role justice." So he said, "I decided to change that and make them average height people," but his initial idea and concept for Luke and Leia was that they would be Little People. That blew me away when I heard that!

Sir Alec Guinness (born Alec Guinness de Cuffe) was born in London on April 2, 1914, to Agnes Cuff and a forever unidentified father. His early life was spent at boarding schools at Pembroke Lodge, in Southbourne, and Roborough, in Eastbourne. At the age of twenty, he entered the acting profession while still in drama school with a walk-on role in the stage play Libel, *eventually being promoted to a small speaking role when the play moved to the West End's Playhouse. Throughout the 1930s, Guinness's stage roles continued to expand, until he eventually performed his own adaptation of* Great Expectations *in 1939, where he was noticed by the then film critic, and future film director, David*

Lean, which would prove to be the most important relationship in Guinness's career.

After serving in the British Navy during World War II, Guinness began taking on film roles, making a name for himself in Ealing comedies such as The Ladykillers *and* Kind Hearts and Coronets. *David Lean hired Guinness for leading roles in 1946's* Great Expectations *and 1949's* Oliver Twist, *before offering Guinness the role he would win an Academy Award for in the 1957 classic* Bridge on the River Kwai. *Future roles in 1962's* Lawrence of Arabia *and 1965's* Doctor Zhivago *cemented Guinness as one of the finest actors of his generation. But by the mid-1970s, his career had slowed, which led to Guinness agreeing to star as the aged Jedi Master, Obi-Wan Kenobi. Of course, Guinness only agreed once 20th Century Fox doubled their initial salary offer, and to pay him 2.25 percent of the royalties George Lucas made off the film—amounting to, in today's dollars, over $95 million for all three films.*

JOHN L. FLYNN

Throughout the many rewrites, Luke Skywalker's thoughtful old mentor who appears as a "shabby old desert rat" was to have been the central role in the piece. Lucas saw the character of Ben Kenobi (aka Obi-Wan Kenobi) as a cross between Gandalf the Wizard in *Lord of the Rings,* Merlin the Magician, and the Samurai swordsman often played by Toshiro Mifune. In fact, Lucas first imagined Mifune in the role of Ben Kenobi, but later went with Alec Guinness when he realized that distinguished actor was available for the part. He wanted Ben to be a kind and powerful wizard who had a certain dignity and could influence the weak-minded. As first envisioned, Kenobi was probably the early General Skywalker and then, in later drafts, Kane Starkiller, an anonymous "seer," and finally the crazed desert hermit who was also a Jedi Master.

PETER BEALE
(UK production executive, *Star Wars*)

The person that I recommended—I wasn't the only person to recommend— was obviously Alec Guinness. I had worked with him on *Lawrence of Arabia* and on *Doctor Zhivago*. He was amazing. On *Zhivago*, he had to play a range of people, so when he arrived in Madrid, he arrived with a chest wig, so that he could work as a young student with his shirt open (I don't think he had any hair on his chest naturally), but he could do it. As you can see from the performance, he treated the performance with enormous respect and care.

It wasn't easy to get him, because up to that point space films and sci-fi were "B" movies. The only "A" movie was *2001* and that was intellect. That was different. It was put in a special category. The word was that we were making a "B" special effects cowboy movie. Alec Guinness's agent didn't want him to be in a "B" movie. It took a lot of careful negotiation and careful meetings and saying we hoped to make something better than that, and obviously financial terms. Later on, he was asked about the part, and he said it wasn't his favorite part, when you look at his body of work, which was so extraordinary. The fact that we remember him for *Star Wars* irked him a little bit, but his *Star Wars* earnings gave him the ability to decide what he wanted in the future.

MARK HAMILL

I asked Sir Alec one time, "Why would you want to do a movie like this?" I couldn't believe that we were able to get an actor of his stature. And he said that he always imagined himself playing a wizard in a film for children. I think you noticed the influence, because later when they did *Superman,* they used that same predicate for an actor with gravitas, Marlon Brando, and then you get away with casting a bunch of unknowns in the leading roles.

DAVID PROWSE
(on-set actor, "Darth Vader," *Star Wars*)

I did all the sword fighting. Alec Guinness did it all as well. We rehearsed it and rehearsed it and rehearsed it for about two weeks. And every five minutes we had, we used to go off and rehearse it a little bit more. It was actually filmed in three specific sequences. We did it three or four times, then we did a master shot. And then his close-up and my close-up. Also, I think we had a long shot of the fight going on. The main problems were that every time the swords [lightsabers] touched, they broke. So, of course, all of that was done practically with the swords hardly touching at all.

ALEC GUINNESS
(actor, "Obi-Wan Kenobi," *Star Wars*)

My role in *Star Wars* had been described as a blend of the wizard Merlin and a Samurai warrior, and you can't beat that. Unlike most space fantasy, the characters George Lucas has created aren't cardboard. And the story is gripping. There's a quest, encounters with other forms of life, and conflict between good and evil.

ANTHONY FORREST
(actor, "Stormtrooper," *Star Wars*)

The part of the stormtrooper mind-manipulated by Ben Kenobi was really a last-minute request from George, as he needed someone to play the scene with Alec Guinness. I was at the hotel when they came to get me and the next thing I knew, I was on the set in a stormtrooper costume and working with Alec Guinness. As an actor, he was a true Jedi and gentleman. Well, Mark Hamill and I had gotten to know each other at the hotel, but working with Alec Guinness out of the blue, that was very special. Even years later when we were both working at the BBC on different projects he remembered, and we would chat. I remember George wanting more dirt on my costume and doing it himself. George has great detail in his work, he was so immersed in the story and what he was looking for visually, something he didn't always share, but he knows what he wants and stays true to his vision.

Carrie Frances Fisher was born on October 21, 1956, in Burbank, California. Daughter to the legendary film actress Debbie Reynolds and singer Eddie Fisher, Carrie's young life was spent as a part of the Hollywood elite. A natural bookworm, Carrie spent her early life writing poetry and short stories—a talent that would come in handy during her second career as Hollywood's unofficial go-to script doctor for everything from Star Wars Episode II: Attack of the Clones *to* The Wedding Singer.

After dropping out of high school to pursue an acting career, Carrie Fisher attended London's Center for Speech and Drama, where she stayed for eighteen months. Fisher's first taste of acting came in 1974, when she appeared as a debutante and singer in the hit Broadway revival Irene *in 1973, alongside her mother, who was in the starring role. Her first on-screen film role came with the 1975 Warren Beatty subversive satire* Shampoo, *which, although it only amounted to two scenes, showcased her ease and charisma in the acting world. But her big break came in 1975, when a young director named George Lucas saw in this diminutive five-foot-two member of Hollywood royalty the makings of the most important war hero of the Rebel Alliance.*

JOHN L. FLYNN

Leia was first conceived by Lucas as an amalgamation of Dejah Thoris from *A Princess of Mars*, Lady Galadriel of Lothlórien from *Lord of the Rings*, and Dorothy Gale from *The Wizard of Oz*. Never really named in the original story treatment, she was an eleven-year-old princess with "goddess-like" powers, who needed rescuing from Imperial troops. Subsequent drafts of the screenplay portrayed her as a sixteen-year-old princess who fell in love with Han Solo, the central male figure, and finally the twin sister to Luke Skywalker. At one point in the third draft, George Lucas even gave Leia the mind-control powers of a witch, but later revised that when she became Luke's long-lost sibling.

PETER BEALE

Obviously one imagined that Princess Leia would have to look attractive, but a lot of the costumes weren't; they were sort of semi-military, disorganized, almost Carnaby Street. We chose John Mollo as costume designer. I first met him when we did *Doctor Zhivago*. He was the expert consultant, he consulted for David Lean in all things to do with the communist revolution. The Soviets, the Russian military, the Cossack military, etc. He became a costume designer and because of his military background, we felt that he would bring something special to that area, and of course, he did.

TODD FISHER
(Carrie Fisher's brother)

Carrie got her first part in *Shampoo* and my mother, of course, didn't like the idea that Carrie was going to say to Warren Beatty, "Wanna fuck?" So my mother went over to renegotiate that deal and said to Warren, "Can't we change that line to like, 'Do you wanna screw?'" And Warren said, "No, Debbie, it's shock value here." At that point, she gave up on trying to change his mind, but she turned to Warren and said, "If you touch my daughter, I'm going to kill you." And Warren confirmed that story to me. After that, Carrie went in to audition for this little B science fiction movie going to be called *Star Wars*.

CARRIE FISHER

I don't remember when I decided I wanted to get into show business, but it was always assumed that I would do it. So I kind of went along with that assumption.

TODD FISHER

Here's the thing: Carrie was being groomed by my mother in a lot of different ways, but first and foremost, even if it was by accident, she was a bit of a Beverly Hills princess. She was born into Hollywood royalty and was raised in a very affluent, privileged life. We both were. So she walks into the room and George Lucas immediately sees a princess. The attitude is all there. I mean, make no mistake, the attitude that Carrie has in life is from my mom. It's her own version of it, because she puts her edge in it. And, of course, Carrie had evolved into an amazing intellect in her own right, but Debbie is Molly Brown. She was brought up a tomboy and punched men in the face. I saw it happen! Ninety-five pounds and knocked a man to his ass with one blow. Carrie grew up around that and you couldn't help but have it rub off on you. So Carrie does this little audition and, of course, later in the film you see it when she steps up into Moff Tarkin's face and says, "I'd recognize that foul stench anywhere." That attitude comes from her upbringing.

BRIAN JAY JONES

I love that Marcia Lucas was teasing George about when he was casting Princess Leia and that he was going to see every starlet in Hollywood coming through there, and Lucas is essentially just like a brain in a jar who could care less. Marcia is teasing him about it and he's like, "I'm going to sit here and look at 1,200 people over three weeks. Just give me a break."

CARRIE FISHER

Although I hadn't read much science fiction before, I had a kind of active space fantasy life all my own. Once I saw a science fiction movie that scared the hell out of me. I don't know what it was, but it took place on the moon. And I used to be afraid of Martians. There was an invisible Martian in that movie who was surrounded by an electric field. If you got thrown into that electric field, it was goodbye forever. It was really scary; scarier than even burglars or snipers. You can't put Martians in jail.

GEORGE LUCAS

I wanted someone tough. I didn't conceive of the Princess as just a damsel in distress. I wanted her very young, younger than Luke, but I knew she had to be able to stand up to the bad guys. She's actually in charge of the Rebellion. She's gotten caught, but she's fighting. That's why I chose Carrie Fisher.

CARRIE FISHER

I wanted to do the role of Princess Leia, because I wanted to have real conversations with people with bubbles on their heads. I just wanted to be blasé about someone sitting across from me being a "small person" or some strange-looking person who was hired through the "Ugly Agency." I love that there's an agency in London called that. I can't tell you how thrilled I was to be casually sitting around with these people as if they didn't have hair-dryer heads and things like that. I wanted to sit next to Wookiees and Jawas and droids.

Mark Richard Hamill was born in Oakland, California, to Virginia Suzanne and U.S. Navy Captain William Thomas Hamill on September 25, 1951. He was one of seven children, in a family that would move between Navy bases from Hawaii to Virginia to Japan. As such, Hamill found his best of friends were the characters in comic books and TV shows: a true fanboy from the very beginning. Hamill finally landed in Los Angeles, where he enrolled in Los Angeles City College with a major in drama.

Early roles for Hamill included a recurring role in the soap opera General Hospital *and a starring role in the short-lived comedy* The Texas Wheelers. *But it was an audition his friend Robert Englund (the future Freddy Krueger) had for the former George Lucas project* Apocalypse Now *that would change Mark Hamill's life forever. As Englund left his audition, he walked across the hall to where George Lucas himself was having auditions for* Star Wars, *and realized this role would be perfect for his friend Mark Hamill.*

Following Star Wars, *Hamill found success on the stage in* Amadeus *and* The Elephant Man, *but he found it difficult to break free of the Luke Skywalker persona on the silver screen. He gradually found work as a successful voice-over actor for animated television and film, and eventually grew to great acclaim for his performance of the Joker based on the famous DC comics character. Unexpectedly, most of all to himself, Hamill resurrected the role of Luke Skywalker in the sequel trilogy that began with 2015's* The Force Awakens.

JOHN L. FLYNN

Luke Skywalker, the hero of this space fantasy, was originally imagined as a swashbuckling freebooter like Flash Gordon or John Carter. Adept with both sabers and blasters, the character had risen to the ranks of general and Jedi Knight. In the thirteen-page summary, General Skywalker leads a rebel band of teenage boys against the Empire. By the first draft screenplay, Luke was still a general in his early sixties and the hero of the piece was now Anakin Starkiller, aged eighteen. Several revisions later, Luke was again the center of the story. He had become a teenager who must rescue his brother, Deak, from the clutches of Darth Vader. George Lucas felt there was much more room for character development if he introduced a young innocent who must grow to manhood, and kept the story central to him. By the next to final draft, Luke had become a farm boy, son of a famous Jedi Knight who must deliver R2-D2 to a rebel stronghold on a faraway planet. The evolution of his character was nearly complete; all he needed was a mentor, which he found in Obi-Wan Kenobi.

MARK HAMILL

I'm the middle of seven children. My father was in the Navy, we moved a lot. I went to nine schools in twelve years, which is a real sort of schizophrenic experience, because once you get settled in, in one school, you'd be moving from coast to coast. You'd be in San Diego and you finally find your niche, and you get transferred to New York where the sensibilities are completely different: "Look, here comes Surfer Joe!" You'd have to change your clothing and your attitude and your thought process, because you know your goal at that age anyway is just to fit in and hopefully avoid being beaten up on a regular basis. That's good enough. So now you know why I am the way I am.

I grew up on a naval base in Japan, which was the greatest film-going experience anywhere. My father was in the Navy, and they had all the movies free and first run there. They had movies even before they came out in the States, and the bill changed every night at the base theater. I learned a lot then. I saw everything. I was so fascinated with the films I even auditioned for the voice of the cartoon character Astroboy, which was made over there. I made it to the finals, but I didn't get the part. But I did get to go down to the studio and I saw giant monster feet and little models of Japanese cities waiting to be crushed. I loved that. I also loved *King Kong*. It was on television every day for a week and it just wiped me out. I was a blob of jelly at the end. My parents finally had to order me not to see it anymore. *King Kong* was to me what *Gone with the Wind* was to girls.

When I heard about *Star Wars,* I thought if they were making a big space fantasy movie, I'd be satisfied just to watch part of it being shot. I even asked my agent if she could get me onto the set. I wanted to see some of the special effects being done. I wasn't thinking of acting in it.

BRIAN JAY JONES

Mark Hamill read very early and he just thinks that he's blown it. It's amazing that, thank God, you've got somebody like Fred Roos sitting in the room who's like, "You remember the kid you saw early on? You might want to talk with him again."

MARK HAMILL

When I was auditioning, I thought, "Are we doing a Mel Brooks–ian send-up of Flash Gordon?" So I tested with Harrison Ford and I thought to myself, "This is like Buck Rogers and Harrison is Buck and I'm his kid sidekick." I didn't even know the story was actually from Luke's point of view.

GEORGE LUCAS

Mark Hamill was young, fun-loving, slightly naïve, and very enthusiastic. He was just like the character he plays.

MARK HAMILL

I was doing the scene where I discovered the robots. I said my lines very big, very dramatic. George came over and went over the lines with me. He didn't give me the readings, but as he explained the intention of the scene, he was very low-key. I just watched him. I don't know why, but something in me told me to observe how he was speaking, to try to pick up his inflection. I even imitated a few of his gestures as he explained to me what he wanted me to do. At one point I thought to myself that he was doing it so small. That can't be right. I thought I'd try it very small and he would see that it didn't work. He would tell me to go back to the way I was doing it before.

So when I played the scene, I did it just like I thought George would react in the scene. When I did it like that, George called, "Cut. Print." I was flabbergasted. I thought, "Oh, I see. Of course, that was right. Luke is George. Even the names are similar, Luke-Lucas." From then on, I followed through on my feelings. I began to really feel like I was playing George. I guess if you sit down and write an adventure like this, you have to think of yourself as the main character. I actually think *Star Wars* is the adventure of George Lucas.

BRIAN JAY JONES

When you watch those audition tapes and even in interviews he does today, Mark Hamill can still recite the technobabble that Lucas gave him; he can still recite that dialogue he was given to this day and it's dialogue that wasn't even used in the movie ultimately. But it's like Lucas gave them what seems like the goofiest stuff to use as their sides on this, and he must've known what he was doing, because it obviously worked. But when you watch them, and you watch Carrie trying to do some of her stuff, it's like every line's a mouthful. Maybe he was doing that intentionally, almost like Harrison Ford said, "If you can say this shit, you'll be fine."

MARK HAMILL

When you went in, you didn't get a script; they just wanted to get a feel for who you were. I noticed there were guys that were sort of teenagers like me, and there were some middle-aged men, so they were looking at Hans and Lukes. After I passed that part, where I just talked to George, who was looking at actors with Brian De Palma, then I got the script scene in the mail and I memorized that and did a screen test on videotape with Harrison. Again, with very little knowledge. Reading the script was amazing, because even though it was a combination of so many different kinds of iconic movies— pirate movies, cowboy movies, and all of those things—it was so original. I just couldn't believe my eyes. People don't realize that when they say, "Oh, it must have been such a shock when you saw the finished film, because you don't see the special effects and all that." It was always on the page. It was a stretch and it was funny.

Ever the man with the swagger, Harrison Ford seemed destined for stardom. Though it wasn't an easy road to get there. Born on July 14, 1942, in Chicago, Illinois, Ford had a fairly traditional upbringing, with his time in the Boy Scouts of America later being an influence in the opening sequence of Indiana Jones and the Last Crusade. *As a senior in high school, he took an acting class to, as he later claimed, get over his shyness. In 1964, Ford moved to Hollywood to pursue acting, eventually being put on a $150-per-week contract with Columbia Pictures as part of their new talent program. Ford obtained small roles in film and television for the next decade, but found it difficult to break into the starring roles. Not happy with the roles being offered to him, Ford became a self-taught professional carpenter to support his then wife and two young sons.*

Ford would eventually take the small role of Bob Falfa in George Lucas's smash-hit American Graffiti, *which would prove to be the turning point in his career. In 1975, Lucas hired Ford to read lines in the casting session for* Star Wars, *with little notion of hiring the actor for a role in the movie. However, after hundreds of line-readings, with Ford bringing his characteristic charm, Lucas could not see any other actor playing the role of Han Solo.*

Ford's everyman quality, combined with larger-than-life charisma, quickly found a home in the public heart. Ford would go on to star in almost as recognizable roles of Indiana Jones, Rick Deckard, and Jack Ryan, as well as successful stand-alone features in Air Force One, Witness, *and* The Fugitive, *among many others.*

JOHN L. FLYNN

Han Solo was first introduced in the initial screenplay as a huge, green-skinned monster with gills and no nose, and only later developed into a human. Lucas probably saw Solo as an amalgamation of all the great sidekicks in literature and film, from Lancelot in the Arthurian legends to Tonto in popular culture, but he eventually evolved into a fully realized leading player. By the second screenplay, Han had been transformed into a burly individual resembling Francis Ford Coppola. Though somewhat comic in appearance with flamboyant clothes and a guinea-pig girlfriend, he was clearly a person to be reckoned with. Lucas later made him a cynical smuggler and thought of him like a James Dean, "a cowboy in a starship: simple, sentimental and cocksure." That persona stuck to Han Solo in the first film, but he gradually emerged as a sexy Clark Gable in the subsequent films.

BRIAN JAY JONES

I've never seen Christopher Walken's Han Solo audition, but it's one of those stories that I'm almost nervous about bringing up, because it's one of those things that's almost too good to be true. But you have enough people who were in his circle at the time who talked about seeing it. But why hasn't footage come out after all this time? You'd think they'd be like, "Just release that one. It's a novelty act." I would love to see Christopher Walken doing Han Solo.

What's really interesting is when you watch Harrison in his takes, you can see that this is a guy who was brought in to sit there and read lines with people and they weren't necessarily going to use them. He looks like he does not need this shit. At the same time, that's the moment where everyone's like, "This is the guy you need, because this is Han Solo; he doesn't need this shit." Because he's very relaxed, he's very nonchalant on this. Every line that gets delivered, he's basically rolling his eyes at the other characters. I mean, it's perfect. Again, largely Fred Roos can claim responsibility for that. Harrison has got this very casual and cool cowboy read to his lines and it's perfect. All these years later he's finally lightened up and accepted, "You know what? You are Han Solo. It's going to be the first line of your epitaph, dude, so get used to it." There is a line in *The Force Awakens* when Han Solo says, "The Jedi, the Force, it's true. All of it." I can't even say that line without choking up. It's fantastic and he's perfect at it, and when I'm watching it, it's the scene where you go, "There's Harrison Ford's moment of acceptance."

Peter Cushing was already known the world over for his genre work in Hammer horror films, and playing the roles of Sherlock Holmes and Dr. Who in both cinema and television, but it would prove to be the relatively small role of the evil Grand Moff Tarkin for which he would be best remembered. Born in Surrey, England, on May 26, 1913, to a quantity surveyor and a daughter of a carpet merchant, Cushing was not destined to be a successful actor. However, the viewing of a stage production of Peter Pan *during a Christmas season of his youth instilled in him the fantastical possibilities of acting—a dream he would never let go of. While in school, Cushing would often skip class to help build sets for school play productions, something he would continue to do for years after as he worked a dead-end job as a surveyor's assistant. It wasn't until 1935 that Cushing pursued an acting career full time, appearing in several small parts and working as a stagehand for the Southampton Rep.*

In 1939, Cushing left for Hollywood with only £50 to his name. He obtained his first role as an on-screen stand-in for 1939's The Man in the Iron Mask, *playing opposite the lead actor, before shooting the same scene again from the opposite position, and then compositing the two takes together to give the appearance of the lead actor playing two roles. Cushing did not receive credit. Cushing's first major role came as the second male lead in the 1940 Carole Lombard vehicle* The Vigil of Night.

He returned to England during World War II and found work on the screen and stage there for several years. Work was hard to find following the war, but Cushing finally gained critical praise in the role of Mr. Darcy in a 1952 television production of Pride and Prejudice *for the BBC and in 1954's controversial production of* Nineteen Eighty-Four. *Following this, he came to notoriety for starring in a number of low-budget horror movies by Hammer Films. His first outing in the starring role of Victor Frankenstein, in* The Curse of Frankenstein, *was such an overnight success that Hammer Films contracted Cushing to star in a series of low-budget horror films, adapting classic works such as* Frankenstein, Dracula, *and possibly his favorite role of Sherlock Holmes in* The Hound of the Baskervilles. *By 1975, Cushing's career was peaking, as he received an offer to star as the villain in a science fiction/fantasy film titled* Star Wars.

PETER CUSHING
(actor, "Grand Moff Tarkin")

Over the years, I've played very few evil and sinister parts. Baron Frankenstein, however ruthless he may be, isn't evil—but Grand Moff Tarkin certainly is. If I remember correctly, I have a scene in which I convince Princess Leia to divulge some information to me, in return for which I'll spare a "planetoid" or something on which some of the rebel army is hiding. Now you know what's coming. She gives me the information . . . and I turn calmly and have the planet blown up. Now that's a bad guy. I don't play too many of them. But on those rare occasions I play one, I don't try to find some way to get out of playing him as the villain he is.

The challenge in that scene was trying to keep the audience from guessing whether I would keep my promise to the Princess, or have the rebels annihilated. It's only a few seconds, but the least wrong move, just a slight change of expression, really, and the audience can catch on. *Star Wars* was made on two levels, really—for audiences who had grown up on the old Saturday matinee serials, and children for whom it was an entirely new experience. But that alone wasn't the key to its success. It was brilliantly made. George Lucas and all the wonderful technicians who helped him create the illusion really knew what they were doing.

CARRIE FISHER

In our first scene together, I had to open by saying, "Grand Moff Tarkin—I thought I detected your foul stench," or something like that, and it took real acting, boy, 'cause two minutes before, Cushing was generously telling me where my key light was, where to stand so he wouldn't upstage me . . . doing all he could to help a nervous actress in her first major, starring role.

PETER CUSHING

Well, there was nothing extraordinary or unusual about the way I was offered the film. George Lucas and his partners offered it to me the same way I am offered every film I appear in. They sent a script and a letter to my agent, with an offer.

CARRIE FISHER

I liked Peter Cushing so much that it was almost impossible for me to feel the hatred I needed to act against him. I had to say lines like, "I recognize your foul stench," but the man smelt like linen and lavender. I couldn't say that to this nice English man whom I adored. So I substituted in my mind the one person I hate.

PETER CUSHING

Dear Carrie was so sweet about it. She later told the press how difficult it was for her to say that line convincingly, since I really smelled like lavender water. You see, I always lavishly slosh lavender water all over myself whenever I'm filming. I will also use a tube of Colgate Dental Cream, because I'm very conscious of bad breath. In fact, if I'm watching a boring love scene in a movie, I can't help thinking, "I do hope they've both brushed their teeth."

MARK HAMILL

When we were making the film, I thought I'd never get to meet Peter Cushing, because I didn't have any scenes with him. So I made sure I went in and got to meet him. I did some research ahead of time and this is before the internet, where you actually had to go to the library and read books. He was really surprised that I knew one of his first movie parts was the Laurel and Hardy film *A Chump at Oxford*. He said to me, "How did you know that?" He was thrilled that I knew that.

PETER CUSHING

The challenge to an actor in these weird parts is enormous, and I like that. The depth of such roles rests on a combination of one's own imagination and the ways in which one looks on a particular character. I stress the human element, the sadness, the loneliness of evil.

MARK HAMILL

When I met Christopher Lee—I was on something that he was in—I kept saying to myself, "Don't ask him about Dracula, don't ask him about Dracula, don't ask him about Dracula," and what did I do? I asked him about Dracula and he pointed out some of the other famous roles he played. I felt terrible, because he was an actor of incredible range and I more than anyone should know what it's like to be so associated with one role.

PETER CUSHING

Horror movies give so much pleasure, and giving pleasure is why I wanted to do *Star Wars*. It's fantasy. People can experience emotions watching it that they can't experience in their ordinary lives.

MARK HAMILL

I always wondered why he had this lavender glove and his dresser told me, "Because when he smokes, he doesn't want to get the nicotine or its fragrance on his fingers and transfer them when he shakes your hand." I said, "Oh my God, we don't have anybody that polite in America." People smoke cigars in elevators.

GEORGE LUCAS

Peter Cushing, like Alec Guinness, is a very good actor. He got an image that is in a way quite beneath him, but he's also idolized and adored by young people and people who go to see a certain kind of movie. I think he will be remembered fondly for the next 350 years at least. And so you say, is that worth anything? Maybe it's not Shakespeare, but certainly equally as important in the world.

PETER CUSHING

By the way, can you possibly tell me what a "Grand Moff" is? Sounds vaguely subversive.

Prior to portraying the most domineering villain in cinema history, the late David Prowse was a bodybuilder from a small housing estate in Bristol, born on July 1, 1935. His early jobs included a dance hall bouncer and a helper at a swim club. His interest in bodybuilding began at an early age, culminating in winning the British Heavyweight weightlifting championship in 1962. The notoriety gained from his bodybuilding allowed Prowse to transition into acting, with roles as Frankenstein's monster in Hammer films The Horror of Frankenstein *and* Frankenstein and the Monster from Hell, *as well as small roles in* Casino Royale *and* A Clockwork Orange, *where he was first noticed by George Lucas. At six foot six, Prowse had the shape and build to be the formidable Sith Lord George Lucas was looking for in his sci-fi epic. Although happy to take the role of Darth Vader, Prowse has notoriously talked down his acting experiences, always feeling he deserved more responsibility and trust than he was given—even as to suggest his potent district West Country accent deserved to be the voice of Darth Vader.*

The voice that would echo through film history, James Earl Jones could never have thought the small voice-over role he took in 1976 would end up being the role he was most identified with. James Earl Jones was born in Mississippi on January 17, 1931, to Ruth (Williams) Jones, a teacher and maid, and Robert Earl Jones, a boxer, butler, and chauffeur. Jones was sent to live with his grandparents in Michigan at age five, as his father had left soon after Jones was born, and his mother found it difficult to financially and personally manage. He found the transition difficult, and developed a vocal stutter—an affliction he still grapples with to this day, despite years of hard work to remove it.

After serving in the military just after the Korean War ended, Jones began to act in several theater shows around the Michigan area. He eventually grew in prominence for his stage work, winning a Tony Award in 1969 for his performance in The Great White Hope. *Jones's first film role came in 1967's* Dr. Strangelove or: How I Learned to Stop Worrying and Love the Bomb. *Starring roles came in both television and film in the years after, for such projects as* The Great White Hope *(an adaptation of the hit theatrical play),* The UFO Incident, Conan: The Barbarian, *and* Field of Dreams, *giving Jones both audience and critical acclaim. But some of his most iconic roles come from his work as a voice-over actor: for 1994's* The Lion King, *and for* Star Wars, *in which he voiced Darth Vader.*

JOHN L. FLYNN

Darth Vader was conceived by George Lucas as the epitome of evil, the Black Knight in the Arthurian tales or Sauron from *Lord of the Rings*. Though he does not appear in any form in the original treatment, the character had two roles in the first draft screenplay: General Darth Vader and Valorum. In early drafts of the screenplay, Vader (under the name Captain Dodona) was an intergalactic bounty hunter who was hired to track down and murder Jedi Knights for the Emperor. Then Vader became a Dark Lord of the Sith, and Lucas created Boba Fett from that early concept of Vader as a bounty hunter. However, in the novelization of *Star Wars* and the final screenplay, the reference to Vader as some sort of bounty hunter remains. According to Obi-Wan, Vader betrayed and murdered the pilot Skywalker, then "helped the Empire hunt down and destroy the Jedi Knights." Darth Vader was also given Kane Starkiller's exoskeleton to help him survive, and a background story was worked up by Lucas to explain his severe injuries—apparently, before the specifics of the prequels were decided on, Ben Kenobi and Darth Vader fought a fierce lightsaber duel and Vader was driven into the molten lava of an active volcano. He survived, but his body was ruined and he was forced to wear an ominous black breathing mask that also hides his disfigurement, like *The Man in the Iron Mask*. Not much more is revealed about his character in the first film.

RALPH MCQUARRIE

George didn't envision Darth Vader with a mask—he said he might have his face covered with black silk. But I got worried for Vader's health, because he had to transfer to another spacecraft through outer space with stormtroopers who had armored spacesuits. George said, "Well, give him some kind of breath mask"—which he wore through all three films. George had mentioned him having to wear a helmet like a Japanese medieval warrior, one of those big flared-out helmets, and I made it somewhere between that and a German World War II helmet. In probably one day, I made all the drawings that defined Darth Vader. I was moving fast and didn't have all week to fool around with him—I had lots of other things to work on. Tusken Raiders, Jawas, and the Sandcrawler were done in those first few weeks. When I was drawing Darth Vader, George described him as someone in an airtight garment with a lot of wrapping and black bands and folds kind of fluttering. He said, "Darth Vader will be coming in like the wind, kind of sneaky, yet big and impressive."

DAVID PROWSE

I didn't have to read for it. I didn't have to do anything. In fact, they offered me two parts. They offered me the part of Darth Vader and they offered me the part of Chewbacca. Peter Mayhew wasn't even considered at that time. I said, "Tell me more about the parts." And he said, "Well, Chewbacca's like a giant teddy bear and Darth Vader's the big villain in the film." I said, "You know what you can do with Chewbacca. I'll take the big villain."

BRIAN MUIR
(sculptor, *Star Wars*)

To create the mask of Darth Vader, the plasterers molded Dave Prowse to create a plaster cast of his head and body. Having cut the head and shoulders from the rest of the body, to make it easier to handle, I used this to start the sculpting process for the now iconic Vader mask. There had to be at least a quarter inch of clay on the head at any point to allow for casting thickness and to know that it would fit on Dave's head. Once I had sculpted the mask to a finish, which was originally designed to have a front and rear section, it was handed to the plasterers to mold and cast in plaster. I then applied clay to the plaster Vader mask and sculpted the helmet.

DAVID PROWSE

I didn't see the finished costume until I arrived on set. When they put the helmet and mask on, George asked me to turn my head from left to right. I did, but the mask stayed facing forward! They took it off and intended to reduce its size. George said, "No, the mask and helmet fit perfectly with your shape and size; we'll pad the mask out with foam rubber." And this is what they did. It was really tight.

BRIAN MUIR

With any sculpt taken from a two-dimensional drawing there is always an input from the sculptor. Every sculptor works in different ways and has their own interpretations of a design. I can always tell my own work.

Prowse admits that as far as he was concerned, he was Darth Vader and didn't anticipate that his voice would ultimately be dubbed by James Earl Jones. Ultimately, Jones would get the lion's share of acclaim for immortalizing Darth Vader in celluloid and eventually an on-screen credit.

DAVID PROWSE

I did all the dialogue all the way through the film. I discussed it with George Lucas. I said, "Well, what are we going to do?" And he said, "Obviously we'll probably, what we call metalize it or robotize it." What I would do is sit down in the sound room and do every line over and then they could do what they wanted to it. But then with the finished film, I think it was a question of George deciding . . . well, I don't know whether he knew what he wanted as far as the voice was concerned. Then they just got James Earl Jones in to do it. I really never got lucky. I wouldn't mind being covered up if people gave you the credit. But now I'm covered up and I'm not getting the credit at the same time. Every time, they mention Carrie Fisher, Mark Hamill, Harrison Ford, Alec Guinness, Peter Cushing, and stop! And then it says, "The big villain of the film with the interesting voice is James Earl Jones," and that's as far as it goes.

"He was very gentle, very sweet, very easy to get along with," George Lucas remembered after the passing of Peter Mayhew. The seven-foot-three British

actor was born on May 14, 1944, in London, England. His early adult life was spent working as a hospital orderly, a position he would maintain throughout his experiences of filming the Star Wars *trilogy—he had little faith in his ability to make a career out of his acting. Mayhew gained his first acting job when the producers of the 1977 film* Sinbad and the Eye of the Tiger *discovered him from a photograph in a newspaper article about men with large feet and cast him in the role of the minotaur. Soon after, he was recommended to George Lucas as a good fit for the role of the towering gentle giant in* Star Wars.

GEORGE LUCAS

A Wookiee is a kind of a cross between a large bear, a dog, and a monkey. And he's very friendly . . . until you get him riled. I'm very fond of Wookiees. I had a Wookiee at home. Well, she wasn't quite as big as the Wookiee in *Star Wars*, but she's a Wookiee just the same. Actually, she was a dog, but she looked just like a Wookiee. She was a very big, furry dog. She looked like a panda bear, but not as big. Her name was Indiana and a Wookiee has certain dog characteristics—a Wookiee is protective, a friend, and kind of cuddly. The word came from Terry McGovern, a California disc jockey who had done some voice-over roles in my film *THX 1138*. He had improvised a line about having just run over a Wookiee in the street. I asked him if he knew what he meant when he said the word Wookiee, and he just told me that he had made it up on the spot. But I liked it and used it in the film. I guess when I was trying to name this new creature, I thought it sounded like a good description of the creature I wanted.

RALPH MCQUARRIE

George said he wanted Chewbacca to look like a lemur, so he had great big limpid eyes in some of my early sketches. George also gave me a drawing he liked from a 1930s illustrator of science fiction that showed a big apelike, furry beast with a row of female breasts down its chest. So I took the breasts off and added a bandolier and ammunition and weapons, and changed its face so it looked somewhat more like the final character and I left it at that.

PETER BEALE

For Chewbacca, we were looking for an enormously tall actor and we put a call out and couldn't find one. One of the casting people was in a pub and there's this tall man sitting on the bar stool, and she went up and talked to him and discovered that he was an actor and that's how our friend got that role. He was found, literally, in a pub.

STUART FREEBORN
(makeup supervisor, *Star Wars*)

George Lucas insisted that Chewbacca had to be eight feet tall. A woman recommended a very tall porter who worked at Croydon Hospital. I called them and they confirmed that their employee, Peter Mayhew, was seven feet four inches. So I told George, "I've found a man who is seven foot four and I think I could build him up to give you eight." George said, "Get him down and see if you think he can handle working the mechanics with his mouth and tongue, and then if you think it's okay, contact me and I'll test him out to see if he can take direction."

PETER MAYHEW
(actor, "Chewbacca," *Star Wars*)

My "acting" career started with a newspaper article. When I was at King's College in London, a reporter came down to do a story on me. He was writing an article on big feet for the *Guinness Book of Records*. He had seen me walking around and thought I'd make good copy. It attracted the attention of the producers of *Sinbad and the Eye of the Tiger* and they asked me if I would be the minotaur and as I knew my height would come in useful for some purpose, I jumped at the opportunity. A lot of the crew on the film would eventually find themselves on *Star Wars* and I'd got to know them really well. One of the makeup chaps forwarded my name to Gary Kurtz when he found out what they wanted for the movie.

STUART FREEBORN

So Peter Mayhew came in and I told him what he had to do. He was quite an intelligent fellow and said, "That's fine, I can manage that." Then I phoned George and said, "He seems great to me." So George sent his assistant down to pick him up, and he tested him. George phoned me and said, "I think he'll do fine." So that's how he came about. And then I built this extra four inches on his head and four inches on his feet and I got him up to eight feet exactly.

PETER MAYHEW

The only problem with playing Chewbacca was the extreme heat of the costume. It was a one-piece suit with a zipper up the back, knitted out of yak and mohair. The mask was fiberglass, which had been cast from my own face. There was no trouble there as it was all ironed out in the planning stages. I could move easily and I soon got used to the heat. In the garbage disposal scenes, there was a ridge built on the set which I stayed on as they didn't want to get this expensive suit wet and dirty.

The late Kenny Baker was born in Birmingham, England, on August 28, 1934. After a time in boarding school, the three-foot-eight Baker was approached by a woman on the street and asked to join a theatrical troupe of dwarfs and midgets. Baker agreed and soon found success as a comedian and performer in ice skating shows. He formed a successful comedy act called the Minitones with entertainer Jack Purvis and played in nightclubs. While working with Purvis and the Minitones, Baker was selected by George Lucas to operate R2-D2, but only on the condition that Purvis would be hired for a role as well, which ended up being the lead Jawa. Baker's other films include The Elephant Man, Time Bandits, Willow, Flash Gordon, Amadeus, *and Jim Henson's* Labyrinth.

PETER BEALE

Initially we thought that R2-D2 would be all mechanical, and when we started doing some early interface between the special effects people pressing buttons and the actors, it just didn't work. There was something missing, and I don't remember whose idea it was to get a midget, a small person, but we did put one inside, and Kenny Baker brought us spontaneousness and interactivity that we could get from a mechanical person.

KENNY BAKER
(actor, "R2-D2")

They offered me the part, but when I work I have to consider my partner. We had been together for fifteen years. At the same time, we were due to appear on the British talent TV show *Opportunity Knocks* and we were convinced stardom was just around the corner. We didn't want to commit ourselves to a film for six months when we could anticipate a lot of lucrative bookings. I turned the film down four times for that reason. Les Dilley, production designer John Barry's assistant, persuaded me to do it. My partner played one of the Jawas who collected the robots for scrap metal.

Being contained in the R2-D2 shell certainly presented some challenges, though Baker was more than able to navigate the exigencies of it.

KENNY BAKER

The head was on a swivel, like a ring on the top that was loose with holes in it so that the spikes on the helmet could slot in. The whole thing moved on graphite. It wasn't fixed, though. If I moved it around quickly, it would lift off. That's why I wasn't in the robot when it fell over in the desert. It was really cramped inside. My elbows were stuck to my sides and I had two grab handles in front of me and two switches, one for lights and one for the motors to power the lights. There was so much buzzing and whirring going on that when Lucas yelled "Cut!," I went on until someone hit me on the head with a hammer to stop me.

With his crisp English accent, it seemed inevitable that Anthony Daniels would have a career as a voice actor. Daniels was born in Salisbury, Wiltshire, England, the son of a plastics company executive. He was educated at Giggleswick School and studied law for two years at university before dropping out to participate in amateur dramatics and attend Rose Bruford College. After leaving school in 1974, Daniels worked on BBC Radio and for the National Theatre of Great Britain at the Young Vic. It was during his time in the theater that he was invited to meet director George Lucas, who was casting for Star Wars. *Daniels at first turned down the interview but was persuaded by his agent to meet Lucas.*

PETER BEALE

There had been robots in films before. There had been, of course, the Tin Man in *The Wizard of Oz*. There had been *The Day the Earth Stood Still*, and my favorite at the time, Fritz Lang's Maria from *Metropolis*. She's remarkably like C-3PO in many ways. The clever one was Kubrick with HAL 9000. What did HAL look like in *2001*? An eye. He was very clever, he only ever had the eye and the voice. He didn't have this problem. In thinking about the solution, I called up Cambridge University and asked the engineering department and was surprised and pleased to find that they had a robotic department. I discussed it with them and sent them a few pages of the script, and sent them the artwork. A few days later they called back and were very excited. "Yes, we can do this." I said, "Great!," and they said, "Three years, five million dollars." So that wasn't an option.

RALPH MCQUARRIE

George brought a photograph of the female robot from *Metropolis* and said he'd like Threepio to look like that, except to make him a boy. There's a lot of similarity in my early sketches, but those were George's instructions. I had a feeling that Threepio should be more elegant and smoothly sculptural, but the truth is he wouldn't have been able to move. The joints and everything had to be solved so he could move. [Production designer] John Barry, George, and I had a meeting where John looked at my early sketches. In a few minutes, he'd drawn on a little pad the look of Threepio's head with the big round eyes. It did have a sort of humorous aspect, and I thought that was very successful.

PETER BEALE

It was pretty clear to me that the option for a humanoid robot was going to be a man or a woman in suits. I felt it was very important that we didn't go back to that obvious thing. Thinking about it, I thought to myself, we need somebody who is ultra-thin, who, when we sculpture the suit, looks natural size. That was the first thing. The second thing I thought of was, well, maybe we need not an actor, maybe we need a dancer, but then I thought a dancer would bring a fluidity, but robots of what we knew about them—because, again, there weren't very many around—weren't going to be fluid, so I thought of Marcel Marceau. I'm a great fan of his and I had seen him recently, he's famous for his window mime, where he's touching the window. I had read that he had trained some English actors, he had an acting school or a mime school, so I penciled in a very thin mime actor to look for that role. Anthony Daniels turned up and he immediately did the window thing. That's it, that's what I'm thinking, and so Anthony was cast.

ANTHONY DANIELS
(actor, "C-3PO")

It's quite amazing to have survived everything, all nine *Star Wars* films. But also looking at all the elements that have come together, to be a part of the things that I've been a part of, starting with George Lucas and his ingenuity and imagination to create the whole thing in the first place. And then to end up with his apprentice, if you like, J.J. Abrams, who has taken that wonderful gift and just run with it in the most exciting way. Plus all the bits in between.

Over all those years, C-3PO remains C-3PO; nobody has really messed with him, except for J.J. and that red arm in *The Force Awakens*. The character is kind of a given. Through it all, it's been an honor to be in all of these films. Even if I didn't have that much to do, at least C-3PO was there. And so was I. I am hugely lucky and strangely lucky to have been given a part where it doesn't matter how aged I'm becoming—and believe me, that's happening on a daily basis. Yet through it all C-3PO retains that very handsome face that we remember from all these years. He's quite lucky, that one.

Casting on the original Star Wars *was arduous enough, but the fact that the film would be shooting in England presented additional challenges for the American cast.*

PETER BEALE

We had a problem with the casting. We obviously had other actors: Peter Cushing, etc. But to get a work permit for an American actor at that time was very, very difficult. The fact is that Equity had to agree. You informed Equity what you were doing and they would always resist. When I tried to get a work permit for Gregory Peck on *The Omen*, they argued against him coming in. We basically said we're not making the film without him, it's your choice. Eventually, we got it. You can imagine if I would have gone to Equity and said, "We're employing three unknown actors in the lead roles, and we've got in minor roles Alec Guinness, Peter Cushing, etc.," I would have had absolutely zero chance of getting a work permit. So I have to confess, first time in public, that I cheated them a little bit. I created a cast list headed by Dave Prowse, Peter Cushing, Sir Alec Guinness, Anthony Daniels, Kenny Baker, and down at the bottom, the minor roles were the three American actors.

Beale took approximately four weeks to complete a budget and a schedule for the film, wary that the budget might not be enough to complete the ambitious production.

PETER BEALE

At Fox, I was paranoid about taking on a film that everybody said was unmakeable, but Laddie said, "Look, if it can be made, you could probably do it. Can you look and see if you can find out?" I was very lucky, because with the script came six pieces of artwork from this man, Ralph McQuarrie. Every visual in *Star Wars* was conceived and drawn by this man. Absolute genius. The first six pieces of artwork came with the script, and without it, I couldn't have possibly done my job. I started to do a breakdown and the breakdown falls into two components. The first component is you have to imagine and list in great detail everything that's going to be in front of the camera lens. It is before computers, so it was a manual job. You had to make long lists and put them into the various categories of props, sets, wardrobes, actors, etc. Effectively you have to direct the film in your own imagination and list it out. Then you have to list everything that you're going to need to take the photographs, starting with the lens, the camera equipment, the camera crew, sound, lighting, lighting crew, grips, props, electrical, insurance, studio, transport, etc. You end up with a very detailed breakdown, and from that you develop an initial schedule, shooting schedule, and from that, you can forecast and do an initial rough budget.

During the process Beale realized one of the major problems was going to be the size of the sets, which he viewed as "enormous." McQuarrie's paintings cer-

tainly conveyed that. For instance, the suggestion for the Millennium Falcon was so large that there wasn't a stage available to build that or the Death Star sets in it.

PETER BEALE

It was quite clear we were going to have to use mattes. We were going to have to use small floor ground sections and stuff. This set, for the end sequence, was the size of St. Paul's Cathedral. Enormous problem. Not to discuss the number of people in it. In England, we've always had great art direction, but the art direction often falls into one of two camps. Either great artists and not very practical, or very practical and not great artists. We were lucky that we have a few that combine the two. Elliot Scott was one of those. A long, long history and he came in and he went through everything, took about a week, made some very important suggestions and improvements. At that point, I felt, yes, the film could be made. I called up Alan Ladd, my boss, and said, "I think we can make the film, but before we go to the next step, I need to have George Lucas and Gary Kurtz in London and really go through it with them in detail." They turned up and we set up an office for them in Soho Square.

I said to them, "I want to read the script line by line." George was very surprised. He said, "Well, that's not what executives normally do. In fact, we don't normally do that even with the heads of departments in America." I said, "The only way I can help you make the film you want is I have to understand everything inside your brain." He wasn't particularly happy about it to begin with, but we spent about two weeks going through the script, line by line, until I really understood, and we made alterations to the way I suggested we go about making the film. I said, "Unfortunately, I've worked in the desert, understood the desert. If we have an actor in some form of suit in the desert, there is no way he or she can stay in the suit for more than about an hour of the time. They'll have to be taken out, they'll have to be cooled down, you'll need at least two people, just to dress C-3PO. Then, not only dress, but also maintain the costume, because you're bound to get damages and scratching." That's just one. Remember, we also had R2-D2 and at that point, we didn't know if we were going to have somebody inside it, or if it was going to be all mechanical (that came later), but we knew that if it was going to be mechanical, probably two people. There were about twenty other robots that had to be managed, and not only the robots, but we had the land cruiser. I had guessed that we would have some form of cantilever system to have it hovering in the air and photograph it, so you couldn't see the cantilever, which is what of course happened. To physically get that structure into the desert needed a truck, lots of people to lift it, to manage it, etc. No small thing. That's on top of special effects or smoke.

ROBERT WATTS
(UK unit production manager, *Star Wars*)

In 1971, I was at MGM Studios in Culver City wrapping up my work as production manager on a film called *The Wrath of God,* starring Robert Mitchum and Rita Hayworth, which was her last film, when a producer called into my office. He wanted to know about filming in England. His name was Gary Kurtz and he was preparing *American Graffiti* with George Lucas. About a year later he contacted me in the UK to ask for a résumé. I sent it and heard nothing. Some three years later I was working on a film in Greece called *Skyriders* for 20th Century Fox, when the head of Fox London, Peter Beale, called me and said they wanted me in London for a day to meet Gary Kurtz. I flew to London and the next day met Gary at Fox in Soho Square. Peter had lined up a bunch of production managers/supervisors to meet Gary. I got the job and I reckon it was because I had met Gary those years earlier.

PETER BEALE

Tony [Anthony] Waye was our first assistant director. The first assistant director really sets the tone on the set. If you asked me what the assistant director's real job is, it is to create a zone of tranquility around the director and the actors, so that all the other activity is minor, and the actors and the director can create this magic, this chemistry. Tony was brilliant at that. He went on to become an executive producer on the Bond films.

The casting of a crew on a film is as important as the casting of the actors. My biggest concern was the art director. I wanted Elliot Scott. I introduced him to George and George said, "Look, we're young and we'd like somebody younger." Elliot was an amazing eccentric. He lived in a house with only electricity in one room so he could have music. He believed electricity made you crazy. He wore open sandals all year round in England. He slept in the garden most of the year. Absolute genius. Wonderful man. Didn't get him. My next choice was Terry Marsh. I invited him to join us for dinner and we discovered that George, who is an absolute genius, has a shyness that at times is painful. On this particular night he was absolutely shy, he wouldn't say a word. At the end of the evening, Terry said, on the way out, "I'm sorry, Peter. I can't do the film with somebody who can't talk to me." I said, "It's going to be a great film." "Sorry, Peter." I told George and he said, "Well, this is impossible. You're 20th Century Fox. If you tell a technician you're employing them, they've got to work." I said, "It doesn't work that way in England. In England, the technicians actually choose the films they want to work on, especially somebody of that level."

GEORGE LUCAS

The trouble with the future in most futurist movies is that it always looks new and clean and shiny. What is required for true credibility is a used future. The Apollo capsules were instructive in that regard. By the time the astronauts returned from the moon, you had the impression the capsules were littered with weightless candy wrappers and old Tang jars, no more exotic than the family station wagon.

PETER BEALE

[John Barry] was recommended as production designer and he agreed that he would meet with George. And this time I said to George, "You've got to talk," and he did and John was hired. And he did an amazing job.

JOHN BARRY
(production designer, *Star Wars*)

George wanted to make it look like it's shot on location on your average everyday Death Star or Mos Eisley Spaceport or local cantina.

Handling costumes was John Mollo, who would go on to win the Academy Award for both Star Wars *and* Gandhi, *which he worked on for director Richard Attenborough in 1982.*

JOHN MOLLO
(costume designer, *Star Wars*)

I started working on films as a historical adviser with particular attention to military costumes. My interest in the latter meant that I took a lot of trouble to make sure they were correct and worn properly. My first five films were therefore historical, but during the shooting, I learned a lot about how the costume department functioned. Sometime after the last of these films, a costume designer friend of mine was asked to do the costumes for *Star Wars*. She had already accepted another job and kindly offered to recommend me in her place. As I had nothing on at the time, I said yes and was almost immediately asked to meet the director, which I did, and got the job.

As Mollo explains, when he began work on Star Wars, *he'd never actually seen a science fiction film, which required a great deal of research on his part.*

JOHN MOLLO

As far as the costumes were concerned, a lot of work had been done in the States and I was given drawings of some of their ideas. These gave me the general idea, but the meetings I had with George Lucas gave me a much better idea of what he wanted, which he summarized by saying that he didn't want anyone to notice the costumes. By this, of course, he meant that he wanted the costumes to look real. In fact, we worked very closely together. He would state what he wanted, I would make drawings of his and my ideas, and we discussed the results, making enormous progress in this rather simple manner.

GEORGE LUCAS

We were trying to get a cohesive reality. But since the film is a fairy tale, I still wanted it to have an ethereal quality, yet be well-composed and also have an alien look. I visualized an extremely bizarre, Gregg Toland–like surreal look with strange over-exposed colors, a lot of shadows, a lot of hot areas. I wanted the seeming contradiction of strange graphics of fantasy combined with the feel of a documentary.

With Star Wars *moving forward, it fell to Gary Kurtz to work out the logistical plan for the challenge of shooting the film on a trio of continents. For the desert planet of Tatooine, the search for a real desert took place in America, North Africa, and the Middle East, but it was southern Tunisia, located on the Sahara Desert's edge, that seemed perfect.*

ERIC TOWNSEND

Principal photography began on March 22, 1976, at Nefta in the Tunisian Desert, and continued for two and a half weeks. On that first day, they shot scenes that included the Jawas selling the droids beneath the giant Sand-crawler tread, which was built on the salt lake of Chott el Djerid, near Nefta. The scene included twelve local children as extra Jawas. A second scene was also shot at the end of the day featuring Luke and C-3PO rushing out of the Lars homestead to search for the missing Artoo. The shot of Luke watching the twin suns set on the Tatooine horizon was supposed to be filmed that day, but had to be scrapped due to unsuitable weather conditions. It started to rain quite heavily.

GEORGE LUCAS

I wanted it to be shot on location. I tried to find an environment that I could make look spacey and unreal and decided desert would be a good thing that I could actually go on location of. It looked realistic, because I was very keen to have immaculate realism. Which is something I learned from Kurosawa, which was to say even though this is a ridiculous story and it obviously has no reality in it whatsoever, I wanted to make a world that looked like it had been lived in; that had logic on every level so that every cultural artifact, every set piece, had a reason for being there. It wasn't just sort of willy-nilly. And obviously, everything had to be designed, and designed around things we could get a hold of.

GARY KURTZ

The long shots of the Sandcrawler are miniatures of the whole thing rumbling along across the desert. We did build a full-size piece of it, and that was about 40 feet high and 125 feet long. We did investigate the possibility of using a real, very large earthmover or some such vehicle. The main problem is they weren't where we needed it to be. They were also very valuable where they are and very expensive to rent. So we felt it was better to build our own. We fabricated the pieces at our studio in London and shipped it all to Tunisia on trucks. We sent four "land trains" (which is what they're called in Europe)—truck/trailer combinations—across the English Channel, across France and Italy to Genoa and across on the ferry to Tunisia. The last group of material—the Landspeeder and costumes and the robots and all the rest of that—went over on a chartered Lockheed Hercules C-130 and unloaded. We shot for three weeks and got back on the charter and flew back to England.

GEORGE LUCAS

The look it had was pretty shocking when I did it, because everybody thought that science fiction is all clean and perfect. We made sure things looked dirty and that there was running water marks down the walls and all kinds of details on the robots. For whatever reason, I've had this relationship with technology. I started out building cars, so it all comes from the point of view of working on a car in a garage where you work on broken cars. In those days when I lived in Modesto and drove to San Francisco, there was pretty much like a 25 percent chance you wouldn't make it, that the car would break somewhere along the line and you'd have to get it fixed somehow. Now, of course, cars are almost invincible, but in those days they were sort of like computers are today where they don't always do what you're telling them to do.

PETER BEALE

The last day before going to Tunisia, late at night, we were still trying to get the gold onto C-3PO (he was black below it), so we had to get gold on there that would stay on there. We were still applying the gold the night before. I say "we" generously; I looked as Bill Welch was doing it, but I was still there.

ROBERT WATTS

The R2-D2 we had on the first film could not turn its head while in the three-legged mode. And although it was radio-controlled, we often had to pull it along on a piece of piano wire. The head could turn in the two-legged mode because Kenny Baker was inside. We made it, but only just. The C-3PO costume was finally put on Anthony Daniels complete on the first day of shooting in Tunisia. That is the scene where Uncle Owen and Luke Skywalker buy the droids from the Jawas outside the homestead set.

MARK HAMILL

The very first shot in the movie is me coming out of that igloo-type dwelling to buy the robots, and I hear Aunt Beru say, "Luke!" What's so funny was, when I went over to that crater and looked down, it was only about two feet deep. When they did the reverse over my shoulder, it was fifty to one hundred miles away at a real hotel. That was the lobby of the hotel. That's the magic of movies. You can pretend. When I was walking out of the igloo house, they said, "Walk about ten feet and then react like someone's calling you," because Shelagh Fraser, who played Aunt Beru, wasn't even on set that day.

GILBERT TAYLOR
(director of photography, *Star Wars*)

It was all a gray mess, and the robots were just a blur. I thought the look of the film should be absolutely clean; also, I was mindful that there was an enormous amount of process work to be done in America after we finished shooting in England, and I knew a crisp result would help. But George saw it differently, so we tried using nets and other diffusions. He asked to set up one shot on the robots with a 300mm lens, and the sand and the sky just mushed together. I told him it wouldn't work, but he said that was the way he wanted to do the entire film, all diffused.

GEORGE LUCAS

Out of nowhere one night, a storm swept in, a very vicious storm, the worst in fifty years (that's what they always say), and knocked down all of our sets. The little homestead on the lake was actually blown five miles away. Especially the big, round plastic top to the garage almost went to Algeria. And the Sandcrawler, which was about three and a half stories high, was completely flattened. And of course, I had to shoot the next day. I was already behind schedule. I couldn't stop shooting just because everything blew away. We managed to get through it. But that day was one I'll always remember.

ROBERT WATTS

That day we were due to shoot the last day on the homestead set in Tunisia. I was out very early that morning and it was raining very hard with a strong wind. I knew that we were in trouble to go on the salt flats as when they were wet the salt would crack. Underneath the salt, there was greasy mud that would stop the vehicles moving, even those with four-wheel drive. I called the assistant directors and told them to tell the crew I was calling a rest day. I then went out to the set with Les Dilley, the unit art director. The roof of the homestead was nowhere to be seen, it had blown across the salt flat heading for the Algerian border. Other bits of the set were damaged. Les got his crew together whilst I figured out what to do. We continued the next day shooting the other sets scheduled for this part of Tunisia. On the last day at this location, we returned to the salt flat to complete the homestead sequence. The last shot was done as the sun was going down. It is the shot of Luke gazing out as the twin suns are setting. One is the real sun, the other was laid in by ILM [Industrial Light & Magic]. Just as we cut it started to rain and we were in a mad scramble to get all our vehicles off the salt flat. We got them all safely off with the exception of the six-wheel-drive crane, which helped the other vehicles. The crane was on hire from the Tunisian army. We left it stuck in the greasy mud. Luckily we did not need it anymore. So all was well.

MARK HAMILL

I remember when Alec Guinness's wife was sketching a mosque when we were in Tunisia, and this was taboo to the religion there. A local official realized what she was doing. He grabbed her paper and tore it up. And Lady Guinness was startled and so was Alec. He looked at me and said, "What was that?" I said, "I have no idea. Unless it was the local art critic."

KENNY BAKER

In the desert, it was freezing in the morning and we all wore anoraks, hats, and goggles. It was like Scott of the Antarctic. Then it changed to violent heat and then wind. All types of weather in one day! The robot conducted a lot of the heat.

PETER BEALE

Over the years, I've read with amusement all sorts of experts discussing it, who had little or nothing to do with it, saying how difficult it was. However, there hasn't been a film made that is not difficult to make. The smallest film, the biggest film—because all of us want to do better. All of us want to try harder to make it better. When you try and do that with robots and all these things in the desert, just being in the desert in itself is a feat. Of course, it's difficult, but that's normal, that's why we're the A-team, that's why we do it properly. I discard all those people that sort of said, "Oh, it was so difficult." It was difficult on location, but we got it done. We got it done on schedule and got it done quite well. When this crew came back to the studio, they had bonded as the actors had bonded.

Star Wars began shooting on March 22, 1976, with the commencement of principal photography in the Tunisian Desert, and would continue there for two and a half weeks. On April 2, scenes of the Mos Eisley Cantina were filmed at multiple shooting locations, the exterior shots obtained in Ajim, Djerba. These included the "These are not the droids you're looking for" Jedi mind trick Obi-Wan pulls on dim-witted stormtroopers, the droids in front of the cantina and the stormtroopers watching the Millennium Falcon take off and blast off. Most of the interior scenes were filmed during April at the Elstree Studios, although there would be additional shooting in Hollywood later on.

Filming moved to Elstree Studios on April 7, where the production shot for fourteen and a half weeks. Finally, on the nineteenth, Lucas did some more work on the script, and it was at this point that Luke Starkiller became Luke Skywalker.

RAY MORTON

As happens in filmmaking, the story continued to evolve during shooting. Luke Starkiller became Luke Skywalker on the day they shot the scene in which Luke first meets Princess Leia. It was then that Lucas decided that Starkiller was too grim a name for his ebullient hero. Most significantly, Lucas decided to kill off Ben Kenobi two-thirds of the way through the story on the way back from Tunisia, where the first scenes of the film were shot. In the shooting script, Ben traveled to Yavin with Luke, Leia, and Han, but then didn't have much to do from that point on. After seeing how strong Alec Guinness's dignified performance as the character was, Lucas decided it would be more powerful to have Ben sacrifice himself to help the others escape (something Kane Starkiller also did in the early drafts) and then return as a supernatural entity to guide Luke during the attack on the Death Star. This was an excellent choice that gave the story a solid emotional punch right at the end of the second act, raised the stakes for all the characters (if one of the heroes can die, then all of them can), and—by showing that Kenobi's mastery of the Force allowed him to conquer death—made an already strong character even more powerful.

MARK HAMILL

I had never been to England. I had been to Glebe Place in a basement apartment and I was near Marylebone station, which was this big train station. And the first time I took the train, I had this overwhelming sense of déjà vu. Why does this look so familiar to me? I couldn't quite place it. Somehow I mentioned it on set, and Gil Taylor, who was the cinematographer on the original *Star Wars*, said, "Marylebone station? That's where we shot *A Hard Day's Night*." "You shot *A Hard Day's Night*?," and he said, "Yes," and of course I turned into Fab Boy. "Oooh, with the Beatles?" Gil had a little bit of the cantankerous C-3PO in him, that tended to see the dark cloud in the silver lining. He said, "Oh, it was terrible. All those screaming girls."

GARY KURTZ

George wasn't happy in England. He doesn't like being that far from home, and there are a lot of little things that are different—light switches going up instead of down, that sort of thing. Everything is just a little bit different, just enough to throw you off balance. And George is not particularly social to begin with. He never goes out of his way to socialize. It takes him a while to know someone to get intimate with, to share his problems. It's hard for him to work with strangers.

GEORGE LUCAS

The studios mostly are filled with television. I needed like eleven soundstages and they didn't have them here. London also had great talent, great actors, they had good carpenters. To do a film like *Star Wars* is really hard and other than Hollywood the craftsmen in England are the best. And their industry was basically falling apart, so the studios were crumbling and they were selling them. They sold Elstree, which is where I was, and turned it over from having a staff to having independent guys come in and work. And as a result, I was able to get a great deal and save a lot of money. Basically, it's always been my philosophy to simply go anywhere in the world I can go where I get the lowest price. On this film, we did the budget and it came out to thirteen million. Laddie said the board will never approve this, we can't do it. It has to be under ten. I said, "I can't do it for under ten." This was not a negotiation thing, which I'm sure everybody's gone through, this is actually a real cost. This is the price. We worked it out, but they are so used to producers and people sort of ripping them off that they don't believe that there's actually a real thing behind it. You know, there's actually that guy who gets paid that much an hour and he's got to work that many days and that's what it's going to cost you. We gave him a budget of $9,999,000 and 99 cents and I said, "I don't think it will come in at that," but we did it anyway. It came up to $14 million because that was what it actually costs to do it.

BRIAN JAY JONES

As the writer of Jim Henson's biography as well, I at least had the perspective I'd gained from it. What I love about this is Jim's across the street the whole time in the television production. When they came over, they were like, "Really? You guys are going to break for tea right in the middle of the day," and we get to the very end of the day and it's like, "We're not done yet. We need to continue." And they were like, "Nope. Lights out." That's a very un-American way of working, so I'm sure they were just getting used to that style. Because of the British unions, you have mandatory tea breaks and you get to 5:00 or 6:00 or whatever you've agreed to, and it is lights out and everyone's gone for the day.

GEORGE LUCAS

You can imagine what I went through. I had long hair, a beard, I was twenty-nine years old, and their industry was sort of crumbling a little bit. And I walked in there and had this really crazy script and the crew was 100 percent against me except for the art department. They were the only guys that stuck by me through the whole movie.

BRIAN JAY JONES

For Americans, that had to be really tough, especially given somebody like Lucas who's like, "We're going to be filming *American Graffiti* and we're filming all night, and we may or may not have a permit for it." It's like, they're going to do it as long as it takes to get it done. And when he's editing the movie, he's going to stay up all night. He's not going to leave the editing studio at 9:00 P.M. because the day is over. So the American mentality of filmmaking is kind of the American mentality of the way we do a lot of things, which is just, "Well, we're on our schedule and everybody just needs to adapt." I'm sure it had to be very tough getting over there and just really having those strenuous union rules clamped down on lights out at the end of the day no matter what's going on. So I'm sure that was very frustrating.

GEORGE LUCAS

It was horrible. At the end of the day, you'd have to go to the crew to get a vote on whether or not to continue. Well, the AD [assistant director] was way against me and the cameraman was way against me. Every time they would say no except for the art department, but of course, they were outnumbered, so I had to get it done at five thirty every night. That was the least of it, but they just had no idea and they thought the film was stupid, which, you know, if you read it, it sort of *does* read kind of stupid.

MARK HAMILL

I have to tell you, the crew that was making it, they were all very professional, but they all thought it was, to put it kindly, rubbish. They thought it was silly. I mean, there wasn't a lot they could compare it to except, maybe *Doctor Who* or the comic strip *Dan Dare*. The idiom was not really something that was familiar to the British crew. So they were really nice and they liked all of us, but they just thought it was ridiculous.

BRIAN JAY JONES

The crew doesn't understand *Star Wars*. The feeling was, "We make great art over here and what is this?" And Huyck or whoever had the great story about, "Get more light on the rug or get more light on the dog." Like, they had these disparaging names for every character in the movie. So, yes, the British clearly just didn't get it. One of the cool stories about *Star Wars* was the process of putting together that film and the story is, again, very American with a lowercase A in this case.

MARK HAMILL

They thought it would be a movie that would be released only on matinees for children in the daytime.

BRIAN JAY JONES

It's hard to be the only person in the room that gets it, because even people like Mark Hamill, who's nerdy enough, I think understands what Lucas is trying to do, but I can't imagine how hard it is to be doing something and somebody telling you, "Okay, later on in production you'll actually see what the planet will be there." There's so much shit that you can't tell what's going on. I think even Peter Cushing talks about it like he didn't know what a god-damn line of dialogue meant; he had no clue what he was talking about most of the time. It's really hard to be the only one there and they're like, "Okay, you're going to be looking out here at the end and you're going to see a planet blow up." And it's like, "So why are we blowing it up?" "Never mind. Don't worry about your motivation." Lucas is one of these guys with actors where he's like, "You're not Brando. You don't get a motivation. Just do the lines that are on the page," and then zero feedback for the actors. I always love those stories where the actors are busting his balls about his direction consisting of, "Faster and more intense." That was the only direction he could ever give anybody.

GEORGE LUCAS

I've been described as a Machiavellian director. I get what I want, but a lot of time I get it indirectly by putting people in situations where it just happens.

MARK HAMILL

There would be moments during the making of the movie where I'd say, "Hey, George, instead of saying this, can I say that?" And he'd go, "Hmmm, no, I like the way it is. Just do it the way it's in the script." And then Harrison would do an ad-lib and he'd get away with it! And I said, "How come you get to?," and he said, "Look, don't ask. Just do it. He's got so many things on his mind that, A, he might not notice and, B, he might like it better if he sees it in performance." So that's another little tip, not to be forthcoming. I've used it ever since.

CARRIE FISHER

"Faster and more intense" were his actual directions. At one stage he lost his voice and we joked about getting two boards fixed up each with their own horn on top and "Faster!" chalked on one and "More Intense!" chalked on the other. He also told me to stand up straight a lot and act more like a Princess. George didn't really have the character well defined. He gave me a lot of freedom and responsibility. The first day I met him, he said that I could change any dialogue that I felt uncomfortable saying. In fact, I changed very little. When I see how I said a lot of it, I wish I had changed more. But that's me just being strict with myself. The only thing you couldn't tell from the script was the style and that was one thing that George communicated really well to all of us. For example, he wanted the dialogue read straight. Like, "I thought I recognized your foul stench, Tarkin." Not thrown away like I was originally going to do: "When I came on board, you know, I thought, the smell. Who is that?" George didn't want us to cheat like that. Go for broke—and I went for broke.

BRIAN JAY JONES

There's a great bit you've probably seen where they show the three of them come running through a room and then they get down and they turn to

Lucas and he tells them it's going well. Well, Lucas said it was pretty good and they're just so excited by this. And he actually looks happy, because Mark Hamill's got this great quote where he says that George always looked like he was ready to burst into tears, which I think we can probably all relate to.

MARK HAMILL

One time when we were shooting some of the action sequences, trying to get the Princess out of the detention cell on the Death Star, one of the British crew members came up to me and he said, "Don't you think that it's just a little phony that you have these forty thousand stormtroopers after you, and you have not been hit once? I mean, can't you just get a little flak on your arm?" By that time I knew, and George had really told me, and Gary had really told me, it's just not that kind of movie. It's a fairy tale, it's sweet, and it's a swashbuckler.

BRIAN JAY JONES

The thing Lucas has to do, and it's huge, is cede control and he has to let the union guys do their stuff, he has to let Gary Kurtz do his thing. And being in charge of all that would have killed him, but I think it also killed him not being in charge of everything, having to put his life in another man's hands, so to speak, at any given moment. That had to make that super hard. But, again, he got physically ill. When you see the pictures of him directing, he actually has gray in his beard. You see photos of Obama, his hair goes white in two and a half years. It's the agony and ecstasy of *Star Wars* is what people always call it. I remember seeing an interview with Harrison Ford talking about pointing guns that don't make any sound and you're just hoping that you've got the gun pointed somewhere in the direction so that when they put in the laser in post, it actually hits what you're supposed to be shooting at. And it's a real leap of faith on everybody's part and it's all hanging around Lucas's shoulders. So, of course, I think he was scared shitless.

Some of that fear must have been assuaged as he watched set designs being brought to life, his imagination finding itself becoming rooted in the real world.

GEORGE LUCAS

John Barry was a really fantastic art director. Really, really great guy. He put together an art department, prop guys . . . the whole little group, and they were completely 100 percent on my side. Very supportive of me in every possible way. And no matter how wacky I got, they would go along with it and came up with other things. They actually contributed a lot by bringing things in. The design work in *Star Wars,* and especially as it goes on to all the other ones, is huge. It's beyond anything that anybody can imagine.

GILBERT TAYLOR

John Barry's sets, particularly the Death Star, was like a coal mine. They were all black and gray, with really no opportunities for lighting at all. My work was a matter of chopping holes in the walls and working the lighting into the sets, and this resulted in a "cut-out" system of panel lighting using quartz lamps that we could put in the walls, ceiling, and floors. I thought I was going to get sacked, but Fox agreed that we couldn't have this "black hole of Calcutta." So, George concentrated on the actors while I took care of my end. This lighting approach allowed George to shoot in almost any direction without extensive relighting, which gave him more freedom. George avoided all meetings and contact with me from day one, so I read the extra-long script many times and made my own decisions as to how I would shoot the picture. I took it upon myself to experiment with photographing the lightsabers and other things onstage before we moved on to our two weeks of location work in Tunisia.

GEORGE LUCAS

Take the stormtroopers. That was, again, John Barry. We were molding plastic, which was like a new thing. Getting a vacuum form machine is a big deal, and we've got the only one in England. It came from some factory; we just grabbed it and we also did another kind of vacuum forming with John designing the sets. I mean, Ralph McQuarrie kind of designed what they look like, but then John took those designs and made them into panels. So we made four-by-eight panels, which is kind of like sheets of plywood, made out of some kind of fiberglass mold that he did. Vacuum formed was a whole different approach to building sets. And that was one of the ways we got it done. It was figuring out new ways to accomplish things without spending.

MARK HAMILL

When we were wearing the stormtrooper uniforms, you couldn't sit down. They put us in piece by piece, and they built us some saw horses to sit on and that's the most we could rest all day. It was terrible. Plus, you get panicky inside those helmets, because it's not like any mask at all which is fitted up against your face. You can see the inside of the helmet and it's all sickly green, plus you've got wax in your ears because of the explosions. You just feel eerie, because with the helmet on you feel that you're in your own little thing because nobody's talking to you. I only once freaked out and said, "Get me outta here!" It was really uncomfortable.

Part of the discomfort came from wearing the stormtrooper outfit in a sequence on the Death Star where Luke, Leia, and Han are in a trash compactor that's being set to . . . compact.

MARK HAMILL

The monster that pulls me under the water in the trash compactor, in the script it said it was a Dianoga. It's never said in the movie. Under our stormtrooper gear, we had scuba gear on. I don't know why. It wasn't that cold. It's just the way it was. What happens is that every time I went underwater, I'd have to go upstairs to my dressing room, take off the stormtrooper gear, take off the scuba gear, change my underwear, put on a new scuba outfit, put on new stormtrooper gear, and have someone do my hair. So it was a real pain. Make sure everything is fine before I go back down underwater!

One time we were sort of just hanging around the trash compactor, and there are all these floating bits of polystyrene—we call it Styrofoam. And George of course was up here; we were down in the compactor. He was twisting his beard and frowning; he was his usual unhappy self. You can imagine that after all these years of imagining this, that he has to realize it on film and that's where your imagination is. He's got to be worried about a bazillion other things. What happened was he and I just linked eyes. We just noticed each other and just to cheer him up I took a little piece of polystyrene off my stormtrooper outfit and said, singing, "Pardon me, George, could this be Dianoga poo-poo?" For younger people there's a song called "Pardon Me Boys, Is This the Chattanooga Choo-Choo?" I thought that would make him laugh. All he did was, he walked up to me like this [head down], put his foot on my chest, and pushed me under the water, [as Lucas calls out] "All right, get him out, up to the dressing room." [Hamill, facetiously waving fist] "Curse you, George, I'll never try humor on you again."

The sequence obviously had an impact on Hamill, who adds that he actually burst a blood vessel during it. Beyond that, there was the Errol Flynn–like sequence on the Death Star, where Leia and Luke make a death-defying leap across a massive chasm.

MARK HAMILL

We were on a platform, and there was a cut-out area where it dropped down lower, where the scuba guy and the scuba gear was, with his hand around my ankle. "I think there's something in here!" And when it came time for me to cue him, I'd just tap my foot and he'd yank me down. For some reason, I thought it'd be a great idea when I was underwater . . . you know how you can make your face go red by forcing blood to your face? I thought it'd be so cool, because once I went underwater, they wrapped the Dianoga tentacle around my neck. When I came up, I was just scarlet red, like I was being choked. And I did it so hard I did burst a blood vessel. And George later said, "Why did you do that? It was really stupid." And I said, "Well, I wanted it to look like I was really being choked." He said, "Well, there's a red filter on the camera to make it look like the red lights, so you're not going to see it anyway." And the problem was, for the next few days they had to shoot me from the other side, because I had a burst blood vessel.

CARRIE FISHER

I was scared to death of swinging across the Death Star chasm . . . but I was sort of sorry we got it right on the first take. I wanted to do it again.

MARK HAMILL

I do remember the "swing across." I was looking forward to that all week long. We were both in harnesses, the way you would be for *Peter Pan*. So we were all on wires. They had our two harnesses linked together, Carrie and I. And so we're ready to go. What I didn't realize was that they had at least four cameras going, in my memory. Maybe three. Normally in a movie, you do a scene over and over. We might spend all day doing that. We swung across once. What a gyp!

One of the most ambitious set pieces of the film in terms of physical production was the final sequence where the heroes (sans Chewbacca) are given their awards for the destruction of the Death Star by Princess Leia.

PETER BEALE

We had this enormous sequence to do. First of all, building it, we were talking about going down to Shepperton Studios and the big "H" stage down there, but to build this was going to cost a fortune. To employ a thousand crowd in England is an enormous undertaking. To have a thousand costumes. To have a place for a thousand people to change. Little lockers to put their possessions. To feed them. To have toilets. We're talking about an enormous scene and we didn't have much of the contingency [money in the budget reserved to cover expenses] left. I went to George and said, "You know, George, when the queen does investitures, she does it a bit more modestly at Buckingham Palace. Could we consider a different form of investiture program?" He said,

"No, Peter, I really want this big thing." So I went to John Barry and Gil Taylor and said, "Can we do an old-fashioned theme? Can we try it? Would you be prepared to do it? Would you design a set where the foreground hides the walls; a couple of fronts of columns and instead of having a thousand crowd, having one hundred and expose them multiple times in different positions." Now, it's done all the time in digital stuff, but in the past, it had been done many years before, but hadn't been done for a long time.

BRIAN JAY JONES

Part of the reason for filming in England is because he needs a gigantic sound-stage, because he's got this goddamn medal ceremony in every draft of *Star Wars*. And it's great, don't get me wrong, but it's one of those things that, like the cutting the arm off in the cantina, were in draft one and made it all the way through. I think had he found a soundstage at Universal, he would have one there, but they weren't big enough, so he's doing it for the vision of that award ceremony at the very end. Of course, he still doesn't have enough bodies to put into that ceremony; he's got cardboard cutouts. But I think that partly defined why he was there. It wasn't necessarily cheaper in England, which is the thing people always forget. Taxes were very high and the cost of everything was a lot.

PETER BEALE

John Barry designed this set where you can see two foreground pieces, not very much of them and inexpensive to build. The background, the lights were matted in, so that one didn't have to be built. We got a very good motion camera and put it and Gil at the very back of the studio at Elstree, on the lighting rail at the farthest back corner. It was locked off so it couldn't possibly move. Put one thousand feet of film in and brought a one hundred crowd in. Gil lit the one hundred crowd and everything was absolutely black. We then moved the one hundred crowd to the next position, rewound the film through the camera with a cap on the lens, and moved the one hundred crowd, relit them to the next position, everything black, and we did that ten times. I said to George, "Let's try it. If it fails, we've spent a day and we'll come up with Plan B. But if it works, it's going to be great." This is what we did and then finally everything was black except the central pathway and the actors walked down the central pathway. I was very nervous and got in early next day to see the rushes. I'm pleased to say that it worked.

MARK HAMILL

When we went to get our medals, Harrison and I came down the steps, walked all along the alleyway, and then up the stairs to where the Princess was. And, of course, all the guys lined up. They didn't give them a script. They didn't know what the movie was about. So during rehearsal, under their breaths, they're saying things like, "Fucking wankers." It was bothering me. Harrison was all, "Who cares?" I said, "I care!" I went over to the guys and I said, "Do you know what this scene is?" and they said, "No, no one tells us anything." And I said, "Well, this is the end of the movie where we've defeated the evil Galactic Empire, destroyed their superweapon, and you guys are all the heroes that helped us succeed." Well, the minute they heard that all of that teasing and razzing went away. It taught me something: you include the background artists, as they call them in England, or extras.

In any case, we rehearsed the scene and I'm in that yellow jacket and Luke is so proud. And, "Action!" Step, step, step, and they said, "Okay, good, but we've got to do it again. Some camera problems." This is rehearsal. So on the second rehearsal, I went step, step, step-step, step, step. Harrison said, "Come here a minute. Is that the way you're going to do it with that little extra step?" Because he was doing the same. We were syncopated. I said, "It's justified, because Luke's anxious. He really wants to get there. Solo's, you know, blasé. He doesn't care." But it was probably stealing the "center of interest." Harrison's a very generous guy, but he will not abide stealing center of interest. And I thought it was justified, I should really do it. But pick your battles, you know? Don't sweat the small stuff, so I didn't do it and Harrison and I have remained friends ever since.

By the beginning of May 1976, the pressure of making Star Wars *wasn't abating at all. It was around this time that Alan Ladd and additional executives from Fox flew to England to view some dailies and get some reassurance about the film's mounting cost. In his memoirs, Ladd wrote of this moment: "I was warned upfront that it was a very rough assembly, and that they were quite unhappy with the editor. The picture started and all I could say was, 'That's interesting; it looks good' and so forth. But, and I never said this to George, my real reaction was utter and complete panic. I didn't sleep that night. But the next day I spoke to George and when I heard specifically what his concerns were, and how things should be changed, I must say I lost the anxiety about it. Had George said, 'Didn't you love it?,' I would have been very scared and very nervous. But he said, 'This is not what I want and this is not what it's going to look like.' He explained that he hadn't even seen a lot of the footage himself yet."*

Between May 13 and 16, the production shifted over to Shepperton Studios to shoot the Death Star attack briefing. The problem, however, is that production had fallen behind schedule.

PETER BEALE

We were coming near the end of the film. We were out of contingency. We were over schedule and my boss, Alan Ladd, called me and said, "Peter, I've got problems. The finance people are putting pressure on me. We have to stop the film in two weeks' time." I said, "But, Laddie, we've got four weeks' work to do, and some of them are important." He said, "Solve the problem." So I went to George and Gary and said, "We've got this problem," and George said, "Well, it's a disaster." I said, "There's always a way. Always a way. Let's have a couple of other units," and Robert Watts, the production manager, directed one and Gary Kurtz directed the other, and somehow or other over those two weeks we kicked the ball and scrambled and we got the work done. A little later, when the studio got a bit more confidence, George was given another week's filming in Hollywood, or up in his area. But we got the film finished.

GEORGE LUCAS

At the end of shooting, we were two weeks over schedule and I was going to need another two weeks to finish it, because I had to finish the whole beginning of the movie. You know, where they come into the ship and Darth Vader comes in and does all that stuff. I had to shoot that, but Laddie said, "Look, you've got to finish it in one week." And I said, "They haven't even finished building the set yet," but he told me, again, we had to finish in one week. I said we could do it, but it means everybody goes on overtime to build the set and to shoot it. It's going to cost you twice as much as if you just give me the extra two weeks. And he said, "I don't care, you've got to get it done." And this is where the reality of making movies comes in. Later on, after I finished the movie, I started talking to members of the board and realized that the board had given him an ultimatum. He was the head of the studio, but basically, this board of directors was making every single decision. Of course, they were stockbrokers and people who didn't know anything about movies. He said they told him, "You will not come back here to the board meeting on Monday and have that movie still shooting."

Filming may have been tough, but Lucas still had to deal with the editing of the film: taking the disparate elements—not even including special effects at this point—and assembling them together in a cohesive whole in what many filmmakers consider any film's final rewrite.

GEORGE LUCAS

When I finished *Star Wars*, I was completely exhausted. Three years of my life and everything was going wrong all the time and everything was half of what I was hoping it would be. I showed an early version that still had all the World War II footage in it to a bunch of my friends, which I've done on all my movies. I invited them to come and see it in a little screening at my house. It was like twelve of them. Now some of them were very vocal like, "Oh my God, what have you done?" They're all directors and writers, so some of them were a little hard, saying, "What's all this Force shit? You can't make a movie like that. This was ridiculous." I had a roll-up at the head that was about twice as long as it should have been. Brian De Palma was like, "Let me help you write out a new roll-up here." So even though he makes horror movies and believes that if you don't cut somebody up with blood splatter everywhere it's a wussy film, he's a good friend and he really wanted it to work. The only one that believed in it was Steve Spielberg. He's the only one. He's the one who said this was going to be the biggest film in the history of movies, and everybody looked at him like he was out of his mind.

PETER BEALE

We had a wonderful editor on the film, and we put a rough cut together and Alan Ladd flew over, and a couple of other executives, and it was very disappointing. There was a long silence. It didn't have the humor. It didn't have the excitement we expected from seeing the rushes—and the rushes were good. Unfortunately, it all was an embarrassment, we had to change editors, and George brought on his wife, Marcia, who had worked for Francis Ford Coppola and had been credited as the assistant editor on *American Graffiti,* but most people say she did the editing. She came on the film and the editing was moved to the States.

PAUL HIRSCH
(editor, *Star Wars*)

My brother Charles produced *Greetings,* a comedy directed by Brian De Palma, and came to me for the trailer. He and I hit it off and he hired me, at my brother's urging, to cut the sequel, *Hi, Mom!* I then cut his next four films and came to the attention of Brian's friends, who included Marty Scorsese, Steven Spielberg, and George Lucas. Marcia Lucas was cutting *Taxi Driver* for Scorsese and when they needed help, called me to work on it, but the studio nixed it. Then, the following year, they again needed help, this time on *Star Wars,* and called me in. George Lucas realized they weren't going to make the release date unless they had another pair of hands at work on the film. The studio went along and the rest is history. I joined Marcia Lucas, who was primarily concentrating on the end battle, and Richard Chew, who had been working on the main body of the film.

I was given a scene to recut, the robot auction where Luke's uncle buys R2-D2 and C-3PO, and changed it to more closely match my sensibility. George liked my work, so I went on to the next. Richard Chew would be working on one reel and I would leap-frog onto the next and so on. Marcia was buried in assembling the end battle. I also suggested, since the effects had not yet been shot, that Vader's ship be made slightly different from the others, in order that his maneuvers stand out. My inspiration for this has a strange origin. As a New Yorker, it struck me as very interesting how people in California begin to be identified with their cars and vice versa.

RAY MORTON

Working with editors Marcia Lucas and Paul Hirsch, Lucas reshaped the Death Star battle considerably. In the script, Luke made two runs at the Death Star's exhaust port, but the footage from both was combined so that in the final film he only makes one. Also, footage of Princess Leia and the rebel leaders monitoring the battle from the rebel control room, which initially appeared only at the top of the battle scene, was interspersed throughout to create more tension. Finally, footage of the Death Star preparing to fire on Alderaan was repeated to make it appear as if the battle station was about to fire on the rebel base—a notion that was not in the screenplay. This added more tension to Luke's final run by making it clear that if Luke fails to blow up the Death Star, the entire Rebellion will be wiped out. These were all very smart choices that greatly enhanced the suspense and drama in the movie's final act.

PAUL HIRSCH

Also, by virtue of working with De Palma for so many years on so many suspenseful movies, I was very aware of the requirements of suspense. For the end battle to work we needed a sense of time running out. To add this, they went and shot some second unit stuff, shots of the Death Star, troopers using a countdown toward the destruction of a rebel planet. All this material gives a counterpoint to Luke's progress in the trench. We then also built up a sequence earlier in the film when Peter Cushing blows up Alderaan, a sequence that duplicates the steps shown later in the film, to give the example of how a planet is blown up. This prepares the audience for the suspenseful effect of the final sequence.

George basically let me do my thing with each scene, and then would give me notes. And he consulted very closely with Marcia, of course. And then at a certain point, he decided he preferred working with just one editor and chose me to finish the film. I was the only editor on the picture over the last five months, during which they reshot the cantina sequence; R2 in the canyon, captured by the Jawas; some of the Landspeeder shots; as well as the gearing-up of the planet-destroying weapon on the Death Star. It was during this period that we completed the blue-screen shots and I watched the space sequences come to life as the backgrounds were filled in.

RAY MORTON

The narrative was further refined during editing. A subplot in which Luke's best friend Biggs tells Luke at the beginning of the film that he is leaving the Empire's space academy and running off to join the Rebellion and then reunites with Luke on Yavin in the film's third act was cut completely (Biggs remains in the film as just one of the several rebel pilots who are killed during the attack on the Death Star, but his emotional connection to Luke is lessened). The subplot was half-reinstated in the 1997 Special Edition, which shows Luke and Biggs reuniting, but not going their separate ways in the first place, a decision that left many viewers scratching their head wondering why Luke was so happy to meet up with some seemingly random guy they had never seen before.

GARY KURTZ

When Alan Ladd saw the footage of the Anchorhead scenes, he said it was like *American Graffiti* in space and he was really unhappy. He started thinking he'd made a serious mistake.

PAUL HIRSCH

Star Wars opens with an initial clash between Darth Vader's troops and Princess Leia's followers. There's a battle going on in space. In the script, and in the original cut, in the middle of the battle, we cut down to the surface of the planet and how Luke Skywalker looks up at the sky with his binoculars and sees the fighting going on—little flashes of light. He gets all excited and jumps into his speeder. Now the rest of this scene, for several reasons, really didn't work. I suggested that we simply ax the whole scene, because other parts of the film imparted much of the same information.

MARK HAMILL

Basically what I liked about those scenes was that it showed Luke in his own environment. He was definitely not the coolest kid in school. His friends ridiculed him for being just a farm boy. It also established that he was a great pilot, but that he was also impetuous and impatient. When Biggs, whom Luke idolizes, is there in his Imperial uniform, Luke is just thrilled. At that point,

Luke wants to join the Empire. When Biggs finally confesses to Luke that he plans to jump ship and join the Rebellion, Luke is totally shocked. It becomes that moment in Luke's life where he first begins to question authority, which I felt was very significant. It's also important, because Biggs is one of the pilots making the assault on the Death Star. He does a suicide move that allows Luke to slip past and is killed in the process. It's like one of those World War II moments where they say, "Let's do it for Johnny!" It added emotional resonance to the scene, none of which is there when you take out that storyline.

PAUL HIRSCH

With that scene missing, we don't get to the surface of Luke's planet until we're brought there by R2-D2 and C-3PO. Now when they're walking around the desert there's an enormous sense of mystery created about where they are. What is this place? When you see the Jawas, you think these may be the only inhabitants of the planet. Rather than cutting to Luke arbitrarily, we're taken there through R2-D2 and C-3PO landing on the planet, being captured, and then delivered to Luke's farm. So we introduce Luke to the story in somewhat of an organic manner.

RAY MORTON

Lucas added a wonderful final touch to his storytelling in the last days of postproduction, when he decided to open the film with a single card that read "A long time ago in a galaxy far, far away" (a phrase adapted from a line that opened the fourth draft of the script—"a long time ago in a galaxy far away, an incredible adventure took place"), a notion that reset the story from the thirty-third century to the distant past and told the audience that what they were watching was not just a movie, but a timeless myth/legend/fairy tale meant to be told again and again around that most modern of campfires—the cinema screen.

3

LIGHT & MAGIC: THE VISUAL EFFECTS

"That's no moon, it's a space station."

The special visual effects of *Star Wars* were a whole additional chapter in the making of the film and the element that so much of its potential success depended on. Back in April 1975, as things were progressing with the project, Fox actually shut down its own special effects department, which ultimately allowed Lucas to create his own visual effects unit for the project. By the time *Star Wars* emerged on movie screens, it had redefined the very nature of cinematic visual effects in much the way that Stanley Kubrick had with *2001: A Space Odyssey*.

GEORGE LUCAS
(executive producer, screenwriter/director, *Star Wars*)
If you hire Douglas Trumbull to do your special effects, he does your special effects. I was very nervous about that. I wanted to be able to say, "It should look like this, not that way." I didn't want to be handed an effect after five months and be told, "Here's your special effects, sir." I want to be able to have some say about what's going on—either you do it yourself, or you don't get a say.

PETER BEALE
(UK production executive, *Star Wars*)
We were talking about special effects and George mentioned Douglas Trumbull. Trumbull had been an assistant special effects person on *2001*, had worked on *Star Trek*, but wasn't available. The name John Dykstra came to mind. I was asked to nip across and see John, and John had developed a different form of motion control, and this was probably one of the great breakthroughs of *Star Wars*. Instead of using a long mechanical clockwork system that was vulnerable and time-consuming, John had taken a stepper motor

off a lathe. Now a stepper motor is an electrical motor that can move forward and back in minute increments, and you can absolutely control it. You take it for granted today, but back then it was fairly new. This was the first time somebody in the film industry had taken one off of a lathe and started using it for motion control. I was very impressed, so we started talking to John about doing the visual effects in America. It hadn't been quite decided, but we were getting close to it. At this point, we really decided that they're going to do the visual effects in the States, so we started interfacing with them, because we needed to have plates for the live-action shooting if we're going to do front projections. John Dykstra started setting up Industrial Light & Magic.

JOHN DYKSTRA
(special photographic effects supervisor, *Star Wars*)

In June of 1975, I was contacted by George Lucas and Gary Kurtz with regard to my supervising the photographic special effects for *Star Wars*. I had been working at the University of California at Berkeley on a project for the National Science Foundation and I had just come back. I got the script and some artwork from the production, which were Ralph McQuarrie's illustrations and they were stunning, and it was the first version of the script, which was really fun. I really enjoyed it. These first meetings with George and Gary outlined effects scenes that involved spacecraft engaged in acrobatics that any stunt pilot would be proud of: three or four ships performing rolls or loops while firing lasers at each other in the classic "dogfight" tradition. I'm kind of an adrenaline enthusiast. I was a flyer and raced motorcycles and cars and surfed and skied and did all that stuff. So this was a great action opportunity for me, especially because of my flying.

GEORGE LUCAS

The one thing Fox was worried about was the fact that this involved a lot of special effects and there were no special effects departments at the studios anymore. There were some matte painters—there were exactly three matte painters in the world and that was it. And they were all in their sixties and seventies. Kubrick could build his own unit, which then turned around and disbanded when he finished. Doug Trumbull was one of those guys and he started a little production company that did a lot of commercials and he was trying to make his own little science fiction film, but there just weren't any special effects and the studio was saying, "Well, how are you going to make this?" So I came up with a phrase called Rotary Chemical Photography and told them that's what I was going to use. "It's very new; it's going to be special. It'll make it work." I didn't know what it was.

I started out in film school as an animator, so I knew a little bit about this stuff. So I took all the money I'd made on *American Graffiti* and I invested in a special effects company, ILM, and hired all these guys. One was a cameraman that worked for Doug Trumbull, John Dykstra; and a bunch of guys that did commercials. None of them had really made a feature film before. None of them had done real special effects except on commercials. So I had money outside the budget of the film that I used to start the company, and then obviously billed the effects back to the studio—Francis taught me how to do that.

Lucas reflected on the fact that back in school he would get into huge fights in the middle of classes with his screenwriting professor, being dismissive of both character and story, stating that that was the sort of thing that theater and books were for, not cinema. That cinema was the art of the moving image.

GEORGE LUCAS

So I was really not a fan of writing, which is ironic, but when it got to that part of it, I knew that I could write what I wanted. I knew still drawings couldn't tell me what I wanted, because I had to do it in terms of motion. I knew that was the secret behind what I was doing in terms of visual effects by that time. The one thing I grabbed onto was that, as opposed to Stanley Kubrick who had two-minute shots in *2001,* and where the thing just sits there and the ships were moving slowly so that you can see every detail and it's perfect, I said, "I'm not going to do that. What I'm going to do is I want to do shots that are only about twelve frames, thirty-two frames at most, and it'll move by so fast that you won't see how it's put together. It'll just be a razzle-dazzle of visual fantasy."

We had no technology to do what we were doing. At film school, I started as an animator and we came up with this idea of basically taking an animation stand and hooking it on rails, and putting the model there and using it just like an animation stand, but an animation stand relies on persistently machined parts so that everything is exactly the same. It really became a thing of metalworking, and making a precision thing that would move down a track and then we could repeat the same move every time and also link it to computers, which was the first time that was done. They were just starting to put computers on animation cameras, and so we just said, "Well, we'll just do it that way." And without that, we could never have done it, because it was literally like eight hundred short shots. It was basically a model on a stick with the camera moving past it and then doing the same thing on the star field and then matching those things together. Even though it's really simple now, it was a big head-scratcher at the time and everything depended on it.

American Graffiti was miserable, while *THX* was fun. But as soon as I started getting bigger and I started pushing the envelope, I started getting myself into real trouble. When you're in real trouble, then you're miserable all day. What happened with this one is that it was literally that I came back from shooting, having a miserable experience, and ILM hadn't done one shot. They had spent half the budget, it was six months later and we only had six months to go before the film was going to be released. We had eight hundred shots and there wasn't one that I had accepted. I realized that I had painted myself into a corner and didn't know what to do.

When Fox accepted the script, I started preproduction with ILM. So they were working when we had to build the whole thing and build the camera from scratch, I'd hired a couple of those guys before that just to start figuring out the technology and how we would do it. I was pushing the envelope with one thing, which was how to make spaceships move fast in the space and pan with them, because I was really obsessed with the kinetic energy of a pan. I said, "If I could just put a pan on a spaceship, it'll really make this thing take off."

On June 1, 1975, that special effects company, ILM (Industrial Light & Magic), officially came into existence in Van Nuys, California, in a warehouse that the recently hired John Dykstra had discovered. Other early employees were model builder Grant McCune, Jerry Greenwood, Richard Alexander, Bob Shepherd, Al Miller, Don Trumbull, model builders Bill and Jamie Shourt, and Richard Edlund, who headed up the camera department.

Their first task was to design and construct a motion control camera, which would allow them to program camera movements and repeat them. In July, ILM would add Robbie Blalack and Adam Beckett as the heads of the optical department. Ben Burtt was hired through USC to head up the sound department, which would, of course, be an integral part of Star Wars.

RICHARD EDLUND

(first cameraman: miniature and optical effects unit, *Star Wars*)

I think we're all a product of experiences. I had a lot of varied experience from being a one-man band, where I did everything myself, to working with other people. All of those experiences that led up to this contributed not only in technical prowess, which I needed to do the project, but also to prepare me psychologically for such a project and to have the opportunity to work with such an incredibly talented group of people that we assembled. I was like, one of the first three or four people that were brought in. At a higher level, anyway. It was John Dykstra, Grant McCune, Joe Johnston, and Dick Alexander.

Basically, I was at Robert Abel and Associates and I was the hot cameraman there at the time. We who were the monks in photographic technology knew about each other all over town. I knew who John was. I'd never met him, but I knew who he was and he knew who I was. So one day I got a call from John, "Come on out and let's talk about this sci-fi movie we're going to do for Fox." So I jumped in my Volkswagen and headed out to Valjean Avenue in Van Nuys, which was this empty warehouse. He was there with Gary Kurtz and I sat down and talked to them and in about half an hour I had the job. Maybe less. I mean, I had all the chops that were required to be the first camera on the show and basically be responsible for shooting all the elements. It was a great opportunity. I didn't start right away; I think I gave Abel two months' notice.

ERIC TOWNSEND
(author, *The Making of Star Wars Timeline*)

Fox had given Lucas a $1.5 million effects budget, instead of the originally proposed $2.3 million. By contrast, the effects shots for the film *2001* cost producers $6.5 million in 1967. The motion control camera was built at a cost of around $60,000. This technology, which was pioneered by ILM, allowed filmmakers to program camera movements into a computer while filming stationary models, giving the illusion of movement.

JOHN DYKSTRA

Jim Nelson was hired by the production to be the producer of the visual effects. Bill Short, Dick Alexander, Grant McCune were all guys who had been working with Doug Trumbull. Doug's dad, Don Trumbull, who did a lot of the optical and camera design work for us, obviously worked at his son's place, too, so I brought those guys in. I brought some people from my educational background into the environment. Then I had worked at Berkeley and that was where Al Miller came from to do the electronic stuff and Richard Edlund came from Bob Abel and he was somebody that I knew from doing commercial work. Robbie Blalack had been operating an optical printer setup and he came in. We were all young. Everybody was in their twenties.

RICHARD EDLUND

Basically, you have to know that you can work with other people and it was a beautiful group of people that we assembled in the first few months there. For example, Robbie Blalack was a talented young guy, just out of Cal Arts, and he had made some kind of a deal with Larry Butler [visual effects artist] over at Columbia who had built a special optical printer for *Marooned* [1969]. So

Robbie had that printer and he brought it out to Cal Arts, but it was a 35mm printer and he didn't have the kind of money to do any work in 35mm at that time. So basically, he wound up taking that printer to the fledgling ILM and Dick Alexander had to spend many months converting it, and our electronic genius came up with a drive system for it and then we got a whole bunch of VistaVision movements from Howard Anderson, Jr.

Howard Anderson, Jr., was a cinematographer specializing in visual effects. He co-owned and operated the Howard Anderson Company with his brother, Darrell. The company, which was started by their father, Howard Anderson, Sr., was an optical effects house that worked on many films and television series, including the original Star Trek.

RICHARD EDLUND

They had an insert stage where they would shoot stuff and they had optical printers and things like that that were in 35mm. When I was at Abel's I discovered that he had a VistaVision printer that had been sitting in a room for years and it hadn't been used and I was trying to talk Abel into buying it. I think we actually wound up buying that printer for *Star Wars* from Howard for $14,000. I mean, what a deal that was and it was a VistaVision printer!

JOHN DYKSTRA

We rented a warehouse next to the Van Nuys airport. It was, I don't know, four thousand or seven thousand square feet—I can't remember which—and we set about putting together the staff to make the movie. There were a lot of questions to be answered. The story of *Star Wars* as presented to me included spaceships having dogfights, which was the most exciting thing, and when I went to talk to George about it, we did a lot of "hands-flying." If you have ever seen people who are pilots talk maneuvering airplanes there is hand-flying and we talked about what existing technology was available to actually execute work like that and what our options were.

All of those effects were to occur while being viewed from a camera platform that itself needed the fluidity and freedom of motion of a camera plane. This visual concept was a far cry from the locked-off camera approach to spacecraft miniature photography seen in the space classics of the past. This was a challenge, to say the least. As the meetings and story breakdown continued, it became clear that this film would not showcase twenty or thirty special photographic effects shots, but would use spaceships, miniatures, and all manner of photographic effects, as you would use automobiles in a film of contemporary time setting. In the entire film, there are some 365 miniature and photographic effects shots. The challenge, therefore, became a task of mammoth proportions. In order to produce the quantity and quality of special photographic effects shots called for in *Star Wars*, a complete in-house system would have to be developed. This system would include miniature design and construction facilities; the design and fabrication of a camera motion control system, electronics, and mechanical facets; and a complete optical house and animation department. I felt that the in-house system would be the only way that consistency of quality and control over each of the separate operations could be maintained.

I had an overall view of what I thought needed to happen and it was based on my experience with Doug Trumbull and his visual effects facility Future General and my experience at Berkeley using computer-controlled cameras for the National Science Foundation. It involved the creation of a complete studio because we needed to do the construction of the miniatures, we needed to construct the camera systems, and we had to develop or construct the optical department because we were going to use a larger film format than conventional. One of the problems with film is that when you duplicate it, which is what you do when you do optical printing, you lose quality. It picks up contrast and the grain gets worse and the resolution gets worse.

So I wanted to do a large negative in order to reduce the quality loss that came as a result of that optical printing step. So we were going to use VistaVision and the reason that the optical printer was purchased was because it was a VistaVision printer. That was our format of choice and of course that required that we build new operating systems for the printers because they were all old-fashioned systems and [we needed] new optics because the quality of the glass had a lot to do with the quality of the image. So we designed and built new lenses and purchased some new lenses for the optical systems and designed a complete photographic system meaning cameras and film-handling equipment around the VistaVision format.

VistaVision was a higher-resolution, widescreen variant of the 35mm motion picture film format. Created by engineers at Paramount Pictures in 1954, the process required new cameras through which the 35mm negative traveled horizontally rather than vertically. The result was a negative image with an area nearly three times that of a standard negative image. IMAX, also a horizontal film system, is a descendant of VistaVision.

RICHARD EDLUND

I remember when we went to see the printer, we had to climb up about three flights of stairs along the side of the stage to get up to the top area where this printer was. Then we go into the room and it had these switches that you turned. They weren't toggle switches. You turned them to turn the light on and everything was kind of battleship green and there's the printer standing there. It was not dusty because the room was closed and actually the last camera report has been written up on *The Ten Commandments* [1956] and was sitting on the write-up table. They basically left the room and never came back and so twenty years later I guess it would have been, we wound up buying the printer.

Howard also threw in two roto benches that were these big contraptions with mirrors and large format. So we could roto at twenty-two-inch field, which is what I decided on and so we had twenty-four-inch cells and these Bell & Howell 2709 cameras, which were very steady cameras that had blanking shutters in them so it would pull twice to make eight—that's tech knowledge, but anyway, we had two of those roto machines and one or two extra 2709 cameras, and then a box of movements. These were VistaVision movements and in compositing, you have to have a positive and a negative movement for each head and the big pin is in a different position for each movement . . .

The issue in compositing for motion pictures is you're lining up with a composite image that's less than an inch wide and that's being blown up to fifty feet. So a thousandth of an inch in a one-inch image is like 3/4 of an inch or an inch when you blow it up. So the kind of precision that's necessary and all that was uncanny and it was miraculous that we were able to put 365 composites together in under two years for *Star Wars*. I mean, we had to actually build the system to start with.

JOHN DYKSTRA

We had to start designing equipment the day we walked in and assembling the team that was going to do it. So we had to have machinists, cameramen, model builders, you know, lighting and grip, all of the things that are required to make a studio that will operate. So we're putting together our team while we were designing the cameras. We were building the cameras while the miniatures were being constructed. We began photography when the first of the cameras and the first of the miniatures reached completion and we had the wherewithal within this studio to start lighting and shooting stuff. It wasn't as quick as the studio would have liked, but we were building cameras from scratch and designing and building a complete numeric control camera system including building the processors that ran it. There were no laptops or desktop computers at that point. The computers that controlled the movement of the camera were individually designed and wire-wrapped. That stuff was all designed and built essentially in the first year. The second year was spent finishing the systems, redesigning and reconstructing some of the systems to meet the new and special requirements of shots that were specified for the movie and then completing the work.

RICHARD EDLUND

When I got there, there was a big empty stage that was like a hundred feet across and fifty or sixty feet wide. That would be the area that I would have for the boom camera that we built and in the beginning, there was nothing on the stage but a card table with a phone on it. And so that's what I started out with and we had to build the Dykstraflex, which had a forty-two-foot track and a boom that went up and down about ten feet, maybe a little more; and it went sideways, it rotated, camera pan, tilt, and roll; that was the camera.

One of the most important early developments was the creation of Dykstraflex— designed by Dykstra, Al Miller, and Jerry Jeffress—which was the first digital motion control photography camera system. Created specifically for Star Wars, *the system used old VistaVision cameras for their higher resolution and allowed for seven axes of digitally controlled movement, which could be duplicated for multiple takes. The trio would ultimately win an Academy Award in 1978 for their creation of the system.*

JOHN DYKSTRA

I had the idea for years. This is just one permutation of the concept. It's not a new concept. It's very old, like blue screen or front projection. It's been around for years, just waiting to be perfected or improved to suit the needs of a particular situation. Al Miller is an electronics designer. We sat down with two bottles of wine during the old Future General days and figured out what the machine ought to do, what it ought to look like, and how to program it. Basically, it is just a combination of all the techniques that have been used for years, combined into a sophisticated device capable of manufacturing techniques.

It started out with the premise that we wanted to have the flexibility to move the camera in free space and have multiple moving subjects. Traditional techniques to do that where you wanted to move the camera and the subject and do it non-real-time, meaning not at twenty-four frames per second, was stop-motion photography and that was the Ray Harryhausen process. One of the problems with that process was the camera was still during the exposure so the subject and the camera move itself had no motion blur.

RICHARD EDLUND

So there's like five or six channels of motion control required there and then you have the model mover which is another track that was perpendicular to the main track and that one went from right to left on the tracking. It didn't have a boom, but it rotated and you could rotate the model. So that was the limitation that we had and we built this very complicated contraption that I compare to a violin that we then had to learn how to play. So we built this very complicated machine and then I had to learn how to play it and then program shots one axis at a time. I usually wound up doing the track first to get the size change and then I'd do various pans, tilts, rolls, and I'd have to position the model right in the right position. We were flying right by the model often with fairly wide lenses to get a real motion dynamic going and every once in a while I'd crash into one. I'd scrape the model and then I'd have to call Grant [McCune] and he'd have to come out and fix it. It was quite a deal.

JOHN DYKSTRA

When you photograph a real subject with a real camera and you are moving the camera during the exposure, the camera displaces and the subject displaces and the image is blurred in the direction of that motion. And nobody had the ability to slow the camera motion down to the frame rates necessary to photograph miniatures with extreme depth of field at that time with the exception of stop-motion, but it stuttered. So I knew that I wanted to be able to move the camera during exposure and the Natural Science Foundation provided me with a means to control the movement of the camera and the subject on a continuous basis. By changing the clock rate, I could vary the speed. I could run the thing at 100 percent and it would be twenty-four frames per second. I could run it at 1 percent and it would be 124th the speed. The idea being that I had the ability to make a continuous move and vary the rate at which that move was exposed with motion blur exposure, which replicated real-world photography in non-real-time and that was the key to making the stuff look real.

The motion blur was what made the spaceships when they whizzed past the camera have that long streak behind them, which is what you are familiar with seeing in actual photography of a car driving by at high speed. In individual frames, the car is actually blurred so that was the key. Full flexibility of motion, variable time base, larger-format camera to compensate for the duplication necessary for optical printing and repeatability, which was one of the elements that was necessary since we had so many ships in the individual shots it was impossible for us to shoot them all at the same time. In many cases, if there were three or four ships in the shot, they would be shot as individual components or as separate elements and the means to do that required that you be able to repeat accurately the movement of the camera. The other aspect of that was that because we were generating these shots as elements and shooting in non-real-time, we had to come up with a matting system that would allow us to extract the images and re-composite them over the backgrounds that we chose to use and that was where optical printing and the blue-screen process came in.

One of the restrictions was, we had to fit this big facility into the space that we had. The stages were limited size, which meant we had to build the miniatures small enough to shoot on multiple stages to complete the work in the time that we had, which dictated the scale and the construction of the cameras to a certain extent.

RICHARD EDLUND

There were all kinds of limitations. I had a forty-two-foot track, but that only gave me about thirty-eight feet that I could use because the carriage on the track took over three feet, and then you had to ramp up to speed and you had to ramp down at the other end. So you only had about thirty-five feet of actual usable track feet at speed.

JOHN DYKSTRA

There was a certain amount of reverse engineering that went into this. The miniatures were much smaller than miniatures were normally made and that was partly based on the effort that we had to make to fit this into the facility that we were working with. Plus, we had to displace the miniatures through great distances because of the speed they carried in many of the shots, so if you built a twelve-foot miniature and you wanted it to travel twelve times its distance, all of a sudden you had to have a 124-foot stage. So instead of building it twelve feet I would build it one foot and we would end up with a stage that was fourteen feet long—not that it was like that—but we were traveling much greater distances so the nature of the photography, the nature of requirements that we had for space, made it so that we used smaller miniatures to get much greater displacement of subject in a much smaller space.

Over the course of those nine months, the facility in Van Nuys was transformed from an empty warehouse into a state-of-the-art visual effects facility. Key to that growth was the talent and integrity of the people involved, and their ability to communicate with each other. But there were definitely problems in terms of logistics between the main production unit of the film in the UK and the efforts of ILM.

JOHN DYKSTRA

Because the photographic effects were to be done in the United States and the live-action filming was to be done in England, some rather severe communication problems had to be overcome. George Lucas, Joe Johnston, and I described each shot in one or more storyboards, and its requirements were established, right to the frame count. Most of this information came from a cut battle sequence, made up of excerpts from war movies. This established the size and speed of the fighters and their positions in frame. With this first set of storyboards in hand, we set about finalizing our miniatures and photographic systems. Concurrent with the assembly of the optical department and model facilities, we continued the development of the photographic and motion control system. Having completed the design in July of 1975, we began construction of the Dykstraflex.

RICHARD EDLUND

We finished the camera and I had about a week to do two tests and then I invited George to come down so I could show him what we could do, what the camera could do, and what the limitations were.

Two of the most impressive moments in the film in terms of visual effects involved the Millennium Falcon. The first is when it makes the jump to hyperspace leaving Tatooine, as well as in the film's finale when it banks while escaping the magnificent Death Star explosion (by the late Joe Viskocil, subsequently modified for the special editions much to Viskocil's chagrin).

RICHARD EDLUND

For the hyperspace effect, I had an idea. It goes back to when I was a kid in Fargo. We used to drive in the car and the snow would streak towards the headlights and I was thinking that maybe something like that would work. So I did a test; I did a streak shot. It was about twenty-four to thirty frames, I think. I shot the stars streak and disappear as a test and I sent it to George and he said, "Oh, I love that!" and he cut it in and so that was it. So it was just take one and that became an iconic shot in *Star Wars*. That cut to a shot of the Millennium Falcon zooming off to infinity, and because I was limited to a forty-five-foot track, or I was limited to being able to do thirty-five feet at speed let's say, what I did was I shot a four-by-five Polaroid of the back of the Millennium Falcon and I cut it out. I shot it diagonally so it was about four and a half inches wide and I stuck it on a piece of glass and shot it in front of a blue screen and did a pull-back from it. And that shot maybe lasted fifteen frames or something like that. So you had the stars streak and disappear and then you cut to the shot of the Millennium Falcon zipping off into infinity and that shot costs about twelve bucks! I just shot this Polaroid against blue screen, but that was all you needed. That's one of the essences of learning how to cheat.

And then with it escaping the Death Star, the Millennium Falcon weighed more than a hundred pounds I am sure. I don't know what it weighed finally, but all the other models—the TIE Fighters, the X-Wings, the Y-Wings—those all had like three-quarter-inch aluminum pipes and all they weighed was like a pound or two, but the Millennium Falcon was this great big mother and it had a two-inch pipe. It was two-inch steel pipe mounting on the back and I had to program this thing to turn and flop around. I can't even remember now, it was really complicated, and I think I remember using all twelve channels to program this and I finally got it programmed. In order to make it work, I had to not only light the ship, but light the docking bay and that was a tough shot. There is actually a picture of me sitting back while the camera is shooting the scene. You can barely see me in there, but I am sitting in the far right side.

And then there's the classic, iconic shot that might be one of the most memorable in the history of motion pictures, in which the Rebel Blockade Runner is pursued by the even larger Star Destroyer blasting in from overhead, which truly astounded audiences when the film was originally released.

RICHARD EDLUND

George would come by and say, "Let's build this miniature on the side wall of the stage," and I would say, "Now George, we only have a forty-two-foot track." So he would ruminate on that and then we would change the subject and talk about something else. I knew he needed a really great shot for an opening and I had an idea that I could try doing a shot of the Star Destroyer that we had. The model was maybe forty inches long and I told Grant, "Put your best guy on detailing the bottom of the ship and especially the little docking bay and let me try a test." Also, I said, "Can you kind of jam together about a three-inch-long Blockade Runner?" The Rebel Blockade Runner, by the way, was originally going to be the Millennium Falcon and George came by one day and said, "You know, that looks too much like *Space: 1999*, you guys have to come up with something else." I don't know if it was Joe Johnston or Grant McCune that came up with the round Millennium Falcon, but that was a brilliant idea and it was asymmetrical so you had the cockpit on one side. It was a great looking ship and it's a monument to *Star Wars*.

So anyhow, I took a paper clip and straightened it out and stuck the Blockade Runner on the tip of the ship and shot the model upside down in front of the blue screen. I pulled back very slowly with a 24mm tilting lens to hold the focus all the way down. I tilted the lens in order to change the focus field like a view camera. I had the tilting lens and I was virtually scraping the bottom of the model with the camera. To get it perfectly level so I could go straight back with the model was not easy either. That took about an hour to get that straightened out. And so I did a test and everybody was flummoxed by the test the next day. It was going to work.

I think I did two or three more takes of the ship until we got to the final shot. But I always felt that that was the most important shot that we did because that was the opening of the movie, and if you want to grab the audience with a shot, that's it. And if that shot doesn't work, the movie doesn't work. It did work and it's another icon to *Star Wars*. And then the Blockade Runner was longer than it needed to be. It was about four feet long and I had to shoot that to make it fit into the bottom of the Star Destroyer. So that huge model wound up being inserted into a four-inch docking bay. So that was the next effect you saw.

In addition to special effects involving spaceships, there was, of course, the introduction of the Jedi Knight's ultimate weapon, the lightsaber, which would come to play so integral a part in the Star Wars *saga.*

PETER BEALE

We had the lightsabers and the obvious first thing I thought of was fluorescent lights, but that would have been too dangerous. Could you imagine trying to duel with fluorescent lights and it breaking and electrocuting the actors? It was obviously not the answer. One thought about animation, but this was before digital animation. It would have been frame-by-frame physical animation, and the cost of that would have been enormous. I didn't have a solution in my mind. What I did is that I put in the budget about fourteen weeks of special effects money, and saying, "That's their problem; maybe they can solve it," and they did. I'll tell how they did it; it was absolutely brilliant how it was solved.

One day, John Stears called me and said, "I think I have a solution for the lightsaber." I got hold of Gary Kurtz and we went up to the workshop at Elstree, up above the carpentry shop, and he was there and he had what looked like an oval wooden blade with some gray material on it, and a fat handle.

He explained that he had put a little electric motor in that handle, so that the blade could revolve. I said, "That sounds interesting." He demonstrated it and the blade revolved.

JOHN STEARS
(special production and mechanical effects supervisor, *Star Wars*)
I devised a spinning sword. It had a lot of flat sides; some were coated with a reflective material and the other sides weren't, which, when spun, achieved a stabbing forward motion in conjunction with a light fixed on the top of the camera. This was photographed through a half-silvered mirror.

PETER BEALE
I thought, "That's not really what we were thinking for a lightsaber." I was a bit worried and disappointed. Then he said, "I'm going to put this light on," and he put a little 100-watt light bulb on and suddenly the lightsaber arrived. What he had used was the front-projection material that we were experimenting with for front projection, he put it onto this blade, this oval blade, and just with a 100-watt light bulb, it glowed and flared. The great benefit of that is that the 100-watt light bulb wouldn't reflect on the actor with the normal set lighting, which is much brighter, and it wouldn't create any shadows. It was an absolute genius solution. It deserved in my mind, that alone, an Oscar. He deserves to go down in *Star Wars* history for that invention. I don't often see people talking about it, but he really deserves the credit.

JOHN STEARS
It didn't look like much if you were an inch away from the camera eye, but through the lens, it looked like how you see it on-screen. In fact, we saw the rushes to this scene the next day. With an optical, it would have taken weeks to see the results. The effect of the light beam emerging from the saber base was due to camera angles and the sword just starting to revolve. I work with very few opticals. I like to do things in one hit for obvious reasons.

DENNIS MUREN
(second cameraman: miniature and optical effects unit, *Star Wars*)
They were actually holding simulated swords made out of front-projection material. A light source near the camera shining onto the front-projection material hopefully would bounce back brightly. However, it didn't quite work. So what George had to do was put an overlay of the glow on top of that through rotoscoping. That's how they got the different colors. I think

the main thing you're seeing is the overlay. A diffusion effect was created by shooting the overlay through a fog filter. [The original] looked too solid, I think. George Lucas wanted something more like energy, something that you wouldn't want to get close to. The image was so bright it was flaring the lens out. Perhaps if they had more time to work on it they could have gotten the desired effect right away, but the entire show was pretty much compromised because of the time factor.

There were 360 composite effects shots made from 1,000 separate elements, something on that order. Most of these 1,000 elements we photographed in five months.

The final day of shooting of Star Wars *took place on July 16, 1976. Needing to decompress before tackling postproduction, Lucas flew to New York to visit with Brian De Palma and then to Mobile, Alabama, to see Steven Spielberg, who was filming* Close Encounters of the Third Kind. *Anxious and nervous about the shape of* Star Wars, *he was reassured by his friend. When he finally did return to California—as has been discussed—and discovered that the special effects team had literally completed only 3 out of 365 effects shots and had already spent over half their budget, Lucas responded by experiencing chest pains and was rushed to the hospital the next day suffering from exhaustion and hypertension. The problems, of course, remained.*

JOHN DYKSTRA

Directors and special effects directors always disagree incredibly because he conceptualizes one thing, but I know what is capable of production. The major problem we encountered on *Star Wars* was being able to apply what George started out with conceptually. From the day we met, we talked about World War II dogfights, footage which involved lots of action, continuous motion, moving camera streak, loops, and rolls. All of the things aerial photography allows you to do in live-action. This is difficult to do in special effects with multiple ships, background planets, and stars, because of the problems with angular displacement, matching shots, depth of field, wiring, etc. It's hard to explain that a concept won't work because of some technological thing, and this becomes a bone of contention. When a director shoots an exterior, he can see the lighting and the setup and the action and hear the dialogue. But when he comes in here all there is to see is a camera running down a track at about three inches a second. You have to be able to determine a spatial relationship without seeing it in front of you or compressing it in your mind's eye. It's more like an animation than anything else.

WILLIAM SHOURT
(camera and mechanical design: miniature and
optical effects unit, *Star Wars*)

We thought that the way we were going about the process was the right way, but it did take a long time before we could really start pumping out scenes.

LORNE PETERSON
(model builder: miniature and optical effects unit, *Star Wars*)

The pressure became really high. When George came back from England, we'd hoped that there [would be] more of those special effects done than there were. The reason that a lot of it wasn't done yet was, we were still building the equipment, the cameras and the rudimentary computers that were used at the time. So they were actually built on the premises and so there were two shots that we did right at the beginning to show George that they were possible to do without going through a lot of optical processes, and that was the detail of the gun firings—the large gun, like this firing on the Death Star. And then the other one was the drop of the escape pod with R2-D2 and C-3PO. They showed me a sketch of it and they said I needed to make the model quick, so I made it in a week.

BRUCE LOGAN
(second unit photography: miniature and
optical effects unit, *Star Wars*)

I had met with George and Gary at the beginning of the production when they were interviewing visual effects people. I found George to be very organized, the man knew exactly what he wanted but not always how to get it. He gave me marching orders and then left me alone to figure out how to do it. I'm not sure that I even watched dailies with him as my unit was at another location across town. He must have liked what he saw because our unit moved to bigger and bigger stages and we shot bigger and bigger explosions. George got back from shooting the live-action in England, and because the signature motion control effects system was being constructed, not a frame of film had been shot. Panicked, he called me up to head up a second effects unit to shoot puppeteers in black suits "flying" miniature spaceships on black rods. Not surprisingly this did not work out very well. So my unit moved on to do some of the signature explosions in the show.

My claim to fame is that I blew up the Death Star. When I think back to the first day of our unit, I remember Joe Viskocil, our powder genius who constructed all the miniature bombs, I realize we were just a bunch of unsupervised kids running the orphanage. Joe came in the first morning and there was a huge explosion and a cloud of smoke coming out of the little room on wheels that was used to load film. Luckily, there was only a loss of hair and a rash on Joe's arms. It was an interesting way to start. But it never really got any better as the explosions got bigger and better. I remember running around the stage wiping burning napalm from my arms after one of our larger explosions. Later, looking at pictures of our shoot, I see that our only fire protection was a single handheld fire extinguisher. Ahh! Simpler days.

JOHN DYKSTRA

The studio sent people in to try and organize the facility in a much more traditional fashion. It was a nontraditional environment. I am sure you have heard the stories. We had a hot tub in the parking lot that we cooled off in. Remember it was triple digits in the San Fernando Valley in the summertime when we were working on stages with thousands of watts of lights. It wouldn't be unusual for the stages to be 120 or 130 degrees and there was no air-conditioning, so we would go out to the hot tub to cool off during the day and people would work in the night time when it was cooler outside and as a result, the stages would be cooler to do the photographic aspect of it. Everyone who worked there was completely engrossed in the making of the movie and they lived there pretty much as a family in a weird way, and I think that was also really difficult for George and the studio, and from the studio's point of view to support because we were obviously going against the grain of the corporate structure.

CHRIS CASADY
(animator: miniature and optical effects unit, *Star Wars*)

I was part of this hiring wave that was supposed to ratchet up production and get this damn thing done by the deadline, and I was part of beefing things up. I understood that George Mather had preceded me not much earlier for the same purpose and that he was sort of brought in to be the hatchet man, or the adult in the room a little bit. Sometimes you'd hear Gary Kurtz talking about what he called "a hippie mentality" at ILM—which is not untrue. My experience of Mather is that he was really sort of there to intimidate us a little bit, and to be the adult and to look after things—particularly these late hires and the night crew and things like that. It felt like Jim brought him on as an adjunct to him.

Mather was the guy who had the ultimate chart. I think he sat down and looked seriously at the calendar and the shots and the shots and the calendar and tried to fit shots into it. "You've got two hundred shots to do, you've got seven months left. That means so many shots per day. That means the stage has got to put out three shots every day. That's two for the day shift or something." So with Mather, my memory was that he was dishing out these assignments. You know, "Dennis Muren, you have to knock out three finished spaceship shots per night if you're going to make this deadline." And so it seemed like we were sort of answering to him. He sort of intimidated us a little bit up in the animation department. Or that's how I felt about it.

DOUG BARNETT

(special mechanical equipment: miniature and
optical effects unit, *Star Wars*)

George asked for one more dollar than Dykstra was making. He got it. Dykstra would just sort of run down George Lucas in the hallways. He had no sense of courtesy with George Lucas. And Lucas just despised that, because George is short and small and Dykstra was tall. Jim Nelson was tall. So they hired George Mather to just push on Dykstra, I think, and make the place work. He'd be there, day or night. He had come from real low-budget stuff, so he really had this idea that we didn't have to spend a dime more.

ADAM BECKETT

(animation and rotoscope design: miniature and
optical effects unit, *Star Wars*)

George Mather, our production supervisor, mentioned the fact that for about six weeks it really looked as though we might get the plug pulled on the picture. That was late in 1976. Hardly any shots were done. Millions of dollars had been spent and we had something like thirty thousand to forty thousand a week in payroll. Production just wasn't there. Can you imagine *Star Wars* not being finished? I think that near-catastrophe is a fantastically romantic aspect of the whole story, though it wasn't exactly pleasant at that time.

DENNIS MUREN

George and Gary are a couple of amazing people to be able to pull off the show like that. I had to say pull off, because that sounds like a card game or something. But it was a real effort they put into it. They never gave up.

In truth, by the middle of production everyone should have realized that the effects were becoming a much bigger problem than anyone realized.

PETER BEALE

We're halfway through, we're a little bit behind schedule, but not much. We've eaten a little bit of the contingency up and we're going to start doing the process work. The day before we're starting, we've got the front screen projection set up, all the equipment set up. I think we're starting with one of the fighters. The front projection plate arrived. We got it up and the first thing we discovered was that it was difficult to synchronize the actors' reaction to the starship flying past. They were going past so quickly that by the time we knew they were coming, woof, they're gone. We had problems trying to anticipate and synchronize the actors' reactions to the background that we were projecting. George Lucas had actually edited the fighter sequence out of footage from World War I and World War II. He had used *Blue Max* and other films, so we had shot-by-shot, and we had to imagine the X-Wing fighter instead of Spitfires, but we had the whole sequence laid out. It was brilliantly done.

Halfway through the first day, I called up and said, "Where are the next day's plates?" Nobody knew. So I called up Dykstra in the States in California—woke him up early—and said, "What's going on?" There was a long silence. They haven't gotten it; they hadn't done it. They had run into troubles and hadn't wanted to tell us, and if they would have told us maybe we could have made a thing, so we've now got the whole thing set up, we're planning to film this for a week and we obviously don't have any other sets ready. We're in trouble. And so we had to jump to blue screen. George was very unhappy, I was unhappy, because we really wanted to have it done, but in retrospect, it was probably a very good thing, because the synchronization of the reactions to the plates was going to be very, very difficult. When we went to blue screen, we caught up on schedule and things got a bit easier. And morale started going up.

Once he was back in the States, Lucas took a decidedly more hands-on approach with ILM, creating conflict between himself and Dykstra.

JOHN DYKSTRA

He looked at the material with us. A good portion of the time he was in England, and then he came back and started editing. We had produced a fair amount of the stuff that was in the movie by the time he was back to cut. But, we used his reference footage from the old war movies, the dogfight stuff, that was sort of the template for what it was we were going to do. We took that and interpreted that into a much more extreme version in terms of how close we got to the subject matter with the cameras and the speeds with which things traveled and some of the choreography of what the spaceships actually did.

So he would come and look at material and we'd run multiple elements together in the Moviola [which allows an editor to watch a film while editing] and discuss the dynamics of the shot and we'd go off and do it and he'd come back and look at dailies. But it was tough because you had to look at the shots elementally. We had a device that allowed us to run multiple strips of film in a projector at the same time, but the film by its very nature was fairly low resolution and didn't have much gray scale to it because of the viewer multipacking. You put three or four strips of film into a projector at a time and in cases where we had more than three or four elements we had to bi-pack or tri-pack or just multiple pack separate sets and then take reference drawings and put multiple sets together to interpret this, which was a long and involved process and he didn't want to be involved with that much. He wanted to be involved in composites where he actually got to see all of the actual elements together in their choreography.

The output from ILM intensified through the latter part of 1976. By November, Marcia Lucas had edited a rough cut of the film that ran about 117 minutes. It was at this point that Lucas decided to cut certain scenes to take the pressure off of ILM as much as he could. He also believed this would tighten and improve the finished film.

Another important aspect of Star Wars, *likely more than most people realized at the time, was the sound design. That fell to Ben Burtt. The son of a chemistry professor and a child psychologist, he was born in Jamesville, New York, on July 12, 1948. Though interested in becoming a filmmaker from an early age, he first studied physics at Allegheny College in Pennsylvania. While attending university, he made his own films, eventually being awarded the National Student Film Award for his short film* Yankee Squadron. *For his next short film, entitled* Genesis, *Burtt was awarded a scholarship to attend the University of Southern California, where he earned a master's degree in film production. He found early work as a sound designer for the Roger Corman film* Death Race 2000 *before being hired by fellow USC alum George Lucas to work on his latest film,* Star Wars. *Never losing sight of his other aspirations, Burtt has directed several documentary films, as well as being an executive producer and writer for the* Star Wars: Droids *TV series.*

BEN BURTT
(sound designer, *Star Wars*)

George and Gary were searching for people at USC to do special effects and costume design, and artists and model builders to design spaceships. This was in June of 1975. Ultimately, Gary Kurtz contacted some professors at USC and asked them to recommend someone who would be interested in working on the soundtrack [sound design]. I was recommended since I was the biggest fanatic down there in terms of sound effects.

My first assignment was to come up with a voice for the Wookiee. At that time, the Wookiee played a slightly bigger role than he eventually ended up with. The story was still evolving at that point. The first thing they said was, "We have this giant creature who's like a big teddy bear. He's a good guy, but sometimes he's ferocious. We need a nonhuman voice for him that's really believable, but not recognizable as a known animal." In a few weeks, it became evident that they wanted a whole repertoire of sounds. I finally saw the script, met George, and talked with them more. They needed all kinds of voices and equipment sounds. They needed sound for weapons and hardware and mechanical devices. Basically what I did was break down the entire script into different categories: special voices, weapons, vehicles, doors, etc. I was trying to find sound that would be appropriate and original. In a film like this, you're creating a total fantasy world. Nothing really exists. None of the equipment makes any sound during filming, or the sound it does make isn't the right one. All the sets look great, but they're totally dead. There's no life to them. All kinds of sounds were needed to give it credibility and to make it exciting. It's not just to make it acceptable. The whole movie is a comic book. It needed really energetic sounds that were visceral.

In terms of Chewbacca, Burtt explains that his research involved a number of things initially. The first was to determine the different methods people have used to modify sound and produce voices. This led him to collect tapes of a variety of exotic languages and study them for alien-sounding, unfamiliar characteristics. From there, he went to language labs of various universities and studied their tapes.

BEN BURTT

The Wookiee had to be approached differently, because he was a real animal. The challenge there was to find some actual animals, record them, and somehow make use of those sounds for his speech. We initially thought that bears would be pretty good and they were. I recorded all kinds of bears that I could find. I rented bears, went to ranches where they had pet bears, and then recorded all different kinds of animals. I went to zoos and recorded sea lions and camels, and tried to determine what animals had certain speech patterns. Sea lions and walruses were terrific. Bears are very good. As it turned out, a lot of the Wookiee was mostly "bear." Even bears of the same species still have different personalities.

In the end, I took recordings of bears, camels, walruses, lions, and a few cougars and extracted sounds out of them that were similar in color. The difficulty in dubbing a language is that you have to be consistent. You just can't cut a dolphin to a walrus. It has to be homogeneous. I picked various bits of those animals, sounds which were consistent, and built word lists out of them. I took each one of them and reproduced it at different speeds, plus or minus, a little bit of one animal or another, sort of like musical notes. Once you have this batch of different sounds, you could draw isolated bits of "words" or syllables. Then you combine them, and try to make up a sentence that gives the desired feeling. The Wookiee ended up not saying a whole lot. He roared when he was angry and he had about five or six "sentences." But there's not a touch of the human voice in there. It's all animal.

A character like Greedo, the bounty hunter, from the cantina scene saw his language "lifted" straight from Peruvian Incan, while the most challenging "voice" to devise was that of the soon-to-be beloved droid R2-D2.

BEN BURTT

Basically, the essential character, as it turned out, was to combine the electronic with the organic, the organic being the warm, lovable, somewhat human side of his personality. The electronic part was generated by a synthesizer. The other part of his voice was derived from human-produced sounds. There was also a fair smattering of mechanical sounds in there, squeaks produced by scraping dry ice against metal, all blended together. What I did was sit down and decide that R2 was going to say something like, "Look out!" when a soldier approached. Then I'd try to come up with a sentence that had some emotional feeling to it. I'd make some beeps and run my voice through a synthesizer and go into my library of cute mechanical sounds and put them all together. I also blew through a water pipe and got this neat little whistle.

Achieving the sound of the Rebel Blockade Runner and the Star Destroyer early on led Burtt to record at the Mojave Air Races, which featured high-speed aircraft flying ten feet above the ground.

BEN BURTT

I took those and slowed them down tremendously. A lot of the very high frequencies would therefore drop down to a more audible range. I then mixed that with the "whoosh" of jet planes and a thunderclap. The first ship was the thunderclap and the jet sounds. The second sound was basically made up of two elements: a low-frequency rumble and part of the sound of the Goodyear Blimp slowed way, way down. I spent a long time recording the blimp. It's one of my favorite sounds. It created the sense of something gigantic moving. The mixers did a lot of special enhancements of low frequencies for that particular effect, too. In other words, when they did the final mix, they would use special filters and exaggerate the rumbling aspect of it. You could do that with 70mm stereophonic sound, but not with an ordinary optical track.

There are also lots of different kinds of lasers. Han Solo's laser was different from the Empire's. The basic concept of the lasers was to come up with something explosive without having it sound like a gunshot. It wasn't going to be Dirty Harry's Magnum. Again, this entailed a lot of research. What really worked well, in the end, was the striking of a long cable suspended from a radio tower. You have to find a tower with just the right frequency, and I found one.

While it would be understandable to assume that much of this was done in conjunction with ILM, it turns out that Burtt actually created his panoply of sounds at home.

BEN BURTT

During the first year of production, they were all in England and the people at ILM were inventing things. I would work at home and spent a little time at ILM shooting computer readouts for the spaceship dashboards. When George came back from Europe, we went to San Francisco where all the editing was done. We worked there for six or seven months just putting the picture together, adding sound effects, trying out different pieces of music, and studying the different versions of the film. We eventually arrived at what we thought was more or less the final product.

Being dubbed as the "Greatest Film Composer of All Time" is no easy feat, yet John Williams thoroughly deserves the title. John Towner Williams was born on February 8, 1932, in Floral Park, New York, to mother Esther and father Johnny Williams, the latter a jazz drummer and percussionist who played with the Raymond Scott Quintet. In 1948 the Williams family moved to Los Angeles where John attended North Hollywood High School, graduating in 1950. He later attended the University of California, Los Angeles, and studied composition privately with the Italian composer Mario Castelnuovo-Tedesco. Williams was drafted into the United States Air Force in 1951, where he arranged music for the U.S. Air Force Band. After his service ended in 1955, Williams moved to New York City, where he attended the Juilliard School and played jazz nightclubs around the city in the evenings to supplement his income.

Williams moved back to Los Angeles after he completed Juilliard, where he became a session musician for television shows and movies, working with such greats as Alfred Newman and Bernard Herrmann. Working his way up through the ranks, Williams would eventually become the composer for television shows like M Squad *and* Lost in Space.

Williams's first film credit for composition came in 1960 for the film Because They're Young. *Williams received his first Academy Award nomination for his score for 1967's* Valley of the Dolls, *and was nominated again for his score for 1969's* Goodbye, Mr. Chips. *He won his first Academy Award for his score for the 1971 film* Fiddler on the Roof. *Arguably, his career-defining moment came when he was asked by Steven Spielberg to compose the score for his 1975 film* Jaws. *This prompted Spielberg to suggest Williams to his good friend George Lucas, when Lucas was on the hunt for a composer who had a grand symphonic style redolent of his idols like Erich Wolfgang Korngold that Lucas felt was lacking in the then current Hollywood norm.*

JOHN WILLIAMS
(composer, *Star Wars*)

I have no pretensions about that score, which I wrote for what I thought was a children's movie. All of us who worked on it thought it would be a great Saturday morning show. None of us had any idea that it was going to become a great world success.

JOE KRAEMER
(composer, *Mission Impossible: Rogue Nation* and *Jack Reacher*)

It's interesting to contextualize the score to *Star Wars* in the cultural landscape of 1977. It really was a throwback to a style of scoring that had fallen out of favor. We take it for granted now in 2020 that the music is what it is, and that it works so well, but at the time, it was a risky choice to do a 1940s sort of Korngold score for a science fiction movie.

People like to point out the similarities in the score to other pieces of music, such as "Mars" from *The Planets,* or the opening of the second tableau from *The Rite of Spring,* but these allusions were deliberate—John Williams felt the principal audience for the film would be children and he hoped that the references to the classics would lead them to explore the original pieces he was alluding to.

George Lucas's original idea had been to use preexisting classical music as the score, much like Stanley Kubrick had done in *2001: A Space Odyssey,* but also like many of the serials from the 1930s that Lucas was inspired by. Williams, concerned that using well-known material would constrict his ability to make the kind of dramatic changes a score would need, convinced Lucas to allow him to instead create original themes for the film. Williams credits Lucas for the instinct that the music for the film should be rooted in the familiar, rather than the exotic, with the belief that the outlandish visuals and "outer-space setting" would be tempered by the classical basis of the score.

JEFF BOND
(editor, *Film Score Monthly*)

John Williams rightly saw the original *Star Wars* as a film for children, and working with George Lucas, he sought to find the most emotionally direct approach to support the film's action and make it understandable to a young audience. Lucas had originally considered licensing Gustav Holst's classical work *The Planets* to give the film a larger-than-life feel; Williams took that as a starting point and also took inspiration from the swashbuckling feel of the movie and looked back to the Golden Age of Hollywood and composers like Erich Wolfgang Korngold and Miklós Rózsa, ultimately giving his score a grand, symphonic sweep and power. Williams also took Sergei Prokofiev's leitmotif approach and composed highly recognizable themes for the film's characters: a heroic theme for Luke Skywalker, a romantic theme for Princess Leia, and a stirring, noble theme for Obi-Wan Kenobi and the Force. Other science fiction films of the era had concentrated on dystopian visions and often abstract, experimental, "futuristic" music, which intentionally created a feeling of alienation. Williams's score was instantly accessible, rousing, and memorable, its themes ready to be hummed and whistled by audiences as they emerged from the theater. The score had a vigorous life outside the film itself and transformed movie music, at least for the blockbusters that followed in the wake of *Star Wars*—Williams and other composers in the following years returned to the grand, symphonic language of classic Hollywood films and created a new era of bold, exciting orchestral film music.

JOE KRAEMER

There is a wonderful nod to Williams's friend, Bernard Herrmann, in the scene where the heroes come up from the smuggling compartments in the floor in the Millennium Falcon when it's in the Death Star hangar. Paul Hirsch, the picture editor, had temped it with a cue from the score to *Psycho*, and Williams quoted the first three notes of the cue in his final score for the scene.

The film has a lexicon of themes, many of which returned multiple times throughout the ongoing saga. There is the Main Theme, considered Luke's Theme in this film. Ben Kenobi has a theme, which grew to encompass "the Force" as the films went on. Princess Leia has a wonderful Korngoldian theme, which had a special concert arrangement featured on the soundtrack LP. The Rebellion has a theme, as well as the Death Star, both of which are brassy flourishes. The Empire has a theme that only appears in this film—in subsequent pictures, Williams used "The Imperial March" for the Empire instead. The Jawas theme is a delightful piece featuring woodwinds in the forefront.

John Williams revealed in an interview during the press for *The Phantom Menace* that he wrote a theme for the Jawas that George Lucas was not totally satisfied with, so he set it aside and wrote a new theme inspired by Prokofiev's "The Love for Three Oranges." The original Jawa theme that Lucas had rejected ended up being used as Lex Luthor's Theme in *Superman: The Movie*.

John Williams had a long-standing friendship with André Previn, who in the 1970s was the conductor of the London Symphony Orchestra. Previn really encouraged Williams to use the LSO to record the score for *Star Wars*, and it began a working relationship that lasts for six years, and included the scores to *Superman: The Movie, The Empire Strikes Back, The Fury, Dracula, Raiders of the Lost Ark,* and *Return of the Jedi*. A wonderful perk of using the LSO was that the British orchestra had different rules about using the music recordings in other contexts, and the soundtrack album was not subject to the same considerations of cost and rerecording that scores recorded in Hollywood were. This meant that the LP could use the actual performances from the film, and could include as much of the score as Williams preferred. The resulting double album was a big success, with a single version of the "Main Title" performance by the LSO actually reaching the Billboard Top Ten.

4

EARLY BIRD SPECIAL: SELLING *STAR WARS*

"I find your lack of faith disturbing."

There is a whole other incredible story to the making of *Star Wars* that is equally groundbreaking. That is the story of how the film was sold to the world, which was the responsibility of the late Charles Lippincott, then vice president of Advertising, Publicity, Promotion, and Merchandising for the Star Wars Corporation. Lippincott pioneered new ways of marketing the film, by targeting the core sci-fi enthusiast demographic, that had rarely been courted as aggressively as it was by Lippincott and Lucasfilm.

ALAN DEAN FOSTER

(author, *Star Wars* novelization and the sequel, *Splinter of the Mind's Eye*)
You can credit Charlie Lippincott with building awareness of *Star Wars*. Charles was in charge of advertising and promotion. On top of that, George was a very astute student of Walt Disney and realized that merchandising was important. The film sparks the merchandising and the merchandising helps feed interest in the film and the franchise, which is even more important. Some films lend themselves to that and some don't. *Star Wars* certainly did.

CRAIG MILLER

(director of fan relations, Lucasfilm, 1977–1980)
Charles couldn't really market the film to the general public: "Come see science fiction!" And there weren't any name stars in it. Alec Guinness and Peter Cushing were well known in England, but Mark Hamill, Carrie Fisher, and Harrison Ford were not well known here. So you weren't going to get them booked on *The Tonight Show*. So he had to come up with ways to market the movie that was not the typical way. One was to go to the fans who are the target audience for this movie and try to build up a grassroots interest.

CHARLES LIPPINCOTT
(publicity executive, *Star Wars*)

I really conceived marketing as a different way of handling science fiction. In a sense, it was like pre-advertising. In the early seventies, I noticed the growing interest in science fiction and comic book conventions and the proliferation of stores like A Change of Hobbit, all of which indicated that something was happening in the genre. My thinking was that we should sell to the science fiction and comic book crowd early on. Why not tailor a campaign and build off of that? Do a novelization and comic book adaptation early. The only science fiction film that we had to go on, really, was *2001*, which had been sold quite differently. For instance, to build awareness, in November 1975 we sold the novelization of the screenplay.

In actuality, Lippincott's efforts began a month before the 20th Century Fox board of directors gave the green light to Star Wars.

CHARLES LIPPINCOTT

Their decision was based on the fact that *2001* had finally broken even in November of '75, and we were to do the film for around the same budget *2001* was done. In January of 1976, Fox held the last of their sales conventions, which up until that point had been an industry mainstay where studios invited exhibitors out to Los Angeles to discuss and preview future production. The presentation was called "Twenty-Six in '76," and we were one of them, though far down the line. The exhibitors weren't interested in *Star Wars* at all. I did a presentation, similar to what I would do at conventions, based on the Ralph McQuarrie paintings and Joe Johnston drawings. I did a slide presentation and they were just bored out of their skulls. However, the younger people in the audience who worked for exhibitors really loved it. Those few thought it was great, but the older exhibitors thought it was terrible.

The film would, of course, be put into production and from that point Lippincott pushed ever forward with the novelization, a Marvel Comics adaptation of the film, and an all-out assault on comic conventions, doing anything he had to do to ensure that Star Wars *was in the public zeitgeist.*

CHARLES LIPPINCOTT

The novel is credited to George Lucas, but it was actually written by Alan Dean Foster. The lawyer for Lucasfilm wanted to put it up for auction, but I wanted to go to the best science fiction publisher and I won out. So we went with Ballantine Books.

STEPHEN SCARLATA
(host, *Best Movies Never Made* podcast)

In 1975, 20th Century Fox had little confidence in the film and were kind of getting worried, so George decided to have a novelization written and he wanted it to be out six months before the film came out—which would never happen today, because of spoilers. So he got Alan Dean Foster, who was a sci-fi writer. I believe George Lucas was a fan of his, or someone was a fan of one of his books called *Ice Rigger*. Alan Dean Foster came and had a meeting with George Lucas and he showed him the Death Star and all kinds of concept art.

ALAN DEAN FOSTER

I had done several novelizations for Ballantine Books, which became Del Rey Books. I had adapted *Dark Star,* the John Carpenter film, and was writing the *Star Trek Log* books, which were adaptations of the Saturday morning cartoon show. I was told by somebody involved with George Lucas that the novel I'd written called *Ice Rigger,* which came out in 1974, was similar in spirit to what *Star Wars* was hopefully going to be. So between that and the successful novelizations I'd done, would I be interested? They contacted my agent and I was asked, "Would I be interested in doing an adaptation of this film that George Lucas was doing plus a second original novel?," and I said yes.

STEPHEN SCARLATA

Lucas wanted him to write not only the novelization, but he wanted him to write a [sequel] book that could be filmed on a low budget. A second novel that could be used as the basis for a low budget sequel just in case *Star Wars* was not successful. They were smart; they held on to most of the sets, props, and costumes so they could reuse them for an inexpensive sequel. It was also rumored that there were going to be three books altogether—two sequel books to *Splinter.* Which, of course, never happened.

ALAN DEAN FOSTER

After I said yes, I was sent over to see Tom Pollock, later head of Universal and George's lawyer at the time, at his office on Hollywood Boulevard, presumably so they could review me and assure George and everybody that I wasn't an ax murderer. Apparently, I passed that test, because I was told to go over to Industrial Light & Magic, which at that time was a rented warehouse in Van Nuys, California, and meet George to see if I got his approval. So I went over and had a wonderful day there exploring and didn't take a camera—there were no phone cameras at the time and probably if there was, would have politely been asked to put it away, but who knows? So I'm bouncing around and there are all these people in this big room putting together spaceships out of cannibalized World War II model kits. And still I'm waiting for George, who's somewhat busy I guess, and this guy calls me over and says, "You want to see something really neat?" So I go over and he's showing me this enormous camera setup. It's the first computer-controlled camera in the history of Hollywood. Then I watched them shoot some green-screen stuff with the original Millennium Falcon model. Then George came out and we had a nice chat; I was really surprised he had any time for me at all to discuss what is, after all, ancillary rights. Spin-off rights, not the film. That went well, he's showing me around saying, "Here's the Death Star," blah, blah, blah. I was approved to write the novelization and the first spin-off, *Splinter of the Mind's Eye.*

Considering this was George Lucas before he was George Lucas, *such a meeting does beg the question of what he was like in those early days before he became Emperor of his own Empire.*

ALAN DEAN FOSTER

There were a hundred people in the room at that time and he'd be the last guy you'd pick to be George Lucas. But he was very focused. I know he had at least ten thousand different things on his mind at the time, which, again, I was surprised he had time for me and I'm trying to make small talk. And because I never met the guy before, I said, "If this film doesn't go, are you going to be all right financially?" and he said, "Yeah, I should have enough money coming in from *American Graffiti* to be okay." And I said, "What if it's a big success?" And he said, "I'd like to do small experimental films." Many years go by and I happened to catch an interview with him on *60 Minutes.* I forget who was interviewing him, maybe Diane Sawyer, and she asked a similar question related to his present circumstances, and he said, "Well, I'd like to make small experimental films." He never lost that idea. He just kind of got sidetracked his entire life.

BRIAN JAY JONES
(author, *George Lucas: A Life*)

He's constantly saying that and has been since the seventies. I love that even Steven Spielberg calls bullshit on him. He's like, "We're still waiting, George." Here's what I'd love to find out: whether or not he's got some weird YouTube channel that's got like nine subscribers and where he's been dumping experimental films on it since the 2000s and no one has found it yet. He's like,

YouTube user GreedoShotFirst and he's got all these little dumb weird films on there. You know, I believe that Marcia Lucas at one point was telling George, "Go make your small art house films. You're a really talented visionary film-maker, make those kinds of things." As I've said, though, it's easy to look back and shit on Lucas, but it's hard to begrudge somebody for success. It's like begrudging a band that makes it big and everyone's like, "You've changed, man." Well, you can give me, again, the dramatic, romantic narrative of, "It's all about the music," which is true, but when you succeed, you're like, "Come on, you can't begrudge success." A lot of people accused Lucas then, because *Star Wars* hit, of dumbing down the market. But that happens regardless. How many people make shitty superhero movies? I love *Mystery Science Theater 3000* and watching everybody trying to capitalize on the science fiction craze, and nobody does it well. That's not Lucas's fault.

ALAN DEAN FOSTER

At the time, George Lucas struck me as a regular guy. Kind of like John Carpenter after a showing of *Dark Star* with some other people related to it. He [Carpenter] came over to me and said, "You want to get something to drink?" I said, "Well, I don't drink," but we ended up going to Hamburger Hamlet. We both had chocolate shakes. I talked about how I wanted to be a writer and John talking about how he wanted to be a director and it's a shame there's no recording of that conversation. Of course, it worked out for both of us, which is nice. And George I thought I could have done the same thing with if he hadn't been overwhelmed with work at the time; we could have had a perfectly nice conversation about movies and film history and literature and everything else, but he didn't have time for that. Then, of course, he did sell *Star Wars*.

To write the novelization of Star Wars, *Foster had access to the screenplay and over a dozen illustrations done by artist Ralph McQuarrie that helped bring the story to visual life, which, he says, was hugely helpful despite the fact that many of the finished versions of things would be somewhat different. Particularly useful were images of the Millennium Falcon and lightsabers.*

ALAN DEAN FOSTER

The feeling of the film was there in the paintings and that's all I had to work with. No shots, no stills from the set, or anything else. No pictures of the principals. I had no idea what anybody would be wearing or what weapons would look like or anything. So certain things like the exact appearance of Chewbacca I had to keep somewhat nebulous along with certain other things.

I mean, I had met Mark Hamill and knew what he looked like, but I guess the first time any kind of promotional thing was done was at the Kansas City Worldcon prior to releasing the film. Charlie did a whole promotion there and Mark was there and so was Gary Kurtz. I didn't participate in that, but I ran into Mark in the bookseller's room. He was looking at comics and I was looking at books and we chatted briefly. So I had some idea what people looked like, but there was no pile of related material like I would get today to use.

I do remember reading the script and looking at the paintings before I started anything, and as I'm turning pages I'm thinking, "That sounds really cool. They'll never get that on-screen, but it looks great. This is actually science fiction; it's never going to be a success." And it was pretty much that way through the whole screenplay. And when I finished it, my final conclusion was that this was going to be a great film, but they're never going to get this stuff on the screen. I knew I could do it in the book, because I had an unlimited budget.

The novelization of Star Wars *was released on November 12, 1976, in hopes to build up anticipation for the movie, set to be released the following May. However, reviews at the time for the novel were . . . less than enthusiastic. Film critique, still mired in the cinema verité, naturalistic aesthetic of the seventies, found this lightweight fairy tale to be less than compelling. One review in an issue of* Cinefantastique *states, "In short, the novel is a huge cliché, and a poorly written cliché at that. A problem is Lucas's poor prose style. He is wordy and almost always overwrites; while saying a lot he oddly fails to give much visual feeling. He is annoyingly arch and self-conscious; he often describes aliens as 'outlandish' or 'monstrous.' Outlandish to whom? Certainly not to themselves or the other inhabitants of this cosmopolitan universe. They are outlandish to George Lucas, who should be in the background where a storyteller belongs." Little did that reviewer know of what was to come.*

With Star Wars *entering postproduction, Alan Dean Foster set to work on the sequel novel,* Splinter of the Mind's Eye.

STEPHEN SCARLATA

When it came to *Splinter of the Mind's Eye,* Alan Dean Foster could not use the characters of Han Solo or Chewbacca, because Harrison Ford was kind of on a movie-to-movie basis, so they weren't sure if he'd return for *Empire* or come back for *Return of the Jedi.* So Alan Dean Foster wrote the novelization, which was a hit, and he wrote the low-budget sequel, *Splinter of the Mind's*

Eye. After *Star Wars* came out and was a hit, *Splinter* came out and became the first novel of the expanded universe.

ALAN DEAN FOSTER

When I worked on the outline for *Splinter of the Mind's Eye* with George Lucas, *Star Wars* was still in production. George didn't know, nobody knew, that he was creating a social phenomenon. We sat down to consciously design a book that could be filmable on a low budget. But [by mid-1977] George no longer has to worry about that.

RAY MORTON
(senior editor, *Script* magazine)

In the midseventies, sequels were not considered a prestige business, but rather as a slightly déclassé way of cashing in on the success of a popular movie. In those days, sequels almost always made less than their parent pictures, so they were usually given a smaller budget than the original film and shot on a tighter schedule, often with a largely different (and cheaper) cast and creative team. 20th Century Fox's *Planet of the Apes* series followed this model—each film in the *Apes* series had a lower budget and a shorter schedule than the one before. Every *Apes* installment did indeed gross less than the previous one, but because of the reduced costs, all of them were profitable. The success of the *Apes* movies is one of the reasons Fox had decided to make *Star Wars,* which the studio felt had similar sequel potential (in fact, one studio executive actually suggested that material for a follow-up be shot during the making of the original film, but as there wasn't the time, the money, or a story idea in place, the idea was dropped). With all of this in mind, Foster was commissioned to write a contained tale that could be made on a much smaller budget than *Star Wars.*

ALAN DEAN FOSTER

On *Splinter,* I was given complete freedom, just using the background I had for the sequel novel. Besides not using Han or Chewbacca, there were two things I had to take out of the book. One was a small thing that I can't even remember anymore, but the other was the first chapter of the book was originally a fairly complex space battle, which is what forces Luke and Leia down onto a planet where they really bond for the first time. George said, "You need to take it out; it'd be too expensive to film." After the success of the first film, I had thoughts in the back of my mind, "Well, *Splinter* would make a nice movie for TV between *Episode IV* and *V*," but it's just one of those things that didn't eventuate. There's a very nice four-part comic book adaptation of the story.

Foster's story picks up Luke and Leia shortly after the events of Star Wars. They are on their way to the planet Circarpous IV to persuade its leaders to join the Rebel Alliance. Along the way, Luke and Leia crash-land on the fog-enshrouded planet Mimban, where they discover a shard from the Kyber Crystal, a mysterious object that can be used to focus and control the Force. After tangling with Imperial forces, the young rebels trek to an ancient temple where they believe the Crystal is located. Unbeknownst to them, they have been followed there by Darth Vader, who confronts them when they enter the temple. Luke and Vader engage in a vicious lightsaber battle during which Luke cuts off Vader's arm. The duel ends with Vader falling into a deep pit, seemingly to his death. Luke and Leia, romance stirring between them, ride off to resume their mission.

ALAN DEAN FOSTER

Of course there were a couple of things in *Splinter* that had to be changed as time went on. There's no mention of the fact that Darth Vader could be Luke's father and there's fairly innocent flirtation between Luke and Leia before anybody knew—including George—that they were brother and sister. This is the way stories develop. There is, of course, that kiss she gives him when they swing across the gap inside the Death Star, which isn't particularly chaste. And then there's the bit in *Empire* where she kisses Luke to make Han jealous. That's all fairly problematic, although this is a galaxy far, far away and maybe they do things differently there. Who knows what the restrictions are?

RAY MORTON

Foster's story was tight and exciting and properly contained—it basically takes place all in one location (and the fact that Mimban is fog-enshrouded meant not a lot of money would have to be spent on sets, since they mostly wouldn't be seen) and would require a minimum of special effects. If filmed, *Splinter of the Mind's Eye* certainly would have made a perfectly suitable, if rather ordinary, sequel to *Star Wars*.

ALAN DEAN FOSTER

Another thing I wanted to do in the novel was deal with Darth Vader. He's subservient to the Emperor, yet he's like, the number two guy. He's a really smart guy and we know nothing about his personal history or anything else. Just that he has these Force powers and he essentially works for the Emperor. But what I really loved about the original conception was his contempt for everybody around him. Mentally he's like, "I can take all of you out with a wave of my hand. I've chosen to work for the Empire, I'm not forced to do this." Of course, nothing had really been defined at the time and I was really interested in the idea of exploring who the Sith were and what was behind the mask. At that point, we didn't even know if he was human. Could have been an alien, but I couldn't explore that. I was asked to keep it within the confines of the first film, unfortunately. Intelligent bad guys are always interesting. Witness *The Silence of the Lambs*—intelligent bad guys are so interesting, but I never got to explore that with Vader.

As far as Luke goes, we don't really know much about him beyond him being a farm boy and wanting to fight for the resistance. I was actually more interested in the character of Leia than I was with Luke. She was a strong woman in the first film and now there are a lot of strong women in film, but none in science fiction before that. They're all pretty secretaries to the scientists or something like that. Even *Forbidden Planet*, she's nothing but decoration and a love object for the male cast. She could have been really interesting, but that wasn't her role in the 1950s. If you want an interesting early strong woman, although it's pushing it a little bit, you look at the character of Maria, the robot from *Metropolis*. But there was only so much I could do.

RAY MORTON

However, when *Star Wars* became not just a hit, but the highest-grossing film in movie history, Lucas abandoned the low-cost sequel idea and began developing much more ambitious plans for a much more ambitious follow-up.

ALAN DEAN FOSTER

Nobody, including me, had any idea George had any kind of long story arc mapped out, even if only in his own mind. And it was obvious he could do whatever he wanted to do.

With the deal for the novelization and its sequel secured at Del Rey, Charles Lippincott turned his attention to what he felt was the next most important component of the film's marketing: licensing a comic book adaptation deal.

CHARLES LIPPINCOTT

I went to New York in the hopes of meeting Stan Lee at Marvel Comics to work out a deal, but Stan kept turning me down. He said, "Once you shoot the film, come in and see me." From there I had a friend introduce me to then Marvel editor Roy Thomas, and discussed the idea with him. He was intrigued, knowing he could get a meeting with Lee, and asked if he could edit and write the comic book if Marvel went ahead with it. I agreed and then we approached Howard Chaykin about the artwork. Then it was the meeting with Stan Lee.

Finally, Stan Lee said, "All right, if you want to do it, fine, but the deal is you don't get any money for the comic book for the first one hundred thousand issues." I said, "Fine, but I want a miniseries of comic books." Nobody had done a miniseries at that time. I said it had to be at least five comic books, because I wanted to present three of them before the film came out and two of them after the film came out. Stan Lee agreed to that. I got the deal through and went back to 20th and they said I was stupid. They didn't care about the money issue. They just thought I was wasting my time on a comic book deal.

Shooting on Star Wars *began in March 1976 and Lippincott almost immediately began doing presentations at conventions. The first was LosCon in late June of that year, followed the next month by that year's edition of San Diego Comic-Con, where he, Thomas, and Chaykin did a presentation on the idea of adapting a movie into comic book form.*

CHARLES LIPPINCOTT

LosCon is where I was heckled off the stage by [writer] Jerry Pournelle. He really gave me a tough time, saying things like, "This is space opera. It's not science fiction." And with Comic-Con, Marvel didn't do anything to push the comic book and the movie had just finished shooting, so nobody knew much about it. But Howard drew a poster which we printed up a thousand of, and we went there with the poster, a little information about the film, and we did our presentation. We had a fairly good crowd show up for it. I talked to a lot of kids, particularly younger kids, about what toys they liked, what models they liked, to figure out what companies we should go with.

CRAIG MILLER

One of the ways I got involved with *Star Wars* was that Charles had come to Wester-Con on July Fourth weekend of 1976. I started consulting with him on other places and ways to take the film to fandom, which was done by going to conventions. So it was Wester-Con, San Diego Comic-Con, Worldcon, and that sort of thing.

At Worldcon in Kansas City, the hardcore convention staff of genre fans was wary of Star Wars, *but they gave the film a room where material and displays were brought in. Also joining Lippincott were Mark Hamill and producer Gary*

Kurtz. After that, fandom began to pick up on the film, fueled in no small way by the support that came its way through Don and Maggie Thompson's The Comic Buyer's Guide *and James Van Hise's* RBCC.

CRAIG MILLER

At Worldcon, Gary Kurtz was afraid people might take the props and costumes if they thought they were something from a movie, even though no one had ever seen the movie. No one was like, a big *Star Wars* collector, but if they thought it was actually from a movie, it was more likely someone would try to take them, so he had all the signs say, "Replica." But there was no money to make replicas for display purposes. They were actually film-used material: props, costumes, photos, matte paintings. Mark Hamill was there, but no one knew who Mark was. He had a small TV career at that point, but he wasn't a star. He was just a guy in a room answering questions for people.

CHARLES LIPPINCOTT

There were the Darth Vader and C-3PO outfits and a number of models, all under a great deal of security. There were science fiction fans who said, "It's just a movie, it's not serious. This is not speculative." On the other hand, we had a lot of people who were very enthused. I would say San Diego and Worldcon were two big moments for the film.

CRAIG MILLER

We spent a year telling people, "We have this movie that's better than what you think it's going to be." Everyone who bothered to come to our presentations came in with the same skepticism and most of them—not all of them—came out with, "You know, if they do this right, it could be good." And I guess we did it right.

Then, rather unexpectedly, the theatrical trailer from Lucasfilm began to develop a following, with word leaking back to the company that there were kids actually buying tickets to other movies so that they could see the trailer.

MARK HAMILL
(actor, "Luke Skywalker")

I remember that Carrie and I, when we heard the trailer was playing in Westwood, we went to the box office and said, "We're two actors that are in this movie *Star Wars* that you're showing the trailer for. We were wondering, can we just go in and watch the trailer and then we'll come right back out, instead of paying the price to see the movie?" And for some reason, they said, "Okay, sure." So we went in and watched the first footage we'd ever seen. There were dubbing sessions where we'd seen bits and pieces of it, but we'd never seen it cut together and they didn't have John Williams's score. And there were very few finished effects. Now sometimes trailers really score and sometimes they fall flat.

In this case, the trailer started and you hear this pulsing "Boom, boom, boom, boom," and the voice of the narrator was somewhere in space. Cut to all this chaos and then back to the "boom, boom, boom, boom." So they're alternating between explosions of action back to the narration. Towards the end—it was only sixty seconds or something—the narrator says, "Coming to your galaxy next summer," and somebody in the balcony yells, "Yeah, and it's coming to the Late Show a week and a half after that," meaning television, because it looked so terrible. It looked like a complete flop, something you shouldn't see in the theaters. But you really couldn't tell anything from it. Who knew?

CHARLES LIPPINCOTT

The novel was published in November of 1976 and sold really well. Normally for a first novel—George had his name on it—there was a print run of 100,000. They had actually done a print run of 125,000 around Thanksgiving. By February, they had shipped all of them out of the warehouse, which was considered unbelievable for a first novel. They were very enthusiastic, but they wouldn't go back and reprint it until the movie came out. That had been a painted cover, not a movie cover. Then, in March of '77, the first issue of the Marvel comic came out and did extremely well in major cities, though it was not an immediate sell-out. But what all of this indicated was that there was already a big buildup among fans—both comic book and science fiction—and that we had a fan following before the movie even came out.

Probably the greatest contributor to the earliest stages of the Star Wars *phenomenon was* Time *magazine. Originally the film was supposed to be the cover story, but it was bumped by the Israeli election.*

CHARLES LIPPINCOTT

Instead, we got a snipe at the top of the cover. This was in May 1977 and it said, "Best Film of the Year." I was stunned. Needless to say, you can never judge the public. They bought *Time* to see what the best film of the year was. The initial genre crowd going in to see it and the people buying *Time* to read about the snipe is what got the whole groundswell started.

STEVE SANSWEET
(chairman and president, Rancho Obi-Wan)

Originally Fox was in charge of the licensing, not Lucasfilm, and there were no records kept. In addition, there were lists of merchandisers and it was impossible to tell if they in fact produced anything.

MARK HAMILL

Nobody was sure how to sell *Star Wars*. There was something like thirteen different proposed ad campaigns. One poster looked like The Little Rascals in Outer Space, and another was a *2001* clone with an important statement to make. There was one that proclaimed *Star Wars*, "The story of a boy, a girl, and the universe," and another that said, "The man who brought you *American Graffiti* now brings you . . ." The one that I liked the best was, "Never before in cinema history has so much time, money, and technology been spent . . . just for fun." That showed that the movie wasn't pretentious. It meant, "Hey, just relax, it's not a big deal." But they didn't think that would work either.

DONALD SMOLEN
(marketing executive, *Star Wars*)

The reports from the early screenings were not very encouraging. We were told not to spend too much money, because the research showed it was just another science fiction movie. They certainly weren't very excited about it, with the exception of Ashley Boone, the vice president of distribution at Fox, who kept touting the film, saying, "It's going to be big." He had an early line on the movie that a lot of us didn't have.

We didn't think anything of the film, because none of the effects were finished. All of the space combat sequences were inserts of World War II airplanes. At that point, there was so much missing from the film it was not fair to judge it, although we did. However, my job was to make sure the film got sold. In that regard it didn't make any difference what the research showed or what anybody thought about the film. We were just trying to sell the film in the best way possible.

January 1977 didn't get off to a good start, with Mark Hamill requiring facial reconstruction surgery following an accident in his BMW. As he was quoted as saying in an issue of Gossip Magazine, *"What happened was that I was on the wrong freeway. I was way out in the sticks somewhere and there were no cars and no traffic, thank God. I was speeding, going too fast, and what happened, I think, was that I tried to negotiate an off-ramp and lost control, tumbled over* and went off the road. I fractured my nose and my cheek. I just woke up and I was in the hospital and I knew that I had hurt myself very badly, but I wasn't really sure. And then someone held a mirror up to my face and I just felt that my career was over."

In mid-February, Lucas screened the latest cut for a number of his director and writer friends, the only one of which was impressed being his stalwart supporter, Steven Spielberg, who continued to believe that Lucas had a massive hit on his hands.

IRVIN KERSHNER
(director, *The Empire Strikes Back*)

During a party at Francis Ford Coppola's house, George said, "You know, I brought some of the footage from this film that I'm shooting, *Star Wars*. I want to show it to you." Our response was, "Oh, boy, that's great." So we all traipsed down to the screening room in the basement and George showed some scenes from what would become *Star Wars*. And we sat there with our mouths open—and not because we thought it was so great. We thought it was junk! We said, "Is he crazy? This is a comic book. These aren't real people. What is he doing?" Then the lights went on and George said, "Well, what did you think?" in his way. We didn't know what to say. Francis said, "I better get upstairs," and he ran out. And I wanted to say the usual thing when you go to an opening of a friend's film and the film isn't very good. You say, "You've got yourself a film, boy!" And he turned to me and I said, "Boy, it's different." He agreed. Then I realized that George loved comic strips, comic books—he collected them—and this is what he was trying for, but there was something that was niggling me. You know, he's trying something and there's no way to know what it's going to be until he finished it.

Interestingly, the Fox executives who watched the same cut actually liked what they saw, which was surprising given their lukewarm response to date.

A flurry of activity followed in the next couple of months. On March 1, 1977, James Earl Jones recorded the dialogue for Darth Vader (much to David Prowse's later chagrin), the character's breathing accomplished by Ben Burtt using scuba diving regulators to provide the sound accompanying his words. A few days after that, John Williams conducted the score with the London Symphony Orchestra. Then, the following month ILM completed work on the assault on the Death Star, while work on the opening crawl was completed—inspired by the one utilized by the 1939 film Union Pacific.

In mid-April, a nearly finished version of the film (including effects and

music) was screened for Fox executives, who loved it. Additionally, Marvel pub-
lished the first issue of the comic book adaptation while ILM finished their last
effect, the Millennium Falcon jumping into hyperspace.

Star Wars *reached theaters on May 25, 1977. Specifically, thirty-two the-*
aters. Across the entire *country.*

MARK HAMILL

The very first day that they opened it in Los Angeles—it was scheduled for
two theaters; those were the 70mm prints and they were still dubbing the
35mm prints to release a few weeks down the road when it went wide, as they
say, because it was just in select theaters. So I said to the driver, "Can you go
by Grauman's Chinese?" I wanted to see where the movie was playing. One of
the big controversies was the back and forth at Fox about how to promote it.
Some of the ad campaigns decided to take it very seriously, calling it an entertainment beyond your imagination. Another said, let's make it more like
a rollicking comedy, like The Little Rascals in outer space, bumping heads,
and accentuate the more goofy side of it. They couldn't really figure this out.
So they missed all the dates and had to release the film with no poster whatsoever. They just stapled stills from the movie lobby cards, but there was no
poster. I don't remember seeing any advertising on television.

CRAIG MILLER

There was supposed to be a series of promotional posters of characters that
we gave away. We only had the Chaykin poster—which it's now referred to by
the *Star Wars* poster-collecting world. It says on the bottom, "Number One
in a series," but it was the only one we ever did. We gave away thousands of
them. But, like all kinds of giveaway things, people didn't save them and they
got damaged. It is now one of the most expensive *Star Wars* posters out there.

CHARLES LIPPINCOTT

People think when *Star Wars* was released in May of '77, it was an immediate
hit. That wasn't the case. If the film was redone today, on the basis of the way
movies are released with thousands of prints, it probably would have been
unsuccessful. Theaters didn't want the movie. We were lucky to get thirty
theaters to open. At that time, Hollywood Boulevard was still very important
for opening films. We only got on Hollywood Boulevard because the new Bill
Friedkin film, *Sorcerer*, wasn't ready yet. It was supposed to be ready by May
25, but wasn't, and we were given a month in the Chinese—it was the only
way we got into Grauman's.

MARK HAMILL

Harrison, Carrie, and I went out on a promotional tour before the movie opened, only it opened while we were on the tour. And we were flying home from somewhere in Canada to Chicago. We landed in Chicago and there were all these people at the airport and I said to them, "Oh, boy, there must be somebody famous on the plane." We're looking around for who it could be and as we taxied in, I went, "Hey, Carrie, look: there's somebody dressed like you with the cinnamon rolls on their head as Leia. There's a guy with a vest like you, Harrison. Oh my God, they're dressed up like characters from the movie!" We couldn't believe that it had caught on like this, because we were sort of in a bubble where you went from a car to a studio to the hotel room to a recording studio to a car and then back to the airport. You don't get out to see this stuff. You certainly don't get to go to the theater and see how it's going down.

CRAIG MILLER

Back then, people might show up and have to wait twenty minutes for the next movie to start—no one stood in line. Even for *Star Wars,* no one was standing in line for days, but, suddenly they were standing in line for like, three or four hours for the next show. And, in fact, that actually helped make the movie a success. Because it hadn't happened before, newspapers and TV news was covering the fact that people were standing in line for all those hours to get in to see *Star Wars.* So suddenly there's all this news coverage and people who had no idea what the movie was, were like, "Hmmm, this must be something special. I should go see this movie."

MARK HAMILL

In Los Angeles, I just couldn't believe my eyes. There were lines around the block. I thought, if anything, it would be a word of mouth hit. People will talk about it and say, "Have you seen this scene? You've gotta see it." People always say to me, "Did you expect it to be so successful?" Well, of course I didn't expect it, but I did think it would be a hit, because we were signed for one film and the contingency was, if it made a certain amount of money, if it was successful, we were obligated to do part two and part three. But I certainly never thought we'd be taken seriously by the mainstream media. We never believed we'd be on the cover of *Time* magazine. Maybe some kiddie magazines or something like that, or *Famous Monsters* and *Cinefantastique,* but never did we think that it would have that kind of mainstream success.

GEORGE LUCAS
(executive producer, screenwriter/director, *Star Wars*)

The night the movie came out, Laddie called me at eleven at night and said, "It's a hit. God, we sold out in every theater. This is fantastic!" I said, "Laddie, you guys have done *Planet of the Apes*. You know that science fiction movies always do well in the first weekend, because of the fans. It's not a hit until the fourth week. You call me on the fourth week and tell me it's working." And he did.

JOHN DYKSTRA
(special photographic effects supervisor, *Star Wars*)

All of this was very much a leap of faith and I have to give George and Gary credit for supporting us during that time, because no one knew what we were doing. We were introducing technology from other arts and environments into the photographic world and into the motion picture industry. It was a convoluted and complex solution that really, unless you worked there, you wouldn't have a clue.

DENNIS MUREN
(second cameraman: miniature and optical effects unit, *Star Wars*)

Science fiction films had usually been low-budget until *Star Wars*. After the impact made by *Star Wars*, it suddenly made the genre acceptable to a new audience. The genre was always around, but it wasn't mainstream, and I think *Star Wars* made it mainstream. It was partly because there was a huge baby-boomer generation that was out there ready for it. You had George Lucas and Steven Spielberg, two filmmakers from that same generation, who wanted to see those kinds of movies. Both George and Steven really had a pulse on what the public would go for. There had been a few things before *Star Wars*, but now the studios would back these big-budget effects films.

JOHN KENNETH MUIR
(author, *Science Fiction and Fantasy Films of the 1970s*)

Today, when the *Star Wars* mythology is so dense and closely tracked by fans, it is easy to forget a few things about this 1977 cinematic landmark. First, its use of a "lived-in" universe, rather than a seemingly new, high-tech one (such as those featured in *2001: A Space Odyssey, Star Trek,* or *Space: 1999*) is revolutionary and different. The connection between the lived-in universe and the opening legend "a long time ago, in a galaxy far, far away" positions the film as a fairy tale or myth, which works to its advantage, and makes the film feel not simple, but rather universal. The setting also opts *Star Wars* out of the dystopian futures of its seventies brethren such as *Zardoz* or *Silent Running*.

GLEN OLIVER
(pop culture commentator)

I was sitting between my mom and dad in a crowded theater watching *Star Wars* for the first time. The size, the sound, the beauty of what was on-screen overwhelmed me from the outset. The Rebel Blockade Runner zoomed overhead, followed by the endless length of the Imperial Star Destroyer chasing it, and my dad said aloud: "If they can do that, they can do anything." At the time I took this as a welcomed affirmation of the movie whose coming had made me mental for many previous months. I was a kid—I wanted my parents to like what I liked. But, over the years, I came to view the statement as a tacit challenge to all movies to come. A manifesto that what can be put on-screen is only constrained by our imaginations and perseverance. Have subsequent filmmakers met this challenge? Some have admirably attempted to do so, some never really tried. Some tried and failed. The results are rather mixed.

In terms of creative atomic bombs whose detonations radiated a blast wave of change? I highly doubt there will ever be another *Star Wars*. It was, in terms of its timing, its innovation, its position in history, and its ability to tap into a hitherto underexposed zeitgeist . . . an absolutely Perfect Storm. There may someday be another sort of exponential surge forward with presentational innovation, perhaps even conceptual innovation. But in terms of seismic shifting? I can't imagine there will ever be another *Star Wars*.

JIM SWEARINGEN
(conceptual designer, Kenner)

We got an invitation to a marketing research screening in San Francisco on the first of May, and by then the film was going to be pretty much what you saw in the theaters. The lights went down and I'm sitting in the middle of this crowd of people. As the words *Star Wars* pops up on the screen and the crawl started, you can kind of see looks of confusion. People had been invited to see the premiere of a movie called *Alaska*, so when *Star Wars* popped up on-screen, they weren't really sure what was going on. The crawl starts and they're reading about this galaxy far, far away. The starfield moves down and the Blockade Runner comes overhead and the "pew, pew pew" starts. Now you can hear this under-the-breath chatter from the audience, and then the Star Destroyer comes overhead and the subwoofers in the theater start going. By the time the engines came, you can feel, "They've got 'em!" The bass is just shaking their seats. By the end, when the Death Star blew up, they were out of their seats, cheering *everything*.

DENNIS MUREN

The first time I saw the film, I was knocked out. Everybody else was knocked out, too. I first saw the original workprint, a private showing for the effects people. Gary Kurtz was there. George was there, too. It was amazing... amazing. We didn't expect it.

JOHN KENNETH MUIR

Many fans have forgotten—or simply don't know—in an age when *Star Wars* films primarily reference themselves (previous chapters and characters)—that George Lucas created *Star Wars* as a pastiche, as a work of art that knowingly and intentionally imitates the work of another artist or artists. The film's opening crawl is not unlike one featured in the 1930s Flash Gordon serials. "Hurled through boundless space they land on an onrushing planet and fall into the clutches of the merciless Emperor Ming," etc. The same pulp-style language and voice is shared by Flash Gordon and *Star Wars* in their opening title cards/crawls. Similarly, as has been noted in many places, *Star Wars* adopts some of the character dynamics and visual touches (namely the visual "wipes") from Akira Kurosawa's *The Hidden Fortress* (1958). The desert planet milieu, and the bones of the giant creature seen on a Tatooine hilltop, remind many of the novel *Dune*, by Frank Herbert.

And of course, the beautifully rendered space combat featured in the latter half of the film is modeled on such World War II aerial combat films as *Twelve O'Clock High* (1949) and *633 Squadron* (1964). It is not stealing being discussed here, it is an act of using other artworks (and elements of those artworks) to build a new one. The new one, however, also encourages a feeling of nostalgia for similar entertainment. If one goes back to the liner notes for the *Star Wars* widescreen special edition laser disc release of the early 1990s, Lucas notes in the behind-the-scenes section that one of the reasons he wanted to see his film succeed was "so everyone will copy it. Then I can go see the copies, and sit back and enjoy them."

Oppositely, it should be remembered that *Battlestar Galactica* was sued for its perceived similarities to *Star Wars*, even though the same liner notes describe *Star Wars* as a "re-creation of the part of his childhood spent in the movies and with comic strip heroes such as Flash Gordon." So, *Star Wars* is clearly a pastiche, in Lucas's mind, a cobbling together of elements of other artworks. But *Battlestar Galactica*, also arguably a pastiche, was viewed legally as having violated creative elements belonging to *Star Wars*, apparently.

It was one copy Lucas apparently didn't "sit back and enjoy," as his liner note comments would have suggested.

RAY MORTON

From a craft perspective, the screenplay for *Star Wars* is really terrific. Although it took Lucas several years to develop a workable script, the eventual result of his labor was a tightly structured, highly entertaining classical adventure set in a wonderfully realized fantasy world and filled with exciting action, engaging characters, and welcome dollops of humor and heart. Lucas's storytelling is highly cinematic—strongly visual, simple but not simplistic, with clear narrative logic and understandable high stakes. The imagination on display in the screenplay is prodigious and the world-building is expert (and greatly enhanced in its believability by the matter-of-fact way in which Lucas presents even his most outlandish concepts). It's a really, really nifty piece of screenwriting.

MARK HAMILL

The film had humor. Women don't normally like science fiction, but it's got a strong female character, it's funny as hell, there's banter, there's sexual tension. On top of that, we had got one of the greatest actors in the English-speaking world, the Academy Award–winning Sir Alec Guinness, right next to an eight-foot guy in a monkey costume flying in space. What's not to like? To me, it was clearly a fairy tale. It's got a farm boy, a wizard, a princess, a pirate. It read like a mash-up of so many other movies I'd seen before, a little *Wizard of Oz*, a little *Dam Busters*, World War II movies, Western films, pirate films. There were so many different cinematic references that everything old is new again. And by using so many recognizable moments, it sort of transmogrifies into something that's seemingly original in and of itself.

RICHARD EDLUND
(first cameraman: miniature and optical effects unit, *Star Wars*)
I always felt that there were four great decisions that George made. One of them was made by Gary Kurtz. First, he discovered Ralph McQuarrie and Ralph produced a dozen or more paintings of *Star Wars* from the script that George had come up with, so that was number one. Number two was—and it was Gary's decision—to hire us to do the visual effects, because I don't think there was anybody else in the world that could have done that at that time. Trumbull was across town working on *Close Encounters* and he had gotten started before we did, so he was amassing all the 65mm and 70mm equipment. We decided that VistaVision was a much better technology to

use, because it was possible, because of the way the film went through the camera, for the top of the camera to be very close to the surface. For example, I could never have shot the opening scene from *Star Wars* with a 65mm camera, because I couldn't have gotten the camera close enough to the model. So it was Ralph McQuarrie and the visual effects team to do the effects, but on top of that you needed an actor with real gravitas to help pull it all off, and I think Alec Guinness was a perfect choice there. And then of course the John Williams music. Those four things were the tipping point for *Star Wars*.

RAY MORTON

The final important creative decision Lucas made was to make his movie *fun*. *Star Wars* is a really entertaining movie—it's exciting, thrilling, funny, imaginative, suspenseful, and sometimes scary. Whatever Lucas's other intentions, he wanted to give audiences a great time and at that he more than succeeded. I'm certainly not the first to make this observation, but after a decade of gritty, realistic, and often quite downbeat films, bringing pure, optimistic entertainment back to the movies was both startling and refreshing, and certainly one of the major reasons for *Star Wars*' incredible success.

DENNIS MUREN

I loved it. George made something superior to everything else that's ever been done in this genre. Imagine, a classic fantasy-adventure film that came out in 1977 that's more creative and imaginative and popular than anything the major studios could turn out in sixty years of trying! We all feel honored to have worked on it. Really.

RICK BAKER
(makeup, second unit, *Star Wars*)

The first time I saw it, I was crazy about it. We were all very excited to see it. The whole crew of people I worked with were all basically fans. They were into films a great deal, and they wanted to see a film like this being made . . . you know, a large budget with integrity. We were all very happy to have worked on it. When I first saw it finished, I was so hyped up over it I couldn't fall asleep that night.

PHIL TIPPETT
(stop-motion animation: miniature and optical effects unit, *Star Wars*)

It's very rare to have an experience like *Star Wars*. We were very lucky to be a part of it. Once every ten years or so, you luck into something that good. I was very aware of the screenplay, and Dennis and I were in wonder of how it would all come together. How would it be possible to make anything that was so complicated? It was very funny how the script read, especially the last act. At the cast and crew screening, which was somewhere in Westwood, I couldn't believe it. Prior to the screening, George had run the sequences of the cantina and the chess game for us, so we could tell from that it was going to be everything we always wanted to see, and of course, we weren't disappointed.

NICK MALEY
(special makeup effects crew: cantina sequence, *Star Wars*)
I heard reports that George was difficult. Not the man I worked with. He was polite, very reasonable in what he wanted. Gave you what was needed to get by. At the end of *A New Hope* [the subtitle given to the first film on rerelease], George and Gary presented key personnel with a signed and dedicated book of stills. Mine said, "To Nick Maley, thanks for your contribution to *Star Wars*, George Lucas and Gary Kurtz." I worked on fifty-three projects and that was the only time a director and producer considered a group of key contributors enough to do something like that. They were good guys and I still cherish that book.

JEANINE BASINGER
(film historian, founder and curator of the Cinema Archives
of Wesleyan University)
All I know is I'm already beyond the age for *Star Wars* when it comes out, but I'm taking my daughter to it. I remember I was there with a headache and thinking it's noisy in here, kids are loud. Lights go down and over my head flies that thing coming overhead on the screen. Oh my God! And then I'm piloting this thing down these canyons and high speeding twisting and turning and I'm like, "Woo!" I'm loving it. The thing is, it's got that combination of newness in terms of technology. It's bringing sound and image and movement and placement of me as the viewer inside this thing I'm flying in. I just thought it used what cinema has that no other art form can give in the same way with cutting and sound and image and movement. It's taking me out of my seat and to a place I've never been.

JOHN KENNETH MUIR
Star Wars connected with people, in large part, for the same reason that *Star Trek* did on TV before it. *Star Trek* was an optimistic view of the future. *Star*

Wars was not necessarily optimistic since it concerned an oppressed galaxy. But it was fun, upbeat, and had a happy ending. That's the basic answer, anyway. A deeper answer goes back to the concept of the Force. In 1966, *Time* magazine ran a cover that read simply, "Is God Dead?" Americans of this era looked at politics, war, equal rights, and the environment and saw problems everywhere. The science fiction cinema of 1967 to 1976 was pretty much an extension of the "Is God Dead?" idea. In the future as presented in *Z.P.G.*, there were abortion appliances in every household, because of overpopulation. In *Logan's Run,* you could have anything you wanted, except your thirtieth birthday. In *Soylent Green,* the oceans were dead and the hot new food product on the market was "people." The *Planet of the Apes* saga posited man losing his place at the top of the food chain, and falling from grace. All these efforts were speculative, smart and grounded in the trends of the times. However, if you were a parent, which of these films would you take your children to go see? I remember seeing *Logan's Run* in the theater with my parents in 1976 and enjoying it. Yet it's not what we would consider a happy kids' movie, is it, what with the "Love Shop" and all?

ALAN DEAN FOSTER

Star Wars is one of those things where everything comes together just right. One of my favorite films is *Gunga Din,* and a lot of people don't know *Gunga Din* was the second-highest-grossing film of 1939. It beat *The Wizard of Oz* and *Wuthering Heights* and *How Green Was My Valley.* Didn't win a lot of awards, but people loved it. I always point to that film when I say, "If you want to see another film where everything works—the writing, the music, the story, the acting and everything else—there it is." There are a lot of qualities to that film that are the same as in *Star Wars* and the same as Indiana Jones.

GARY KURTZ
(producer, *Star Wars, The Empire Strikes Back*)
We were resigned to the fact that the film would be badly received because of its light-hearted entertainment value as critics tend to be too serious and too analytical. Surprisingly, they accepted the film for what it was and enjoyed it on that level. The immediate public reaction took us aback. We were relying on good word of mouth, but what happened was phenomenal. I guess we hit the right time of year. It may have been clearer to us if we'd had the time to preview the film, but we worked on it solidly until a week before its opening. Also, the eighteen-to-thirty-five picture-going market has been analyzed, but not the six-to-eighteen-year-old one, so that was another factor.

JEANINE BASINGER

It's an old story. It could have been a Western story, whatever, but it's given to me in a strong new way visually. So it's moving us forward historically into adding the bold use of technology into a strong saga kind of story that has the old things you want: good versus evil, interesting characters, a little humor mixed with danger—all of that was there. And what's not to like? What's not to like about *Star Wars*?

GEORGE LUCAS

Fun. That's the word for *Star Wars*. At that time, young people didn't have a fantasy life anymore, not the way we did. All they had was Kojak and Dirty Harry. There were all of these kids running around wanting to be killer cops. All the films they saw were movies of disasters and insecurity and realistic violence. I wanted to open up the whole range of space for young people. Science fiction is okay, but it got so involved that it forgot the sense of adventure. I wanted *Star Wars* to make them think of things that could happen.

The reason I made *Star Wars* is that I wanted to give young people some sort of faraway exotic environment for their imaginations to run free. I wanted them to go beyond the basic stupidities of the moment and think about colonizing Venus and Mars. And the only way it was going to happen was to have some kid fantasize about getting his ray gun, jumping in his spaceship and flying off into outer space.

THOMAS PARRY
(studio executive, United Artists, 1974-1977)

When the movie was done, Tom Pollock [George Lucas's attorney] called me up because I had shown interest in *Star Wars* as an executive at United Artists and said, "Would you like to come to the cast and crew screening?" They held it at the Academy Theater, and I walked out of that thinking I had just seen the best movie I'd ever seen. I called up a woman who was a friend of mine, who also happened to be a stockbroker, and I said, "Is it possible to buy 20th Century Fox stock?" And she said, "Well, why would you want to do that? Movie studios stock is a horrible stock to buy—it's too risky! How much money do you have?" And I said, "I have no money!" She said, "Well, you could buy it on margin." I said, "What do you think, Fran?" "Well, you know . . . maybe if you want to take the risk, you could buy a thousand dollars of stock on it." So I did that, and I paid off every single debt I ever had.

5

TOY STORY: MERCHANDISING
STAR WARS

"In my experience, there's no such thing as luck."

When George Lucas was ready to move forward with the sequel to *Star Wars*, *The Empire Strikes Back*, he sent lawyer Tom Pollock back to the negotiating table with 20th Century Fox. "When we made the sequel deal," Pollock tells Deadline.com, "the deal we came up with and proposed to Laddie, and maybe it was Dennis Stanfill or Marvin Davis at that point, is that George made the decision to self-finance the film. Lucasfilm made a lot of money on *Star Wars* and would reinvest the money in the movie. The deal that was offered to Fox was, you get distribution rights theatrically and video around the world for seven years, and we retain everything else. And, by the way, we want the merchandising back. Fox had started with the merchandising in that first year, or two, and did very well, too. He wanted the merchandising back as of the time *Empire* came out. That meant soundtrack albums, music publishing, television, all rights other than the rights we were granted to Fox under this deal."

The studio wasn't really in a position to argue: as Pollock points out, they would have taken *Empire* elsewhere. "Even then," he notes, "while the merchandising was doing well, it hadn't become the phenomenon it would become. We agreed to do it that way on the next one. In fact, we had the same relationship on the next one and the three prequels, they were made at basically the same terms. They had certain rights for a certain time and got a distribution fee, and George put up all the money. And owned it."

KYLE NEWMAN
(director, *Fanboys*)

I remember the *MAD* and *Cracked* covers, and wanting the action figures of the aliens they had in the cantina on the *Cracked* cover and thinking, "Kenner's gonna make that. They *have* to make that." I was obsessed with the aliens. That's how I learned to draw. It was just looking at these magazines and the images, and I just started drawing, and *Star Wars* inspired that.

On September 4, 1974, as discussions and negotiations between Tom Pollock and Fox continued, Lucas was granted creative control of the Star Wars *name in conjunction with the merchandising. In 1976, the license for action figures and toys based on characters from the film was initially offered to the Mego Corporation, a leader in the field with their popular* Planet of the Apes *and* Star Trek *toy lines. When they turned it down, the license was picked up by Kenner, which at the time was a subsidiary of General Mills.*

JIM SWEARINGEN
(concept designer, Kenner)

Star Wars had already been turned down by all the major toy companies. The bigger guys. The way *Star Wars* worked was, we didn't get the script until sometime before February of '77, the script came into Kenner. It was either late '76 or very early in '77. And it came in through the marketing department, and they just handed it over to the advanced design department. I had read in the November issue of *Starlog* magazine that the movie was coming out, and I knew that *American Graffiti* was Lucas's previous film. When I was in college, I saw *THX 1138* at the student center at UC, so I was kind of tuned in to George Lucas from that.

When the script came in, Dave Okada, my boss, said, "Well, we've got this script, who wants to take it?" I volunteered. I practically grabbed it out of his hand, "I'll do that one!" Because I knew of George Lucas. So, I got to take it home that night. We got the script and a book of black-and-white stills from the live-action shoot—that was already done—a photograph of an X-Wing and a TIE Fighter, some snapshots, and that's what we started with. So, I took it home and read it. Took it back the next morning and went to Dave Okada and said, "Go in your office and shut the door for two hours. Read this." I was convinced from the moment I read it that it was something that we had to do. The advantage I had was I didn't have to worry about schedules, or how much money it would cost or any of that stuff. Dave agreed we needed to present it to management. So, we started doing presentations of what we would do with this property. The marketing people were less convinced—for the same reasons all the other companies had turned it down. Because George [Lucas] didn't want word to get out about his new movie, he had kept a lot of stuff secret, so when he was showing the toy companies, it was late. Everybody was looking at it and going, "Well, we couldn't have product out until the next year, until '78." The movie was dropping in May of '77. And *Star Trek* had already screwed up the marketing for science fiction, because they did such crappy stuff early on so everybody else had said no. I guess it was a good thing I was naïve enough to say, "But we gotta do it!"

BRIAN VOLK-WEISS
(producer, *The Toys That Made Us*)

George Lucas only got 2.5 percent on the Kenner deal. It wasn't that he fell for it, it's that he had no choice. Everyone else said no. That's another part of the story that is insane. I still never was able to get a straight answer; I asked everyone the same question and everyone gave different opinions, but either Kenner was genius that they went into production without a contract, or maybe because they literally only had one lawyer, and they were so "mom & pop" it happened by accident. Had they not gone into production, Lucas would've been like, "Whoa, whoa, whoa! No deal! No deal!" and gotten a better deal. It was only because the stuff was on shelves and in factories that they were able to get it done.

In 1972, Swearingen had started working for Kenner, a midsized Midwest toy company that was begun by two brothers in the 1940s. By the 1970s, prior to their producing action figures, they were the creator of products like Spirographs, the Sit 'n Spin, and the Betty Crocker Easy-Bake Oven—a big seller for them.

JIM SWEARINGEN

They had built up a pretty good small toy company. The thing that started them in licensing, at least in the Boys Toys line, was that they got the rights to do *The Six Million Dollar Man* in '74 or '75. By that time, I was in the preliminary design department, which was kind of the advanced concepts area. So, we looked to develop our own product, but we'd also look to license properties. So, the license for *The Six Million Dollar Man* came by, and the marketing department decided we should take a look at it.

Once that decision was made, the company would start reading scripts and looking at visuals that had been provided by different studios to try and get an idea of what could be done in regards to toys. In essence, this was Kenner's first foray into licensing Hollywood properties.

JIM SWEARINGEN

My claim to fame for *The Six Million Dollar Man* was giving him his bionic eye. There was a bunch of other people who put skin on his arm and gave him power grip—it all came from different places within the department. We saw the show before it went on TV and it ran for a number of years. We had *The Six Million Dollar Man* and then we had *The Bionic Woman,* so it was a couple of years. I think we introduced them in '74. That was the big foray into licensing properties. We did it at the twelve-inch scale to be competitive with *G.I. Joe.*

That was what got Kenner on the list of, at least, TV properties. We looked at *Man from Atlantis,* and a couple of other things. At that time, TV shows were more relevant to the toy business, because they generally dropped in September—that was when they premiered new TV shows—and then they ran for thirteen or twenty-six weeks, which usually got toy companies through Christmas.

As Swearingen describes it, once a product was given a "go" order, it took about a year to go from his desk to production. In other words, concepts would be presented to marketing and management, and once approved they would be turned over to the production design and engineering groups. From there the plans would be sent to China or the Far East for production. But with Star Wars, *tooling was done in Asia, while injection molding was done in the United States. The action figures were produced overseas, but the X-Wing, TIE Fighter, and Millennium Falcon were manufactured in Cincinnati.*

JIM SWEARINGEN

I got to be the liaison between Lucasfilm and Kenner for the first, probably, six months. I was kind of on my own for at least the first few months, and then the marketing people were still trying to figure out if they could do the thing or not. So, I got to go back-and-forth with the people at Lucasfilm and ask for stuff—trying to get more information from them. Because really, all we had was the script we saw, and the snapshots of the X-Wing and the TIE Fighter, but neither were very good pictures. So we were kind of figuring it out as we went. We put together all kinds of stuff, action figures, games, and puzzles and all of the things that we could do. Dave Okada and I flew out to California, and the first presentation we did was to 20th Century Fox in March of '77. We went out to try and convince 20th Century Fox that this little Midwest toy company could do a job on it. And at the same time, we were trying to convince the Kenner management that they should do it. About that time, we did our presentation in March, they were kind of talking money, deal points, and such. Which I wasn't involved with. We presented to Alan Ladd, and Marc Pevers and a bunch of 20th Century Fox guys. Lucas didn't see that presentation; I don't think he was there. But they were doing the release and licensing on the movie, so they had to see everything first.

Because Lucas had played things so close to the vest due to fear of his ideas being ripped off by others, there was no way Kenner could have the first wave of action figures ready for a May 1977 release and, frankly, not even Christmas of that year. Instead, they came up with an innovative plan to placate what had become a growing legion of fans hungry for anything Star Wars: *they created and sold what was described as an "Early Bird Certificate Package," which featured a certificate that could be mailed to Kenner and redeemed for four* Star Wars *action figures. Luke Skywalker, Princess Leia, Chewbacca, and R2-D2 were the first four figures to be distributed. Also, a part of the box was a diorama display stand, stickers, and a membership card for the official* Star Wars *fan club.*

JIM SWEARINGEN

We sold the empty box/envelope at Christmas of '77. Also at Christmas of '77, we had a board game that was all paper and I think we did Dip-Dots and some paint stuff that didn't require any retooling. Then the first four figures shipped in February or March and the rest of the line picked up from there. We went to Toy Fair in '78 with a full line, including the X-Wing and TIE Fighter.

In terms of the design process, the way we did it then was, I went through the script, picked out the characters, and made a presentation board, which is basically black line drawings with marker renders of the characters. That was the first presentation with the characters. From that point, I'd start modeling the first kit-bashed figures.

There's a quaint story about the 3 ¾-inch-size action figure and Bernie Loom from Kenner is saying, "Make them this big." But in reality, which is often a little different, I needed something to model these things—and I'm not a sculptor—but we needed to do figures, so I happened to find "the Adventure People" from Fisher-Price. We used that as the principal base for the kit-bashed models, and they just happened to be 3 ¾ inches tall. Bernie may have said, "Make 'em this big," but it turns out that just by chance the Fisher-Price Adventure People were the right size. So those early models were basically, I took [the Adventure People] and used body putty and an X-Acto knife and made most of the figures that way.

These figures were turned over to engineering and they would take it from there. A sheet was worked up with a breakdown of what material the arms would be made from, what material the body would be made from, the minimal paint operation, and a rough estimate of what the expected cost would be.

JIM SWEARINGEN

The X-Wing and TIE Fighter was a similar process. First thing was taking what little information we had, early on, and do a simple rendering, black line again with marker. Then, we stepped up from that to an articulated board where we could see the wings opening in the X-Wing, and we made a TIE Fighter where a panel would pop off. And in the next step up from that, I did layout drawings and the model shop—preliminary designs had their own model shop—and they did what they needed to do to make their own models. We had an engineer working with me to figure out the mechanisms, the wings opening, and all that stuff, and then we made the model. They weren't fully accurate, because we didn't have any blueprints or anything, but it looked fairly similar—and then the same process, we'd do a cost sheet, and then the engineer would take over and do a hard cost sheet, and figure out how to actually make it work. The figures are all done with ABS [acrylonitrile butadiene styrene], the ships were injection molding styrene—the models we did for those ships were pretty close, but done with cut plastic, so none of that was done with injection molding.

For the lightsabers, at the model shop, we experimented with different ways to make them. The original model had a monofilament fishing line and a spool in the back of the character's body, then we'd cut a channel in the character's arm, and it'd come out through the hilt in the hand, and pulled the monofilament out, and then reeled it back in. That was the original solution, but monofilament has a natural bend to it, so it was always coming out in some different direction. We didn't have the material that would coil up and return straight. Maybe we could do it now.

Those models were probably presented in April or May [of '77] and once the movie dropped, we were in a big hurry. So, what got turned over was, we had this monofilament line with the spool in the back—when it went to engineering, it didn't seem to be a practical solution, so that was when they did the telescoping lightsabers, and then the fixed ones. That all happened in production design.

Even with the time delay, there was no denying the impact that Star Wars *ultimately had on Kenner, transforming the scope of the company.*

JIM SWEARINGEN

We staffed up pretty well. I mean, the company had to grow. When *Star Wars* was out and taking off, shortly after it was on in theaters they took everyone in Kenner to go see it. The Boys Toys group and designers had to staff up some, because they had a lot to do very quickly. They did bring in some freelancers, but a lot of people got pulled into *Star Wars* that may have been working on other projects. For the first couple of years, it was the biggest thing that was happening at Kenner. And it changed us. We were no longer at the bottom of the list for movie and TV properties. Suddenly, we were at the top of the list when it came to looking at new projects. I looked at *Alien* (1979); I went to England to see the film's sets. I came back from looking at the sets and monster and recommended we not do *Alien*. But they did it anyway. They wanted to keep the relationship up with 20th Century Fox. It was a good movie, but I didn't see it as a toy for kids.

And part of our deal with Lucasfilm was that Kenner had first right of refusal for any product that had the *Star Wars* license on it. So, if Lucasfilm wanted someone to make bedsheets, we had to say okay. I got to critique anything that they were going to do. If I'd kept all the samples I'd gotten, I'd be a rich man right now. I got a sample of every product for a couple of years. We weren't going to let anyone do any toy product, and George was very set on keeping things close to the movie, so things like Funko Pop! and some of the other kind of things going on now, would never have happened until George wanted to make more money.

BRIAN VOLK-WEISS

The first check that Lucas got from Kenner was seven figures. I think it was three million. They went to lunch and they gave him a check. Lucas opens the check, closes it, puts it in his pocket and doesn't say anything. And the reason is, he's calculating: if 2.5 percent is worth three million, what 18 percent looked like, what 20 percent looked like, and so on.

GLEN OLIVER
(pop culture commentator)

I think this happened for one chief reason: when many people encountered *Star Trek* and *Space: 1999* and *Apes* toys, it was somewhat posthumously; the future of those franchises was essentially unclear. Their times had more or less passed or at least fallen into a protracted stasis. What was unique about *Star Wars*, in my circle at least, is that the toys represented a "buy-in" to a larger experience of an ongoing franchise. We knew there was going to be more *Star Wars*. Its toys were a means of not only celebrating a film we loved and were deeply impacted by, but carrying us towards future movies as well. That felt relevant. It made us feel like we were a part of something holistic. The Powers That Be were, and remain, very aware of this dynamic, hence the various high-profile, highly publicized merchandise reveals . . . Force Friday events, and whatnot. Yes, they are all capitalistically motivated, but they're also very much geared towards keeping us adherent to the franchise and stoking our sense of wanting to be connected to it. Shrewd? Absolutely. Negative? Eh. There are probably a million salient arguments against *Star Wars* commercialism. In a very strange way, though, I can't conceive of *Star Wars* without it.

ANTHONY DANIELS
(actor, "C-3PO")

Yeah, I've done some really stupid things like the C-3PO breakfast cereal; a truly disgusting product, it tasted so sweet. I have the last remaining box on earth . . . unopened . . . and one day, when I get really bitter, I will go to a high place and open it . . . [with a deep, dark voice] and destroy the planet. The world will crack when I open it. The box is beautiful, what's inside is, well . . . C-3PO has lent himself to many products, some good, some bad. My proudest thing is that I have been in an anti-smoking commercial.

BRIAN JAY JONES
(author, *George Lucas: A Life*)

Prior to *Star Wars*, there weren't a lot of sequels out there, there weren't a lot of film franchises, especially in science fiction. So I think the main thing the people looking at toys and merchandising, and toy sellers and department stores that sold the toys—and it's hard to believe nowadays—were just like, "There's no shelf life for this beyond just the life of the movie." You couldn't move merchandise, because people were like, "Well, the movie's going to be out of the theaters and then we're going to be stuck with a whole bunch of C-3PO figures and no one's going to care in five months." But he very brilliantly gets the rights to both of those. I don't know that he necessarily knew what he had with that, but, again, there's a lot of control going on there. He wants the sequel rights, because he doesn't want to leave those with Fox, makes the movie and if, God forbid, it does well, he doesn't want them handing the rights of the sequel off to somebody that he doesn't approve of, which is the card that they played on him with *American Graffiti*. He almost got stung by that. Universal was like, "Well, we actually have the sequel option on this, so you can either play or don't." And so he does get involved in that, but that stung. So I think part of getting those sequel rights is to ensure that if something happens, he is in control of the narrative again.

RAY MORTON

(senior editor, *Script* magazine)

Once Lucas decided to go big, his creative thinking for the sequel was as bold and unconventional as it had been for the original picture. Lucas's most striking creative choice in devising his sequel was to eschew doing a traditional follow-up. Instead of making the new film just another stand-alone adventure of Luke Skywalker in the same way that each new Bond movie is just another stand-alone adventure of agent 007, Lucas decided to make *Star Wars* the first part of a much larger overall tale. *Star Wars* would now be act 1 of an epic three-part saga and this first sequel would be act 2.

Star Wars *would not be the first cinematic series to tell a single, unified tale. The* Planet of the Apes *series had also presented an ongoing narrative, but it had done so accidentally. The original* Planet of the Apes *told a self-contained story that was not meant to continue. The tremendous success of that film motivated the studio and the producers to make* Beneath the Planet of the Apes, *another (mostly) self-contained tale. Since* Beneath *ended with the planet blowing up, obviously no continuation was intended at that point either. However, when* Beneath *was also a sizable hit, 20th Century Fox and producer Arthur P. Jacobs decided to make a second sequel. In his script for* Escape from the Planet of the Apes, *Paul Dehn, the series' primary screenwriter, gave the archaeologist/historian chimpanzee Cornelius a speech that detailed how apes supplanted man as the rulers of Earth. When the success of* Escape *prompted Fox to request yet another follow-up, Dehn then dramatized that backstory in* Conquest of the Planet of the Apes *and then continued it in* Battle for the Planet of the Apes, *the final film in the original series. Dehn went to great lengths to tie the events of the last two movies to those in the first three, thus transforming the five separately made movies into a single saga (albeit one with lots of loose ends and continuity issues).*

Star Wars *would, however, be one of the first movie series to deliberately and purposefully tell a single story in multiple parts. The notion of creating a trilogy of films that told one unified tale—something that is commonplace now—was strikingly original and innovative at the time.*

DALE POLLOCK

(author, *Skywalking: The Life and Films of George Lucas*)

The success of the first *Star Wars* gave Lucas, for lack of a better term, "fuck you" money, and that was really important to him. His father, I believe, had incorporated into him the idea that a small businessman, the person who acts on his own instincts and runs his own company and has his own vision for what he wants to do, that is the secret of American success. The thing is, *American Graffiti* made him rich, but now he was wealthy in an entirely different way. And his response is to get completely out of L.A. and build a base where L.A. can't touch him; where he's separate from the industry and shows them how it should be done. Wealth, as opposed to simply being something he could accumulate, brought with it this idea of true independence and the concept that he would own his own work. He was a good businessman, as it turned out, and that isn't true of most creative people. Look at Francis Ford Coppola or Charlie Chaplin. [Look at] how much money Chaplin pumped into United Artists and it ultimately failed. So there's a long line of these kinds of figures in the entertainment industry. But Lucas was something different. Number one, he's separated himself from Hollywood. And number two, he bet only on his own vision. Wasn't interested in market research, wasn't interested in what the fans wanted. He knew what *he* wanted and he finally had the money to do that.

GEORGE LUCAS
(executive producer, screenwriter, *The Empire Strikes Back*)
I just said, "I will now take over and start financing my own pictures," because then they cannot touch me. They cannot come in and recut it afterward. They can't make notes on the script, they can't do anything. I will say I've been very lucky in my career. When I did *Star Wars,* I was in England and it all came down to the very end. At the same time, Fox was very, very good to me. The board hated the movie, but Alan Ladd, Jr., who was the head of Fox, gave me all the help and cooperation I needed. He gave me some extra money to do retakes and he never wanted to cut anything. It was like, "Hey, this is the way it's supposed to work." But I realized that that is such a fantasy, though I actually got to live it. But you're never going to find a studio executive like that. After that, the studio executives all decided that they were Irving Thalberg and that they were really in control of everything. That they're the ones making the movies, not the director. The director's just some hired person, right? Like the plumber who comes in and does the work. I don't know what they do, but plumbers do the work that makes it happen.

Writers have always felt that way and they've been treated badly. So you kind of just say, "I don't want to be a part of this." And so I went off and invested everything I had and more into *The Empire Strikes Back* and took out a big bank loan. There was a thing where we went over budget and the bank wouldn't extend our loan, so we had to get another bank loan. So we did it, and the film worked and I made that money and invested into the next film. So I kept investing everything I had into the next movie and in the company.

What this also meant was expanding the scope of ILM—which had begun as a small group of people working in a warehouse—to the premier visual effects company not only working for Star Wars, *but other projects like E.T. or the* Star Trek *feature films, among many others. And then there was Skywalker Sound, created for sound mixing purposes that greatly expanded its output.*

GEORGE LUCAS

We built that and I got to do what I really wanted to do with Francis and with American Zoetrope, to be able to build a bigger studio. I was just working at a house in San Francisco, which was not red zoned to be a studio or anything, but that's where we made *Star Wars*. But after that, we built a bigger studio and had a great state-of-the-art mixing facility and ILM. We were bringing it along to be state of the art, because I wanted it to be great. But you don't make any money in those businesses. Anybody who says they make money in postproduction is lying. Anybody that says they make money in visual effects is lying. It's about action figures. All the money's in the action figures. Yes, you own the movie, which I came to do, and you make a lot of money, but you have to own everything. And that means, again, you have to put the money in, so you have to take the risk.

LORNE PETERSON
(chief model builder: miniature and
optical effects unit, *The Empire Strikes Back*)

The success of *Star Wars* was pretty unusual; we didn't expect it to happen. There was no expectation that it would become a blockbuster. My partner and I and the people at ILM, we rented the equipment back from George Lucas and did *Battlestar Galactica*. George wasn't really happy about that, doing a film that was a little bit similar to *Star Wars*, but we had to make money. Then, *Star Wars* did make a lot of money and George Lucas asked six of us to move up north to start over again in an empty warehouse, so that's what we did. We went up, there weren't even walls inside the building. We laid out two by fours like where we wanted the rooms instead of doing a drawing. We just basically took a bunch of two by fours and made different rooms in the hallway and then had the carpenter start to build after that.

You know, when we were doing *Empire*, I had saved a bunch of questions for George about the models and he was coming to the model shop that day, so I wanted to ask him what he wanted on this model, what he wanted with that. I started asking the first question, and he stopped me. He said, "Well, that sounds like your job to me." It was like, that isn't what he wants. You didn't think of that as his job. He already hired me because he liked what I did and you do whatever you want. "I like whatever you want to show" is a real joy to work with. You didn't feel he was micromanaging anything.

Thanks to the success of Star Wars, *Lucas could now abandon the idea of a low-budget sequel, as postulated in the* Splinter of the Mind's Eye *novel written by Alan Dean Foster (and published in March 1978). In November 1977, he wrote a handwritten treatment for the film that he was already referring to as* The Empire Strikes Back. *To flesh it out, he began meeting with screenwriter/ author Leigh Brackett, believing her writing represented the perfect sensibility for what he was looking for.*

Leigh Douglass Brackett was born on December 7, 1915, in Los Angeles, California. Beginning at an early age, she began writing science fiction and fantasy stories, with her first short story, "Martian Quest," being published in the February 1940 issue of Astounding Science Fiction. *Brackett was also an active member of the Los Angeles Science Fantasy Society and contributed to an issue of* STF-ETTE, *an all-female science fiction fanzine.*

Brackett published her first novel, No Good from a Corpse, *in 1944. A hard-boiled mystery novel in the tradition of Raymond Chandler, this work would prove instrumental in getting Brackett her first work as a screenwriter. Hollywood director Howard Hawks was so impressed by her novel that he had his secretary call in "this guy Brackett" to help William Faulkner write the script for the 1946 film* The Big Sleep. *A sad testament to the time, women writers, and particularly women screenwriters, were a rarity, making the achievements of Leigh Brackett an inspirational tale of her generation.*

She would continue to write science fiction novels for the next thirty years, and be called upon by Howard Hawks to write screenplays for such films as Rio Bravo, El Dorado, *and* Rio Lobo. *When George Lucas set to the task of creating the* Star Wars *sequel in 1977–78, he wanted an expert writer who could tackle Howard Hawks–like dialogue of the forties and fifties—and so he called upon the then sixty-one-year-old Leigh Brackett.*

RAY MORTON

At this point, it must be stated that Lucas's oft-repeated claim that the entire three-part saga had originally been contained in his first draft of the *Star Wars* screenplay, and that he cut that first draft into thirds and made each section separately, is simply not true. Lucas's first draft of *Star Wars* does contain some locations, concepts, and rudimentary versions of set pieces that eventually appeared in the trilogy (and later in the rest of the series), but it did not tell the same story that the trilogy told. Following *Star Wars,* Lucas had to think up the rest of his saga.

As things developed, he decided to build the trilogy around Luke's journey to becoming a Jedi Knight. Having become aware of the Force and embracing it in the first movie, in the second Luke would formally begin his Jedi training under the tutelage of a Jedi Master. Meanwhile, the Galactic Emperor—having become aware of how strong Luke is with the Force—orders Vader to capture young Skywalker. The Emperor wants to turn Luke to the dark side so that Luke can help him complete his conquest of the galaxy. Vader takes up the search, but has his own reasons for wanting to turn Luke. Luke makes excellent progress in his training, but his impetuousness and immaturity become a problem when Vader captures Han and Leia and uses them as bait to lure Luke into a trap. Desperate to save his friends, Luke runs off before his training is complete and thus faces Vader woefully unprepared. During a titanic lightsaber duel, Vader does all he can to goad Luke into giving in to his anger and hatred, which will trigger Luke's turn to the dark side. We learn that Vader wants Luke to embrace evil not to help the Emperor, but to help him overthrow the Emperor so Vader can rule the galaxy himself. Vader almost succeeds in turning Luke, but young Skywalker manages to escape (barely) before he does. In the third film, Luke would complete his training and become a full-fledged Jedi. He would face Vader again, resist the temptation to turn to the dark side, and finally defeat Vader and the Emperor and save the galaxy.

STEPHEN SCARLATA
(host, *Best Movies Never Made* podcast)

What ended up happening was that George Lucas was really burnt out from *Star Wars* and didn't want to tackle writing the script. He was also working on *More American Graffiti* at the time. He was sinking everything into *Empire,* so he just wanted someone else to tackle writing duties. Enter Leigh Brackett.

LEIGH BRACKETT
(screenwriter, *The Big Sleep, The Empire Strikes Back*)

Early in my career I did a script, and actually got something that I was pleased with. But I discovered [producers] don't know anything about science fiction. They're afraid of it. They just wanted a good, warm family picture. Science fictional, but no monsters, no hardware, no spaceships; in other words, nothing science fictional; just a good, warm family story. It was hard to do. Every time I'd throw in something that was the least bit technical, I'd get, "Oh, the audience isn't going to understand that." They'd be surprised, because the audience is generally miles ahead of them. I think *Star Wars* is a great thing, and I think *Star Trek* is a great thing, too. Perhaps it's gotten to be a little too much of a cult item, though.

JOSH MILLER
(screenwriter, *Sonic the Hedgehog*)

I didn't know much about her as an author, but she cowrote *The Big Sleep* adaptation with William Faulkner, *Rio Bravo* with John Wayne, Robert Altman's *The Long Goodbye*. So she had this kind of hard-boiled Western background.

BONNIE BURTON
(senior editor, StarWars.com 2003–2012)

Which makes sense, because *Star Wars* is a Western. I always called it that, a Western soap opera.

KYLE NEWMAN

It's interesting, though, Lucas's choice to work with her. People say he was a fan of her. Same thing with Irvin Kershner, who would direct and who was his mentor and teacher at USC. But that's what George was like. He puts his ego aside and finds who's going to bring out things that he didn't have the time or patience to do. Like Kershner finding those little comedic moments, or things like Artoo stepping on his tippy toes to peek into something. That's not scripted. Those are all things the director is finding. Like, "I love you." "I know." Just finding those people that are about making it better and not about their ego. With Leigh Brackett, I know the script didn't work out, but he said, "I didn't like this script at all, but I'm giving her credit, because she recently passed away." He wanted to work with people he admired. I think he eventually went to Lawrence Kasdan out of desperation, because he was frustrated with writing, but he was a fan of Kasdan, who was a tremendous writer. At the same time, it is interesting to see what Leigh did before George and other people got involved.

ERIC TOWNSEND
(author, *The Making of Star Wars Timeline*)

One of the most significant ideas to come up during these meetings was the concept of Yoda to essentially replace Ben Kenobi as a mentor to Luke. At the time, Yoda was seen as a crazy, tiny little creature known only as "the Critter." The writers saw the Critter as an almost frog-like creature with a wide mouth, no nose, bulbous eyes, thin spidery arms, short legs, and very large, floppy feet. An idea of Darth Vader in a black castle surrounded by lava was also thrown around. Unused ideas of a water planet with an underwater city, and a "city planet," that was to be the home of the Empire, were also discussed. The backstory of Han Solo was fleshed out during these meetings. Solo was an orphan raised by Wookiees on their planet. The character of Lando Calrissian also grew out of these meetings. He was to be a slick gambler, possibly a clone from the Clone Wars.

LEIGH BRACKETT

I think that this is because Lucas cut his eyeteeth on science fiction; he's been reading it for years and years. He's one of the few in Hollywood who knows science fiction. Not "maybe he's read one book by Isaac Asimov or one by Heinlein," but he's read the whole field, and he came to it knowing all the things to throw in, the stuff which is all a part of the matrix. And he threw it all in with no apologies whatsoever.

Star Wars was just a great film, I thought; just beautiful. He didn't try to teach anybody anything; it's not beating people over the head with what terrible people they are and how they're ruining the environment, or telling us we must all get down and wallow in our shame and beat our breasts. With no apologies to anybody, he just took us back "a long time ago" to "a galaxy far, far away," and did one hell of a rousing adventure story. Beautiful! So much of it was "throwaway" lines or shots. You know . . . momentary shot of a skeleton of a sand-worm; "Hello, Frank Herbert."

BONNIE BURTON

Leigh Brackett was groundbreaking. Just speaking as a woman screenwriter myself, I'm breaking into this field now and am looking at the history of women who shaped Hollywood, and she was definitely one of them. It's so mind-boggling to me that a lot of women in the forties to the seventies earned these great chances to show their stuff. Now it's like Thunderdome; it's such a battle. You have to have a brand and a social media following and a fan group that can attest that we're worthy talents as screenwriters. It's just a lot harder for female directors and screenwriters now than it was then, where you had more collaboration. Also, in sci-fi you had a lot more women back then who were working in that industry. But a credit to George for not making it all a boys' club.

JOSH MILLER

It's also interesting that people kind of remember Kasdan, but not Brackett, who was the veteran on this. Clearly John Carpenter, a big Western fan himself, named a character in *Halloween* after Leigh Brackett: Sheriff Brackett.

STEPHEN SCARLATA

Also from the forties to the seventies, she wrote an insane amount of short stories and novels. She was regarded as the Queen of the Space Opera and writing stories like *Martian Quest, The Beast Jewel of Mars, The Dragon Queen of Venus, Eric John Stark: Outlaw of Mars,* and *Purple Priestess of the Mad Moon.*

PETER HOLMSTROM
(cohost, *The Rebel & the Rogue* podcast)

Most big-budget films have nine or ten writers who work on drafts and never receive a credit. There's stuff in the Brackett draft that stays through to the end, but it's mostly ideas, concepts, not the actual script. I doubt it would get a credit in WGA arbitration. Lucas gave Leigh Brackett a credit to honor her, even though he was the main writer on the film. He wrote most of the drafts, and Kasdan just did dialogue punch-ups. That's the sort of humble guy George is.

ALAN DEAN FOSTER
(author, *Star Wars* novelization and the sequel, *Splinter of the Mind's Eye*)

Empire is a science fiction film written by a science fiction author, which almost never happens. Even though Kasdan did rewrites, I think Leigh Brackett had a lot to do with a lot of the elements of *Empire.* I can't prove it; I don't know what was written by whom, but it resulted in a very different film with a very different tone.

GARY KURTZ
(producer, *The Empire Strikes Back*)

We wanted someone with a background in science fiction who also understood screenwriting; we didn't just want a novelist. Leigh had done *The Long Goodbye* for Robert Altman, and he mentioned her to us. Then, after we talked to Leigh, she really seemed like the ideal person. She had the right sensibility about space as an adventure genre, and she loved the idea of the *Star Wars* characters. George gave her a rough overview of the story, and she was very easy to work with.

ERIC TOWNSEND

By February 23, 1978, Leigh Brackett had completed the first draft of the script. The idea of Luke Skywalker having a twin sister first appears in these early drafts, although it wasn't necessarily Princess Leia at that point. The topic of Luke's father was also a bit unsettled. In this first draft, his father appears to Luke as a Force ghost alongside Ben Kenobi. "The Critter" was known for a time as Buffy, but was eventually given the name Minch Yoda. And Lando was introduced as Lando Kadar.

JOSH MILLER

Vader is not Luke's father in this draft; he's purely trying to make a power play. What's interesting is that Vader was such an iconic villain in the first movie, but you can see in this draft, if they hadn't added the father element, he kind of starts to feel less interesting.

KYLE NEWMAN

He just becomes generic. In their early meetings talking about Darth Vader, I know at one point George is quoted as saying he's a disposable villain when they're talking about *Splinter of the Mind's Eye*; I think the story session with Alan Dean Foster or one of the early story sessions with Kasdan—there's transcripts of it. It's like, "He's a nothing villain. He's a throwaway." He obviously revisited that, because he became the iconic supervillain, but sometimes you have to adapt to the way the movie is accepted into the consciousness.

JONATHAN RINZLER
(author, *The Making of The Empire Strikes Back*)

Each movie has their own interesting and sometimes bizarre backstory. George Lucas movies are particular in that they have their own George Lucas idiosyncratic backstory—which is more like a kaleidoscope. If you ask George Lucas today if Darth Vader was always Luke's father, I'm 99 percent sure he'd say yes. And he would be justified, because in the rough draft of the original *Star Wars*, the main character was Annikin Starkiller, and his father was Kane Starkiller, who was a Jedi Bendu, and he was half-man, half-machine. So he's there in the very earliest draft—except he wasn't Darth Vader, he was this other guy—and then things shift around so many times, that it was no longer true, really. But maybe it was! There is this gray area where maybe he's justified in saying that it's true. But frankly, while he was making the movie, it wasn't true. Darth Vader was the bad guy, Luke the good guy, the two were not related.

STEPHEN SCARLATA

If you watch *Star Wars*, Vader is second fiddle to Peter Cushing in that, and in this one [*Empire*], he's the main villain. It's interesting that with the second draft Lucas brought in the idea of Vader being Luke's father. That's also when the film is changed from being called *Chapter II* to *Chapter V*. It's when it really dawned on him, "Oh my God, combining this character . . ." Because he was looking at Father Skywalker and Obi-Wan, and it's like all three of these people are kind of the same thing. It's redundant. "So if I put Vader and Anakin together . . ." In the first movie, Luke Skywalker had a dad, so seeing these two Force ghosts planted the seed in his head to combine the characters. Now when you watch the first movie, it kind of makes sense. It's pretty amazing. And it also planted that seed that he could do a prequel trilogy by blending them together. So it's like a really big, monumental event.

KYLE NEWMAN

It's discovering story. Discovering the power of simplification and how things can be symbolic when reduced to their core. Which is ultimately why you have to get through these drafts. The good thing is that he took the time to do this. He knew it wasn't right; he had to keep pushing for it to be better. Whereas some people would have been like, "Eh, it's pretty good as is."

JOSH MILLER

It gets reported that Leigh Brackett turned in her script, Lucas didn't like it, and Kasdan rewrote it. Well, she probably would have rewritten it, except she died mere months after turning it in. That script is basically *Empire*. There's a reason she still gets credit for it. It's basically the movie we all saw, minus the big twist, but the building blocks are all there.

STEPHEN SCARLATA

Lucas didn't want to write this. But she passed away and immediately in April he wrote like, two drafts. It's pretty amazing what he created with those two drafts in terms of the changes.

BONNIE BURTON

He always outlined and always knew what he wanted. But the nitty-gritty of the stuff he always found a pain in the ass. He was always criticized for writing dialogue that no one wanted and he knew that. He knew what he wanted, he just had a hard time getting there.

KYLE NEWMAN

But when you look at the Brackett script, the foundation is there. The narrative thrust of it is there. The beginning of the major conflict is there. A bit of the triangle conflict is there. They introduce Lando. They introduce Minch/Yoda.

They introduce the Emperor as a controlling figure—Vader always has a controlling figure in his life in every movie. He's never been the primary villain, which allowed them to liberate him and for him to become a protagonist. All of these things are congruent, but it's the details. It's the details that made this movie special. And warm and as human as you can get with Wookiees and droids. And traditionally in anime stuff. You've got to start somewhere and this is a competent first draft to get all of your ideas on paper so Lucas can go, "Oh, this sucks. The ideas are here, but we've got to do a lot more." I mean, every first draft, if you've ever written anything, sucks. If you're making your first draft, you're probably in trouble. You have to think about things and look at it from multiple levels. And he did this and went off and collaborated with other writers.

In March—after Time *magazine had stated Lucas's plans to film a total of twelve* Star Wars *films, the last to be completed in 2001—he found himself disappointed in the draft of the screenplay that Brackett handed in. When he attempted to contact her, he was told that she was hospitalized in a battle with cancer, which she lost on March 23, 1978. As a result, he decided to rewrite the script himself.*

RAY MORTON

Then he hired Lawrence Kasdan to do the final two passes. After selling two highly regarded spec scripts—*The Bodyguard* and *Continental Divide*—Kasdan had recently begun his professional screenwriting career by penning the screenplay for Lucas's then upcoming collaboration with Steven Spielberg, *Raiders of the Lost Ark.* Kasdan, who would go on to become one of the most prominent writer/directors of the 1980s and 1990s, was an extremely talented craftsman who was highly adept at structuring stories, developing characters, and crafting sharp, witty dialogue. Lucas liked what Kasdan had done with *Raiders* and asked him to help out on *Empire.* Working closely with Lucas and Irvin Kershner, who would sign on as director, Kasdan carefully reworked Lucas's drafts and got the piece into excellent shape for shooting.

GARY KURTZ

We were scheduling a meeting with [Leigh Brackett] to go over the script for a polish, when she died quite suddenly [in March 1978]. She was only in the hospital for four days. She had just barely finished her first draft, up to the last two pages. The pages weren't even typed, but they were done. Larry Kasdan, who was working on *Raiders of the Lost Ark* for George at the same time, came in and did the polishing work on the script. He did a very good job on the final draft. It remained very close to the original script, in terms of the action. It was just the tone or emphasis of a particular scene that might have been altered slightly.

LAWRENCE KASDAN
(screenwriter, *The Empire Strikes Back*)

Had Leigh Brackett lived, she could have made the changes that George wanted in an excellent way, but my responsibility was to understand the *Star Wars* galaxy, not the basic concepts of science fiction. I had to develop *Empire*'s screenplay based on my perception of the characters in *Star Wars* and what George wanted them to do in its sequel. I had to write it much the same way I have to live my life—I don't know how it will end, but I have some way of dealing with my personality the way it exists right now.

GARY KURTZ

We looked at Leigh Brackett's first draft and it was fine. George took it and made some minor modifications, fleshing it out a bit because, obviously, Leigh didn't have the chance. She was going to do two drafts and a polish, but passed away just as she was about to start the second draft. The difference between her first draft and the second one completed by George is fairly minimal. George had to readjust the emphasis slightly.

RAY MORTON

To transform a single film into a three-part saga, Lucas had to retcon many of *Star Wars*' core narrative concepts. This was inevitable, because a properly conceived and constructed dramatic tale should be complete in and of itself—its story should conclude definitively, with no loose threads or open ends. In other words, there really should be no possibility of a sequel. So, in order to extend *Star Wars* into a triptych, Lucas had to create some viable new avenues, which he did by making some significant alterations to a number of ideas that were introduced in the first film. The first was continuing the war. At the end of *Star Wars,* we are left with the distinct impression that the rebels have won and that the Empire had been defeated. As *The Empire Strikes Back* begins, we learn that the Empire has not been defeated, that the war is still going on, and that, while the destruction of the Death Star was definitely a blow to the Empire, it was not the death strike it seemed to be in the last film.

The second was making Vader the story's principal villain. In *Star Wars,* Darth Vader is just a henchman (albeit a really cool one)—Grand Moff Tarkin is that movie's big bad. In the second film, Vader becomes the main antagonist. This decision deepened the character of Vader, transforming him from an exotic version of Oddjob [from the Bond film *Goldfinger*] into a complex figure who poses as a loyal servant to the Emperor while simultaneously plotting to overthrow his evil master and steal his throne. In *Star Wars*, Obi-Wan Kenobi and Darth Vader are the last remaining practitioners of the Force and the Emperor is a fascist politician—the head of a technology-based empire that has become so mechanized that it has completely lost touch with its spiritual side. It is only by tapping that spirituality that Luke is able to defeat the Empire's awesome machinery. In the ongoing narrative, the Emperor also becomes a Force practitioner—an evil Sith Lord who has mastered the dark side of the Force and whose malevolent spirituality now permeates every corner of his Empire.

Luke was an only child in *Star Wars*, but in *Empire*, Lucas gave him a secret sister who is located elsewhere in the galaxy and is just as strong with the Force as Luke is. During the writing of *Empire*, the sister was not meant to be Leia, but an entirely new and different character to be introduced in the final film of the trilogy. The sister is mentioned explicitly in the first draft of the screenplay but referred to only obliquely in the finished film as "another" ("That boy is our last hope." "No, there is another").

JONATHAN RINZLER

I didn't find anything in my research, or any of the script version or fragments that I read, to support that George even knew [Leia was "the other"]. I'm sure he had some idea in his head who the other was, anything's possible—but I think he just put it in there because it was a good story point. It keeps audiences on their toes. He figured, "I'll answer that when I have to."

In George's kaleidoscope way of doing things, it was in the second draft of the original *Star Wars*, where Leia's not a Princess, she's a cousin of Luke and she's off on the farm on Tatooine—so George could arguably say "the other" was always related to Luke and had been from the beginning. But he also didn't argue with the fact that when I did the *Jedi* book, I found a fragment where he wrote LEIA! And that's where it crystalized in his mind. Again, always the kaleidoscope—oh yeah, Leia's the other, Luke's sister. But I don't think until that point it was crystalized. I really *don't* think you'd have that kiss in *Empire*, if he knew.

RAY MORTON

Star Wars was presented as a stand-alone story, but when Lucas decided to make it the jumping-off point for a continuing saga, he reconceptualized the title. *Star Wars* would now be the title of the entire series. Taking further inspiration from the serials, each individual film would now be designated as an episode and given both an episode number and title. In all new prints of the movie, *Star Wars* would now be known as *Episode IV: A New Hope.* The sequel would be known as *Episode V: The Empire Strikes Back.* The final film in the trilogy would be *Episode VI.* (Numbering the trilogy as episodes *IV–VI* instead of *I–III* was an indication to viewers that they were being plopped down into the middle of a narrative that had already been going on for a long, long time, as well as a cheeky tease that they might someday get to see these earlier adventures.)

MARK HAMILL
(actor, "Luke Skywalker")

We went to North Africa on the first film and in some downtime I said to George, "Why are we doing *Episode IV*? Why aren't we doing *Episode I*?" And he said, "This is supposed to be like the old Flash Gordon serials." Serial chapter plays were even before my time, but that would be a serialized story that you would go to the movies to see each week. You'd see the feature film, you'd see some cartoons, you'd see a newsreel and you'd see a chapter play, usually with a cliffhanger ending. You know, the cargo ship is sailing off the cliff to certain death and then they'd say, "Next week, Chapter 12."

GEORGE LUCAS

In choosing the episode to be filmed first, I chose the chapter I felt the most secure with and which I liked the most. The episode number and title were dropped due to the length and the confusion they might have caused.

GARY KURTZ

We got cold feet [on the first film] at the last minute and took [the *Episode IV*] title out. 20th Century Fox was worried, and to be perfectly honest, so were we. Most people wouldn't have understood what that meant. They would have been asking themselves, "What happened to the first three episodes?"

MARK HAMILL

So it was his intent to mimic the Flash Gordon serials, and he thought that if he called it *Episode IV*, they would just have that written scrolling preamble, much like the serials filled you in on what happened the previous week. You know, Flash and Dale are in the clutches of Ming the Merciless and have to escape. He would say really profound things that later I would think, "Boy, that was so perceptive of him." I remember I wanted to go in the day they were filming Darth Vader's arrival onto the spacecraft where you first see him at the beginning of the film. They were going to blow a hole in the door and he's going to step through. I said to George, based on the script, "Aren't you going to cut to two characters saying, 'Who is that?' 'That's the Dark Lord of the Sith.' You know, for some exposition?" And George just casually said, "No, he's dressed in black and we'll play some scary music. They'll know he's the bad guy." Brilliant!

6

TO BEA OR NOT TO BEA:
THE STAR WARS HOLIDAY SPECIAL

"We have to get Chewie home for Life Day."

Throughout much of 1978, things were ramping up behind the scenes in terms of bringing *The Empire Strikes Back* to the big screen. Ralph McQuarrie was working on a variety of illustrations that would ultimately be brought to life while George Lucas and Lawrence Kasdan were revising the screenplay. There were other elements coming into play as well. With Lucas maintaining merchandising control of *Star Wars*, there was some real question of how much interest there would be in the potential franchise, especially with toys from Kenner coming toward the end of the year. It is worth pointing out that in the late seventies, conventional wisdom said a franchise was only viable if the sequels came out every year or two at most. Lucas's notion of every three years had a lot of people worried. To "help"—if ultimately that was the end result—was the creation of a television event debuting on November 17, 1978, titled *The Star Wars Holiday Special*.

It has proven to be the stuff comic-cons are made of. A terrible, abysmal, yet oddly enchanting chapter of the *Star Wars* franchise. *The Star Wars Holiday Special* is a made-for-TV movie cum variety special that aired on the CBS network. The main storyline of the film transpires on the Wookiee home planet of Kashyyyk. Chewbacca and Han Solo visit the planet to celebrate the Wookiee holiday Life Day with his family, which includes his wife Malla, his son Lumpy, and his father Itchy. George Lucas himself was not really involved with the production, but did attend some production meetings, and encouraged the creatives on the special to include the character of Boba Fett in the cartoon segment (the only part of the special really worth watching).

CBS wanted to utilize the then popular variety show format, which leads to odd, almost surreal segments with Bea Arthur, Harvey Korman, and the Jefferson Starship. The *Holiday Special* was an epic failure, both critically and commercially, and was never aired again, nor made officially available on home video. This lack of availability helped the special achieve a "cult" status among fans, with bootleg copies becoming trophies at conventions.

STEVE BINDER
(director, *The Star Wars Holiday Special*)

The *Star Wars* movie was released and became this huge success, and Lucas evidently made a deal with Kenner toys to sell merchandising as soon as he got those rights. As a result, in order to sell toys, he made this deal to do *The Star Wars Holiday Special* with CBS aimed at kids to buy toys. But they didn't tell the public this.

MARK HAMILL
(actor, "Luke Skywalker")

Do you know that after all these years Lucasfilm is still saying, "Mark, we shouldn't be talking about the *Holiday Special*." I said, "No, we've got to own it." I knew when I read it, I thought it was awful. You know, "Why are we doing this?" Then I said, "I'm not doing this," but George called me and explained, "Do you realize when that came out we'd been in the movie theater for almost a year and a half?" *Star Wars* opened in the summer of '77 and this is the fall of '78, so George said, "Look, it's just a way to keep the merchandising fresh in people's minds and it's really a favor to me for those merchandisers." So I said, "Oh, all right, but I'm not singing."

BRUCE VILANCH
(screenwriter, *The Star Wars Holiday Special*)

They started with George. He hadn't made *Empire* yet and he was concerned that the franchise—they didn't talk about franchises that much in those days—had a lot of public interest and needed something to stir the pot in the two years between *Star Wars* and *Empire*. So he had in his trunk, he told me, ten stories. He was going to make six movies, which he eventually did make, and that he had another story that became a novel and another that became something else, but he had one story left that he sold to CBS as a variety special. I don't know how that happened. They talked him into it or something. It was a genre of the day. This was back when there were just the three networks and everything was an event, and if you could create an event on one of them, you'd get a lot of eyeballs. It wasn't crazy to take something like *Star Wars* and use it as a framework for a special. What was unusual was to take a fully formed George Lucas *Star Wars* story and turn it into a variety special.

GLEN OLIVER
(pop culture commentator)

Even when removing from the equation how innately shitty it ended up being, the notion of the *Holiday Special* was, at its core, far too disconnected from the "universe" that had already been established around the *Star Wars* brand. Sure, it was a fledgling brand at that point, but it was, nevertheless, bold and dramatic and defined. Suddenly songs and comedy sketches are added into the mix from out of nowhere? The whole affair was tone-deaf and ill-conceived and doomed not to work from the outset. But not simply because it was connected to *Star Wars*. A project like this would've been problematic when weighing any number of established properties for this kind of adaptation and treatment—especially one as newly established as *Star Wars* was at that point. Some ingredients simply aren't meant to be mixed together. Ever. And can't coalesce at a core, fundamental level. This is one of those instances.

BRUCE VILANCH

The story they had started had the Wookiees as central characters and, unfortunately, they spoke in a language not known to man in this universe or any other known or unknown universe. So everything had to be subtitled, which at the time you couldn't do, because nobody would read subtitles. Now, of course, the *Star Wars* movies are half-subtitled, because they're all speaking Klingon—sorry, that's a different universe. So we had to have people translating for them. We had guest stars who would listen to the Wookiees talk and explain to the audience what they were saying. That's how it began.

They called the usual suspects who write variety shows, like me, because there were going to be a lot of variety performers on it as well as the characters from *Star Wars,* Han Solo and Princess Leia and Luke Skywalker. But they were only going to give us a day, I think, to shoot. Maybe two. So their dialogue was limited, and that's the way it started. The show was not being executed by Lucasfilm; it was being executed by people who did variety shows. So there was an immediate sort of culture clash. It was supposed to be held together by a director who was handpicked by George, a young Canadian guy named David Akuumba, who had never done anything in this genre before. This guy was on the floor directing, as opposed to sitting in the booth saying, "Camera three." We're just having a traditionally put together variety show, so the battle lines were drawn. Okay, they weren't really battle lines, it was just people who spoke different languages and didn't really know how to communicate what they wanted in the middle of it.

STEVE BINDER

The big production team in the sixties and seventies in the variety field was a terrific director friend of mine named Dwight Hemion, and his partner was Gary Smith. Dwight, I had known because he had done the New York version of the Steve Allen New York show originally. I was kind of the generation behind Dwight, who got accolades for his direction of just about every show he ever did, including Liza Minnelli and Baryshnikov on Broadway and so forth. Gary was my original producer on *Hullabaloo* and they're the ones who signed the contract to do *The Star Wars Holiday Special*. Lucas evidently chose his own director when they started production. I got a call from Gary Smith telling me that the entire production was shut down, because they were running out of money. Also, the director that Lucas hired wasn't familiar with multiple-camera directing.

BRIAN JAY JONES
(author, *George Lucas: A Life*)

No self-respecting Lucas or *Star Wars* fan is going to let him get away with not talking about that. I was ten when it aired and watched it live and I've never forgiven him for it. Boy, he was smart enough to see the wheels are coming off of this thing early enough that he can get his name off of it. But poor Harrison Ford looks absolutely miserable in every frame of that thing. Hamill is a mess, because he's just come off of his car accident, so he's heavily made up, looking like a member of KISS or something. Carrie Fisher I think is baked, but having a great time because she gets to sing, which she really wanted to do. Everybody else is just happy they're wearing masks. I watched it again just last Christmas and, I'm sorry, it's still terrible. It's just one of those moments where you have to ask, What were you guys thinking? I loved variety shows as a kid, but trying to turn this into some weird comedy variety show special? But it was a huge effin' deal. I mean, it's *Star Wars* on TV, even though *Star Wars* is only there about 18 percent of the time.

BRUCE VILANCH

It was a big network variety show and the network had things that it needed to do to make the sponsors happy and needed to stock it up with star names and give them all showcases. And they were all interruptions in George's story.

STEVE BINDER

They had built this enormous, beautiful Chewbacca set on one of the big soundstages there, but the problem was that it never had a fourth wall, so it was a 360-degree set where you couldn't get the cameras in. Anyway, they had shut it down and were in jeopardy of the entire project going away. Would I be willing to come in and at least get the show shot if they could convince CBS to restart the production? I said yes and the next thing I know I got a call from Gary Smith asking me to meet him at Warner Bros. and that they were mailing me a history of the Chewbacca family background. I think I donated it to UCLA or USC, but I wish I had it with me. Evidently, Lucas had done a twenty-five-page guide to the Chewbacca family from the time they were born to the present. So I went over to Warner Bros. and they had hired the cream of television people behind the scenes. We all knew basically if you're doing mainstream variety network television, there weren't that many of us that were really doing all the shows, especially in the sixties and seventies. Same camera crews, same art directors, and so forth—just a handful of people in each area. I knew just about everybody on the crew. Who I didn't know were the Lucas people.

When I came in and saw the set, I said, "We've got to open up this set. We've got to cut out one of the walls or we've got to cut out the set and make a wall that you can bring in and bring out so everybody can get inside" and so forth. So that was step one. Step two, Gary and Dwight got permission from CBS to start the production again, but before I even got there, they did the bar scene and they did the Harvey Korman scene, which was a take-off on Julia Child and so forth. I also think the Jefferson Starship had done that musical piece. And then I came in and I had tons of script to do in a limited number of days with no money to speak of. There was no time to do any prep whatsoever other than my own homework at home. On top of that, the opening scene was the Chewbacca family, the mother, father, and the baby—and it was all silent with subtitles. So immediately I said, "Wait a minute, is this going to work?" And it goes on and on and on and on. And I couldn't change a word of the script. I couldn't do anything.

My job was to just go in, act as the fireman and just get it shot, get it so they could put it together. And it's the only show in my entire career that I didn't have time to edit the show when I finished shooting it; I had to go on to another project.

RIC MEYERS

(author, *For One Week Only: The World of Exploitation Films*)

When I was with *Starlog* magazine, I was on the set of the Richard Donner/ Christopher Reeve *Superman* at Pinewood Studios. There I was befriended by production designer John Barry (not to be confused with the James Bond film composer of the same name), editor Stuart Baird, makeup man Stuart Free-born, stop-motion animator Phil Tippett, and even on-set stills photographer

Bob Penn. Over the years they and their friends, and their friends of friends (and their friends of friends of friends), would become my unofficial, off-the-record source for many rumors, reasons, and rationales. Little did I know that their input would be required so quickly. My first major cry of "wtf" came the minute after *The Star Wars Holiday Special* aired. Instantaneously I figured that whoever made this probably hadn't seen the movie it was based on, or certainly hadn't reacted the way I had. The result was an abomination that I credited to standard operating ignorance on the part of the television network.

GLEN OLIVER

Beyond this fundamental disconnect, it didn't seem to appreciate or respect *Star Wars,* which brought about a double doom. The moment, and it happens very early on, we see a Wookiee in an apron, we know we're in trouble. The Wookiees themselves—who drive the show—are bizarrely, unimaginatively anthropomorphic, living amidst decidedly human home appliances and fixtures. It doesn't make any sense. Their world is just this side of those cheap-ass cartoons which show kids stuff like sharks sitting on a couch in their living room watching flatscreen TVs. Which, by the way, these Wookiees pretty much do. But kudos to whoever was willing to have the Wookiees not speak English, which must certainly have been a temptation given the overall nature of this ramshackle affair. Although this adheres to the concept is bizarre and remarkable considering the shoddiness of the narrative and storytelling on the whole.

STEVE BINDER

I came in and I had a ball. I got to work with all the original cast, we got it all shot on time. I really wasn't objective and not to take a step back, but I definitely felt somebody should know this is not *Star Wars II* the movie. The budget was low, but probably pretty high for a television special and especially a children's special. I knew all the *Star Wars* fans were expecting to see a follow-up to the *Star Wars* movie. After I finished it and left, they put it together and although I didn't see it when it aired, I started getting feedback from people in terms that Lucas wanted to buy the master tapes to get it off the market. He was so embarrassed by it and he pretended he didn't have anything to do with it, practically. He was involved evidently, and approving everything from day one.

BRIAN JAY JONES

You know, the one thing I have to say about this is that when that special is on the draft table inside Lucasfilm, he is up to his eyeballs in *The Empire Strikes*

Back at that point already. I mean, it's 1978, but he is in deep development of *Empire*. He doesn't have time to really pay attention to this special that he signed off on. And as we all know, the modus operandi of George Lucas *is* control. But he does with *The Star Wars Holiday Special* what he has never done with anything associated with *Star Wars* up to that point: he turns control over to everybody else. I mean, he's not doing anything. His hands are off of it, so he turns it over to producers who should know what they're doing, and writers who should know what they're doing. But without Lucas's hand on the wheel, the car goes into a ditch immediately and by that point, he's already washed his hands of it. So as the dailies come in, it's like, "I'm taking my name off of this." Again, I believe the result from his turning control of that project over to someone else is that it taught him a valuable lesson: it was a mistake he was not going to make again.

STEVE BINDER

Lucas's people were great to work with, but the actors playing Wookiees could only be in those costumes for forty minutes out of the hour; the rest of the time they had to be given oxygen offstage with their "heads" taken off. Those were very heavy, hot, and intricate. So my shooting time was always cut down, because I wasn't getting the full hour to shoot. Every time we geared up and when you stop and start, it takes time just to get the momentum going again and so forth. From my perspective, I got to work with great people and I don't remember any confrontations onstage with anybody complaining about anything except a few of the actors were concerned that *Star Wars* was such a big thing and they initially worked for so little money. Now the story is that Lucas actually gave a lot of them small points in the movie, which was great. I also remember when I got to the final scene with all the actors and all the extras—I think it was called "Light Day"—I had no money for anything.

I had this huge stage at Warner Bros. that was just empty. So I asked my art director, "Can you afford to just go into every store in Studio City and buy every candle you can get your hands on?" And that was the set. We just lit candles all over the set and it was pretty effective, because we went black camo around it.

There is, however, one element of the Holiday Special *animated segment that provides a redeeming quality: the introduction of bounty hunter Boba Fett, who would be seen in* The Empire Strikes Back *but never really gets the chance to shine in that film or its follow-up,* Return of the Jedi. *It isn't until his appearance decades later in TV's* The Mandalorian *that the character's promise is truly fulfilled.*

BRUCE VILANCH

The one part of the special that was pure George Lucas from beginning to end was Boba Fett, which was an animated segment in the movie that he and his people supervised. That character later became a real *Star Wars* thing, and a very popular one. The rest of it was his idea, but heavily peppered with what the network required.

RICH HANDLEY

(*Star Wars* author, both comics and short stories)

George Lucas was very involved with the special, despite his repeated statement that he'd like to burn all existing copies of it. Back in the 1990s, I wrote an article for Wizard's *TOONS* magazine and I interviewed Nelvana executive Clive Smith about the cartoon. According to Smith, Lucas wrote the cartoon's story and handed his animation team a nine-page outline, along with a rough scene-by-scene breakdown created by Rod Warren. Lucas's team then sent Smith a low-quality black-and-white video of the Boba Fett costume, shot in someone's back garden, which Smith used to design the animated version of the character—which explained the color differences between Fett's outfit in *The Empire Strikes Back* and in "The Story of the Faithful Wookiee." It's kind of astounding to consider that Lucas himself wrote the basis for the Fett cartoon, given his widely known dismissal of the *Holiday Special.* Interestingly, Smith told me Lucas chose to give Luke Skywalker the most screen time with Fett in the cartoon rather than Han Solo and Chewbacca, misleading the audience into believing Chewie had injured Han when he was actually protecting him from the talisman's deadly radiation. Making Chewie out to be a bad guy, as well as fooling viewers into thinking Fett was a friend with good intentions, kept the audience wondering what was going on. And according to Smith, it was all Lucas's idea.

ALEX NEWBORN

(journalist, *Star Wars* chronicler)

Here's where Mark Hamill's participation really shines, foreshadowing his later success in voice-over perhaps. But name another cartoon that got Hamill, Ford, Fisher, James Earl Jones, and Anthony Daniels as voice talent. Daniels was having quite the week as animation voice-over artist, with his turn as Legolas in Ralph Bakshi's version of *Lord of the Rings* coming out in theaters just two days before the *Holiday Special* aired. Besides introducing Boba Fett nearly two full years ahead of his big-screen debut in *The Empire Strikes Back,* the animation artists actually got Luke's outfit right! I might not have liked the squash-and-stretch style they applied to the rigid characters like the droids, but to see *Star Wars* translated into another medium (besides the film and Marvel comics) was very mind-broadening. I also like the link between it and the *Droids* cartoons from the mideighties, both being done by Nelvana studio.

JOHN CELESTRI

(animator of the Boba Fett sequence, *The Star Wars Holiday Special*)
I just happened to be animating at Nelvana studios when the production started. I very much enjoyed seeing the first *Star Wars* film when it came out in the summer of 1977. I had watched reruns of the old Flash Gordon and Buck Rogers serials on TV back in the early 1960s, and knew firsthand Lucas's movie references. It was a ton of fun watching cutting-edge effects being layered over a classic storyline. So, I was excited to get a chance to work on a non-Saturday-morning animated adventure. I knew we didn't have the budget to produce the quality of the Max Fleischer Superman cartoons, but we could give it our best shot! Villains are always the most fun to animate. I was originally cast to animate the Devil in *The Devil and Daniel Mouse* and animated several scenes of that character, but I had to switch over to Daniel Mouse because that animator drawing him dropped out of the production; so, I made sure the Nelvana producers made up for it. I jumped at the chance to animate what we at the studio thought would be a major villain in the sequel.

GLEN OLIVER

Bizarrely, Boba Fett is more interesting, fully developed, and compelling in the *Holiday Special* than he was in any of the *Star Wars* features in which he appeared. It's regrettable that this iteration of Boba Fett was never canonized or cannibalized.

BRIAN JAY JONES

That's its only saving grace. It's like certain comic books are complete crap, but they also mark the first appearance of a character, so there was something that makes it special.

RICH HANDLEY

The Boba Fett cartoon (title "The Story of the Faithful Wookie" on its script— one "e," though most people don't know this since the title wasn't shown on-screen) was, hands down, the best thing about the special. This fifteen-minute Nelvana cartoon, about the Rebels' first contact with Fett, is worlds above the live-action scenes in terms of both writing and production value. This single short story had a profound effect on *Star Wars* fandom and viewers during the only televised airing; all of them immediately fell in love with the mysterious bounty hunter. Fett was cool in *Empire*, but he was a minor character at best in that movie, with very few lines. The mystique that has grown around him throughout the past decades is largely due not to *Empire*, but to "The Story of the Faithful Wookie." Fans often debate what makes Fett a popular character, and the reasons are as varied as Ackmena's alien regulars during the cantina's night shift. But one thing most agree on is that "Faithful Wookie" is among the more enjoyable Fett tales available, so it's a shame no professional copies are available. Perhaps one day, if Lucasfilm ever gets around to releasing the full *Droids* and *Ewoks* series on Blu-ray, they can bull's-eye two Womp rats with a T-16 by including the *Holiday Special* cartoon as a bonus. In the meantime, *Star Wars* fans will have to make do with worn-out bootlegs.

"The Story of the Faithful Wookiee" would eventually see an official release, but only as an Easter egg on The Empire Strikes Back *Blu-ray release from 2011.*

GLEN OLIVER

I vividly remember the excitement surrounding the introduction of Boba Fett in the animation section; in many ways, that cartoon—as uneventful as it was—was the chief positive takeaway from the whole mess. And his introduction is handled reasonably well here, taken on its own merits. At the end of the day, perhaps the Powers That Be would've been better off merely running the thirty-minute Boba Fett cartoon in its own timeslot, dispensing with the swill around it and be done with it. I can't help but wonder if, at any point, this approach was ever actually considered.

JOHN CELESTRI

It was George Lucas who requested that the studio I worked for design the look of the cartoon in the style of French artist Jean "Moebius" Giraud, whose work could be seen in *Heavy Metal* magazine. That direction and a black-and-white home movie showing a person wearing Boba Fett's prototype costume were basically all the cues we had to work with. All the color models and basic designs had to be okayed by Lucas before production of the cartoon proceeded. Regarding the animation itself, the biggest challenge was how to give a performance without facial expressions. I had to use hand gestures and body attitude. Not so broadly as a pantomime artist, but with an economy of movement. I approached playing Boba Fett as a Clint Eastwood–style character in a spaghetti Western, with mannerisms expressing a sense of extreme self-confidence. I used macho posing, tossed his rifle across his body from one hand to the other. In one particular scene, I had Boba adjust the fingers of his glove before gesturing with his hand. I timed tilting Boba's helmeted head to go up and down, side to side to change the arc of the helmet's rigid eye-opening to reflect the tone of his dialogue delivery. All of these were some of my touches.

GLEN OLIVER

Based on his appearance in the *Holiday Special,* I recall being incredibly amped to see how Boba Fett fit into the live-action universe. This was stoked considerably by the ability to special-order the Boba Fett action figures. You know, the ones which were supposed to have a firing missile, but didn't? All factors being equal, this was such a strong introduction for a character. He had to be interesting, right? Thus began a five-year arc towards disappointment as the young me slowly, stubbornly came to terms with the fact that the live-action Boba Fett was never going to do a great deal more than stand around, and be swallowed by a Sand Rectum.

JIM SWEARINGEN
(conceptual designer, Kenner)

The last *Star Wars* project I worked on at Kenner was the "Rocket Fire Boba Fett." I went out to California and met with George Lucas and Gary Kurtz. They brought out the first Boba Fett costume and I got to take turnaround photographs of it; this was probably the first time I had a camera there and allowed to take pictures. So I took pictures of the model and then they came back and made the first twelve-inch Boba Fett, which I kit-bashed.

The reason we were doing this figure at all was between the two movies—it was three years—Kenner management was getting really nervous and convinced George into doing one character from the new movie that we could use as a promotion. The timeline gets a little fuzzy—it was forty-some years ago—but the Boba Fett character was already planned for the movie, though he wasn't a major character at that point. And then he showed up in *The Star Wars Holiday Special.* And we needed a cool figure we could use and they came back with Boba Fett. I don't know how important he was to start with, but for us, we needed something to drum up business for '79 before the new movie came out.

The other big surprise about the special was the fact that it featured Harrison Ford, Carrie Fisher, and Mark Hamill reprising their roles as, respectively, Han, Leia, and Luke—and singing!

BRUCE VILANCH

You'd think that everybody was on there for a reason, but it seems like nobody was on there for a reason. They all had a motive. Harrison was dragged into it. George dragged all of them into it. Carrie was kind of out of it most of the time; we were very close at the time and were snorting the Sweet & Low. Of course, the *Star Wars* actors were also in there, Peter Mayhew, Anthony Daniels, and Kenny Baker, because George owned all of them. They only had to work a day or two. Carrie wanted to do a number; she wanted to do Joni Mitchell's "I Wish I Had a River," which I thought was hysterical. Why Princess Leia would sing that song anyway we weren't exactly sure. At the end, there was a number that everybody sang and they were all sports about it, and knew it while they were doing it. Carrie was more invested, because she comes from a family of showbiz people who did these shows all the time. And for her own self it was a way to do something different. But you can't do anything different, it's Princess Leia. George wasn't going to let her mess with the character; she had to live in six more movies or something.

RICH HANDLEY

It was painfully clear that none of them wanted to be there, and that they were only doing the special out of contractual obligations. Hamill's Lucille Ball wig, necessitated by his car accident, looked absurdly silly, especially combined with his self-conscious grinning. Meanwhile, Ford appeared to be embarrassed and/or annoyed in every scene he was in, and Fisher seemed . . . well, let's say medicated. The *Holiday Special* got low marks in pretty much every category, but some of its lowest are in regard to the acting of all involved, even the leads. All three of them are wonderful actors . . . just not here.

MARK HAMILL

I personally love to sing. I did a Broadway musical, but I didn't feel it was right for Luke to sing. Carrie had a wonderful voice and she did a great job. She was all about having fun. It was impossible not to have fun around her. That's the way she was and she appreciated the absurd, the craziness.

ALEX NEWBORN

Funnily enough, one night after *The Star Wars Holiday Special* aired, Carrie Fisher hosted *Saturday Night Live,* with musical guests the Blues Brothers. Her opening monologue was in costume as Princess Leia, which segued right into a skit called "Beach Blanket Bimbo," where the November 1978 television viewing audience got to hear her sing again, this time a peppy little number about being the new kid on Earth, which had a chorus that repeated the name Obi-Wan Kenobi like it was a fifties doo-wop song. Can you imagine seeing the *Holiday Special* on Friday night and then watch Carrie kissing Bill Murray on Saturday night?

BRUCE VILANCH

There are two things you have to remember. First, it was the 1970s and a lot of us had chemical additives. It's trippy. You know, "Oh my God, the show I'm working on is so trippy!" There was also, of course, the mad dash to appeal to youth, which was endemic of Hollywood at that time in general. "How do we get the youngsters into the seats or how do we get them watching the shows?" So there was a combination of all of those things to make it, the thinking being the crazier, the better. Also, these variety shows were pretty lighthearted. They were lightheartedly led by comedy, or extremely, elegantly, led by music, and this was seen as a show that was going to be dragged around by its comedy nose, because we had these big comical characters. In this concept, you weren't going to watch Chewbacca fight off the enemy. Chewbacca fighting off a stormtrooper was not a number we were going to do.

GLEN OLIVER

The moment that really drives me crazy is when Malla and Lumpy run to their front door, open it—excited to hear the Millennium Falcon approaching for landing—only to find two stormtroopers standing outside, their blasters pointed at the door. What the fuck were those stormtroopers doing out there? Were they waiting for someone to open the door because they couldn't figure out how to get through . . . a wooden door? Did they not want to barge in and interrupt the Wookiees' family time? Was the door their enemy? Such blocking is sloppy, lazy madness, and nicely exemplifies much of what is wrong with this show. There simply wasn't much heart or thought put into it—the notion of whether or not it should have ever existed to begin with notwithstanding.

BRUCE VILANCH

This was going to be Chewbacca's tender domestic life of Wookiees. He had a fried-blonde Wookiee wife who was a cook and who was watching Julia Child on TV, and Julia Child in our universe, of course, was an alien played by Harvey Korman with four arms. And there was a kid. George's other gigantic idea was virtual reality, which was unknown at the time, and was in the form of a helmet that you put on, it plugged into your brain and your fantasies came to life. Just in front of you, of course. So a number of production numbers were fantasies happening in virtual reality. It was a lot for the audience to take. George's genius is that he doesn't run away from these ideas; he takes them and turns them into something. It was one of the interesting ideas of the show and became a way that we got production numbers into it, which allowed us to feature Cirque du Soleil and Diahann Carroll and the Jefferson Starship.

GLEN OLIVER

The prevailing vibe of the show is cheapness and disconnect. Without a doubt, a little more thought and effort and soul and budget would've, at the very least, helped the project to feel less whorish. This doesn't mean it would've been any good, not by a long shot. But at the very least it could've been rendered a little less skanky. As is, we get a cruddy variety show, which often plays like the score for a comedic, Mel Brooks–ian parody, than music intended to actually drive any kind of respectable narrative. The tacky video "look" of the show, along with its production values, doesn't even rise to the quality of the lesser-budgeted TV projects that aired around, or before, this time. Imperials play as hammy *Spaceballs*, OTT parodies of archetypes which are already decidedly unsubtle in (what would become known as) *A New Hope* before it. If they'd just given these bozos mustaches to twirl, it would've been perfect. A slinky, sexy, vaguely interactive Diahann Carroll appears as some sort of neutrally driven VR experience, immediately calling into question what the hell Itchy is doing over in this chair where the other Wookiees aren't around (and possibly even when they are around). It feels unhealthy. Carroll's song sounds like it was rejected from a 007 title sequence. It all feels Sid and Marty Krofft on a blandly colored, bad trip.

JOHN CELESTRI

I eagerly awaited the original TV broadcast of the show. Honestly, after watching the first fifteen minutes of the live-action, I was worried that all the viewers would switch channels before our animated segment, which was the best part of the show, had a chance to be seen. But I feel quite proud that the animation stands on its own as being the seed that helped grow the character of Boba Fett. Fact is, the Nelvana studio staff was very young and inexperienced, myself included. I had been in the animation business a mere three years and had been a professional animator for only a year and a half when I did that animation. What it lacks in finesse is made up for with energy and commitment to doing my best, and then it was the only performance associated with Boba until *The Empire Strikes Back*. I was extremely disappointed that the live-action Boba had so little screen time in *Empire*. Truth be told, I wish the animated sequence in the *Holiday Special* was officially acknowledged as being part of the *Star Wars* "canon," but that's not my call.

DAN MADSEN
(owner, the Official Lucasfilm/Star Wars Fan Club, 1987-2001)

There's definitely an interesting story in the making of [the *Holiday Special*]. It's funny, because the *Holiday Special* has become a cult film. I can remember back in the day when I was running the fan club, somebody got me a bootleg on VHS. And I can remember thinking, "Wow, this is awesome!" Because you couldn't see it—there was no way to watch it anymore. So, I got some sort of bootleg copy, I don't know how I got it, and I was able to kind of watch it over and over again. It was kind of like, "Wow, this is kind of special to be able to see it, because all you could otherwise was to remember it from the first time when it aired." It's nostalgia. It's the first appearance of Boba Fett. It's almost freaky to watch Bea Arthur and Diahann Carroll singing and dancing—it's like, "Whoa! What were they smoking when they came up with this?!"

[The cantina costumes] look fake and phony—no denying it. But in the magic of cinematography and the right lighting, for *A New Hope*—it worked. It didn't have any of the campiness that you saw in the cantina scene in the *Holiday Special*. It made a whole different effect on you.

RIC MEYERS

In retrospect, I realized it was the first ominous reference to a mantra that would haunt the film series, and me, to this day: "George thinks *Star Wars* is for kids." Don't know who first said it, and even doubted it was said that early, for Lucas had to be hip deep into prepping *The Empire Strikes Back* at that point.

GLEN OLIVER

It's a mixed blessing. Wookiees jabbering and grunting and growling and barking for long stretches wears thin very, very quickly, no matter how cute they may be. Which, again, demonstrates how out of touch the filmmakers were with the show they were crafting. Little Lumpy stops to watch a cartoon as the Imperials are searching his house (as one would). The program of choice? A cartoon about the Rebel Alliance, using established *Star Wars* characters. A bizarrely meta development essentially stating that the *Star Wars* lore and heroes we're familiar with are also cartoon characters within their own universe, doing more or less the same things in animated form that they do in "real life." This kind of wackadoodle thinking might actually be impressive or agreeable in any other context, but I'm reticent to give the Powers That Be too much credit in this instance, as I'm certain the implications of the set piece never crossed anyone's minds at the time.

STEVE BINDER

It was truly a miracle that we pulled it off. Now, of course, I see Harrison Ford on *The Tonight Show* saying what a disaster it was, and I know before she died Carrie Fisher said, "I hated doing it," and so forth. That's all new news to me. I mean, when we were there doing it, I never heard anything negative. I was thrilled that I got the opportunity to do it. It's amusing to me and I wouldn't say anything negative about it. I mean it was there to sell toys to little kids. That was the purpose of this *Star Wars Holiday Special*.

GLEN OLIVER

This, along with *Droids* and *Ewoks*, must certainly have impacted Lucas's trajectory towards becoming a control freak, um, auteur.

7

ICE, ICE, BABY:
THE EMPIRE STRIKES BACK

"Do. Or do not. There is no try."

Doing his best to make *The Star Wars Holiday Special* a distant memory, Lucas remained firmly focused on *The Empire Strikes Back*. Returning crew members included Robert Watts as associate producer, Paul Hirsch as editor, Ralph McQuarrie as design consultant, Stuart Freeborn as makeup supervisor, John Mollo as costume designer, and John Williams as composer. Among the newbies were Peter Suschitzky as director of photography and Brian Johnson as the supervisor of mechanical special effects while the film was shooting, and then joining ILM in the creation of other special effects. Most importantly, though, Lucas had elected not to serve as director. Instead, he turned to a friend, his former USC professor and filmmaker Irvin Kershner.

Kershner was born on April 23, 1923, in Philadelphia. His parents instilled in him at an early age a love of the arts, which led to him pursuing numerous arts degrees, finally landing at the Arts Center of Design in Pasadena, California. He served three years in the Air Force during World War II, before returning to Los Angeles to study cinema and become a professor of photography at the University of Southern California. Kershner then became a still photographer for the State Department, traveling around the world to take still photographs for the United States Information Service.

Throughout the late fifties and sixties, Kershner worked in television, creating series like *The Rebel* (1959–61), as well as the pilots for *Peyton Place*, *Cain's Hundred*, *Philip Marlowe*, and others. Kershner then moved on to features, with such films as *A Fine Madness* starring Sean Connery in 1966, and *The Return of a Man Called Horse* starring Richard Harris in 1976. During this time, he would also work as a professor at the University of Southern California, where he taught, among many others, a young aspiring filmmaker named George Lucas.

IRVIN KERSHNER
(director, *The Empire Strikes Back*)

George chose me because he wanted a film in which the people really came alive. I was afraid of the challenge at first, because *Star Wars* was such a unique film and I didn't want to try to follow it. *Empire* has many more special effects, tons more sets, and much more complexity in the characters than *Star Wars*. I had my hands so full that I stopped worrying about trying to make it better than *Star Wars* and just tried to make it right.

When George came to me at first, I said, "Wow, what the hell can you do with the second one that you didn't do with the first one?" And I worried that maybe the audience had already had enough and they'd view a sequel as something just to make a few bucks. I'm not especially interested in sequels. I had made one before, *Return of a Man Called Horse*, but I did that because I really loved the subject and felt they failed in the first film. Fortunately, George didn't want a typical sequel—which made it a bit frightening, because it was a much bigger picture than *Star Wars*. We had sixty-four sets, which was unheard of, and they were big. I would work on a giant set for two days and they would rip it down overnight and start building another one, because we had to put those sixty-four sets on seven stages. The film was all shot inside with the exception of the first ten days in Norway. We started shooting there and then went into the studio and never left. Everything was done inside. The woods, the water . . . everything. It was incredible.

DALE POLLOCK
(author, *Skywalking: The Life and Films of George Lucas*)

I think on *Empire* Lucas wanted to see what would happen if he didn't direct. He hated directing *Star Wars*. It physically, mentally, and emotionally took an enormous toll on him and he was tremendously frustrated. You know the old Woody Allen line, you're lucky if you get 40 percent of what you want onscreen. Well, Lucas thought he had gotten 20 percent, so I think he really said, "That was not an enjoyable experience for me. Let's see what it's like to have somebody else on one of these films."

IRVIN KERSHNER

I've heard from all over the world that many people consider *The Empire Strikes Back* to be the best film of the trilogy and I am gratified, because I worked so damn hard on the film for two and a half years. What made it easier was being backed up by someone like George Lucas, who stayed in California while I worked in England. We communicated on the telephone constantly. Whenever I had a problem that I couldn't get solved there—which wasn't often—I knew I could call him. I knew I always had the ear of some-one who understood the production, which is not true in the studio, because those people are raised as accountants and agents and attorneys.

DALE POLLOCK

Lucas did not like how independent Irvin Kershner was. Once he started directing, he wouldn't really listen to George and wouldn't kowtow to him when it came to every creative decision. As a result, when it came time to do *Return of the Jedi,* he picked a very pliable director in the form of Richard Marquand. I was on the set of that film and he feared Lucas. After ivery take, he would look over at Lucas, so I think George said, "Oh, I'm not hiring somebody that independent [like Kershner on *Empire*] again." Then when *Return of the Jedi* was released and got weak reviews, he said, "Well, fuck that. I'll do the next ones myself."

IRVIN KERSHNER

When George decided he wanted me to do the picture, he was very, very kind. He said, "Look, I want you to make a better picture than I did," which is a nice way of saying, "Hey, this is important to me." You see, if *Empire* didn't work, then there is no third one and it's all over. We didn't know if the audience was still there for a second one. We had no idea. We assumed it was, but we didn't know for sure. And George was putting up his own money. Fox didn't put up the money. When I went up to seek approval for something, George said to me, "Do you know why you're making this picture?" And he showed me all these detailed plans for Skywalker Ranch, and he said if the picture is successful, this is what he is going to build. George is fantastic. He invests all the money he makes into moviemaking and no one else does that. No one else who makes a lot of money in movies puts it back into the medium. Look at ILM and the other stuff he had developed. It is incredible. I really have tremendous respect for him.

BRIAN JAY JONES
(author, *George Lucas: A Life*)

I don't know enough about the discussion that went into hiring Kershner, but you've got Gary Kurtz who knows directors as well as Lucas does and is willing to sit down with them and then go to Lucas and say, "You need somebody who completes you. You need somebody who's good with actors. You need some-body who's going to get out of themselves on the set." Things that Kershner is really good at, and Lucas had had Kershner on the list of possibilities anyway. And the only person making the decision at that point is George Lucas.

GARY KURTZ
(producer, *The Empire Strikes Back*)

A lot of the pictures Kersh has made have been strong character pictures, and we were interested in someone who had the feel for creating strong character parts. He also did some good pictures, like *The Return of a Man Called Horse, The Flim-Flam Man,* and the TV movie *Raid on Entebbe*—they all have relatively strong action sequences. Probably the most important thing is that he believed in the fantasy. A lot of contemporary filmmakers are very cynical about life in general. Because of that it comes through in their work.

IRVIN KERSHNER

I analyzed *Empire* before production and came to the obvious conclusion that it was not just a sequel, but the second act of a three-act space opera. Now, the second act does not have the same climax as the third act or even the first act. The second act is usually more ambiguous. It is quieter, but the problems are accentuated; you get into depth. It is not fast, like the end of a three-part drama. So therefore I knew that I would never have the climax, because if it comes to a complete climax, where do you go with the third one? It is about revealing character.

RAY MORTON
(senior editor, *Script* magazine)

As all of them further developed the story, it had to be constructed around two unusual accommodations. On his way to shoot pickups for the original movie, Mark Hamill was severely injured in a terrible car accident and had to undergo facial reconstruction. As a result, he no longer looked the way he did in *Star Wars*. To explain this discrepancy in appearance to the audience, Lucas devised a scene in which Luke was attacked and smashed in the face by a local monster at the very beginning of the movie.

Harrison Ford did not have a sequel clause in his contract for the original film. He had agreed to return for *Empire,* but had not agreed to do the third film and had indicated to Lucas that he was not likely to. To explain Solo's impending absence, Lucas decided to write Han out of the story at the end of *Empire.* The original notion was to have Solo leave to search for his stepfather—a wealthy oligarch with the power to help the Alliance. Han would be away for the bulk of the third film and return only in the final scenes of the saga (Lucas was confident he could get Ford to agree to come back for a day or two to shoot a cameo). Later, it was decided to have Han captured by a bounty hunter pursuing him for the debt incurred to Jabba the Hutt (the Tatooine gangster who was after Solo in the first movie). The dashing smuggler would be frozen in carbonite at the end of *Empire* and shipped off to Jabba and then rescued and thawed out in the final scenes of *Episode VI*.

Writing out Solo meant Lucas had to come up with another character who could take Han's place in *Episode VI*. This led to the creation of Lando Calrissian, a gambler, con man, and old running buddy of Solo's who initially betrays Han and Leia to Vader, but later has a change of heart and becomes one of the good guys. Any confusion as to why Calrissian was brought into the story was cleared up at the end of *Empire,* when Lando—wearing Han's costume from the first movie—literally takes Han's seat in the cockpit of the Millennium Falcon next to Han's copilot and then flies off in Han's ship.

IRVIN KERSHNER

George and I worked closely with Lawrence Kasdan for three months getting the script right. Then, when the script was right, I went off to London alone, where the production was set up. I spent about a year locked away doing storyboards for the script so that every single effect, every scene that had anything unusual in it, was storyboarded. By the time I went to shoot, I wanted to know every single scene. In fact, I knew every word in the script by that time, so I didn't have to even think, "Now what am I going to do next?" Not that I followed the storyboards that religiously. I did follow them, but where things didn't work I could change it, because I knew where to go. So I could concentrate on the characters. You see, the biggest problem with epic productions like this is the special effects take so much attention that you tend to let the acting slip by. I didn't want that to happen. And Harrison Ford was constantly calling me on it. If we did just two takes and I'd say, "That's great," he would say, "Wait a minute, wait a minute. What's great? Was it great for the special effects or for me?" And I'd say, "Harrison, I wouldn't say, 'great' unless it was for you. It really was great." And he would give me that wonderful look of his, that wry look, and we would move on. We had a great relationship.

LAWRENCE KASDAN
(screenwriter, *The Empire Strikes Back*)

It always starts with George: George talking to an artist about his conceptions, and encouraging the artist to come up with his own ideas. A great many of the things in that initial draft were things that were already in the painting stage with Ralph McQuarrie. I would sometimes see a painting of something in that draft before I had written about it at all. There were certain large events in the movie that were always part of the general structure, and how exactly they would look had much more to do with Ralph and the effects people than they did with me or Kershner.

DALE POLLOCK

Kershner was an independent filmmaker and that appealed to Lucas. He had what he considered to be a studio hack; he wasn't really looking for an independent director. But what Kershner brought was a fresh pair of eyes and he saw this incredible potential in the ultimate father/son story. He realized he had gotten the good chapter and understood the mythic implications, which is what really made *Empire* so strong. But the "problem" was that he approached it like a director and he hated somebody telling him what to do. If my memory's correct, Lucas spent the first two weeks on the set and Kershner really bristled at his presence. I seem to remember a conversation where he said, "Either you trust me to make this film or you don't. And if you trust me to make this film, I really can't have you on the set every day, because everybody looks at you after every take." I think Lucas respected that as a filmmaker and he left. But in the end, he did not want to make another movie with Irvin Kershner. He felt that Kershner made it too much his movie and not enough of what Lucas would have done with it.

JOHN MOLLO
(costume designer, *The Empire Strikes Back*)

Star Wars had been a pleasure to work on, but George Lucas passed the job of directing its sequel over to an old friend who had taught him filmmaking at university. He needed a lot of help from George, who was now in the States all the time and was not able to supervise things as he had on the first film. I was very glad when it [*Empire*] was over, and even happier when I was already employed on another film when number three commenced.

All of the familiar cast returned to their now iconic roles including Mark Hamill, Carrie Fisher, Harrison Ford, as well as the men in the masks: David Prowse, Anthony Daniels, Kenny Baker, and Peter Mayhew. Even Alec Guinness returned after being killed in the first film for a cameo, which helped introduce the film's most popular character that continues to enchant audiences to this day, Yoda, performed and voiced by Frank Oz.

IRVIN KERSHNER

All of the actors surprised me; they were far more interesting than I expected them to be. I got Mark, Carrie, and Harrison together, and we talked and talked. I explained things, told them what the characters were doing, what they could try, and how they could try to feel out their scenes and physicalize whenever possible. This was their language, they responded to that approach. If I hadn't done that, I think I would have been in trouble. The way we worked made it fun; we really had fun doing the takes.

A newcomer to the cast was the man who brought the smooth to the swagger with the character of Lando Calrissian, played by Billy Dee Williams. Williams was born in New York City on April 6, 1937. Acting was in his blood from an early age, and he appeared in the Broadway show of The Firebrand of Florence *in 1945. Much of his childhood was spent studying to become an actor, with a film debut in 1959 with the film* The Last Angry Man. *He won acclaim for his role in the 1971 made-for-TV movie* Brian's Song, *which earned Williams an Emmy Award nomination. In 1972, Williams shot to worldwide acclaim with the Billie Holiday biopic* Lady Sings the Blues, *starring Diana Ross. By 1980, Williams was labeled by media as the "black Clark Gable" for his suave demeanor and smooth voice.*

BILLY DEE WILLIAMS
(actor, "Lando Calrissian")

Before *Star Wars* I did a whole bunch of movies. I gained the reputation of being a charming, roguish individual. I imagine he took that into consideration. I was pretty popular back then. Nobody had ever seen someone like me before.

Another fan-favorite character, Boba Fett, came to life on the big screen thanks in part to the late British character actor Jeremy Bulloch. Bulloch was born February 16, 1945, in Leicestershire, England. At the age of twelve, Bulloch entered the screen acting world with an appearance in a breakfast cereal commercial. After several uncredited screen appearances, Bulloch's first regular role was in the 1960 TV series Counter-Attack! *and (the same year)* The Chequered Flag. *He went on to have a recurring role in* Billy Bunter of Greyfriars School *in 1961, and a regular role in* The Newcomers *from 1965–67. He earned the role of Boba Fett because his half-brother, Robert Watts, was working as an associate producer on* The Empire Strikes Back *and was looking for someone who would fit in the suit. The voice for Boba Fett was originally provided by character actor Jason Wingreen, and in the updated versions by* Attack of the Clones' *Temuera Morrison—to strengthen the connection with the prequel trilogy, and who reprised the role in* The Mandalorian *and its spin-off series,* The Book of Boba Fett.

JEREMY BULLOCH
(on-set actor, "Boba Fett," *The Empire Strikes Back*)

I think the popularity is due in a large part to the costume, which is just wonderful. I also think people are attracted to what they see as Boba's code of honor. He's ruthless. He's money-oriented. He probably was a very good soldier, but something makes him turn into a bounty hunter. His code of honor is that he'd never tread on anyone else's feet to capture a bounty. He does it his ruthless way, but he wouldn't cross anyone.

They asked me to put the Boba Fett costume on, which I donned and thought: "This is strange." There was an odd sort of Wookiee scalp hanging from my shoulder, which I originally put under my helmet, because I thought it was some kind of hairpiece. My first meeting with George Lucas was actually in the costume. "You look fantastic." Everything seemed to stop and there was this marvelous feeling of a presence of somebody else. All the crew looked around at this new character. I thought, "Hey, this character obviously looks good. He's the one who got away. There are bullet holes all over his armor. And he has a shredded cape. He's got these Wookiee scalps. So, he has obviously done pretty well over the years in the galaxy."

STEVEN MELCHING
(screenwriter, *Star Wars: The Clone Wars*)

Boba Fett was built on mystique. He was the first major new character introduced to the *Star Wars* universe in the 1978 *Holiday Special*. Then Kenner released the mail-away action figure, so he was someone we "first generation" fans speculated about and endlessly obsessed over in the years leading up to the release of *Empire*. When we finally saw him in action, he was this laconic, badass bounty hunter who was smart enough to track down Han Solo where the entire Imperial fleet failed and tough enough to stand up to Darth Vader. Plus, he had an awesome costume, was outfitted head-to-toe with all kinds of weapons, and wore Wookiee scalps as trophies. The guy killed Wookiees!

CHRISTIAN GOSSETT
(comic book artist, *Tales of the Jedi*)

What's not to love about Boba Fett? He's the guy, the only guy, who thinks like Han Solo. He's Solo without a soul. He's the Lee Van Cleef of the *Star Wars* galaxy.

KEVIN J. ANDERSON
(author, *The Jedi Academy* trilogy)

Boba Fett just looks cool. Darth Vader defined evil for everybody, but for me, Boba Fett defined a bounty hunter. He looked like a bounty hunter, he acted like one, he was smart, he was cold and ruthless, but he's only got three lines, which makes him even more impressive.

STEVEN MELCHING

I think a big reason why Fett became so popular was because we really didn't know a whole lot about him. He was described as a "Mandalorian Shock Trooper." Who the hell were *they*? Did they fight in the Clone Wars? Could he be this "other" that Yoda spoke of? All this anticipation made his ignominious demise in *Return of the Jedi* all the more crushing.

CHRISTIAN GOSSETT

The prequels screwed that all up, because they basically made him some kind of clone spawn which is one of my main problems with the prequels. *Star Wars* is such a great ensemble piece, and just as Luke's dark side is personified in Vader, so is Boba Fett the path that Han could have chosen at any point in his youthful days as a smuggler. Showing that contrast was one of the functions Boba Fett served, and he served it damned well. The fact that Lucas dropped him in the Sarlacc pit was a sign of poor choices to come.

STEVEN MELCHING

In those years before *Empire* and really until the release of *Episode II*, we fans fleshed him out in our own imaginations, and poured all our fantasies into him, fueled by the Expanded Universe. Only much later did we learn that Fett was supposed to be the main antagonist in *Episode VI*, with the bulk of the Luke/Vader/Emperor storyline intended to be the spine of *Episodes VII–IX*.

Frank Oz could be described as the most famous actor that you've never seen. Prior to his role as Jedi Master Yoda in the Star Wars *saga, Frank Oz had already made a career for himself as a puppeteer and performer for Jim Henson's* The Muppets *and* Sesame Street—*providing the much-beloved personalities for the roles of Miss Piggy, Grover, Sam the Eagle, Bert, and many more. He would go on to portray those roles and characters for over thirty years. While Jim Henson was himself first asked to portray the role of Yoda, Frank Oz would step in and become instrumental in the creation and characterization of this beloved character.*

Oz would eventually add writer/director to his résumé, codirecting the 1982 film The Dark Crystal *with Jim Henson (and George Lucas on as a supportive producer), the 1986 film* Little Shop of Horrors, Dirty Rotten Scoundrels, *as well as many others. But he has continued to portray the character of Yoda and an occasional role on the Muppets when the circumstances arise.*

One of the most surprising success stories of The Empire Strikes Back *is the way that the character of Jedi Master Yoda—a puppet manipulated off-screen by a team and voiced by Frank Oz—interacts with Mark Hamill as Luke Skywalker.*

IRVIN KERSHNER

The floor of the Dagobah set was about five feet above the actual floor of the stage. We built it up and put Yoda there, and there were splits in the floor so that they could manipulate him. Below the floor were about five TV sets and Frank Oz and his crew. One person would control the ears, one person would blink the eyes, another person would move the mouth, one person moved one arm, another moved another arm. It was all scrutinized carefully and all they could see were the television sets around them.

FRANK OZ
(puppeteer/voice actor, "Yoda")

I just do the voice and I get all the credit. It's amazing how people don't understand that I'm the guy who gets all the credit for just doing a day of work, and for the character itself. I don't work in a vacuum. Back then it was remote control, but it was always me and three other people and we had to perform him. One person was on the left hand, the other guy the right hand, and another guy with a cable was RCing the unibrow. I remember one guy was doing Yoda's blinking hard before the eyes met. The other guy doing the eyes knew he couldn't move the eye until after the blink. But for me, it was a piece of cake. I was just doing the voice.

IRVIN KERSHNER

Because we were getting sick from all of the smoke on the set, I was wearing a gas mask with a microphone in it and I had a speaker, through which I would talk to Frank and Mark and the crew. And Frank would use a speaker for rehearsal, so that when Mark would say to Yoda, "Can you tell me where I can find the Jedi Master?" he would hear, "Why do you want to know?," which was Frank answering him through a speaker somewhere. But when we actually did the take, Mark didn't hear anything; Yoda's dialogue was put in later. We rehearsed until we got the rhythm and then we'd do the take and he'd say, "Can you tell me where I can find the Jedi Master?," there was a pause and then he'd say, "Well, I want to know . . . ," pause . . . "It's my business." And so on. See what I mean? Mark would know exactly how long to pause. He did a wonderful job of reacting to nothing but memory. Though Mark couldn't hear him, he could see him. I wanted Yoda to look like he was Luke's equal. I wanted Yoda to look like he could climb around. I wanted to give the illusion that he had emotion. It was not something that was put into stop-motion like King Kong, which is a miniature put in later. This was actual time.

FRANK OZ

With Yoda, you can't perform spontaneously, because you drag three other people along with you. If I tried spontaneity, they wouldn't know when to do the eyes when I do the ears. In this kind of situation, the satisfaction you get working with two or three other people occurs after you rehearse and rehearse and suddenly the role opens up to you. It's a living organism. It just happens. It unfolds like a flower, because you are so in tune with each other. It's a wonderful moment.

IRVIN KERSHNER

These challenges are what make films so exciting, when you have interesting, believable characters and you see how they react to each other and their surroundings. The characters have to be real, no matter how fantastic the situation.

Although shooting started in Norway on March 5 (more on that to come), filming moved to Elstree Studios on March 13, 1979, where all eight existing stages were used and a new one was built for footage on the ice planet Hoth and the jungle planet Dagobah. Things progressed, though the production was delivered a setback when production designer John Barry (who had worked on Superman: The Movie *and parts of* Superman II *between* Star Wars *and* Empire*) collapsed on the set and died as a result of meningitis. Stepping in to replace him was Norman Reynolds, whose previous credits include, as art director,* Star Wars *and* Superman. *Some of the sets, or their elements, offered particular challenges.*

PETER SUSCHITZKY
(director of photography, *The Empire Strikes Back*)

There were some very tricky setups indeed. We had one set with a glass tube in the middle of it, with Luke Skywalker suspended in a kind of liquid [a bacta tank]. For it, I had to devise a method of lighting this tube so that it would be very bright and the rest of the scene would be extremely low-key—the tube would be the main source of light in the set—and I hit upon the idea of suspending a large mirror halfway up the studio above the set and a searchlight down below. The light from the searchlight would bounce off the mirror, which worked marvelously well until the mirror shattered once or twice, I believe, from the heat of the searchlight. There were other sets which presented their own difficulties.

LAWRENCE KASDAN

I visited the set in England, but only briefly. I had done almost all of my work by Christmas of '78. That's when they took off for England. We continued to correspond with drafts through early '79. The changes that happened after that were during shooting—most of them are in the line of dialogue changes, which often happens on the set. I feel those are of varying degrees of success, but every screenwriter is dissatisfied with what happens by the time the words get to the actors' mouths. The only other area of change (during production) was a certain amount of condensation of sections of the movie that were dictated by logistics or mechanical problems.

NORMAN REYNOLDS
(production designer, *The Empire Strikes Back*)

On *Empire*, I didn't actually have a day off, I worked every weekend for a year, because it was such a horrendous picture in terms of volume of work. There were sixty-four sets on *Empire*. I don't know a way of avoiding that. It's like doing a painting: You have to look at it, and if it works for you, it works. If it doesn't, then you have to do something else to it. If you're responsible and you want it to look a certain way, you have to be there and be looking at it. There's no shortcut. You really have to like what you're doing.

RALPH MCQUARRIE
(design consultant and conceptual artist, *The Empire Strikes Back*)

The interiors are very effective. The British carpenters and plaster workers are really good. I'm afraid if I was designing the film, I wouldn't have had the nerve to go as far as Norman did, because he had more of an idea of what these guys could do. While I was working on it, George urged me to just forget about how hard things are to do on film, but make up anything. The stuff I did was used as reference material—it's there for the designer to look at.

PETER SUSCHITZKY

There was another set in which a sword fight was to take place between two of the characters. When I looked at that set, it struck me as being rather like a model for a stage set. In other words, it looked unfinished. It certainly had no walls at all; it was a series of ramps and discs and blackness. I was extremely concerned about that set and I thought about it a lot, about how I was going to make it work and look believable and look dramatic. Then I decided to light the whole thing from underneath, as the floors had been made translucent. In the black areas I had shafts of light penetrating the darkness. Then the whole set was filled with steam, which made it photographically very impressive, but physically very uncomfortable, since it was like working in a Turkish bath. We were quite high up in the stage and we all suffered for quite a number of weeks, but it was one of those sets which made me feel uneasy before I entered into the shooting of it, because it looked so unreal, so unworldly and unlike anything I had ever done before.

I was concerned about it looking dull, in fact, because although there seemed to be plenty of material in the set, it was all either on the floor or on the ceiling. The fact is that unless one goes for extreme angles (and you usually can't do that right through a long sequence), the camera is pointing straight ahead and not up or down. There was nothing for the eye to look at straight ahead except blackness, because all the set elements were on the floor or the ceiling. I was concerned about the scene looking interesting and about the eye having something to look at—but, in the end, I think we succeeded in overcoming those problems—all of us working together.

IRVIN KERSHNER

We sometimes had to begin shooting on one of the big sets even before the construction crews were finished building it. We'd be off shooting in one corner of it, and they'd be hammering away somewhere else. Whenever I could, I would go to the set the night before we were to begin using it. I'd take a camera with me—and have the film quickly developed that night—and I'd make drawings. Our objective though, was not to show how wonderful our sets were; it was to tell a story. I used very low-key lighting. It's a lovely, aesthetically satisfying effect.

PETER SUSCHITZKY

We did have one set which is probably the most awkward set I have worked in for many, many years. There were plenty of difficult sets, but this one was really physically awkward. It was the house belonging to the Wampa creature, played by a Muppet, and as he was quite small, they built the house to suit him and not to suit a human being. Then we had to place Luke Skywalker (a human being) in the set and he could only sit down in it. Even so, he just barely escaped knocking his head against the ceiling. The set had three sides and virtually nowhere to conceal the lights. It had a fire going and that's about all. I found it very difficult and painful to light and I had to crawl on my hands and knees into it, as one would in a mine at the coal face.

One of the things that delighted Kershner was a true highlight of The Empire Strikes Back *and cinema in general: when, during a lightsaber battle between Luke and Darth Vader, Vader tells Luke that he's his father. For audiences, it was a stunning revelation that added depth to the saga's growing mythos.*

IRVIN KERSHNER

I wanted to enhance the characters in *Empire,* because I knew I couldn't depend on the action, since I didn't have a grand climax. It's like the second movement of a symphony, the slow movement. It presents the problem, but doesn't solve it. In *Star Wars,* George came to a grand climax and the third one came to a grand climax, too. I had to have a climax of people and mine came about with two people: the father and son.

ERIC TOWNSEND
(author, *The Making of Star Wars Timeline*)
During filming, that Darth Vader was Luke's father remained a secret, even to most of the crew and actors, throughout most of the production of the film. The famous "I am your father" line was not written in the production scripts. David Prowse filmed the scene by telling Luke that Obi-Wan killed his father. Director Irvin Kershner and Mark Hamill were the only people on set during shooting that knew the actual dialogue of the scene. James Earl Jones was also let in on the secret as he had to record Vader's dialogue.

MARK HAMILL
(actor, "Luke Skywalker")
At the time *Star Wars* was being filmed, I had no idea Darth Vader was my father. I don't think Alec Guinness did, either, because in the scene where I ask him who my father was, he hesitated. I don't know how George made him do that. I didn't hear him saying, "Maybe you don't really want to tell him." I remember very early on asking who my parents were and being told that my father and Obi-Wan met Vader on the edge of a volcano and they had a duel. My father and Darth Vader fell into the crater and my father was instantly killed. Vader crawled out horribly scarred, and at that point, the Emperor landed and Obi-Wan ran into the forest, never to be seen again.

RAY MORTON

This is arguably the greatest, most unexpected, most shocking plot twist in the history of cinema when Darth Vader announces that he is actually Luke's father. It's not certain when and how Lucas came up with this bold and astonishing notion. When asked, he prefers to maintain the fiction that it was part of the story from the very beginning, which it wasn't. In the rough and first drafts of *Star Wars*, Annikin Starkiller's father Kane resembled Vader in that he was half-man/half-machine, but that's as far as the resemblance went—Kane was and remained a good man throughout. In the final drafts and film of *Star Wars*, Anakin Skywalker and Darth Vader are two different people. Vader was not Luke's papa in *Splinter of the Mind's Eye*, nor was he in Leigh Brackett's first draft of *Empire*, in which Luke's father (identified as "Skywalker") appears as a ghost who administers the Jedi oath to Luke. The notion of having Luke's father turn to evil and become Darth Vader, and then to later be turned back to the light by his son, first appears in Lucas's earliest notes for the sequel. However, Lucas did not incorporate the concept into the script until he did his initial rewrite of Leigh Brackett's first draft. It is in Lucas's handwritten second draft that Vader first informs Luke that, "I am your father."

ALAN DEAN FOSTER

(author, *Star Wars* novelization and the sequel, *Splinter of the Mind's Eye*)

I didn't really agree with the idea of Vader being Luke's father, but it worked for a lot of people and you go with it. It just seemed so out of the blue. I saw that and was just as shocked as anybody else, because I had no involvement with the film and didn't know what was coming. And it just struck me as we'd have to find something to really shock the audience and stun the audience and make them want to come back. I think that was the impetus for that rather than something that flowed naturally from the story. And I knew as soon as that happened, as soon as I saw that on-screen, it was like, "Well, we've lost Darth Vader as a great villain, because no matter what else happens, he's Luke's father now and there's always going to be that tinge of his father that has to be redeemed and can't be all bad." It just diminished the character for me.

RAY MORTON

Forty years after the fact, Lucas's decision to spin his core material in such a radical and unexpected direction remains a breathtakingly brilliant and daring one. The concept of a young hero who discovers his allegedly dead father is not only still alive, but has turned evil and become his greatest foe, is positively Shakespearean, and elevates the comic book narrative of the first movie to the level of Greek tragedy. However, as cool and dramatic as Vader's revelation is, it has a negative impact on Luke's personal storyline. When Luke first meets Yoda, the Jedi Master identifies Luke as being impatient and impetuous. Throughout his training, Yoda warns Luke not to give in to this impatience, because doing so will make him vulnerable to being turned to the dark side. Luke initially heeds Yoda's warning, but after he has a vision of Han and Leia being threatened by Vader, he impetuously decides to leave Dagobah before his training is complete to rescue them. Both Yoda and Ben beg Luke to reconsider, but he refuses.

ALAN DEAN FOSTER

I think the entire prequel trilogy is an attempt to justify the ending of *Empire*, and that's a lot of material needed to justify it. It's not that Anakin wasn't an interesting character, and this is a personal thing, I just think Darth Vader works as a really bad guy.

RAY MORTON

The setup in *Empire* strongly suggests that when the unprepared Luke faces off against Vader, it is inevitable that he will be turned to the dark side. This suggestion is borne out in the course of the lightsaber duel between the two as we watch Vader steadily beat and batter Luke before finally cutting off his hand and trapping him far out on the end of the platform in the Cloud City shaft. At this point, the narrative has arrived at the key dramatic question in the story of Luke Skywalker: Will Luke turn to the dark side of the Force? Having posed the question, the film then fails to answer it.

MARK HAMILL

I've told this before, but when we were shooting that climactic scene with Darth Vader in *Empire*, Irvin Kershner, the director, pulled me aside one day. He said, "I'm going to tell you something. Now I know it. George knows it. And when I tell you, you'll know it. And the reason I'm putting it to you this way is that if it leaks, we'll know it was you." I'm thinking, "What is it?," because the original scene was David Prowse doing the dialogue about, "Join me and together we can rule the universe" and "Obi-Wan never told you the full story," or whatever it was. I'm paraphrasing, of course, and I say, "He told me you killed my father," and in the script that was printed for the crew and for David Prowse, who was playing Darth Vader, the climactic twist was, "Obi-Wan killed your father," and I go, "No!"

And when you think of it, it's a pretty good twist as it was, but then

[Kershner] said, "What we're going to do is record that and then we're going to put in the line, 'I am your father.'" I was stunned. I was, "Really? Oh my God, I can't believe it. What a great twist." And I had to keep it a secret for . . . I don't even know how long. Between filming it and it coming out the first time it was screened, Harrison turned to me and said, "You never told me that." I was afraid to tell anybody, because the consequences would have been so extreme. In the time between *Star Wars* and *Empire,* we went from a film that nobody cared about when we were making it to one where there was incredible pressure for information and quietly leaked script pages.

DAVID PROWSE
(on-set actor, "Darth Vader")
I didn't actually know I was Luke Skywalker's father until I saw it in the cinema.

RAY MORTON
Just when we expect to learn whether or not Luke will turn, Vader makes his surprising revelation. When he does, the focus of the drama shifts from Luke to Vader, and the key dramatic question of the narrative now becomes: Is Darth Vader really Luke Skywalker's father? At that point, Luke's story is put on hold. *Empire* sidesteps the issue of whether or not the young Skywalker will turn evil by having Luke essentially run away before it can be dealt with. Physically and spiritually devastated, Luke drops from the platform and falls down into the shaft. He ends up hanging on an antenna on the bottom of the floating city. He is rescued by Leia, Lando, and Chewie, and together the band escape Vader's clutches and make it to safety with the Rebel fleet. The film ends with the question of whether or not Luke will give in to the dark side unresolved and indicating to the audience that we will need to wait until the final film in the trilogy to learn the ultimate answer.

Character-wise, there's no question that The Empire Strikes Back *was in good hands between the script, direction, and performances. But then there was the spectacle element, the unprecedented special effects having to take a quantum leap forward from even the first film.*

RON MAGID
(journalist, visual effects historian)
In the wake of *Star Wars,* audiences quickly became less forgiving. Within just a few years, as a wave of effects movies suddenly changed the industry, ILM was feeling the pressure to top itself; to keep pushing the envelope as effects that had been ahead of their time quickly began looking old-fashioned

to audiences. Dennis Muren, for one, was able to explore the dynamics of motion control with his next project, the *Battlestar Galactica* pilot.

GARY KURTZ

[*Empire*] was about double the budget we had on *Star Wars*. We built a lot of new equipment for *Empire*. It may not sound like it when you spend $22 million on a film like this, but the techniques that we used allowed us to do effects much cheaper than were possible before *Star Wars*. That was one of the apprehensions about *Star Wars*. They thought the special effects couldn't be done for a reasonable amount of money using the old techniques that were utilized in the fifties.

DENNIS MUREN

(visual effects director of photography, *The Empire Strikes Back*)
Empire was a much, much bigger show. I probably spent two months trying to figure out the logistics of the schedule so we knew what background elements we could use twice, to get the show done on time. We reused the backgrounds from the big Snow Walker scene and the asteroid sequence for shots of the background looking out the windows of the speeders or the *Falcon*, which was important, because every shot we used twice saved us a day. So on one hand *Empire* was more to manage, but on the aesthetic side, I think that we attempted to give much more artistry to the shots than we had on *Star Wars*. The shots were better composed, better designed, better-made use of lighting and color and had more dynamic motion to things.

Of course, not making the situation any easier was the fact that Lucas, who kept his base of operations in San Francisco to maintain independence from Hollywood, decided that ILM should move from Van Nuys to Marin County in Northern California. It was part of the reason that John Dykstra was among others who did not make that transition.

JOHN DYKSTRA

(special photographic effects supervisor, *Star Wars*)
Well, first of all, I wasn't invited. It wasn't my choice to not go to ILM. But I wanted to do work here in Los Angeles and had taken on a role on *Battlestar Galactica*. At the time we had finished the work for *Star Wars*, there was a hiatus and those of us who worked on *Star Wars* came together to work in the same facility to do the work for *Battlestar Galactica*. Then George figured out what he wanted to do in San Francisco and started building his facility up there. I didn't want to move to San Francisco, although I wasn't invited. It's

not something I would have chosen to do anyway, because I wanted to work with the people who I had been in partnership with during the production of *Star Wars* and to pursue additional visual effects work in Los Angeles.

RICHARD EDLUND
(special visual effects, *The Empire Strikes Back*)

The most important consideration in setting up Industrial Light & Magic, the facility that produced the special effects for *The Empire Strikes Back*, was finding a staff. We have an organization that is really dependent upon the interaction of departments on a fairly immediate basis and our building is small, as compared to normal studios in the motion picture industry at large. It's somewhat of a disadvantage to have a space that is not quite big enough, but, on the other hand, it is an advantage in that it forces you to compact the departments closely together and to utilize this little nook and that little nook. The positive result is that all of us worked close to each other and passed each other frequently in the course of doing our work, which is very complex in nature. The coffee machine was our most important meeting place, and when we passed each other in the hallway we could say, "What about the density in this scene?" This kind of thing happens in the normal course of getting from one place to another in the building, so we don't have the problem of departmentalization.

If the matte department were a block away from the optical department and the shooting stage were somewhere in the distance, we would lose that contact. If you are a block away, you may as well be miles away, because the work we do is so intricate and detailed and you get so involved in your aspect of it that unless you automatically tend to bump into each other, you don't communicate.

RON MAGID

One difference between *Star Wars* and *Empire* is that Lucas wasn't directing, which allowed him to be around much more when it came to the special effects than he had been the first time around—despite the fact filming was going on in England. Dennis Muren knew that the film's FX Waterloo, so to speak, was going to be the battle on the ice planet Hoth between the Empire's Snow Walkers—or AT-ATs—and the Rebels' Snowspeeders. There were so many shots to do, so very little time to do them in, and there was talk that the Walkers should be automated using motion control, which worried Muren.

DENNIS MUREN

It would've taken forever just to film it. So I introduced stop-motion animation back into the *Star Wars* series with the Walkers. That was something the technical group didn't want to do. But stop-motion was tried-and-true and George thought it was a good idea, because it made everything look more mechanical, and because it helped us get the movie done.

RON MAGID

Which, to no one in particular's fault, still finished late and about $10 million over budget. That being said, Muren in particular was excited by the opportunity to use stop-motion animation again, but in the end, he wasn't the only one. There were some big hurdles. One of the few saving graces for the FX crew on *Star Wars* was that most of the effects were composited against the blackness of space, which hid any dark matte lines around the blue-screened spacecraft. But the pristine white, ice planet Hoth at high noon would give no quarter. Having overcome the new technology folks on the motion-control issue, Muren now had to shoot the Walkers in a miniature snowy landscape, rather than compositing blue-screen Walkers into live-action snow background plates.

DENNIS MUREN

The technological guys wanted to do it all blue screen. I thought the technology we'd developed for *Star Wars* should not be applied to those scenes, because blue screen doesn't work well in daytime. So I managed to wrangle it in the other direction, the idea being that looking through the camera we could see what was wrong with the shot, and once it was shot it was virtually finished.

With the music of Star Wars *being heralded as one of the great crowning achievements of cinema, the need for a strong follow-up was of paramount importance. Once again, Lucas turned to John Williams to compose and conduct the music for* The Empire Strikes Back, *for which he wrote one of his most beloved pieces of music, "The Imperial March," which he continues to play in concert to this day.*

JOE KRAEMER

(composer, *Mission Impossible: Rogue Nation* and *Jack Reacher*)
John Williams returned to score the sequel to the original *Star Wars,* and he brought with him the London Symphony Orchestra and the library of themes he had composed for the first film. He also added new melodies to the lexicon, including the iconic "Imperial March," which also served as a theme for Darth Vader. Equally impressive were the new themes for Yoda, the Jedi Master, and for the tragic romance between Han Solo and Princess Leia. There

was also a quirky theme for the robots C-3PO and R2-D2, a regal melody for Lando Calrissian and Cloud City, and a mysterious motif for low woodwinds that underscored the bounty hunter Boba Fett.

There was a great deal of music composed for this film that ended up being dialed out of the final mix. The spotting of the film had music virtually nonstop for the whole picture, but significant portions of it were dropped, including music for Han Solo walking through the rebel base at the start of the film, Luke training to be a Jedi Knight with Yoda, and the opening scenes of the lightsaber battle between Luke and Darth Vader. Interestingly enough, the music can be heard on the 1997 Special Edition soundtrack, and can be synced to the final film, allowing fans to get a glimpse at what the film might have been with all the music intact!

Themes from the first film that returned for this sequel included Luke's Theme (which was quickly growing to encompass the saga as a whole), Ben Kenobi's Theme (which was expanded to be The Force Theme), and Princess Leia's Theme. The love theme for Han and Leia was a clever development of Princess Leia's Theme, taking the central motif of her melody and taking it in a different, tragic direction.

Yoda's Theme was written in the Lydian mode, an alternate scale that lent a magical sound to the melody. The theme made a cameo appearance two years later in Steven Spielberg's *E.T. the Extra-Terrestrial*, when the title character sees someone in a Yoda costume on Halloween.

John Williams made a new recording of the 20th Century Fox Fanfare for this film, since the one used in *Star Wars* was actually the original one conducted by Alfred Newman decades earlier, and was not of similar fidelity to contemporary recordings.

As The Empire Strikes Back *moved into the postproduction stage, the marketing and merchandising machine was gearing up, though it would seem to have been much easier to sell the sequel than it had the original.*

STEVE SANSWEET
(head of fan relations, Lucasfilm: 2006–2011)

It was just as hard for the licensing arm at Lucasfilm to sell licenses on *Empire* as it was to sell them on *Star Wars*, and that was a pretty difficult sell. Despite the amount of money that they made on the first film, the licensees were dubious because there had never been a sequel made that brought in anywhere near the kind of money the first movie made. So clearly, licensing and merchandising didn't drive *Empire*.

CRAIG MILLER
(director of fan relations, Lucasfilm Ltd.)

Of course in '76 almost no one knew what *Star Wars* was. Comic-Con was much smaller back then. We had Roy Thomas and Howard Chaykin do the presentation. We figured people at Comic-Con would know why they were there. They were big-name comic book people and they were doing the *Star Wars* comic. And we had a few hundred people show up at the panel. Comic-Con was maybe 5,000 people back then. We were not unhappy that we got a few hundred to show up, but that's all. Three years later, in 1979, Comic-Con was 7,500. I went down to do the presentation and we filled the 4,000-seat room. The dealers were telling me that the place was a ghost town. Just everyone had gone to the *Empire Strikes Back* stage. People now knew what it was. It wasn't hard selling *The Empire Strikes Back*. We did a lot of marketing for it. It wasn't like selling something that people weren't already in the market for.

As Lucasfilm's director of fan relations on the first two films, Craig Miller was tasked with coming up with new and innovative ways of reaching out to the fans and flaming their passion for the franchise in its earliest days. One of the innovative ideas he came up with for Empire, *which today would seem simple, was at the time actually a really big deal.*

CRAIG MILLER

Back in the early eighties, "800" numbers were relatively new, as were answering machines. I came up with this idea for *The Empire Strikes Back* where you could call an 800 number from anywhere in the U.S. and get a message from one of the characters telling you what's going to happen in the movie when it opens. I wrote and produced all of those, and we recorded Mark Hamill, Harrison Ford, Carrie Fisher, James Earl Jones, and Tony Daniels doing their messages. Then, at the beginning of January 1980, you could call and get a message from one of them. This was a kind of marketing that no one had ever done before. In the first week, so many people called that it completely shut down the 800 system in the state of Illinois. It just completely overwhelmed the equipment. And we ended up getting so much more publicity for that than if we tried to generate publicity for it.

While the reaction from viewers curious about the first Star Wars *and standing in line for several hours at a time had been surprising, it was nothing compared to the response that* Empire *got.*

CRAIG MILLER

The Empire Strikes Back was going to be opening on Wednesday night, but on Monday morning I was driving into work at Lucasfilm and my route took me past the Egyptian Theatre in Hollywood, and there were four people standing in line at eight thirty in the morning. I was curious, so I stopped and went over and found out they were in line for Wednesday; they wanted to be the first people to see it. And they were not all there together. Two of them were together and two of them were individuals. I thought we could get some good press out of that, so I introduced myself and gave them my card and told them that, if they didn't mind, I was going to let some reporters know and maybe they would be interviewed for why they were there so early. Later I called some reporters. The line grew, the press covered it, and local businesses were coming out and selling these people sandwiches and drinks, so it worked out for everyone. The movie opened at midnight Wednesday, which is actually Tuesday night, I guess, with a 12:01 showing. And there were people there for the 2:30 or 3:00 A.M. show and the 6:00 A.M. show—whatever the times were.

We all went in for the first showing at midnight, stood in the back and it was great. First, it was a great movie, but this audience was super primed for it. And they were cheering and applauding, and they were having a great time and I stayed for the start of the next showing and the audience was still reacting the same way. And the audience had a great time in other shows, too.

The Empire Strikes Back was released on May 21, 1980. Admittedly Lucas, who again was financing the production himself, had mounting concerns (having seen his mentor Coppola nearly bankrupt himself several times with runaway costs on his films) when the film's budget spiraled from $18 million to $33 million. But with a global gross of $548 million, as it turned out, he needn't have worried. To this day, the film is still widely regard by fans and critics as the best film in the entire saga.

BRIAN JAY JONES

When Lucas was preparing *Star Wars*, he takes all of his money from *American Graffiti* and dumps it into this project that nobody understands; that he really has a terrible elevator pitch for. He can't really explain it. Nobody really gets it except for Alan Ladd, who kind of gets it, but he's dumping all of his own money into this and dumping until the money runs out. Marcia is taking jobs editing to pay the bills. But then once *Star Wars* hits and he wants to make the sequel, it's like, "By the way, I've got this Shangri-La of a film company I want to build, too." He takes all of the profits from *Star Wars* and dumps them right down the pipe again, right back into this project. Again, really reckless when you think about it.

But what finally happens is he dumped so much money down that pipe that he's got to go back and get a line of credit for *The Empire Strikes Back*. And that's when Fox was like, "Ha, ha, ha. Okay, we'll get to sign off on that." So it was him again, trying to take control of his own destiny in that way, but he constantly risks everything. That, to me, is really incredible and one of the big surprises of his narrative. He does it probably for the first time as a young man when his father is like, "George, just come run the company," and he's like, "Nope, Dad. I'm going to be a millionaire before I'm thirty and I'm off to film school in Southern California. See you later." A really bold move.

JEANINE BASINGER
(film historian, founder and curator of the Cinema Archives
of Wesleyan University)

The Empire Strikes Back is like a whole new movie. It's a whole new world and it doesn't feel like a sequel. It does give you the things you wanted or liked from the first one, but you're getting in a totally different experience. Remember, *The Godfather II* was a huge success also for the same reasons. Usually, sequels are a less good version of the first one, with the characters and actors a little bit older, everybody a little bit more tired. Your anticipation, when you went to the first one you maybe didn't expect a lot and you got a lot. Now you're going to the sequel and you're expecting everything, and maybe you don't get so much. But the great thing that *The Empire Strikes Back* did give you was a new and different level of story and it took you in a deeper and more character-driven direction. And it didn't count on the technology that had made the first one so wonderful. Not that the first one didn't have other things, but it didn't rely on that. It had to give you something more. It knew that to really keep this going, you would have to involve the audience at a deeper, more character-driven level. I think that's what worked there. That would be my sense of it. But it began to drift after *The Empire Strikes Back*. I liked what would be the completion of the trilogy with *Return of the Jedi*, but, again, I started to drift.

BRIAN JAY JONES
Look at a film like *The Last Jedi* and people shit all over it until the next one came out and suddenly everyone's like, "Oh that middle piece was such a great one; the dark one. It's sad." And remember there were probably not

critics as much as fans, but fans who were just as pissed when *Empire* came out because it ended on a cliffhanger. Well, that's called a story arc, but I remember as a thirteen-year-old walking out of there without any closure. My brain hurt.

RAY MORTON

Lucas decided to end *Empire* on a cliffhanger—on several cliffhangers, actually. The story ends with all of its central narrative threads unresolved and leaves us wondering if Vader is really Luke's father; if Luke will be able to resist temptation, complete his training, and become a Jedi; or if he will turn to the dark side and become an even greater villain than Vader; what will happen to Han; how the romantic triangle between Luke, Leia, and Han will be resolved; who the "another" is; and if the rebels will defeat the Empire or will the Empire vanquish the Alliance?

ALAN DEAN FOSTER

Nobody saw the cliffhanger coming, and for what they wanted it to do, it worked perfectly. It set everybody up who wasn't already set up to come to *Jedi*. It's like, "Wait a minute, I want to see what happens." So it did everything it was supposed to do from the standpoint of getting people to want to see the third part. Whether it works 100 percent as a story, I don't know. But it's not my universe.

RAY MORTON

Leaving the audience hanging like this was a risky move—on the one hand, it was completely in the tradition of the Saturday morning serials that were part of Lucas's original inspiration for *Star Wars*. On the other hand, ending the movie with so many plotlines unresolved and making viewers wait three years for the answers could cause the audience to reject the film. That didn't happen of course, but in the conception stage, it was quite a gamble.

HARRISON FORD
(actor, "Han Solo")

What obligation is there to tie up every question with an equal answer? [*Empire's*] cliffhanger is because the trilogy is really constructed in the classic form of a three-act play. Naturally, there are going to be questions in the second act which have to be resolved in the third. I figure that there was at least $11 worth of entertainment in *Empire*. So, if you paid four bucks and didn't get an ending, you are still $7 ahead of the game.

RAY MORTON

One of *Empire*'s greatest achievements is that it expands and deepens the world of *Star Wars*. The first picture introduced us to a unique new galaxy and this sequel shows us there is much more to that galaxy than we previously realized—more worlds, more races, more cultures, more creatures, more weapons, more intrigue, more dimensions—and invites us to imagine that there is even more to come in the next movie. *Empire* leans more into pure fantasy than its predecessor; the Dagobah scenes especially have a Tolkien-esque feel to them and Luke's trial in the cave is more mystical than anything seen in the parent picture. We are in a land of dreams (and nightmares) in this picture and it is in *The Empire Strikes Back* that George Lucas's ancient space-age fairy tale transcends its Flash Gordon/space opera origins and moves into the realm of myth and magic.

JOHN KENNETH MUIR

(author, *Science Fiction and Fantasy Films of the 1970s*)

This film works so beautifully, in part, because it eschews the pastiche approach of *Star Wars*. It proceeds from the notion not that the film is a combination of old elements reshuffled in a new setting, or pattern. Rather it proceeds from the assumption that the universe is real, and the characters themselves exist not as stand-ins for serial heroes like Flash Gordon, but on their own two feet as real characters. The pastiche approach is gone, and the characters take on new depth and meaning. Solo and Leia find that they have more in common, perhaps, than they would have thought possible, and that these qualities are the basis for a romantic attraction. Luke's journey, he discovers, will not be as easy as he had hoped or believed it would be. In every way, the characters are deeper, and challenged to a greater extent in *The Empire Strikes Back*. Sure, it was tough to destroy the Death Star at the end of *Star Wars*, but in *The Empire Strikes Back*, Luke learns the real battle will be to overcome his own character limitations, biases, and beliefs. The universe in *The Empire Strikes Back* becomes a whole lot more grounded, and real, and less about the "movie-ness" of the enterprise.

RAY MORTON

The characters are more complex in *Empire* than they were in *Star Wars*. Thanks to strong writing and more confident, nuanced performances by the actors, Luke, Leia, and Han transcend their archetypal origins and present as real, three-dimensional people. The supporting characters have also been better fleshed out, Chewbacca especially (his poignant howl as the doors of the rebel base on Hoth close, stranding his friends Han and Luke out in the fatal cold, is one of the most touching [and human] moments in the entire trilogy). Yoda combines humorous eccentricity and dignified wisdom to create a truly memorable character (that this multifaceted persona is portrayed completely convincingly by a puppet makes the accomplishment even more impressive). Darth Vader, an unforgettable but undeniably one-dimensional villain in the original movie, becomes a much more formidable personage in this film—one with a surprising and complicated backstory and a complex Machiavellian ambition hitherto unsuspected.

STEVE SANSWEET

Empire is absolutely my favorite. It was a dark, complex, initially trusting movie that made me think of more than the other two ever did. And it was unexpected, because I had planned on seeing a thrill ride like in the first one. I wasn't expecting to put much thought into it. Suddenly, there was a whole new layer of complexity. The mysticism that Yoda added to *Empire* really made it a more adult picture that stayed with me a lot longer.

RAY MORTON

Many critics and fans describe *Empire* as being a "dark" film, certainly when compared to its predecessor. I've never liked this description—to me, dark implies something that is grim, violent, and depressing. Instead, I see *Empire* as a film that plays for keeps: it's a fantasy, but it takes itself seriously. The stakes in the story are high and consequences are not backed away from. It's a scarier film than *Star Wars,* more subterranean and primal and much more psychologically complex. Many consider *The Empire Strikes Back* to be the best film in the entire series. For the most part, I tend to agree. My only hesitation is that *Star Wars* is the original movie—the prototype—and therefore can stand alone, whereas *Empire* can't exist without *Star Wars.* Therefore, the first movie may have an edge in claiming the title. With that said, *Empire* is certainly my personal favorite of the bunch.

IRVIN KERSHNER

I felt *Empire* was the best film. And that's not meant to be disrespectful to George with *Star Wars,* because that was the first one, which is usually the most difficult. I give him a lot of credit. It's his concept.

If there was a "casualty" in the success of the growing Star Wars *franchise, it would undoubtedly be Alan Ladd, Jr., the executive who believed in George Lucas and, because of it, fought to have it brought into existence in the first place. Yet, with no small sense of irony, it was that relationship with Lucas that ultimately cost him his job at Fox.*

DALE POLLOCK

George couldn't have kept his vow of independence if Alan Ladd had not said yes, or fought his board of directors to protect the project. How did Lucas reward him? "I never want to make another movie for you again." And Alan Ladd tried like crazy when he was at Orion after he left Fox to get Lucas to do something for him, and Lucas wouldn't. And yet it was Laddie who protected his movie from the Fox board of directors, who would've shut the film down. Obviously, loyalty to people in the business was not very important to him. And without Laddie there would not have been a *Star Wars,* or at least not the *Star Wars* we came to see. Might've been a very diminished, not very good film given that he wouldn't have been able to realize his entire vision. Alan Ladd went on to his career as a producer; he didn't need Lucas, but I believe he was deeply hurt when he wanted to have Lucas come and help make a film for his company and help put it on the map, but he wouldn't. After the book [*Skywalking*] came out I heard from many of the people I interviewed, and Laddie in particular said, "I'm so glad you showed the way that he really just dumped all of us."

BRIAN JAY JONES

Lucas had other problems as well. You have to remember that *Empire* was all of Lucas's money. He's the one paying every crew member on that set and for every minute that they run overtime. You read that little paperback on the making of *Empire* . . . The movie's not even done yet, and Lucas is already grumbling about how much time this thing is taking. So I think he knew that Kersh was the right director, but at the same time he's kind of like, "What are you doing, man? Stop being an artist and just finish the goddamn film!" I think he was pleased with the way it came out, so there were no complaints on that front. But he was really angry as far as I can tell that the thing just kept going. What's funny is that unlike other directors there isn't a studio breathing down his neck; Fox will take it whenever they can get it. The timeline at that point is Lucas's timeline, but, again, it's his money.

In between The Empire Strikes Back *and the ultimately-titled* Return of the Jedi *(after some dalliance with the name* Revenge of the Jedi, *which was dropped when someone realized that the Jedi don't seek revenge), the Star Wars universe had begun an expansion in a new medium. NPR (National Public*

Radio) debuted a thirteen-part radio dramatization of the first film (broadcast between March 9 and June 8, 1981), with Mark Hamill and Anthony Daniels vocally reprising their respective roles of Luke Skywalker and C-3PO. They were joined by Ann Sachs as Princess Leia, Perry King as Han Solo, Bernard Behrens as Obi-Wan Kenobi, Brock Peters as Darth Vader, and Keene Curtis as Grand Moff Tarkin. The Empire dramatization, which was broadcast between February 14 and April 25, 1983, added Billy Dee Williams voicing Lando Calrissian and John Lithgow as Yoda. Return of the Jedi, produced by Blackstone Audio, made its debut on November 5, 1996, after a thirteen-year delay due to NPR abandoning the radio drama format due to budget cuts, and saw cast changes in the form of Joshua Fardon as Luke and Arye Gross as Lando, with the additions of Edward Asner as Jabba the Hutt, Paul Hecht as the Emperor, Ed Begley, Jr., as Boba Fett, and David Birney as Anakin Skywalker.

The radio dramas got their start when Lucas "sold" the rights to his Star Wars films to National Public Radio station KUSC-FM, which was connected with his alma mater, the University of Southern California, for the exorbitant fee of . . . one dollar. With rights to the scripts, the trilogy's myriad of sound effects, and John Williams's score, NPR in turn went after science fiction author Brian Daley, whose credits include a trilogy of novels focused on Han Solo, as well as other radio dramas, to take on the adaptation. But rather than doing a straight adaptation, Daley expanded the original story, adding new elements and reinserting old ones—expanding Star Wars to a six-hour radio drama, and The Empire Strikes Back into a four-hour drama (minus three to four minutes per episode for credits). Years later Return of the Jedi was also produced, no longer under the aegis of the not-for-profit NPR, and as a result Mark Hamill, who had been so great in the first two radio adaptations, bowed out.

KYLE NEWMAN
(director, Fanboys)

The Brian Daley radio dramas were something massive for me, because there were these gaps in the movie, but you could listen to these things and they filled them in. They're well performed, and what they do is they showed you extra little corners of the galaxy, ancillary parts of the story, little expanded bits—like, the scene ended in the movie, but, "What? I can hear more about this about how Princess Leia got the plans to the Death Star?" and there's all these back stories, and Luke's friends? I'm like, "What's going on?" I just thought that was incredible. That's what made you realize Star Wars was more than a series of movies. It was a story. It was a legacy. We even did a radio drama at *Star Wars* Celebration. I wrote an original Han Solo thing, a throwback. That was, to me, so magical, hearing it and realizing that your mind just filled in all the gaps. Once you had those key Ben Burtt sounds and—anything that could bring me closer to *Star Wars*, I just gobbled up.

PETER HOLMSTROM
(cohost, *The Rebel & The Rogue* podcast)

The radio shows are a fascinating look into what could have been with *Star Wars*. The Jabba deleted scene, the Biggs/Luke backstory, even hearing Mara Jade appear in the *Return of the Jedi* adaptation due to it being produced after the Thrawn trilogy was done—these were real treats for fans. I love radio dramas, and it's a shame they didn't stay popular in America like they did in Europe. NPR took a chance on this old medium with their adaptations—as well as a few other radio dramas at the time—in the hope of boosting NPR's ratings, so they could receive more funding, but they didn't boost the ratings like NPR hoped they would, so they abandoned the concept before *Return of the Jedi* was produced.

BRIAN DALEY
(writer, *Star Wars* radio dramas)

It was like exploring different corners of a room you already knew well and finding different things. I had a copy of the script and some pictures from the film. At first, I had three meetings with Lucasfilm per script, but that eventually became three scripts per one meeting. They really trusted me with the material.

ANTHONY DANIELS
(actor, "C-3PO," *Star Wars* radio dramas)

Brian really expanded the films. It sometimes seemed that we cut out portions of Brian's scripts to make the movies, rather than the radio scripts being adapted from the movies. When I do advertising or other projects with C-3PO's voice, I often have to stop and say, "Threepio wouldn't say that line of dialogue," but never with Brian's work. He knew Threepio at least as well as I do.

MARK HAMILL

The *Star Wars* radio show appealed to me, because it wasn't money-oriented. I feel bad that all kids can't afford to buy a glow-in-the-dark Yoda or whatever. This was one way to pay back the fans, since it was free over radio. The radio shows are great because you can take them into your mind. For visual effects, you need a budget of millions of dollars. There is no budget on imagination. And you don't have funny matte lines in your imagination.

BRIAN DALEY

The first time around it reminded me about the joke with the two boxers. The ref says, "I don't want to see any gouging, biting, or kicking." And one fighter sighs, "There go all my best punches." When you're writing a novel, you have all sorts of time for expository prose. With this medium, it's the dialogue, music, and sound effects that really make it.

Overall, Daley was given an immense degree of freedom, though there were certain things that he wrote that came under scrutiny and ultimately were excised.

BRIAN DALEY

The only scene I remember getting cut occurred at the end. In the next-to-last episode, Han is about to leave the rebel base. I must have been watching *Mutiny on the Bounty* at some point that day, because I had Han with his shirt off, and Leia sees that his back is terribly scarred. I imagined that he'd been hit by a laser cat-o'-nine-tails or something. That part seemed a little graphic and was left out.

I also included in my script the scene in *Star Wars* with Jabba and Han in the docking bay on Mos Eisley that was cut from the film. When I learned that they had other plans for Jabba, we changed the character's name to Heater and kept the scene. Some lines got cut that I just put in more for my own amusement than anything else. Narrative lines like when Luke goes in to see Aunt Beru, and she's cooking away with her billion-gigawatt, DNA-replicating saucepot. There were also some mistakes that got in, particularly with Leia's father, who I named Prester, as a tribute to Prester John. His name I found out later is Bail Organa.

As he was writing the scripts, Daley came to an important realization about the impact of Star Wars *in the annals of the genre.*

BRIAN DALEY

I've had other novels out, but then I look at *Star Trek* novels appearing on the *New York Times* bestseller lists and I realize that a vast amount of the public is really keyed into science fiction only through the images they see on TV and in the movies. There are some hard feelings from science fiction writers who don't realize how marginalized science fiction was before *Star Wars*. After *Star Wars*, the whole world wanted science fiction and fantasy. For myself, getting involved with the *Star Wars* trilogy was one of the best experiences in my life. It was better than drugs, and damn near as good as sex. You cannot buy those kinds of experiences.

8

CELEBRATE THE LOVE:
RETURN OF THE JEDI

"I'll never turn to the dark side. You've failed, Your Highness. I am a Jedi, like my father before me."

The success of *The Empire Strikes Back* immediately led to the third installment of the *Star Wars* saga being put into development. *Empire*, of course, was conceived with the idea of a follow-up in mind, but when it came to *Jedi*, virtually every decision was based on the fact that the film had a release date of May 25, 1983, that couldn't be missed. The necessity was to work backward from the release date. As a result, every choice from hiring a director to writing the final draft of the script revolved around the date the film needed to land in theaters in the summer of 1983.

JONATHAN RINZLER
(author, *The Making of Return of the Jedi*)

It was really interesting reading the early outlines, pages of notes and then the script [for *Return of the Jedi*]. There are things I really like about that rough draft that George Lucas wrote, that was before Larry Kasdan was involved. In some ways, it's better than the final film. There's a much more exciting battle. Princess Leia is a much more active character, pretty much all of act 1 is devoted to Princess Leia. She's alone on the Ewok planet and spearheading this Rebel incursion. They need to grab control of two guns—one of the big guns was going to knock out communications to the Death Star, and the other big gun was going to do something to the city planet that was below. There was this whole city planet—Coruscant was in the first draft, it doesn't make it to the final draft at all—but the Emperor was in some sort of lava lair below the city planet. It's not called Coruscant, it's called Had Abbadon.

When Leia's on the forest moon through act 1, there's another alien species called the Yuzzum, who are tall with spindly legs. And the Ewoks are short, so it would've been this great contrast, Leia having to deal with both of them. She's the one who spearheads getting the Ewoks on the side of the Rebels. She's the one on the rocket bikes, what became the speeder bikes; Luke isn't involved, it's just her. It would've been really cool.

Leia wasn't involved [with rescuing Han from Jabba]; she stays on the Ewok planet through the whole movie. Luke begins outside on Tatooine and is plotting with the droids on how to rescue Han—but in the early version, Han has already been unfrozen. We don't see him frozen on-screen. They had unfrozen him, and now they were going to kill him, so there was more of a time-lock too. So they have to go rescue him. There's more banter between Luke and Han Solo, which is kind of lost in the final film.

And in a way you can kind of see how Leia gets almost shoehorned into the final version—because they never actually say anything to her in the final film. She's a prisoner, half-naked and chained to this giant slug. When they actually shot that scene, "cut," and Carrie Fisher said, "Hi guys!," you realize there must've been some dialogue missing, 'cause there's no recognition on their parts at all that, hey there's this person you know real well. Because it kind of got shoehorned in from this other part of the story, they didn't quite visualize what was happening. And on set, Richard Marquand I guess didn't have enough latitude, or didn't really care, whatever.

I think the rough draft was George's "blue skies" version. He did the same thing with the rough draft of *Star Wars*. He didn't do that for *Empire*, but he did it for *Star Wars* and *Jedi*. I think if he had all the money in the world, this is what he'd do. I don't think he ever intended the rough draft of *Jedi* to be filmed. It's very interesting to see how it changed in different ways.

RAY MORTON
(senior editor, *Script* magazine)

The writing of *Return of the Jedi* was a somewhat protracted process. Lucas generated notes and a preliminary outline prior to the start of preproduction, but it took a long time for him to pen even a rough draft. Preproduction and creature, set, and prop design were begun off of Lucas's initial outline and proceeded parallel to the writing of the rough draft, with the design work sometimes influencing story development. Some action sequences were originated in storyboards and then written into the script, rather than vice versa as is the usual procedure.

STEPHEN SCARLATA
(cohost, *Best Movies Never Made* podcast)

There's also this cool concept in the rough draft where when Luke defeats Vader, Vader falls into the lava, and it's almost this flashback for him to the

Obi-Wan fight, but here Luke saves him from the lava. Something about that I really dug.

JONATHAN RINZLER

The whole battle [between Luke, Vader, and the Emperor] takes place in this lava lair underneath the city. It's very interesting, it's almost a four-way battle, where Vader is much more at odds with the Emperor. That's another reason why I really like the rough draft, because—at the end of the *Empire Strikes Back*, Darth Vader is ruling the universe, the Emperor is an afterthought. "Join me—we're going to bring down the Emperor." The rough draft is much more like that. The Emperor and Darth Vader are at each other's throats. They're plotting against each other. Whereas when the finished film starts, something has happened off-screen, and Darth Vader is this domesticated Sith. In the rough draft, Vader is trying to convert Luke still, so in the final battle, it's a battle of wits, to a certain extent, between Vader, Luke, and the Emperor. Finally, the Emperor realizes Vader isn't going to kill Luke, and Luke isn't going to kill the Emperor. The Emperor starts unleashing his lightning, and Obi-Wan and Yoda show up, and act as shields for Luke to the lightning. First Obi-Wan shows up, and the Emperor is like, "Eh, I can deal with you, you're kind of a light-weight." Then Yoda shows up, and the Emperor is like, "Holy shit!"

An approach that could be expensive, historically speaking, it proved to be an intelligent approach to write through the preproduction process, allowing early material to guide physical creation.

DALE POLLOCK
(author, *Skywalking: The Life and Films of George Lucas*)

If the success of *Star Wars* gave Lucas "fuck you" money, *Empire* just reinforced his feeling that he was doing the right thing by being outside of Hollywood and doing things himself.

HOWARD KAZANJIAN
(producer, *Return of the Jedi*)

Some people thought I was crazy to set dates for the different phases before we had a script, but that was the only feasible way to approach a production of this magnitude. As things progressed, naturally there were some changes that had to be made, but the original calendar remained accurate to within a day or two throughout production and postproduction. If you don't follow a calendar, you're not following the budget. If you're a week late starting the mix, it means you have a week more of offices and cutting equipment or whatever. The budget was $32.5 million because of the special effects work done at ILM. It would have cost fifty million if anyone else had tried to make it. You have to think in terms of money all the time. Should we build this set or should we use miniatures or a matte painting? If we just move the vehicles over this way a little bit more, we don't need that big a set and we can paint that in.

You know, it might cost $20,000 at ILM to composite a blue-screen shot with a matte painting, but it's going to cost you $28,000 to build a set, money to strike it, and more money to fill it with a bunch of extras. And maybe you're taking space on the stage that you could use for something else. At one point we were going to move the Millennium Falcon from the big *Star Wars* stage to another location for a scene, but then I told George it was going to cost $40,000 to move it and he said, "Let ILM paint it in." So it became a blue-screen shot and I don't think anyone realizes it's a painting when they see it in the movie. So that was a way we saved money and that was George's idea. At the same time, you have to know when to forget about the budget and spend more money on the set or for an actor or on the shooting schedule or on a hundred different areas where you might spend more money. Then you have to look at it and say, "Now where can I save money? If I give an extra $15,000 to a particular actor that wasn't budgeted, is it possible to save by having twelve less extras in a particular scene?," or whatever.

JONATHAN RINZLER

One thing you have to remember with *Return of the Jedi* is, George Lucas was really disappointed with *Star Wars*. He was not happy with the way *Star Wars* turned out. It was very disappointing in two very important ways for him: he didn't get the cantina scene that he wanted, and he didn't get the attack on the Death Star that he wanted. So in doing *Return of the Jedi*, at a certain point, he thought, "Now I've got the money, now I've got the control, I'm going to redo those scenes." So Jabba's palace is kind of a redo of the cantina scene, with as many aliens and creatures as he wants, and the Death Star attack—it is pretty cool. ILM did a fantastic job. They took what was kind of a B film and made it into an A film with those visual effects. At the time it was just mind-blowing. The Millennium Falcon flies into the Death Star, you've got 150 TIE Fighters coming at you, it was just unbelievable. It really was much, much more of the attack on the original Death Star. As great as that is, *Return of the Jedi* is much more visually striking.

STEPHEN SCARLATA

The amount of spacecraft during that battle, it was amazing. I saw it at the right age—and it was just mind-blowing how much was coming at me in that theater.

JONATHAN RINZLER

With the first [cantina sequence] Stuart Freeborn got sick, they moved it up in the schedule, they only had seven or eight aliens ready when they shot it at Elstree, and then they did pickups and they didn't have enough money. Fortunately, Rick Baker came to the rescue with dozens of masks and such, but it was really kind of a hodge-podge thrown together, and mixed together in the editing room, but I think it was immensely frustrating for George.

DALE POLLOCK

Another lesson Lucas learned from *Empire* is that when it came time to pick a director—because he certainly wasn't interested in directing—he didn't want as independent a director as Kershner, so he hires a lower-rank director with Richard Marquand. He made, I believe, one good movie before he did *Jedi.*

HOWARD KAZANJIAN

We were looking for a director that was rather young, that was flexible, that had not established himself as a great independent filmmaker, that would follow the tradition of *Star Wars,* that would let George be as closely attached as he likes to be on these projects. We wanted someone who believed in *Star Wars,* who really believed that Wookiees and Darth Vader exist and who was a fast-thinking director capable of making a decision and moving on if something wasn't working.

Richard Marquand was born in Cardiff, Wales, on September 22, 1937, to Rachel and Hilary Marquand. His father, Hilary, was a Labour Party member of Parliament, and his older brother, David, would also later become an MP to the Labour Party. Richard Marquand was educated at Emanuel School, London, the University of Aix in Aix-en-Provence, France, and King's College, Cambridge. During National Service he studied Mandarin and was posted to Hong Kong, where he also read the news on the English-language Hong Kong Television. By the late 1960s, Marquand had begun directing documentary films for the BBC, such as 1972's Search for the Nile. *Later, Marquand would utilize those lessons from documentary filmmaking in the 1979 TV movie* Birth of the Beatles *about the early days of the Fab Four. His first dramatic fictional feature was the Donald Sutherland thriller* Eye of the Needle, *which earned him enough acclaim to attract the attention of George Lucas, as Lucas was looking for a director for his second* Star Wars *sequel.*

RICHARD MARQUAND
(director, *Return of the Jedi*)

When I went to see *Star Wars,* I was completely bowled over by the experience, by the mythological storyline as well as the incredible creations in the story and the way it was technically made. I had never seen anything like it as an emotional human being or as a moviemaker. I felt an enormous surge of pleasure when I discovered there was going to be another one; it was as though a group of long-lost members of my family had phoned to say they were stopping by the house. I believe in the Force and I believe in Luke Skywalker. I absolutely take the myth seriously. I believe in the same way as I believe in the story of Arthur and the Round Table or in the stories of Robin Hood. You don't approach this type of movie, or indeed any movie, with cynicism, because if you do, you're dead. You can see it on the screen: you can smell the cynical director. And if you can tell it in any movie, then you can certainly tell it in *Star Wars,* which is a movie about innocence. I'm constantly being told by friends that I'm an innocent. I take people at face value and then it turns out they're crooks. It happens to me all the time, but I just think that's the only way you can get through life, actually, by being starry-eyed. I wear rose-colored spectacles.

And I don't think it would have been possible for me to do what I did on *Jedi* for two and a half years of my life so intensely without being a total fan. Now when I say "total fan," I don't say I'm the type of person represented by other total fans. I don't put myself in that category. I couldn't indulge to that extent. I like the films and stories as they exist on the screen. I don't need to take it further than that.

BRIAN JAY JONES
(author, *George Lucas: A Life*)

You read the quotes from Richard Marquand and he's a fanboy. It's like if J.J. Abrams came to me and he's like, "Do you want to direct the movie?" I'd be like, "Yes, please." Like, I'd do whatever they asked and that's why I could kind of sense from Richard Marquand that he was just so excited to be there that he was going to do whatever Lucas wanted.

RICHARD MARQUAND

I fit the bill in that it seemed like they were looking for a younger man who has a great deal of experience, can work hard and fast, make up his mind and stick to it, and run a crew very quickly. I knew then what George was searching for was not the old-school movie director who would wait for the weather to get the shot he wanted. He wanted someone who could improvise, think on his feet. And he was in London doing the music for *Raiders of the Lost Ark* at the time and it was a very convenient moment for him to come see what was then a rough cut of my *Eye of the Needle*. His people called my cutting room and asked if I would screen it for him. I said, "By all means." At that stage, you don't particularly want to show your movie because it's still in a very embryonic stage, but I thought he was a moviemaker who I admire, so let's show it to him. And I was proud of *Eye of the Needle*. I felt I had achieved for the most part what I wanted to achieve.

GEORGE LUCAS

One of the most important things is to create an emotion in the audience. The movie can be funny, sad, or scary, but there has to be an emotion. It has to make you feel good or laugh or jump out of your seat.

BRIAN JAY JONES

Return of the Jedi was also when Gary Kurtz was like, "I'm done. We did the Death Star once. I'm not doing that again."

GARY KURTZ
(producer, *The Empire Strikes Back*)

I'm not making a sequel unless the script is good, and I approached it from the premise that it's got to be as good or even better than the original.

BRIAN JAY JONES

Lucas had told Kershner, "You make the movie and I'll leave you alone," and then of course he didn't. I think he intended to do the same thing with Richard Marquand, but he liked the fact that this guy came from TV, because the lesson he had learned from Kershner is everything was taking too long and he was burning up his money. Coming from TV, Marquand was used to keeping it snappy and quick, but, more than anything, he would actually listen to Lucas. I don't think Marquand was a bad decision, but he's definitely a very different kind of director.

RICHARD MARQUAND

When we met, I felt extremely comfortable. It was one filmmaker talking to another filmmaker. It was very good. We talked about our films and how we dealt with certain problems. It was not in any sense an interview or the kind of thing that happened in Hollywood where you must put on a tremendous performance to impress somebody. Then came a series of different meetings during which I supplied Howard Kazanjian with films of mine and also began to be aware of the other names on the list. There were many names. And the number slowly whittled down until it was just me and an American director. At that point, I realized that I must get this job, because I really cared about it.

I told George that, if I was going to direct this adequately, I would need loyalty and support in the areas that were new to me. In a way, being the director of a film of this size is rather like being the president of the Ford Motor Company. You don't necessarily have to know how to weld a car door, but you must make damn sure the guy who is doing it for you is someone you know, that you know his skills and that he'll do a good job. If you are the director, you are really the man who says what goes. There are always stories in the movie industry about directors getting pushed around by producers, but all those producers are people who really don't understand how movies get made. You can only really have one person doing that job. The good thing about George Lucas is he knows that fact. All you can do is tell the story your way. The best way that you can.

DALE POLLOCK

Being on set, you could see that he was so subservient to Lucas that it wasn't really a Richard Marquand film, but it was a sort of George Lucas film through another director and that's when I think Lucas decided, "I'm going to do the prequels by myself." He's also the same guy who told me he hated the process of being on set twelve hours a day and having to communicate with everybody. He would actually say, "People keep coming up to me and asking questions." So I think he just had to really swallow hard and say, "You know what? I'm not using other directors. I'm going to do the prequels myself."

RICHARD MARQUAND

I must say, I like the way George made *Star Wars,* the way he set it up and did it was extremely clever. He made it seem to have a very simple surface, but, in fact, it had a very dense, complex background to it. I preferred that surface naïveté to the much more sophisticated way Kershner told his story. His style very much suited the rather more dark, metallic second section of the saga. I think this third segment has a different kind of glow and flavor to it. But I tried to make it simple, because the textures in *Jedi* are so very complex.

There's a world of new people and some of them are incredibly difficult to appreciate at first meeting.

IRVIN KERSHNER
(director, *The Empire Strikes Back*)

Let me tell you: after seeing the third one, I was kind of sorry I didn't do it. It didn't hold together. It flew off in all directions and I felt the continuity was disruptive. It would move in one direction and then it would skip in time as if they had cut sections out. I don't know what really happened, because I never even read the script, but it didn't seem to follow a logical dramatic progression. There were jumps, cuts, jumps, cuts. They got out of situations in kind of miraculous ways, which I didn't like.

RICHARD MARQUAND

I like the way George made the three movies that he actually directed. He's a very deceptively simple stylist. His movies have a look of ease about them, and I now can say with truth it's very difficult to be that simple. It's surprisingly complex, but looks easy. That's part of what makes *Star Wars* so available to children, and I wanted to go back to that sort of presentation in *Jedi* rather than the highly sophisticated, sexy way in which Kershner made *Empire*, which I enjoyed—I thought it looked like an incredible, glossy, glorious sort of machine—but I prefer the other way.

GEORGE LUCAS

The truth of it is, that the third one is much more like the first one than the second one is. It's just the nature of the story, the way it is laid out.

RICHARD MARQUAND

Having George Lucas as executive producer is like directing *King Lear* with Shakespeare in the next room. Kershner told his story. His style very much suited this rather more dark, metallic second section of the saga. The actual *Star Wars* saga from chapters one through nine is a total symphony, if you like, though it's actually just a movie. I wasn't making a sequel, I was doing the third movement of a piece of music. I also don't see it as a science fiction film. Many people get completely carried away by the superficial, the science fiction aspect of the movie. That's like being completely enthralled with the frame around a Picasso. Science fiction is not really what it's about. It happens to be set in that world, because that's where the saga works best. I don't want to get pompous here, but *Jedi* does set up some echoes in your mind and in your heart. It deals with life and death of man, which is very important stuff.

To capture that sentiment, Marquand made the decision to often keep the camera stationary rather than moving it around, even with technology paving the way for Steadicam and Laumas Crane shots in the early eighties. He preferred to film the movie in a much more static fashion.

RICHARD MARQUAND

You can cover a multitude of sins by doing some wonderful crane shot that turns into a tracking shot, but it's like the tendency to say that the music will sort out a problem. I'd rather solve the problem in the stage of interpretation of the scene itself. It's really exciting when you can get it right in a medium shot without doing anything with the camera. I like it when the camera doesn't move. I try to keep it as simple as possible. I believe I was chosen to direct *Jedi* because I do have a cinematic eye. I don't shoot what I call movies for the blind. Also helping was my background in documentaries—by documentary films, I mean films about real people, where you follow them around with a handheld camera and really get inside their lives. I don't mean reportage or newsreel stuff. You see how people behave, you watch them when you're not filming them and you become very aware of what reality really is—the rough stuff of life, not the well-honed performances.

While these elements were being brought together, Lucas began the "rough stuff" of screenwriting. Between February 20 and June 12, 1981, he turned out three rough drafts of the movie. Doing so, he knew there were several things he had to achieve, most notably completing Luke's journey from farm boy to Jedi Knight. He also had to resolve the conflict between the Rebels and the Empire, and he had to tie up loose ends left hanging in Empire, including answering the question as to whether or not Darth Vader was really Luke's father.

RAY MORTON

To accomplish all this, Lucas wrote the initial outlines and a rough draft of the screenplay, then brought Lawrence Kasdan in to pen another draft. Lucas did a cut-and-paste revision of Kasdan's draft, after which Kasdan did a polish. Lucas did the final revisions himself. For me and many others, the result was a significant disappointment. The main reason I found the screenplay for what was originally called *Revenge of the Jedi*, but was ultimately renamed

Return of the Jedi, disappointing was the way it dealt with the material that should have been its main storyline.

As developed over the course of Star Wars *and* The Empire Strikes Back, *the primary narrative of the trilogy was about Luke Skywalker and his adventures on the path to becoming a Jedi.* Empire *brought that narrative to a crisis point and left Luke seemingly on the verge of turning to the dark side of the Force. At the conclusion of* Episode V, *audiences were left with the expectation that the third film would pick up Luke's story at that crisis point and then tell the rest of his tale. Extrapolating logically from the narrative elements established in the previous two films, the expectation was that Luke would indeed turn to the dark side and then fight his way back to the light in time to defeat Vader and the Emperor (this is certainly what Mark Hamill assumed would and wanted to happen). The final draft of the screenplay for* Return of the Jedi *did indeed include this material, but rather than make it the film's primary narrative, it instead compressed it all into a relatively brief segment in the movie's third act.*

MARK HAMILL
(actor, "Luke Skywalker")

I don't think this chapter confounded and confused people. It's the logical resolution to what had gone before. It's very traditional storytelling. It's not meant to have an O. Henry type of twist. The trilogy is structured as a fairy tale set to a classical three-act play. *Star Wars* was act 1. It introduced the characters. *The Empire Strikes Back* was act 2. It developed the characters and gave them problems, with tragic overtones. *Jedi* is act 3. It's the big finish, and everything is brought to an end.

The storyline is set up with two scenes at the end of act 1, where Luke learns Vader is in fact his father, and the only way for the rebellion and "goodness" to win this conflict, according to Obi-Wan and Yoda, is for Luke to kill his father and the Emperor. Later, the third act begins when Vader brings Luke before the Emperor, who sets Luke on the path to the dark side by encouraging Luke to attack him. At this point Vader intervenes to save the Emperor and he and Luke begin another lightsaber duel. During this fight, Luke tries to convince Vader to turn away from the dark side, and in response, the Sith Lord pushes Luke to turn to the dark side by threatening Leia. Enraged, Luke finally gives in to his hate and uses his aggression to beat Vader back, knocking him to the ground, and then hacks off his mechanical hand. Luke is on the verge of actually killing Vader when he realizes what he's become. At this point, Luke makes a conscious decision to rebuff the dark side, a decision which nearly costs him his life. It is only when Luke is near death at the hands of the Emperor that Vader himself turns away from the dark side, and kills the Emperor to save his son.

RAY MORTON

While we are pleased to see Luke's story concluded so definitively, it is disappointing that it has been disposed of so quickly. What should have been an entire feature film's worth of drama is crammed into just a few minutes of screen time. They are a very good few minutes—the best, most dramatic, and most satisfying in all of *Jedi*—but the sequence still feels abrupt and truncated and leaves us wishing much more had been done with this very fertile material and that Luke had been allowed to complete his arc in a much more extended and developed fashion. The other major story component *Jedi* needed to address was the truth about Darth Vader: was he indeed Luke's father and, if so, what Luke would do about it—would he kill Vader, join him, or find a way to redeem him? The screenplay for *Jedi* did incorporate this material, but once again compressed most of it into a short segment in the third act.

At the top of *Jedi*'s second act, Yoda confirms that Vader is Luke's father. Following two brief scenes also in act 2—one with the Emperor and the other with Luke—that suggest Vader has become ambivalent about his commitment to the dark side, the Sith Lord's actual return to the light is set in motion when the Emperor—furious at Luke for refusing to kill Vader—attempts to slay Luke by shooting him with lightning. At this point Vader decides he loves his son too much to let him die and so kills the Emperor by tossing him into the Death Star II's reactor, which causes the evil ruler to explode. The blowback from the explosion mortally wounds Vader. The now-dying former Sith Lord asks Luke to remove his helmet, revealing the scarred old man beneath the monster. Thanking his son for believing in his inherent goodness, the once and future Anakin Skywalker dies.

This exciting and effective sequence is another of Jedi's dramatic highlights. The reason Lucas chose to compress these two important narrative elements and consign them to Jedi's third act was to make room for an idea repurposed from his first draft screenplay for Star Wars.

RAY MORTON

In [the] early script [for the original *Star Wars*], the Rebels land on a planet populated by primitive Wookiees and eventually enlist the furry giants to help them in their fight against the Empire. Because Chewbacca had been developed to be an advanced, sophisticated creature, Lucas needed to come up with a new race of primitives [for *Return of the Jedi*]. Since Wookiees were giants, Lucas decided to shrink them down, turn their name on its side, and change the jungle planet to a forest moon and thus were born the Ewoks. The Wookiees help the Rebels by training to be space fighter pilots and then taking part in the climactic aerial raid on the Death Star. Lucas decided to retain the final attack on the Death Star, even though he had already used it in *Star Wars*. However—perhaps because the idea of training primitive creatures to fly spaceships may have seemed too outlandish—he decided to have a separate squadron of Rebels attack the giant battle station. The Ewoks would assist the rebels in a ground assault, using their primitive traps and weapons to defeat Imperial forces stationed on their sylvan home.

In the final Jedi *screenplay, Han, Luke, Leia, Chewie, and the droids land on the forest moon of Endor on a mission to disable a generator that projects a protective force field around a still-under-construction Death Star II, but the Emperor is well aware of their plans and intends to capture Luke. What the Emperor doesn't foresee is the aid of the furry Ewoks in helping the Rebels defeat the garrison of stormtroopers on the forest moon, allowing the Rebels to destroy the shield generator and attack the now vulnerable Death Star.*

RAY MORTON

The seed of this sequence grew out of the research Lucas had done on the Vietnam War for *Apocalypse Now* (Lucas was the original director of that film before Francis Ford Coppola directed it himself many years later). Impressed by the way the Viet Cong—equipped with relatively simple and even primitive weapons—had defeated the far-better-equipped army of the United States through sheer tenacity and commitment, Lucas incorporated the notion of a primitive society vanquishing the technologically superior Empire using the same spirit and dedication into his space opera. However, as the narrative for the original film developed, Lucas replaced the primitive culture with a spiritual one—in the final script and movie the overwhelming technology of the Empire was defeated by the mystical power of the Force rather than the power of primitive tenacity. However, Lucas was still enamored by the notion of a stone-age culture using rocks and sticks to defeat a technological giant and so decided to resurrect it for *Jedi*.

The problem was that the idea didn't fit into the trilogy's overall narrative as it had been developed through the first two movies. When Lucas wrote his first draft of *Star Wars*, he was crafting a single, stand-alone movie that could well have been focused on a "primitives versus technology" theme. Eight years later, however, the narrative of the trilogy had evolved into a tale about fathers and sons, the potential for both good and evil contained within each of us, and the power of destiny. A "sticks versus lasers" storyline was both thematically and plot-wise irrelevant to the trilogy's overarching narrative, and there was no way to incorporate it into that narrative without shoving the tale's primary elements to the side, which is what Lucas essentially did. Unfortunately, he didn't find a way to make the Ewok material pertinent to the main storyline. Although the Endor sequence is well structured and contains a number of entertaining elements (the speeder bike chase, the Ewoks worshipping C-3PO, the climactic battle, etc.), the only element in the entire segment relevant to the trilogy's main plotline is the destruction of the shield generator. The rest of the material is essentially just filler and so during all the scenes featuring the Ewoks the movie tends to feel as if it's just spinning its wheels.

After the hiring of Richard Marquand, Lawrence Kasdan—who, following the scripting of Empire, *had written* Raiders of the Lost Ark—*was brought back as screenwriter. At that point, he, Lucas, Kazanjian, and Marquand met in San Francisco to talk about and further develop the story over the course of a couple of weeks.*

HOWARD KAZANJIAN
For five days George, Larry Kasdan, and myself sat in story conference meetings where George laid out the plot. Larry asked most of the questions. We all made suggestions. There were several drafts delivered both by Larry and George and by George and I, and one time Marcia Lucas discussed what worked and what did not. I will tell you now that Darth Vader never was to appear at the end in ghost appearance with Yoda and Ben. Two days before we shot that scene I suggested that Vader be there as well. George didn't answer, but just looked at me. The next day George told me to prepare to shoot Vader with Yoda and Ben. Later that day I had second thoughts about what I had suggested. After all, two good guys were standing next to a very bad guy. But in the end, there was redemption on Vader's part, and forgiveness on Luke's. It worked, and I am still very pleased with my suggestion.

JONATHAN RINZLER
There was this big story conference—but it's basically George saying, "I can't do this big city planet, it's going to be really expensive." They only had the one soundstage at ILM, and the city planet was going to take up the whole soundstage for the whole shoot, which was going to be problematic. It was just logistically impossible. Lawrence Kasdan was actually arguing to keep it, and George was saying, "Even if we keep it, how can we explain that we can just destroy this whole planet? The Rebels can't destroy a planet." And Kasdan

was saying, "Well, you don't have to destroy a whole planet. You could just have a power station on the city planet, and have the Rebels pinpoint that, and all the power goes out, and the Rebels won." But George nixed it. Somewhere in the story conference, they decide to put the Emperor on the Death Star, and that's the thing that changes everything.

ERIC TOWNSEND
(author, *The Making of Star Wars Timeline*)

Kasdan was pushing for major characters to be killed, including, at one point, Luke Skywalker himself. The team also wrestled with the issue of Ben Kenobi's declaration in the first film that Darth Vader had killed father Skywalker and how to explain the films' new revelations.

RICHARD MARQUAND

I recall two items that I feel are indicative of the kind of input I was able to have at that point. First of all, I felt very strongly that the opening shot of the film should be modeled after the openings of the first two films, starting in outer space and revealing something that has to do with the Empire so that it would begin on a dark note of threat. Plus, I wanted to include Yoda. The story originally began after Luke had completed his training with Yoda and Yoda was no longer in the movie. I thought the audience would feel cheated if there was no scene with Yoda, because the importance of Luke's return to Yoda to complete his training was set up so strongly in *The Empire Strikes Back*.

As Kasdan began rewriting the script—and would do a number of drafts in a relatively brief time period—Marquand flew to England to oversee the design of the film's sets. The need for flexibility became obvious in a scene involving the set for Darth Vader's bridge on the Star Destroyer.

RICHARD MARQUAND

I thought going in that I could manage with a very, very reduced set because I wanted as much as possible to keep a tight control on the budget. I thought I could manage with a small section of that set; but as the day grew nearer and nearer to shoot the sequence, I began to realize more and more that actually, we'd have to build some more and paint some more. Ironically, Norman Reynolds, the production designer, had already thought to himself, "I don't think he's going to get away with this." When it came down to my actually saying to Howard and Norman, "Look, I think we're going to have to have a little bit more," Norman said, "Oh, I've got some extra pieces. I had them made anyway. We'll paint them overnight and you can shoot tomorrow."

I would say my experience in television taught me a lot about preplanning. If you work on tape with four cameras, you have a shooting script with every single angle mapped out. You've rehearsed for three weeks with actors on a set with a little viewfinder against your eye so that you've actually got it all completely knocked out. You can't do that in movies, but I don't think it does any harm to make up your mind ahead of time, particularly if you're able to change if you have to. I mean, you've got a situation there where you really are creating something. You are actually saying, I think this should look like this and I think that should happen. If you're any good, that's how it's going to look and it can look terrific, because you've got a whole army of people all working toward that goal. Suppose you want an archway with a huge door and light that comes pouring in the moment the door opens. If you can say that three months ahead of the shoot, you're going to get it. You ain't gonna get it if you decide this afternoon that you'd like that tomorrow morning at eight thirty, because it's just not going to be there. So what do you do then? You postpone everything or you put up with something that somebody else thought up. I'm astounded by the stories I hear of directors who actually walk on the set in the morning and work out roughly what they're going to shoot and start shooting in the middle of the afternoon. I'm just amazed, I'm not bragging; I just don't have the guts to pick up a fat fee without being prepared.

The shooting schedule of Jedi *lasted a total of eighteen weeks, six less than they had on* Empire. *Seventy-eight days were spent at Elstree, which was followed by a one-week break and then two weeks on location in Yuma, Arizona; two weeks in Crescent City, California; and a week and a half of blue-screen work at ILM in San Rafael. Additionally, a second unit was utilized to work behind the main unit, capturing pickup shots, and, finally, there was a day of photography in Death Valley.*

HOWARD KAZANJIAN

We wanted to start photography in January of 1982 so we could maximize the time available for postproduction and special effects work, even though we were rushing into production before everyone was fully prepared.

RICHARD MARQUAND

I chose to start with one of the toughest sequences. I've always liked to plunge immediately into a very tough week's shooting, because I've discovered that if you slide in the way a lot of directors like to do, you set up a very slow pace for the crew. If you've got an easy day's shooting on the first day, then it's hard to pull up the speed. And the bigger the crew, the harder it gets. So I was very anxious to find some really tough things to do first, which surprised everybody. They thought I was crazy, but since we were starting in January and the weather did not permit shooting in Crescent City and the set was not completed in Yuma, we went straight into an enormous shoot on what is probably one of the more complex and demanding sequences in the movie. I could see halfway through the week that either the crew and I would be destroyed or we would get through the week on schedule and feel so terrific that we'd be in good shape for the rest of the production. A professional crew is like a racehorse. You can't take it easy coming out of the gate, because you'll get brushed aside and that'll be the end of it.

As the director, you're the focus of everybody's attention. It's important that they feel that you know where the scene is going. The moment it's over and you're happy and you say "Print," if the very next thing you say is, "Now we're over here on the 35 and I want to be on a low angle," if you immediately know where the next scene is going, everybody can feel this horse racing under him and they know it's carrying them to the finish line. It's a nice feeling, but it can easily be broken by an actor having a temperament or by a first assistant who thinks that everything should be done through a bullhorn. We need to concentrate, but I like the set to be infused with a sense of humor and fun. I don't mean outrageous fun and swinging from the chandeliers, but fun where you can crack a joke or talk about a given character in endearing but amusing terms—rather than feeling that you're in a temple of art. Because you're not in a temple of art. This is show business. You're hoodwinking an audience. You've got this cheap three-ply door which is supposed to look like a monstrous golden metal thing and you're using gauzes and smoke and God knows what to make them think that they're in some magical fairy-tale place. It's all hoodwinking the audience, so I think you can enjoy the fact that you're doing that and I think you can take pride in it if you're doing it well. I think it's good to have a sense of humor about it.

To some, the screenplay for Return of the Jedi *"hoodwinked" the audience in certain ways as well, particularly in terms of elements of narrative irrelevancy. This was obvious in the way it was decided that the film should open.*

RAY MORTON

In *Jedi*'s early planning stages, Harrison Ford agreed to play a major role in the film after all. Therefore, Lucas opted to begin the screenplay with an elaborate sequence in which Luke, Leia, Lando, Chewie, and the droids rescue Han from the clutches of Jabba the Hutt, the galactic gangster on whose behalf Boba Fett pursued and captured Han in *Empire*. This was a perfectly fine and necessary idea, but as executed, the segment is very awkwardly constructed.

The notion of all of the main characters assembling to rescue Han is terrific, but rather than have the group travel to Jabba's palace on Tatooine en masse and get on with it, the script instead has the principals arrive at Jabba's one at a time: Lando infiltrates Jabba's lair in disguise before the movie starts; the droids arrive next, followed by Chewie and Leia; Leia then defrosts Han from the carbonite; and then—twenty-two minutes into the movie—Luke finally arrives. With this one-by-one approach, it takes what feels like forever to get the gang assembled and we grow restless waiting for them to do so.

By the time the old friends are all together, we are more than ready for the rescue to finally begin. Unfortunately, we have to wait even longer while Luke takes time out to battle Jabba's pet monster, the Rancor. While this is an exciting bit on its own, in the context of the overall sequence, it just delays the heart of the scene—the rescue—even further. Finally, thirty-two minutes into the movie, the rescue finally begins as the gang battles Jabba's forces over the deadly Sarlacc pit. Although it's not completely clear what Luke's rescue scheme is (was his plan really to get captured and sentenced to walk the plank over a giant yonic symbol?!), it is at this point that the movie finally comes alive with an exciting sequence full of fights, stunts, and explosions, climaxing with the gang's exhilarating escape and Jabba and his minions going down in flames. It would have been a terrific way to kick off the movie had it actually kicked off the movie.

There are some great bits in this first act: Jabba is a terrific character both in concept and in execution, the Rancor is scary, nobody minds Carrie in her slave-girl costume, and, as just mentioned, the Sarlacc battle is just thrilling. However, this entire section of the script and the film has the same basic problem as the Endor sequence does: it contains only one element that is relevant to the trilogy's overall narrative—the defrosting of Han Solo and his return to the fold. As on Endor, everything else is filler, which is why—as exciting as the act eventually becomes—in aggregate it's pretty boring. As a result of all of these decisions, the screenplay as finally assembled begins with a long, awkwardly structured sequence that is fundamentally irrelevant to the plot, which is then followed by another long, better-structured segment that is also irrelevant to the plot. The material that is relevant to the plot doesn't come into play until the third act and then is given extremely short shrift. This poor construction is the main reason why the script for *Jedi* is such a disappointment, especially in light of how well structured the scripts for the first two movies in the trilogy are.

Once again the main cast was back including Mark Hamill, Carrie Fisher, and, of course, Harrison Ford, albeit begrudgingly. Also back was Billy Dee Williams as Lando and Frank Oz performing Yoda.

RICHARD MARQUAND

Carrie Fisher gives a tremendous performance in this film, and I, as an actor's director, really pride myself on being able to help actors over what are problematic areas. I actually feel that she and I together brought out depths in Princess Leia's character hitherto unseen. She became very well founded metaphorically and physically as a character in this movie. At last, you got to see what a good actress she is. In the past, by necessity, there often wasn't very much room for depth of character. She really has some emotionally deep scenes which she handles wonderfully well.

I call myself an actor's director, because many directors direct cameras. I think the actors felt very lost and almost neglected on *Empire*. The special effects sort of rode through that movie in terms of the actors being left alone. I was lucky in this film. The major actors who carried the story and dialogue were by now very experienced at this nightmarish way of working. They were used to it and knew how to deal with it. I tend to shoot rehearsals. The reason I do that is because it makes the crew suddenly realize we are actually shooting film. There's a different quality to the way people act when they know film is going through the gate than if it's just a rehearsal and we're moving the camera around. Very often you find that the first take has a quality to it; it's a sort of angst, that the adrenaline is really pumping and often you get some wonderful stuff. It's money well invested to get as much on the negative as you can in one day.

KENNY BAKER
(actor, "R2-D2")

George knew exactly what he wanted. He told me where to look, what to do. Richard Marquand hardly ever used me, he said he was going to, but he didn't. George said to him that when I was in R2, R2 came to life. Still, Richard never used me a lot. Irvin Kershner was good; he was easy to work with.

BILLY DEE WILLIAMS
(actor, "Lando Calrissian")

When we shot *Return of the Jedi* I remember doing the scene where Harrison was saving me from the Sarlacc pit. He was so wrapped up in his acting that he didn't realize right away that I was actually hurt. A squib went off in my foot and we had to cut the scene. Harrison was so into his part. We of course did get the scene done.

One of the surprise returnees in terms of cast was Alec Guinness as Luke's mentor, Obi-Wan Kenobi, though it was once again in the form of a Force ghost.

RAY MORTON

Jedi presents the formerly wise, dignified, and immensely capable Obi-Wan Kenobi as a screw-up and a liar who not only doesn't apologize to Luke for not telling him the truth about his father, but also offers a lame justification for why it's okay that he did. Alec Guinness didn't like playing ghosts and had originally agreed to reprise Ben after Lucas promised to return Kenobi to life and have him play a substantial role in the narrative. Early drafts had Obi-Wan reemerging and aiding Luke during the boy's climactic fight with the Emperor and Vader. However, as script development proceeded, Ben's part was whittled down more and more until all that was left was one scene in which he delivered a bunch of exposition and showed himself to be a failure. Churlish comments that appeared in Guinness's posthumously published diaries revealed he was not at all happy about how things turned out.

Although the Emperor had previously been a character in The Empire Strikes Back *(Clive Revill had provided his voice with mask-wearing actress Marjorie Eaton physically playing him along with a superimposed pair of monkey eyes), in* Return of the Jedi *he was played by Ian McDiarmid. The thirty-seven-year-old, Scottish-born McDiarmid could hardly have imagined the small role of an aged, hooded, pure personification of evil, Emperor Palpatine, would end up becoming his crowning achievement in cinema and one of Star Wars' most iconic characters—or that he would return decades later in the culmination of the Skywalker Saga, 2019's* Rise of Skywalker, *reprising his role as Emperor Palpatine. McDiarmid's early life found him as a great theater aficionado at local theaters in the east coast of Scotland. McDiarmid's early work as an actor began in British theater. He starred in several Shakespeare plays, including* Hamlet *in 1972,* The Tempest *in 1974,* Much Ado About Nothing *in 1976,* Trevor Nunn's 1976 Macbeth *(and in the television version in 1978), and* The Merchant of Venice. *But the role that won the attention of George Lucas was a small one as a sacrificial priest in the 1981 fantasy film (for which Lucas's company, ILM, did the special effects sequences)* Dragonslayer.

IAN MCDIARMID
(actor, "Emperor Sheev Palpatine")

One day, I got a phone call. Someone said they were looking for an actor to play the Emperor of the Universe. That's how I ended up in *Star Wars*. They thought of me because the film's casting director had seen me as Howard Hughes in *Seduced*, a play by Sam Shepard. In it, I played an older part under a lot of makeup. At that time, they were looking for somebody who was a bit younger to play older, because the special effects and makeup were rather strenuous. In fact, someone who looked exactly like the Emperor of the Universe walked into the office after I did. He was the right age and everything, although I'm not sure if he had the yellow eyes, or indeed, teeth. It looked for a while as if he would play the part, but in the end, it was decided that he was too frail, so I got it.

Once I was cast, I only received my section of the film, which is unusual. Normally, you get a full script, but it was George's intention that no one should know what happened. For example, he very much wanted to protect Vader's story. If those secrets had gotten out, the surprise would have faded.

The makeup required for the character was explained to him in detail, beginning with a look at images of the Emperor as he appeared in Empire. *On top of that, he was shown drawings as well, and assured by Lucas that he would be able to "keep" his mouth and possibly his nose.*

IAN MCDIARMID

They're fairly distinguishing features, which quite pleased me. He also said my eyes would be mine, but they would change the color. All these things helped me suggest a person other than someone who just ran things. They gave the character an added dimension, which is what I was really looking for in playing the part. They added things, like echo and reverb and on top of that, of course, it's in multitrack stereo. But they didn't do anything with its natural timbre. It was I who dropped my voice down to what comes out on-screen. I spent a great deal of time working on that. Because I knew it would have to be done again in the dubbing, I practiced. I also listened to Clive Revill's voice from the previous movie. While I was allowed my own interpretation, if I had chosen a pitch different from his, people would have felt cheated and thought that something was wrong. They might have required an explanation, like did the Emperor have a throat operation? So, I had to get the rough area of his voice. I listened to a tape of Clive, got my voice in the same vicinity, and added my own stuff.

What was most interesting was to try and get hold of the satanic side in a broad, simple way that is the easiest way to get hold of it. I thought, "My task is to go one step beyond Vader, and see how black and uncompromising I can be." The script was there, of course; a very tight, very good script by Larry Kasdan and George. You wouldn't have wanted to change the script. And the film's scheduling was so precise that there wasn't too much leeway. But within that, I had complete freedom to create the character. I found the voice, which was keeping of my own, and this slightly humorous interpretation, that I was encouraged to go to now and again.

The first scene we shot was the hangar, where I come down a ramp to meet Vader. That's one of the biggest studios in Europe, and I hadn't been in it before. A friend of mine, Michael Pennington, who plays one of Vader's lieutenants, was there. I walked into this room, in makeup for the first time, my eyes slightly hurting, and trying very hard to adjust to what was happening. I saw what looked like three thousand people—I don't know how many there were, but they weren't painted on!—and I said to Michael, who was standing next to Vader, "You didn't tell me. I thought it was going to be a quiet party just for the three of us!" But it was an extraordinary first day on a movie. Doing it was a fantasy for me. As a kid, I had always wanted to play villains, they're always the most interesting characters. But I never imagined I would play one of the greatest villains of all time.

McDiarmid leaned on producer George Lucas for a better grasp of the character, which helped him craft the role, but never really put too much thought into it. In a way, he wasn't much more than Snow White's Evil Witch with his robe, chilling laugh, and crooked teeth.

IAN MCDIARMID

I didn't come up with much of a backstory, as I recall. I remember joking with George about Palpatine. Richard Marquand directed *Jedi,* but George was around a lot. And he actually directed the sequence in which Darth Vader threw the Emperor down the hole. I got a chance to spend some time with George then, and I said, "I know how this guy started out. He had a very trying English public school education." George laughed very loudly. He thought it was a good joke. Of course, it has nothing to do with Palpatine's history. In fact, that was probably the nearest I came to speculating about how Palpatine turned into this terrible creature. So, I had no idea. I just played him as the oldest, most evil figure in the galaxy.

In some ways, it was very easy to do that, because all the apparatus was right there for me. In *Jedi,* we had this throne room and that great swiveling chair. There was a large expanse of studio. And I had those wonderful robes. It all made me imagine Richard Nixon in the Oval Office. Also, I had tunnel vision because of the contact lenses. Tunnel vision is probably a good thing to have if you're playing an Emperor. So, I could only see straight ahead. As a result, people had to help me around a lot. I used that, as an actor, to play the old man's frailty in the physical sense. We knew that he was frail, but he still had a laser-like mind.

Production of Jedi *was plagued by a number of problems, best described by* American Cinematographer *magazine: "There were problems with the operation of the creatures as well as the robots. There were complications and delays caused by the fact that a set for the Ewok village was twenty feet above the stage floor. There were problems with the special effects device designed to enable Boba Fett to shoot a rope from his arm to ensnare Luke. There were even problems with the perforations in 100,000 feet of raw stock which did not meet ILM's specifications for special effects photography."*

These problems were nonetheless manageable. Special effects devices for Boba Fett were replaced with simple monofilament and a camera running in reverse. Rather than rely on a French plan, raw stock was obtained by an American manufacturer, and delays involving the Ewok village and Jabba's followers were obtained through additional second unit work and adjustments in scheduling. Despite everything, things wrapped on schedule, with the production's focus switching to special effects and the nine hundred shots required by ILM.

Visual effects of Return of the Jedi *were shown off in several scenes in particular, among them Luke's battle with Jabba's Rancor beast, the high-speed chase on speeder bikes involving our heroes and stormtroopers on the moon of Endor, the Empire's AT-STs on Endor, and the Rebel Alliance's assault on the Death Star II.*

RICHARD EDLUND
(visual effects, *Return of the Jedi*)

This show was more of a refinement of the things we've been doing than a great deal of new invention. *Star Wars* was the initial invention period where we put the whole system together in basic terms, utilizing new electronics, making motion control available to a large production where a lot of elements and a lot of material can be shot in a reliable way, day after day, to produce the complex battles and other effects. In *Empire*, it was phase two of equipment development and refining of techniques so that the shots outshone those in *Star Wars* to a large extent, because everyone had had more time to learn how to play the instrument, so to speak. The cameras and printers were built so that we could get great quality on the screen and achieve parity with the original photography, so that when we cut to an effects shot you don't suddenly see something that's grainy and makes you wonder what's going to happen now—a problem with effects over the decades. The idea of using the larger format and being able to reduce and composite without generation loss so that we don't have a drop in quality when we go to an optical was the basic reason for building the printer. The techniques of stop-motion also achieved a good state here. There's really some great stuff in *Empire*, but the stop-motion in this picture has gone beyond that because now we had *Dragonslayer* under our collective belt, and it was some of the best that's been done.

Time really determined how we operated. Almost all of the elements you saw in *Jedi* are take-ones, because we had less time than we would like to have had. We were just finishing three big pictures: Dennis Muren had *E.T.*, Ken Ralston had *Star Trek II*, and I was still shooting *Poltergeist*. The pictures backed up on one another and nobody had time for much of a breather between pictures. Though we were short on time, we were long on experience and we have an excellent group of camera people who know what they're doing. When we'd see a shot in the dailies, we'd just make sure it didn't have any scratches or digs or technical problems that meant it couldn't be used, because we knew it had to be used to get the show done.

RON MAGID
(journalist, visual effects historian)

Edlund believes that achieving conviction had a lot to do with the proper editing of effects. In *Star Wars* the visual photographic effects don't exceed fourteen moments, and *Empire* only went up about six minutes from there.

RICHARD EDLUND

George has a way of putting them in at the right points so that the impression is that they're always there. They're not; they're in the right places for just the right amount of time, because he has a gift for knowing how long to leave a shot on the screen before you start seeing the seams. Any visual effect, if left on the screen for a long period of time, will give itself away. What we go after is an impression, and often that impression can be achieved in less than a second. *Jedi* has at least a hundred more effects shots than *Empire*.

During production, one of the challenges facing the film was actually keeping plot points under wraps, not easy when it came to certain actors—most notably David Prowse, returning in the Darth Vader costume, who had a well-documented penchant for giving in to the lure of publicity.

RICHARD MARQUAND

The actors who needed to know, knew well in advance of shooting what was going to happen. They had their scripts. Any actors who we felt were security risks were given other [fake] scripts. There was one particular actor who gave an interview to the English press about the movie's plot, which extremely upset us. But we knew that actor was a security risk and had actually not given him the correct lines of dialogue. He fell completely into the trap. And there he was, having lunch with the English press one day. The next morning, the paper came out, having printed all this totally misleading information.

Howard Kazanjian called the actor into his office for a talk, explaining that there were certain secrets which must be kept in order for the story to remain "fresh." We were very disappointed he did it. He was very apologetic and said that he was a very weak man. When the press phoned him, he found it very hard to turn them down.

ANTHONY DANIELS
(actor, "C-3PO")

I dozed off and woke up hearing Carrie say, "He's my brother." I thought I'd better keep still, because they would kill me. Although you get the script, there are always pages that they don't want anyone to see because then there would be certain problems with the actors or people in the cast telling things to the press. This is stupid and something no professional should do. So, they worked on a "need-to-know" basis. I didn't need to know that information. Generally, I had an idea of what was going on, but I didn't think about it. I was kind of amused they were brother and sister, just as in years to come after that when George told me I was made by their father.

ERIC TOWNSEND

Filming began on *Return of the Jedi* on January 11, 1982, on nine stages at Elstree Studios in London. In order to throw fans and media off the track, the project was given the working title of *Blue Harvest: Horror Beyond Imagination* during production. The first scene shot was a later deleted sandstorm segment. As soon as Marquand yelled "action," the problems with the malfunctioning R2-D2 started all over again. After three days, the scene was completed. What's funny is that when actor Dermot Crowley arrived on set to play the role of General Crix Madine, the crew handed him a fake beard. Kenner had already begun production on action figures based on his character and the toy had a beard. So, Crowley had to wear a beard to match the toy.

DALE POLLOCK

Return of the Jedi feels almost like a merchandise-driven film. I mean, they had high hopes for the *Ewoks* TV series and they were really going to market the hell out of the Ewoks, because they figured it would bring along the younger *Star Wars* fans. It gives them a character they could relate to, because it looked like a teddy bear. On top of that, the film felt like the weakest film of the trilogy. It begins to feel repetitive, which is why I think Lucas jumped backward in time to do the prequels. He didn't want to face where he had to go with the current trilogy. It was easier for him to go back.

WARWICK DAVIS
(actor, "Wicket," *Return of the Jedi*)

The Ewoks, if you look in the designs and how they were developed, were initially very strange, very primitive looking. Eventually, they ended up being very cuddly and very cute. I think that was a very deliberate decision by George to do that, because it really helped bring children into the movie. The adults and the fans already had something to look at.

BRIAN JAY JONES

Toys are definitely on his mind with *Return of the Jedi*. I mean, Harrison Ford has that great moment where he's telling Lucas that he needs to let Han die, and Lucas says, "There's no money in Dead Han toys." I don't want to call it the lowest common denominator, and I'm speculating a little bit here, but I think he remembers where he really made his money on the first *Star Wars* was merchandising. Merchandising is what built Skywalker Ranch. Merchandising is what built Lucasfilm. I said at one point in the book, that the entire empire is built on three-and-three-quarter-inch action figures. So I think at that point he's hyperaware of it to the detriment of the story. With the Ewoks, it's conscious effort to cater to the toy industry, which is why there's more ships coming out at that time and things like that. Another great story is the guy from Kenner talking about things that are toyetic and talking to Lucas about ideas. And then going to talk with Steven Spielberg about *Close Encounters* and Spielberg is showing them all the things that they're doing in *Close Encounters* and the guy goes, "This isn't really toyetic. It's no *Star Wars*."

I remember there was a great cartoon in *MAD* magazine that said, "E.T. in the theater was cute. E.T. all over your home was not." It's like Spielberg didn't quite have the knack for merchandising that Lucas did. Lucas, like Jim Henson, was incredibly protective and hands-on, almost to a fault, on merchandise. They wanted to see everything, to sign off on it, approve it and make sure they weren't putting out junk. Lucas sort of maintained that through the original *Star Wars*, whereas Spielberg, I'm guessing, was more lenient, so bad decisions were made on things. Lucas never really did that. Lucas at one point said one of the reasons he merchandised is because he wanted the R2-D2 cookie jar. Lucas likes toys, he's aware of the power of merchandising.

MARK HAMILL

I'm convinced that if George had signed for a three-picture deal, he might have saved the Death Star for the third picture. But he wasn't sure he was going to be able to do all three, so he sort of blew it all out on the first one. How in the world were we going to top that? It's not so much a matter of copying it in *Return of the Jedi*, it's finding new ways to thrill people.

RICHARD MARQUAND

I think *Return of the Jedi* is an extremely unusual film. I don't think there had ever been a movie quite like that one before. It's big in scope, big in dimension, big in the extraordinary multiplicity of the characters. It's just amazing; a huge, huge movie that's like *Star Wars* and *The Empire Strikes Back* rolled into one. It's not a cartoon serial. For me, it's more akin to an agnostic religious experience.

RAY MORTON

The script for *Return of the Jedi* disappoints on a number of fronts. For starters, it does a poor job of tying up *Empire*'s loose ends. In *Episode V*, much emphasis is put on the need for Luke to complete his Jedi training and on the fact that—because he has not completed his training—Luke is not yet a Jedi. However, when Luke first appears in the third film, he looks and acts like a full-fledged Jedi (e.g., using the Jedi mind trick on Bib Fortuna) and even identifies himself to Jabba as being one. This suggests he has completed his training. However, after Han is rescued, Luke returns to Dagobah to complete his training, which suggests he has not completed his training. But then Yoda—the one who was constantly telling Luke he needed to complete his training—tells him that he doesn't need any more training after all. But then a few minutes later, Yoda scolds Luke for not completing his training. It's all very confusing and it's never clear exactly where on the road to becoming a Jedi Luke actually is.

IAN MCDIARMID

I've heard that fans consider *Return of the Jedi* to be the weakest of the three movies. At the time I was working, however, I couldn't have told you that. I filmed my scenes in three weeks in total secrecy, as everyone else did. I knew that Palpatine was a very powerful person and I obviously knew a little bit of what was ultimately going to happen between Vader and Luke. But I didn't know all of it. I didn't know, for example, the tremendous revelation at the film's end. I didn't know that Sebastian Shaw would be in the film as the dying Darth Vader until I saw him at the studio while I was getting my makeup on. I knew Sebastian for years. We had worked together at the Royal Shakespeare Company and so on. He was a delightful man. I said, "Sebastian, what are you doing here?" And he said, "I don't know, dear boy. I think it's something to do with science fiction." I thought that was a very good line and

I considered using it myself when people asked me the plot of *The Phantom Menace*. Sebastian was in a state of blissful ignorance. Most of us knew at least a little bit about what we were doing.

MARK HAMILL

During *Star Wars*, I was in a white floppy rag doll outfit. Then for *The Empire Strikes Back*, I wore a militaristic-looking khaki-colored costume. In *Jedi*, I wear the black uniform of a trained Jedi. But the question is: What kind of Jedi? Is he a wizard, a religious figure, or just a glutton for punishment?

RAY MORTON

Much of this confusion is due to the fact that in Lucas's early outlines and script drafts, Luke had returned to Dagobah and completed his training in between *Empire* and *Jedi*, so when he entered at the top of *Episode VI* he already was fully trained. At this point, he was then told that the only thing left for him to do to become a Jedi was to kill Vader, although why this is necessary is never made clear (do all Jedi have to kill a Sith in order to be let into the club? Seems like a pretty dark entry bar). In the final draft, Luke has not completed his training but apparently Lucas did not want to drop all the cool stuff (and it is pretty cool) where Luke acts like a Jedi, so I guess we're just supposed to assume that eager student Luke is just showing off with some of the tricks he learned before he quit his training. But then why does he still identify himself as a Jedi? Like I said, it's confusing.

Audiences, he notes, were forced to wait three long years to find out if Darth Vader was, in fact, Luke's father. As a result, the expectation was that the truth would be revealed in some big, dramatic fashion.

RAY MORTON

But instead, Yoda confirms that Vader is Luke's dad with a brief, almost off-hand "Yeah, he's your dad" statement. There's no buildup, no big dramatic re-veal. It feels as if the writers couldn't wait to get the whole matter over with as quickly as possible so that they could move on to the Ewoks. Then there's also the fact that the identity of "another" is revealed in the same let's-get-this-over-with-as-quickly-as-possible manner. Yoda mentions there's another Skywalker, Luke asks Ben who it is, Ben tells him it's his sister. That's it. The revelation that the sister is actually Leia is presented even more lamely. There's no investigation, no dramatic discovery. Instead, Luke simply "senses" it, which is the worst kind of fantasy-writing cheat. As I mentioned previously, Luke's sister was never meant to be Leia—as originally conceived, the sister was supposed to be an entirely different character who Luke would meet and train in some future episode. It was only in the writing of the final drafts of *Jedi* that Lucas decided the sister would be Leia. One presumes he did this to provide a neat wrap-up to the Luke/Leia/Han love triangle (an earlier idea was to give Luke a girlfriend, who would presumably cause him to lose interest in Leia) and also to provide some sort of resolution to the "another" concept, which—after receiving such a big buildup in *Empire*—ultimately didn't come into play in *Jedi*.

I've never liked the idea of Luke and Leia being siblings. First of all, it's lazy. Lucas introduced the idea of another Skywalker, a concept with tremendous dramatic import and potential, in *Empire*, but obviously didn't have a clear idea of what he was going to do with it. Since he ultimately decided to do nothing with it, one wishes he had just dropped the notion entirely, because to just fob the whole idea off onto an existing character feels like he just wasn't trying very hard. Also, as many jokesters have pointed out, making Luke and Leia siblings retroactively adds an incestuous undertone to their flirtations in the first two movies. And that's really creepy. It was then, it still is now, and the whole idea casts an uncomfortable pall over some key scenes in the earlier films. I didn't like it when I first saw the movie and to this day I still wish Lucas hadn't done it.

The script in many instances fails to properly service the regular characters, none of whom are written with the same sort of depth and complexity as they were in Empire; *in fact, many of those characterizations are inconsistent with how they had been previously presented.*

RAY MORTON

Luke is the protagonist of *Star Wars* and *The Empire Strikes Back*. His role in *Jedi* is more inconsistent. He makes an impressive entrance into the film with a confident display of his newfound Jedi powers and is the driving force through the remainder of the rescue sequence. In the second act, however, Luke becomes just a passive recipient of exposition in the Dagobah scene and then a tag-along in the Endor section of the film. He returns to the lead position in the throne room sequence, but as soon as he rejects the dark side, Luke stops being the protagonist once and for all. He is reduced to a passive supporting character in the redemption segment, in which Vader is the protagonist. Luke is often described as saving Vader in the end of Jedi, but he does not—Vader saves himself. Luke is simply the catalyst that prompts Vader's turnaround and then later serves as a sounding board when Vader/Anakin confirms that he has reformed. While it's good that *Jedi* allows Luke to complete his arc, even if only in truncated fashion, it's a shame he wasn't allowed to drive the action of film consistently from beginning to end, as a strong protagonist always should.

PETER HOLMSTROM
(cohost, *The Rebel & the Rogue* podcast)

The thing you have to remember is, *Star Wars* was always meant to be Vietnam in space. George Lucas has said so many times. You see his first draft for *Star Wars*, it's there—and I think part of the reason he says "I only got 30–40 percent of what I wanted" from *Star Wars* is that. It became a story of good versus evil, which isn't what he wanted. He finally sets up the conflict in *Empire,* and you see the theme first emphasized in *Return of the Jedi.*

Luke's arc in that film is one of the great arcs in cinema history. It's beautiful. He starts as a hero—literally a swashbuckling hero, saving the day; but then the crux comes during the scene at Dagobah, where both his previous mentors tell him he must do the thing he was told never to do. "A Jedi only uses the Force for defense, never for attack." Yoda's own words from *Empire.* But here, Yoda and Obi-Wan tell him no—tell him the only way to be a Jedi is to murder his father and the Emperor by any means necessary. In other words, saying, "To do good, you must do something evil."

Luke struggles with this through the whole movie—knows it's wrong, even if everyone around him says it's right. Then, in one of the most brilliant moments in film history—a moment mirrored in cinema greats like *Citizen Kane, The Searchers, Batman v. Superman, Schindler's List*—Luke gives in to anger, defeats Vader, and has him at his mercy, moments away from slashing through him. And *then* Luke stares down at his gloved hand, then to a shot of Vader's robot stump of a hand Luke just cut off—and in that moment, Luke has a pure reflection of what he has just become. It's a moment where a mirror is shoved right up in the character's face, and they are forced to see that they've become the monster they have so longed to destroy. It's beautiful. Luke throws his lightsaber away and embraces a path that neither the Emperor nor Yoda set out for him—and that's what makes him the best of us all.

ALAN DEAN FOSTER
(author, *Star Wars* novelization and the sequel, *Splinter of the Mind's Eye*)

Darth Vader was a terrific character until he was redeemed. It's like, you know, Hitler's on his deathbed and he says, "I'm sorry," and all is forgiven? I couldn't get past that.

RAY MORTON

Vader's character changes significantly in *Return of the Jedi*. In *Empire*, Vader was a dynamic, complex personality—a ruthless, ambitious actor full of secrets who would let nothing stand in his way as he schemed to overthrow his master and seize the ultimate power in the galaxy. In *Return of the Jedi*, Vader is . . . a lapdog. Whereas Vader was the main villain in *Empire*, in *Jedi* he is once again a henchman as he was in *Star Wars*. In that first film, Vader was at least a feisty henchman, willing to argue with Tarkin and give the Grand Moff a hard time if they disagreed. In *Jedi*, that fire is gone and Vader is obedient to the Emperor to the point of obsequiousness. This Vader doesn't seem capable of questioning his boss, much less of plotting to overthrow him. He appears to have lost the ambition that drove him in *Empire*, as well as his intense, determined nature. *Jedi*'s Vader isn't even very ruthless: the dark angel who tortured and Force-choked people left and right in *Star Wars* and *Empire* doesn't crush a single larynx in *Episode VI*. He doesn't do much else either. Apart from intimidating Moff Jerjerrod in the opening sequence, Vader spends most of the movie just passively standing and saying, "Yes, my master," whenever the Emperor croaks out some pronouncement. He only jumps into action at the very end of the movie when he jumps in to stop Luke from killing the Emperor.

In early drafts of the screenplay, the Emperor was actually aware of Vader's desire to depose him and of his attempt to enlist Luke to help him do so. Angry, the Emperor lets Vader know that he is aware of this treachery and that Vader is on thin ice with him. He treats Vader badly—removing him from vital assignments, mocking him, and assigning a condescending Moff Jerjerrod to serve as his minder. At one point, Vader pushes back and the Emperor Force-chokes him, *reminding Vader which one of them is the more powerful.*

RAY MORTON

It's not clear why Vader was de-balled so significantly in *Jedi*, but it seems likely that Lucas feared that audiences might not accept Vader's transformation into a good guy if he spent the bulk of the film running around being evil and killing people. Whether that would have been the case or not is hard to know, but what is certain is that the Darth Vader in *Return of the Jedi* is a much less formidable (and, frankly, less interesting) character than the Vader of *Star Wars* and *The Empire Strikes Back*.

When Vader is redeemed by saving Luke from the Emperor, and is dying on the Death Star, Luke removes his helmet to reveal the kindly face of Sebastian Shaw as Anakin Skywalker—which came as a shock to David Prowse in particular.

DAVID PROWSE
(on-set actor, "Darth Vader")

I hated it. I thought it was the worst possible thing they could have done to me, as far as the movies were concerned. I had terrible problems with them all throughout the movies. They overdubbed my voice without telling me. It was all very underhanded. They gave me false dialogue in the second movie, which I thought was stupid. There was no need for the secrecy. It wasn't as though I was going to go around blabbing things to the press. Then they decided to unmask somebody else, without telling me, without even discussing it with me. I really thought that was the dirtiest of tricks. They tried to film it all before I started work on the movie, so I wouldn't know what was going on. The only reason I found out about it was because one of the reporters from a newspaper in Britain asked if I knew that they were killing me off in this movie. I said, "You must be joking! They won't kill Darth Vader off!" And he said, "Not only are they killing you off, they're killing you off in another studio and using another actor so that you don't know what's going on in the movie!" All these decisions came right from the top, right from Lucas.

IRVIN KERSHNER

I would never have shown the face of Darth Vader. When that helmet was put on his head in *Empire*, it was about a half-second blink. I wanted to show that there was a human being in there and that there was something wrong with that human being, but nothing more. The audience had to imagine what the face looked like. When they showed just an ordinary man lying there talking with a couple of little marks on his head, I felt it was a cheat. I would not have done that.

RAY MORTON

And then there's Leia. In *Star Wars* and *Empire,* Princess Leia is a feisty, determined leader of the rebellion. In *Jedi,* she is no longer a leader—for reasons never made clear, the character of Mon Mothma assumes Leia's role in the Alliance's ruling hierarchy, reducing the Princess to Han Solo's sidekick. Leia also loses her feistiness, which has been replaced by . . . nothing. Leia is a very vague character in *Jedi*—it's not clear what she is thinking or feeling at any point in the movie. Carrie Fisher is on record saying she didn't recognize the character anymore when she read the screenplay and couldn't figure out how to play her.

Han has lost all of the complexity he was given in *Episode V.* He's not only one-dimensional in *Jedi,* but he also seems to have lost quite a few IQ points. Apart from a brief shuttle ride, Han Solo, the greatest daredevil pilot in the galaxy, doesn't even do any flying in the film, thus robbing the character of the one area in which he is guaranteed to shine. Harrison Ford famously wanted Solo to die in *Jedi*—to make a noble sacrifice of some sort in order to complete Han's arc from selfish loner to selfless hero—but Lucas didn't want Solo to die, because he felt audiences wouldn't accept it, so Han lived and Ford responded by unenthusiastically phoning in his performance. Beyond "Someone who loves you," the reverse "I love you/I know," and some brief kissy-face at the end, the romance between Han and Leia is not only not developed in *Jedi*, it is barely acknowledged. And with Han returning at the beginning of the story, there isn't much for Lando to do in *Jedi*. After taking part in the opening rescue, he is shunted off to the Millennium Falcon for the rest of the movie for what is basically an extended cameo. Why Lando, whose piloting skills have never been established, would be chosen to lead an aerial attack instead of experienced pilot Han Solo is never explained.

After stealing the show in *Empire*, Yoda is inexplicably killed off in *Jedi* following an appearance in only one scene. In *Empire*, he's approximately eight hundred years old and hale and healthy. A few weeks later in *Jedi*, he is suddenly old, sick, and dying. What happened? What happened is that Yoda wasn't originally supposed to appear in the movie at all. As previously noted, Lucas's original notion was for Luke to have returned to Dagobah and completed his training between films. Without on-screen training to be done, there was no role for Yoda to play. However, Richard Marquand insisted he appear, assuming (correctly) that audiences would want to see more of the diminutive Jedi Master after his film-stealing appearance in *The Empire Strikes Back*. In some early drafts, Yoda was still alive and made an appearance at the end of the movie; in others, he died off-screen. He was finally killed off in *Jedi* when Lawrence Kasdan insisted one of the principals had to die in order to convince audiences that the stakes in *Jedi* were for real. Had Yoda died making some noble sacrifice, that might have worked, but to just have him catch a cold and croak feels like a waste of an incredible and beloved character.

While some people disliked the additions to the Rebel Alliance, the new additions of Mon Mothma, Admiral Ackbar, and General Crix Madine would become fixtures in the iconic Star Wars *Expanded Universe for many years to come.*

CAROLINE BLAKISTON
(actress, "Mon Mothma," *Return of the Jedi*)

I was in a television series working in Manchester. When they needed to make the costume that I am wearing as Mon Mothma, they came to Manchester to do a costume fitting in the hotel where I was staying. I was told to keep that a secret. I couldn't tell anybody about the design. We even discussed my hairdo, but in the end my own short red hair was used. They thought it was just fine. I had no idea what a Bothan was—then I discovered later, of course. I didn't understand the story, I didn't know the story. I had just a page with my lines. Everything was secret and I had to sign for that. So I learned what I had to learn and I went to the studio and they told me my lines had changed. I had to learn new lines, which was difficult as the language that was used is not the language we speak. After a day and a half there was the intimidating big scene with Harrison Ford, Carrie Fisher, and all the extras and the film crew. I worked in that studio many times because during the sixties and seventies many series like *The Avengers* were made there.

TIM ROSE
(on-set actor, "Admiral Ackbar," *Return of the Jedi*)
I was already working in Phil Tippett's workshop at ILM designing animatronics for the characters of *Jedi*. I knew that when preproduction was finished I would be going to England to perform Sy Snootles and Salacious Crumb. We were never given copies of the script for reasons of secrecy, so I had no idea who Admiral Ackbar was. I had done a lot of the design work for his close-up version and when I asked Phil who he was he said, "Oh, he's just another background character that appears later in the movie." So I asked if I could perform him, as I was familiar with his controls, and Phil said okay. It was as simple as that.

As the film entered into its final days of production, John Williams set to work on the final chapter of this trilogy of the Star Wars *franchise.*

JOE KRAEMER
(composer, *Mission Impossible: Rogue Nation* and *Jack Reacher*)
The completion of the final film in the original trilogy would not have been the same without John Williams returning to write the score. For this film, he created new themes for Jabba the Hutt, the Ewoks, and the Emperor, as well as the tender "brother-and-sister" love theme for Luke and Leia. This score was recorded in Studio One at Abbey Road studios in London, the same studio where John Williams would return nearly twenty years later to record the *Star Wars* prequel trilogy.

Returning themes from earlier *Star Wars* films included the Main Theme, the Force Theme, "The Imperial March," Yoda's Theme, Han and Leia's Theme, "The Rebel Fanfare," and action music from the "Attack on the Death Star," as well as the "TIE Fighter Battle" from the Death Star escape sequence. Despite having more music recorded for the film, the soundtrack LP was actually the shortest of the first three films, being a single disc made up mostly of concert arrangements of the new themes rather than underscore from the film itself. Of the album's eleven tracks, only five were from the actual score, with the rest being at least partly made up of material specially written and recorded just for the LP.

One of the most charming scenes in the movie also had one of the highlights of the score—the sequence where C-3PO tells the Ewoks the story of the *Star Wars* trilogy. Williams took the opportunity to create a medley using many of the themes from the series for a small woodwind ensemble and percussion, and it solidifies the fairy-tale quality the films and scores had achieved by this point in pop culture.

Williams had adapted the score to the original *Star Wars* for symphony orchestra for use in concerts around the world, and one of the changes he made in doing so was to add a very short timpani roll to the opening chord. This finally made its way onto a soundtrack album with *Return of the Jedi*, although in the film, the "Main Title" was actually the recording made for *The Empire Strikes Back,* since it started without the percussion roll. This was the last of the scores John Williams recorded with the London Symphony Orchestra until he returned in 1999 to record *The Phantom Menace.*

John Williams's son, Joseph, followed in his father's footsteps as a musician, and worked on several pieces heard in the film as "source music," including the music the Max Rebo Band performs after Jabba the Hutt purchases Chewbacca from Boushh the Bounty Hunter. This piece can also be heard in the documentary *From Star Wars to Jedi.* It remains unreleased on any soundtrack album, as the master recording is rumored to be missing from Lucasfilm's vaults. Joe Williams also served as the lead vocalist for the rock band Toto for many years.

Although *The Empire Strikes Back* used a choir for the Millennium Falcon's approach to Cloud City, this film was the first *Star Wars* entry to really feature choir in a significant way, using low male singers for the Emperor's Theme, as well as the stirring, "religioso" treatment as Luke rages against Darth Vader in lightsaber battle. Finally, in the original version of the film from 1983, a full choir sings in both English and the Ewok language for the final celebration music. In 1997, the full choir was replaced by a group of children singers.

For the first time in the saga, an entire action sequence was rescored. The fight at the Sarlacc pit had first been accompanied by all-new music, but it was later decided to instead write a score based around action themes from the original *Star Wars* score from 1977. The original version can be heard on the 1997 Special Edition release of the soundtrack. During the Rebels' attack on the second Death Star, Williams incorporates a clever development of the Medal Ceremony music from *Star Wars*.

Return of the Jedi was released on May 25, 1983, to mixed critical reaction— actually, the worst reviewed of the original trilogy, not that the audience seemed to mind very much. Made at a production cost of $35.5 million, it eventually earned a worldwide gross of over $475 million.

RIC MEYERS
(author, *For One Week Only: The World of Exploitation Films*)

Let me go on record right now. I have absolutely no problem with creators who make things for kids. Walt Disney made things for kids. Roald Dahl made things for kids. Stan Lee made things for kids. Warner Bros.' Looney Tunes made things for kids. Dr. Seuss made things for kids. But they all made things for kids they liked and respected. They all made things that didn't speak *down* to kids. They all didn't treat kids as if they were stupid. They didn't make things for kids that were "good enough for garbage." *Star Wars* was not for dumb kids. *The Empire Strikes Back* was not for undiscerning kids. So what the hell had happened? I was told that Lucas was upset by the overwhelming reaction, and, in addition, this cerebral, art film–loving director was having a hard time accepting that his heartfelt homage to Flash Gordon was becoming his inescapable legacy to cinema.

I could buy that. To me, *Return of the Jedi* was the work of a numb producer— one who now cared so little for his creation that, when the plotting gambits he had used in *Empire* to give him options in case any of the stars refused to return for *Jedi* (Boba Fett, the "other one," and Obi-Wan lying), he simply dropped the plot twists without developing them in any exciting or involving way. He didn't even care that the Ewok suits were rudimentary and not credible, or that the characters "borrowed" from H. Beam Piper's *Little Fuzzy* and worshipped C-3PO for no apparent reason. The final result was, for me, the work of a film-maker who just didn't seem to care, or worse, didn't care if the audience cared. Little wonder one of the film's most overused lines was "I've got a bad feeling about this." That bad feeling would only increase as time, and *Star Wars* films, went on. But, for the moment, I put my love of the first two, and my heartsick disappointment in the third, behind me. For what it was worth, the *Star Wars* trilogy was over, and both its maker, and I, had other fish to fry.

BRIAN JAY JONES

One thing to keep in mind is that when Lucas gets to *Jedi*, his entire life is falling apart. He's getting divorced from Marcia, and the fact is he's selling off portions of his company, including Pixar, at fire sale prices for the divorce settlement. At the time Lucas is producing *Indiana Jones and the Temple of Doom,* and there's a moment in there when someone gets their beating heart ripped out of their chest. I really think Lucas is putting that on-screen intentionally. His life is a mess at this point and he really does need to step back to try and get his shit together. And in the divorce, what's really astounding to me, is that he and Marcia get shared custody of their oldest child. He ends up with the kids. He's raising the kids and then he adopts two more. So he's raising the family, and he wants to be a dad at that point. And more power to him. He steps out at that point and it just shocks people that he's willing to walk away. But when you've got fuck-you money, you can do that.

RAY MORTON

On top of *Jedi*'s other problems, there's too much repetition of old ideas; too many elements recycled from *Star Wars.* This includes the Star Destroyer flyover in the opening scene. While *Jedi* showed us more of Luke's home planet, Tatooine, than we saw in the first movie, there was no escaping the fact that we'd been here before. Once again, Luke and Leia swing across a vast expanse on a rope. In terms of monsters, the cantina scene in the original *Star Wars* is a classic bit of weirdness featuring a delightfully odd collection of intergalactic creatures. Jabba's court is essentially the cantina scene on steroids with triple the number of monsters. While there are certainly a number of really cool creatures in these scenes (including Jabba himself), the higher quantity of monsters can't make up for the concept's basic lack of freshness.

It was inevitable (and correct) that *Star Wars* had to end with some wars in the stars. However, to conclude *Jedi,* Lucas opted not to devise a new type of space battle, but to instead simply repeat the climax of *Star Wars* by presenting another dogfight in space between the Rebels and the Empire ending with the Rebels blowing up an important Imperial object. To differentiate it from the battle in the original picture, Lucas made the dogfight in *Jedi* bigger and more elaborate, but there was still no escaping the fact that it was a retread. And the fact that the object of the Rebel attack was another Death Star didn't help matters. Early in the writing process, some thought was given to making the target of the Rebels' attack in *Jedi* the Empire's capital planet—a polluted world completely covered by cities called Had Abbadon (Abaddon was an angel of death in the book of Revelation). Eventually, it was decided it would be too unwieldy and unbelievable for the Rebels to blow up an entire planet, so Lucas fell back on the idea of using another Death Star. To make it seem less repetitive, initially, the idea of using multiple Death Stars was considered, but that notion was eventually dismissed because it was too difficult to dramatically focus the final attack if the fighters had multiple targets. Ultimately, Lucas decided to proceed with a single Death Star, albeit one that was not finished (although not, as the Rebels would discover in one of the story's better twists, nonoperational). The filigreed look of this unfinished battle station was quite striking, but not striking enough to hide the fact that we were basically seeing the same thing all over again.

ALAN DEAN FOSTER

It's a good movie that showcases everything that the people involved learned about making *Star Wars* movies in the first two films. It kind of harkens back to the spirit of the first film and was a lot of fun. At the same time, you build everything up to such a peak of anticipation after the first two films that it's virtually impossible to bring off a third film. *Lord of the Rings* does it, but there's no problem coming up with a storyline for *Lord of the Rings*—it's all there in the three books. The one problem I have with *Jedi*, which I've already mentioned, is the redemption of Darth Vader. Nobody asked my opinion, but what I wanted was at the ending of *Empire* when Vader says, "Luke, I am your father," I thought you should find out in *Jedi* that he's really Luke's evil older brother who killed their father, making him doubly worse. Then you'd have no problem killing him and the audience would cheer it on. It all would have fit with the storyline at that point, too, but, again, nobody asked me.

JONATHAN WILKINS
(editor, *Star Wars Insider*, 2009–2017)

The thing you have to remember as well is, there were lots of things in the original trilogy that people aren't necessarily enamored with. Like Boba Fett getting walloped in the Sarlacc pit by a blinded Han Solo. After all that build-up, "Oh wow, he's *such* a cool character . . . Oh, wait. That's it?" I remember saying to Jeremy Bulloch once, "How did you feel about that?" And he said, "Well, if Boba Fett had a cool fight and been dispatched in a cool way by being shot by Han Solo, whatever. It would've been a cool moment in the film, but people still talk about what happened."

The Ewoks for example, there was a period where people really didn't like the Ewoks. I think we've kind of gone past that now. It would be very boring to end *Return of the Jedi* with a space battle of ships and another big battle of spaceships, and not have any sort of fun with it. Nothing unique or original. Where else are you going to see a tribe of savage teddy bears defeating an Empire? It's a *Star Wars* thing. When people were criticizing *The Phantom Menace*, I remember George Lucas having to say, "It's *Star Wars*. It's not *The Terminator.*" There's a lightness to it.

RICHARD MARQUAND

It was an enormous responsibility getting the ending right. Endings are always a problem. This film has such a complex ending that your problem as a director is to make it clear, make it work, and make it emotionally satisfying. Your job is to enable the audience to overcome some of the sadness of the film. And there are some deeply sad moments in this movie.

RAY MORTON

It's hard to fathom why Lucas—after displaying so much imagination and originality in the first two films in the trilogy—would be okay with recycling so many ideas in this one. Some accounts suggest that Lucas—who has been quite vocal over the years about how disappointed he was in *Star Wars,* because budget and technical limitations didn't allow him to fully realize his expansive vision for the project—redid many of the concepts he was unhappy with in the original movie—in particular the monster rally and the space battle—in *Jedi* so that he could finally get them "right."

KYLE NEWMAN
(director, *Fanboys*)

I know people malign *Return of the Jedi,* which is sad. I think it's one of the boldest independent movies ever made. The guy took the greatest villain of all time and he said, "You know what? I'm not going to do a layup. I'm going to humanize him. I'm going to create an even scarier villain," which he did. Then he did this whole Luke rejecting his elders, embracing love—none of this was easy terrain for a sequel. *Empire Strikes Back* was a crazy sequel. That's why I think people have issues with *The Force Awakens.* That's why George has issues with *The Force Awakens,* which J.J. Abrams has openly admitted is a heavy retread. George committed to bold sequels and he put all of his own money into it. That was a $35 million investment out of his own pocket that would make or break him. That's pretty crazy stuff. What filmmaker is putting $35 million—today that's like a hundred and fifty—of their own money into a sequel? And they're like, "I'm going to break the mold and not do what is expected." That's pretty crazy.

RAY MORTON

Lucas may have been suffering from burnout. As J. W. Rinzler's excellent 2013 book *The Making of Return of the Jedi* makes perfectly clear, after six years of nearly constant work on *Star Wars,* everyone in the company from Lucas to the actors to the visual effects teams were running on fumes. Concerns about the repetition of elements were raised frequently during the story and script conferences between Lucas and Kasdan (and producer Howard Kazanjian and director Richard Marquand)—often by Lucas himself. Fresh alternatives were discussed, but most of the time it was ultimately decided to redo that which had already been done. It may be that Lucas was simply too exhausted to come up with anything new.

JOHN KENNETH MUIR
(author, *Science Fiction and Fantasy Films of the 1970s*)

A crushing disappointment. *Return of the Jedi* is a film made not for the young at heart, like the previous two films, but for very young children who wish to consume product (meaning purchase toys). Cue the burping Muppets. Cue the teddy bear aliens. Every concept that might have been treated with maturity and intelligence in the film is instead handled in perfunctory, let's-get-this-over-with fashion. The Luke-Leia-Han triangle? Forget it, Luke and Leia are siblings, and she claims she's always known (which makes their previous on-screen kisses double creepy). Obi-Wan lied to Luke about Vader? Well, no, it all depends on your point of view. Watch Yoda squirm when confronted with the fact that he was in on all the lies: "Rest I must. Tired I am," or thereabouts. This is how the Jedi Knights behave? Lying, obfuscation, and deflection? And even the film's big threat is a rerun, a second Death Star. Han Solo, meanwhile, is portrayed as a bungler and comic relief, as though Harrison Ford were being punished for doing too good a job with the character in *The Empire Strikes Back*.

RAY MORTON

Apart from making large chunks of *Jedi* feel uninspired and tired, all of this repetition reduced the scope of the saga. Whereas *Empire* told us that there was much more to the world of *Star Wars* than we initially imagined, the recycling of locations and events in *Jedi* told us no—the world of *Star Wars* was actually no bigger than the one we saw in the first movie. Given all of the marvelous, expansive world-building in the first two films, this was quite a letdown. The finale of *Return of the Jedi* is not at all satisfying. After three epic films, we were expecting an epic finish: a galaxy-wide celebration of the defeat of the Empire; Leia being named the leader of the New Republic; Han and Leia getting married; and Luke becoming a full-fledged Jedi Knight and setting off on a lifetime of new adventures. Instead, we get a campfire at which the heroes we had been following through three films literally sit on the sidelines as a bunch of teddy bears dance. Crushing, crushing disappointment would not be too light a description of my and many others' reactions to this conclusion.

JOHN KENNETH MUIR

On a personal note, I saw the film when I was thirteen and I was left gasping, when it ended, at the *emptiness* of the entire film. This was it? This was how it all ended? Dancing Ewoks around a campfire? This film was the canary-in-the-coal-mine for later *Star Wars* films, stressing either burping or cute aliens, merchandising opportunities, and facile storytelling. As Mark Hamill noted in an interview with *Time* magazine ("Great Galloping Galaxies") at the time: "Let's face it, we made a film for children." He might have added, "at the expense of everyone else."

PETER HOLMSTROM

I've been a die-hard fan my whole life, and I honestly never knew there were people who hated this movie until a couple of years ago. Guess it's the difference between growing up with something, and growing up with something else and seeing this as something different. Structurally, there are some problems, sure—but there are some amazing moments, best of the franchise. When Lando blasts out of the Death Star with fires right behind; Luke's battle with Vader; the fight on Endor; all of Jabba's palace—this is the stuff dreams are made of! Boggles my mind how anyone can say this movie is anything other than amazing.

BRIAN JAY JONES

After that, Lucas steps out for almost a decade. He's producing friends' films, art films that he wishes he could make. I don't regret him stepping back at all and I really do think he believed with *Return of the Jedi,* it was done. And what sort of puts a final note on that is that he makes an appearance at some award ceremony or on a talk show, and when he walks out onstage, they play the *Raiders of the Lost Ark* march, and not the *Star Wars* theme. It wasn't just Lucas. It seemed like the world was moving on as well.

With the release of Return of the Jedi, *the trilogy was complete and Lucas was ready to move in different directions—not the least of which was rebuilding his personal life. That being said, there were attempts to keep* Star Wars *alive, though admittedly in ways the vast majority of fans may not have been expecting. They'd already seen the results of* The Star Wars Holiday Special *some years earlier, but this time it would be in the form of a pair of movies about the Ewoks as well as the Saturday morning animated series* Droids *and* Ewoks. *None of these, needless to say, have stood the test of time.*

What all of this represented for those who had turned the big-screen trilogy into such a sensation, and embraced it as a kind of religion, were future directions, and what was unfolding was not encouraging.

GLEN OLIVER

All of the early TV stuff, as crappy as it often was, suggested a breadth of storytelling—the presence of possibility and flexibility of narrative within the *Star Wars* universe—which would've worked nicely if any, or all, had been more strongly realized. These shows weren't exponential leaps forward for either *Star Wars* storytelling or televised science fiction/fantasy in general. But they did help to lay the groundwork for bigger, bolder, more interesting shows to come: *The Clone Wars, Rebels, Resistance, The Mandalorian,* the Cassian Andor series, Obi-Wan . . . I kind of look at those early efforts as being a first-ever date. Someone's first-ever date doesn't necessarily go so well, and is awkward and exploratory and filled with unease and maybe even regret. But it almost always opens the door to a larger world . . .

DAN MADSEN
(owner, the Official Lucasfilm/Star Wars Fan Club, 1987–2001)

I did cover [the Ewoks films] for the [Lucasfilm Fan Club] magazine. I didn't personally cover them, I hired some other writers to cover those. It was a lean time for Lucasfilm when I took over running the fan club. Because *Star Wars* was over, we had *Willow* and Indiana Jones—but those were years apart from each other. So, we had things like *Maniac Mansion,* which was a TV series that Lucasfilm did, and *Tucker,* which was a movie about the car designer that Jeff Bridges was in. So we had to try and do the best we could. Every issue I tried to throw in something *Star Wars.* It wasn't like all this amazing new stuff available for us to cover at that time. We did the best to try and keep interest alive in the whole Lucasfilm/*Star Wars* franchise, while there was literally nothing new of *Star Wars* to come out for ten years.

9

ISN'T THAT SPECIAL?: WARS AFTER *JEDI*

"Prince Xizor, who knew?"

The word "renaissance" would seem superfluous when it comes to the *Star Wars* franchise, yet as it turned out, that was exactly what was needed in the aftermath of *Return of the Jedi*. Interest in all things *Star Wars* seemed to rapidly cool off with the saga apparently wrapping up with the *Ewoks* and *Droids* animated series, the pair of live-action Ewok TV movies, and the emergence of new blockbuster franchises like Tim Burton's *Batman* arriving on the scene. Howard Roffman, who at that time was the vice president of licensing for Lucasfilm, Ltd., having moved into that position from Lucasfilm general counsel, recognized along with George Lucas himself that while the brand had enchanted hundreds of millions of people—and not just children—it needed to be nurtured and developed into an enduring classic a la *The Wizard of Oz*, or risk going the way of Flash Gordon itself.

HOWARD ROFFMAN
(former vice president of licensing, Lucasfilm)

When I moved to licensing in 1986, *Star Wars* merchandise was at a virtual standstill. We had gone through this tremendous period with *Star Wars*. When it was new, it was a mass market phenomenon and toys were by far the majority of the product being sold and revenues being generated. Things like that normally have a limited life span and the question always is, is there something about them that makes them more enduring or are they a one-shot phenomenon? But in 1985, the toys were over. You couldn't even mention *Star Wars* to retailers. There simply wasn't a lot happening.

BRIAN VOLK-WEISS
(executive producer, *The Toys That Made Us*)

Things were dead for two reasons, one of them 75 percent responsible, the other 25 percent. It was 25 percent dead because the audience had become smaller and the demand had diminished. Basically, everybody was into *Star Wars* up until about six months after *Return of the Jedi*. A year later, it was just hardcore fans, so instead of having a market base of a hundred million people, you had a market base of fifteen to twenty million people. The 75 percent of it is that George didn't want to do anything.

GEORGE LUCAS
(creator, the *Star Wars* franchise)

I ran out of energy to do it. Once you have done it a couple of times, then the thrill of it wears off and you really want to get into different territory.

JOE BONGIORNO
(webmaster, starwarstimeline.net)

While *Star Wars* was not quite the "dead" property that many claim, it was getting close. Four years earlier the Marvel *Droids* and *Ewoks* comic book series that told new stories based on the two animated series (both of which had ceased production the year prior) ended, but West End Games had a thriving *Star Wars* role-playing game that started in that same year in 1987. Through various sourcebooks, supplements, and role-playing adventures, West End Games provided names, races, planets, and backstories for everything seen in the films, as well as new stories and characters set in the universe.

BRIAN VOLK-WEISS

At the time, Kenner had made a gigantic proposal to Lucas and Lucasfilm, and had made mockups of vehicles and extra characters and all of it based on the Clone Wars, and this was before the TV series. Kenner on their own initiative made a run at figuring out what that line of dialogue from *A New Hope* about the Clone Wars was all about and presented it to George, and George declined it. The way the contract worked was Kenner was entitled to do the toys and merchandise for anything based on the movies or TV shows, but if Lucas wasn't making movies or TV shows, they couldn't really do anything.

JONATHAN WILKINS
(editor, *Star Wars Insider*, 2009–2017)

There was that period where *Star Wars* was so intense, and then about '84 or '85 there was just this massive drop-off. There were no new films, or projects coming. I just remember it being a sudden thing—kids around my neighborhood, we all moved on to *Masters of the Universe*. I'm so sorry to say that. Then *Star Wars* had a sort of resurgence in the early nineties, and they had those action figures where Luke Skywalker had the body-building look. I didn't collect those.

BILL SLAVICSEK
(game designer, West End Games)

West End Games' *Star Wars Role-playing Game* line was actually the first thing to show Lucasfilm Licensing that they still had a viable property even without new movies. I was at WEG when we were awarded the license. This was late 1986. The movies were finished. The novels were done. The Marvel Comics line and Kenner toys were winding down. The following year, for the tenth anniversary of the original film, there were only two new *Star Wars* offerings: *Star Tours,* which opened in Disneyland, and *The Star Wars Role-playing Game* from West End Games that debuted in October 1987.

BILL GEORGE
(visual effects supervisor, Industrial Light & Magic)

I started working on the reboot of *Star Tours* in 2008, and have ended up working a lot of WDI—Walt Disney Imagineering—since then. It was a project I really thought was interesting, mostly because it was in stereoscopic 3D, but I have completely fallen in love with working on theme park rides. Because it takes the challenges of production, 2D production, and takes it into this whole other world where you have to pay attention to so many different things. It's compressed, it's usually in high resolution, you have a story to get across, you usually have a simulator that's going, you got the stereo. What I call the three S's. They've got this complex melody that is really, really challenging and fun. And then we've got the branching storyline with *Star Tours,* where we've got the opening, a detour, the transmission, and an ending—and those can all fit together in different combinations. So that's really fun.

JOE BONGIORNO
Another important thing that happened was in 1990, when the original trilogy was packaged together for the first time on home video by CBS/FOX, which introduced and reintroduced a generation to the saga who hadn't previously owned or even seen them. While this wasn't the first time *Star Wars* had been on video, it's significant because the eighties' releases were cost prohibitive. A VHS tape from that era could run around $80 each. This same year saw the releases of the new Ewok films and various episodes of the *Droids* and *Ewoks*

animated television series, ramping up interest in what was soon to be called the Expanded Universe. In 1992, the first widescreen (letterbox) VHS set was released in a gorgeous box set boasting a lenticular hologram cover. Derived from the laser discs that had debuted two years prior, it introduced the concept of widescreen as a preferable format, not just for the theatrical experience, but for home viewing. It was an exciting release and the first of many to come.

BRIAN VOLK-WEISS

The first new toy in about ten years was in 1993 with the Luke Skywalker and *Star Wars* Bend-Ems, and they were garbage. But I bought them all, because there hadn't been a *Star Wars* story in ten years. I would argue—and this is not fact, just my opinion—is that the reason Kenner fell to Hasbro in the first place was because George didn't want to do anything else. With the Bend-Ems, I can't stress this enough: they're possibly the nastiest, grossest things toy-related that *Star Wars* ever did, but they flew off the shelf. One of the things about Lucas is that he was always testing things. Like, *Howard the Duck* was a gigantic test for animatronic technology. *The Phantom Menace,* and Lucas says it himself on the film's documentary, was a giant test to do a photorealistic character that ILM would then be able to make for other companies and other movies. So, again, the Bend-Ems were largely a test. Lucas hadn't approved a new toy in ten years and he approved it just to get some sales data. I don't know if he intentionally approved the worst toy to say, "Well, if they buy this garbage, imagine what they'd buy if it was good." Now in case you can't tell already, I have a sweet spot in my heart for the Bend-Ems, but they're also an irrelevant piece of history that's not as sexy to talk about as the Timothy Zahn novels or West End Games.

HOWARD ROFFMAN

With the success of the West End Games, Lucasfilm began to formulate a plan that would take the franchise into new territory, which would not only include games, but novels and comic books as well. It was not an attempt to repeat what had been done before when *Star Wars* was hot in 1977, and we slowly began building it. It started with the novel, Timothy Zahn's *Heir to the Empire,* the first in a trilogy, which like many of the novels became bestsellers.

BILL SLAVICSEK

By the time Lucasfilm, Ltd., decided to expand back into novels and comics, WEG's products were provided to the other licensees as reference material. Tim Zahn tells the story of how he received a box full of game books when he started writing *Heir to the Empire.* At first, he was a little insulted, but as he dug into the material we had produced, he saw that there was a wealth of material he wouldn't have to create, including ships, weapons, and aliens. That allowed him to really focus on his story.

JOE BONGIORNO

Howard Roffman correctly ascertained that one of the first things to turn everything around for *Star Wars* was the Timothy Zahn novel. He would know as he was the one who proposed the idea to Lucas, along with Lucy Wilson, Lucasfilm's finance director and one of Lucas's first employees, who literally typed the screenplay of the first *Star Wars* film in George's house. Wilson had been longing to see *Star Wars* return as the publishing venture it had once been, and knew it could be even greater. Although former publisher Del Rey was no longer interested, not seeing the financial value in it, serendipitously, the head of Bantam-Spectra, Lou Aronica, was very interested, having just sent a proposal to them.

HOWARD ROFFMAN

One of the things obvious about *Star Wars* was that, like *Star Trek,* it's a very rich universe with very well-defined characters and situations and creatures and politics. It was very fertile area to let gifted science fiction writers come and play in. Timothy Zahn's first book turned out to be a smashing validation, if you will, of the theory that people would be interested in good new fiction based on the *Star Wars* universe.

JOE BONGIORNO

Clearly the Force was at work. *Star Wars* was meant to expand into a literary saga. The idea was to set new stories after the events of *Return of the Jedi.* Lucas liked the idea; after all, he was the one who set up Carol Titelman and her team to oversee the expansion of his saga in the pages of Marvel's *Star Wars* comics, newspaper strips, and Del Rey novels. However, it had now been five years after his last film and with no new films on the immediate horizon, he had doubts it would sell. Nevertheless, he green-lit the idea, saying that the time period before *A New Hope* was to be left alone, since if he did ever return to *Star Wars* on film, it would be in the form of prequels.

TOM DUPREE
(editor, Bantam Books)

The success of the novel surprised everybody. *Heir to the Empire* hit number one on the *New York Times* bestseller list, which was almost unheard of for a science fiction novel. We were stunned to hear stories about customers at bookstores helping clerks open boxes to find the books. Also, a key difference between our program then and, say, the *Star Trek* program is that *Star Trek* is episodic, while ours was part of a larger mega-story. In a typical *Trek* novel, everything's okay at the beginning, there's a problem, they fix it, and then everything is okay at the end—just like an episode of the TV show. We were making our stories work together in the larger *Star Wars* universe, so if Han and Leia get married in Zahn's book and you write a book that happens after that, they are married. Each publication added a little bit to the mythology.

TIMOTHY ZAHN
(author, *Heir to the Empire, Dark Force Rising, The Last Command*)
When I got the news that I would be writing the first new *Star Wars* adventures since *Return of the Jedi*, my reaction was, "Wow" and, then, "Argh!" I had to do something that felt like *Star Wars*, but wasn't the same thing as the movies. Part of my goal was to give the feeling of a real universe, which is what George Lucas did with the films. Part of that is the political aspect. Bear in mind that I had a lot more room in three books than Lucas did in the movies, so I could have a lot of exposition. I could do things beneath the surface. In a movie, everything has to be visual or in dialogue. I realized that since it was set about five years after the last movie, in this case the Rebel Alliance had to create a government. That's not as easy as people like to think. I wanted to get a feel for some of that challenge without letting it take over the whole book.

JOE BONGIORNO
In *Heir to the Empire*, Zahn eschewed the less popular aspects of *Return of the Jedi* to focus on a more adult-oriented story, careful to capture the voices of Luke, Han, and Leia as well as to introduce readers to memorable new characters in the form of the still famous Grand Admiral Thrawn (who, along with the Noghri Rukh, would years later transition to the *Star Wars: Rebels* animated series and perhaps future live-action TV shows). The Emperor's Hand, Mara Jade, would go on to significant fame: starting out as an assassin intended to kill Luke Skywalker, she would after many years go on to become his wife, and the mother of his son Ben. Zahn's story was compelling and epic, adding into the mix a mad Jedi named Jorus C'baoth who was a wild card, adding to the edge-of-your-seat tension brought on by Thrawn's meticulous, Machiavellian, Sherlockian maneuvers.

TIMOTHY ZAHN
When I was developing Thrawn, I wanted someone the reader could understand, someone who would be interesting and someone I could enjoy writing

about for three books. In the back of my mind was the original *Star Trek* episode "Balance of Terror," the first one with the Romulans, and the Romulan commander's last line to Kirk was, "In another reality, we might have been friends." I wanted to put some of that into Thrawn—that in another reality this guy could have really kicked butt for the Rebellion. He understands his people. He understands how to be a leader.

JOE BONGIORNO

Debuting in December 1991 was the first issue of a six-part comic book series by Tom Veitch and Cam Kennedy called *Dark Empire*, from Dark Horse Comics. With no shortage of momentous events, it featured the return of Emperor Palpatine in a cloned body, and Luke Skywalker going to the dark side in an attempt to defeat him. Released only six months after *Heir to the Empire* debuted, the films on VHS, the book series, and the comic book were a triple-punch knockout that solidified the return of *Star Wars* in a big way.

PETER HOLMSTROM
(cohost, *The Rebel & the Rogue* podcast)

The Dark Horse era of *Star Wars* was a really beautiful time. Every comics publisher in the world was vying for the rights—for obvious reasons—but George Lucas chose Dark Horse because, at the time, Dark Horse was one of the few independent publishers out there. This was before the Image [Comics] Revolution, and the explosion of small publishers. So George was mirroring what he did with NPR years before—supporting the little guy. Advocating for decentralization of the entertainment industry. And those years had some really creative stuff flow out. For many kids, those comics were *Star Wars*, just as much as the movies.

I know when Lucasfilm sold to Disney, the breakup with Dark Horse was not pleasant. Rumor was that before the sale occurred, there was a handshake agreement to say Dark Horse would keep their license to publish even after the sale, but Marvel would publish the new continuity of stories. Couple of years go by, and that deal goes away. Then the 20th Century Fox sale, and Dark Horse loses the *Aliens, Predator, Buffy, Firefly* licenses—suddenly their paydays aren't looking so good anymore. The rich get richer and the poor get poorer.

JOE BONGIORNO

When Zahn discovered *Dark Empire,* he was aghast at the idea of Palpatine's return. Whether he generally disliked the idea, or worried that it might upstage his Grand Admiral Thrawn, he contacted his publisher requesting that he ignore it, or that it be deemed a separate continuity. When he discovered Lucasfilm's intent to establish a single canon across media, he refused to include mention of its events. In fairness to him, having to set *Heir to the Empire* after the very big events of *Dark Empire* would've necessitated a complete rewrite. So, not wanting to delay its publication, Bantam and Lucasfilm conceded to switch things up and place *Dark Empire* after the events of Zahn's forthcoming trilogy. Apart from a few hiccups in *Dark Empire* that the editors missed (e.g., referencing the Rebellion instead of the New Republic), it worked well enough.

Blissfully unaware of the behind-the-scenes drama, audiences devoured the continuation of the *Star Wars* saga, which now branched out to new time periods and characters, including those set four thousand years in the past with the *Tales of the Jedi* series, also written by Tom Veitch and Kevin J. Anderson, who followed the Thrawn trilogy (as it's now called) with his own excellent *Jedi Academy* series, building on Luke's promise to Yoda to "pass on what you have learned," tying it directly to the *Tales of the Jedi* arc being developed. Lucas was consulted about the ancient Jedi and Sith, as he was with several important aspects of the saga along the way.

Bantam-Spectra also took advantage of the desire for more *Star Wars*. Despite several missteps along the way (e.g. demanding too many rewrites of Margaret Weis's *Legacy of Doom* novel and failing to publish Kenneth C. Flint's *[The] Heart of [the] Jedi*), Bantam put out some excellent *Star Wars* stories by authors as diverse as Kathy Tyers, Barbara Hambly, Vonda McIntyre, Kristine Kathryn Rusch, and A. C. Crispin (including editors Carol Titelman, Lucy Wilson, Sue Rostoni, and Bantam's Shelly Shapiro—who in their right mind would think that there wasn't already female representation in *Star Wars*' content creation?), as well as Kevin J. Anderson, Rebecca Moesta, Roger MacBride Allen, Michael Stackpole, Michael P. Kube-McDowell, John Whitman, and others.

ROGER MACBRIDE ALLEN
(author, Corellian trilogy)

I had been looking to a post-Imperial period in the *Star Wars* universe where the Empire had collapsed and there is chaos in spots. One of the things in the real world that I was interested in were the so-called "hot spots" around the world where civil wars were popping up because the authority imposed on the population is no longer there. Basically, the story was inspired by what happened in the former Yugoslavia and Soviet Union. It's Bosnia in space. I also wanted to explore the character of Han Solo. I've always felt he was the most intriguing character, because he's the most flawed. He was never the perfect knight in shining armor. Luke is very difficult to write for, because he's so powerful and so perfect. It's tough to come up with a problem that he can't solve by waving the Force at it, while Han has to sort of muddle through like the rest of us.

KEVIN J. ANDERSON
(author, *Jedi Academy* series)

My first concept was an Imperial Weapons Research Lab that is so secret that it's locked away and doesn't even know that the war is over, kind of like Japanese soldiers on islands after World War II. I didn't want to do another one of those "last remnants of the Empire" ideas, which get tedious after a while. I thought a good way around it would be with people who are so isolated that they don't even know Darth Vader is dead. Since I worked for many years in a government nuclear weapons research lab, it seemed natural to have a secret weapons station hidden within a cluster of black holes, something so remote that nobody can get in or out unless they have a specific hyperdrive route plan. These are the people who developed the Death Star, and now they're working on something even more fun—a weapon that can blow up stars. The second plot has Luke Skywalker working to bring back the Jedi Knights. Having recognized the power of the Force in himself, Luke realizes there must be more potential Jedi out there. Obi-Wan Kenobi implied that everybody can learn how to use the Force if they have the right training. And it would seem like an obvious thing for Luke to want to bring the Jedi back.

HOWARD ROFFMAN

With all of this, continuity was an important issue to us. We felt there had to be an integrity to the program or it's not worth doing.

JOE BONGIORNO

Into this environment came something rather unique, a multimedia crossover event that would incorporate a novel, comic book series, video games, action figures, short stories, soundtrack, toys—pretty much everything except the film. It was called *Shadows of the Empire*.

Launched in 1996, just three years before the arrival of the first of the Star Wars *prequels,* The Phantom Menace, Shadows of the Empire *established a storyline set between the events of* The Empire Strikes Back *and* Return of the Jedi. *The* Shadows *storyline revolves around the galactic underworld's attempts to assassinate Luke Skywalker and get closer to the Emperor in order to take control of the Empire, as well as deal with feuding bounty hunters. The project involved the following components: a novel by Steve Perry; a video game for Nintendo 64 as well as computers; a six-part Dark Horse Comics series by John Wagner, Kilian Plunkett, and Hugh Fleming; a trading card series from Topps featuring art by the Brothers Hildebrandt, who created the famous one-sheet poster for the original* Star Wars; *the Mark Cotta Vaz trade paperback,* Secrets of the Shadows of the Empire; *and a soundtrack album composed by Joel McNeely.*

"Prince Xizor, who knew?" remarks Eric McCormack's Mark in the 1999 feature film Free Enterprise, *in the toy aisle of a Manhattan Beach Toys "R" Us, which may be the only time this* Shadows of the Empire *character ever made it to the big screen.*

BRIAN VOLK-WEISS

This is a great example of the kind of things Lucas does that I feel he doesn't get enough credit for. I've never heard of anyone else doing something like *Shadows of the Empire* in the history of original content, for lack of a better term. Lucas makes movies that are intentionally designed to have holes in them that need to be filled later. Think about it: *Clone Wars* and then *Rebels* were designed to fill in the holes between *Episode II* and *Episode III*. *Shadows of the Empire* was basically designed as a test to see how the fan base was doing. Do they still love us? But it was also designed to help keep the storytelling going. It was a multimedia play before the term even existed.

BILL SLAVICSEK

This project was one of Lucasfilm's first attempts to create an event for *Star Wars* by utilizing all of the licensees they had at the time. I was no longer actively working on *Star Wars* during this period, so I only know what I saw and experienced as a fan. They brought together novels, comics, video games, toys, and the RPG to craft an event that took place across these different mediums. It certainly generated excitement at the time and added things to the canon that are still being used today, including the Black Sun criminal organization.

PETER HOLMSTROM

I don't think people realize how revolutionary that was—the notion of cross-media storytelling. It had never been done before. There had always been tie-in material, but this was different. You could watch *Friday the 13th: Part IV,* for example, and not *need* to read the novelization to get it. Here you did. Novel, comics, video game, action figures, its very own soundtrack—each told a different angle to a larger story. That's fantastic! Fans ate it up.

STEVE PERRY

(author, *Shadows of the Empire*)

Tom Dupree at Bantam had given me a movie tie-in, *The Mask,* to write. The money wasn't great and there was a short deadline, so when I turned it in, he figured he owed me one. He offered *Shadows of the Empire* to me, if Lucasfilm thought I had the chops. Meanwhile, Mike Richardson, at Dark Horse, had me doing the first couple of *Aliens* novelizations based on their continuing graphic novels, and he bragged on me to Lucasfilm and sold them—Dark Horse was doing the *Star Wars* comics—so that's how I wound up with the job.

HOWARD ROFFMAN

We had been using three different media to spin new stories in the *Star Wars* universe and the fans were really enjoying them; it was all working really well. Even though we were paying a lot of attention to continuity so that they weren't contradicting each other, it hit us: Wouldn't it be interesting if they all complemented each other, so that we had all these media united into a single, galvanizing story? To do that, it had to be a very special story set in the time period of the original trilogy. We looked to the movies to give us our clue as to what would be interesting to explore in that time period. That's where we came up with the idea of the underworld, the organized crime empire within the *Star Wars* universe. We glimpsed it in *Empire,* where Vader hires bounty hunters.

When we thought it through, it just got more and more interesting, because if there was a head of an organized crime world, he would most likely need to exercise great influence with the Emperor. So, suddenly you have a shadowy figure who is all-powerful, head of the immensely powerful criminal organization, and who has the ear of the head of the Empire. Naturally that person could be an ally of Darth Vader—or a political infighter. It's more interesting to have him as a political infighter.

STEVE PERRY

I think Vader is more interesting in this book than he'd ever been before. I got to play with his motivations and reveal why he's doing what he's doing. I also had to show the transition of Luke from where he was in *Empire* to the beginning of *Jedi,* where he is a good enough Jedi to walk into Jabba's palace unarmed and come out alive. I also had the chance to develop a new villain, Xizor, who had to be on par with Vader. I sat down with members of Lucasfilm and developed a history for the character and his Costa Nostra–like organization, Black Sun. He's kind of like Marlon Brando in *The Godfather*, though more physically capable than Brando was in that movie. He wants to be the number-one man in the galaxy, but he's about number three. Obviously he's got a couple of major impediments in Vader and the Emperor in his efforts to get to the top. If you've seen the third movie, then I don't think it's ruining anything to say that he doesn't quite make it to the top.

HOWARD ROFFMAN

Shadows of the Empire also spawned a toy line, but we weren't looking to turn the concept into a merchandising free-for-all. That was not the idea of *Shadows*. I saw it much more as a platform for a lot of creative people to express their love for *Star Wars*. I saw it as a better version of what we'd been doing all these years with books, comics, and games. As far as I'm concerned, if a product isn't contributing something new and creative, then it's not going to happen. You look at everything we were doing, where we were making extensions, they're all areas that allow very gifted people to bring their own creativity to bear on the *Star Wars* universe.

STEVE PERRY

We had a big meeting at Skywalker Ranch, with all the players in the various departments. We had a general idea Lucasfilm wanted to explore the character of Xizor, and we went back and forth, all of us offering story ideas. I took notes, offered some characters—we couldn't use Han, so I came up with a guy who was kind of like his wild younger brother, Dash Rendar. There were certain elements the various folk wanted—the game guys wanted a motorcycle chase, the comic book guys wanted to use Boba Fett. I went home, hammered out a long outline, and then everybody read that, made notes, and eventually signed off on it. It became the basis for the toys, game, comics, musical CD, etc. I wrote a draft of the novel based on that outline and we repeated that process on the draft. I did a rewrite, and that was my part of it.

JOE BONGIORNO

It's odd that despite the huge success of *Shadows of the Empire*, Bantam didn't repeat. That would come after the license was snagged by Del Rey in 1999. Del Rey had produced seven excellent titles, *Splinter of the Mind's Eye* and Han Solo and Lando Calrissian trilogies released in the seventies and eighties, and finally came to their senses, outbidding Bantam for the license when their contract expired. Now that they regained it, they took their own bold steps to push the universe forward, not only building titles around the prequel trilogy on the way, and especially *The Clone Wars,* but pushing the narrative forward into a sprawling multibook series that would have large consequences for the main cast, starting with the death of Chewbacca in the first book of the *New Jedi Order* series, *Vector Prime.* Well-written and fueled by controversy, it proved to be another big success. This series was followed by the excellent *Legacy of the Force* and *Fate of the Jedi* series, along with several unrelated single volumes.

HOWARD ROFFMAN

The idea was that if we were going to bring *Star Wars* back as a classic, we had to give people something that adds value to the property. It's not just putting the name on something in an effort to pump up a mass market success. Everything had to have a reason for being. You really needed to be sensitive to the quality demands of your audience. In everything we were doing, that was a big concern. And we approached toys very cautiously. We had no idea if you could sustain any kind of toy presence at mass market, because the two things that seem to drive toys very much are either television and movie exposure, or television advertising. What we learned is that there was a pretty big pent-up demand for *Stars Wars* in the toy category. Overall, there were two different goals. We wanted to treat *Star Wars* the way it deserved to be treated, preserving its status as a classic. That is what we were entrusted with, and it was a long-term goal regardless of whether there would be sequels or not. The other is making sure that everything would lead into the marketing of new films. It was an interesting challenge, because it's combining something old and something new while continuing to make it relevant to people.

Meanwhile, there was an additional element that played an integral role in what would lead to the rebirth of Star Wars: *ironically it was derived from another Lucasfilm franchise, the ABC 1992–93 television series* The Young Indiana Jones Chronicles. *That show took Harrison Ford's character from the popular trilogy of feature films and told adventures of when he was a child (Corey Carrier) and a young adult (Sean Patrick Flannery). Shot all around the world with a huge budget, it revolutionized digital effects and, even more importantly, seemed to reignite Lucas's passion for filmmaking.*

By 1992, Lucas had become intensely interested in education and was developing interactive technology that would make it more interesting for young students to learn history and geography. He came up with an idea for an educational CD-ROM he called Walking Through Time with Indiana Jones, *but he liked it so much that he decided to turn it into a television series, writing the story for the pilot episode and outlines for the rest of the series himself.*

GEORGE LUCAS

I'm known for doing big-budget projects. What most people don't understand is that I'm usually doing a $70 or $80 million picture for $40 million. A lot of this [*Young Indiana Jones* series] was an experiment because of the problems in feature production in keeping costs down. It was a way to work through certain ideas and experiment on a smaller scale.

NICK LAWS

(assistant director, *Young Indiana Jones Chronicles*)
The producer Rick McCallum took so many bold, innovative decisions and it's amazing what was achieved. He and George Lucas wanted to get away from the feature film "circus" of a big crew and wanted to do it with a small "guerrilla" team going in to each country using local crew and resources. I worked on episodes in Spain, Italy, Kenya, Turkey, and what was then Czechoslovakia. Even now on productions, I try to think of how a production can work more simply and efficiently. That is the legacy of *Young Indy*. In the beginning it was fun, and we worked really hard in amazing locations and situations.

FRANK DARABONT

(writer, *The Young Indiana Jones Chronicles, The Shawshank Redemption*)
I think his passion for the project grew out of a new-found liberty. I think he and Lucasfilm had finally reached a level of prosperity—both creatively and financially—that would allow him to step from CEO duties and concentrate on being a filmmaker again. I think he was coming out of ten years' worth of, "Okay, I've got to build this empire and make sense of it. I've got to make this machinery run." Without such guidance, companies like Lucasfilm tend to erode after a while and it needed a steady hand at the tiller. I think he was now putting on his filmmaker hat again after waiting awhile, and this was his means of getting his feet wet. This was my understanding from talking to George and others at Skywalker Ranch during the creative process. *Young Indy* was George really hopping up on the horse, picking up the shield and sword, and saying, "We're filmmakers again! We've been businessmen for too long!"

While many today look at the period of '83 to '99 as a quiet time for Lucasfilm, it was actually one of their most productive. Lucas served as active producer and financier for a number of ambitious film projects, from Willow (1988) *and* Labyrinth (1986) *to the continuation of the Indiana Jones franchise in film and television, as well as founding the now legendary film company Pixar.*

There would, however, be one more stop on the journey to those films: the so-called Special Editions of the original Star Wars trilogy. It's no secret that Lucas is and always has been a perfectionist. In the 1970s he had battled studio indifference combined with budget and time constraints and come out the other side with the film fantasy that changed the face of Hollywood. But even with the glowing reviews and Oscar nominations he'd received for Star Wars and the film's mammoth box office take, he was always pained by what he perceived as its flaws. It's why, in 1997, twenty years after the initial release of the first film in the saga, he released a $10 million update as the Special Editions, which presented the original trilogy with enhanced miniature and optical effects and editing changes that also allowed him to do R&D for the potential prequel trilogy that lay ahead.

In a strange way, the seeds for the Special Editions were being planted shortly after Lucas had completed work on the original Star Wars trilogy. It was at that point that he established the Lucasfilm computer graphics division, though its intent was originally very different than creating virtually anything you could imagine.

GEORGE LUCAS

I put together the computer division in 1978 or '79 to develop a nonlinear editing system, a laser printer, and a more efficient rendering technology. We were able to do all of that, which allowed us to actually begin using computers to do 3D animation, rather than just wireframes, which was the level of the technology then. We were trying to develop an efficient system for getting the images in and out of the digital domain, as well as technology to manipulate the images once we got them into the digital domain, and a postsystem that would allow us to edit everything together and tell the story. We were basically trying to digitize the entire process. I don't know that I had a complete idea of the level at which things would shift. You take one step at a time. I knew that the editing process and the postprocess were very antiquated and cumbersome, and that doing it electronically was much easier.

DENNIS MUREN

(visual effects supervisor, Star Wars Special Editions)
The Star Wars stuff was state of the art then, but by the 1990s it was looking a little shaky. George said on Star Wars that we achieved 30 percent of what we really wanted to do and I'm not sure we even achieved 30 percent. Looking at it, the film had the same kind of funkiness that time has given our perception of King Kong.

GEORGE LUCAS

You know, if you go back and you check the interviews of when I made the movie, and everybody said, "Oh, this is so . . . ," I said, "Well, it didn't turn out very well. It's only about 40 percent of what I wanted it to be. I'm really disappointed in it." In every interview, relentlessly, right through the thing.

DENNIS MUREN

I remember first hearing that they were going to rerelease the movies in anticipation of the new series of films. A few weeks later, I heard that George was going to add some scenes that he had always wanted to do, and fix some things up. I felt we could improve the matte edges on some shots that had been done at the last minute—particularly those involving explosions. But there were also a number of shots in the space battle where the movements just weren't right. If we could smooth them out, the action would have more clarity, and viewers would also be able to follow the movie a little better. I suggested digitally redoing shots in which the models were moving incorrectly.

RICK MCCALLUM
(producer, *Star Wars* Special Editions)

On *Young Indy*, we wanted to set a template for a way to make features, and with the Special Editions we were applying that template to the existing *Star Wars* trilogy and the prequels. For the redo, we didn't change anything more or less than what George wanted. There have been special editions of other films that directors have gone back to, to restore the cut the studio took away from them, but nobody's ever gone back to reshoot and augment those things that they clearly saw, but couldn't achieve at the time. It's such a romantic vision.

BRIAN JAY JONES
(author, *George Lucas: A Life*)

From a fan perspective, I've never really been happy with the Special Editions. But then I'm going to walk that back a little bit, because I remember sitting in the theater watching the original *Star Wars* and loved it. But the problem with Lucas is he can never leave well enough alone. He has to go back and screw with it again and again and again. He just keeps doing that with these movies. So from a professional standpoint, it's brilliant, because what Lucas is doing is he's sending out his new digital technology on a test run in a movie that he knows isn't going to lose any money.

JEANINE BASINGER
(film historian, founder and curator of the Cinema Archives
of Wesleyan University)

People tend to want directors to make the same movie again and again. Like if Hitchcock tried something different, they were always mad at him. I always say, let them play and experiment and we may get something better. But here, it didn't make things better. I want my movie experience, I'm not interested in the new director's cut, except intellectually. I want to go to see my movie that I saw when I saw my movie. I once had an experience with Frank Capra when I was showing *Mr. Smith Goes to Washington* to my class and was projecting for myself in the booth. He came in during the scene where Jimmy Stewart's finding the letters, one of the great scenes of American movie history, right? And he goes up to the window in the booth there and he starts talking to himself, muttering and stamping his feet and getting mad. I mean, I could see him getting mad and I was like, "Have I not got it in focus?" I asked him what it was, and he said, "I never should have cut that way, I should have done it this way . . . ," and he was already remaking the movie in his head. One of the great movies and a great scene, but now he's seeing a different way to do it. But should you remake them? I think you should just let them be. I respect George Lucas; let him do what he wants with his own movie. But you know what? I'd rather have my movie.

DALE POLLOCK
(author, *Skywalking: The Life and Films of George Lucas*)

What artist goes back and continually alters their work? Who does this to their movies? And in his mind, he would keep doing that as long as he felt like it, because they were his work. This was really kind of his degree of selfish proprietor. It's like, "This is one of my films. I paid for it. I earned the money for it. I could do what I want with it. And if I want to keep changing it, I'll keep changing it." What work of art has been finished, released, and then starts getting altered? No novelist does that with their book. No painter does that with their painting. Beethoven doesn't say, "You know, I'm pulling that back and changing it." And the more people were outraged, I think in a perverse way the more he enjoyed it.

PETER HOLMSTROM
"Art is never completed, just abandoned." Plenty of novelists, painters, musicians, etc. go back and alter their work through the years, always in search of perfection. Frank Herbert's *Dune* added a whole chapter when it was first published in novel form; the alterations to *Lord of the Rings*, *The Hobbit*, and *The Chronicles of Narnia* are well documented; *A Room with a View* added a whole nihilistic

ending as the author aged; Da Vinci is said to have wandered the countryside and touched up his work up until his death. And how about the Bible? Filmmaking is different, because artists aren't given complete control over their work. Investors control the art, not the artist. George Lucas didn't have that problem. So I applaud him for creating his final cuts. And you know what? When you really dissect the motivations for those changes down—they come from a place of story. He creates an active ticking clock for Han Solo with the Jabba the Hutt scene, he populates Mos Eisley to justify the very populated cantina and create a firm start to act 2—literally, "entering the larger world." He turns Cloud City into an actual city in the clouds as opposed to the underground bunker it was before, and fills out the world with the end celebration in *Jedi*.

GEORGE LUCAS

Special effects don't make a movie. The story makes the movie. And all the special effects do is allow you to tell a particular story.

TOM KENNEDY
(visual effects producer, *Star Wars* Special Editions)

George had said, "As long as we're going to rerelease *Star Wars*, I always wanted to redo the shots in Mos Eisley, because we had this one shoot in this little town and it just wasn't big enough." So we went back initially to redo Mos Eisley and then we decided to do one matte painting of the Sand Crawler and then to add Jabba's scene with Han Solo—that was the scope of what we started with. We started out doing about two dozen shots.

GEORGE LUCAS

In the case of the Jabba the Hutt scene, it was a scene that worked and could've been in the movie, but at the same time, at that point in history, ILM was coping with so much work, and it was a brand-new company and we were way behind schedule. To add that sequence, which was a stop-motion sequence which we hadn't done too much of at that time, just would've broken the back of the operation. We could never have finished the film.

RICK MCCALLUM

The Jabba the Hutt scene took over four months to do, with all the resources that we have available to us. And to take four, five, or six months at that time would have been suicide.

While the Jabba the Hutt from Return of the Jedi *was a giant slug-like puppet, the original Jabba that was filmed with Harrison Ford and then cut from* Star

Wars *was a portly Scottish actor, Declan Mulholland, in a furry vest. Lucas realized the only way to add the grotesque extraterrestrial of* Jedi *into the deleted* Star Wars *shots was via digital technology, and to do so he turned to animator Steve "Spaz" Williams and CG supervisor Joe Letteri. Their first meeting with Lucas about the rebirth of Jabba led to some interesting alterations of the character as he appeared in* Return of the Jedi.

JOE LETTERI
(CG supervisor, *Star Wars* Special Editions)

George wanted to put Jabba on a floating anti-gravity couch, because that's how we saw him in Jedi. But there were two problems with that: one, in the original scene Harrison Ford was talking to this guy who was shorter than him, so his eyes are looking down. And, two, having Jabba just sort of floating around was not quite so interesting. So we thought, "Why not just put him on the ground?" A sea lion was the model we used, because Jabba had to throw his weight forward, bring his tail up and then push off with it in order to move. We wanted him to have this big, thrusting-his-weight-forward movement, like his tail was just solid muscle, so he'd feel really massive and really menacing. Steve Williams and I were partners on this. We tend to work like the director and director of photography. It fell on me to figure out what the inside of Jabba's mouth and his tongue would look like, how much drool there should be on his chin—all that kind of stuff. I used the *Return of the Jedi* Jabba's textures for reference. I adapted the "shaders" I designed for *Jurassic Park*'s T. rex for Jabba's skin and surface textures. I wanted his eyes to be totally different. I used some new eye techniques I came up with for *Casper* to give him cat eyes. That varied from the original Jabba, but I wanted something a little more organic than those glass eyes the *Jedi* puppet had. George just said, "Go for it!" He liked the eyes.

Lucas made one last-minute addition to the sequence: As Jabba rejoins his henchmen after his conversation with Han Solo, a familiar bounty hunter (Boba Fett) follows the overlord out.

JOE LETTERI

One day, when we were midway into the shot, George said, "I woke up last night and thought, 'Boba Fett should walk on right about now!'" So we dug up the Boba Fett costume, put it on one of our animators, and then set up a blue-screen shoot and put him in there. That seemed like a good time to introduce Boba Fett. George was definitely going back and reweaving the threads.

And then there's the most controversial change of all. In the Mos Eisley cantina, Han sits at a table with the alien Greedo and, recognizing his life is in danger, shoots him from under the table. In the Special Edition, suddenly Greedo shoots first so that Han doesn't seem like such a bad guy. Decades later, it seems that Lucas is the only one satisfied with that change that most everyone else found very "maclunkey."

GEORGE LUCAS

It was always meant that Greedo fired first. And in the original film you don't get that too well. And then there was a discussion about, well, it's good that it's left amorphous and everything. But basically in terms of Han's character and everything, I don't like the fact that when he was introduced, the first thing he did was just gun somebody down in cold blood. We had three different versions of that shot. In one, he fires very close to when Han fires. And one was three frames later. We sort of looked at it and tried to figure out which would be perceivable but wouldn't, you know, look corny.

While Star Wars *boasted the majority of the changes, a succession of smaller changes marked the subsequent installments, including swapping out the Clive Revill–voiced Emperor for Ian McDiarmid, who had portrayed the nefarious Palpatine in the flesh for* Return of the Jedi.

IAN MCDIARMID
(actor, "Emperor Sheev Palpatine")

George felt that it was just and proper. When he made *Empire,* we hadn't met and he didn't have a particular idea of who would play the Emperor or how the character would develop. And he had no notion that he would do the backstory—*Episodes I, II,* and *III.* So whoever played the Emperor in a mask and added to Revill's voice wouldn't seem authentic to the people who are going to watch the entire saga in the right order. It wouldn't make any sense. Since I was the Emperor in the other films, it felt appropriate that I should be inserted in *Empire,* and that's what George did.

In addition to the visual effects work, the Special Edition of A New Hope *allowed John Williams to revisit some themes previously abandoned in the original film.*

JOE KRAEMER

(composer, *Mission Impossible: Rogue Nation* and *Jack Reacher*)

A couple of fascinating glimpses into "what might have been" can be found on the Special Edition soundtrack CDs from 1997. The first is a set of alternate takes of the "Main Title," including one that would have an orchestral chord that starts in the black and builds to the cut to the title *Star Wars*—this chord was actually used in the opening credits of *The Making of Star Wars* TV special that aired after the film came out. The second is Williams's first version of the music for the iconic scene where Luke looks at the twin sunset. The music in this original take is much darker, and although I firmly believe that George Lucas did not intend for Darth Vader to actually be Luke's father until he was well into writing *The Empire Strikes Back*, this music would almost lead one to believe it had been in the cards all along!

A piece of music had been written for the first half of the trash-compactor sequence, where Luke is dragged underwater by the Dianoga, but it went unused in the final version of the movie. However, it was repurposed in the Special Edition of the film in 1997 for the extended footage of the Landspeeder ride into Mos Eisley.

For the restored scene of Han Solo and Jabba the Hutt, music from *Return of the Jedi* was edited and tracked into the soundtrack, allowing the film to use Jabba's Theme, even though it hadn't been composed at the time the film was originally released.

While finishing unfinished art was paramount in George Lucas's mind, the Special Editions also allowed for some much needed R&D for the proposed new trilogy of films—ones that were always going to be more visually demanding than their predecessors.

JOHN KNOLL

(visual effects supervisor, Industrial Light & Magic)

I think probably more than half the reason for doing this in the first place was as a trial run for the prequels. If you look at the kinds of things George had us working on, they were experiments about, "What's it going to be like doing a show with this many extras in it? What does a typical space battle shot cost? What does it cost to take a live-action scene and put two big CG creatures in the background?" They were very carefully tracking the actual production costs of doing that work, I think to accurately budget the *Star Wars* prequels.

GEORGE LUCAS

One of the reasons I did the *Star Wars* prequels was that the technology had gotten to the point where there was, again, a lot of thrill involved. I've loved movies and making films and telling stories all my life, but I've struggled with special effects and all of the photographic problems. To suddenly have those things solved and be able to change things with a computer is like being set free after having been tied down for [so many] years.

In retooling The Empire Strikes Back, *Lucas exercised the right of executive privilege and chose not to consult director Irvin Kershner on the changes he had planned for the film.*

GEORGE LUCAS

He didn't have any input, but I told him what was happening. Of the three films, *Empire* is the one that has the fewest changes. Some of the alterations were things that Kersh had suggested back when the film was made, when I had been forced to say, "Kersh, we're out of money, we're out of time, we've got to come home, I'm sorry."

IRVIN KERSHNER
(director, *The Empire Strikes Back*)

I don't like the idea of upgrading the effects, because I feel that they are already in a way primitive and they're beautiful because of it. Look at *Forbidden Planet*: it's a primitive film as science fiction, but the story is exciting and you look at it as an artifact. I think it's wrong, but George always has his reasons and his ideas. He's very, very bright and certainly a showman.

Changes for the Special Edition of Return of the Jedi *allowed Lucas's original vision for the sequence in Jabba's palace to be more fully captured, which was far more extensive.*

There was perhaps the most visually impressive inclusion of all: a montage of planetary celebrations after the defeat of the Empire, with masses of CG extras carousing on the planets of Bespin, Tatooine, and Endor. There's also a fourth world that audiences will view for the first time, one which plays a dramatic role in the upcoming trilogy: Coruscant. The Metropolis-*style galactic capital, which the Emperor of the Universe calls home, was originally visualized by concept artist Ralph McQuarrie.*

TOM HUTCHINSON
(computer graphics supervisor, *The Empire Strikes Back*)

We start up high, looking down at the Emperor's city—a huge, spread-out metropolis. Then we tilt down through the buildings until we reach the ground plane, where we see crowds, confetti, and a huge parade. One of the things we were told right up front was that we would hopefully be able to apply some of the things we learned on *Empire* and *Jedi* to the new prequels. While budget and time considerations didn't really allow the Special Edition films to serve as R&D projects, I think George wishes we could have taken more of that kind of approach. Still, we learned tremendous amounts of information that we could use in the R&D stage on the prequels.

At the time of the release of the Special Editions, it wasn't clear exactly what would happen to the original versions, though they've never been officially rereleased. The last sanctioned releases were on THX laser disc and a substandard DVD reissue as a bonus feature, which was a remaster of the previous laser disc reissues. Industrious fans, however, have re-created and remastered the original cuts off vintage film prints and the laser discs to make them available on illegal file-sharing sites throughout the galaxy for other fans who are clever enough to find them.

JASON WARD
(webmaster, makingstarwars.net)

After *Return of the Jedi,* I think one of the factors for George Lucas not continuing at the time was exhaustion. And then, and I'm not sure how much of this is true, but there is a rumor that in the divorce Marcia Lucas got half of the money from Lucasfilm, which crippled the company and prevented them from making *Star Wars* movies comfortably. It's supposedly the reason that *Willow* was done with a studio. Another rumor is that when he did the Special Editions, that actually cut some of her divorce payments. Money from those versions supposedly doesn't go to her anymore. That's one of the reasons the films were changed and will never go back. I've heard this so many times; I don't know if it's urban legend, but supposedly the divorce agreement was for the original films and the Special Editions do not count towards that.

GEORGE LUCAS

For people who ask me what will happen to the original versions of the films, there will only be one version. And it won't be what I would call the "rough cut," it'll be the "final cut." The other one will be some kind of interesting artifact that people will look at and say, "There was an earlier draft of this?" The same thing happens with plays and earlier drafts of books. In essence, films never get finished, they get abandoned. At some point, you're dragged off the picture kicking and screaming while somebody says, "Okay, it's done." That isn't really the way it should be. Occasionally you can go back and get your cut of the video out there, which I did on both *American Graffiti* and *THX 1138*; that's the place where it will live forever. So what ends up being important in my mind is what the home video version is going to look like, because that's what everybody is going to remember. The other version will disappear. Even the thirty-five million tapes of *Star Wars* out there won't last more than thirty or forty years. A hundred years from now, the only version of the movie that anyone will remember will be the Special Edition, and you'll be able to project it on a large screen with perfect quality. I think it's the director's prerogative, not the studio's, to go back and reinvent a movie.

BRIAN JAY JONES

It's funny, but I was working in the U.S. Senate around the time of the Special Editions. One of the big moments in digital technology was when they did the vacuum cleaner commercial with Fred Astaire dancing with a vacuum cleaner. They had removed, I guess, his partner; I can't remember the whole story, but people were like, "This is dangerous technology. They're going to make it look like things happened that never did." They had people who were actually nervous about this technology from both a copyright standpoint and a creative standpoint. You actually do hit this moment where people are like, "I'm not sure if this is a good idea."

Part Three

THE PREQUELS

1999–2005

10

DUEL OF THE FATES:
THE PHANTOM MENACE

"And you, Young Skywalker, we will watch your career with great interest."

There was a decade of relative quiet in the *Star Wars* universe following the 1983 release of *Return of the Jedi*. But then, in the early nineties came a variety of new products, not the least of which was Timothy Zahn's bestselling novel *Heir to the Empire*, culminating with the release of the Special Editions in 1997. In between those events, George Lucas had taken the first steps in bringing the long-awaited prequel trilogy to the screen (though many doubted it was something he would do or they would ever see).

DAN MADSEN
(owner, the Official Lucasfilm/Star Wars Fan Club, 1987–2001)
I got word from Lucasfilm [that they were doing *The Phantom Menace*]. Funny thing is, I did so many interviews with George for the *Star Wars Insider* magazine. As you can imagine, every interview, one of the questions that was there was, "When are you going to get back to *Star Wars*?" And, every time, he'd kind of look at me and laugh, "Oh, I'm planning on eventually getting back to it. I'm playing around with this and that." And I always remember leaving his office thinking, "Crap." I was hoping he'd say, "I'm starting on it next year!" Well, "When, George, when?!" It was always kind of a disappointment. So I finally got the word from Lucasfilm that he had actually gotten serious, and was going to do prequels—which surprised me, to be honest, because I thought he was going to do sequels. So, when I first got word he was going to do prequels, I was like, "*Really?*"

Official work on the prequels began in 1994. Though their general concept had been in existence since the original films, Lucas actually started writing the screenplay for the first film in November of that year, taking about two years to complete it. Unlike the original trilogy, the prequel trilogy would need to have more continuity between episodes, meaning that the first film had to set up its two sequels. This trilogy would allow Lucas the opportunity to flesh out the themes of balance and symbiotic relationship between man and nature that he had briefly touched upon in the originals. On top of that, it would provide the opportunity for him to tell a story the way he wanted to without any studio interference, and chronicle how the innocent, young Anakin Skywalker became the Dark Lord of the Sith, Darth Vader.

GEORGE LUCAS

(executive producer, screenwriter/director, *The Phantom Menace*)

This is the one time I was able to sit down and basically let my imagination run wild and not be hampered by, "Oh, I can't do this, I can't do that, I can't go to Coruscant, I'll never be able to do the buildings, I can't do a podrace, because that's impossible." I dream up whatever I wanted and for the most part, was able to pull it all off.

It was basically my movie that I had been working on for twenty years. I was telling a story I wanted to tell. I did things that in certain cases might seem unconventional, that I knew I might get killed for, but I was doing what *I* wanted to do and making it the way *I* wanted to make it. I work in this great odd genre that doesn't really exist. It's a miniseries done with feature-length films, and it's not done as one unit—it's done as what would eventually be forty years. It was ultimately twelve hours of just one story, broken into a bunch of pieces, but it's just one book. Nobody had ever really done that.

There was another undeniable fact about 1994: it was the year when it became clear a new Star Wars *trilogy would actually come to fruition—consisting of* The Phantom Menace *(Episode I, 1999),* Attack of the Clones *(Episode II, 2002), and* Revenge of the Sith *(Episode III, 2005)—not only for those who grew up on the original films in theaters, but those whose experience had been limited to VHS or broadcast airings without a* Star Wars *they could call their own. What this would ultimately mean for the films themselves in terms of reception was unclear at the time, but the ability to move forward came down to advancements in visual effects pioneered by Lucasfilm's Industrial Light & Magic.*

First, there was The Young Indiana Jones Chronicles *television series and* The Radioland Murders, *which served as proof positive for Lucas that virtual sets—either fully CG or extended versions of practical ones—could be created that looked as genuine as the real thing. Even more importantly, in 1993 there* was Steven Spielberg's Jurassic Park, *which brought prehistoric creatures to un-precedented life. Not only would this lead to the* Star Wars *Special Editions, but the CG creatures that would populate the new trilogy, an example being* The Phantom Menace's *Jar Jar Binks—who would turn out to be a polarizing figure . . . to put it mildly.*

GEORGE LUCAS

At the time I went into the [*Young Indiana Jones*] TV series, on the [feature] film end it just costs so much to do everything, because film has about seven times more resolution [than video], which brings it up to roughly ten times the cost. But on the TV series, I was able to work in a much lower-res medium; we were able to move things around much more quickly and cheaply, so I could use [digital technology] more often. I said, "I want to be able to do a couple hundred shots in every hour-long episode and still have a budget that's under $50,000." I wanted to be able to play with this stuff and see how it worked. In the end, we made twenty-two "feature films" in the space of five years, and we experimented with all kinds of things. Some things worked, some didn't. We learned a lot in the process. The TV show was really a test bed for the *Star Wars* Special Editions.

RICK MCCALLUM
(producer, *Young Indiana Jones Chronicles*, prequel trilogy)
We were trying to set up a template in the early nineties with *Young Indiana Jones*. It was about figuring out how we were going to make the prequels for the money that we wanted to spend. We were financing them ourselves, just like we did the marketing and distribution all by ourselves. When we were working on the Special Editions, it was about how far we could push things like ILM in terms of the things that we wanted to do. It was wonderful, but weird.

GAVIN BOCQUET
(production designer, *Young Indiana Jones Chronicles*, prequel trilogy)
TV production is a much faster process than film, which is something we brought over from *Young Indy*. You shoot one hour of film in two weeks, whereas with a feature film you generally shoot two hours of film over a twenty-week period. So, the speed and application of the design work is much faster-paced on a TV show. You are living very much on instinctive decision-making as there isn't much time to pontificate about ideas. Also, you have a different director for every two-week shoot, so you are continually making decisions about locations and sets on different episodes with different

directors and often in different countries. I think on all the *Young Indiana Jones Chronicles* shows we touched down in over fifty different countries, so it was a mad two years.

DAVID TATTERSALL
(director of photography, *Young Indiana Jones Chronicles*, prequel trilogy)

Young Indy was a fruitful testing ground for CG effects work. On that project, logging hours in a Quantel Harry [editing] suite proved far more frugal than working practically. The main lesson we learned on the series was that we had a lot more control over our locations in that with a little digital help, we could erase or replace what we had. For instance, a lot of the episodes were shot in Prague, in what is now the Czech Republic. We could use it as a double for most European cities, like Paris or Vienna, simply by having the skyline changed. Another important thing was learning how to replicate crowds: to make twenty-five soldiers look like an army, for example. That type of thing seems very straightforward now, but it was a great innovation at the time and cost-effective.

BRIAN JAY JONES
(author, *George Lucas: A Life*)

Lucas was like, "Everything I've been doing up to now was prelude." He was running his experiments in public, which is actually a dangerous thing to do. He did *Radioland Murders* and it didn't work; that movie bombed horribly. There's a decent movie there, but they were trying to do too many things. One of those things was digital technology and it really shows in there. It's kind of like when he was doing *Red Tails* years later. If you watch *Red Tails*, it doesn't look finished. The effects of it are just awful for a story that he thought was so important to tell. It looks like somebody did the CGI over a weekend; it's just terrible. The whole point is that it's dangerous to do your experimenting in public, but Lucas did it. And then Spielberg is the one who's like, "Wait till I get my hands on that technology!" And *he's* the one that proves that audiences were going to go for it.

GEORGE LUCAS

With ILM, we were pushing digital animation, which really reached its culmination with *Jurassic Park*. We did a test for Steven Spielberg and when we put it up on the screen, I had tears in my eyes. It was one of those moments in history like the invention of the light bulb or the first telephone call.

RICK MCCALLUM

I remember a wonderful moment when George was supervising *Jurassic Park*. He saw the first Dennis Muren run-bys of the T. rex and he was just *so* excited, because, finally, a character could be created that could interact seamlessly with live actors; a character that you *believed* was real and terrifying. He knew that was the start of creating creatures that you could actually care about and empathize with, that had all the human qualities and fallibility that we do. Once that happened, he said, "Okay, I am ready." *That* was the turning point.

GEORGE LUCAS

A major gap had been crossed, and things were never going to be the same. You just can't see them as anything but real. It's just impossible. Maybe years from now they'll look clumsy, but I'm not sure even that will happen. I think we may have reached a level here where we have actually created reality, which of course is what we've been trying to do all along. That was when we sort of jumped the fence and said, "My God, we can do this." And since then, the issue of digital animation and creating characters and being able to manipulate and move things has completely changed the way we think about film. It's just a completely different medium than it was before, and that's very liberating; it's a better, more efficient way of using the resources.

LIAM NEESON
(actor, "Qui-Gon Jinn")

The digital aspect is exciting and I think it was a new toy. *The Phantom Menace* would be assessed in terms of how the relationships work. When you think of *Mary Poppins* and such, you think, "Wow, isn't that cute! Look, Dick Van Dyke is dancing with a penguin." Then there's the next stage and there will be another stage. But I don't think that actors and actresses will ever be done away with.

KEVIN J. ANDERSON
(author, *Jedi Academy* series)

Lucas's mindset has always been to change the way cinema works. A lot of it has been behind the scenes, like with the THX sound system and film transfer technology. One of the scariest things for me when I thought of them working on a new trilogy is that they would have such enormous shoes to fill. I could imagine how that might have been a part of the reluctance to doing the next movies. What could you do to top the existing trilogy? Special effects are one aspect of it, but not all.

ALAN DEAN FOSTER

(author, *Star Wars* novelization and the sequel, *Splinter of the Mind's Eye*)

Everybody has their own personal *Star Wars*—no matter how many times you've seen the existing films, or read relevant books. It's like when you're reading a comic strip, and you're imagining the voices of the characters in your head, and then somebody does an animated version of it and the voices are never right, because they're not the voices you hear in your head. It's the same in *Star Wars*—characters never seem to react the way that you want. It's a wonderful thing that the viewers get so involved with these characters. And these are characters—they're not real people.

ASHLEY ECKSTEIN

(voice actress, "Ahsoka Tano," *Star Wars: The Clone Wars*)

The prequel trilogy introduced *Star Wars* to a new generation. And the reason *Star Wars* is so popular today is because you have the original-generation *Star Wars* fans. Then you have the prequel generation of *Star Wars* fans, and now you have the *Clone Wars* generation of *Star Wars* fans.

No matter what anyone wants to say, the prequels are so special to that generation of fans, and that's why everyone gets so passionate, is because it was the same experience people had back in 1977. There were kids that had the same experience with *Episode I, II,* and *III.* And then kids that haven't even seen the movies have the same experience with *Clone Wars.*

RICK MCCALLUM

George is very ruthless about technology just supporting the story. We were going through an evolutionary stage in filmmaking where people (directors, writers, producers) were just learning how to deal with the things they can actually achieve on-screen. It's just like when sound or color first came out. You get so obsessed with what you can do that often you've got a great script, but you get so hung up about the twenty-minute action sequence that nobody's ever seen before, that everybody's efforts go to *that.* You're not sure how to make it work and it gets to be a huge thing and everybody is obsessed by it, because they don't know conceptually how it's all going to come together. Even today, if you have a fantastic set-piece, but you've forgotten about the characters, the story, and the themes of the movie, you've lost the audience.

KEVIN J. ANDERSON

Think about the opening scene of *Star Wars*: Those were some nice effects, nice moving ships and everything, but I think it was the artistic eye that Lucas brought to it that made it the cinematic moment it was. *Flash Gordon* couldn't have dangled a ship that kept coming and coming and coming in front of the camera. The Star Destroyer sequence wasn't any fundamentally new technology, it was just a different way of looking at something.

BRIAN JAY JONES

In a way, what was scary about the Special Editions as far as paving the way for the prequels is when he goes into them, when we're on Tatooine and they're going to Mos Eisley. Ben Kenobi is talking to people and they're now robots, with little droids buzzing around his head. Then there are creatures in the background floating, Jawas falling off creatures. This is exactly the way Lucas operates. This is why, when you get to *The Phantom Menace* and especially in *Attack of the Clones*, which I just think is a terrible movie, there was *so much* on the screen—so much shit going on—that you can't tell what's happening. You can't follow the story. You can't follow the chase sequences. You don't know what's going on, because Lucas is just throwing everything he can up on the screen. He's so excited to have that technology finally working—God bless him, he invented it; it's *his* technology—that he's having the best time as a filmmaker.

JONATHAN RINZLER
(nonfiction editor, Lucasfilm, 2002–2017)

I hope for people who study his work, they come away with knowledge of something that is so often badly done today in movies—which are action scenes. The action scene is just as important as any other scene. It almost seems like people's brains go out the window when it comes to action scenes [these days]. Just the fact that somebody's fighting doesn't make an action scene exciting. Obviously, there has to be emotional content. One of the things I love about George is—and I've watched him do this, I've sat with him for hours and hours and hours as he directed the animatics on *Episode III*—is that every shot, even if that shot was less than a second long, it was designed to the nth degree. It wasn't that he put too much stuff in it, it's just that it was wonderfully designed in terms of how it connected to what came before, how it connects to what came afterwards. He was very concerned that the audience understands what was happening. He'd be telling the animatic guys sometimes, "Well, they have to go from left to right, or it has to be bigger so people can follow it." He was really concerned that the eight-year-old in the audience could understand what was happening, and why it was happening, and how it advances the story. It's very rare for there to be an action shot in the Lucas action scenes that is not somehow advancing the story of that action scene.

PETER HOLMSTROM
(cohost, *The Rebel & the Rogue* podcast)

Lucas was first out the gate with digital technology and he was really thrown under the bus for that. It's a shame. You go back and look at the early sound films, and the acting is terrible by today's standards. Even *Citizen Kane* has some cringy performances. Because actors had been trained in the silent era to convey emotion with their body, or on the stage to project their voices for the people in the back. It took time. But we forgive those efforts, because we see them in the context with which they were made. People don't give Lucas that. Actors were on blue screen for the first time, with all new technology—it'd throw anyone. But now Robert Downey, Jr., hasn't worn a scrap of metal since '08, and no one blinks an eye. We wouldn't have Marvel films if it wasn't for George Lucas.

JOHN KENNETH MUIR
(author, *Science Fiction and Fantasy Films of the 1970s*)

I felt that this flaw—Lucas's desire to fill every shot with CGI creations—was more evident in the Special Edition releases of the original trilogy in the late nineties. Perhaps because I was so familiar with those films, I found it very distracting, for example, in the Special Edition of *Episode IV: A New Hope,* to see all those additions. The prequels had the same problem, but perhaps because I hadn't seen the films, I didn't find the flaw as distracting.

KYLE NEWMAN
(director, *Fanboys*)

The prequels came out right after *The Matrix,* and all of a sudden *Matrix* was pushing all these technological boundaries and you were seeing all types of new visuals, and then you get a *Star Wars* movie and it's gone back to kind of objective kind of framing. And everyone that summer was like, "Oh, I wanted it to be cooler." You're twenty now. You're twenty-five. You're twenty-eight. You're thirty-five. Shut up. You're being selfish. Look at it as a kid.

The writing of the Star Wars *prequels officially began on November 1, 1994, with Lucas taking the fifteen-page outline he had written in 1976, which was actually intended to allow him to track the backstories of the different characters and events that took place prior to the original trilogy—some of which had been hinted at in those films.*

GEORGE LUCAS
When I have an idea for a character, usually the character comes alive and metamorphoses into something else, or another kind of character. If you take

the first draft of *Star Wars,* you can find the central characters that always existed, but they had different names, shapes, or sizes. But the core of the character is still there and growing. It's just trying to find the right persona to carry forward that personality.

RAY MORTON
(senior editor, *Script* magazine)

When Lucas subtitled the films in the original trilogy *Episodes IV to VI,* he created the expectation that we would someday get to see *Episodes I to III.* In interviews done at the time of the original trilogy, he stated that he had all of the stories for these early episodes worked out in detail. This was not true—he had many *ideas,* but no concrete narratives. In ensuing years, Lucas would sometimes suggest different possibilities as to what the first three films might be about. At one time he mused they would be stand-alone stories, with *Episode I* telling the origin of the Jedi Knights. In the early 1990s, when he was finally ready to make new *Star Wars* movies, Lucas decided that *Episodes I to III* would be a trilogy about the early years of Obi-Wan Kenobi and Anakin Skywalker/Darth Vader.

The story outlined by Ben Kenobi in the original *Star Wars* would have been a strong tale to tell: Obi-Wan Kenobi and Anakin Skywalker are Jedi Knights and best friends. Obi-Wan takes on a young apprentice named Darth Vader (perhaps over Anakin's objections) and begins to train him to become a Jedi. At some point, Vader turns to the dark side of the Force and becomes evil. He then kills off most of the Jedi, including Anakin (thus orphaning Anakin's infant son). Vader and Obi-Wan fight and Vader eventually falls into a pit of lava and is horribly scarred. However, Vader survives and is encased in a permanent life-support system. Feeling responsible for Anakin's death, a guilt-ridden Obi-Wan goes into hiding to watch over his friend's young son while Vader helps the Emperor conquer the galaxy. Someday, Obi-Wan and Vader will meet again for a final showdown. Again, *that's* a strong tale.

However, that story became an impossible one to tell once Lucas decided to make Vader Luke's father. At this point, it became inevitable that any prequel film or films would have to tell the story of how noble pilot and Jedi, loyal best friend, and loving husband and father Anakin Skywalker became the evil Darth Vader.

ALAN DEAN FOSTER

I feel that the first three episodes—*Episode I, II,* and *III*—are an attempt to justify the end of *Empire* when Vader tells Luke he's his father. That's a lot of material needed to justify *one* story twist. It's not that Anakin wasn't an interesting character—this is just a personal thing—but I like Darth Vader. He was really a bad guy. It's like, I enjoy *Garfield* better when he's just a cat talking about stuff, laying around like an actual cat. But that's just me.

JOHN KENNETH MUIR

The first film [*The Phantom Menace*] is much more intriguing and successful than many other reviewers claim or viewers consider. Virtually every key relationship in the film is defined in part or completely by Lucas's concept of symbiont circles—the idea that people and their fates are connected. This is the idea that such symbiont circles involve connections that aren't always seen (hence the "phantom" of the title). Sometimes the real symbiont circles are merely hinted at, or only partially detected. Lucas's leitmotif of symbiont circles allows him to reach beyond the binary "light side" / "dark side" dichotomy of the original trilogy and aim for some fascinating material.

For instance, Qui-Gon and Obi-Wan attempt to convince Boss Nass, on Naboo, that their fate will be the same as that of the humanoids under Federation rule, because they share the same planet. Later, Amidala also presses this concern with them. The fate of Naboo is one that is shared, because the Gungans and the humanoids are linked. The underwater chase, with the big fish eating the smaller fish (which is attempting to eat Qui-Gon's sub) also suggests this kind of symbiont circle. Certainly, in more familiar territory, the dominance of the Jedi has caused the fall of the Sith. But the arrogance of the Jedi has also given the Sith room to plot in secret and reassert themselves. Again, a symbiont circle. I don't think I've ever read any analysis of the film that points out this theme or acknowledges how it runs through the film's drama.

RAY MORTON

Using Ben's revisionist speech and other revelations in *Return of the Jedi* as a jumping-off point, the tale Lucas decided to tell in the prequel trilogy was that of how Obi-Wan Kenobi meets ace pilot Anakin Skywalker, senses the Force is strong in him, and decides to train him to be a Jedi Knight. Meanwhile, Senator Palpatine, a member of the Senate of the Galactic Republic—who is secretly an evil Sith Lord called Darth Sidious—manipulates events to facilitate his rise to power and the formation of a military he can then use to create an evil empire with himself as its head. When Palpatine becomes aware of Anakin—who in the meantime falls in love with and marries Queen Amidala of Naboo—he seeks to turn the Jedi apprentice to the dark side so that Anakin can help him kill the Jedi and carry out his nefarious plans.

Palpatine succeeds just as Padmé gives birth to twins. Learning Anakin has turned evil, Obi-Wan confronts him. The two fight and Anakin is horribly injured. Surviving, he is encased in a permanent life-support system, becomes Darth Vader, and continues to help the Emperor destroy the Republic and create his empire. Meanwhile, Padmé dies and Obi-Wan separates the twins and places them in foster homes to hide them from Vader and the Emperor. Obi-Wan then goes into exile in anticipation of the day when the twins will come of age and be ready to join the fight to save the galaxy.

From the start, this was going to be a challenging story to tell, especially since Lucas's intent was to make Anakin (rather than Obi-Wan) the protagonist of the narrative. Had the reverse been true, the overall story would have been about a man with the best of intentions who inadvertently creates a monster and must then defeat and destroy that monster. The decision to make Anakin the central character made that much more problematic.

RAY MORTON

Lucas's stated intent was to craft a classical Greek tragedy about a good man who brings about his own downfall. While a valid concept, the difficulties of it stemmed from the fact that in a Greek tragedy, the damage the protagonist does is to himself, where in *Star Wars* the damage Anakin would do would be to others—which doesn't make him a tragic hero, but an outright villain. In essence, Lucas's story would be about a good man going bad.

RICK MCCALLUM

All told, it's the story about one of the most extraordinary kids who ever had the power of the Force. It's the story of Anakin and what happened to him and that inevitable moment when he chose between good and evil. Why did that happen and *how* did that happen? Where did he come from and how could he have made that choice? *That* was the real saga. The ultimate moment is when you see Darth Vader reveal himself—the impact of that moment was incredible.

HAYDEN CHRISTENSEN
(actor, "Anakin Skywalker")

Putting on the Darth Vader costume was exhilarating. I was really hoping that I was going to get to put on the outfit when I got cast in these films. When we got to Sydney for *Episode III,* George told me that I would have the chance of finally getting to put on the helmet and what not. It was really one of the coolest things I'd gotten to do. And it was a very emotional experience for me. *And* empowering. There was a certain hint of sadness as well.

RAY MORTON

This would be a tricky story to tell, because it would require Lucas to create a character who was *so* likable and sympathetic and whose motivations were so relatable, that viewers would be willing to invest themselves fully in him and his story at the beginning and then stick with him as he grows worse and worse and worse. It would also be a tricky story to tell, because a properly conceived and constructed dramatic narrative should contain both a protagonist and an antagonist—a protagonist to drive the story and an antagonist to oppose him. In this tale, Anakin would be protagonist *and* antagonist, a nearly impossible concept to make work both dramatically and structurally. And it would be a tricky story to tell, because it wasn't clear there would be enough narrative in this concept to fill three entire feature-length films. These were issues he would wrestle with as he made his way through his new trilogy.

GEORGE LUCAS

Throughout the writing and making of *Episode I,* I always stayed focused on ten years later when the new trilogy would be completed. Then people would be able to watch all six films together as they were intended to be seen. The *Star Wars* saga is, in a way, symphonic in nature. I have certain musical refrains that I am purposely repeating in a different chord, but still repeating. In the first three films, I told a specific story. With the new trilogy, I was telling nearly the same story, with many similar emotional, psychological, and decision-making moments.

Some people may not even understand that sort of thing. They think it's just *Star Wars* with a shorter Luke Skywalker. But it was all done on purpose to create a certain feeling when you watch all of them in order. Certain lines become more meaningful. It changes the first three movies rather dramatically. That was my whole reason for doing it. If it didn't change them, I wouldn't be doing it. I like the idea that you can take something and look at it one way, then you turn around and you are given more information and you look at it completely differently.

RAY MORTON

The question of whether or not there was enough narrative in Lucas's story to fill three movies became apparent as soon as he began to write this first episode. The answer? No, there wasn't. As a result, the plot Lucas developed for this first episode would essentially serve as a prologue to the main story he was planning to tell in the new trilogy. It would introduce the main characters and the primary situations, but the only plot points that would be relevant to the trilogy's overall narrative would be Obi-Wan meeting Anakin and deciding to train him to be a Jedi; Anakin and Padmé meeting for the first time; Palpatine meeting Anakin and taking notice of how strong he is in the Force; and the notion that Darth Sidious is working in the shadows to manipulate events to his sinister benefit.

GEORGE LUCAS

What I started with was just a little story outline with bits and pieces. But it had a structure that hasn't changed much in all these years. Everybody then started asking, "How many are you going to make?" So I thought I *could* go back and do the backstories of the original trilogy. When people saw Darth Vader, they didn't know what he was. Is he a monster? Is there a guy in there? Is it a robot? They didn't know. He was just the villain and he was such an iconic villain, although at the time I didn't have any idea any of this would work or have the impact that it did. You just don't think that way. You just do your best and it comes out and maybe in the end you do the first three movies. I had this whole backstory, because I wanted to start with *Episode IV*, because I wanted to be like a serial. "I don't know what's happened before. What's going on? Who are these people?" So I wanted to throw you right into the middle of something you don't have any idea about. But then later on I realized that the tragedy got lost in that. And if I told the backstory, which was obviously written before the actual film, that it would make sense. You know, he started out as a nice little kid and turned bad.

RICK MCCALLUM

It's basically that crucial moment that everybody usually has in their life that Anakin is dealing with in these films. Once you've been educated, you basically have a choice to make in what you are going to do with your life. Anakin makes one choice, Obi-Wan makes another. Once you've made that choice, it's very hard to turn back. Some people can, at that very last moment, like we saw with Darth/Anakin in *Return of the Jedi*. But it's basically that whole dramatic situation: the choice that you ultimately make between good and evil, right and wrong. What George had to struggle with on the first three *Star Wars* films was to create a universe of people and places and their relationships and the way the story was going to go and how they all interrelated. It's somewhat easier now, because he knows all those characters and where they came from, but there was still the essence of what makes a powerful, dramatic story that had to be dealt with.

GEORGE LUCAS

It's a story about Ben Kenobi and Anakin Skywalker and how we got to the point where Obi-Wan Kenobi was waiting in the middle of the desert for something to happen. It's also about how Darth Vader got to be who he is, and how the Emperor came to power. It starts out with the Emperor *not* in power and then it keeps progressing.

RICK MCCALLUM

It's the story about one of the most extraordinary kids who ever had the power of the Force. It's the story of Anakin and what happened to him. Why did that happen and how did that happen? Where did he come from and how could he have made that choice? That's the *real* saga.

GEORGE LUCAS

The backstory started when Anakin was young and with the issues of where he came from. The fact that he was a slave, the fact that he suffered—these kind of things are important story points. I had to start at a young age. Originally I had him about twelve years old, but then when I started writing the screenplay, I realized that the issues of him leaving his mother and these things weren't quite as dramatic as they needed to be, and I wrote him down to ten years old, and I felt it worked better.

RAY MORTON

Lucas began work on *Episode I* by repurposing the first half of his original 1973 treatment for *Star Wars*. In that treatment, the galaxy is in the midst of a civil war. The evil Emperor puts a price on the head of rebel Princess Leia. The veteran General Luke Skywalker is tasked with escorting the Princess and her retinue of courtiers to a safe haven on the planet Ophuchi. Escaping Imperial ground forces in a stolen spacecraft, the Rebels are attacked by an Imperial warship. Their ship is damaged and crash-lands on the planet Yavin.

In the reworked version, the planet of Naboo is under siege by the evil Trade Federation. Under the direction of the mysterious Darth Sidious, the Trade Federation's droid army invades Naboo and take the planet's queen, Padmé Amidala, and her entourage hostage. Veteran Jedi Knight Qui-Gon Jinn rescues Padmé and agrees to escort her and her entourage to the

Republic's capital planet of Coruscant so she can ask the Senate for help in repelling the invaders. They escape from Naboo on Padmé's royal ship, but the ship is damaged as they break through the Federation's blockade and it crash-lands on Tatooine.

While trying to obtain spare parts to repair their ship, Qui-Gon and Padmé meet nine-year-old slave boy and expert podracer Anakin Skywalker, who Qui-Gon quickly determines is not only very strong in the Force, but is quite possibly the "Chosen One" prophesied to bring balance to the Force. Qui-Gon makes a bet with Anakin's owner, a junk dealer named Watto: if Anakin can win a big podrace, Watto will free him and give the travelers the parts to repair their ship. Anakin wins the race, bids farewell to his mother Shmi, and leaves Tatooine with Qui-Gon, who intends to train the young boy to become a Jedi.

Following a fight with Sidious's evil apprentice Darth Maul, who has been sent by Sidious to kill Padmé, Qui-Gon introduces Anakin to his current apprentice, a young Obi-Wan Kenobi. The royal band travels to Coruscant, where Padmé begs the Republic's Chancellor Valorum and the Senate to help her planet. Palpatine manipulates Padmé into calling for a vote of no confidence that results in Valorum's resignation. Palpatine is chosen to be his replacement. Meanwhile, Qui-Gon asks the Jedi ruling council—led by Yoda and Mace Windu—for permission to train Anakin. The council denies the request because it fears Anakin will be susceptible to the dark side of the Force. A defiant Qui-Gon says he will train Anakin anyway.

As the Senate dithers, Padmé decides to return home to save her planet. The Jedi Council orders Qui-Gon to go along to protect her. Qui-Gon brings Obi-Wan and Anakin with him. Back on Naboo, Padmé persuades the Gungans—a race that lives under Naboo's waters—to join with her people to repel the Trade Federation invasion. A great ground battle ensues. As it does, Qui-Gon engages in a lightsaber battle with Darth Maul. Meanwhile, Anakin gets trapped in a space fighter that travels automatically to the Trade Federation's orbiting battle station, from which its droid army is controlled. Through a series of mishaps, Anakin accidentally blows up the entire battle station. The loss of central control causes the droid army on the surface to shut down, allowing Padmé's forces to win the day. Unfortunately, Maul mortally wounds Qui-Gon and Obi-Wan retaliates by cutting the evil Sith in half. His life slipping away, Qui-Gon asks Obi-Wan to train Anakin. Obi-Wan promises he will and Qui-Gon dies. The story concludes with a celebratory parade on Naboo at which Palpatine—impressed by what he's seen of Anakin's abilities—assures young Skywalker that he will keep an eye on him from now on.

RAY MORTON

Lucas incorporated a number of ideas originally devised but not used in *Episodes IV* to *VI* into this new story: the notion of Padmé using a decoy was one Lucas considered for Leia in his early work for *Star Wars*; an underwater city and an underwater adventure were both originally suggested for *Empire*; the idea of a young slave boy originated in Lucas's notes for *Star Wars*, where it was originally Han Solo's backstory; and the concept of a city that covered an entire planet was initially proposed for *Jedi* (in that film, the Imperial homeworld of Had Abbadon was to have been covered in a decayed and polluted city, as opposed to the clean, gleaming megalopolis that was the Coruscant of *Menace*). In fact, Lucas developed the Jedi and the Sith in far more detail than he had in the original trilogy.

In the first three films, the Jedi were described as having once been the guardians of peace and justice in the galaxy, but beyond that all we knew was that they were adept at using the Force and that their weapon of choice was a lightsaber. The impression we got was that they were priests/warriors akin to Samurai—roaming the galaxy, helping people and righting wrongs where they found them. In *Menace*, we see that the Jedi are actually a more formally organized group, a sort-of-a-religious order with a ruling council and an official headquarters, and that they are closely aligned with the government of the Republic, which they serve as a combination diplomatic and law enforcement entity. The knights recruit new members as children, teach them in a school contained within their headquarters, and when a pupil is old enough, apprentice him or her to a master Jedi to finish their training. *Menace* also tells us that the final step in becoming a Jedi is to successfully complete a series of undefined trials—a step that apparently was dropped by the time Luke came around. In the prequels, Jedi are not allowed to have intimate personal relationships or marry, another change, which does not jibe with the fact that the Anakin Skywalker of *Star Wars* had a son.

GEORGE LUCAS

The Jedi are like negotiators. They aren't people that go out and blow up planets, or shoot down things. They're more of a one-to-one-combat type. In *The Phantom Menace* I wanted the form of the fighting and the role of the Jedi Knight to be special. More spiritual and more intellectual than just something like a fighter or a superhero.

In the original trilogy, all viewers knew about the Sith was that they were in essence the bad guys who used the Force nefariously. In The Phantom Menace, *Lucas provided more detail on the sinister-sounding dark Force wielders.*

GEORGE LUCAS

Palpatine *is* the Devil. There's no fall from grace there. He's the evil one. Palpatine is a Sith and there are usually only two Sith. And that's because if you put more than two Sith together, two of them always conspire to kill the third one. So you'll notice through the whole series that the apprentice Sith is always trying to recruit somebody else to join him, to kill the Emperor so he can be the Emperor and his partner can be *his* apprentice. That's a constant. It's greed, a greed for power. It's, "I'm second and I want to be first." These aren't quiet little apprentices who say, "Oh, I respect you and I want to serve with you." They basically want to kill the other guy and take over.

RAY MORTON

Lucas's imagination, which seemed to have flagged during the creation of *Jedi,* is firing on all cylinders in *Menace.* He dreamt up a whole bunch of new races, cultures, and worlds (including a lush pastoral planet, a vast city planet, and an underwater civilization), all of which were developed with lots of intricate and eccentric detail. He took us back to Tatooine yet again, but showed us new aspects of life on the desert planet, including the unique sport of podracing. Lucas showed us the grand Senate of the Republic and introduced us to Darth Maul—a nifty (and scary-looking) villain with an awesome dual-blade lightsaber.

DAN MADSEN

Rick McCallum invited me out to Skywalker Ranch, and he took me up to this top room in the main house—like an attic room, I'd describe it as—where all the designers were working on the designs for *Episode I.* When we got to the door to get in to this room, he literally had a special knock. I don't remember what it was like, but you had to have a special knock to get in the damn room. So, we got in the room, and there are all the designers working on sketches and drawings and storyboards, and things for *Episode I*—this was two years before the film opened. I'm walking in there with my eyes wide open, like "Holy Mackerel . . . I'm seeing this stuff for the first time, nobody even knows about this!" There's maquettes and statues of Jar Jar Binks there, and telling me what this character is, and what that character is, and showing me some early special effects work on the computer, and VFX stuff, and introducing me to Doug Chiang and some of the designers who are working there with art on their desks and such. But, you know, you can't report on all of this stuff—you're just here to get an idea of what's going on.

JOHN KENNETH MUIR

While these things are in the story, eventually *The Phantom Menace*'s visual design transmits much of the film's underlying theme about the rise of fascism and fall of an enlightened republic. It's about life here on Earth in the mid-twentieth century, particularly the years between the two world wars. This was, on Earth, a gilded age of Art Deco architecture and art, and apparent prosperity in the United States. Yet, economic ruin was around the corner, racism thrived, and the "phantom menace" of fascism and tyranny grew in the shadows. *The Phantom Menace* reflects this time with its chrome spaceships, and Art Deco spires and skyscrapers. Notably, Art Deco is a form or design often described as being purely decorative. It is the art of a people satisfied with the social status quo. In the film, we see the Futura or Art Deco touches primarily applied at Coruscant, the capital city of the Republic. What we glean from the architecture is that the Republic and its people are satisfied with their high level of society. They don't perceive the phantom menace outside. They don't correct the wrongs that diminish them, like the slavery on the outer rim planets. The film's design carries all this information beautifully. The people of the Republic, including the Jedi, are self-satisfied and blind to the suffering of those beyond their borders.

Visually, Lucas equates the fall of Naboo's capital city with the fall of Europe to the Nazi scourge. At least twice in the film, his camera photographs a sculpture/monument in that city that resembles France's Arc de Triomphe. In 1940, of course, Nazi troops invaded Paris, and marched the Champs-Élysées as a sign of their domination. In 1944, France was liberated and the Allies had a parade at the same monument. *The Phantom Menace* features two moments under that Arc-like structure, one at the commencement of the droid army/Trade Federation occupation, and then again after their expulsion, during a triumphant parade. These shots are not an accident, or a coincidence. Lucas's galaxy far, far away is undergoing the same tumult that our world did in World War II.

JONATHAN RINZLER

George at one point wanted to do this book, *Star Wars and History*. Which we did. So I got to learn firsthand from George all the historical situations that inspired various things in *Star Wars*. We went out and got a bunch of historians to write about *Star Wars*, and they could write about anything they wanted to. They could just do whatever they wanted. And I think 70 percent of them wrote about the prequel trilogy. Not the original trilogy.

RAY MORTON

Unfortunately, some of Lucas's new ideas were not so cool: In his cosmology, Jedi training is supposed to begin when the candidate is young, so Lucas intended to start his new trilogy with a youthful Anakin. In his initial notes and treatments, Anakin was a teenager, but Lucas later decided to make him even younger—in the final script drafts and the film, Anakin would be nine. This was important, because the separation of Anakin from his mother would be a key factor in decisions Anakin was going to make later in the trilogy. The problem with making Anakin so young was that Lucas planned to portray him as an expert pilot and have him play a key role in some of the story's main action sequences—specifically the podrace and the climactic destruction of the Trade Federation's orbiting battle station.

While it was already a bit of a stretch to think that a teenager can be an ace pilot and both win a podrace *and* make an attack run on an enemy space station, it was just plausible enough to be believable. However, it wasn't at all believable that a nine-year-old could do any of these things—especially take part in combat or blow up a spacecraft. Lucas seemed to recognize this, because he reworked the final attack to unfold essentially as an accident—Anakin gets locked in a space fighter and accidentally activates the ship's remote control, which flies the fighter up to the battle station, at which point Anakin makes a series of missteps that fortuitously result in the station exploding. While this may have been marginally more plausible action for a nine-year-old, it was all far too convenient and farcical and thus spoiled what should have been a very exciting climax.

Then there was perhaps one of the most controversial elements of the story, the introduction of the idea of the midi-chlorians, microscopic creatures living inside living cells that connect the host to the Force (and can also apparently create human life given Anakin's seeming immaculate conception), in an ill-fated attempt to give Qui-Gon a concrete reason for believing Anakin was the "Chosen One" fated to bring balance to the Force.

GEORGE LUCAS

Midi-chlorians are a loose depiction of mitochondria, which are really necessary in order for the cells to divide and probably had something to do with the beginnings of life, and how one cell decided to become two cells with a little help from this other little creature. Life could not exist without it and it's really a way of saying we have hundreds of little creatures that live with us and without them, we'd all die. There wouldn't be any life. They are necessary for us and we are necessary for them. And I'm using them in the metaphor to say that society is the same way; we must all get along with each other. And the planet is the same way: we must treat the other creatures on this planet with respect, otherwise the planet will die.

RAY MORTON

Apparently Anakin has a higher level of midi-chlorians than any other person, making him more Force-powerful than anyone else. This attempt to provide a scientific explanation for the Force severely lessened the spiritual and mystical aspects of the energy field generated by all living things that was so appealing in the original movies.

JOHN KENNETH MUIR

Along comes *Star Wars* and it features the concept of "the Force." Lucas devised this "thing" that binds the universe together, and binds us to one another. And his Force is nicely bifurcated among light and dark, good and bad, so not much deep thinking is really required to guess who to root for in the battle. But the Force is, on a deeper level, about faith. Those who believe in it, can use it. I can be a Jedi, if I try. You can be a Jedi. We have only but to concentrate . . . and believe. In the "Is God Dead?" world, post-1966, this assertion of belief in something we can't see, something supernatural, let's say, was nothing less than a revelation. That's why Lucas goofed so badly with midi-chlorians in 1999. Suddenly, you had to have the right bloodline to be a Jedi. It was no longer something that could inspire everyone. But in the summer of 1977, *Star Wars* championed a nondenominational testament to the power of faith and the availability of spirituality to everybody who embraced belief. If the culture's "lack of faith" was "disturbing," the swashbuckling, spiritual *Star Wars* was the antidote.

TIMOTHY ZAHN
(author, *Heir to the Empire*)

I do not like the midi-chlorian idea at all. It sounds like an attempt to make a scientific basis for something that really was more mystical to begin with. I'm not sure of the purpose of it, but the idea that you can scan for a Jedi with a blood test bothers me for some reason. I've always thought of the Force as more than a talented art, that it is something that "if you've got it, you know it and you can develop it," but it's not something that you can look at a person and say, "Okay, he's got that talent." It's just cold.

BRIAN JAY JONES

The midi-chlorians absolutely ruin it for me. That's the big antithesis of the Force as Lucas himself articulated it. Having a biological foundation for the Force really bothered me and my wife is like, "You need to get over that; I don't want to listen to you bitch about that anymore." But I *really* hate that. This is a little off the reservation, but that's why I really liked what Rian Johnson was starting to do with it in *The Last Jedi*. When Luke is saying to Rey, "All that stuff you've heard about the Jedi Knights, forget all that. The Force doesn't belong to them. The Force belongs to everybody. It's not a royal blood thing. Anybody can tap into it." *That's* the way I want the Force to be. I want Han Solo to be able to be "forceful" if he wants, not because he has the right blood count.

PETER HOLMSTROM
(cohost, *The Rebel & the Rogue* podcast)

Obi-Wan's description of the Force in *A New Hope*: "The Force is what gives a Jedi his power. It's an energy field created by all living things. It surrounds us and penetrates us; it binds the galaxy together." Qui-Gon Jinn's description of midi-chlorians: "Midi-chlorians are a microscopic life-form that resides within all living cells, and we are symbiotes with them. Creatures living together for mutual advantage. Without the midi-chlorians, life could not exist, and we would have no knowledge of the Force. They continually speak to us, telling us the will of the Force." Where's the problem? Midi-chlorians are not the Force. They have never been described as the Force. They're symbiotic life-forms that bind all living things to the Force. The Force has always had wills and desires and an agenda of its own ever since the beginning. So the Force having more interest in one person over another, would naturally mean they would have more midi-chlorians within them.

Also, again, it's meant to be a plot point. The Jedi have their temple in a major metropolis, and care more about the inner political machinations than their own spiritual growth—they're measuring things on science, and kidnapping children at the age of two to be Jedi—this dogmatic approach to spirituality is something Lucas wanted to highlight, because he's saying the Jedi are flawed. This isn't Good Guys versus Bad Guys—again, this is meant to be Vietnam in space, and we're seeing the seeds of that highlighted here, to be explored later.

RAY MORTON

The other thing about *The Phantom Menace* are some of the new characters. Jar Jar Binks is a dreadful character. Many people have attacked the floppy-eared

Gungan for being what they perceived as a racist, Stepin Fetchit–style carica-ture. Those complaints are certainly understandable, but equally offensive is just how stupid the character is, both in conception and in presentation. As the Ewoks in *Return of the Jedi* demonstrated, Lucas seems to have an affinity for broad, overly cutesy characters who perpetrate ridiculous slapstick antics. I suppose such characters and behavior have their place in the appropriate type of movie, but in my opinion, they have no business being in the "serious" fantasy of a *Star Wars* movie. The hyperactive Jar Jar, who speaks in a hard-to-understand dialect with an annoying high-pitched voice, is a thoroughly irritating creation and his omnipresence in the movie makes him unbearable. The supposedly comedic bit in which he steps in (bantha?) poop is arguably the nadir of the entire series.

JONATHAN RINZLER

My daughter loved Jar Jar—it was made for kids. They didn't know it was going to be interpreted the way it was going to be interpreted.

RICK MCCALLUM

For kids, there is no doubt that Jar Jar is their favorite character [of the pre-quel trilogy]. This is something that we not only saw in research, but in exit polls. People love Jar Jar! I think there was too much criticism of him. There were even racist accusations about Jar Jar. That is ridiculous. Jar Jar was cre-ated with great care and affection and was meant to be a lovable, innocent character. To read anything more into his creation is ridiculous and absurd.

SAMUEL L. JACKSON
(actor, "Mace Windu")

Jar Jar *wasn't* racist. That was Ahmed's [actor Ahmed Best] interpretation of who he was, and it was what George wanted. It's stupid to say, "Okay, that's like Stepin Fetchit and he talks that way." I can watch Stepin Fetchit, Willie Best, and all those other guys do what they did. It was their job at the time. If you want to feel that way about something, you can. If you watch Jack Benny, even if you think Rochester is his manservant, watch it really closely and you'll see that Rochester is the smart guy. He's the one in charge. Jack Benny kind of defers to him. But you don't *need* to do that in a *Star Wars* movie.

DAN MADSEN

Claims of racism in the prequel films were just ridiculous accusations. George Lucas doesn't have a racist bone in his body. I always was really offended by that accusation that went out there. Not even Ahmed Best—he poo-poo'd that—he said the same thing, that that's just ridiculous. There's no truth to that whatsoever.

FRANK OZ
(puppeteer, voice of "Yoda")

I *love* Jar Jar Binks. I don't know what the whole flak was about. When I read the script, I thought, "Oh, Jar Jar is going to be a terrific character." I was surprised at the bizarre reaction to him. I love Jar Jar. He's hysterical.

GEORGE LUCAS

In *The Phantom Menace* there was the whole issue of two symbiotic societies living next to each other, but not cooperating. Jar Jar was the key element in tying these societies together. He was a bumbling, fumbling outcast, and his purpose plot-wise was to bring the Jedi to these two societies and bring them together. As a plot device, Jar Jar was very important to the film. He *wasn't* just comic relief.

AHMED BEST
(actor, "Jar Jar Binks")

Most adults are taking it too seriously. When people slag on *The Phantom Menace*, it's like, "What do they expect? What are you looking for?" Jar Jar *is* for the kids. He was created to balance Darth Maul. Darth Maul and Jar Jar are probably the two extremes in the movie. I know many adults want to pick it apart, but if they're doing that, then they're missing the point. I don't take it personally as a criticism of my performance. I performed to the best of my ability. Overall, the film is George's vision. I have a certain amount of distance from it. I can remove myself from it. The kind of person I am, though, I really don't listen to what other people have to say . . . unless it's good.

PETER HOLMSTROM

I never had a problem with Jar Jar as a kid. He's fun, and has a poignant story. If the original trilogy was Cowboys versus Indians, where the Indians win—the prequel trilogy is Cowboys versus Indians, where the Indians are corrupted by the white man, and destroyed. Sadly, more true to real life. And Jar Jar represents that. He's the innocent corrupted and turned into an unknowing agent of evil. Objectively, I can see he's not the comedic character Lucas meant him to be. I think the problem is he didn't have a steady straight-man to play off of. He keeps jumping around in the role of sidekick, from Qui-Gon to Anakin to Padmé to being on his own—so there's no rise in comedic pressure that's needed for slapstick roles. But look at his role in *The*

Clone Wars—he's hilarious! Nothing's better than Jar Jar and Mace Windu on a mission together. He's not as funny as he was meant to be in *Episode I*, but you know what? Most Will Ferrell movies don't work either, but no one's out there saying, "Will Ferrell raped my childhood," because of *Holmes & Watson*.

GLEN OLIVER
(pop culture commentator)

The merchandising of action figures and vehicles can sometimes be interesting indicators of which characters and devices will find popularity over the long haul. One instance of this I witnessed during a late-night opening of Toys "R" Us. They were unleashing *Phantom Menace* merchandise for the first time, so it was a pretty big deal all around. [Toys "R" Us] had dumped huge quantities of action figures into baby pools—the hordes of fans had to kneel or squat to fuss through which figures they wanted to get. I saw a dude—I think he was probably in his midthirties—topple into a baby pool full of action figures. People were half-heartedly trying to help him, but they were generally more concerned with getting *their* own action figures before someone else did. This guy flopped around in a baby pool of *Phantom Menace* figures. After a few moments, I realized I should probably try to help the poor bastard—to preserve the packaging of the figures he was squishing, if nothing else. When I moved over to him, I quickly realized that this baby pool had already been stripped clean by the Geeky Locusts and that the only figures left behind in the pool—the figures in which this guy was flailing about in—were exclusively Jar Jar Binks.

RAY MORTON

Qui-Gon Jinn, on the other hand, is a very cool character—the perfect embodiment of what we expect a Jedi in his prime to be. Unfortunately, his presence severely weakens Obi-Wan's character and his role in the story. To begin with, introducing Qui-Gon contradicts an important story point established in *The Empire Strikes Back,* namely that Yoda was the Jedi Master who trained Obi-Wan. In *Menace,* Qui-Gon is Obi-Wan's teacher, which dilutes the close connection between Obi-Wan and Yoda that is so vital to *Empire* and *Return of the Jedi.* It also dilutes the connection between Ben and Anakin. In *Star Wars,* Obi-Wan describes Anakin as having been his "good friend." In *Jedi*, Obi-Wan explains that when he first met Anakin, he was struck by how strong Anakin was with the Force and so undertook to train him to become a Jedi, only to eventually lose him to the dark side. These speeches establish that Obi-Wan is the character who sets Anakin's story in motion and then must deal with the fallout when things go awry.

However, in *Menace*, Obi-Wan is *not* the character that sets Anakin's story in motion—Qui-Gon is. Qui-Gon is the one who first meets Anakin, who senses his power and decides to train him. Obi-Wan isn't even present when all this happens. He is eventually introduced to Anakin by Qui-Gon, but has no meaningful connection with him (and in fact feels—along with the Jedi Council—that Anakin is actually dangerous). It is only after Qui-Gon is killed that Obi-Wan agrees to take Anakin on as his apprentice and only because Qui-Gon asks him to, not because he has any personal interest in the boy or his potential. This waters down the drama of what happens later on in the trilogy, because when Obi-Wan finally confronts the now evil Anakin in *Revenge of the Sith*, it is to rectify Qui-Gon's tragic error (of choosing Anakin) rather than his own. Finally, having Qui-Gon be the one who discovers Anakin and chooses to train him leaves Obi-Wan with next to nothing to do in this particular movie—if he wasn't in the film it would make almost no difference at all to the final product.

All of which has to do with the evolution of the story and the screenplay, which needed to be ready for a production start date of June 1997. But even before then, McCallum was tasked with getting things into development, starting in April 1994. Needless to say, an unorthodox way to make a movie. But any behind the scenes look at the making of the prequel trilogy has to begin with a look at Rick McCallum, who was essentially filling the role that Gary Kurtz had on the original trilogy.

Born August 22, 1954, in Heidelberg, West Germany, McCallum would come to collaborate on and oversee The Young Indiana Jones Chronicles, *then produce Lucasfilm's* Radioland Murders *(1994), and was privately informed by Lucas that he was planning on making the prequel trilogy and wanted him to be a part of it. Lucas noted that they would test the technology they'd be using on the Special Editions. Needless to say, McCallum decided to stick around, establishing a solid working relationship with Lucas.*

RICK MCCALLUM

Every summer I used to work in a perfume factory when I was a kid. Even though I have a huge nose, I found out it wasn't right for me. A friend of mine was working for a news show and asked me if I wanted to come over. They were doing an interview with Henry Kissinger the day I was there. I stood in for one of the camera assistants who got sick and at the end of the day I thought it was fun. When I got back to New York to finish college, I met a wonderful group of filmmakers, including James Ivory, and then I was hooked.

Later, I did a film called *Dreamchild*. I was shooting at Elstree Studios in England. It was a tiny film; there were only about twelve of us working on it and we had a budget of only one million pounds. We had to shoot it in three weeks. This was back in 1984. Jim Henson had agreed to make the creatures for us. It was his first [outside] film other than working on Yoda for *The Empire Strikes Back*. Our film was about *Alice in Wonderland* and the complex relationship between the author who wrote the book and the little girl he based Alice on. It was a really fun picture to do. We had huge sets, but they were all made out of cloth and were painted. We had virtually no money. One day, producer Robert Watts, who has worked on many Lucasfilm projects, came on the set. I met him and we started talking and he loved the idea that twelve people could actually make a movie. Robert was working on the film *Return to Oz* at the time. So we met at that time and basically connected. Robert went back and told everybody that we were making a film that looked big, but only had twelve people behind the scenes and I think that kind of stuck in George's head. You have to remember, George comes from a tradition of making small, independent films. That's where his heart really is, not to the huge blockbusters that he is so associated with.

In 1989, Lucas had the idea for The Young Indiana Jones Chronicles. *Following the completion of* Who Framed Roger Rabbit, *Watts wanted to pursue his own projects, so there was an amicable split between him and Lucasfilm. He called McCallum and told him they were trying to get a group of people together for the series and introduced him to Lucas.*

RICK MCCALLUM

I thought the series sounded fun and it was more than fun. It was *brilliant*. It was one of the most enjoyable times of my career. In fact, oddly enough, I hardly saw my family during the four years that we were making the show. I would see them once every couple of months, but it was long periods between those times. My wife could deal with it, though, because she knew it was a special moment in everybody's life.

It's very interesting the relationship directors and producers have, especially when they last a long time. I believe that the job of a producer is to enable a director and the writer to do whatever they want to do within the limits of the money and the schedule that you have. Our job is to make it happen for those guys. When it works, it works beautifully. It's all about the dynamics in the relationship between the producer and director. I've spent almost my entire career working exclusively for writer/directors. So, it's just two people who set up the movie. The director's job is to make sure his story comes out the way he wants it while mine is to spend all the money, resources, the tools to make sure the movie is the way the director has in mind. That's how it really works. When it doesn't work, when you look at people's careers and they haven't worked with the same people, it usually means they haven't found someone they can get along with.

Is there someone you can get along with too well? That's the feeling that some critics have had regarding McCallum as producer, particularly in comparison to Gary Kurtz. It's similar to the difference between the direction of Irvin Kershner on The Empire Strikes Back *and Richard Marquand on* Return of the Jedi. *The former knew when he had to push back and would, while the latter usually acquiesced to everything Lucas wanted.*

BRIAN JAY JONES

Gary Kurtz was a good collaborator for Lucas, because they had worked together on *American Graffiti*. The big difference between the first two films and then once the prequels come along is that Gary Kurtz is the one guy who's willing to get in Lucas's face and tell him, "No!" That's the strength of your line producer. Kurtz is the guy who's like, "Whatever you need, George, I'm going to get it. I'll go back to the studio, I'll go in on bended knee and I'll ask for the money you need to reshoot this," and then he'd have to come back to Lucas and say, "They're only going to give us twenty grand or forty grand or whatever it is, so you can get your cantina scene. I'm sorry. I know it's not what you . . . ," and he has to disappoint Lucas.

DALE POLLOCK
(author, *Skywalking: The Life and Films of George Lucas*)

As much as George wanted his independence, he needed somebody to say no; to argue with him. His best work came when he was married to Marcia Lucas and she was that person. She was the one who pushed him on *American Graffiti*. She pushed him on *Star Wars*. She pushed him on *Empire Strikes Back*, but they split up by *Return of the Jedi*, which is where you begin to see the bad filmmaking start. Obviously, he didn't direct that, but he was all over the back of Richard Marquand, who he could control. Irvin Kershner didn't want to hear it, and that was a very unpleasant experience for Lucas, even though *Empire* is still the best one. The prequels would not have been the same had she been around. There was nobody there he would either listen to or respect enough to listen to.

BRIAN JAY JONES

Kurtz is the one who's kind of willing to be the reality check, that is going to bust his ass to try to get Lucas everything he needs, but when it doesn't work, he's going to tell Lucas, "You know what? No." And even going through a script, he's the one that's able to tell him, "This isn't going to work. You probably need to have somebody come in and punch this up." That's the difference, I think, between the original films and the prequels. The prequels were Lucas putting everything into it and nobody's going to tell him that he can't do it that way.

DALE POLLOCK

It's the difference between a Gary Kurtz and a Rick McCallum. Gary Kurtz knew the universe. Gary Kurtz was the only one Lucas communicated with on the initial *Star Wars* film. He would barely speak to anybody else. I mean, read the interviews with the actors. If he gave them four words of direction a day, it was a good day. Usually his direction consisted of, "Faster. Louder. More intense."

BRIAN JAY JONES

The lack of a Gary Kurtz is why the prequels become quite a bit of a mess. Lucas is really engaged in both the technology, which of course he loves, and world-building, which he *really* loves, to the detriment of the films at times. I think for him having a Gary Kurtz is hugely important, because you can see the difference between a Gary Kurtz and Rick McCallum. It's the difference between having a yes man like McCallum and somebody who's willing to say, "I don't think that's the right thing to do and it's a bad decision," and is willing to walk away even when he thinks the decision is bad. To use a Beatles analogy, it's like McCartney needs a Lennon. You need somebody there to say, "You know, that line's a clunker" or somebody who says, "That's the best line in the song." You *need* somebody to do that. Remember, Kurtz came in at the beginning of his career and when you're there on the ground floor, you feel freer to speak your mind. I don't know if Rick McCallum was worried about telling George Lucas "No!" and that's why he was such a yes man. Or maybe he really *did* believe everything Lucas was shitting was marbles. Clearly you can see the difference when you *don't* have Gary Kurtz around. Kurtz was a great person willing to call bullshit on Lucas when he needed it.

As far as the film was concerned, McCallum began pulling together an early team to bring together concepts and designs based on Lucas's ideas—about seven months before any actual writing was done. He also attempted to apply lessons learned from the extensive production schedule of Young Indy, *such as planning on signing the cast to long-term deals, seeking talent from art and architecture schools, using digital technology to create sets and landscapes, and securing soundstages.*

*Early hires included director of photography David Tattersall (*The Wind in the Willows, Con Air, Soldier*), production designer Gavin Bocquet (*xXx, Stardust*), concept artist Terryl Whitlatch (coming from a background in zoology and anatomy, and who was in charge of creature designs), and ILM's Doug Chiang as design director (he currently works as vice president and executive creative director of Lucasfilm). Actual art development began in January 1995.*

RICK MCCALLUM

Gavin Bocquet and our cameraman, David Tattersall, and the basic shooting crew from *Young Indy* were all brought on board for the prequels. Their dedication and attention to quality was something we wanted to bring to *Star Wars*. Our philosophy has always been that this is a family, it's teamwork. We're totally interdependent on each other. We're only interested in people who can pack their egos long enough to work for a single individual dream. That's why I wanted the people who were with us on *Young Indy*. They worked on the longest location shoot in the history of film or television. They are the ones who suffered to make *Young Indy* a great project. Being away from home so long created great hardships on their lives, yet they never complained— they did it all for the series. But nothing they ever suffered on *Young Indy* came close to the experience they had on the *Star Wars* films.

GAVIN BOCQUET
(production designer, *The Phantom Menace*)

I was always interested in film throughout my school days. The two films that were strong influences on me were *Jason and the Argonauts* and *2001: A Space Odyssey*. Maybe that's why I have ended up working on the type of films I've been working on? However, at that time there was no obvious career path that would lead me into the world of films. So being quite creative, I went to art school and studied product design. Firstly, at undergraduate level and then at postgraduate level at the Royal College of Art in London. During my time at the

Royal College of Art, the first *Star Wars* film came out, and that again started to bring forward my interest in the film world as a possible career.

RICK MCCALLUM

We had a couple of artists working at the ranch since the second week of January [1995]. They were conceptualizing George's ideas. We met with George once a week and he'd go through some of the ideas that he had been thinking about that week and then they started developing sketches of various characters and worlds and certain action props and vehicles. This would get more and more intense as we got going, but it was basically the ideas that are on his mind that he wanted to get a visual handle on. They'd come up with the sketch and then, the next week, George looked at it and made adjustments to it. We cataloged and archived and photographed each piece of work that they did.

GAVIN BOCQUET

The most important thing that the art department and I tried to achieve when we started on *The Phantom Menace* was to keep the visual spirit and identity of all the previous *Star Wars* films. We wanted the fans to really believe this was part of the same saga visually, and apart from pleasing George, which of course was our professional aim, that was our major *personal* aim. George has very precise ideas about what he wants, although you have to put the ideas in front of him for him to react to. So by a process of elimination you would slowly get your ideas closer to the visions George had in his head.

RICK MCCALLUM

It was exciting just watching these meetings every Friday with George and the artists, even though they could be very brief, sometimes a half hour to an hour. I was usually with George all day, but when we got up there, just watching him begin to weave the characters together was amazing. Each week saw a dramatic increase in that. That's where his real genius is—the ability to take ordinary things and names and characters, events, and stories and then put a new twist on them. They're right there in front of you, but you can't quite see it until George fleshes them out. It's like a cubist painting—he looks at reality in such a special way and makes the connection between the imaginary worlds and the people and the things that they need to survive and live. It really was quite amazing to sit back and watch this happen.

GEORGE LUCAS

I think somewhere in the dark recesses of the company's files there is something with every creature and everything about them, but I've never seen it.

And I don't really know. Even though I live this and I know the worlds very well, and I know what everything in them is, half the time I'm in the fortunate position of just getting to make it up. So when somebody asks me a question, I know what's consistent with a particular environment and what isn't. And, really, that's the job of the director, to keep everything in line. I can do that on the movie, but I can't do that in the *Star Wars* universe.

GAVIN BOCQUET

There are certain elements—whether it is hardware, characters, costumes, or specific pieces of furniture—that have a lot more connection to images and ideas that people have seen in *Episodes IV* through *VI*. It could come down to very small pieces of furniture or details in sets. You see it in certain types of ship designs from Doug Chiang and the concept group. It is certainly not overplayed; it could be quite subtle. Fans who have knowledge of that will probably see where we place them. Apart from Tatooine and Coruscant, there wasn't too much initial connection in *Episode I* to the other films. I think George was quite happy with that on *Episode I,* but on *Episode II* and *III* we were getting closer and closer to the storyline in *A New Hope,* as well as visually closer.

RICK MCCALLUM

As George was working on sequences, he would stop by the art department and say, "I have an idea for this," or "Hey, wouldn't it be great if we had this?" and so on. Then the artists would do their conceptual drawings and he'd come in the next week and say, "No, I was thinking this would be a little longer and the engine should be a little bigger," etc. It *was* difficult designing things without a script, but since we were dealing with the guy actually writing the story, it was very clear. He'd tell us the sequence and we'd know the characters within the sequence. The sequence might change, the dialogue might change, the shift of the focus might change, but the characters wouldn't. So we needed the locations where it would take place and we needed the characters. Once we had those, we could begin to design them. No matter what happened with the script, some of the new characters will remain and some will be deleted, but we had this armory of characters that could allow us to make those shifts.

Over the next two years, the Chiang-led team created and went through thousands of different designs based on Lucas's concepts. In terms of look, it was Lucas's determination that the new trilogy take a different stylistic approach from the originals, more like a "period piece" that, between the three films of the trilogy, would transition to the look of Episode IV. As an example, the battle droids were viewed by Lucas as a precursor to the stormtroopers. Ultimately, Chiang and his team would work closely with production designer Gavin Bocquet, director of photography David Tattersall, and ILM's John Knoll to bring the different environments to life. Aiding in that was the use of animatics to capture story sequences.

RICK MCCALLUM

We did not travel down the traditional storyboard path. In 1995 we started by doing animatics on two large sequences. Animatics are a 3D representation of our storyboards. We also started the storyboard process on some of our larger action sequences. As each storyboard got completed, and George refined it and made his changes, we output them in animatic form. We used a computer program that allowed us to create vehicles and landscapes in 3D. We then began to output them in shots and started to edit a sequence; we had about seventy minutes that George had cut before we even shot a single frame of film. It's a communication tool more than anything else. For me, it helped enormously with budgeting and scheduling and we used it as a tool to express to both cast and crew what was going on in every blue-screen shot. Everyone knew what the background looked like, what the props were that they were interacting with.

While the script was being honed and the designs coming together, the process of casting the disparate characters began with casting director Robin Gurland, McCallum, and, of course, Lucas.

RICK MCCALLUM

The casting process began two and a half years before we started shooting. I hired a really nice woman from San Francisco named Robin Gurland as our casting director. Her first year was spent trying to find a young boy for Anakin, because we knew it would be very tricky. An eight-year-old is very, very tough to find. You can meet them when they're seven and by the time they're eight, they're a totally different kid, depending on their environment and what happens to them. So, Robin started looking at six-year-olds and tracked them, to see how they maintained certain characteristics at eight that were attractive at six. That was a long process to find Jake Lloyd.

GEORGE LUCAS

I'm always looking, first and foremost, for very accomplished actors, people who are extremely talented and know their craft very well. So I'm looking for the best possible talent I can find, and I've done that in all my movies. Next,

I'm looking for people who have the stature and, more importantly, the demeanor of the character.

RICK MCCALLUM

A year and a half before we started shooting, we locked in on the main cast. That was pretty painless. George had written very specific things for us to look for and find. Robin did an incredible job and we cast the whole movie in less than six months. They're all such easygoing, laid-back, professional actors. There was no star behavior that came out of any of them.

Liam Neeson, an actor with a certain set of skills, was cast as Jedi Master Qui-Gon Jinn. Prior to The Phantom Menace, *his films included* Schindler's List *(1993),* Nell *(1994),* Rob Roy *(1995),* Michael Collins *(1996), and* Les Misérables *(1998).*

RICK MCCALLUM

Liam is such a great actor. He has an enormous stature and he's just a wonderful guy when you meet him. He has a lot of authority, but with a real gentleness at the same time. He is extremely wise and always a surprise to me. He has all this dramatic weight behind him—I always think of him as Schindler from *Schindler's List.* Something happens to him on film; the dignity, the power that he has without saying a single word comes through.

GEORGE LUCAS

Liam Neeson's character is a master Jedi, the center of the movie just like Alec Guinness was in the first movie. You think, where are you going to find another Alec Guinness, where are you going to find someone with that kind of nobility and that kind of strength and that kind of calm? Liam is the guy. There isn't anybody else who can do that. When you start looking at other actors, there are very few who actually have the same quality in them. When you see him in the part, it's like, "Of course!" It's a natural. From my point of view, he seems to have been born to play that role. He's very quiet. He's very big. He's very powerful. But he's very contemplative.

LIAM NEESON

I've always been a fan of George's. The quality of *American Graffiti* was rough, very energetic, and infused with his love for automobiles. I got my driver's license at age thirty. I drive a car that I *may* remember the make of. There was something about the love and care that he had for cars that's conveyed in *American Graffiti.* And then to see *Star Wars*—that it was from the same guy!

It was reminiscent of—God rest him—Stanley Kubrick. He did something entirely different every time, with a different dynamic, energy, and rhythm.

IAN MCDIARMID
(actor, "Senator Sheev Palpatine")

I knew Liam a bit before the film. He did a play called *The Judas Kiss* for my theater company, the Almedia. Liam and I actually had very few scenes together in *Episode I*.

PERNILLA AUGUST
(actress, "Shmi Skywalker")

I loved working with Liam. When you meet him on the set, you just go with it. He's so there, so supportive and so polite. I'll do anything with him. He's also such a great actor who arrived on *The Phantom Menace* set right after wrapping *Les Misérables*, directed by Billie August.

NATALIE PORTMAN
(actress, "Padmé Amidala")

Liam is very kind and reserved. He's a very classy man and such a great actor. He had just finished filming *Les Misérables* and he hopped over and started *Star Wars* the next day. It was amazing to watch him work. He was very good to me.

By the time he would pick up Obi-Wan Kenobi's lightsaber for the first time, Ewan McGregor had already established himself as an actor to be reckoned with in films like Shallow Grave *(1994),* Trainspotting *(1996),* Emma *(1996), and* A Life Less Ordinary *(1997). He is also the nephew of Denis Lawson, who played Wedge Antilles in the original trilogy.*

GEORGE LUCAS

The first thing Ewan McGregor said when he came in for his audition was, "You've got to give me this, because my uncle was Wedge." I said, "Okay, that's a good reason."

RICK MCCALLUM

Ewan is playing the young Obi-Wan. A fantastic Scottish actor who can play a variety of roles; he's like a chameleon. To have somebody be in *Trainspotting* at the beginning of one year and *Emma* at the end of the same year, shows amazing versatility. He is really a mercurial, multitalented, multifaceted human being. He just seemed to us the perfect Obi-Wan.

GEORGE LUCAS

Ewan McGregor is the perfect young Harrison Ford, but he's also a great young Alec Guinness. He's extremely relaxed and very strong. All the things that Alec Guinness is. Ewan is very witty and enthusiastic and young and impatient, and those things come through.

EWAN MCGREGOR
(actor, "Obi-Wan Kenobi," *The Phantom Menace*)

I knew I wanted to be an actor when I was nine years old. Denis used to come out to Crieff, my small, conservative town in Scotland, where I lived. He didn't wear any shoes and he had long hair, and I would say, "Who's that weird guy?" He was so different from the people I was surrounded by and I think my wanting to act had a lot to do with that. I wanted to be different as well. There was that *and* I was obsessed with old black-and-white movies from the twenties, thirties, and forties, from Hollywood, Ealing, or wherever. They were so beautifully shot and the acting was very straightforward and amazingly underplayed. They had very good stories, which we seem to have forgotten about these days. The third reason I wanted to be an actor was that in Britain we had a tradition called the Principal Boys. If there was a production of *Jack and the Beanstalk,* Jack would always be played by a woman. It was all about sex. Whenever I would go to the theater, I would fall in love with whoever was on stage. And it's still absolutely about sex.

But Denis didn't give me much advice. He was actually very bored doing the *Star Wars* movies. He had a tiny part in all three and I think he's rather bemused that he still gets fan mail from people. He has done some very good work, but it's always "Denis Lawson from *Star Wars.*" He didn't think it would be a good idea for me to do the *Star Wars* film, really. Everyone asks if he'll have a cameo in the prequel films, but he can't because Wedge wouldn't be born yet. George was joking about having him play Wedge's father and age him up a bit.

IAN MCDIARMID

I've known Ewan for quite a few years. His uncle, Denis Lawson, and I are great friends. We've been friends since we were at drama school together rather further back than I care to admit. I remember that Ewan first came into my theater when he was studying acting at Guild Hall. He came to see his uncle and me in *Volpone.* That's when I first met him, and I've watched his meteoric rise ever since. I've seen him now and again, on and off. As I say, though, we weren't often together in *Episode I.* We actually had one day together where we worked *very* close, with Ewan, Jake, and myself. Ewan and I swapped old stories. We're both Scots, so there was an immediate bond.

EWAN MCGREGOR

There's no doubt that *Star Wars* is the hugest thing there is. When I was getting ready to start, I realized I hadn't thought about that kind of thing—how huge it was—since the time they had offered it to me. It took me a long time to say, "Well, maybe this isn't the right thing for me to do." No, it *really* was, "Do I want to do *Star Wars*?" Well, yes. *Yes!* But I couldn't think about playing Kenobi, because I was kind of in *Star Wars* denial. Essentially it was like making any other film.

When she assumed the role of Queen Padmé Amidala in The Phantom Menace *in 1995, fifteen-year-old Natalie Portman had already had a great deal of success in Hollywood. Five years earlier a Revlon agent tried to get her interested in being a child model, and while she turned* that *opportunity down, she did use it to acquire an agent for acting. In 1992, she (along with aspiring singer Britney Spears) auditioned for the Off-Broadway musical* Ruthless!, *and both became understudies. In 1994 she played a child who's a protégé to Jean Renoir's assassin in Luc Besson's* The Professional, *which was followed by roles in Michael Mann's* Heat *(1995) and, in 1996, Ted Demme's* Beautiful Girls. *She sings in Woody Allen's underrated musical* Everybody Says I Love You *and fights aliens in Tim Burton's* Mars Attacks! *Just prior to becoming part of the* Star Wars *universe, she appeared on Broadway in the adaptation of* The Diary of Anne Frank.

NATALIE PORTMAN

When I was offered the films, I took a long time to decide whether I was going to do them or not. That was for two major reasons. One was the commitment—I was signing at age fourteen for at least ten years. That's a *huge* thing to do at *any* age. When you're fourteen and you don't know what you're going to do the next day, you're not really jumping at the opportunity to sign away your life until you're twenty-four. That was the first consideration. The second one, obviously, is that *The Phantom Menace* is so big. When you do any sort of big film, it changes your life. The recognizability—I really couldn't prepare for that. You can imagine what will happen, because you see other people being so excited, but it worried me that people would be more interested in me and my private life. It makes your life much more difficult, but it presented so many opportunities. It seemed like I would have the best summer ever, so I said yes.

RICK MCCALLUM

She's like Audrey Hepburn: serious, deeply committed, and focused. She was only fifteen when we started the movie, but there's just something electric about her. She is a lovely actress. She was always our first choice for this role.

GEORGE LUCAS

The perfect queen! She's very strong. At the same time, she's very young. She plays a fourteen-year-old queen in *The Phantom Menace* and it's the same problem I had in the first film with Princess Leia. Natalie is very intelligent, has a lot of presence, and is a very strong person. I needed somebody to play a fourteen-year-old girl who could basically be elected to rule a planet and make that believable.

Early on in his life, Ray Park devoted himself to studying the martial arts, though by the late 1990s he had turned his attention to acting. He was a stunt double and played Raptor #3 and Baraka #2 in Mortal Kombat: Annihilation *(1997), and would follow* The Phantom Menace *with* Sleepy Hollow *(1999) and* X-Men *(2000), playing, respectively, Headless Horseman and Toad. In the first of the Star Wars prequels, of course, he memorably portrayed Sith Lord Darth Maul, who would ultimately go into combat against both Qui-Gon and Obi-Wan.*

GEORGE LUCAS

I was looking for the kind of sword-fighting we had already done, but I wanted a more energized version of it, because we actually never really saw Jedis at work—we'd only seen old men (Obi-Wan), crippled half droid–half men (Darth Vader), and young boys (Luke). To see the Jedi fighting in their prime, I wanted a much more energetic and faster version of what we'd been doing.

RAY PARK
(actor, "Darth Maul")

My wanting to act was one of the reasons I started with martial arts. Also, my dad was a big fan of movies. We watched a lot of martial arts and science fiction movies. I saw *Star Wars* when I was about seven years old. It was one of the first movies I saw after we moved to London. I got all the action figures. I was a big fan. My dad cried when he saw the trailer for *The Phantom Menace*. Anyway, I was into movies and martial arts. My heroes were Jackie Chan, Arnold Schwarzenegger, and Jet Li. *Mortal Kombat: Annihilation* was my break. It was where I learned about the industry. Before I got that, I was going to set up a gym and teach full-time. I met people on the film. I got to perform stunts. It was a good experience, but it made me feel even more that

I wanted to be an actor out there *in front* of the camera, doing stuff for myself and not for someone else.

RICK MCCALLUM

One of the problems we had when we were casting for Darth Maul was that Robin Gurland was really looking for an actor, and I wanted an actor, too. But the truth finally came to us that an actor could only go so far in the role, because it was so physical. When I saw Ray in the first makeup test, that was when I actually did the deal with him to be Darth Maul. There was no point in going with anyone else. It's not a major speaking role. It was really about attitude and stunt performance. He has all those gifts and more. He made total sense for this role. We got him into the stunt union—everything was a first for him on this film. He is a really focused and caring guy and he's quite stunning in his makeup for the role.

RAY PARK

People can't quite take it in that I played this character in the movie or that I am who I am. They can't comprehend how this nice guy could have played this evil character. Some people don't believe me at all when I say, "I played Darth Maul." When I was on *Phantom Menace*, I was concerned about the kids I used to teach gymnastics to, because I was the bad guy and I didn't want them thinking, "My coach is a bad guy in real life." But it's great when people come up to me and say they were eight years old when they saw *Phantom Menace* for the first time and it got me into tae kwon do and karate. It's nice to hear that it was an inspiration. I grew up with Jackie Chan and Bruce Lee, so it's really nice that the character had an impact on kids to want to do martial arts. I also played Snake Eyes in *G.I. Joe,* so I'm aware that I've relived my childhood. Like, G.I. Joe was the first toys I played with. Then it was *Star Wars* and *The Empire Strikes Back* that really got me into martial arts and gymnastics. I saw Luke Skywalker do a handstand with Yoda and I was like, "That's what I need to do. I need to learn." I even asked my dad, "Can you build me a lightsaber?" So *Star Wars* really had a big impact on me as a kid as well.

I didn't know what to expect. I kept an open mind about what might happen. I knew that once people saw the movie, they would realize that I wasn't an extra. But I didn't realize just how cool Darth Maul would look and how popular he would be.

A newcomer was needed to play the role of young Anakin Skywalker, and the production cast Jake Lloyd, who began his acting career at age seven on four episodes of ER, *in the film* Unhook the Stars, *as Arnold Schwarzenegger's son in* Jingle All the Way, *and* Apollo 11.

JAKE LLOYD
(actor, "Young Anakin Skywalker," *The Phantom Menace*)

After *Jingle All the Way,* my mom was like, "Okay, you worked with Arnold Schwarzenegger. Are you done now?" I was like, "No, Mom, I'm still up for the new *Star Wars* film." She was like, "We'll have to talk about that." Then my agent called me and she was like, "Oh, how would you like to go to England for four months?" I started yelling and then I took a deep breath in, and I was like, "Oh my God, I got *Star Wars.*" And then I started crying.

RICK MCCALLUM
We went through two years of searching for the right kid to play Anakin. Jake has a very interesting personality. He's smart, mischievous, and loves anything mechanical. He was really a good kid. He had all the right qualities that George was looking for in Anakin.

GEORGE LUCAS
With Jake, he was this wild little Tom Sawyer kid who was exactly the kind of thing I was looking for in Anakin.

PERNILLA AUGUST
I tried to be a motherly friend to him. I got to know his parents, because they were always with him, which was good. He's so relaxed. I've worked with kids quite a lot, and you have to be patient with them. They are so sensitive. I think it's important that child actors always have one person to relate to, and George was that person for Jake. He would talk to George about the character and our relationship. I thought what I could do to help Jake was just to show that I'm professional and that I'm doing it for real, to be open and be there when we were acting.

NATALIE PORTMAN
Jake was a little elf on the set, just running around, being happy and playing. When you work with kids that young, you get scared that they'll be obnoxious stage kids corrupted by the business. And Jake wasn't like that at all. He's a total kid. He was playing with droids and constantly telling us riddles.

JAKE LLOYD
I wasn't nervous. I treated the other actors like they were just regular people. And they treated me the same way. They were all really nice. I really enjoyed working with everyone. I worked a lot with Ahmed Best and he was always

making me laugh. And I worked a lot with Pernilla August. We all became really good friends. George was really nice to me, too. He helped me a lot, as any director would help an actor. I think that his being a nice guy helped me. He treated me as he did the other actors, and that felt good.

Prior to his work as Jar Jar Binks in The Phantom Menace, *musician and actor Ahmed Best cowrote and coproduced three albums for the Jazzhole, and was a part of the cast of* Stomp, *which toured the United States and Europe. It was this show that brought him to the attention of casting director Robin Gurland, who thought he would be perfect for the CG character.*

AHMED BEST

Stomp is very different from *The Phantom Menace* in terms of what I do as a performer. *Stomp* was an incredible training ground. You could try anything. If it worked, if it got a reaction, you swam, and if it didn't, you sank. So I learned how to play off people. In doing *The Phantom Menace,* I looked at George as the audience. I just bounced ideas off of him. *Stomp* was also a very personal show. It's very much about putting your personality, who you are, out there. I tried to approach Jar Jar as a personal character. It was more than a surprise; it was a shock that they cast me in the movie. I had no idea, no inkling. I had no motivation, even, to seek out this movie in any way, shape, or form. After I got it, I just knew it would be cool.

RICK MCCALLUM

We made a very conscious choice up front to always make sure that whatever digital character we were doing, the actor who would do the voice would be present when we were shooting those sequences. In the case of Jar Jar Binks, we had a wonderful actor named Ahmed Best from the stage show *Stomp*. He was in a suit that resembled the CGI character. Ahmed was on the set every day. We would always rehearse with him and we would actually shoot sequences with him. That was not only for the actors, so they would know where their eyelines were, but so that we would have reference for everybody at ILM to understand the lighting conditions he was in. So, we took a great deal of time and effort. George wanted to make sure that the actors felt comfortable, that they wouldn't be talking or interacting with sticks of ping-pong balls or any crude or artificial markers. They always had an *actor* to work with.

AHMED BEST

I wore a costume that made me look *exactly* like the character does in the movie, aside from the ears and the neck. The arms were made of foam latex.

They had the same design, the same flesh tone and fingers. The costume was made out of leather; it's the same thing Jar Jar has on in the movie. I would do scenes with the actors in rehearsal and then shoot them with the actors. Then I would go back to the bench and George would do shots without me in them, too. The costume got pretty hot, especially when we were in Tunisia, but I survived.

GEORGE LUCAS

He's a very hard character to figure out; very hard dialogue to understand and make work. Kind of Yoda times ten. But Ahmed Best just sort of took to it. It takes a very particular kind of personality. A lot of people couldn't figure it out. They couldn't equate what they were saying with real life, but he really got it and turned it into a real language and a real character. When you're doing a digital character, you end up having the actor on the set. I do, anyway. I cast Ahmed Best, because he was a talented actor and also because he was focused a lot on movement and dance. He knew how to move his body and create a character with his body. I wasn't sure if I would re-voice him or not. That wasn't a concern. I just wanted to make sure he was up to acting with the other actors in the movie. Could he create a character? As it turns out, Ahmed was terrific. I used his voice. He turned in a great performance on the set.

AHMED BEST

I was very happy they decided to use my voice, but I always knew they would. I just had to convince them. I guess I did a good job of it. It was always in the back of my mind that they *wouldn't* use it. That's reality, but it didn't stop me from doing the best I could do. And then they used it.

RICK MCCALLUM

Every day when we'd do a sequence and set up for a shot, George would re-hearse with him and the actors. They would make sure that they blocked out all the movements they had, and then we'd always film Ahmed with the actors. We'd do one or two takes and finally get to the take that we liked, and everybody knew what the behavior was. Then Jar Jar would get out of the shot and we'd reshoot it, very fresh, where everybody knew where his position was and knew where they needed to be looking in order to see Jar Jar. So that's how we did it throughout the whole movie. ILM needed to see the lighting reference, so they always have their plate with Jar Jar in it and the animators know what the basic movement of Jar Jar is. Then they also have the lighting of Jar Jar; what he's got to look like and the shadows that he casts on other people. Then on the empty plate, without Jar Jar, they take their wire model of Jar Jar and animate it. That's where they create his performance. It's an amalgam of what Ahmed did on the set and their imagination. George directs that performance in animation for huge periods of time.

GEORGE LUCAS

Now with a digital character, not only do you have to hire that actor, but you have to hire a second actor with the same techniques, the same skills, the same talents—plus some. That actor is called an animator. He works in collaboration with the original actor. They work together in terms of motion capture and spend time together. He takes the performance the actor on the set did—and the voice performance he did—and turns it into minute facial expressions, eye movements, and things that really create the character on the next level. With digital characters, you're basically paying two actors to create one character, so it's twice as expensive that way. With an actor, you shoot it and three hours later, you're finished. With a digital character, it takes three or four months.

Swedish actress, director, and screenwriter Pernilla August, and frequent collaborator with director Ingmar Bergman, was cast as Shmi Skywalker, Anakin's mother. As established in the film, Anakin, it seems, was the result of an immaculate conception.

PERNILLA AUGUST

I'm not surprised George added the immaculate conception scenario. It's a little controversial.

LIAM NEESON

There's a virgin birth in every mythology and in every culture. Sometimes people just attribute it to Christianity. That's not true. It's ancient. But Pernilla and I had a few giggles when she had to say her line. When it came to my close-up, I thought, "How do I play this? Do I do a double-take? Do I say, 'You're still a virgin?'" I just had to take it in stride.

GEORGE LUCAS

I've been very conscious about *not* making the movies religion-specific. When I brought *Star Wars* out, it seemed most religions used it to demonstrate their own beliefs—not only Judeo-Christian, but also Eastern. And in many cases, people have said they're much more Eastern than Western in nature. The ideas of a virgin birth, the freeing of slaves—the issue of immaculate conception is a motif that runs through all religions, all stories about the local deity or the local hero. It's the same thing with Hercules. Most heroes are conceived in an unusual way. And in this particular case, it's actually not immaculate conception, it's conception by metaphor.

PERNILLA AUGUST

George actually didn't give me any more backstory than we know from the movie. Shmi and Anakin have been slaves for a while, probably about three years. George gave us a lot of space and I felt we were building the character together. It was a give and take. He didn't talk too much, but I never hesitated to ask him if I was wondering about something. I liked working with him. I think Shmi is "the" mother. She's very brave and supportive of her son. She's not selfish. She lets Anakin go and she's thinking of the best way for him. She also taught him to go with his feelings.

RICK MCCALLUM

We'd known Pernilla August for a long time. She had worked with Ingmar Bergman a lot. She's a great Swedish actress. We first worked with her on *Young Indy* where she played Princess Sophie's nanny, Emillie, in the "Vienna 1908" episode. She's a lovely and wonderful actress. She has all the dignity and power that you could ever want for the role of Anakin's mother.

PERNILLA AUGUST

I was nervous at the beginning. I'm not used to speaking in English. I didn't know if it would work, if I could speak another language *and* do the acting at the same time.

Longtime Star Wars *fan Samuel L. Jackson made no secret of the fact that he would love to be a part of the franchise, and, of course, he got his wish when Lucas cast him as Jedi Master Mace Windu. Prior to* The Phantom Menace, *he starred in* Jurassic Park *(1993),* True Romance *(1993),* Pulp Fiction *(1994),* Hail Caesar *(1994),* Die Hard with a Vengeance *(1995),* The Long Kiss Goodnight *(1996), and* Jackie Brown *(1997).*

SAMUEL L. JACKSON
(actor, "Mace Windu")

I didn't call George Lucas and make it known that I wanted to do *Star Wars*, but I might as well have. I was doing a talk show to promote something and one of the questions I got asked was, "If you could work with any director you haven't worked with, who would it be?" Usually I say, "The directors tend to come with the film and I usually choose my jobs based on the film." But suddenly I realized that George was about to do a *new Star Wars* trilogy. I love the genre. I wanted to be in a *Star Wars* movie. So the next time I was asked, I said, "Well, I would *love* to work with George Lucas. I would love to be in the next *Star Wars* movie."

GEORGE LUCAS

When I talked to Sam, he said, "Oh, I want to be in *Episode I*." I said, "Well, I've got this role in *Episode I,* but it's not much now. In the next one, he actually gets to swordfight." Sam said, "Ooooh, okay. I'm in." He wanted to be in it anyway.

SAMUEL L. JACKSON

I said it often and apparently I said it on some British talk show while George was in preproduction on the first film. Somebody in his office heard and told him what I said. They called me and asked me if it was true, and I said it was. While I was shooting *Sphere* George was back at his ranch. They invited me to the ranch and I went out to talk with him. He said, "Sam, I don't know what to do. I haven't written the script yet. I'm not quite sure what the story is. I've seen some of your work and you're a very good actor, but you could wind up yelling, 'Look out! Go this way! Run that way!'" I said, "I don't care. I just want to be in a *Star Wars* movie." Sure enough, he found something for me.

RICK MCCALLUM

In terms of the other cast members, Sam is just a consummate professional. He's one of the actors for whom making a film is like digging a ditch and he loves being in the ditch. He doesn't make the ditch more comfortable. He doesn't want to turn it into something it isn't. He just loves coming to work. Sam's extraordinary. He never had any adjustments to make, even on *Episode I.* He also understands blue screen incredibly well. In that regard he's more like a theatrical actor. We showed him the artwork. He saw the animatics. And he just gets it. He only worked on *Episode I* for a few days. In *Episode II,* all together, we had him for about ten days. He also got to pick up a lightsaber and use it. For someone like Sam, who's a big *Star Wars* fan, that was a huge deal.

SAMUEL L. JACKSON

I'm there and some guy comes over to me and opens up a case. Inside there were nine lightsabers and he would say, "Choose yours." I would be there, hyperventilating. I would say, "I'll take *that* one." That was *very* cool.

RICK MCCALLUM

Sam sets the standard for everybody in terms of work ethic, focus, dedication, and what he brings. Stardom didn't happen for him early. It happened for him later on, and so he worships and loves every single day he's on a set, every day he's working.

SAMUEL L. JACKSON

I had five pages of scenes and that was it. Nobody gave me a whole script. It was a *very* cool experience. Frank Oz was cool. George was so low-key it was incredible. To understand the kind of pressure that surrounds that film, to know it was George's baby, that he hadn't directed in twenty years, and to see him so calm was amazing. It was great.

Returnees to the franchise include Ian McDiarmid as Senator Palpatine/Sith Lord Darth Sidious, Frank Oz as the voice of Yoda, and Anthony Daniels as C-3PO. On top of that, of course, there are many supporting performers as well.

IAN MCDIARMID

I was happy that he wanted me. George is a wonderful storyteller. Look what he did with *Star Wars*. It's the supreme evidence of his brilliance. He started right in the middle of the saga. *Star Wars* was *Episode IV*. That was always the way he imagined it. Richard Wagner spent a large part of his life when he set out to write *The Ring*. *Star Wars* is, in some ways, comparable to *The Ring*.

George actually mentioned Shakespeare quite a lot during my conversations with him. The whole panoply of the *Star Wars* films is very Shakespearean. It's also very much Mark Twain, Buck Rogers, and Wagner. But it's somehow not a ragbag. There are allusions to classics past, but the vision is a governing one and it is George's. At the end of the day, *Star Wars* is *not* Shakespeare, Wagner, or Buck Rogers, but George's own precise and clear story, even if you can trace back his influences. I'm sure there's some Akira Kurosawa and D. W. Griffith in there, too.

RAY PARK

On my first day of shooting, I worked with Ian and he was very nice to me. I asked him for a few tips, because I was very nervous. I asked, "Do you think I'm doing this right?" It was my first time acting and I didn't want to look stupid. Once I started speaking, acting out the part and doing the moves, I felt really comfortable. It was just that I had put a lot of pressure on myself because I wanted to do well.

NATALIE PORTMAN

Ian was awesome. He's such a *great* actor. I loved what he did in the movie. We really didn't talk a lot about *Return of the Jedi*. We talked more about theater and his acting company in England. He was very supportive.

IAN MCDIARMID

Also, the thing about George is that he makes strong, instinctive decisions. You feel that you're cast because he thinks *you* are the person who can play the role. You already have that confidence. And if anything didn't feel right or appropriate, we would discuss it as any actor and director would. George and I hardly discussed anything at all, actually. We didn't *need* to discuss much. That kind of straightforwardness makes for a very relaxing relationship between a director and an actor. I was very pleased to see him take full charge on *The Phantom Menace*.

FRANK OZ

Rick McCallum came to me and we talked about how they wanted to do Yoda. It surprised me that they decided to do Yoda as a puppet. I thought that they would go with CGI. But I love the character and I like working with George. So I was happy to do it. George intimated to me that there's something about Yoda as he is now that's more organic, that worked somehow. I'm comfortable with CGI, *if* it's used properly. I think Yoda—and this is my own opinion—should not be *too* high-tech, because you'll lose the warmth.

RICK MCCALLUM

Frank Oz has reached a whole other level of performance as Yoda that I absolutely admire and love deeply. Frank is involved in much more than just doing Yoda's voice. He worked with Rob Coleman, our director of animation, who actually does Yoda's CGI performance. They collaborated very closely together.

FRANK OZ

In the beginning, operating Yoda was through cables and later it was remote control. You still have the same basic situation, though—four people trying to make one character work subtly. There are always good parts and bad aspects to technology, but you're doing essentially the same thing and still trying to achieve a common goal. And the other thing is that at least half the success of Yoda comes from the people who are working with him. Sam, Ewan, and

Liam were very good with Yoda, and the scenes with Yoda in *The Empire Strikes Back* would not have been nearly as good if Mark Hamill didn't do as fine a job as he did. And at the time I wrote Mark and Irvin Kershner notes telling them that.

ANTHONY DANIELS
(actor, "C-3PO")

I was genuinely surprised when the *Star Wars* Special Edition came out, because I *wasn't* involved in any of the upgrading. It was all done digitally. I didn't have to do any new acting. But I thought it was pretty neat and very good, obviously. Then they told me that they were going to make *Episode I*. I was glad, because there were always meant to be three more movies. The fans had been waiting for them. But there was a time when I didn't know whether or not Threepio existed in the world of *Episode I*. I had very mixed feelings about the prospect of being left out—partly because I wasn't sure if I had a job, but really because I was hoping to be in *all* of the movies. It's like collecting beer caps. So I asked some questions and they said, "We don't know yet." Then, *finally*, George asked me to go to Leavesden Studios in England.

George and I sat down and he told me the story. The real joke was when he told me, "You're made by Anakin Skywalker." I thought that was really neat, and I was very happy. Then, two days later, I realized that Anakin is the *baddie*. So I was genuinely surprised—partly by my own stupidity, but also at the twist in the story. I thought to myself, "If Threepio ever finds out who his father is, he's going to be traumatized." Maybe that's why this guy is so weird—maybe he found out the truth. I never even thought of that. So although I was only briefly involved in *Episode I*, it was just terrific to be a part of it, and to keep my connection with the movies.

George told me that Threepio would be made of wires, and he explained to me how it would be done. I thought it was a tremendously inventive and clever bit of scriptwriting. We all know C-3PO as the golden robot, and I had always assumed that he was a million years old, so it really tweaked my interest to discover that he started out as a box of junk. That was very clever, and the puppet was a tremendous piece of engineering. It managed, visually, to have a personality as well. I learned that it was very, very difficult to operate, though, because I actually took over the operation of it for *Episode II*.

One thing about doing the films this time around is that we all suffer from thinking of Threepio as a main character in the other trilogy. George made it very clear to me that *Episodes IV* to *VI* were really Threepio's main movies. In *Episode I*, it was a meet-and-greet. It wasn't a big deal. Here are two robots meeting and—with some dramatic irony—you know what's going to happen to them.

Filming on The Phantom Menace *began on June 26, 1997—nearly three years after Lucas started writing the script—and continued until September 30 of the same year. The big news, and it wasn't always clear that it would be the case, was that Lucas stepped behind the camera as director. Although he had done uncredited work as a director on every Lucasfilm project from* More American Graffiti *all the way through* Young Indiana Jones *(and directing the one Harrison Ford appearance in the series), he had avoided fully stepping behind the camera as sole director since he directed* A New Hope *in the 1970s. That was all about to change.*

GEORGE LUCAS

Making movies is very much like being in a war; you're responsible for *everything*. I mean, you hire a great crew, but a crew is 250 people, and there's probably fifty of those people that are *really* connected to the important part of designing things and doing things. So you have to work with fifty people and you have to make sure they're always on the same page every single day, all day long. And then what you do is you direct the actors and you direct the crew and before that you've directed the sets and the costumes and all these other things. And when you're shooting, that's when all that comes together. I say it's sort of like surgery, because if you make a mistake you have to live with it forever.

RICK MCCALLUM

I think he thought, "If I'm going to do these movies, why not do it right?" He needs to be able to set up the tone, style, and look, and the way it's going to be done. I'm thrilled that he finally agreed to direct.

GEORGE LUCAS

The divorce from Marcia kind of destroyed me. She had another man who was ten years younger than me . . . the classic situation. But my former wife and I adopted a daughter and, as I held her for the first time, it was like having lightning hit me, a transforming joy I'll never forget. Until then, I had loved movies most. After that, movies became second. Fortunately, I was forty and already successful and that put me in a place where I could enjoy the pleasures of children. I have three kids now. I adopted the other two as a single father. There's Amanda, Katie, and Jet. So I was raising kids, running companies, and making movies at the same time. I drove my kids to school every day. I had them on the set with me when I was working. I was Mr. Mom and Mr. Dad combined. I even made them waffles. I make *great* waffles. I really wanted my children and I love being with them.

BRIAN JAY JONES

There were probably a couple of reasons he chose to direct again. For one thing, he can have his family on set with him. That makes it worth it right there, when you can have the kids with him by his side. He's actually lightened up.

GEORGE LUCAS

I found getting back to directing was like I hadn't stopped and in some ways I *hadn't* stopped, because I'd been directing second unit, I'd been very involved in the creative process in everything I'd done since I stopped directing. When I stopped directing, part of it was the explosion of *Star Wars*. It meant I had to put some focus into my company on how I'd maintain this franchise that sort of grew up in my backyard. And directing it, I wasn't going to be able to oversee everything. The films are very big and hard to do, and I felt that I could serve them better as executive producer overseeing an entire production than I could trying to run right back in and be a director. As it happened, I just ended up going off on a different path and being executive producer. I had some other projects that I had sitting on the shelf; told one to Steve Spielberg [*Raiders of the Lost Ark*]. He said, "I wanna do that, I wanna do that." So I thought, "Well, okay, I'll produce this one." Jim Henson came. I just ended up with a lot of projects and went down this path of making all these other movies. Nobody says you *have* to be a director.

DAVID TATTERSALL

With George directing, two cameras were generally used to cover every setup—one wide and the other tighter, but at the same angle. The first camera would cover for the storyboard, while the second would get something else. It was fairly conventional. The first unit would start with George and then the second unit, with cameraman Giles Nuttgens, would follow up behind to pick up their material. Giles shot several episodes of *Young Indy*, so, again, he was somebody familiar with our proceedings. George was very hands-on during shooting, and every sequence was planned and detailed with the storyboards or animatics that we'd refer to over the day. Also, because we had so many standing sets, we were able to spend a good amount of time walking through them and working out how we'd be shooting things.

BRIAN JAY JONES

The other factor in his directing is he's got digital technology at his fingertips and he's much more relaxed, because he feels like he can make the movie he wants to make. Doesn't matter if there's an effects shop that can or can't build his effects or turn them in on time. He can do everything in the computer now. There's a great George Harrison story where he talked about the time after the Beatles broke up and he releases the triple-album *All Things Must Pass*. He described it as being like diarrhea where you've had to hold it for so long and then you finally get down on the bowl. That's the way Lucas is with *Episode I*. It's like he can finally get down on the bowl and let loose with everything he has. This movie, again, is almost overwhelming visually at times, but he's just having so much fun with it.

STEVEN MELCHING
(screenwriter, *Star Wars: The Clone Wars*)

The Matrix on the surface was very flashy and groundbreaking, but I think *Phantom Menace* was actually more groundbreaking in terms of its filmmaking. It was just more seamless and invisible, whereas *The Matrix* used a lot of techniques that we're all familiar with and using the bullet-time stuff, which I had been seeing in Gap TV commercials.

BRIAN JAY JONES

There's actually a great meme showing Lucas in 1983, standing among all the spaceships and everything they built. Then they cut to 1999 and he's standing in front of the green screen, but that's really what he's done at that point. I mean, I think he feels like he's earned this. He's the one that invented the CGI technology. He's the one that had the faith that it would work and he's having a great time.

Most of filming took place at England's Leavesden Film Studios, a former Rolls-Royce aircraft factory. In 1994, unable to get access to Pinewood Studios, Eon Productions, the company behind the James Bond films, leased the space, gutted the factories on the property, and turned them into soundstages for the first Pierce Brosnan 007 film, GoldenEye. *After that, Lucasfilm took over the property for the duration of production of* The Phantom Menace. *And while Tim Burton's* Sleepy Hollow *would be filmed there, in 2000 it began serving as home base for* Harry Potter and the Sorcerer's Stone *and all of the subsequent films in that series. Warner Bros., Potter's producer, ultimately purchased Leavesden outright, turning part of it into a permanent* Harry Potter *exhibit open to the public. But at the time, it was ideal for the return of* Star Wars.

RICK MCCALLUM

It's an old Rolls-Royce aircraft engine factory which was bought by a company called Millennium, which is a Malaysian consortium. The thing that makes it unique and extraordinary is that it has the largest backlot in the world. One hundred and eleven acres and over 850,000 square feet of stage space. What was great is that we had it all to ourselves for a very long time. We had an extensive area for special floor effects, we had a huge area that we turned into our special creatures effects, which is where we were making our creatures. We also made every single costume ourselves. We had an enormous construction area, because we were building close to fifty sets. We had our own rigging department, our own fire department, etc. It was like a small city. It's basically the same *Young Indy* template. We did everything ourselves and didn't depend on the kindness of strangers.

DAVID TATTERSALL

The advantage for Rick and George was that they could lease the entire facility; they didn't have to share anything with other productions, which is the usual situation in a studio setting. Because of that, many sets could be built at once and left standing indefinitely. Our production designer, Gavin Bocquet, had about fifteen quite large spaces to work with, which gave us the room to have some twenty-five fully constructed sets to shoot on. Meanwhile, all of the wrapped sets at Leavesden would be replaced with new ones—we'd then return to shoot, using the *next twenty-five* sets, including the Jedi Council Chamber, the starfighter hangar in Theed, and the palace's generator complex. The advantage to this plan was that we had time to pre-rig and pre-light before we began shooting again, which allowed us to just go from one set to the next.

While the studio was secured, extensive scouting by McCallum, Bocquet, and David West Reynolds, the author of numerous Star Wars *reference books, was done to find locations that would be unique to the film.*

RICK MCCALLUM

We scouted locations in Morocco and Tunisia. We invited David West Reynolds to join us on this trip. He's not only an intelligent guy, but he was fun to be with. In terms of archaeology and science and the movement of races, he is very knowledgeable. He saw things on this trip he had never seen before. He was the first to spot Ben Kenobi's house, although we found it totally by accident. It was by the ocean and we said, "It can't be by the ocean," but it *was*! We also found the entrance to Mos Eisley, which is completely covered over now and looks totally different. We found an area in Tunisia called the Ksour. These are fortified grain areas. They were used in this one section of Tunisia where the Berbers would store their grain. Ksour have unusual shapes and have existed for hundreds of years and almost all of them remain intact. They are very difficult to get to, so it's not something that tourists end up seeing. You really need a four-wheel drive and be committed to spend at least a week finding them. Nobody has been there. Basically what I wanted to do, since none of us had worked on the previous three films, was to make sure we really understood Tatooine well. All my life, I've always wanted to see this area of the Ksour. I thought it might be a good place for Jawas or slave quarters or something else that would relate to the prequels. The trip was *very* worthwhile.

GAVIN BOCQUET

We traveled a lot on those scouts, mostly through Mediterranean Europe and North Africa. Sometimes it was just myself, sometimes a small group with Rick McCallum. Extraordinary travels and a once in a lifetime experience. For the Naboo environments, I traveled to most of the grand and impressive buildings that southern Europe has to offer, from cathedrals, palaces, monasteries, grand houses, etc., and eventually we decided on the palace at Caserta in Italy for the Naboo palace. We covered both Tunisia and Morocco for the Tatooine locations, and decided to stay with Tunisia. Rick McCallum and I initially did a tour of all the old *Star Wars* locations in Tunisia, to see what we might be able to use again, which was almost like an archaeological expedition, and we even saw remnants of old set pieces still lying around on many of the locations, which was extraordinary twenty-five years later.

RICK MCCALLUM

What's interesting is that the countries we were going to didn't know much about *Star Wars*. In fact, when we were in Morocco, they didn't know much about *Star Wars* or Indiana Jones. They didn't even know who Indiana Jones was. I think the films were made before they really started seeing a lot of movies. David West Reynolds said that nobody in Djerba knew anything about *Star Wars*, even though they had huge portions of the series all over their backyards and in the streets, nobody knew what they were for.

GAVIN BOCQUET

There was probably no average workday, and that is what can be so exciting about the film business in general, and even more so with *Star Wars*. Every day is a surprise and different. You could be in the office all day designing on the drawing board, you could be on-location scouts in different countries or closer to the studio, or you could be supervising set builds and also supervising all the other design work being done in the art department.

Other locations included Cassiobury Park in Watford, Hertfordshire, to serve as the forest of Naboo; a return to the Tunisian desert for scenes on Tatooine, with the outside of the city of Tozeur serving as Mos Espa; and the interior of Theed City's Naboo palace at the Reggia Palace in Caserta, Italy.

DAVID TATTERSALL

The long-term lease at Leavesden worked well with the production's general shooting schedule. We had three distinct phases on the production. The first was to work our way through our initial twenty-five sets at the studio, including the Galactic Senate chamber, the Mos Espa arena, Watto's junk shop, and Anakin's home on Tatooine. In the second phase, the company moved on to Italy and then Tunisia for location work depicting the Queen's palace on Naboo and scenic desert exteriors on Tatooine, respectively.

For the palace, all of the large palaces in Europe were scouted, but Reggia Palace in Caserta, Italy, just north of Naples, was selected because it featured the types of space we were after. George was looking for something on a massive scale and which featured classical architecture that could then be digitally enhanced and extended to seem even bigger. Unfortunately, Reggia Palace is also a popular tourist attraction and could only be secured for a handful of shooting days from the late afternoon into the night. Shooting in Reggia Palace was difficult for other reasons as well, primarily because we were shooting in anamorphic. The architecture there is almost entirely vertical, so composing shots that really took in the structures was sometimes hard, and we were limited in what we could do in there because it was a historic place.

In one key scene there, Queen Amidala and her assault team are pinned down by the platoon of battle droids within a vast corridor of polished stone. To escape, they blast through a large window and use grappling-type hooks to climb to the next level of the castle-like structure. Unfortunately, we couldn't get permission to use squibs—explosive charges—while shooting in Caserta. But Gavin did a brilliant job of reconstructing that corridor from Reggia Palace back at Leavesden after we returned to England for just one day of shooting. That let us blow chunks out of columns and shatter the windows, but it had to match what we'd shot at Caserta.

Back at Leavesden, there were a number of extensive sets and situations that were challenging but also impressive to the cast. One of them was the Jedi Council sequence.

SAMUEL L. JACKSON

The first time I stepped on the set for *Episode I*, it was a little daunting, but only because I didn't have a clue what I was doing until I got there. Even when they told me I was playing a character named Mace Windu, I didn't know what he did until I went to costumes and they started putting Jedi robes on me. "Really? I'm a Jedi?" I looked at the script and saw my first conversation with Yoda. "Okay, how do I wrap my mind around this?" Apparently, this guy is pretty important and they've already been working on the film for two months. Here I am just showing up and I'm going to Liam Neeson's funeral and we're having a conversation there.

It was daunting to go into a situation where everybody had been there for a while. People had been in makeup for three hours and they had big heads and long necks. But by the time Lucas said, "Action," it was like, "Huh? Oh, what? Yeah." It was hard to keep a grin off my face sometimes, because I was looking around and thinking, "Look at this. This is great." You *do* get used to it, though, and then you go into a very comfortable space where you walk in, you command it, and you feel like you're a Jedi. You walk into the Jedi Council meeting, sit down, and pull out your robes. It happens.

While the movie was shot on 35mm, it would be the only entry in the prequel trilogy to do so. Some portions of it, however, were shot in high definition digital, which both Lucas and McCallum believed was pointing toward the future of production. Additionally, the fact that The Phantom Menace *had no less than three visual effects supervisors—John Knoll, who handled on-set production, the podrace, and space battle sequences; Dennis Muren, in charge of the underwater sequence and the ground battle; and Scott Squires on lightsaber effects as well as with teams on miniature effects and character animation—says so much about the scope of the film. There were a little less than two thousand effects shots in* The Phantom Menace *(by comparison,* Avengers: Endgame *and* The Force Awakens *contain 2500 VFX shots each, whereas* Jurassic Park *in 1993 had just 63).*

RICK MCCALLUM

Some of the effects technology we were trying to utilize was really beyond state-of-the-art. It was pushing the envelope in a new way, especially in terms of character animation and digital set technology. Those two areas were really being pushed heavily. But we also wanted to have the right amount of time to explore and continue the way in which we did *The Young Indiana Jones Chronicles*. The production template for us was that we'd shoot in a very nonlinear form. We'd shoot the bulk of the film, then we'd edit, then George rewrote and we'd go back and shoot, then we'd reedit, rewrite, and reshoot again. We kept on doing that; fixing and placing all the bits of the puzzle right up to the very last moment that the picture was being released.

RON MAGID
(journalist, visual effects historian)

Given that they had the ability to endlessly tweak and repurpose like this, the question was whether or not there was such a thing as having *too* much control over the images.

GEORGE LUCAS

Having lots of options means you have to have a lot more discipline, but it's the same kind of discipline that a painter, a novelist, or a composer would have. In a way, working in [digital] is much less frustrating than working in film, but it's not as though it's limitless no matter how you go. The artist will always push the art form until he bumps up against the technology—that's the nature of the artist. Because cinema is such a technological medium, there's a lot of technology to bump into, and I think as more people use digital they're going to find [it has] a lot more limitations. Some of those limitations will be [equivalent to] the limitations they had with film, and some of those limitations will just be because they've gone so far that they finally bumped into the technological ceiling.

DAVID TATTERSALL

Because so much of the picture would be completed in postproduction, I found myself working on a largely virtual production. The extensive use of blue screen on *Episode I* is what made shooting it so very different from any other I've done. The sheer amount of blue-screen material was amazing.

And for many of the cast members, it could be overwhelming given that there was actually very little for them to interact with. Some enjoyed the process, others clearly did not.

EWAN MCGREGOR

It was a different process from anything I had done before, only because it was a special effects movie and I had never made a big film set in space before. It's a different process; a much more arduous, time-consuming process to make one of these films. It's really hard work. When you're in front of a camera, it's the same deal wherever you are and whatever the budget is. What changes is how big your dressing room is, if you have a fridge that's stocked up every day. That's all superfluous and it doesn't mean *anything* in terms of the work. But in a film like *Star Wars,* compared to *A Life Less Ordinary,* let's say, it's a very different process for an actor. I knew that would be the case. You're just another player amidst a large amount of people. That's why I love movies. It takes hundreds of people to make them. In one respect, you are just another worker on the set.

LIAM NEESON

At the end of the day, you still have to act, whether it's with Jar Jar Binks in *The Phantom Menace* or Aidan Quinn in *Michael Collins.* There's something you still have to convey and share. Acting for me is about reacting, so it is very difficult to act with something that isn't there. Yet there *is* a technique to it. My main consideration was that I didn't want to be like someone in those early, early science fiction films where you see the hero with a glassy-eyed stare trying to fight some huge ant. Subconsciously, as an audience member, you say, "That guy is not looking at anything."

So we were conscious of that in *The Phantom Menace.* There were actors in back of the camera just to give us some kind of input. Sometimes we had little colored balls. We just needed something to help focus our eyes. I admired what all the actors did in *A New Hope* in regards to their attitudes towards the technology. It was very matter-of-fact. This is the universe they're in. Mark Hamill jumps into his speeder and—*phooph!*—he's off. He sold it as much as the special effects magicians did afterward. I loved that the actors used all of that. To them, it was everyday stuff, and I tried to do the same thing.

EWAN MCGREGOR

When [Alec] Guinness was interviewed about playing Kenobi, he said, "There wasn't a great deal of psychological preparation to have to do." I have to deliver the lines and hope they do the backgrounds nicely. In a way, that's all it was. It's not as demanding as other parts I've played in terms of emotions. It was a long shoot and very tiring. It's just a slog making a film like that. Science fiction movies are very taxing.

NATALIE PORTMAN

When I saw the movie, I didn't recognize 99 percent of the settings. It was really weird to do and I didn't realize how weird it was until I saw the movie.

I saw myself walking around places I had *never* been to, places that had been totally fabricated. It was a really different skill to master as an actor. It's a huge exercise in imagination. Not only do you have to imagine what your character is thinking and feeling, but you have to imagine what's around you. It's like a kid playing with a cardboard box and pretending it's a horse or a spaceship. That's what I was doing.

One of the key scenes in the film—which was obviously inspired by Ben-Hur's *chariot race—was the podrace scene on Tatooine, which young Anakin participates in hoping to win his freedom from servitude. The two-headed podrace announcer was Fode and Beed, voiced respectively by Greg Proops and Scott Capurro. Both were filmed in heavy makeup and blue bodysuits, but were ultimately replaced by full CGI.*

GREG PROOPS
(voice actor, "Fode")
George Lucas has his vision and I was but a prawn in the salad. The face makeup was quite good and took several hours.

SCOTT CAPURRO
(voice actor, "Beed")
I was surprised how much the CGI still looks like us. Sorry, I was alarmed at how much I actually resemble an alien. I guess our heads didn't match our bodies, but I could've told them that on the shooting day.

GREG PROOPS
I think it is a classic sci-fi homage to the chariot race in *Ben-Hur* and, of course, the most thrilling part of the picture.

SCOTT CAPURRO
It's fast and thrilling. Proops is very funny. For myself, for the lines in Huttese, I asked for cue cards. I tried to memorize the lines, but I was nervous and wanted to be exacting, because I'm both lazy and anal. It's a curse.

DAVID TATTERSALL
The podrace represented an interesting situation in which we dealt with large blue screens and interactive lighting came up while we were filming Anakin's ship during the podrace. We shot that with Jake Lloyd sitting in a full-scale pod mockup, which was on a gimbaled rock-and-roll base. We had a map that showed the route of the race, so we knew when he would be flying across

wide-open spaces with plenty of sunlight, through narrow canyons, under stone arches, and through tunnels. We then had to re-create the interactive lighting characteristics of those different areas on the race circuit, including nearby explosions caused by other pods crashing into canyon walls and so forth.

RICK MCCALLUM

Digital technology is an extraordinarily powerful tool, but it is just one part of the complex process of making a film. Digital effects were in their infancy. They still needed very complicated software and code that had to be specifically written to be able to achieve each result. That's what makes ILM so special. They were able to develop the technology and write the code to achieve everything we asked of them in-house. We presented them with what I had thought of as insurmountable problems, and yet they continued to amaze me by solving all of them.

JONATHAN RINZLER

Not only did George do big battles [in *Episode I*], but the shots are so beautifully composed. The tanks coming over the hill with the grass blowing underneath it—that is a *fantastic* shot. But also, people forget—or maybe they don't forget, but some people need to be reminded—George did not shut down the model department. The physical model department was in all of its glory. He's shone this PR spotlight on the digital side, because he was pushing that agenda very, very hard. Without a doubt. In some ways there was backlash against him for that. But he never actually shut down the model department. Until post–*Star Wars*.

By the time filming wrapped (not counting postproduction) on September 30, 1997, Lucas had shot 1.25 million feet of film—that quantity, in part, was shot because of his preference for master-shot coverage, allowing for maximum flexibility in the editing room. Due to the fact that Lucas and editor Paul Smith were editing throughout production, and because many of the sets were able to stand long after scenes utilizing them were wrapped, it was not difficult at all for the first unit to return to any given scene for additional footage if necessary.

DAVID TATTERSALL

The first shot of the day was always the master. After that, it was a matter of moving in to get two-shots, over-the-shoulders, and close-ups. We then switched to the reverse angle and repeated the process. It's really a classical way of getting coverage and so many other directors tie themselves in knots, from an editing standpoint, by not doing exactly that. The great thing about doing a wide master first is that nobody on the set is in any doubt about what's going on in the scene, which is important when there are so many effects. Confusion can very easily occur.

As things entered the final stages of production, Lucasfilm began to unveil its marketing push for the film. An unprecedented show of force, only galvanized by the large success of the brand during the 1995 "Power of the Force" action figure line, along with the continued success of the Star Wars *books and comics, showed what a potent brand* Star Wars *remained in popular culture after nearly two decades. To say anticipation was high for the film's eventual release is something of an understatement. While today movie trailers are eagerly awaited, with their very own PR campaigns to entice the hordes on social media, in 1998, theater owners were shocked to find showings for* The Waterboy, Meet Joe Black, *and* The Siege *were sold out, only to discover their numbers drop appositionally after the previews ended—all because of fans wanting to see the trailer for* The Phantom Menace.

DAN MADSEN

There's never been another time, and there never will be in *Star Wars* history, that was as exciting to live through, as the time leading up to *Episode I*. Everybody had been waiting for so long—for something new of *Star Wars* to come out. Never knowing if George was ever really going to get back to making it or not. Suddenly, everything is top secret. They're starting to work on it. The excitement, the anticipation around that. Even [leading up to] *The Force Awakens,* there was never a time in *Star Wars* history that was so exciting, and had such anticipation as that period leading up into *Episode I*. Unlike any time period I think I'll ever experience again.

Even a year before the movie came out, I flew out to Skywalker Ranch again, and Rick met with me—I met him in his office, I think we were doing one of his updates for *Star Wars Insider* magazine in person there. And he took me into this room, and there's George sitting in this editing bay, and he's literally editing the trailer, the very first trailer for *Episode I*. And Rick says, "George, look who's here." And George greets me, and I get to sit down. I get to sit there and watch the very first trailer—that George is literally editing at that moment—for *Episode I*. Rick is on one side, George is on the other, and they let me watch it. Then they're questioning me, "What did you like? What didn't you like? What worked, what didn't work?" So, I was giving my feedback for the very first trailer that was ever going to go out there for *Episode I*. I got goosebumps from the very first scene with the [text] that comes up with the "Every generation has a legend" kind of thing. And then you see that Gungan riding in on that Calf through the mist, and I'm thinking, "Holy Mackerel, this is incredible."

I can remember people going [to the movies] just to see that trailer, and then going again—they didn't really want to see the movie again, they were going just to see the trailer. That's how exciting it was. I don't know if I've ever known a movie that had so much excitement for it, that people went to go see a movie they didn't care about, just so they could see the trailer before it. That was an unusual situation as well. It was a time period that was so unique, and there was such excitement about the fact that *Star Wars* was coming back. And whether you liked the movie, or didn't like the movie, the whole buildup to that time period was truly an amazing and wondrous time to be a *Star Wars* fan. We're spoiled now, we have so much *Star Wars*—it's not as rare as it used to be. I'm grateful that I got to be at ground zero during that time. Because I got to be there in the trenches.

The trailer alone garnered tens of millions of views, which, in the days of dial-up internet, was no small feat.

Licensing for this film was at an all-time high—unlike the events that occurred in '77, Lucasfilm no longer had to beg and scrounge for licensees. They had to turn people away. Like the previous films, a comic book adaptation was completed by Dark Horse Comics.

HENRY GILROY
(comic book writer, *The Phantom Menace* adaptation)
Probably about five years before [adapting *The Phantom Menace* to comics] I started doing some short *Star Wars* stories for *Dark Horse Presents* and *Star Wars Tales*. Somebody at Lucasfilm said, "Hey, we should get a guy who did the *Star Wars Tales*, but also knows how to write a screenplay, to maybe do *The Phantom Menace* adaptation." It was funny, because eventually that became the same reason I became involved with the *Clone Wars* project: "Hey, this guy knows animation, he knows *Star Wars*, why don't we bring in someone to help us bring this all together?" I'm very fortunate to have been chosen by the producers, and George, who approved me early on.

They weren't letting any footage out at the time I was writing *The Phantom Menace* comics adaptation, so the material we were given were the scripts, a few storyboards, but mostly it was going to be still-frames. It was very important for George that the artist, Rodolfo Damaggio, draw the characters to look like the actors. I think, in previous adaptations, they aren't as specific about it—and George, in his mind, he wanted the comic book to be the movie on a printed page. I tried to add thought balloons, and narration here and there, and he was like, "No, no—just adapt the script."

Today, in the era where Lucasfilm waits six months to release a comic book adaptation (when at all), it's novel to look back to 1999, when Dark Horse put out The Phantom Menace *adaptation before the film was even released.*

HENRY GILROY

I asked actually that we push the release of *The Phantom Menace* comic adaptation back, and Dark Horse laughed. They go, "No, no, no, we want to do as much sales as we can beforehand. That's a huge part of it." Another part of that, a little insider story is, I had been sent *The Phantom Menace* script, and it had my name engraved on it, whatever, the watermark. Once it had been announced I was doing the adaptation, I think [in] '97, people started to try and find out where I lived. I was so paranoid about the script, that actually, before I left the house, I would hide it in the attic underneath insulation. So I probably inhaled all sorts of fiberglass particles, getting this script out and putting it back. I was so paranoid after I heard, "Oh my gosh, Henry Gilroy is adapting *The Phantom Menace.* We need to go find where that guy lives so we can go get information." I figured it was harmless enough that they just wanted to ambush me to try and get a copy, or get spoilers.

As the film entered the last few months before its release, John Williams returned once more to compose the music for a galaxy far, far away.

JOE KRAEMER
(composer, *Mission Impossible: Rogue Nation* and *Jack Reacher*)
The score to *The Phantom Menace* marked John Williams's return to the London Symphony Orchestra for the first time since *Return of the Jedi.* Like that score, this, too, was recorded in Studio One at Abbey Road. The centerpiece of the new score was "Duel of the Fates," a dynamic orchestral piece featuring choir. In a first for the saga, the choir would sing text. In choosing what words the choir would voice, John Williams chose a Celtic poem about an ancient, ongoing war between trees, focusing on a particular couplet that he felt resonated with the context of the film: "Under the tongue-root, a fight most dread, while another rages behind in the head." Williams had a linguistic expert at

UCLA translate the phrase into a variety of languages before settling on ancient Sanskrit, picking and choosing key words from the translation for the choir, based on the strength of the vowel sounds, which lent themselves most effectively to singing. Although the final "lyrics" are not a direct translation of the phrase, the result is an effective derivation that resonated with the film and audiences around the world. Lucas was so happy with the piece that he told Williams, "You've already scored the end of *Episode III*!"

Williams created a new theme for the character Anakin Skywalker, who is introduced as a nine-year-old boy in this film. Knowing his eventual fate would be to become Darth Vader, Williams chose to incorporate that villain's iconic melody into Anakin's Theme, tying the film to the original trilogy in a fundamental way. Anakin's Theme starts as an innocent, slightly magical tune (using the Lydian mode as he did in Yoda's Theme), but as it develops it darkens and finally reaches its conclusion—a melodic presentation of Darth Vader's Theme with altered chords.

New themes were written for Jar Jar Binks, the Trade Federation army of battle droids, Darth Maul, and Qui-Gon Jinn, as well as a sinister motif for Darth Maul, a set piece for the Flag Parade that introduces the podrace, and funeral music for Qui-Gon that would return for the climax of *Revenge of the Sith* and bookend the prequel trilogy. Anakin's mother Shmi also has a theme, which will return in the next film, *Attack of the Clones*.

Returning themes included the Main Theme, the Force Theme, Jabba the Hutt's Theme, and Yoda's Theme, as well as subtle references to "The Rebel Fanfare" and the secondary theme from the "Main Title." The Emperor's Theme makes a significant impact on this score, recurring several times to underscore Darth Sidious. A quote of Darth Vader's Theme is also explicitly heard at the end of the film when Yoda warns Obi-Wan of the danger he senses in training Anakin to be a Jedi.

The final scene of the film is a victory parade through Naboo, and the music is a clever use of the Emperor/Darth Sidious music in disguise, reinforcing the victory of the true menace of the film, the phantom Sith Lord. Williams takes the Emperor's Theme from *Return of the Jedi* and moves it into a major key, while also transposing it from low male choir to children's voices, turning its funereal dirge–like quality into happier, more triumphant music. The title of the track on the soundtrack album, "Augie's Great Municipal Band," is a reference to an obscure early recording by "Johnny" Williams called "Augie's Great Piano."

Reel 6 of this film is the battle of Naboo, and has a very strong connection to Lucas's first draft of *The Star Wars* from 1974. There are four simultaneous battles happening at once: The Gungans face the battle droid army on the plains; Padmé leads a team into the palace to capture the trade ambassador; Naboo pilots strike the Trade Federation ship in orbit around the planet; and the Jedi face Darth Maul in a thrilling lightsaber duel. This sequence underwent several major revisions in picture-editing, based on feedback Lucas received at different times from different directors, and as result, the music written and recorded for the scenes needed a lot of editing to fit the final flow of the picture. Additionally, Lucas had asked Williams to write a "religioso" choral piece for the duel with Maul, and upon hearing it, he reportedly liked it so much that he began inserting it into reel 6 in lots of places where it hadn't originally been intended. As a result, a large amount of highly detailed action music went unused in the final film, something that would come in handy for the music team on the next film.

Another sequence that underwent some significant changes in music was the podrace, which in the finished film bears little resemblance musically to the way it was originally conceived by John Williams. The soundtrack album offered a better look at his musical intentions for the exciting scenes.

The Phantom Menace, *the first* Star Wars *film in sixteen years, was released on May 19, 1999, produced at a cost of $115 million, and has a cumulative gross of a little over $1 billion. Reviews were mixed, with many fans being particularly critical over the oftentimes kid-friendly tone, Jar Jar Binks, and a seeming obsession on Lucas's part with visual effects and virtual sets.*

RAY MORTON

Unfortunately, the assets do not outweigh the movie's deficits, chief among them the very weak storyline (more an episodic collection of sequences than a fully realized plot); the many feeble story elements; the excessive slapstick; Jake Lloyd's performance as young Anakin (which, unfortunately, is quite amateurish and conveys neither the promise Qui-Gon is scripted to see in him nor the potential menace that supposedly concerns Obi-Wan and the Jedi Council); the frequently juvenile tone; and Jar Jar. Many critics and fans consider *The Phantom Menace* to be the worst film in the entire series. For me it's the second worst behind *The Rise of Skywalker*. However, for all the film's faults, one has to admire Lucas's attempts to expand the *Star Wars* universe by introducing so many new worlds, cultures, characters, and concepts, as well as his determination to not repeat himself. *The Phantom Menace* is an extremely flawed movie, but it's not a rote, predictable retread of any of the films from the original trilogy. Many fans were disappointed by this, but I think it's something for which Lucas should be commended.

RICK MCCALLUM

There is a hardcore fan base. It might be a million people. It might be two million people. It might even be three million people. But it's *not* what drives *Star Wars* at the end of the day. It's no different from the mantra of marketing. When you're at a studio, the studio executives and the marketing division think that they've made the movie if it's a hit. And if it's not a hit, then it's the filmmaker's fault. The truth is that you've got to market and spend an enormous amount of money just to get people to even know that your movie is out there.

At the end of the day—and I don't care what the research shows or what the marketing bullshit is—a film *only* works by word of mouth. A movie may work the first weekend, but then if it doesn't deliver, if people don't go back to work or back home and discuss it, or talk on their cell phones or the internet, then the movie just doesn't work. You might get it to $100 million with hype or to $150 million. But anything after that is a movie that works. Once you get a movie that makes $200 million, $250 million, you're in the stratosphere of people liking the movie. You're talking about people who like it so much that they're going back and seeing it two, three, four, five times. That's the only way you get to $450 million. You can have all the hype out there, all the bullshit, but that's not what drives you to those numbers.

KYLE NEWMAN
(director, *Fanboys*)

When I came to watch, say, *Phantom Menace,* I embraced the spoilers because I didn't look at *Star Wars* anymore as a movie, so much as it was the mythology and the story. So maybe I was ruining it for two years by following every little tidbit story, but I kinda felt I had an idea what it was, so I didn't go in and I wasn't shocked like some people. I accepted it for the mythology more than I was judging it all at once.

LEWIS MACLEOD
(actor, "Sebulba")

It is a movie without technical equal for its time. There are scenes where there are upward of four thousand digital effects interacting on-screen. An awesome achievement. I didn't like some of the dialogue or the Obi-Wan Kenobi accent, but otherwise it was good, if a tad overlong. The John Williams score is breathtaking. My character even had its own track. Number 9 on the CD is "Anakin Defeats Sebulba." I was thrilled. And the opening cue sounds like "Scheherazade," which was my father's favorite. He died before the movie was completed. It is very special to me.

RAY MORTON

The script's biggest problem was that it doesn't tell a story. Because *Episode I* is essentially a prologue, it is basically an expository piece. There is a lot of incident in *The Phantom Menace*, but very little plot in the traditional meaning of the term. The script is more of a chronicle—a presentation of events in order of occurrence—than a drama. There is little dramatic progression, momentum, or build, and the result is often a bit dull. *Episode I* also lacks a clear protagonist. Anakin is the protagonist of the overall trilogy, but in this particular film he is just a supporting character. Qui-Gon is the lead character in the film's first act; he splits this role with Padmé in the second; and there is no main character in the final act, which cuts back and forth between three different subplots led by three different people without ever focusing in on any of them.

JONATHAN RINZLER

George really took a beating after *Episode I*. Really took a beating. He never said this to me, but I got the impression that it took a bit of the wind out of the sails, in general. I wasn't at Lucasfilm yet, I went to see a preview of *Episode I*, because I was reviewing movies at that time. I took my older daughter, she was ten, and there had been nothing about it. There had been no buzz, I didn't know if it was good, bad—I assumed it would be good, because it was George Lucas's *Star Wars*, how bad could it be? And I was just blown away. I absolutely loved *Episode I*. And I will stand by that. I thought it was really interesting. When Qui-Gon says, "I didn't actually come here to free slaves," that's an amazing bit of writing on many levels. The fight at the end was amazing. I thought John Williams's music was incredible, and Liam Neeson? C'mon. And the podrace? George started filming the movie with no idea how they were going to film the podrace. John Knoll just figured out himself how they could do it, and he showed it to George on his laptop. And they were already shooting *Episode I*! I just love that. George was just constantly pushing the envelope on so many levels.

RICK MCCALLUM

The criticisms of *The Phantom Menace* are of value insomuch as everybody has the right to express their opinion. But do they affect us in any way? Not at all. They really don't. I did all the Special Editions and the fan base got totally whacked out. I remember getting literally hundreds of emails and reading dozens and dozens of articles from people worried to death that we were changing this unique and extraordinary mythological and sacred thing. But they forgot that it was George who was changing it. It wasn't some studio that was doing it. It wasn't some marketing division doing it. It was us. And the only reason George wanted to change the Special Editions was that he wanted to make them exactly the way he wrote them.

NATALIE PORTMAN

The Phantom Menace was a very difficult film for me to make. It was probably the hardest film experience I've ever had. I wasn't used to working with blue screen and I was sixteen years old and had no people my age around for an entire summer. This was back when my working schedule was my summer break vacation, so I always tried to find things that would be more fun than camp. That was my standard. In terms of the finished product, *Phantom Menace* is a really fun film and many people liked it. I personally would have preferred if there was a little more story, but I think it's great, because we set up this background for these characters, which served the second film well.

RICK MCCALLUM

I do admit and I can concede that—especially to the hardcore fan base—*Episode I* is a disappointment to them. It deals with an eight-year-old kid. It's the beginning film and it has to set up almost everything for the rest of the saga. And I *do* understand why certain people hated it. It's the same thing with Jar Jar Binks. If you're between six and twelve years old, Jar Jar is probably your second most favorite *Star Wars* character behind R2-D2. But if you're over twelve or thirteen years old, Jar Jar is repugnant to you. There's no in-between there. If you actually go back to the original reviews of *A New Hope,* C-3PO was *hated.* Just absolutely loathed. It's definitely worth checking out. People said he was obnoxious, that there was something about his voice and manner that really, deeply offended them.

LIAM NEESON

The wonderful thing about the first *Star Wars,* I felt, was, from an acting point of view, these actors believed the world they were in. In that universe, you have to converse with things that fly and strange animal-like creatures and humanoids and stuff, and that's an everyday occurrence. And just to keep it absolutely simple and try and believe absolutely everything you're saying.

RAY MORTON

Menace (and the prequel trilogy in general) does not draw as much upon the classical tropes and archetypes of the world's myths, legends, and fairy tales as the original trilogy did. There's not as much of the mystical or of "serious" fantasy in these new films, and the only element from the universal myth prominent in the prequel narrative is the notion of a "Chosen One," which unfortunately is one of the hoariest and most clichéd concepts in fantastic literature. The prequel trilogy did lean more into religious elements than the earlier trio, most notably with the notion that Anakin's birth had been a virgin one (although using a concept so closely associated with the Christ story for a character destined to become a mass-murdering monster seems an odd choice), as well as the design of Darth Maul, which was meant to evoke biblical images of the Devil.

KYLE NEWMAN

It was never going to be the movie in your head for sixteen years, and if you step outside of that—that's my point—to look at it, you realize that there are merits. Would I have chosen to have Anakin be nine years old? No. I would've rather seen the same actor through all three films. There's just little things I would've rather seen happen, but I get it, and then I can look back at it for the story outside of the film.

I'm crazy with *Star Wars*. I look at it like it's history, and that's how I break it down. I can step out of the movie. And I always look at people like, "If you like three *Star Wars* movies out of six, then guess what? You give *Star Wars* an F, that's a failing grade. You're not even a *Star Wars* fan. Get out of here."

GEORGE LUCAS

Many people commented on the fact that *The Phantom Menace* was kid-friendly. I don't think it is any more kid-friendly than the other films. When I did the other films, I said, "This is for twelve-year-olds, and it's a kid's movie." At the time, everybody said, "Fine," and that was, I think, one of the reasons we got a lot of bad reviews. But then somehow over the years, people have sort of drifted away from that and tried to make it into something other than what it actually is. Look, this is a Saturday afternoon serial for children. *The Phantom Menace* was the perfect title for a film like this. You have the roll-up, you have *Episode I*. People forget what the movies actually are.

11

SEND IN THE CLONES: ATTACK OF THE CLONES

"Begun, the Clone War has."

In the aftermath of the release of *The Phantom Menace*, some might say that George Lucas was left in a state of confusion and, according to others, was reluctant to sit down and start writing the follow-up, *Episode II: Attack of the Clones*. It certainly wasn't because of the film's box office: *Episode I* did remarkably well and proved that there was very much an appetite for new *Star Wars*. But the critics weren't kind and the "fans" were merciless in their vitriol, a common online refrain being, "George Lucas raped my childhood." Ouch.

GEORGE LUCAS
(executive producer, screenwriter/director, *Attack of the Clones*)
With *The Phantom Menace*, I gave people as much as I could. I gave them 110 percent. Even though it became the most successful *Star Wars* film of all time, the second most successful film in the history of the movies, and 60 percent of the critics thought it was fantastic, people say, "Why did you do this?" I knew when I made the film a lot of fans weren't going to like it, because I wasn't making the movie *they* wanted me to make. They wanted me to start with *Episode II*. They wanted to see Jedi fighting, they wanted to see battles. They wanted to see *The Matrix*.

I knew that I was telling a story that I wrote thirty years ago and I had to start at the beginning *and* I had to do all the groundwork. Which means you have to lay all the pipe for all the characters for the world you are creating. What is the Republic and how does it operate? What is the Trade Federation and how does it operate? How did Anakin become a Jedi? The relationship between Anakin and his mother, the fact that he has special skills. *All* these things had to be laid out. Otherwise, the second one doesn't work that well. You take them all together, they will work better than any one individual or even this first trilogy. It's a six-part story that I wrote thirty years ago that I'm just finishing.

KEVIN J. ANDERSON
(author, *Jedi Academy* series)

Dune was Frank Herbert's second book he published. It was a fabulous book, one of the best I've ever read. He went on to a long and distinguished career, and wrote dozens and dozens of really special books. And each time one of his big ambitious books came out, instead of people recognizing that it was a really good book, all they ever said was, "This is good, but it's not as good as *Dune*." It's like you're cursed by doing something good. I think it's too bad that we can't just celebrate the fact that the first trilogy was monumental and look at the next one to see how good it could be. Let's accept the fact that these new movies are *Star Wars* prequels, but look at them as independent movies in and of themselves rather than having this predetermined attitude of, "It can't possibly be as good as the first."

SAMUEL L. JACKSON
(actor, "Mace Windu")

I think what happened is that people had expectations they didn't feel were met, because they didn't *understand* what George was doing, and George is the only person who knows how all of this stuff fits together. So when he made the first one and it was a kiddie film, the adults who fell in love with *Star Wars* when they were kids had forgotten what they were like when they saw *A New Hope*. They couldn't appreciate that *The Phantom Menace* is a story about a little boy who's going to turn out to be Darth Vader. George was creating a new audience and hoping the old audience would enjoy it, too. And all these children who didn't know anything about the original trilogy found this kid, Anakin, they could relate to and then they moved on to the next film.

GEORGE LUCAS

All of the films were intended for twelve-year-olds. They're aimed at adolescents. They're aimed at that period of time where they're transitioning from being young to being mature, and maturing into adolescence. Mythology is designed to take the values and information and knowledge from one generation and move it on to the next. That's what it's all about. It started out as a storytelling medium and it was an oral storytelling medium. It had a lot of psychological meaning as it was presented live to people. It had to resonate, otherwise the storyteller wouldn't get their dinner. In *Star Wars*, the mythology part is the motif; the sort of underlying psychology of the whole thing.

DAN MADSEN
(owner, the Official Lucasfilm/Star Wars Fan Club, 1987–2001)

I ceased publication in 2001, and I sold the company to Wizards of the Coast. Part of the reason that happened was because I had invested so much money into the *Star Wars* action figures from Hasbro. I had three warehouses full of that product. And then the movie opens. You know, *Episode I* was both a blessing and a curse to me, because everybody had those action figures and toys—everybody from Walmart to Toys "R" Us, everyone's mom-and-pop shop to Walgreens, and unfortunately, the Walmarts and Targets were just able to buy in much greater bulk than I was, so I couldn't sell at the prices they could.

We had the Jawa Trader inserted into every issue of *Star Wars Insider,* and it was just full of all we sold. We sold every product from the licensees. We also were the first ones to do the *Star Wars* online store at StarWars.com. We did all the backend of that. We did all the product fulfillment for that. Prior to the movie opening, we were just going gangbusters, and then the movie opens, and a week to two weeks after, sales just *dropped.* Unfortunately, a lot of times with those action figures, you know, we'd get a case of them, for every five Jar Jar Binks figures, we'd get one Darth Maul. And everybody wanted Darth Maul, I couldn't sell enough Darth Mauls, but Jar Jar was everywhere, I couldn't get rid of them! The fan club had to go on, so that was the only alternative. It was a painful time, but it was the right decision to make as I now know.

At any rate, I got stuck with so much inventory, and I couldn't sell it, and once the movie came out, the reception was a little less than what we had all hoped it would be, and the sales started to decline, and I was stuck with this huge debt to Hasbro. So I had no other choice but to sell the business, so that it could go on and it could survive. Wizards of the Coast had just been purchased before that by Hasbro, so it was a subsidiary of theirs, so it was the only way to keep the fan club going, to make it survive. So as much as it was painful for me to do it, it was the only way to do it.

KYLE NEWMAN
(director, *Fanboys*)

It became cool to hate *Star Wars.* Before the Special Editions, it was still underground, and then the Special Editions repopularized it, and then by the time of the prequels it was Pepsi and it was Taco Bell. It was everywhere. And then it became cool to hate it. I remember I was living in New York at the time, and I went to film school, so everyone that was at film school at NYU was like, "*Star Wars* is the stupidest thing in the history of cinema ever. It's so dumb." And they intellectualized it in a way. I was like, "Whoa, let's chill out. It's not that bad. I've seen many, many bad movies." It's still fashionable. People still say George is evil. "George raped my childhood. George only puts out movies because he wants money." George didn't trick us into buying toys. We wanted the toys.

DAN MADSEN

Everything kind of changed after *Episode I* came out. All that anticipation and eagerness changed. Critics were panning the movies, and some fans hated it, and some fans liked it. There was a lot of negativity, and then there was this whole "Jar Jar Binks is racist"—it's just one thing after another. It wasn't what everybody had expected it would be. I don't know what people's expectations were, but at the time, it wasn't what people wanted it to be. And it created some disappointment.

SAMUEL L. JACKSON

In the *next one,* you have a story that these kids probably can't go and see yet, but they can catch up with it later. *Revenge of the Sith* is a *very* dark tale. The fans really didn't understand the progression of these prequels; that this pivotal person, Darth Vader, had to start somewhere. These films change the way you view the first three movies, because you can look at Darth Vader as a sympathetic character, whereas before he was simply the personification of evil. We've seen Anakin grow up and now we know how he went to the dark side and how he was duped by this evil person into going to the dark side.

HAYDEN CHRISTENSEN
(actor, "Anakin Skywalker," *Attack of the Clones*)
As an actor, you look for characters who change and who are affected by the stimuli around them and grow and don't stay on the consistent plane they're introduced at. Anakin probably goes through the most change of any character I could possibly imagine.

BRIAN JAY JONES
(author, *George Lucas: A Life*)
After *The Phantom Menace* is released, Lucas kind of throws his hands up and walks away from the internet, and I don't blame him. But he actually co-opted the internet film nerds for *Attack of the Clones* and brought them in on the process, because I think getting shit on for *The Phantom Menace* hurt him terribly. But by the time he gets to the next one, *Revenge of the Sith*, he was

like, "I don't even care what Bleeding Cool has to say, because I'm not reading *anything*," which is probably not entirely true.

The irony is that you can go on YouTube and type something like "*The Phantom Menace*, First Preview," and that was the time when people were paying to see *Happy Gilmore* or whatever it was just to see the trailer. You can hear the crowd just going ape shit as soon as the Lucasfilm logo comes up; the place burst into this spontaneous applause. *That's* where Lucas is at that point, and that's an *amazing* place to be. It just doesn't last.

RAY MORTON
(senior editor, *Script* magazine)

The box office success of *The Phantom Menace* ensured the prequel trilogy would continue. Lucas began preproduction on what he initially called *Jar Jar's Great Adventure* (a mischievous poke at the legions who disliked Mr. Binks so intensely) and what would eventually be titled *Attack of the Clones* not long after *Menace* was released.

JOHN KENNETH MUIR
(author, *Science Fiction and Fantasy Films of the 1970s*)

At the time of its release, *Attack of the Clones* was felt to be a step up from *The Phantom Menace*, perhaps because it featured a more breakneck/even pace. However, the film did not feature the deep allegorical visual design or plot that had bolstered *The Phantom Menace*. Instead, George Lucas seemed dedicated to paying homage to his friends and his own work. This means that the planet of the Cloners was populated by the aliens from his buddy Steven Spielberg's movie, *Close Encounters of the Third Kind*. This means that Obi-Wan visits a 1950s diner straight out of Lucas's own *American Graffiti*.

RAY MORTON

As he did on *Return of the Jedi*, Lucas wrote a basic outline for the movie, but put off writing the actual screenplay until well into preproduction. He did not complete a rough draft until three months prior to the commencement of filming. Lucas then produced a first and second draft in quick succession before bringing in the British writer Jonathan Hales, who had written a number of scripts for Lucas's *The Young Indiana Jones Chronicles* television series, to help him craft the script's third and final draft, which Lucas then polished.

GEORGE LUCAS

I've used cowriters a lot. The first *Star Wars* I wrote myself, but the other two were cowritten. *Phantom* I wrote myself, but when I finished it, I was tired and burned out and I took a vacation for about a month. As a result of that, I did four or five drafts of *Attack of the Clones*. It was to the point where I could show the script to the crew and they could start working on things, but it was one week before we were to begin shooting and I was about to direct the movie. So I brought in Jonathan Hales, whom I had worked with before in *Young Indy* and whom I trusted. We sat down and I said, "This needs to be fixed." I turned into a director and let him be the writer.

RICK MCCALLUM
(producer, *Attack of the Clones*)

I would describe the George Lucas–Jonathan Hales collaboration as great and easy. Once George was done with the first draft, he needed a little help, so I called Jonathan and he was waiting on standby. He came in and spent about four or five weeks on the film, helping us focus on the thematic issues and plot points. And then we were on our way.

JONATHAN RINZLER
(nonfiction editor, Lucasfilm 2001–2016)

The general idea was, you had to have *Star Wars* in your blood. I know George had problems with the films and the prequels in particular in finding writing collaborators. His problem was he couldn't find someone like Lawrence Kasdan and Willard Huyck and Gloria Katz to come in and polish his scripts. There was Jonathan Hale, but I don't think he was able to do it. I'm not sure exactly what happened there. He's a very good writer, but you know, sometimes it just doesn't click. George wasn't the kind of person who would have a long, "this is my philosophy" kind of thing. You either learn by doing it and pick it up, or you didn't.

GEORGE LUCAS

Obviously, I'm telling a story about a good guy's descent into the depths of evil . . . In the second act, the plot thickens. That's always more interesting, because things start to happen, things start getting revealed and, in this case, you descend into both the evil of the Empire and Anakin's struggle to maintain his goodness. In the third one, we get to conclude that.

HAYDEN CHRISTENSEN

The film is, in some ways, a coming-of-age story for Anakin, because we meet him as he's fully evolved in his Jedi training and learning to master the Force. And then he falls in love with Amidala when he's on this mission to protect her. It's a conflict of interest for him. Does he choose love or his responsibilities and obligations as to the way of the Jedi, which are really in direct conflict? The Jedi *aren't* supposed to know any sort of romantic love. At the same time, Anakin's a very passionate character and unwilling to make any compromises. He wants both to play prominent roles in his life. He wants to be a Jedi and he also wants to develop a romantic relationship with Amidala.

GEORGE LUCAS

Film is generally plot-heavy. Television is character-heavy. So, in television, you move characters in and out depending on their popularity. I can't do that in *Clones*, because the plot is very important. In this case, the main story—which is the first three films—and the backstory—which I'm telling now—are, ultimately, to me, one story. Again, it's one six-part, twelve-hour story and all the characters who are there in *Menace* and *Clones* are really only there to move the plot along. They have a very *specific* reason for being there in terms of making the plot. So, they're not there arbitrarily. People tend to think I just put characters in for the fun of it. I *can* create personalities for the characters for the fun of it, but every character has to revolve around the plot.

JOHN KENNETH MUIR

The resulting plot of *Attack of the Clones* is unnecessarily complicated, too, involving a Jedi who died and mysteriously put in an order for a clone army before doing so. This was a strand introduced and never really followed up in the subsequent film. The film's action is very cartoon-like as well, particularly the aerial car chase on Coruscant, which involves Anakin defying gravity, falling hundreds of feet, and landing without being hurt. Obi-Wan and Anakin defy gravity, get electrocuted, and come out no worse for the wear, which is baffling. Jedi are still supposed to be mortal, I believe, not superheroes.

RAY MORTON

Lucas began writing *Attack of the Clones* in the same way he began writing *The Phantom Menace*—by returning to his early work in *Star Wars*, in this case, his rough and first-draft screenplays. In those drafts, the Empire attacks Princess Leia's home planet Aquilae. General Skywalker assigns his Jedi apprentice Annikin Starkiller to collect the Princess from her school and protect her as he and Skywalker help Leia and her siblings escape from the invasion and make their way to safety in the Ophuchi system. In the course of their adventures, Annikin and Leia fall in love.

JOHN KENNETH MUIR

As the script evolved, he kept the love story, which *should* have been the heart of the trilogy, but has been criticized by many for the bad dialogue in it, particularly Anakin's line to Amidala about how much he hates sand. Fair enough. However, this was the year 2002, a time when movies were still in the post-*Titanic* [1997] blush of young, doomed love affair stories.

PETER HOLMSTROM
(cohost, *The Rebel & the Rogue* podcast)

I liked the sand line. It was a character beat, to say Anakin hadn't gotten over his PTSD from being a slave and leaving his mother behind. Tatooine has a lot of sand . . . if you didn't know. That's beautiful writing.

NATALIE PORTMAN
(actress, "Padmé Amidala")

Anakin is at the center of it all—it's his story—but then there's this love story in the middle of this great action movie.

GEORGE LUCAS

That was challenging in its own way, because *Star Wars* films have a tendency to be very action-oriented. To be able to slow that down a little bit and tell a love story in the middle of it was a challenge to make happen. I had managed to do this philosophical lesson plan in *The Empire Strikes Back*. I was very worried about, "How do I have Luke and this little green man sitting around and philosophizing about the Force?" I thought it would really stop things dead, because it was going to be about twenty minutes of the movie. But by intercutting with Han Solo and Leia, I was able to make that work. On this film, I thought I would use the same technique, because it worked then. Essentially a love story *does* stop things. But I figured I would have the film noir mystery of Obi-Wan trying to find out who the assassin is, and I would intercut that with the romance. Even though it's not as action-oriented, I thought I could get away with it, because it has a suspense through-line. It was a little tricky, but it seems to work.

NATALIE PORTMAN

I'd never worked with the same cast and crew a second time, so that was really wonderful. Padmé wasn't a queen anymore; she was a senator. And because of that, she was allowed to wear less-formal clothes, have more free time, doesn't have as many formal dues—which gave her the time to fall in love with Anakin, who in this film came back as her protector. All of a sudden, this kid is a strapping young gentleman and they hit it off. They also have this tension, because their formal roles don't allow for both of them to fall in love, but they can't help it. You can't put those kinds of restrictions on love. It's the classic duty-versus-love story and obviously love always wins out.

JOHN KENNETH MUIR

I remember reading a review of *Titanic* asking how many young people could enjoy a love story with such obvious clichés and wooden dialogue, when it had all been done a million times before. The answer was that for thirteen- to fifteen-year-olds, it was all new. They *hadn't* seen it all before. It was that simple. I think this also explains the success of the *Twilight* saga. Filmmakers, including Lucas, were aiming at a generation of moviegoers who would take the love affair between two attractive young people at face value, rather than as something that had been seen before—*and* in better films.

NATALIE PORTMAN

Anakin and Amidala meet up on *Clones* and they haven't seen each other since the audience last saw them together in *Phantom Menace*. It's a fossilized relationship that has been resurrected. It was caught in a time capsule—not unlike film—and now it's back and they're bringing it to life again. It has changed, though. It's *not* the same relationship. Now it's about a woman and a man. And it takes a while especially because Anakin hasn't matured as much as she has. But he has this real passion and it excites her, because it's very much like her own passion for what she does and her intensity, although there's something much more sinister about his. Hers is a very youthful, idealistic, save-the-world kind of passion and his is not quite as clear-cut and sunny. Also, for someone who thinks she can make everything better and save everybody, obviously Anakin's issues are very attractive to her.

RAY MORTON

Lucas took those early plot strands and reworked them for *Clones*. In the new version, it is ten years after the events of *The Phantom Menace* and many systems are seceding from the Republic to join a separatist movement led by one Count Dooku. With the galaxy in turmoil, the Jedi are having trouble keeping the peace and a faction in the Senate is pushing to create a grand army of the Republic to help in this task. No longer a queen, Padmé Amidala is now Naboo's representative in the Senate of the Galactic Republic and she opposes this proposal, certain it will ultimately lead to war.

As the story opens, an assassination attempt is made on Padmé's life as she arrives on Coruscant to vote against a proposal to build a grand army of the Republic. Padmé survives the attack, but is still clearly in danger. Obi-Wan Kenobi, now a Jedi Master, and his apprentice Anakin Skywalker, now nineteen, are assigned to protect her. Anakin has not seen Padmé since they parted a decade before and reveals to Obi-Wan that he has been carrying a torch for her ever since. Obi-Wan warns Anakin not to pursue these feelings, since Jedi are forbidden to marry. Following a second attempt on the senator's life, the Jedi Council orders Anakin to escort Padmé back to Naboo, where she will be safe. During the journey, Padmé finds herself growing attracted to Anakin. During their time in hiding in Naboo's lake country, Padmé and Anakin fall deeply in love.

Lucas joined this material with a parallel plotline, in which Obi-Wan investigates the assassination attempts on Padmé to discover who is behind them. Obi-Wan's search for answers leads him to a secret cloning facility on the ocean world of Kamino, where he discovers that an army of clones made from the DNA of a bounty hunter called Jango Fett has been created, supposedly at the request of a long-dead Jedi Master acting on behalf of the Republic. Realizing that Jango commissioned the hits on Padmé, Obi-Wan follows him to the planet Geonosis, where he learns that Jango is working for Count Dooku, a former Jedi who once trained Qui-Gon. Dooku is conspiring with the leaders of the villainous Trade Federation previously seen in The Phantom Menace, *and other big business leaders, to create a droid army that his separatist movement can then use to attack the Republic. Dooku captures Obi-Wan and tells him that the Republic Senate is corrupt and under the control of the Sith. Dooku invites Obi-Wan to join him so they can destroy the Sith. Not trusting Dooku, Obi-Wan declines.*

Padmé and Anakin travel to Geonosis to rescue Obi-Wan, but they themselves are captured. Dooku has Obi-Wan, Padmé, and Anakin placed in an arena, where they are set upon by a pack of vicious monsters. The trio do their best to hold off the beasts, but even after succeeding, Dooku orders destroyer droids to finish the job. Just as the droids move in for the kill, the Jedi—led by Mace Windu—arrive.

A battle ensues—the Jedi against the monsters and Dooku's droid army. At first, the Jedi do well, but eventually, they are cornered by the droids. Just as the mechanical soldiers are about to open fire, Yoda arrives with the clone army from Kamino. The clones battle and ultimately drive the droids to retreat. Dooku tries to escape, but Obi-Wan and Anakin pursue him and wind up engaging in a lightsaber duel with the crafty Count. During the fight, Dooku chops off Anakin's arm and knocks Obi-Wan unconscious. Yoda then arrives and faces off against Dooku in another lightsaber duel. This duel also ends in a draw and Dooku escapes again.

Dooku travels to the far side of Coruscant—a dark, grimy, industrial landscape—where we learn that the Count is actually a Sith Lord in thrall to Chancellor Palpatine / Darth Sidious, who has manufactured the separatist conflict as an excuse to gain emergency dictatorial powers over the Republic and to create a massive military he can use to conquer the galaxy.

Palpatine/Sidious's plan works. As the story comes to an end, the Senate votes to give him emergency powers and to create a fleet of star destroyers, which are used to take the clone army into battle against the separatists—the Clone Wars have begun. Meanwhile, Anakin is fitted with a new mechanical arm and he and Padmé marry in secret.

JOHN KENNETH MUIR

As a start to the Clone Wars, the film is relatively disappointing. So many questions are unanswered, or more aptly, un-asked. Why does Yoda accept an army, built and gift-wrapped for him? Why does Amidala accept Anakin's massacre of the Sand People without at least suggesting, let alone pursuing, the idea that maybe he should see a therapist?

RAY MORTON

The screenplay for *Attack of the Clones* is a definite improvement over the script for *The Phantom Menace*. It has a stronger movie-specific narrative—both Obi-Wan's investigation and the Anakin/Padmé love story have more drama and forward momentum than the largely plotless *Menace*. The story also has more action and its tone is less juvenile. Thankfully, Jar Jar's role has been significantly reduced (although not enough—in the brief time he appears on-screen he manages to destroy the Republic). However, in relation to the storyline of the overall prequel trilogy, *Clones* is still mostly prologue. The only elements relevant to the trilogy's larger narrative are Anakin and Padmé falling in love and Anakin's fear of losing more of his loved ones.

JOHN KENNETH MUIR

On a positive note, certainly one can see Lucas weaving the War on Terror, post-9/11 worldview into the film, since it opens with Amidala under threat from terrorist attacks. But not much is done with that real-world issue. In my judgment, *Attack of the Clones* is the weakest of the prequel series. It is less uneven than was *The Phantom Menace,* but even if it doesn't have that film's lows, it gets nowhere near its highs, either. For instance, the Dooku lightsaber duel is a relatively disappointing affair, especially after the elaborate "Duel of the Fates" battle with Darth Maul in *The Phantom Menace. Clones* is probably the low-point of the saga, at least until *Rise of Skywalker* was released in 2019.

RAY MORTON

Apart from these bits, *Clones* is just more filler and backstory. And so, while it is a more energetic tale than *Menace,* like the earlier movie, *Clones* is pretty much irrelevant. This, however, is not the screenplay's biggest problem. The script's biggest problem is Anakin. As conceived, Skywalker is supposed to be talented but headstrong and impulsive. This by itself is not a problem—many young heroes start out this way. However, as scripted, Anakin is also arrogant, angry, and reckless, as well as whiny, petulant, and frequently obnoxious. In the movie, these problems are compounded by Hayden Christensen's acting. Although Christensen has done good work in other films (especially in *Broken Glass*), in *Clones* his awkward performance amplifies Anakin's negative qualities without providing the charm and charisma that would make them tolerable. So, from the get-go, Anakin is a hard character to like and to feel much sympathy for.

HAYDEN CHRISTENSEN

To be honest, I more or less knew what the reaction to *Attack of the Clones* was going to be when I first read the script, because Anakin was a petulant, sometimes whiny teenager. That's how he was scripted, that's how George wanted me to play him, and that's how the character needed to be. So, I had no problem with it in that respect, but I *knew* that it was going to receive some criticism when it was released. I just hope that when people saw the next film, they were a little more sympathetic to some of the qualities and characters that they had a hard time with in the first two movies. But, hey, it has never been a popularity contest for me. I wanted to fully realize the character George envisioned and I feel like I accomplished that.

RAY MORTON

In the middle of his romantic interlude with Padmé, Anakin has a dream about his mother, Shmi, whom he has not seen since he left Tatooine ten years before. Feeling Shmi is in danger, Anakin decides to go to Tatooine to find her. Padmé insists on accompanying him. Seeking out his former owner, Watto, Anakin learns that his mother was sold to a moisture farmer named Klieg Lars, who later freed and married her. Anakin and Padmé travel to the

Lars farm, which we recognize as the same place where we will eventually meet Luke Skywalker in *Star Wars*. There, Anakin learns that Shmi happily married Klieg, but then a month ago was kidnapped by a savage band of Tusken Raiders. Anakin rides out to find the Sand People's camp and rescue his mother. Upon reaching it, Anakin discovers Shmi—who has been brutalized by the Raiders—on the verge of death. A few moments after he finds her, Anakin's mother passes away in his arms.

One of Anakin's primary motivations for turning to the dark side in *Revenge of the Sith* is to save Padmé's life after he dreams of her dying in childbirth (by then Palpatine will have persuaded Anakin that the dark side gives one the ability to bring the dead back to life). So the narrative point of having Shmi die in *Clones* is clearly to have Anakin experience an early significant loss that makes him determined not to suffer another one later in his life. Although the entire Tatooine sequence feels like it has been plopped down in the middle of a movie that it otherwise has nothing to do with, if this was as far as the sequence went it certainly would have been acceptable and might have actually made Anakin a more sympathetic character. However, right after his mother dies, a vengeful Anakin mercilessly slaughters every single Tusken Raider in the camp, including the females and the children. Anakin has just committed mass murder.

The purpose of the prequel trilogy is to tell the story of how Anakin Skywalker, once a noble and virtuous Jedi, came to embrace the dark side and become Darth Vader. This terrible event is supposed to happen at the climax of the entire trilogy. Instead, with this incident, it happens halfway through.

All through the original trilogy, Luke was warned not to give in to his hate and his anger and his aggression—if he did, he was warned, he would travel down the path to the dark side and it would forever dominate his destiny—he would become a villain now and forever. Anakin does exactly what Luke was warned not to do—he gives in to his hate and in his anger commits multiple killings. With this act, he has turned to the dark side and become a villain. Surprisingly, though, instead of the script treating Anakin like a villain, it actually treats him far more sympathetically.

RAY MORTON

After the murders, Anakin returns to the Lars homestead and tells Padmé what he has done. Rather than condemn his actions or running from him in horror, she is understanding and sympathetic. Without explicitly saying so, she justifies his actions and forgives him. And not long after, she appears to have forgotten all about it. As does Anakin. As does the movie. The script and the film proceed as if the entire Tatooine episode was just a minor bump in the road—as if Anakin has not yet turned to the dark side. And here is where having a protagonist who is also an antagonist becomes a problem. Just a few scenes after Anakin confesses, he (along with Padmé) is off to rescue Obi-Wan. He gets captured, declares his love for Padmé, fights off monsters, duels with Count Dooku, gets his arm cut off, gets his arm replaced, and finally marries Padmé. These are all the actions of a heroic protagonist, which is how the movie regards him and wants us to regard him also.

But this is impossible. Because Anakin has committed mass murder. And because we've seen him do it. And because we can't forget it. From now until the end of the trilogy, our feelings about Anakin are forever in conflict—we know we're supposed to regard him as a hero, but how can we when we know he is a villain? With this conflict ever-present, we can no longer invest our emotions or our sympathy in Anakin's story. From now on, we can only watch it unfold.

Thirteen months after the release of The Phantom Menace—*on June 26, 2000, to be exact—principal photography began on* Episode II: Attack of the Clones. *There were definitely a few behind-the-scenes changes made. For starters, production had shifted away from Leavesden Film Studios in London to Fox Studios Australia (with some additional shooting at Elstree Studios in England). Beyond that, Stephen Jones (*The Well, Red Planet*) was brought on as production manager. Exterior locations would be shot in Tunisia; the Plaza de España in Seville, London; China; Vancouver; San Diego; and the Villa del Balbianello on Lake Como, and the Reggia Palace of Caserta in Italy. Principal photography would wrap on September 20, 2000—less than three months after it began.*

RICK MCCALLUM

The reason for the move to Australia, actually, was a combination of a couple of things. One, Fox had just built a huge studio there and that was an opportunity that we just couldn't miss. It was a fantastic deal to be able to work at that studio with a great infrastructure and a great film community. We brought a few English heads of departments to the studio, and we had some of our English crew working on various locations as well. So the decision to film the next two pictures in Australia was really a combination of things, but primarily it was a great opportunity to work at Fox's brand-new studio.

Production on *Episode II* was low-key and done with great precision. We shot very quickly and tried to film the bulk of the movie in an intense period of sixty days. We shot in five countries and it was great, because there were no problems. We didn't have anything on location that screwed us up on any level. There were no storms like the ones that destroyed some *Phantom Menace* sets. There was plenty of rain, but it never stopped us from shooting. Everything went really well. But it was relentless, because we always shot a minimum of thirty-six setups a day, but he was into it. I think he had a great time.

GAVIN BOCQUET
(production designer, *Attack of the Clones*)

We were on a similar schedule for *Episode II* as we were on *Episode I*, because of the time of year we were shooting. On the other hand, we were probably getting the information [we needed] later than we did the last time, but then we also had environments we already knew a lot about, which had to be developed a great deal last time. So, the initial conceptual work on *Episode I* needed to go back to "base camp," so to speak, whereas on this one we felt, despite the slightly delayed information gathering, there was a sort of comfort level with the fact we had all worked together before, and we understood the major environments of *Star Wars,* how we work, how George works, and how we put all of these things together. Half of our environments we had knowledge of. There might be different rooms or spaces in these environments, but a lot of the initial conceptualizing was done. So on the one hand we were getting the information later, which made us work a little bit faster, and we were in a new country, which also made it a little bit more hectic. But then there is an awful lot of familiarity with the people we were working with and what we were doing. And the new people fit in as well.

The biggest change in terms of production on the film came from the fact that, whereas portions of The Phantom Menace *were shot digitally,* Attack of the Clones *was completely digital. This allowed them to break with the norm and shoot interiors first prior to going on location.*

RICK MCCALLUM

Those days were long gone. The reason that you used to have to do your exteriors first was so you knew what your lighting conditions would be like for the interiors. In the digital world it doesn't matter. We can change the exterior to anything we want to match the interior, so you deal with what you want instead of what you get. And then what you want, you re-create. And even if it's a rainy day, it doesn't matter. Personally, I love location. It's much more exciting for me, because anything can happen. You just never know. It doesn't matter how well you plan, you live by the serendipity of weather.

There are so many different kinds of exigencies in production that can fail. Perhaps your actor drank too much the night before and gets in a car accident or the driver doesn't see anything, including the oncoming bus. The person who owns the house where you got permission to shoot gets a divorce and suddenly the permission vanishes. Anything can happen and every day it does. Whereas here you know you can control your day. It's a very controlled atmosphere. Technologically we need to be in an atmosphere like that, and also because we have so many different worlds and so many different sets. We were shooting for fifty-six days but we had sixty-seven sets, so you can imagine some days when we are moving from one area of the stage to another. And if it's raining, that's about as much drama as we get.

GEORGE LUCAS

The problem with digital is that if you have a leaf wiggle in a tree, you have to figure it out and go program for that. It's a totally different kind of art form in that if you want water, you have to work on it and work on it. We had water left over from *The Perfect Storm,* so we licked the water thing. But working digitally is a big challenge. It takes a lot of people, a lot of money, a lot of time just to develop a realistic . . . anything.

RICK MCCALLUM

For example, you shoot the real rain, and then, when you want something that is a bit more powerful, that doesn't look as naturalistic as you want, then you add the CG. There is stuff called particle animation. It's what made *Twister* work. It was taking particles and animating them to a performance level. That's what was done on *Perfect Storm* and also on *Twister* and to a large degree, we pushed it to a whole new level in the podrace sequence in *Episode I.* When a CG element crashes on the ground and you see it break apart and pieces fly all over, *that* is all performance-driven. There is somebody who is actually creating the performance of a particle. That is really amazing to see come to life. I mean, *Perfect Storm* almost cracked it totally with water; some of it so unbelievably realistic. That couldn't have been made two or three years earlier. It would have been impossible. So, each film pushes the technology a little bit further.

Seven and a half years were spent attempting to develop the technology, the final prototype of the camera arriving two days before they began shooting. Which just happened to correspond with the time the crew received the shooting script from Lucas and Hales.

RICK MCCALLUM

For us to shoot a movie that lasts about two hours and ten minutes and has about twenty-two hundred or twenty-three hundred shots in it—and every single one of those shots has a digital effect in—it would have been ludicrous to shoot on film and scan it all into a computer before we could even cut or begin to manipulate it. That was one of the major reasons why we wanted to be able to acquire our images digitally.

But the most important reason was to push the technology so that, finally, audiences could see a film in the theater that is duplicated exactly the way in which we made it. It's a very simple, compelling idea, but getting an audience to see the actual movie you've made is still one of the most difficult things out there to achieve. Moviegoers usually don't see a film that even comes close, visually, to representing what we've shot. And most of the time you can't hear a film the way you should after we've spent millions of dollars trying to get a sound mix for it. It's very hard to do.

GEORGE LUCAS

I've always [said], "This is like the film industry in 1902," so the advances are going to be huge, because what we did on *Episode II*, we did in essence by ourselves. We had to talk Sony into it, [but] they built the cameras and they tried really hard to make this work; we also had to talk Panavision into committing a lot of money to build those lenses. Both companies really went out on a limb. This was a giant experiment for everybody, and nobody knew if it was going to work or if they were pouring money down a rat hole. The whole medium was opening up, there were lots of lens manufacturers out there building lenses and lots of other camera people building cameras, so you had competition. It was the same with digital editing—for the seven years that we had EditDroid [almost] nobody would use it, and even after we sold the company to Avid another two or three years passed before they got anybody to use it. All [digital technology] does is give you more to work with. It's a much more malleable medium than film, by far; you can make it do whatever you want it to do, and you can design the technology to do whatever you want to do.

RICK MCCALLUM

We weren't trying to change everybody else's world, we were just trying to change *our* world. There was so much controversy about us filming *Episode II* digitally. There was so much fear being projected all over by cameramen and by studios. As far as we're concerned, we were not trying to convince the world that they need to go a different way in making movies. We probably got 10 to 15 percent more setups per day, because of the ease of the camera.

GEORGE LUCAS

Audiences can't tell the difference. We knew that right from the beginning because we shot [parts of] *Phantom Menace* digitally, and nobody could tell which shots were digital and which weren't.

RON MAGID
(journalist, visual effects historian)

As *Episode II* unfolds, it seems as though a new style of filmmaking is evolving, particularly in terms of the stunt and effects sequences, which felt more believable because there was less cutting around to hide the trick. Digital tools allowed them to develop a different style.

RICK MCCALLUM

It's a whole different medium on one level and it's a whole different skill set on another. For us, I love it. It's so easy and you know exactly what your movie's going to look like. Our real problem was going to be in exhibition, once we tried to take what we knew was the future and tried to force it into the analog world that existed then, with poor projectors and horrible presentation. But that was all changing.

GEORGE LUCAS

I refined the process of working more visually; I shoot for a period of time, about sixty days or so, and then I stop and work on the film for a while. Then I come back and shoot for another ten days or so, and then I stop and go back and work on the film, rewrite and change things, and then I come back and shoot for another week. I do it in pieces rather than in one long shoot. That way I can actually look at what I'm doing, cut it and study it. The previsualization process [allows me to] put scenes together without having to shoot them, see how they fit in the movie, and then, if they work, I can cut them in and actually go out and shoot them. There's a lot of freedom and malleability that didn't exist before. It's easy to move things around in the frame, to change various visual aspects of the film, which just wasn't possible before. It's the same kind of thing that you find in still photography if you use Photoshop.

RICK MCCALLUM

That camera was only an interim step. High-def isn't the ultimate answer, just the way you acquire images. And if you acquire them digitally, you have the ability to manipulate every frame with total control.

RON MAGID
One reported problem was the decision to use high-def instead of VistaVision for miniature effects photography.

GEORGE LUCAS
We had to reinvent the system. We had to get new cameras and build the system rather than just use the system we had. But I wanted *Episode II* to be consistently digital; I didn't want to have to use film. Film ultimately is very cumbersome. It's like working with the lights out—you can't see the work until the next day. Being able to look at what you're doing while you're doing it, without having to run to the lab or [hurrying] because you want to break down the setup and all that, makes high-def a much more efficient way of shooting visual effects.

Beyond new supporting players, those joining the main cast include the legendary Hammer horror star Christopher Lee as Count Dooku; Temuera Morrison, who had wowed audiences in Lee Tamahori's Once Were Warriors, *as Jango Fett; Daniel Logan as his son, Boba; NYPD Blue's Jimmy Smits as Bail Organa; and, of course, Hayden Christensen stepping into the role of Anakin Skywalker, which Jake Lloyd had played in his pint-sized version in* The Phantom Menace.

Christensen was born April 19, 1981, in Vancouver, British Columbia. Prior to Attack of the Clones, *he starred in the TV series* Higher Ground *(2000) and appeared in the films* In the Mouth of Madness, No Greater Love, *and* Street Law *(all 1995),* The Hairy Bird *(1998),* The Virgin Suicides *and* Free Fall *(both 1999), and* Life as a House *(2001).*

RICK MCCALLUM
There are never star vehicles in the *Star Wars* films. That isn't what drives the films at all—and we didn't need it, especially with the character of Anakin. It's better to meet him and have as little baggage as possible attached, because then you can watch that person just purely as someone out of nowhere. Hayden was a wonderfully decent, incredible kid, unbelievably focused. But there was something—I wouldn't say damaged, but there is something in there that's really interesting, something in his look, something about him that you don't quite understand. And if you use it, it makes things very interesting, because he's such a likable and decent guy.

I think we all saw different things in him. I don't think we all agreed on *what* we saw in him, but ultimately, we came to the same decision that he was the one. I didn't necessarily see the dark side in him and I find that interesting. George and Robin [Gurland] could see that easier than I could. You know, you could easily come to the conclusion that, "Oh, yeah, I see the bad seed in him and what he could become." But it was much more complicated than that. It's the process of being Anakin Skywalker and the eventual fall to the dark side that I think requires an enormous amount of acting ability, and Hayden has that. He has infinite potential. It was pretty much a slam dunk. We didn't know that until we saw him and tested him, but once he did the test, it was pretty obvious.

GEORGE LUCAS

We saw hundreds and hundreds of people. You work very hard to cast your picture. You look for the very best, qualified actors—the ones with the best craft and real talent—and then you find people who fit into that role as you envision it to be. In this case, we went through lots of testing with many people, and finally we brought it down to a few. I then tested them with Natalie Portman to see what the chemistry was, because, after all, this is a love story.

NATALIE PORTMAN

George asked my opinion and my opinion was Hayden. I don't know if he was thinking along the same lines as I was or how much he took my opinion.

GEORGE LUCAS

The thing that got Hayden the role was that—beyond being an extremely talented actor—he had this boyish quality that was necessary for this impatient young kid, who's very similar to Luke. Anakin's roughly the same age in *Clones* that Luke was in *A New Hope*. Hayden also had a great capacity to have a brooding dark side. He's very good with anger and those kinds of qualities—which aren't only important to this film, but even more important in the next one. So, I was casting for two films and for the arc of this character, not just how he behaves in *Clones*.

HAYDEN CHRISTENSEN

It was a process that ran four or five months. First, it was just a meeting with the casting director, Robin Gurland. I flew myself into Los Angeles—I was in Vancouver doing a TV show, *Higher Ground*, at the time. I went to meet with Robin and that was an hour-and-a-half videotaped conversation, not about *Star Wars*, but more about my approach to how I work. George saw that and I was supposed to fly out to L.A. again, because that's where he was going to meet with twelve of the kids whom he had seen on tape and liked. I was invited to that, but I couldn't go because of scheduling commitments to my show. Three weeks to a month later, I got a call saying that if I wanted to go out to Skywalker Ranch, he would meet with me on my own there. I did that and met with him. Again, we didn't talk about anything specifically related to *Star Wars*. It was just a chat. A month and a half after that, I went in and did a screen test with Natalie Portman. And that was it, really.

I was on Cloud Nine for about a week, and then it settled in that I had to actually *play* the part. How I was going to do that was sort of daunting, considering George could have had his pick of actors. So, I got to work and tried not to project my thoughts too much about *why* I was playing the part or what it was about me that George thought I could bring to the role. I just tried to figure out the best way. That was really where my focus was throughout the entire filming process, trying to break the character down.

RICK MCCALLUM

It was one of those weird prophecies when you're casting, a dynamic that happens. The minute he walked in the room, he and Natalie just clicked. Although he was very nervous, there was something about the way he read. It was one of those things. It's so subjective. The way he read the part, the way he got along with Natalie, this thing that's in him—it just worked. We just knew.

SAMUEL L. JACKSON

The first time I asked George about who was going to play Anakin, it was interesting. He said, "I found this kid with this great face and great character about him. He has an edge that lets you know he can be Darth Vader." I said, "Are you serious?" When I met Hayden, I thought he was a nice kid. Fortunately for him, the majority of his scenes were with Ewan and Natalie, two people who had been through the process and understand the seriousness with which we approach the job. He had a chance to watch them and how they came to work every day and did what they did.

Christopher Lee entered the Star Wars *universe with much the same grandeur and gravitas as Alec Guinness and Peter Cushing had in the original trilogy. Lee's personal history is in many ways more interesting than the characters he played on-screen. Born May 22, 1922, to father Lieutenant Colonel Geoffrey Trollope Lee and his wife, Countess Estelle Marie, Lee's childhood was one of high-end schools and grand occasions with Europe's elite. Acting was an early passion: he appeared in several plays as a child, and the world of fiction was always near to hand. Lee's cousin was future James Bond author Ian Fleming, and he attended school with actor Patrick Macnee and studied under famed ghost* story writer M. R. James while attending Eton. While his education at Eton and Oxford was focused on the Classics, he never lost his love of the theater.

With the onset of the war with Germany in 1939, and his family now penniless, Lee enrolled in the military academy and volunteered to fight for the Finnish army against the Soviet Union during the Winter War. During the next few years, Lee would move from country to country, and assignment to assignment, eventually working within the intelligence service on assignments he would refuse to speak of to his dying day. After the war he spent a brief period hunting Nazi war criminals across war-torn Europe before finally returning home, deciding to leave the bloodshed of war behind in favor of becoming an actor.

The next decade, he slowly made his way up the ranks of the British film world before his first breakthrough role in Hammer Films' 1957 film The Curse of Frankenstein, alongside future Grand Moff Tarkin actor Peter Cushing. Hammer's films were known for using and reusing actors, and Christopher Lee, with his "stiff-upper-lip" British mannerisms combined with a man who's seen much of the world and remembers what he's seen, made him the perfect match for roles in Hammer's Dracula and Frankenstein franchises, and many other gothic horror films of the time. For the next several decades, Lee would attract acclaim for roles in various Sherlock Holmes films; as James Bond villain Scaramanga in The Man with the Golden Gun (1974); and for his role in the horror cult classic The Wicker Man (1973). His career, which seemed to fall into B-villain roles and the occasional guest spot, saw a major resurgence in the early 2000s with the role of Saruman in Peter Jackson's adaptation of J.R.R. Tolkien's The Lord of the Rings trilogy—as well as that of Count Dooku in George Lucas's Attack of the Clones (2002), Revenge of the Sith (2005), and Star Wars: The Clone Wars (2008).

CHRISTOPHER LEE
(actor, "Count Dooku")

To be Saruman in Lord of the Rings and Dooku in Star Wars . . . it's a wonderful experience for me. Between them, these are six stories in the two greatest and most successful franchises, which is not something you really expect at my age. I consider myself very fortunate.

RICK MCCALLUM

Christopher Lee is someone who came out of the blue for me. It was a choice that Robin and George made. George has always liked his work, always wanted to work with him, and thought this was the chance and that he was the perfect person for the part. I was looking for somebody who was traditionally more evil, but it made sense to me. We worked with him on

Young Indy and really enjoyed the experience. So, it was a great idea and he is fantastic.

CHRISTOPHER LEE

My agent called and said, "George Lucas is going to call you from Australia in connection with the next *Star Wars* film." The script was sent to me and then George called and said, "I'm doing another *Star Wars* film and I would very much like to have you in it. We'll have a lot of fun." That was what really did it for me, that three-letter word—*fun.* That's so immensely important. You can work extremely hard, you can give the best performance you can, you can satisfy the director, the producer, the public, and yourself, and you *can* have fun doing all that. That sense of fun has disappeared in the making of most pictures today, and to such a degree that it's quite depressing. It's all "time is money" now. But there's no reason why I shouldn't have a laugh with the director or anyone else on a film, for that matter.

GEORGE LUCAS

With Christopher Lee, I was looking for a villain, a Sith Lord who wasn't Darth Maul, who wasn't Darth Vader, but who was more elegant, who had been a Jedi, who was more sinister than he was scary. I was getting away from the Frankenstein Monster kind of character and into the more elegant Dracula brand of character. I realized I was setting myself up to go there, and I dared *not* go there. But I wanted a more sophisticated kind of villain. Dooku's disenchantment with the corruption in the Empire is actually valid. It's all valid. So, Chris plays it as, "Is he really a villain or is he just someone who is disenchanted and trying to make things right?"

CHRISTOPHER LEE

I would be more inclined to describe Dooku as a person, but I think most people would consider him a villain. He's not, however, your traditional black-hearted villain, although he's extremely dangerous and lethal and pretty cold-blooded about everything that goes on. But the most dangerous people are the ones who are casual about everything. Dooku is quite casual about the things he does, which leads to trouble for other people. He appears to be casual, though he really isn't.

Dooku's a former Jedi, so at some point in his life he was a valorous and honest knight, but he became disillusioned with the establishment and decided he could do better. So, he joined forces with other people. I don't think it's quite clear whether he wants to take over, as Saruman does in *The Lord of the Rings,* or whether he's simply obeying his master. By the way, I would say that there's really no comparison between Saruman and Dooku, except that they're both seeking power. Saruman wants to be number one and Dooku, as I said, is certainly quite content to be number two in this story.

RICK MCCALLUM

Christopher Lee is someone we hired before *The Lord of the Rings* and he was perfect for the part. There's a baggage that comes with Christopher and his relationship to this role was perfect. It really didn't have much to do with his connection to Peter Cushing. We needed somebody who had a great, great voice, who came with a subtext of menace. And Christopher Lee fulfills that.

CHRISTOPHER LEE

We sat around and talked, the members of the cast. It was the same thing on *The Lord of the Rings* and *Sleepy Hollow*. That was the great joy for me of working on these films. You give your best when George Lucas, Peter Jackson, or Tim Burton says, "Okay, now we're going to shoot," but during rehearsals, during breaks in the shooting, they encouraged you to talk, to tell jokes and to relax.

SAMUEL L. JACKSON

Talking with Christopher Lee was a real defining moment. When I stepped into that space and say that line, "This party's over," I almost wanted to stop and say, "How are you doing, Mr. Lee?" It was like, "Ooh, Fu Manchu." He's a *very* cool man.

Besides being the father of the young Boba Fett (who would be an iconic part of the original trilogy), Jango Fett is a bounty hunter whose DNA serves as the basis of the clone army introduced in Attack of the Clones. *Playing the character is Temuera Morrison, whose credits prior to the* Star Wars *film include* Once Were Warriors *(1994),* Barb Wire *(1996),* The Island of Dr. Moreau *(1996),* Speed 2: Cruise Control *(1997),* Six Days, Seven Nights *(1998),* Vertical Limit *(2000), and* Crooked Earth *(2001). Morrison returned to portray his son, Boba Fett, in* The Mandalorian *and its spin-off,* The Book of Boba Fett.

TEMUERA MORRISON
(actor, "Jango Fett")

To be honest with you, I really didn't know anything about Jango Fett or Boba Fett or *Star Wars*. I don't know what happened to me in the late seventies and early eighties with the whole *Star Wars* saga. I guess I was in New Zealand trying to find jobs. I had a lot of jobs, actually, and little time to see the *Star Wars* movies. So, I didn't know who Jango Fett was and, when Robin said, "Look, you're playing this Fett character"—I think she said Boba Fett's father—all I comprehended at the time was Boba Fett. I went, "Yeah, yes, yes," but in the same breath I was wondering, "Who the hell is *that*?"

GEORGE LUCAS

Boba Fett had a connection to the stormtroopers. I sort of built him out of the stormtroopers and I knew the stormtroopers were clones. Exactly what that relationship was I hadn't really established yet. I knew Boba was a clone, but I didn't know how all of that fit together. I knew that the clones were made out of a bounty hunter and when I got to this story, I thought, "Well, gee, the best bounty hunter is Boba Fett. And rather than him maybe being a clone, he could be the *originator* of the clones." Most of the pieces were there, but I actually put them all together in this one.

TEMUERA MORRISON

Everybody told me, "Boba Fett is one of the most popular characters around," though, and so *that's* when I got excited. But I didn't use what I saw of Jeremy Bulloch as any kind of reference. When I got to the set, I just did what came naturally and asked what time lunch was.

George didn't say too much about the character. He just told me, "Stand over there and look that way. Look up there. And look over there." I just tried to hit the mark where he told me to stand. He also told me to relax a little bit. Initially, during my first scene, it was quite intimidating because of the scale of the sets and the enormity of the production.

My first scene on my first day was with Ewan McGregor, when he walks into my apartment as Obi-Wan Kenobi. It was very intimidating, but fortunately for me, I knew some of the crew guys from *The Island of Dr. Moreau*. That put me partly at ease, and then George was very nice and cordial. He said, "Just relax" and told me, "You're like the olive grower." Those were his words, actually. What he meant was that, for Jango, it should be like just another day growing olives. Jango should be relaxed and think that it's no big deal that this Jedi Knight is here. I'm just trying to put him off the trail. So it was intimidating, because of the sets and meeting George for the first time on the set and there being hundreds of people around. Man, I'm surprised I looked any good. I didn't find the character interesting. It was all in the costume. That was the *only* interesting thing about him.

For Natalie Portman, her return as Padmé was a demonstration of her maturation from The Phantom Menace, not just as an actress, but in life as well. This, of course, would be reflected in her portrayal of the character.

RICK MCCALLUM

Natalie Portman was fifteen when she started on *Episode I*. She was nineteen on *Episode II*. She had gone to her first year at Harvard. She had friends of her own and her parents weren't around, so it was a totally different thing for her. She was a whole different person. Imagine being fifteen years old and being the queen, the hairpiece, and the costumes . . . Now she gets to wear sexy costumes and is more attuned to who she is and what she wants to be as a person. Her life was balanced. She had a great academic career, so she didn't take stardom or any of that seriously on any level. But it freed her with her work so that was really fantastic.

For the returning Anthony Daniels, Attack of the Clones *presented a different sort of opportunity to play Threepio. As initially conceived, Threepio was to still be in his "naked" wire state, as he was last seen in* The Phantom Menace, *only to finally have a metal covering put on by Padmé while Anakin was in search of the Tusken Raiders. Lucas eventually scrapped the idea, and reshot the footage of Threepio with only the gray metal covering. However, during the initial shoot, Anthony Daniels was able to learn a new skill in the art of creating Threepio.*

ANTHONY DANIELS

I not only played Threepio on *Attack of the Clones,* but I also handled his puppeteering. I said I would like to do it. On *Phantom Menace,* somebody else did it while they listened to me saying my lines. The problem with that is, if you've ever watched someone on TV who is wearing an earpiece and doing a remote, there's always a little satellite time delay and a bit of brain-shifting going on. Though much of that was corrected in postproduction on *Menace,* there was a sense of it not being me or, in a way, not being Threepio. So, I told Rick McCallum and George that I would like to try it. I didn't know if I *could* do it, even though I had done some puppeteering on *The Empire Strikes Back.* I did all of the stuff when Threepio was in pieces, but that involved old-fashioned tricks—like me kneeling through a piece of furniture so it looked like I didn't have any legs, or me being half-dressed with my arm going up C-3PO's chest and into his head, where I acted like a kind of ventriloquist. They were Victorian melodrama tricks and that was fun, because it wasn't just a normal performance.

For *Episode II,* I had a Steadicam harness to support C-3PO. I worked out a rig which put the weight on my hips rather than down my spine, because it was rather heavy. Threepio really did become a demon puppet at one point—like in a horror movie, where the puppet takes over its master and strangles him. I had to do strengthening exercises so I would be able to support him, and also so I could get back into the suit. It was a challenge, to use that boring word actors use. But it *was* a horrible challenge. There were a couple of times when I thought I had bitten off more than I could chew, but I got away with it—just in the nick of time.

One of the highlights for the cast was the battle in the arena between the Jedi Knights and Count Dooku's army of droid soldiers on Geonosis in the finale.

SAMUEL L. JACKSON

I had spent so much time as a child in my room fighting imaginary pirates and Basil Rathbone and all those guys, and running from the Cyclops and all those other fantastic things, that when George put me in that big, empty room and said, "Okay, lots of things are attacking you. Fight them off," I went straight to that place. I turned the *Star Wars* theme music on in my head, started looking around and said, "Okay, let's go." It was great. George would say, "Okay, there's a big thing running around in the arena." I would say, "How big is it?" "It's kind of like an SUV and it hits you and you lose your lightsaber. And it runs away and you start doing things." It was fun. It was the biggest kid's game in the world. Just open your mind and have some fun.

KYLE ROWLING
(fight choreographer, actor, "Jedi Master Joclad Danva,"
Attack of the Clones)

We actually filmed that scene a week or two before we came back and did the second unit shoot on that set and it was just the principals in that scene. One of the things [stunt coordinator] Nick Gillard did for me is he put me in that scene as one of the last surviving Jedi. It was a fast two-day shoot, so you didn't really have time to hang out with the stars while they were working, although I was already in rehearsals with Hayden and Ewan, so we had the occasional chat. But everyone was very professional and polite. It was very funny, actually: a huge soundstage with sand on the floor and a blue curtain that went all the way around and people shouting at you, "Now these things are walking in and shooting at you, and these things are flying around over-head, this monster will run past you here, when you hear your number, fall down," etc. If you look carefully, Joclad is on the floor one minute and fighting the next. "I'm alive! I'm dead! I'm alive! I'm dead! Or am I?"

ZACHARIAH JENSEN
(actor, "Kit Fisto")

We had soundtracks playing and there were lots of "being a Jedi in the back-yard as a kid," but with awesome costumes and lots of cameras. There were individual sessions where George had some specific directions as well as group scenes and lots of improvising. It was a long and tiring day, but fun!

LILY NYAMWASA
(actress, Jedi "Stass Allie," *Attack of the Clones*)

I liked the action and I was so happy that I could use my martial arts moves. But, it was very sad to watch a lot of Jedi dying. During the shoot, I swear I had tears in my eyes—although I could see that it was acting—but I really felt sad to see them all dead. I would like to play a strong female warrior. I like to challenge myself, so anything that takes me outside my comfort zone would do it for me. Also, I think it's becoming trendy to have female action heroes, so I wouldn't mind playing a female action hero, saving some innocent people somewhere in the world. Although this won't be as challenging as playing an evil person, because, naturally, I regard myself as a philanthropist or a people person, so it's easier for me to act a good person than playing a bad person. I found it challenging when we were filming the arena scene. George Lucas kept saying to me, "Lily, put on your angry and serious face, you're supposed to be killing enemies," and I thought I was trying my best, so something like this would be really good and challenging for me.

"Challenging" is probably an appropriate word for what most of the cast felt as they filmed the vast majority of Attack of the Clones, *as a large majority of the sets were virtual, meaning that they were essentially acting against nothing in front of a green screen.*

EWAN MCGREGOR
(actor, "Obi-Wan Kenobi")

Shooting was boring as hell. What bothered me most was that everything was so deliberate. It's all about, "We're going to go and do this now . . . ," as opposed to getting under the skin of what the character's thinking. There's no spontaneity; your job, as an actor, is just to get it out. There's not a lot of psychological stuff goes on when you're acting with things that aren't actually there. If I wanted to be polite when people inquire about it, I'll say, "It's not quite as performance-based as the films I've been doing in the past" or I'll say something diplomatic like, "I've never done a movie that big before. I've never done anything with effects or that kind of blue-screen work, so it's a different process." But, quite honestly, after my initial excitement, the filmmaking process turned out to be the epitome of tedium. The work was so complex with all the special effects and stuff, that I found myself just hanging around for days and days and days. When you realize that George Lucas and his people went into eighteen months of postproduction after two years of preproduction and three and a half months of actual shooting, you can judge for yourself exactly how important the live-action actors were to the film. We were just a small part.

NATALIE PORTMAN

The technology and effects are definitely part of the enjoyment for me. I mean, there's *so* much technology and you can learn so much by talking to the special effects people or the camera people who are measuring the distance between different spots and the blue screens so they can get the right dimensions for the light and the shadows. It's just incredible and also makes you feel like you're part of something much bigger. When you're working with three hundred people on a movie and everyone has such an important role, it's nice to know that you're part of a crew more than being the center of attention.

HAYDEN CHRISTENSEN

It definitely required a leap of faith, because when you watch it on playback, you're not sure what it will be like when they mesh the live-action and CGI elements. So, it's a risk, but you know you're in good hands. To be honest, if there was a feasible way of getting those ridiculous environments on Earth—so we could actually act in them—it would be counterproductive for the actors, because we would be so much in awe of our surroundings and thinking, "I'm this character and this is my world and my norm." Not knowing what it will actually look like makes you not take in your surroundings as much as you ordinarily would. The blue screen forces you to use your imagination. So it was helpful in almost every way.

EWAN MCGREGOR

The process makes it difficult to maintain momentum in the performance, it being all in my imagination. It's very important for it to be very, very sharp and very quick, because these creatures would be coming from all over the place. I had to imagine where they were coming from and look in each different direction. It's all quite complicated and at the same time it was exciting.

CHRISTOPHER LEE

It was a very interesting experience. So, George was sitting in front of one monitor, and a special effects king was sitting in front of another. One was looking at one thing and the other was looking at something else. And there were blue screens. But the two of them knew what was going to be on that screen. They knew what was going to be in front of us, behind us, below us, and above us, but we didn't. It was described, some of it, in the script. But even then, it wasn't crystal clear, because we didn't know what kinds of characters they were going to put in, what these characters were going to look like. So even though I acted in the movie and had the script, I couldn't tell you what happened ahead of time. What's on the screen could have looked so much different from what I actually read. I was always a little nervous talking about the film—aside from the fact that I signed a confidentiality agreement, because I had *no idea* what will be going on around me.

HAYDEN CHRISTENSEN

You don't have any real environments to be affected by with blue screen, and the majority of sets *were* blue screens. In many ways, it's not that dissimilar from doing theater, where you don't have those real environments and it demands much more of your imagination. I was excited by the challenge and by the fact that when I finally saw the film, I would have a fresh experience, because I *hadn't* really seen any of those places I was supposed to be in. At the same time, I was pretty accepting of the blue-screen work, probably because I hadn't been a part of too many films in general and especially none that worked like this one. I was twelve when I did *In the Mouth of Madness*. I got to meet Sam Neill and that was neat. Other than that, the other films were all sort of hobby projects more than anything else. I was more interested in other aspects of my life at that time. Acting was a way to get out of school.

CHRISTOPHER LEE

I must say I didn't find blue screen a problem at all, because I have a very vivid, powerful imagination. If I know what's supposed to be there—although I may *not* know what it looks like in the physical sense—I can deal with it. In this kind of film, you're working and getting nothing back from the other person. Well, I've been through that many times with some of my colleagues, if you get my point. So I'm used to it, let's put it that way. In a war movie made forty years ago, a single line in a script could say, "And there's a battle." Well, that could take three weeks to a month to shoot. And you don't know what it's going to look like, because you're just one part of it. So much of it has to do with trust.

Additional shooting took place at England's Ealing Film Studios during March 2001, for which Lucas had come up with a new action sequence taking place in a droid factory in an effort to add more action to the film's final act, which for many came across as a glorified video game sequence.

RICK McCALLUM

It's a lovely little studio. It's very compact and it is very easy to work out of, because it has two reasonably small stages. All of the workshops are around it so you don't have to walk miles to get to them. We didn't have to share it with anyone; we basically had the whole place to ourselves. When you're doing this kind of intense work, moving back and forth from one stage to another two or three times a day, it is important to have interconnecting stages. It is a wonderful place to make a movie. It also happens to be the place where Alec Guinness first started his film career. He filmed all the Ealing comedies at this studio, so it is kind of sweet and nice to be here.

When you are doing a film as complicated as *Star Wars,* what happens is that you shoot the bulk of the film all at one time. You want to try to get through all the difficult stuff, all the major set pieces, the major special effects—all the really complex stuff, location work, etc., on the main shoot. You want to get through that as quickly as you can. You then edit the film and it's like rewriting an article—you cut and paste and change things. When you are writing, you just have to make up the dialogue, but when you are filming, you have to go back and reshoot. It is actually not so much reshoots, but additional shooting. Often when you are shooting, things are out of continuity; you film the ending first and so on. Everything is filmed out of order.

What happens as a result of that is that some actors never meet each other and you watch it in the editing process and you realize that there were scenes you could have filmed which would have made that scene more intense, or you think, "Gee, I would like to develop this character a little more or add more of that." Sometimes you think, "Maybe this action sequence isn't long enough" or maybe it's too long or you need another dialogue scene to cement this relationship. We've always done this. We did it since day one on *Young Indy,* we did it on *Episode I*—we went back and shot three or four times. They're just little bits and pieces, things which make the film that much better.

JONATHAN RINZLER

George was always tinkering. On *Episode II,* I was there, George decided he wanted this shot of Anakin's mechanical hand taking Padmé's flesh hand when they get married. The movie was finished, it was literally the day before the movie was coming out. I was in Rick McCallum's office, the producer, and there was a guy there who was like, "We can't do it." And Rick says, "You want me to tell George you can't do it?" And the guy says, "We can't do it for the celluloid version, but we can do it for the digital release." You know, it's digital, you can send them that one thing and they can make the change. And that guy went running out of the office. There was some high-pressure stuff going on. They got that shot in for the digital release, but not the film release. George was always changing things.

The pioneering effects work from ILM entered new territory completely with the wholly CGI character, in the form of Yoda, replacing the puppet that had been used to great success in The Empire Strikes Back *and* Return of the Jedi . . . *and to lesser success in the theatrical release of* The Phantom Menace.

JONATHAN RINZLER

Before, they had done Jar Jar, and they really had high hopes for him. That's before my time, but I know it was a fact. Then, of course, Jar Jar became detested by a large number of people. But, the CG character existed—whether you hated him or not—the fact that they pulled it off at all. So now they were taking it to the next level with Yoda.

My first full day I was on the job, they said, "Here's a VHS cassette of *Episode II*—the latest cut—stick it in the machine, we'll close the door, and don't tell anyone what you saw." It was amazing! There was lots of temp stuff in it, because ILM hadn't completed all their shots, and Yoda was a little animated spec fighting Count Dooku, it looked terrible. I rapidly learned everyone thought this fight between Yoda and Count Dooku was not going to work, that it was going to look terrible.

As the film entered postproduction, John Williams set to work once more crafting the film's glorious soundtrack. Returning for the first time since The Empire Strikes Back *to the themes of romance, and revenge.*

JOE KRAEMER

(composer, *Mission Impossible: Rogue Nation* and *Jack Reacher*)

The major new theme in this score is the Love Theme for Anakin and Padmé. It's a fascinating theme because in many ways it is a minor-key version of the Main Theme (Luke's Theme), bearing a strong resemblance to the melodic contour and rhythm. It's also interesting because as it passes through its many twists and turns it actually modulates to a lower key, which has a subconscious effect of darkening our psychological response to the tragic and doomed love affair. And by titling the concert version of the theme "Across the Stars," Williams draws an association to the old cliché of star-crossed lovers.

The other significant theme is the Separatist Theme, which is essentially the Love Theme with a different first note. But what's really cool is that Williams takes that central melodic idea and modulates in a parallel chord sequence to the Emperor's Theme, which creates a subconscious connection between the two seemingly disparate elements: Anakin and Padmé's Love, and the Emperor, inextricably tied together by the war with the Separatist movement.

Williams evokes the music of Bernard Herrmann and his score for *North by Northwest* in the terrific chase through Coruscant early in the film, with its wonderful pulsing rhythm and imperative xylophone. And even though it went unused in the final mix, there is some electric guitar heard on the soundtrack album that demonstrates how, even five films into the saga, Williams was still trying to find ways to inject new ideas and textures into the fabric of the scores.

Reel 6 of this film, like *The Phantom Menace,* was a large action reel, this time showcasing the prolonged fight sequences in the Geonosis Arena, first between our heroes and the monsters, and then between the Jedi forces and the battle droids, before moving to the deserts of the planet for a large-scale ground battle between the clone troopers and the mechanized forces of the Separatists. From the moment Mace Windu arrives at the battle until Anakin, Obi-Wan, and Padmé take off in pursuit of Count Dooku, the score is all created editorially from the mostly unused action music from *The Phantom Menace* that had been dropped in favor of "Duel of the Fates." This was a major deviation for a *Star Wars* film, and it was apparently the plan from the beginning. I can only imagine how much work had gone into the composing of this music in the first place, and the disappointment that it went unheard must have been palpable, so it was a win-win situation for everyone involved. Funnily enough, the music Williams wrote for the first half of the arena scene in this film was dialed out, Ben Burtt finally able to have a sequence in the film driven by sound effects, well deserved. But this unused music would come in handy on *Revenge of the Sith.*

The final two minutes of the film consist of a dialogue-free visual sequence showing the clone army heading off to war and the wedding of Anakin and Padmé. The clone army sequence features the first full presentation of "The Imperial March" in the prequel trilogy, something Williams had been intending to save for the appearance of Darth Vader. His original scoring of this moment in the film has no reference to that famous theme at all, relying instead on a variation of music associated with Count Dooku and the clones. But apparently, when they recorded the cue, Lucas was surprised not to hear "The Imperial March," and so Williams rewrote the sequence in his hotel room after work and then recorded the new version as an insert. A small snippet of Williams's original version can be heard in the music video for "Across the Stars" in the final moments of the piece.

Themes that make a return appearance in this film include the Main Theme, the Force Theme, and Yoda's Theme, as well as the aforementioned "Imperial March." Shmi's Theme makes two haunting reappearances in the score, first when Anakin discusses the nightmares he's been having about her with Obi-Wan, and then again when he is reunited with his mother in the Tusken camp. Surprisingly, considering how strongly the score for *The Phantom Menace* relied on it, Anakin's Theme only appears once, when he sees Padmé again for the first time in ten years. Also, the Emperor's Theme is only heard once, at the end of the film, in the single scene explicitly featuring Darth Sidious. The Trade Federation march is heard during the reveal of the clone army on Kamino, which is a curious choice, since the clones are, at least on the surface, the enemies of the Trade Federation. I suspect that placement was at the direction of Lucas. Interestingly, Jar Jar's theme is nowhere to be heard . . . Of course, lots of other themes are reused in the edited battle music for reel 6, but none of that was actually composed for this film.

Attack of the Clones, *produced for $115 million and cumulatively grossing $654 million, was released on May 16, 2002. It was considered by some as being superior to* The Phantom Menace *but was also greeted by mixed reviews.*

RAY MORTON

The script has a number of issues. The nature of the relationship between Obi-Wan and Anakin isn't clear. At one point, Anakin tells Obi-Wan that he is the closest thing Anakin has to a father. However, we never see any example of that allegedly close relationship—mostly we see Obi-Wan criticize and correct Anakin and Anakin resents Obi-Wan and push[es] back against his instruction. So, it's not clear where these two really stand with one another. Also, Anakin is shown to have a close relationship with Palpatine—he goes to the Chancellor with his problems and Palpatine encourages Anakin and predicts great things for him. This relationship seems to be more of a father/son relationship than the one Anakin has with Obi-Wan. How did this relationship develop? Isn't it unusual that the leader of the entire galaxy has time to chit-chat with a lowly apprentice on a regular basis? Is Obi-Wan aware of this relationship? (He does not seem to be.) If he is aware, what does he think of it—is he fine with it? Is he jealous? Is he concerned that someone else has this much influence over his Padawan? None of this is clear.

The love scenes between Anakin and Padmé are really, really terrible. Really. They are the Jar Jar Binks of this movie. The notion that someone as smart and capable and experienced as Padmé would entrust her position in the Senate to a dopey character like Jar Jar is simply not believable. And the notion that this same dopey character is permitted to make a proposal that ultimately brings down the Republic is so ludicrous and unbelievable that one almost suspects Lucas was deliberately trolling the audience by including it. There's an odd, pervy vibe to some of the material in this script—Padmé getting the hots for a man whom she first met when he was a nine-year-old boy; Anakin's constant leering at and suggestive remarks to Padmé; Klieg Lars buying an enslaved woman and then marrying her. It's all just a bit . . . yucky.

As was the case with *The Phantom Menace, Attack of the Clones* contains a number of prequel elements. Meeting the Lars family at the old moisture farm is a reasonable enough nod to the original trilogy, although the entire group seems passive when it comes to rescuing Shmi, a woman they all profess to love. In *Episode I,* the notion that Threepio was created on Tatooine was ridiculous. In *Clones,* the notion that he is still there and is working as some kind of farmer is equally ludicrous. And the fact that he is working on the very same farm he will return to in the future stretches credulity to the breaking point. It also raises the question of why Owen doesn't recognize Threepio when he turns up again years later—just how many fussy English butler droids does a backwater moisture farmer on Tatooine run into in the course of his life?

Indeed, Lucas's idea that the stormtroopers we saw in the original trilogy and Boba Fett are all clones of the same guy is certainly novel, but it somehow makes them all retroactively less interesting. In a sense, this makes the Star Wars *universe feel significantly smaller.*

RAY MORTON

The backstory relating to the ordering of the clone army from the facility on Kamino is confusing, mostly because it involves a character (the late Jedi Master Sifo-Dyas) we have never met and events we have never witnessed. We're never really sure if Sifo-Dyas was a real person or if he was just Palpatine in disguise (the script hints at both), and so when Obi-Wan and the Kaminoans are discussing it all, we never get a clear understanding of what they're talking about. Along the same lines, it's hard for us to figure out what Dooku is doing, because none of the action involving the Separatist movement is shown on-screen. Instead, the characters just talk about it, and since they're talking about things we never see, it's hard to follow (movies are a visual medium—if you want people to get it, you've gotta show, not tell). We eventually learn that it was Nute Gunray from the Trade Federation that invaded Naboo in *Menace* who put the hit on Padmé, but we never learn why. We assume it was in revenge for repelling the invasion and having him arrested all those years ago, but this is never stated for sure. And so the incident that kicks off the movie remains vague.

PETER HOLMSTROM
(cohost, *The Rebel & the Rogue* podcast)

Lucas always had it in his mind that the ideal movie was around two hours long. James Cameron talks about it on the *Aliens* audio commentary, when discussing the studio-imposed deleted scenes for the film. Basically, before megaplexes, most theaters only had one or two screens—and if you kept a movie around two hours, you could have an additional showing a day. So, literally, to keep a movie around two hours could mean 20 percent of your box office. And Cameron just shrugs it off, "I totally understand." But I'm like, "What are you talking about?!?! They cut out the most important scene in the movie!" Lucas always believed that logic wholeheartedly, but these movies needed to be longer, and he had the material to fill it. You read the scripts, storyboards, even deleted scenes—Lucas had no shortage of ideas. Every episode in the entire eight seasons (seven aired) of *The Clone Wars* was based on abandoned concepts for the prequels. Eight seasons. And it's a shame we lost those. Even the deleted scenes for *Episode II* would've gone a long way to flesh out Padmé's character, and the gradual fall of the Republic into Palpatine's larger plan. Instead, whole subplots are reduced to one line. Fans pick up the intricacies through books, comics, and watching behind-the-scenes material, but for the general public a lot of these nuances are lost.

RICK MCCALLUM

Episode II ends with two paths, but you pretty much know which is going to be taken. They may go in different directions, but they are going to end up at the same place. If you do that successfully, you can't wait to get to the third episode in terms of storytelling. If you care about Hayden and Natalie, then you really can't wait. It's like when you have been in a car crash or something like that, there is a moment that is quite extraordinary. If you have ever been in an out-of-control car, it's absolutely breathtakingly beautiful. The senses, the experiences, the images that come to you; then there is a moment that you know when you are going to hit the wall that becomes unbearable. That's the painful, physical side of it in terms of life and living and things like that, I think that is the fun part about *Episode II* if you really like them.

GEORGE LUCAS

My hope was that *Episode III* wouldn't be too intense for kids. It's grimmer, but in a *Star Wars* context, which means it's obviously *not* horrible. It may be emotionally more difficult, but I went there in *The Empire Strikes Back*. I was very nervous for kids about, "I am your father," and then cutting Luke's hand. I thought, "Have I gone over the line here?" I discussed it with people, basically many psychologists, and came to the conclusion that it was okay. I'll probably be pushing the envelope a little on this one, but if kids see all six films, they will discover everything gets redeemed and everything is okay. Over the course of the six films, there are scary moments and it's tough that I'll have to end *Episode III* on a scary moment, but that *is* the story. There's not much I can do about it. For parents, if a child does have a problem with the next one, there *is* hope in it—in the sense that there will be all these babies. So, a parent can say to a child—if the child hasn't seen the other ones—"Don't worry, the babies grow up and save their father."

RICK MCCALLUM

You *know* what's going to happen and it's not good. He's a nice boy. But you know, you see it at work, you see it every moment of your life. You see it when you go out driving, you see it in a movie. When you see someone who's an awful person, you know he's not awful all the time. There is somebody out there who loves him. It's really interesting when you know somebody and you can't help them. They have a destiny and they are going to do it and you want to shake them. Even if you can get to them, it still doesn't help.

NATALIE PORTMAN

As an actor, when you know the end, it's inevitably in your mind. But you try to keep it out, because as a human being in real life, you don't know how or where things will end, and so to act that way you have to pretend like you don't know, even though you have read the full script and know what will happen in *Episode III*—and even though you know that there are three stories that come after you stop.

RAY MORTON

The script has too many endings—there are two rescues (Jedi rescuing Obi-Wan, Padmé, and Anakin; Yoda and the clones rescuing the Jedi), an escape (Dooku from the arena), a chase (Obi-Wan, Anakin, and Padmé chasing Dooku), two lightsaber duels (Obi-Wan and Anakin versus Dooku; Dooku versus Yoda), and another escape (Dooku from the duels). The climax just goes on and on and on until we're completely exhausted.

HAYDEN CHRISTENSEN

Watching the finished film, I was blown away. Seeing my face in a *Star Wars* movie just made me very self-aware the whole time. It makes you realize what

George created visually. You can read it on the page, but there's *nothing* like seeing the detail on the screen. I had no idea what so much of it would look like. I remember when I first read the script, I was really excited. I thought the story had so much promise. There are more humanistic elements in this film, more human interaction. It's far more dialogue-intensive, as it relates to building relationships—especially in terms of the scenes between Natalie and myself. The fight scenes put anything else you've seen in a *Star Wars* film to shame. And Ewan does a wonderful job of bringing Obi-Wan closer to Alec Guinness's Obi-Wan.

12

SITH HAPPENS:
REVENGE OF THE SITH

"I have waited a long time for this moment, my little green friend. At last, the Jedi are no more."

Episode III: Revenge of the Sith was the culmination of the trilogy and the final cinematic entry in George Lucas's vision for the Skywalker Saga, providing the story that would theoretically tie all six films together by chronicling Anakin Skywalker's full transformation into Darth Vader, the Dark Lord of the Sith, and his final lightsaber duel with Obi-Wan Kenobi. This alone promised that it would be the darkest entry in the first six films of the series.

RAY MORTON
(senior editor, *Script* magazine)

Revenge of the Sith is the best movie in the prequel trilogy. This is because it's the one that finally tells the story the trilogy set out to tell—the transformation of Anakin Skywalker into Darth Vader. This is what we've been waiting to see since this trio began and this makes it the most satisfying of the prequels as well. However, it's also a movie with some significant issues.

RICK MCCALLUM
(producer, *Revenge of the Sith*)

I'm *not* going to be defensive about it, because I know there's a large group of people out there, especially hardcore fans, who *don't* like the first and second films. To be honest, and it's a very interesting thing, when George and I were starting to do *Young Indy*—which was really set up to be the template for the production techniques that we were going to use to make the new *Star Wars* movies—George began to tell me what *Episode I* would be like. He warned me, "We're going to get killed for this, because this *isn't* the film our hardcore base wants to see." They wanted *Episode III*. And, as I've said, the story they wanted to see first is the third film we made.

RAY MORTON

In contrast to his last-minute scripting of *Attack of the Clones,* Lucas began working on the screenplay for *Revenge of the Sith* while *Clones* was still in production. His jumping-off point was a speech written for Obi-Wan in *Return of the Jedi* that was cut from the final release. In the speech, Obi-Wan tells Luke that after Anakin turned evil, Obi-Wan confronted him. They fought and Vader ended up falling into a "molten pit" and getting so horribly injured that he had to be permanently encased in a robotic life-support system that would keep what was left of him alive. Lucas knew this sequence would be the climax of the third movie and so constructed his narrative to move inexorably toward it.

RICK MCCALLUM

I think, deeply, that the fans hoped *Episode II* would be an extension or the start of *Episode III,* and they wanted *Episode III* to be even further down the line. But, at the same time, this was a story George wanted to tell for a long time. And it's the saga of this family. He was particularly interested in creating a new audience that was young. Remember, however people want to rewrite history, that the first three films were pretty badly reviewed when they first came out. Everybody said the acting was appalling and wooden. Not much has changed, but there's a whole other audience. There are kids who saw *Episode I* when they were eight or nine years old, who were then fifteen, sixteen, seventeen years old, and that's a very serious potent group of people who love *Star Wars.*

This movie was never a tricky task, because we always knew what *Episode III* was going to be. For hardcore fans, it's the film that everybody wanted *Episode I* to be and, at the same time, we knew that we had to, in a very brief time, set up everything that happens in *Episodes IV, V,* and *VI.* We also had to take the cumulative ideas from *I* and *II,* of where Anakin is and what he's becoming, and figure out what pushes him to the dark side. The biggest problem was: How do we show Anakin's turn dramatically in two hours? What's the *real* reason for his transformation, that makes him do the turn? But it wasn't a major thing we fretted over. It really is part of the overall structure that George had set out thirty years ago. We kind of knew where the film was going and what we needed to do.

GEORGE LUCAS

(executive producer, screenwriter/director, *Revenge of the Sith*)
It would be a problem if I were following the market testing and all that sort of thing. On the first film they said, "Oh, you can't do this, this is going to

be a suicidal mission, you're doing *More American Graffiti*." My reaction is, "Great, I'm going to do *More American Graffiti*, I'm doing something that is basically against the marketing wishes of what you would normally do in a film like this." I needed to tell a story and in the end, if you watch all six movies, that's the way I see this. I see this as one movie in six parts, and if you see it from the beginning to the very end, where the father is redeemed by the children, it all works. But you have to accept the middle, and the middle is pretty grim.

RICK MCCALLUM
Revenge of the Sith is total mayhem and destruction. And, of course, it's a complete and utter and sad fall from grace for Anakin. That's really the basics of what *Episode III* is about. The heart of the story is the downward spiral of Anakin—how people can be so blind to what it is they do and what effect it has on other people. But dark is good. Darkness is illuminating. Sometimes you have to go pitch black to be able to see anything. That's what happens with Anakin. Because, remember, at the end of the day he *does* fulfill his destiny. At the end of the day he chooses the dark side, but he ultimately does redeem himself.

GEORGE LUCAS
It's just the nature of the story. I knew where this was going all along, that in order to connect the story up, you have to go to a rather dark place, because in this one Anakin goes bad. As a result, everybody around him feels the tragedy and obviously *IV, V,* and *VI* are bringing him out of that tragedy.

JOHN KENNETH MUIR
(author, *Science Fiction and Fantasy Films of the 1970s*)
Since we know what will occur in the time period after this film is set, *Revenge of the Sith* feels like a grand, tragic opera, a near *Godfather*-style epic about the fall of a good man and a noble society. There is an epic, unstoppable sweep to the film that carries the audience away. In bringing about Anakin's downfall, the film ties in visually and thematically with the beginning era of the saga, *A New Hope*. So, the film's relentless drive makes it powerful (and indeed tragic), the theme (giving away ideals for security) speaks powerfully to the culture that produced this art, and *Star Wars* fans got to see everything tied up in a neat, if sad, package. The film's final moments, with the return to Tatooine and the double suns, is tragic, nostalgic, and weirdly hopeful at the same time.

RICK MCCALLUM

If the audience cared enough about Anakin, what happens would be unbearable. Because it's no different when you love somebody; all of us in our personal lives have had that problem with some member of our family. That's what the whole movie is about. It's a saga of the family. Sooner or later from one generation to the next there is somebody who screws up badly. And you never understand. And if you are a close family, you love them anyway and nothing is more unbearable when you can't help them. This is a family saga that takes place over twelve hours. It is in six parts. If you watch all six together, then you realize that you aren't left with darkness, you are left with something much more positive. You have to watch *Star Wars* as an entire series.

JOHN KENNETH MUIR

Revenge of the Sith is the best and the most widely accepted of the prequels. It is a "War of Terror Age" parable about people surrendering liberty in the face of fear, and the consequences of doing so. For the first time, the central theme of the prequels really comes together. That idea is that people who are afraid or fearful tend to make bad decisions. People who are scared of losing their way of life give away the things they should *never* give away. Benjamin Franklin once said, "Those who would give up essential liberty to purchase a little temporary safety deserve neither liberty nor safety." In the *Star Wars* universe, free people give away their Republic to be safe from a boogeyman, the Separatists. And one man, Anakin, gives away his goodness—part of his identity—in the mistaken belief that by embracing the dark side, he can protect his family. The Chancellor is voted into power as Emperor by the very people who need protection *from* an Emperor. The scared masses practically beg a "strong man" to protect them. And he does so, at least after a fashion. Palpatine tells Darth Vader: "Go bring peace to the Empire." Unfortunately, it is the peace of subjugation, the peace of oppression, that he provides.

BRIAN JAY JONES

(author, *George Lucas: A Life*)

Revenge of the Sith gives Natalie Portman one of the greatest lines Lucas has ever written, which is, "This is the way liberty dies, with thunderous applause." I think especially nowadays, every day that line gets better and better. Again, one of the finest he's ever written, whether he meant to do it or not.

Production on Revenge of the Sith *began in June 2003 in Sydney, Australia, also shooting in Thailand, Switzerland, China, Italy, and the UK. With much of the cast of* Attack of the Clones *returning, the production welcomed back Peter Mayhew as Chewbacca, much to the joy of fans.*

PETER MAYHEW
(actor, "Chewbacca")

Rick McCallum called completely out of the blue. I almost dropped the phone. It was a pleasant surprise. Rick was calling from Australia to ask about dates and availability. I think my answer was, "When can you get me on a plane?" So it was a very enjoyable and welcome conversation. The last time I had actually worn the costume was for the MTV Movie Awards, which was an interesting event. There were loads of Hollywood and music people there, and Chewie sort of stole the evening. He got the only standing ovation of the night. It was a ball and I had a great time. But I had a *better* time, I must say, on *Revenge of the Sith*.

The change between films in special effects makes a hell of a difference. First of all, it's faster now. It's much quicker to use a blue or green screen, where certain items represent certain things. And with modern cameras, you get instant replay and can see what has been shot, whereas before you had to wait for the footage to come back from the processing plant. That usually took a day. Now you have everything *instantly*. So if anything goes wrong, you can shoot it again right away, while everyone's still there. The whole process is *much* quicker.

RICK MCCALLUM

It was fantastic to work with Peter Mayhew and have him return as Chewbacca. He's such a consummate gentleman and a decent guy, and he wanted to be back in that suit so bad.

PETER MAYHEW

So far as acting against nothing—which is what you do when you have the blue and green screens—that's where the skill of the actor comes in. You are told what's going to be around you and—if you use your imagination—you know what has come before and what occurs afterward. You work out what you're going to do in your mind.

Comfort-wise, I had a water-cooled suit underneath the original. It kept me pretty comfortable when I wasn't working, and when I was working, I would just unplug it from the power unit, tuck it in under the costume and stay cool for fifteen or twenty minutes. However, certain scenes were done with CGI, but the majority of Chewie's stuff *is* me.

I saw Ewan, Hayden, and everyone from the *Sith* cast when we were shooting in Australia, and I also shot with a couple of other Wookiees. That was interesting, because being the older and more experienced actor who had played a Wookiee before, I could sit back and know what I was going to do, whereas some of the others were a bit tense. I was the boss man, the Wookiee boss man, apart from George. It was nice to be back. It was also weird not standing next to Harrison Ford. How do you describe it? It was odd, but it was also nice that Chewie could become the personality he has always been. Under Han Solo, Chewie was a little bit daunted. But in *Revenge of the Sith*, we saw much more of Chewie and learned more about him than you did in the last film, *Return of the Jedi*.

A unique challenge was given to ILM and the Lucasfilm design team at the start of production: to create a fully CG villain . . . with four lightsabers. General Grievous—a deadly being who abandoned his physical body in favor of the perfection that is metal and machine, the supreme commander of the Separatist droid army—would go on to become a fan favorite, appearing across multiple TV shows, video games, and novels. The man behind him is the film's animation director, Rob Colman; he is voiced by Lucasfilm sound engineer Matthew Wood.

RICK MCCALLUM

He's a really interesting digital character, but he isn't a crucial player in the whole film. He's a bad guy who has to be eliminated at a certain point in the story. Obi-Wan is sent out to destroy him and then Grievous becomes a major plot point, but only his destruction is important.

ROB COLMAN
(animation director and motion capture actor for
"General Grievous," *Revenge of the Sith*)

Grievous was fully computer-generated. What was neat about him from both an animation and acting point of view was that he has no mouth or eyebrows. He only has these eyes that are sort of hidden behind his mask. Several of my animators were concerned and asked, "How do we make him expressive?" It was a great acting exercise getting him to emote through his body performance. I was fortunate enough to take Chuck Jones out to dinner a few years ago, and one of the questions I asked him was, "Which character was the hardest to achieve—and that you were happiest with?" It turned out to be Marvin the Martian. He told me that Bugs Bunny was a little bit of him and a little bit of the other guys, and that Bugs was actually easy to animate. But Marvin has no mouth and yet he's constantly talking, so they really had to focus on his performance and movements.

WARREN FU
(concept artist, *Revenge of the Sith*)

My main inspiration for tone and attitude with General Grievous was Michael Meyers from *Halloween,* although the final character in the movie didn't act like that. If you study the face, you can find a few other influences: The Crow, Shrunken Heads (in the mouth), and some shapes stolen from the Desert Skiff [from *Return of the Jedi*].

ROB COLMAN

When we were doing Grievous, I said, "Okay, here's our opportunity to animate a character with no mouth, but who talks a fair amount." Grievous's eyes look great and we went through a whole elaborate investigation as to how he should move. Originally, Grievous was going to be very powerful and tall, but George said, "Nah, I don't want him to be too Vader-like. I want to make him more sinister. He's ill. He's grievously ill." And the subtext there is that Grievous is the first generation, the Alpha version of this creature-droid technology blend. So he's sort of this sickly prototype. The same technology would then, in George's mind, be used to build Darth Vader.

WARREN FU

The MagnaGuards turned out closer to how I envisioned them. I pictured Grievous being a silent but deadly character that spoke through its intimidating presence, so I was a bit surprised to see how animated and talkative he turned out. But at the end of the day, my work as a conceptual designer was in service of greater story, so it doesn't matter how I envisioned him, I'm just happy I was able to contribute the design to this great universe. I'm actually pleased to see that he's still a prominent character in the universe. It's pretty surreal to think that he'll be around longer than I will.

Revenge of the Sith *is set three years after* Attack of the Clones, *beginning with an action sequence involving Anakin and Obi-Wan working together—which, as far as Hayden Christensen is concerned, nicely establishes how things are between them since the last film.*

HAYDEN CHRISTENSEN
(actor, "Anakin Skywalker")

They're like brothers now, and that's a great setup for where the relationship goes and how it unravels. Anakin becomes slightly suspicious of everyone around him, including Obi-Wan. The seedlings of dismay are planted and their friendship begins to spiral from there. We know where the relationship is heading. We know that it's going to all resolve itself in this lightsaber duel at the end. But it's very much like a Butch Cassidy and the Sundance Kid partnership at the get-go. So you're really emotionally invested in their friendship, and when things fall apart, you're affected by it. Anakin isn't doing so well with his relationships in this film. Padmé senses that something is up.

The Clone Wars are still raging and the Republic is starting to crumble. At the behest of the Separatist leader Count Dooku, the Separatist droid army, led by General Grievous, has invaded Coruscant and kidnapped Chancellor Palpatine. Anakin and Obi-Wan set out to rescue the Chancellor by boarding Grievous's ship and fighting their way to the chamber where Palpatine is being held by Dooku. The two Jedi engage in another lightsaber duel with the count, during which Obi-Wan is knocked out. Anakin bests Dooku and holds two lightsabers to his neck to subdue him. As Anakin stands over Dooku, Palpatine shifts into his Darth Sidious persona and urges Anakin to kill the treacherous count (who, in one of the film's best moments, is visibly shocked to discover that the master he has been completely loyal to has betrayed him). Anakin hesitates for a second, but then complies and beheads Dooku.

RAY MORTON

And here is where the first of the script's major problems arise. The most problematic aspect of *Clones* is that in the middle of the film, Anakin—who up until that point is portrayed as the film's hero—slaughters an entire tribe of Tusken Raiders. He does what Jedi have always been warned *not* to do: he gives in to his hate, anger, and his aggression, turns to the dark side and becomes a villain. But the movie almost immediately forgets about this transformation and resumes portraying Anakin as a hero, as if the incident never happened. While the movie ignores the murders, moviegoers couldn't and were left with very conflicted feelings about him—at best there's an unease about him; at worst they despise him for being the villain he has chosen to become. The three years between films could have helped them forget about all this and return to viewing Anakin as a sympathetic protagonist (something that is necessary if they're to see his transformation into Vader as a tragedy). However, *Sith* sticks the dilemma right back in their face in this opening sequence.

And after this happens between Anakin and Dooku, we once again see that Anakin is a murderer. While an argument can possibly be made that we should have some sympathy for Anakin after the killings in *Clones*, because he was distraught over the death of his mother and so wasn't thinking clearly, in *Sith* the killing is in cold blood—Anakin slays Dooku simply because Palpatine tells him to. So while this film is supposed to be about the descent of Anakin Skywalker into Darth Vader, as far as we're concerned, that descent has already occurred. However, once again the script doesn't see it that way. Moments after he has killed Dooku, Anakin goes right back to being a hero—fighting off the droid army, trading quips with Obi-Wan, smart-mouthing Grievous, commandeering the general's ship, crash-landing it back on Coruscant, and returning the Chancellor to safety. The movie cheers Anakin, but *we* can't. Not after the evil we've seen him do. And this makes it hard for us to experience the joy the film clearly wants us to feel in the next sequence: upon returning to Coruscant, Anakin reunites with Padmé, who tells him she is pregnant. He is thrilled and the movie expects us to be thrilled for him, but we aren't because it's hard to feel happy for a guy we just watched murder someone in cold blood at the behest of the worst person in the galaxy.

A short time later, Yoda travels to the Wookiee homeworld of Kashyyyk to help the Wookiees repel an invasion by Separatist forces. Not long after that, Obi-Wan is sent on a mission to find General Grievous on the planet Utapau, where, accompanied by a group of clone troopers, he will eventually track down the droid general and, after a vicious fight, destroy him and finally bring an end to the war.

JONATHAN RINZLER
(author, *The Making of Revenge of the Sith*)

Episode III had more miniature shots than all the original trilogy put together. That might've been true for *Episode I,* but I know it was true for *Episode III.* And I saw it firsthand. It was incredible—they were building the sinkhole planet (Utapau), and I saw from day one to the end, the whole volcano miniature going up right next to where the dailies theater was. And there was Lorne Peterson working on it, and a bunch of other guys. It was fantastic. It wasn't like, "We're going to do all CG, screw models."

One unaccredited position on Revenge of the Sith *went to Steven Spielberg, who wanted some firsthand experience working with the new digital technology and motion animatics his friend, George Lucas, had developed. The preliminary form of directing for CGI sequences, animatics, are motion storyboards that have since become industry standards for big-budget movies, and was first developed for* Attack of the Clones. *Directors Guild of America rules—which Lucas had left in 1977 along with Hollywood—prohibited Spielberg from actively working on the project, so his work went uncredited. Though rumors persist as to which section of the film Spielberg worked on, the one confirmed section was the Obi-Wan Kenobi / General Grievous chase sequence through the tunnels of Utapau.*

JONATHAN RINZLER

One thing is that Spielberg was involved with some of the animatics for *Episode III*. He had planned quite a bit of stuff. Not much made it into the final version of the film.

George liked to play around with ideas. Originally when Obi-Wan falls off the creature [in the Grievous fight on Utapau] and into a sinkhole into the water, there was going to be this whole thing where he comes out into a cave, and there's this creature in the cave, and he makes friends with the creature—and then there were these troopers following Obi-Wan and the creature eats them. So, there was all kind of stuff.

Lucas created the two Obi-Wan and Yoda subplots to separate Anakin from Yoda and Obi-Wan, so that there would be no one to stop Anakin from going over to the dark side. As Obi-Wan is about to depart on his mission, he and Anakin bid each other a warm goodbye, which is the last time they will be together as friends. With Obi-Wan and Yoda out of the way, the narrative now focuses on Anakin's final descent.

RAY MORTON

Still wanting to present Anakin as a tragic hero, Lucas sought to give him a sympathetic reason for his transformation—some motivation that would allow us to retain enough compassion for Anakin to see his fall as an epic tragedy rather than just as a guy going bad. Lucas was able to come up with a motive that had the potential to generate this compassion: soon after learning Padmé is pregnant, Anakin begins having nightmares in which he sees her die in childbirth. Already haunted by his failure to save his mother, Anakin becomes determined to keep Padmé safe. Palpatine—seeking to convert Anakin so he can utilize his powers for his own nefarious ends—uses the boy's fear to his advantage. Revealing that he is a Sith, Palpatine suggests to Anakin that the Sith possess the ability to keep loved ones from dying and hints that he can teach Anakin how to save Padmé. Anakin is initially horrified to learn the Chancellor is actually a Sith, but when Mace Windu attempts to kill Palpatine, Anakin, fearful of losing the knowledge that will help him save Padmé, foils Windu, saves the Chancellor, and finally embraces the dark side. Had Anakin still been a sympathetic hero—if we hadn't seen him commit mass killings and cold-blooded murder—this motivation would have worked perfectly to frame his turn as a tragic fall. However, because we have already seen Anakin access the dark side, it is not as effective as it could have been.

For Ian McDiarmid, one of his favorite scenes in the making of Revenge of the Sith *(and ours) was the one taking place at the Galaxies Opera House between himself and Christensen, which is more or less the seduction of Anakin Skywalker in which Lucas received an uncredited assist from playwright Tom Stoppard.*

HAYDEN CHRISTENSEN

The toughest part was making the poignant transition scene believable, where Anakin and Palpatine make their pact to be allies—in a sense. That was the difficult one. For the most part, though, all the other evil doings that Anakin is involved in were more enjoyable than arduous. It was where I was looking to go in *Episode II*. Finally, George said, "All right, you've got free rein. Let it loose." So it was not that challenging.

IAN MCDIARMID
(actor, "Emperor Sheev Palpatine")

Of all of my deliciously evil scenes, and there are many—I can't think of one scene that *isn't* deliciously evil—was when we go to the opera. The reason I liked doing that so much is that I'm a theater actor, too, but more than that, Hayden and I could really sit down and, from my point of view anyway, have an evil chat. And I think it's one of the longest dialogue scenes in the whole saga. I was allowed to tell a story, so that was really exciting.

KYLE NEWMAN
(director, *Fanboys*)

What's interesting about the politics of *Star Wars* is the Emperor is fascinating as a character because he's so patient—that's how he rose to power. It just wasn't pure, sinister, murdering people. He almost never uses the Force in the prequels. And the interesting thing about the Sith in the prequels—they always tell the truth when they're in key positions, where the Jedi in the original trilogy are always lying. There are a lot of these really cool parallels. The scenes are almost hitting emotionally at the exact same timing as in their movie and the character's mood, Anakin going through these parallels. So, there are these fascinating things the way Lucas applied it.

GEORGE LUCAS

Ian is the nicest, kindest, sweetest guy in the world. *Nothing* like the Emperor.

HAYDEN CHRISTENSEN

I think Ian McDiarmid is one of the greats. He does such a fantastic job of playing the puppeteer. Palpatine is very charmingly, but still very evilly pulling at all of Anakin's strings, so to act opposite him was sometimes distracting. He would do a speech and suddenly I would break character, because I was in awe of him.

IAN MCDIARMID

Anakin has an appetite for power which he feels is being denied him as a Jedi. He believes his skills aren't appreciated and that his talents aren't being fostered in the way that, say, in earlier days his mentor Obi-Wan's were fostered. And so he's full of resentment and impatience, and these are qualities that Palpatine seizes on. He also detects in Anakin an appetite for power quite apart from his psychological flaws, and he feeds that. Palpatine completely *exploits* this young man. He's always looking for a new apprentice and in this young man he finds the ideal. And then this thing happens—Anakin is badly wounded and scarred, and as a result of that, he becomes half-man and half-machine. That wasn't, I don't think, part of Palpatine's plan. But as a great pragmatist, he's able to take advantage of that and he gets something that's even better than he hoped. Palpatine gets someone who's half-human, but who's now the perfect instrument of his will.

HAYDEN CHRISTENSEN

Anakin is much more battle-worn when we meet him in *Episode III*. He has really come into his own as well. Anakin has always been a conflicted character, but now even more so, as the stresses and anxieties of his life are really weighing on him. And he's looking at his options. Hence the seduction to the dark side.

IAN MCDIARMID

The dark side is a big, potent power and it's as strong as the power of light. The question is, Can it be resisted? And the conclusion at the end of the *Star Wars* films is, Yes, it can, but it isn't easy. Resistance doesn't happen without a great deal of pain, suffering, and soul-searching on all sides, and I think that's fundamentally what George is saying in these movies. He's saying it lies in wait for all of us. It's so easy for people to persuade us—and it seems increasingly so these days—to surrender our freedom, our natural rights, our sense of morality and so on, and we need to be on our absolute guard to make sure we *don't* capitulate.

Palpatine rechristens Anakin as Darth Vader. Once he does, the events the audience have been waiting for over the course of three movies begin to unfold. Now in full Darth Sidious mode, he contacts the clone troopers and instructs them to carry out Order 66, the trigger for the clones to assassinate the Jedi Knights. Palpatine then orders Darth Vader to go to the Jedi Temple and eliminate any knights remaining within. Vader complies and kills everyone—even the younglings.

RAY MORTON

Lucas crosses an unforgivable line when he shows Anakin murder a group of children. Yes, the action makes it clear that Anakin has truly become evil, but it is such a heinous act that it wipes away all vestiges of tragedy—Anakin is now just a monster and we hate him for it. Plus, it's just a repellent thing to present to viewers in what is supposed to be a mainstream entertainment, as well as a horrible traumatic sequence to include in a movie series that Lucas frequently claims is made for little kids. Disney this sure ain't. Finally, it makes it much more difficult for us to celebrate Anakin's redemption at the end of *Return of the Jedi*, because it's hard to feel happy that a guy has regained his soul after we've watched him commit poli-infanticide.

PETER HOLMSTROM
(cohost, *The Rebel & the Rogue* podcast)

You have to remember, *Star Wars* was Vietnam in space. The heroes become the villains, the villains become the heroes—and Lucas is trying to say there's a path down the middle which is the key to enlightenment. Balance. But this isn't the film that shows you that—this is the film that shows you the opposite of that. The midpoint in the six-part film.

So, Anakin kills children. Yeah. American soldiers killed children during the Vietnam War. Were they heroes or villains? Soldiers throughout history have done terrible things in every conflict. Do you think those people were monsters from birth? Killing puppies with barb wire and [censored] into their mother's skull? Sorry, it's not that simple. They loved and were loved, they laughed, they cried, they felt the spectrum of human emotions, and they were coerced to believing that killing children and doing terrible things was the right thing to do.

In the beginning of the film, Anakin's hero persona is hit when his mentor, Palpatine, tells him to kill Dooku in cold blood. "He's too dangerous to be kept alive." He knows it's wrong, but he does it. (Unlike Luke.) Then, at the end of act 2, that line is mirrored by Mace Windu. Palpatine is now too dangerous to be left alive. The keepers of peace, who only use the Force for defense, never for attack, are about to murder. Lucas's thesis was always that if you only ever strive to do good, you end up becoming an agent of evil. The Jedi had become agents of war, not keepers of the peace. They attacked, they didn't defend. Luke is presented with the same conundrum in *Return of the Jedi*, where his mentors tell him the ends justify the means, and he must murder his father. He denies this, and embraces compassion and love over hate. Anakin doesn't—and in the moment of attacking the Jedi Temple, he becomes like the soldiers in war, doing "what needs to be done" to establish peace. He sees the Jedi as murderers and traitors, and he does what he must to establish peace. It's Hobbes-ian philosophy fulfilled, which is exactly what Vader always was.

That's not to say Lucas was saying Anakin was right to kill children. It's unpleasant to watch—it should be. Vader is a monster and you see him, both physically and metaphorically, become a monster. But he's also reflecting the world around him. Mace Windu was a murderer, the Jedi had abandoned their ways, and Anakin was lost. But like a symphony, this moment is meant to be reminiscent of the moment in *Return of the Jedi*: Luke, too, had to choose between mentors—to kill or to let his friends die. Luke finds a third option, which is why he is the first to live within Lucas's main theme of the films, which is like the Buddhist form of Nirvana: "There is no pure right, there is no pure wrong, there is a middle, gray path that must be walked."

After the Jedi have been eliminated, Palpatine sends Vader to the volcanic planet of Mustafar to kill the leaders of the Separatist movement, who are no longer of use to Palpatine. In the meantime, Palpatine appears before the Senate and declares himself galactic emperor. His declaration is greeted by cheers and clapping from the senators, half of whom are corrupt and half of whom have been easily duped. This leads Padmé to utter one of the best lines in the series: "So this is how liberty dies—with thunderous applause." Given the current state of our world in 2020 under Donald Trump and a corrupt and clueless Republican Senate, this line has even more resonance now than it did in 2005.

Yoda and Obi-Wan are the only two Jedi who survive the massacre. Quickly realizing that Anakin has turned to evil, Yoda orders a reluctant Obi-Wan to confront and destroy Vader. The thought of this devastates Obi-Wan, but he knows it must be done. He goes to Padmé and tells her the news. She can't believe it and denies knowing where Anakin is. Soon after, Padmé travels to Mustafar to find her husband. Unbeknownst to her, Obi-Wan has stowed away on her ship. Arriving on Mustafar, Padmé reunites with a power-mad Anakin/Vader, now fully consumed by the dark side and already plotting to overthrow the Emperor so he can rule the galaxy himself. Padmé realizes that Obi-Wan was right and that Anakin has turned into someone she no longer knows and can no longer be with. At this point, Obi-Wan reveals himself. Convinced

Padmé has betrayed him by bringing Obi-Wan to Mustafar, an enraged Vader uses the Force to choke his wife into unconsciousness. Obi-Wan then confronts Vader and the two begin an epic lightsaber duel. Each combatant brings their best to the duel, but Obi-Wan ultimately gains the advantage (he has the high ground) and severs Anakin's legs. This leaves the nascent Sith helpless on the bank of the lava flow as the molten liquid gradually engulfs him. Anakin's body catches fire as Obi-Wan sadly walks away.

ROB COLMAN

The volcano world where their battle takes place is amazing. That was mostly about combining the environment and the actors, Hayden Christensen and Ewan McGregor. There was some animation, some effects shots where we animated stunt doubles, but that was it. To sit there in the theater and watch those beautiful shots was fantastic.

JONATHAN RINZLER

There were sets, and there were tons of models on *Revenge of the Sith*. ILM was functioning full-throttle for that film—not just for the digital side, but for the model side. Then they had the whole lava planet, which was created using mostly a huge miniature, which took up the whole ILM soundstage, and that was something to behold. We would all meet outside two times a week to go in for dailies, and sometimes the door would open and we'd see them working. It started as just this huge blob of material, and every couple of days it would look more and more like a lava planet. And then it was actual flowing lava—it wasn't real lava, it was some red milkshake substance—but still, it was incredible. Lorne Peterson was part of the team, hacking away at Styrofoam—the same guy who was doing it in 1975. All the stops were pulled out for that film.

STEPHEN SCARLATA
(cohost, *Best Movies Never Made* podcast)

I think that's why the effects largely hold up for those films. He was using miniatures and effects together.

JONATHAN RINZLER

John Knoll, who was the visual effects supervisor for those films, said many times, "When you're doing visual effects, you have to use every trick in the book." If it makes sense to build a set, you build a set. If it makes sense to build a miniature, you build a miniature. You don't throw away all these tools people spent decades perfecting, just because you could do it digitally. Because often, it won't look that good digitally. And if it doesn't look that good, the audience subconsciously detaches from the movie, because they're just watching an animated movie.

KYLE ROWLING
(fight director, *Revenge of the Sith*)

In all honesty, it was one of the greatest experiences of my life. Choreography and rehearsal for *Episode III* was three months in total. Ten-hour days, six days a week, and Hayden and Ewan were both there from almost the very beginning. Both of them wanted to work on the fights as much as possible. The most important thing for everyone involved—[stunt coordinator] Nick Gillard, Hayden, Ewan, and myself included—was that this fight really told the story of what was going on inside their characters' hearts and minds.

Both of the guys are incredibly talented, not just as actors, but their sword skills are amazing. That made them really easy to work with. They both learn choreography really quickly, and quite huge chunks of it, too, not just a few moves and cuts.

HAYDEN CHRISTENSEN

The lightsaber battle was only different from the one with Count Dooku in *Attack of the Clones* in the respect that Ewan and I were fighting each other, which was just too much fun for us. The battle itself was much more involved, because of the duration. It's a very long duel that covers diverse geography. Not that we actually got to witness it because it was shot against a green screen. It's every kid's dream to fight with a lightsaber, and I don't want to say Ewan and I got giddy, but we suddenly became six-year-olds as soon as we took up our lightsabers. We would make the sound effects and had a good time with it. So it was incredibly fun to fight against each other.

NICK GILLARD
(stunt coordinator, *Revenge of the Sith*)

When I started out their final battle, I didn't want there to actually be any hits at all. I wanted it to glide the whole time, where there wasn't any time for them to move their sabers away from each other because they each knew what was coming next. You know, they're reading these hits like in a chess match, three or four moves ahead. That's how I saw it: someone fighting themself. Not only that, but you're talking about the light and the dark here. This is Anakin; this is where he is going to go. So he's technically fighting his own personality. His bad side is about to kill his good side through this fight, which is represented by Obi. And for Obi, even though he's been sent there to kill him, he doesn't want to do that. This is his boy; he loves him. I saw Obi just trying to absorb it long enough for Anakin to calm down.

HAYDEN CHRISTENSEN

The burn makeup was probably the toughest part, because it was a long process, in which they used a latex-like material. First they had to cast my body and then it was a big ordeal to get the burn suit right. Getting into it took a couple of hours, and getting out was a couple of hours as well. So it was time-consuming.

RAY MORTON

Because of the change in backstories from *Star Wars* to *Jedi*, the addition of Qui-Gon in *Menace*, and the often prickly nature of the relationship between Obi-Wan and Anakin in *Clones*, the exact nature of the personal conflict between Obi-Wan and Vader here is a bit fuzzy. Is this a fight between once good friends who have taken different paths? Between principled teacher and wayward pupil? A grudge match between an angry younger man and a mentor he has grown to resent? There's a bit of all of it in the mix and so it's never quite clear.

What *is* clear is the emotional and physical nature of the duel—this is a titanic battle between light and dark, good and evil, Jedi and Sith—a fight across a river of lava upon which the fate of the galaxy depends. Wonderfully visualized and choreographed (allegedly with help from Steven Spielberg), this duel is the action highlight of the prequel trilogy.

After the fight, Obi-Wan takes Padmé to a hospital, where she gives birth to twins, a boy and a girl she names Luke and Leia, before—having "lost the will to live"—she dies. As Luke and Leia are being born, Vader is being reborn. Having somehow survived his dismemberment and immolation, Vader is rescued by the Emperor and permanently encased in a cybernetic body that also functions as a walking life-support system—a system he can never remove, lest he die.

RAY MORTON

This is the film's most horrifying moment, as well as the dark heart of the prequel trilogy. No matter how much sympathy one does or does not feel for Anakin at this point, the terrified look in his eyes as the iconic mask is lowered down over his face is heart-breaking. He seems to have finally realized what a dreadful mistake he has made as the helmet clicks into place with a sound reminiscent of the sealing of a tomb. The sight of the atmospheric smoke being displaced as the ventilator first exhales chills us to the bone—this truly is the sound of doom. Lucas then seals the moment by raising Vader up into a room that looks like Dr. Frankenstein's lab from a 1930s Universal horror movie, which is most apt, since we have just witnessed the birth of a monster.

HAYDEN CHRISTENSEN

Wearing the Darth Vader mask and costume was orgasmic. It was everything you could ever imagine. It was a little boy's dream come true. It was overwhelming. It's hard to put into words, because it was a new sensation for me: a mixture of elation with this amazing sense of empowerment. To get to act behind a mask is a great freedom, but to act behind an entirely enclosed character like Darth Vader is *really* neat.

RAY MORTON

Speaking once again in the voice of James Earl Jones, Vader asks about Padmé. With a hint of mischievous delight, the Emperor informs Vader that Padmé is dead and that he—Vader—killed her. Since the Emperor has already informed Vader (after he turned to the dark side) that he does not actually possess the power to save people from death after all, Vader realizes there is no hope. He has lost Padmé forever. The telepathic blast of pain and fury Vader unleashes as he tears through his restraints and takes his first halting steps in his new body finally generates the tragedy Lucas has been after from the beginning. Although the drama wasn't quite able to deliver it, this frightening and poignant moment certainly does. Even Vader's ill-advised "Nooooo . . ." can't detract from the horror and the sadness of what has become of Anakin Skywalker.

As the film and the trilogy come to a close, Padmé is buried; Yoda goes into exile; Vader and the Emperor begin supervising the construction of the Death Star; Leia is adopted by Bail Organa and his wife; and Obi-Wan brings Luke to Tatooine and gives him to Anakin's stepbrother Owen and his wife Beru to raise.

RAY MORTON

This last bit is a rather odd choice, considering that Obi-Wan is trying to hide Luke from Vader. Not that we expect Darth to visit for the holidays or anything, but leaving Luke in the custody of Anakin's closest relative does seem to be tempting fate a bit (in *Star Wars*, Owen was the brother of the non-Vader Anakin—who, of course, had no connection to Vader—and in early drafts of *Jedi*, Owen was identified as being Obi-Wan's brother—not exactly no connection to Vader, but at least a remote and unlikely one).

HAYDEN CHRISTENSEN

There *are* a few odd things in the films, like the Skywalker name or the idea of leaving baby Luke with the Lars family on Tatooine, since it's a place Anakin is already familiar with. Why don't Aunt Beru and Uncle Owen recognize C-3PO when they first see him in *A New Hope,* considering they met C-3PO and Anakin in *Episode II*? So there are a couple of fun loopholes for the die-hard fans to pick up on. George is human and we all make mistakes.

GEORGE LUCAS

There was a whole sequence in *Revenge of the Sith* that I cut out. The scene with Obi-Wan, Bail, and Yoda went on for quite a while and there was this whole discussion. Obi-Wan says, "I'll take Luke to Tatooine," and Yoda replies, "Well, yeah, you take him to his family, to Tatooine. That is such a painful place for the Sith that they will never go back there, and they'll never think about it again." So we had details like that, but in the end, you don't need that stuff. It's a *big* universe. There are billions and billions of stars, and millions of millions of them are inhabited. Why would anybody have any knowledge that anyone would be in any one place? Hell, there's another George Lucas right here in San Francisco. What makes you think he and I have any connection with each other? And I live on Lucas Valley Road, which has no connection with me at all. So you can't go around the universe looking for Skywalkers.

As originally shot and edited together, there was definitely something missing in Anakin's narrative, which resulted in Lucas having to do some additional shooting for better clarification.

RAY MORTON

Lucas's showcasing Anakin's descent probably could have worked reasonably well despite the earlier issues pointed out, except that the screenplay then gave Anakin more motivations for his turn: he is angry at the Jedi Council for refusing to make him a Jedi master; he is arrogant and greedy—Anakin sees himself as a great Jedi who feels he deserves more acclaim and power than he has yet been given; he is loyal to Palpatine, who has been mentoring him since childhood, and he supports the Chancellor's authoritarian ideas. When the Jedi threaten Palpatine's rule, Anakin sides with his mentor. He is angry at Obi-Wan, whom he suspects of undermining him and of having romantic designs on Padmé. Unlike the unselfish desire to save Padmé, these additional motivations are self-centered and driven by arrogance, ego, and a desire for power. These are not sympathetic or tragic motives, just the usual despicable ones that drive most run-of-the-mill bad guys. They only confirm the negative aspects of Anakin's character that we have already seen and frame his fall not as a tragedy, but as an inevitable outcome of bad character.

These multiple motives generate confusion. In a properly constructed dramatic narrative, a character should have a single, clear motivation for doing what he does. In the script for *Sith*, Anakin has so many reasons for his turn that his ultimate motivation for turning to the dark side just isn't clear. Lucas recognized this when he was editing the picture, so he enlisted the acclaimed playwright and screenwriter Tom Stoppard (who had previously done an uncredited rewrite of the script for *Indiana Jones and the Last Crusade*) to write several new scenes that emphasized that Anakin's main reason for turning to the dark side was to save Padmé. Lucas then recut several sections of the film to stress the point even further. Unfortunately, the changes weren't sufficient. While they do make Anakin's determination to save Padmé more pronounced, the other motivations are still prominent enough that his true incentive remains unclear.

DAN VEBBER
(producer, *The Simpsons*)

I think it would have been more interesting had Anakin found out that Obi-Wan was having an affair with Padmé. His jealousy and sense of betrayal would lead to the dark side and also justify Obi-Wan's self-imposed exile for the next few decades, blaming himself for the death of Anakin and rise of Darth Vader.

PETER HOLMSTROM

Every screenplay, the hero has more than one motivation for doing what they're doing. The macro and the micro. Look at *Lawrence of Arabia*, how many motives does that guy have? (Hint: it's more than four.)

JONATHAN RINZLER

They had filmed this whole subplot of Padmé forming up what becomes the Rebel Alliance. But then they cut those things out because Francis Ford Coppola said, "You got to just have Anakin. Anakin is your throughline, you don't need all this other stuff. It can't be three hours long." So . . .

EWAN MCGREGOR

The third one was the best. There's no question. I was really happy with this last movie. It satisfactorily ties up all the plot points leading into *Episode IV*. I was very pleased with *Revenge of the Sith*, and I thought it was the most competent as a film.

HAYDEN CHRISTENSEN

George was very excited by the story he was telling, and you could see that in his eyes. He was extremely involved, more so than the last one. He was up from behind the monitors after every take and he had a bounce in his step.

RAY MORTON

Some of *Sith*'s problems are similar to those in the other two prequels: Hayden Christensen is simply not good in the role of Anakin Skywalker / Darth Vader—he looks far too young for the part (there is no way the fellow we see here could possibly have aged into the elderly man revealed when the mask is removed at the end of *Jedi*) and his callow performance fails to convey the depth and complexity the character demands. Natalie Portman's performance is also weak—as Padmé, she is stiff and shallow and is never able to reconcile the character's many contradictory traits (although, to be fair, the writing works against Portman at just about every turn in this regard). The dialogue, while not as risible as that in *Clones,* is still pretty awkward. And—while technically impressive and often quite stunning—there's just too much CGI in the movie. Too many of the shots are overly busy to the point of being frantic and the result is often quite distracting.

However, the narrative—even with the problems outlined above—is much stronger than those in the other two films. The movie contains a single plot rather than a collection of subplots; it's tighter; has less filler; is more focused; and has much more dramatic drive, momentum, and build. Ewan McGregor continues to shine as Obi-Wan and Ian McDiarmid delivers his most effective performance as Palpatine—his treachery in this movie is truly hissable and the venom he furiously spits as the Emperor reveals more and more of his true evil nature and is pretty terrifying. Lucas's imagination is as fertile as ever, the production and costume design continues to impress, and the major action sequences—especially the opening rescue and Obi-Wan's pursuit of Grievous—are quite thrilling. Also, Jar Jar only appears in one shot—and is silent.

BRIAN JAY JONES

At the end of *Revenge of the Sith,* when Vader breaks free of his shackles and screams, "Nooooooo!"—people laughed. Exactly the opposite of what Lucas intended. And it *is* a terrible decision from a storytelling standpoint and from a character standpoint. But what I love about Lucas—and this is where you've got to admire him—is that when people say a moment like that is inconsistent or bad storytelling or they say Vader wouldn't do that, he's like, "Fuck you.

What do you know about Vader? *I* created him. It doesn't exist until *I* say it does. And *that's* the way Vader behaved." What a great place to be.

RAY MORTON

It is in its final act that *Sith* impresses most. Epic, riveting, terrible, and poignant, it is here that the prequel trilogy finally recaptures the dark, mythic, playing-for-keeps fantasy of *The Empire Strikes Back* and in doing so connects itself stylistically, thematically, and narratively with the original trilogy.

In the final days of production on Revenge of the Sith, *John Williams returned for what was presumably the final time (not realizing there were still the sequels in his future) to compose the score for the final installment in the story of Anakin Skywalker.*

JOE KRAEMER

(composer, *Mission Impossible: Rogue Nation* and *Jack Reacher*)

Six movies in and John Williams is still taking risks: for this film, his original idea was to interrupt the Main Title with battle music as Anakin and Obi-Wan fly to the rescue of the kidnapped Chancellor Palpatine. The soundtrack CD has this music the way he meant it to go. In the end, the final movie plays things more traditionally, allowing the Main Title to play to its natural conclusion, then segueing to the battle music through editorial convolutions. To be honest, I prefer the film version, but it's so fascinating to see Williams still trying new things.

This film's major new theme is the "Battle of the Heroes," written to underscore the climactic lightsaber duel between Obi-Wan Kenobi and Darth Vader. Apparently, Lucas was surprised not to hear "Duel of the Fates" scoring the entire sequence, but Williams saved that theme's return for the fight in the Senate between Yoda and the Emperor. There is also a new theme for General Grievous, scored for orchestra and choir, which some likened to the Harry Potter theme. It appears a handful of times in the film, but the structure of the movie doesn't really lend itself to allowing Williams to develop it significantly.

Of course, the "Main Title" and the Force Theme make appearances in the score, as well as Yoda's Theme in its most original-trilogy-like usage yet, and at the end of the film, Princess Leia's Theme. A particularly nice use of the Main Theme can be heard in the final scene on Tatooine, as Obi-Wan delivers the infant Luke Skywalker to Owen and Beru at their homestead. The Emperor's Theme can be heard strongly in the final reels of the movie, and some nice quotes from the score to *The Empire Strikes Back* underscore his fight with

Yoda in his office under the Galactic Senate. "The Rebel Fanfare" even makes a surprise appearance when R2-D2 pulls off a heroic deed. The previously mentioned "Duel of the Fates" and "Funeral Music" from *The Phantom Menace* also return, as does the love theme for Anakin and Padmé from *Attack of the Clones,* though never in its full romantic glory—their relationship is long past that now. Anakin's first assignment as the newly christened Darth Vader is an attack on the Jedi Temple, which is underscored by the unused music from *Attack of the Clones* for the battle with the monsters in the Geonosis Arena. Anakin's Theme from *The Phantom Menace* is heard once in this film, during a moment where Anakin confides to Padmé that he's been having nightmares of her death during childbirth.

Perhaps the most satisfying theme to return was the funeral music for Qui-Gon Jinn, now underscoring the death of Padmé and the rebirth of Darth Vader in his iconic black suit. Williams cleverly interpolates "The Imperial March" into the sequence as counterpoint, and reprises the approach for the final moments of the film when Padmé's funeral is juxtaposed against the construction of the Death Star.

There is a fascinating dive into Sith history between Palpatine and Anakin during a live performance of a water ballet, and the music for this sequence is a spooky atmosphere of bass choir and synthesizer eventually joined by orchestra and a subtle Sith melodic motif that returns when Sidious anoints Anakin with his new name of Darth Vader. This choral texture will be revisited in the Disney-era *Star Wars* movies for Supreme Leader Snoke.

There are a few sequences in the film that, similar to what was done on *Attack of the Clones,* utilize tracked music from previous scores on purpose, with no intention to replace that music with new cues. The crash landing of Grievous's ship on Coruscant is one such sequence, as are the fight scenes between the Wookiees and the battle droids (and also, the aforementioned march on the Jedi Temple by Vader and his troops).

This score is probably the darkest score of the entire saga, in keeping with the tone of the film, which is an unrelenting tragedy in its second half. It's remarkable that the film's ending is in any way satisfying given the oppressive gloom that precedes it, but the score does a good deal of the heavy lifting there, with its placement of iconic themes from the original film to bring the audience to some feeling of homecoming and resolution.

Revenge of the Sith, *which was released on May 19, 2005, was produced at a budget of $113 million and enjoyed a worldwide gross of $868 million. The best-reviewed entry in the trilogy, it nonetheless had its detractors. In the end,* *though, Lucas had told the story* he *wanted to in the way he decided, and ulti-mately* many *people paid money—repeatedly—to see it unfold.*

GEORGE LUCAS

If anyone else had done *Sith,* it would have been a $250 million movie. The interesting thing is that we did an inflated/adjusted estimate of all the films. *Return of the Jedi* came in at $100 million, and I think the first *Star Wars* was $44 million. *Empire* fell somewhere in between at $70 or $80 million. But on these prequels, we've managed to make three of them at relatively the same cost. That's quite an accomplishment when you're talking about sequels, because they have a tendency to grow. I used my TV crew, whom I've worked with for a long time. We also used much of the technology that we've developed over the years. And Rick McCallum is an amazing producer. He really keeps a lid on things. Plus, we relied on digital technology, which probably saved us $20 to $30 million.

EWAN MCGREGOR

I don't think of the *Star Wars* trilogy as being "event movies." The *Star Wars* pictures are way beyond studio pictures. They're enormous. Whatever issues I had with them, I couldn't say no when George Lucas called . . . There's nothing cooler than being a Jedi Knight.

DON BIES
(model builder: droid unit supervisor, *Revenge of the Sith*)

It has been an amazing opportunity, and not something I ever dreamed would happen to a little kid from Chicago like me. I look back on my time with those projects fondly and proudly, and will probably continue to bore my children (and eventually grandchildren) with all my stories repeated over and over.

NALINI KRISHAN
(actress, "Bariss Offee")

I think you have to understand that these movies were made in a different era in the eighties, the target audience for the trilogy had grown up and weren't maybe into the next three as were the teens of today's society. Different people reacted differently. I think everyone watched it because it was *Star Wars* and it had played a part in so many people's childhoods and it was one of those movies that would be remembered forever! The first three were far more superior, but, having said that, I have spoken to the younger generation and they are saying that the last three are better. I think it depends who identifies with the movies and everyone has had a different experience, there is no such thing as one was better than the other, it was *Star Wars*!

HAYDEN CHRISTENSEN

It's strange to be a part of the *Star Wars* phenomenon. My whole relationship to these films is very surreal. My knowledge and involvement in the science fiction world prior to this was minimal. I wouldn't necessarily call myself a huge fan of the genre. I wasn't the first person in line to see *Episode I*, but I've definitely become a fan since becoming a part of it. You have to find a way to enjoy it. In anticipation of shooting the film, I spent a lot of time on the internet immersing myself in the culture of *Star Wars*, because it has such a huge following. Some people have put the belief system associated with *Star Wars* into their lives. It's pretty amazing.

KENJI OATES

(actor, "Saessee Tiin," *Revenge of the Sith*)

I think the prequels were really a new style of movie, and maybe those people weren't ready for it. If you think about what made the original *Star Wars* movies so popular, the gritty, Wild West reality of it, with busted-up, broken spaceships, etc., you can see how the completely unreal, shiny, almost cartoony quality of the prequels could rub old fans the wrong way. I actually quite like the cartoony look, and the absolute freedom it gives the director to make the world look exactly as they like. The story that was being told would not be possible using any other method, so I think perhaps people's real argument is that they didn't like the style of the CGI, not that it was used.

BRIAN JAY JONES

When I go out and talk about Lucas and *Star Wars*, I always get asked about the prequels. I think people desperately want me to shit on them and there are times when I want to, but my response is usually that they're not made for me. I *have* my *Star Wars*. I'm an original trilogy guy and the prequels are not made for me. I'm not going to tell some seven-year-old something different. Stephen Colbert or Jon Stewart said, "My son told me *The Phantom Menace* is his favorite *Star Wars* movie. I had to explain to him he was wrong." You really try *not* to do that. Let them have their *Star Wars*. At the same time, I'm trying to figure out if Lucas deserves credit for not providing fan service, though he may be—for instance, for the most part, a lack of Jar Jar Binks—in *Attack of the Clones*. I feel like he sort of rights the ship by the time he gets to *Revenge of the Sith* . . . but I find that film unwatchable.

JOHN KENNETH MUIR

Anakin's story adds to the saga significantly. It adds weight and tragedy to the saga in a more explicit way. For instance, the betrayal and execution of the Jedi makes palpable the Emperor's evil in a way that is less cartoon-like than the "evil" we see in the original trilogy. The prequel, for all the fan gibes about trade routes and blockades, is a political story about a ruthless dictator's rise to power, and the good man at his side who, basically, loses his soul to serve him. The prequel trilogy "rhymes" with the original trilogy, but also deepens it in many ways.

GEORGE LUCAS

Science fiction is a literary medium. It's a medium that depends on creating worlds in your imagination. The audience is half the process. In film, it doesn't work like that. You have to create the impression or illusion that it's the real deal. Otherwise, it won't work and people are more sophisticated, so you really have to be pretty good at it. It used to be *King Kong* where he moved and everyone said, "Wow, that's great." Unfortunately, we live in a very different world now and the art form has become very sophisticated. The demands of what is credible and what is not credible are much more difficult.

BRIAN JAY JONES

The trilogy is Lucas putting everything up on-screen and those are the moments where you're like, "Oh, *this* is Lucas's weakness as a writer." If you go back and read those early first drafts of *Star Wars*—it's the prequels. Lucas spent all his time world-building. He's giving us every backstory, every motivation. You read those first drafts of what becomes *Star Wars* and, my God, every character has to have their entire backstory told. You've got to know *everybody*. It's what he loves to do and, again, that's when you need somebody like Gary Kurtz or Willard Huyck and Gloria Katz. People who can say, "This is boring. You need something funny here." He needed an angel on his shoulder.

GEORGE LUCAS

I made these films, because I like to make movies. I wanted to finish this. I had been very frustrated before when I made the first series, because I had an imagination that created a kind of world that I could never get on film; it was just technically impossible. I was stuck with creatures in rubber masks that couldn't move very fast, and it was very hard to direct a movie and tell the story that I wanted to tell. I was stuck with environments that were extremely limited in what I could do. Part of coming back, one was to finish the story.

I kind of like working in the *Star Wars* world, because I put in so much time and energy to create it. But part of it was that it was a chance to make it more the way it was in my mind when I created it.

When I finished *Star Wars,* I figured that was it. And once I finished *Return of the Jedi,* I never really expected to go back and turn the backstory into a movie. But as time went on, I realized that being an icon of evil so overwhelmed the Darth Vader character that the idea he is actually a tragic character kind of got overwhelmed. So by going back and telling Darth Vader's story, telling the whole story right from the beginning, I was able to get the full range of all the things that were going on and how everything fit together.

JOHN KENNETH MUIR

I believe, in light of the lackluster Disney trilogy, the prequels are being re-assessed by all generations. Although the prequels are uneven, they do feel original and as if there is a direction or plan behind them, which is something many fans do appreciate. The sequel trilogy, by comparison, is scattershot, lacking direction and inspiration, despite the presence of some great characters and performers. So in that sense, I think the prequels are finally being assessed for what they are (flawed but intriguing movies from the mind of *Star Wars'* creator) rather than what they are not (adventures that continue in the exact same spirit as the original trilogy). Also, my son grew up with the prequels, and like many of his generation, they are his favorite of the *Star Wars* films—although he is thirteen, he dislikes the Disney trilogy vehemently. This is very much a generational thing. Those who grew up with *Star Wars* seem to have rejected the prequels for being different and for being aimed at younger audiences. But those fans should be asked a question now: Would they rather have the prequels, with their creator's integrity and vision behind everything, or would they rather continue to see the wholesale strip-mining of the saga at the hands of a big corporation that doesn't really understand the magic of these films?

JONATHAN RINZLER

I think all the prequels will have their day. They all have flaws—people have examined those flaws ad-nauseam—but I don't think as many people have gone and looked for positives. I've never understood why the things with the Senate bothered people. I've just never understood that at all. What's wrong with having a scene in the Senate? I don't get why that's a bad thing. Even in *Episode IV,* they talk about how is the Emperor going to rule. There were politics. Even in the very first one.

RAY MORTON

The prequels are ultimately a very mixed bag. They told a story that perhaps didn't need to be told. Maybe we really *didn't* need to know where Darth Vader came from—maybe it would have been better to have just let him be that dark, mysterious figure who emerged from the smoke way back in *Star Wars* to scare the living daylights out of us. If the story *did* need to be told, perhaps it should have been only one movie—a single tightly constructed tale rather than three largely episodic tales weighed down with a lot of irrelevant filler. And certainly the trilogy could have been better written and (in some places) better acted.

GLEN OLIVER

Were the prequels disappointing? They were imbalanced, and ill-considered in a number of ways, but they were on the way to creating a reasonably interesting framework for the three-feature trajectory. This is especially true if you factor in *The Clone Wars* TV series, which was a largely more successful undertaking both conceptually and narratively. At the end of the day, though, I think what most hamstrung the prequels is that their heart simply doesn't beat correctly. They represent a warm and tragic story, often told robotically and coldly.

Many performances are stilted, directing is often stagey and muted, the scripts are abrasively clunky at times, and poor John Williams works his ass off to enliven material which is often doggedly tepid, and sometimes even turgid, at best. The prequels felt extravagant and excessive in many regards, while also feeling underbaked and sloppily conceived in other ways. When weighed as a three-picture cycle, there's probably enough genuinely inspired material between the three pictures to equal one rather good movie. On the whole, however, they ring as spotty. Their broader contribution to filmmaking technologies and crafting, however, are without dispute.

RAY MORTON

But for all the negatives, there is no doubt that *Revenge of the Sith* concludes the prequel trilogy exactly where it should conclude: with Owen and Beru cradling an infant Luke Skywalker as they gaze at those twin setting suns, leaving them and us looking forward with (a new?) hope toward *Episode IV*.

GLEN OLIVER

One area in which the prequels truly do shine is imagination: the technologies, some planetary environments, some of the creature work, the weapons of warfare—all felt unfettered, and that is fun to behold. The "universe" and world-building often feel quite reasonable and were sometimes even interesting and provocative. Sadly, these contributions are frequently not supported by story or performances.

GEORGE LUCAS

The story is ultimately a discussion about how fragile democracy is and how democracies sometimes get turned over to tyrants with applause. We should always be vigilant as citizens to make sure that doesn't happen. We have to look inside ourselves and see what kind of a person we are. Are we a good person or an evil person? We all have both of those components in us and we can *choose* to be more evil than good. And if that happens, we should look at ourselves and think, "Am I doing the right thing? Am I harming others? Am I doing this for selfish reasons? Am I only concerned about myself or am I compassionate and caring about other people?"

HAYDEN CHRISTENSEN

It's about a lack of options. Anakin is at a crossroads in his life and in this last film all of his frustrations and anxieties are becoming too much, and he's looking for other avenues, so the dark side seems appealing to him. And it doesn't *seem* that dark, you know? That's sort of the point, that good people turning bad don't necessarily know it.

JOHN KENNETH MUIR

There are a number of interesting factors about *Sith* that relate directly to America in the 2000s (the time the prequels were made and released). In *The Phantom Menace* audiences witnessed precisely how the Emperor began his ascent, chipping away at democracy a piece at a time (in doing so, functioning as an unseen or phantom menace). A Dark Lord and his allies, using the *technicalities of the law,* removed the Supreme Chancellor (Valorum) from office, consequently gaining power for themselves. They did so by claiming that the Senate's bureaucracy had swelled to unmanageable and nonfunctional levels—an antigovernment argument—and that Valorum himself was a weak man beset by scandal. The antidote was a self-described "strong leader," someone who could rally the Senate and get it to work again, someone, for instance, such as Palpatine. In real life, of course, George W. Bush ascended to the presidency promising to restore "honesty and integrity" to the White House after the scandal-plagued Clinton. And after the attacks of 9/11, terrified Americans willingly accepted a massive new surveillance state with the passage of the Patriot Act. And Bush had this to say to the World on November 6, 2001, about the War on Terror, "You are either with us or against us." In May 2005, George Lucas explicitly put the following words into Anakin Skywalker's mouth: "If you're not with me, you're my enemy." And Obi-Wan's rebuttal? "Only a Sith deals in absolutes."

SAMUEL L. JACKSON

Star Wars is still a classic story of good versus evil and that's always been a common theme of a lot of films. George has put it in a pretty fantastic place that people kind of imagined, but your imagination gets overloaded by watching what he's done. You place yourself in that particular situation. And you're amazed by all of the creatures and people that show up. And very seldom do you think about the politics of the galaxy and the ramifications that the films have in terms of what's really going on around us. George started over forty years ago; the world has changed so drastically since then and it's still essentially the same story. So it kind of lets you know that the more things change, the more they stay the same.

During a THX 1138 retrospective prior to its release on Blu-ray at the annual Telluride Film Festival, Lucas mused on the nature of politics in the prequels with moderator Elvis Mitchell, confirming that they were indeed intended as a rebuke of the Bush administration and, specifically, Dick Cheney. "George Bush is Darth Vader. Cheney is the Emperor," Lucas famously remarked.

JOHN KENNETH MUIR

Clearly, George Lucas crafted Revenge of the Sith as a direct rebuke to the path America took post-9/11. Those who whine that there is no political message in Star Wars are, well, blind to the evidence. What remains clever and artistic about Lucas's metaphor is not merely that it is timely (and frightening), but that Lucas tells his story on two parallel tracks. First, in terms of the Republic, and second in personal, individual terms. Anakin travels the same path personally that the Republic citizenry undergoes on a wide scale. Anakin too is "terrorized," or rather, the victim of a terrible attack. Not by the Separatists, but by the Sand People on Tatooine. They kill his mother. That loss hurts him deeply, and he pursues his revenge against the agents who hurt him. But then Anakin begins experiencing visions that he will also lose his beloved wife. So, like the Republic itself, Anakin willingly exchanges freedom and liberty for safety and security. He surrenders his ideals and turns to the dark side because he fears more "attack"; he fears the loss of his family. He does not heed Yoda's warning that "fear of loss is a path to the dark side." Again, in the 2000s-era America, the government launched a preemptive war against Iraq because it feared America would suffer a second 9/11, or terrorist attack. It gave up our values to prevent experiencing such a terrible hurt again. Anything was justified—including torture—in the name of safety and security.

RAY MORTON

In the years since the release of the *Star Wars* prequels, admittedly a much less creatively successful set of films than the original trilogy, it has become fashionable in some areas of movie fandom (the "George Lucas raped my childhood" crowd) to deride Lucas's talents and minimize his contributions to the success of the original movies. This line of thinking posits that Lucas had a few good ideas, but that his execution of them was weak, clumsy, or just plain bad, and that the real credit for the series' success belongs more to Lucas's more talented collaborators—Gary Kurtz, Marcia Lucas, Gloria Katz, Willard Huyck, Lawrence Kasdan, Irvin Kershner, John Williams, etc.—who more often than not saved Lucas from his own worst creative impulses.

KYLE NEWMAN

I wrote a good article in *Star Wars Insider* defending the prequels, and we did a panel, too, at *Star Wars* Celebration where we defend the prequels—not so much defend the prequels, but we talk about the saga as a whole and how all the episodes work together and how they enhance each other. If you sit down and revisit them, you find that there are these rhythmic patterns and story patterns in the structure, and it's really deep and really smart, so they're better films than people give them credit for.

RAY MORTON

Giving more credit to Lucas's collaborators is a truly bizarre notion—one that demonstrates a profound lack of understanding of so many things: film history, Lucas's accomplishments, the collaborative nature of filmmaking, the role of the director, and the way the movie business works. Lucas's collaborators made vital contributions to the original trilogy; that has never been disputed, least of all by Lucas himself. But George Lucas was the prime mover of the initial *Star Wars* films. To think anything else is simply bonkers and anyone who continues to perpetuate this idea needs to be seriously slapped upside the head.

GEORGE LUCAS

The first chapter is basically how Anakin becomes a Jedi, and I wanted to see him as an angelic little kid. *The Phantom Menace* is really about setting everything up. How does he meet Padmé? What are the basic politics of the Republic? How does he become a Jedi? All those things are set up, which is what usually happens in a first act. So that's the story. When I went to do the prequels, everybody said, "Oh, great, he's going to do the prequels! Oh boy, more *Star Wars*!" and all that kind of stuff. But then I said, "The first one is about a nine-year-old boy, and it does not have Darth Vader in it." Everybody said, "Oh my God, this is going to destroy the franchise. It's going to be terrible. You can't do this."

People were telling Rick, "You've got to stop him. You've got to change it. We need to see Darth Vader killing everybody." And I said, "That's *not* the story. I'm telling a story. It's not a marketing piece. Let's remember where we are here." I didn't fight to get my freedom in order to do what the studios would do. Because I'm sure if *Episode I* had been made at a studio, they would have said, "You're not shooting that picture. We're going to do a sequel with Darth Vader, the same thing you did before, only it'll be . . ."

That's what I worked very hard for—so I *wouldn't* have to do that. And, at that point, everybody was concerned. Nobody really worries about what people are going to think of the movie, but everybody worries about whether it's going to make money. And there was a chance, at that point, that I could have lost everything. *The Phantom Menace* could have not made much money. So many sequels have died off and *Episode I* was after a sixteen-year hiatus. That's why it got overhyped: everybody was extremely concerned that it wasn't going to work and that nobody would see a movie about a little boy. But I did *The Phantom Menace* the way I thought I *should* do it. I made *that* movie because I wanted to *tell* that story, not because I wanted to make a sequel.

When it came to the second one, people were more panicked. They said, "Everybody hated the first one, and they're going to hate the second even more because you're doing a love story. Bring Darth Vader in now!" I said, "Look, it's a story. For God's sake, let's tell the story. We'll make it to the third one, and then Darth Vader will show up. Everybody will be happy and then the story will be finished. If we don't make any money on it, fine. I've got to make my movies and tell my stories."

RICK MCCALLUM

I say this in the nicest possible way, but *Star Wars* is a curse and a blessing. George started off as a really small filmmaker. If you track his career, his relationship with Francis Coppola—this incredible, dynamic relationship that the two of them have had—Francis is the one who forced George to go out and write his own movies. And then George wrote and directed something that, not in his wildest dreams, did he think would work or, much less, give him a chance to do *six* of them. Money is one thing, but that has never been

George's main motivation. The ability to control the destiny of his own life, to be completely independent of the Hollywood machine—and in a way no other filmmaker has ever really been—those are the important things to him. And he has achieved that.

GEORGE LUCAS

I'm not sure if my career would have gone in a different way without *Star Wars*. *Star Wars* is a very big, consuming thing. I'm a little surprised at how big it got and how much it has dominated my life. I don't regret it. It has been a very interesting experience and very rewarding. I didn't go back and do another film. I stopped after *Jedi*, because I was burned out on it. I didn't want to do it anymore. It's a nine-year commitment. And when I went to do this one, I knew I had another nine-year commitment. And that's a big deal. People say, "Well, why didn't you do another nine-year commitment?" I just didn't want to. I said, "This will be fine. This will be fun. And this will be it."

At the time of the release of The Phantom Menace, *Lucas was asked if he planned on doing* Episodes VII, VIII, *and* IX, *to which he responded, "I will not do VII, VIII, and IX." The follow-up was, "You will not? Will they be made by somebody else?" and he replied, "No. They will not. This is it. This is all there is." Well, as time would show, he was right about one thing: he wouldn't make them . . . but there would be more* Star Wars *adventures. A lot more.*

Part Four

THE SEQUELS
AND BEYOND

2012–

13

FORCE FED: *THE FORCE AWAKENS*

"Chewie, we're home."

Back in 1980—at the time *The Empire Strikes Back* was released—George Lucas gave an interview to Jim Steranko's late *Prevue* magazine regarding *Star Wars*, and acknowledged the fact that he had plans for a total of nine films in the saga. He detailed that what he started with was an "overlong screenplay" for the first film, so he took that script and divided it into three stories, then rewrote the first one. "Then," he said, "I had the other two films, which were essentially split into three parts each, two trilogies. When the smoke cleared, I said, 'This is really great. I'll do another trilogy that takes place after this.' I had three trilogies of nine films, and then another couple of odd films. It's a nine-part saga that has a beginning, a middle, and an end. It progresses over a period of about fifty or sixty years with about twenty years between trilogies, each trilogy taking about six or seven years."

MARK HAMILL
(actor, "Luke Skywalker")

When I first did *Star Wars*, it was supposed to be four trilogies. Twelve movies! And out on the desert, any time between setups, George was talking about this whole thing. I said, "Why are you starting with *IV, V,* and *VI*? It's crazy." He said the first trilogy's "darker, more serious." And then he said, "How'd you like to be in *Episode IX*?" This is 1976. "When is that gonna be?" "2011." I defy anyone to add thirty-six years to their lives and not be stunned. Even an eight-year-old is like, "No, I'll never be forty-seven." So, I did the math and figured out how old I'd be. I said, "Well, what do you want me to do in *Episode IX*?" He said, "You'll just be a cameo. You'll be like Obi-Wan handing the lightsaber down to the next new hope." So, I went, "Sure." But I thought that he'd just realized he's going to be doing it the rest of his life and he'd rather not do that.

A few years later, Lucas spoke to Starlog *magazine, noting, "It's a long way from the plot to the script. I've just gone through that with* Return of the Jedi *and what seems like a great idea when it's described in three sentences, doesn't hold together when you try to make five or six scenes out of it. So, plots change a lot when they start getting into script form."*

Many things change as time goes on. For instance, when he completed production of Episode III: Revenge of the Sith, *Lucas made it pretty clear that as far as* Star Wars *was concerned, he was finished; the story had come to its proper conclusion. Flash forward to 2011. Disney CEO Bob Iger had approached him about selling Lucasfilm to the Walt Disney Corporation. Although Lucas had considered retiring, the timing to do so just didn't feel right to him. Instead, he asked producer Kathleen Kennedy—at that point working on Steven Spielberg's* Lincoln—*to lunch. Cutting to the chase, he asked her if she was interested in joining Lucasfilm as cochair, with leadership being transferred to her the following year. Ultimately Kennedy said yes and she started with Lucasfilm on June 1, 2012, tasked with developing new films and managing existing assets.*

KATHLEEN KENNEDY
(president, Lucasfilm, Ltd.)

When George asked me to have lunch with him and he said, "I'm retiring and I'm thinking about moving on. I'd like somebody to come in and carry on this legacy," I thought he was going to ask me recommendations on who might do that. I said, "Who are you thinking about?" He said, "Well, I was thinking about you."

GEORGE LUCAS
(creator, *Star Wars*)

I've spent my life building Lucasfilm, and as I shifted my focus into other directions, I wanted to make sure it was in the hands of someone equipped to carry my vision into the future. It was important that my successor not only be someone with great creative passion and proven leadership abilities, but also someone who loves movies.

KATHLEEN KENNEDY

George and I talked about the opportunities that lie ahead for the company, and as George was moving toward retirement, I was honored that he trusted me with taking care of the beloved film franchises. I feel fortunate to have had George working by my side as I took on this role—it's nice to have Yoda by your side.

GEORGE LUCAS

When Kathy came on, we started talking about starting up the whole franchise again. I was pulling away and I said, "I've got to build this company up so it functions without me, and we need to do something to make it attractive." So I said, "Well, let's just do these movies [the *Star Wars* sequels]."

RAY MORTON
(senior editor, *Script* magazine)

In the early 2010s, George Lucas began writing the outlines for a new trilogy of *Star Wars* films that would serve as a sequel to the original trilogy. In interviews, he has stated that his stories focused on the grandchildren of Anakin Skywalker—a girl and a boy sometimes described as being teenagers and sometimes as being in their twenties. The girl was strong with the Force and definite Jedi material. Luke, Han, and Leia would also appear in the movies.

PETER HOLMSTROM
(cohost, *The Rebel & the Rogue* podcast)

Like the prequel trilogy before, Lucas had the idea to rerelease the previous films, this time all six of them being in 3D, and use the box office earnings to fund the new trilogy. Again, he's an independent filmmaker, and didn't want to be beholden to studios holding the purse strings. *Episode I* came out in 3D in 2012 and didn't do well. I don't know if that was the nail in the coffin that convinced him to sell Lucasfilm, but it probably didn't help.

It's important to remember—2012 was a drastically different time in our pop culture. Today, you see every cheerleader and jock wearing a *Star Wars* or Marvel T-shirt, but in 2012, being a nerd was still kind of a bad thing. This had been slowly changing, but it really wasn't until the spectacle films of Marvel and DC dominated the box office schedules, post-*Avengers*, that that really occurred. But also, the public consciousness in 2012 was darker. People wanted *The Dark Knight*, they wanted the dark, gritty tale of murder and revenge. *Breaking Bad*, *Mad Men*, anti-heroes, and villainous villains. Where does *Star Wars* fit into that? That soon changed, but it's easy to see why George's projects weren't as successful at the time.

GEORGE LUCAS

The original saga was about the father, the children, and the grandchildren.

The initial concept for the new trilogy reportedly would have focused on Anakin Skywalker's grandchildren, to be about twenty years old. Offers the website Polygon.com: "In the book The Art of The Force Awakens, *one of the characters, a Jedi named Kira, is described as a 'loner, hothead, gear-headed badass.' The other teen was most often referred to as Sam, and mostly appears depicted with a blaster, which seems to indicate that he didn't have Force powers himself.*

Kira and Sam eventually morphed into Rey and some of Finn, which makes sense . . . Another major character who appears to have gotten a similar arc to their original version is Luke Skywalker."

In the pages of the art books for both The Force Awakens *and* The Last Jedi, author Phil Szostak says of the Luke character, *"The late-2012 idea of a Luke Skywalker haunted by the betrayal of one of his students, in self-imposed exile and spiritually in a 'dark place,' not only precedes Rian Johnson's involvement in* Star Wars, *but J.J. Abrams' as well."*

Later, concept artist Christian Alzmann posted an image of Luke that he created on Instagram, of which he said, *"[In] January of 2013, Luke was being described as a Colonel Kurtz type hiding from the world in a cave."* Again, it was Lucas embracing themes of Heart of Darkness/Apocalypse Now.

KATHLEEN KENNEDY

I've known George a long time and I've worked with him, so it's not as though we were sitting down and having a conversation for the first time. Everything George has done with *Star Wars,* right from the beginning, has been very personal, and I could clearly see that what was really important to him—and certainly important to me—was story. It really required getting inside his head and talking a lot about it. And we are very fortunate to have a lot of incredibly great people still within [Lucasfilm] that have spent a lot of years working with George and have had these kinds of conversations over the years. They greatly respect the stories and respect the franchise, and they're still extremely involved in the decisions we make creatively. That's probably the best way to describe how we began; it was over a period of time and many conversations.

George Lucas confided in James Cameron for his Story of Science Fiction *documentary on AMC that "[the next three* Star Wars *films] were going to get into a microbiotic world. But there's this world of creatures that operate differently than we do. I call them the Whills. And the Whills are the ones who actually control the universe. They feed off the Force. Back in the day, I used to say ultimately what this means is we were just cars, vehicles for the Whills to travel around in . . . We're vessels for them. And the conduit is the midi-chlorians. The midi-chlorians are the ones that communicate with the Whills. The Whills, in a general sense, they are the Force."*

George Lucas elaborated more recently on his plans for his abandoned sequel trilogy to journalist Paul Duncan. "I had planned for the first trilogy to be about the father, the second trilogy to be about the son, and the third trilogy to be about the daughter and the grandchildren. Episodes VII, VIII, and IX would take ideas from what happened after the Iraq War," he revealed. "Rebuilding afterwards is harder than starting a rebellion or fighting the war. When you win the war and you disband the opposing army, what do they do? The storm-troopers would be like Saddam Hussein's Ba'athist fighters that joined ISIS and kept on fighting. The stormtroopers refuse to give up when the Republic wins."

Filling the power vacuum left by the demise of the Empire would be a famil-iar villain: Darth Maul. "There's a power vacuum so gangsters, like the Hutts, are taking advantage of the situation, and there is chaos." Taking advantage of that chaos would be Darth Maul, whose resurrection was chronicled in The Clone Wars *and the* Rebels *TV series. The character was also reintroduced in live action in a brief cameo in* Solo *as the head of the Crimson Dawn crime syn-dicate, which would have explored similar territory had the movie succeeded and led to sequels.*

JOHN KENNETH MUIR

(author, *Science Fiction and Fantasy Films of the 1970s*)

I have read about it a lot, and it sounds weird and strange and unconven-tional. Those are all qualities that might have moved *Star Wars* into a new and genuinely thrilling chapter, and allowed it to continue innovating in the cinema. Everyone would go to see those new movies, so Lucas could have made the most expensive, daring, experimental film ever and introduced it to a vast audience. I champion Lucas for wanting to take his conceived third trilogy in a new direction, rather than rehash and give us another Death Star. I would rather have something weird and different, having seen the mish-mash, generic-blockbuster films of the Disney trilogy, frankly.

PETER HOLMSTROM

Information about George's notion for the sequel trilogy is a bit vague—but what we've been able to glean throughout the years is as follows. Luke was missing. The Republic and the Empire still exist, but aren't at war. However, they both had splinter groups which were hell-bent on keeping the war alive through acts of terrorism. Again, reflecting the world we live in, if the origi-nal trilogy was George's sci-fi take on Vietnam, and the prequels was his take on the rise of a Donald Trump–like dictator, then the sequels would be his take on the war on terror. Both sides had superweapons, and our heroes are in the middle, advocating for a middle path. Again—balance. Peace.

Thea (who would eventually be called Rey) lived on a junk planet, but was always a princess in hiding. Hidden Fortress–style. Luke is in hiding, not because he's ashamed of some mistake or whatever, but instead knows the universe would be better off without the exploration of the Force. He knows

Force-users are potential weapons of mass destruction, and wants to snuff it out. The enemies of the trilogy are not remakes of Vader and the Emperor, but are instead corporations—scientists—who have devised a way to artificially manipulate the midi-chlorians within life-forms to create their own supersoldiers. Artificial Jedi/Sith, if you will. Thea (who we're pretty sure was always Han and Leia's kid) arrives to convince Luke to rejoin the fight. The metaphorical battle between spiritualism and those who would co-opt spiritualism for selfish purposes would follow. Also, the notion of spiritual morality and intellectual morality. No one was to die until Luke becomes one with the Force at the end of *Episode IX*, after completing Leia's training.

Those are interesting ideas to chew on. Reflective of our current world, and expanding on what *Star Wars* means. Anakin was the Chosen One, Luke fulfilled what it meant to bring balance to the Force, and the new generation would have to learn to live and carry on with that.

RAY MORTON

Lucas intended to develop the midi-chlorian concept more than he had in the prequel trilogy, introducing an ancient life-form called the Whills that use the midi-chlorians to control the actions of Force-sensitive individuals and thus rule the galaxy. Then, in 2012, Lucas hired Academy Award–winning screenwriter Michael Arndt (*Little Miss Sunshine, Toy Story 3*) to develop his outlines into full treatments. He also approached Mark Hamill, Harrison Ford, and Carrie Fisher about appearing in the new films and they agreed to participate. Lucas intended to direct at least the first film in the new trio.

DALE POLLOCK
(author, *Skywalking: The Life and Films of George Lucas*)

And, who knows, if Disney hadn't come along and offered him $4 billion, he might've directed these last three films himself. He was certainly starting to prepare them and he had no intention of hiring another director. Now would those films have been better had they been directed by George Lucas? Who knows. In the last one, he may have been able to pull up a certain emotional component, because it was all so personal to him. It might've worked, but on the whole, based on the prequels, I think they would have been worse.

RAY MORTON

That was around the same time he hired producer Kathleen Kennedy, with whom he had worked on the *Indiana Jones* movies, to become Lucasfilm

Ltd.'s cochairman. Lucas wanted Kennedy to help him make the sequels and then take over the company after Lucas retired, which he planned to do at the conclusion of the new trilogy.

KATHLEEN KENNEDY

First of all, it was a big decision on his part that he was ready to see sequels made; I think he'd really decided at that point that there weren't going to be any more. Just making that decision was a big one, and we spent quite a bit of time talking about it. It was George who actually made the first inquiries to Carrie [Fisher], Mark [Hamill], and Harrison [Ford] about whether they would be interested, and, obviously, if any or all of them had said no, then it would have been a very different conversation creatively. But luckily, they all said yes, and that [prompted] some decisions about how far [in the future the story would be from the time frame of *Return of the Jedi*], and what it might include. George also felt very strongly about this idea of creating other *Star Wars* stories inside the universe, and he had actually written up a few different ideas.

GEORGE LUCAS

I turned seventy and my whole life centered around me doing these avant-garde experimental films. Films that you don't know whether they're going to work or not, or you're kind of playing with the medium, which is what I wanted to do. All my student films are like that. Everything I did for a long time was like that. Even *THX* is vaguely like that. And I always say, "Well, if this fails, I'm going to go back to doing my experimental films." Right now, all of my friends—Marty and Francis and Steven—are like, "Well, what are you going to do?"

Well, I got caught in this tar baby called *Star Wars* and lots of opportunities, a lot of things that accompanied it. So, I said, "Well, I like *Star Wars*. I fell in love with it and I want to complete it." And then after I completed it, I produced films and did things. At the same time, I came back and did the backstory to the whole thing. Then I felt, "Well, at some point there are three more stories," but it takes ten years to do all three of them. I didn't think I could do that. I wanted to go do my little experimental films. I was commuting between Chicago and San Francisco and all of that stuff, and I just said, "I'm going to take my life and make it so I can live in Chicago, a little in San Francisco, make my little art films, build a museum, and take care of my daughter." That's what was important to me.

The other thing is that at the height of my career, after *Jedi*, I had a daughter who was a year old. I was married and we got divorced and I was left with a baby, who was adopted. When I first held her in my arms in the hospital, lightning bolts went through me. I said, "This is the best thing that's ever happened to me." So, when she left, I just took the baby and I said I was going to retire; I'm not going to direct any more movies, because you can't raise kids and direct movies, because it's literally four in the morning until ten at night, working weekends and working all the time. So I said I think I'm going to retire from directing movies and I'm simply going to try to work my company a little bit, because I can go to work at eleven in the morning and come home at three in the afternoon and not work weekends.

Then, after that, I ended up adopting another baby on my own, and then another baby on my own. So I had three kids that I raised for fifteen years. Then I came out of retirement and started directing again. At the same time, I think I reached the end of what I could contribute to *Star Wars*.

It was that revelation that resulted in a seismic shift in a galaxy far, far away when, in October 2012, it was announced that Disney actually did acquire Lucasfilm in a $4 billion deal that would see Lucas selling the company and all its assets, with Kathleen Kennedy shifting over to be "brand manager" (just as Kevin Feige was so successfully on the Disney-acquired Marvel Entertainment).

BRIAN JAY JONES
(author, *George Lucas: A Life*)

I think Lucas walked away from Lucasfilm with his head held high. What I always say about Lucas, *Star Wars* movies, and fandom is that he's not disposed to worry about your emotional well-being. If you like it, great. If you hate it, he doesn't really care. But his decision is something that I wish I had a good answer for. I don't necessarily know what prompted it, but I think partly it was the fact that he'd get to pick his heir apparent. I don't think he wanted to have the Jim Henson problem where he would die and then the company went into insolvency and lawyers got involved and they got to decide the direction of Lucasfilm and what happened to the characters. Again, it gets right back to his need to control things. He wants to be the one who's like, "I'm approaching my seventies, I'm not going to be around forever. I want to be sure I'm in charge of where this company goes, where it lands, who's taking care of it."

JONATHAN RINZLER
(author, *The Making of Star Wars*)

It's funny how many times George tried to divest himself from his own company. From the very beginning, George was trying to get rid of the company he himself had started. It's kind of funny to go through and see: 1977 he said he was retiring, 1980 he said he was retiring, 1983 he said he was retiring. '84, '85, '86 . . . So finally, he's done it.

BRIAN JAY JONES

With Disney, he knew it was a company he could kind of trust: "I'm going to bring Jim Henson back into it"; I think Disney was a big part of it for him. Disney was a very different company even in the seventies, and Jim Henson at the time knew that. He was like, "Look, they managed *Mary Poppins*." They manage a million characters and it's like, this is where you park your icons. And Lucas, we've got to remember, had been with Disney with [former CEO Michael] Eisner, he's got projects going on in the theme parks. That's the other thing people forget as well. When Star Tours first went in the Disney parks, it had absolutely nothing to do with Disney; it was just one of the attractions completely outside the Disney purview. It was like *Star Wars* literally dropped in from another galaxy into the middle of the Disney park.

It doesn't relate to anything Disney owned, but they were smart enough to know that. The whole point of this is that Lucas has been puttering around with Disney. He's comfortable, I think, with Disney and the people and they're deferential to him, which he likes. At one point he had expressed interest when people forget how badly Disney was doing before they sort of revitalized themselves with cartoons like *The Little Mermaid* and *Beauty and the Beast* in the early nineties. He actually considered at one point running that company, so Lucas was comfortable with Disney and, again, they've been around a lot longer than Lucasfilm and they really know how to handle their icons. He knew it was a good place to put them and that they had the resources to promote them and distribute them, which was always the biggest fight he had with his movies. So I think he knew that that was the place to go where everything that he thought was important about the suit side of the equation would be well cared for.

TODD FISHER
(brother of Carrie Fisher)

When Carrie heard that Disney bought Lucasfilm, her first reaction was her rolling her eyes like, "Oh my God, I can't believe this." So the initial reaction was not like, "Oh, this is great." The initial response was lukewarm at best, if not cool. But then when she saw the script and saw how it was being treated, she thought, "Oh, you know, this isn't too bad." And, of course, when she saw how much they were going to offer her to do it financially, that also made it brighten in her eyes. Let's face it, actors do do things for cash.

ROBERT A. IGER

(chief executive officer, Walt Disney Company)

George Lucas is a visionary, an innovator, and an epic storyteller—and he's built a company at the intersection of entertainment and technology to bring some of the world's most unforgettable characters and stories to screens across the galaxy. He's entertained, inspired, and defined filmmaking for almost four decades and we were incredibly honored that he entrusted the future of that legacy to Disney.

GEORGE LUCAS

One of my greatest pleasures has been to see *Star Wars* passed from one generation to the next. And it was time for me to pass *Star Wars* on to a new generation of filmmakers. I've always believed that *Star Wars* could live beyond me, and I thought it was important to set up the transition during my lifetime. I felt confident that with Lucasfilm under the leadership of Kathleen Kennedy, and having a new home within the Disney organization, *Star Wars* will certainly live on and flourish for many generations to come.

KATHLEEN KENNEDY

I feel a huge responsibility to that. I think about it all the time. In fact, looking at *The Lord of the Rings* and *Star Wars*—[J.R.R.] Tolkien and George Lucas—that kind of defines modern mythology for our generation. What George has created is a meaningful mythology, a history to draw from. I have often said that there's a fragility to it, too. We have to take everything we do seriously; we put a great deal of effort into what it is we're creating.

RAY MORTON

The sale of Lucasfilm had a definite impact on the development of the sequels. When the sale closed, Lucasfilm ceased to be a stand-alone company and became a division of Disney, alongside Pixar and Marvel. Lucas retired and Kennedy became the president of the division, reporting to Disney Studios chairman Alan Horn. With all of these changes, it was initially unclear what would happen to the sequels Lucas was developing. Disney bought Lucasfilm primarily to acquire the *Star Wars* brand, so it was definitely interested in making a sequel trilogy. However, it did not want to make Lucas's sequel trilogy. Lucas did not want to repeat himself and wanted to push the *Star Wars* concept into new territory, so, as he had done with the prequels, he intended to give his sequels their own look and feel and take the story in unexpected directions. This is exactly what Disney did not want. Feeling that part of the reason so many fans were dissatisfied with the prequels was because *Episodes*

I to III didn't look or feel like *Episodes IV to VI*, Disney wanted the sequels to look and feel as much as possible like the original trilogy.

When Lucas retired from the company, he also retired from making any more Star Wars *movies—he would no longer be the creative force behind the sequels, nor would he direct* Episode VII. *Kennedy would now be in charge of developing and producing the new movies, on which Lucas would serve only as a consultant. When Disney bought Lucasfilm, they also bought Lucas's outlines and treatments for the new trilogy. The impression Lucas got from Iger was that Disney would be doing so. Disney CEO Robert Iger wrote in his memoir,* The Ride of a Lifetime, *"We decided we need to buy them, though we made clear in the purchase agreement that we would not be contractually obligated to adhere to the plotlines he'd laid out."*

PETER HOLMSTROM

George sold the company with the handshake agreement with Disney that Lucasfilm would "carry on business as usual." And he's not completely wrong for thinking that—Disney bought Marvel and more or less let them carry on with their plans for a while. But here it was not the case. Lucas said at the time that he sold Lucasfilm because he couldn't see a way to produce new $150 million films, and keep his two thousand Lucasfilm employees employed. So he sold the company because he felt people keeping their jobs was more important. Then we see what Disney/Lucasfilm does to those employees after the sale. Lucasfilm threw out George's plans for the sequel trilogy, canceled *The Clone Wars* TV show and declined to broadcast *Detours*—firing both staffs along with them—closed LucasArts, ended the long-standing relationship with Dark Horse Comics, and fired a large amount of the Lucasfilm staff. They cleaned house and firmly stated, "There's a new sheriff in town."

RAY MORTON

When Lucas later found out the company was going in its own direction, he became upset and withdrew from the project entirely. Iger later admitted that he was not as forthright with Lucas about his intentions as he should have been.

In his memoir, Iger further illuminated the growing chasm between Lucas and Disney. "George immediately got upset as [the plot of the new film was described] and it dawned on him that we weren't using one of the stories he submitted during the negotiations," he wrote. "George knew we weren't contractually bound to anything, but he thought that our buying the story treatments was a tacit promise that we'd follow them, and he was disappointed that his story was being discarded. I'd been so careful since our first conversation not to mislead him in any way, and I didn't think I had now, but I could have handled it better . . . George felt betrayed, and while the whole process would never have been easy for him, we'd gotten off to an unnecessarily rocky start."

BRIAN JAY JONES

I think with *The Force Awakens* Lucas had a bit of seller's remorse. You watch your company, you watch your characters, and they're in someone else's hands; someone else is controlling it. You can't do anything about that. They're somebody else's responsibility now. That had to be hard for him, but on the other hand, he was paid very well to shut up and walk away. And even with that payout, *The Force Awakens* comes out and he takes a few shots at it. It wouldn't surprise me if he picked up the phone and is like, "What did you do? What are you doing?" "Shut up. You were paid very well to be quiet."

RAY MORTON

Of the three *Star Wars* trilogies, the sequel trilogy is the worst. It's the worst, because it is based on a really terrible premise, which is that all of the heroes in the original trilogy turned out to be screw-ups or failures and that none of their victories were real. *Return of the Jedi* ends with the Rebel Alliance vanquishing the Empire; a redeemed Darth Vader killing the evil Emperor; Han and Leia in love; and Luke finally becoming a full Jedi Knight and poised to restart the Jedi order. Yays all around!

But then the sequels tell us the Alliance did not defeat the Empire—while the destruction of Death Star II dealt the Empire a pretty strong blow, apparently enough personnel and equipment remained that it was able to quickly reconstitute itself as the First Order. Vader did not kill the Emperor—sure, he fell down a miles-high shaft into a reactor and exploded, but to paraphrase Monty Python, apparently he got better. Attempting to revive the Jedi, Luke decided to take his nephew Ben as his pupil. However, when Luke sensed Ben might possibly turn evil, he decided to try and kill him. Luke's action understandably upset Ben, who then did turn evil and ran off to help the First Order destroy the New Republic. Having unleashed this terrible monster on the galaxy, Luke did the brave thing and ran away.

After siring the worst person in the galaxy, Han apparently couldn't hack it and also ran away. Throwing away all of the character growth he experienced in the first trilogy, Han abandoned all his responsibilities and went back to being an itinerant smuggler. In addition to giving birth to a monster, Leia apparently wasn't able to create a New Republic that was strong enough to withstand whatever it is that the First Order did to undermine it. She loses her government and so is once again on the run and leading a resistance movement.

These are really depressing concepts that make losers and cowards out of Luke, Han, and Leia and completely invalidate all of the triumphs of the original trilogy. It's hard to fathom why the sequel creators felt these ideas were good ones or that anyone who enjoyed the original movies would embrace or be entertained by them. The sequel trilogy certainly has its good points, but it is harder to emotionally invest in these newer films when their narrative foundation is built entirely on negating so much of what made the original films work (and beloved).

When Star Wars Episode VII—ultimately titled The Force Awakens—went into development in a fairly accelerated manner, and with Disney's mandate to create a new trilogy that closely resembled the original films in mind (at one point, Disney attempted to pressure J.J. into resurrecting Darth Vader, which they felt was the key to the success of the franchise), Kennedy turned to J.J. Abrams to develop and direct the first of the sequels.

RAY MORTON

Abrams got his start as a screenwriter in the 1990s, writing and cowriting features such as *Taking Care of Business* (1990), *Regarding Henry* (1991), and *Armageddon* (1998). He then moved into television, creating, producing, and directing series such as *Felicity, Alias,* and *Lost.* He returned to features as a director in 2006 with *Mission: Impossible III.* Abrams followed that film up with *Star Trek* (2009), *Super 8* (2011), and *Star Trek Into Darkness* (2013). His specialty as a film director has been to take ideas from older movies and TV shows and reboot them into energetic new packages, which made him the ideal person to helm Disney's back-to-basics-mandated approach to *Star Wars.*

J.J. ABRAMS
(cowriter, director, *The Force Awakens*)

The obvious challenge with *Star Trek* was that we wanted to make our own brand-new thing and at the same time embrace and honor what had come before. As a director who didn't know and love the world of *Star Trek* by default—*Star Wars* was much more my thing—I ended up telling a story for people like myself that love fun movies, but are not necessarily familiar with the archaic details of the *Star Trek* canon. If you look at the *Star Wars* films and what technology allowed them to do, they covered so much terrain in terms of design, locations, characters, aliens, ships. So much of the spectacle has been done and it seems like every aspect has been covered, whether it's geography or design of culture or weather system or character or ship type. Everything has been tapped in those movies.

The challenge of doing *Star Trek,* despite the fact that it existed before *Star Wars,* is that we were clearly in the shadow of what George Lucas has done. The key to me was to not ever try to outdo them, because it's a no-win situation. Those movies are so extraordinarily rendered that it felt to me that the key to *Star Trek* was to go from the inside out. Be as true to the characters as possible, be as real and as emotional and as exciting as possible, and not be distracted by the specter of all that the *Star Wars* films accomplished.

KATHLEEN KENNEDY

There is an aspect of that which is really important for directors who step into this kind of storytelling. You do want it to feel authentic and genuine, and that is very much the way that we've looked for directors—[though] I wouldn't say it has to be 100 percent absence of cynicism. I think with someone like J.J., I also felt that his sense of humor is so great, and I think that's a really important ingredient in *Star Wars* movies. They've always had a buoyancy and a lightness to them that makes them fun and purely entertaining. That was a very important characteristic and continues to be important with the directors we consider.

Abrams admits that he was initially reluctant to take on the daunting task of relaunching Star Wars, *and it was actually his wife who convinced him that it was the right decision.*

J.J. ABRAMS

I said no partly because it was an incredibly daunting thing, partly because my family and I had this plan of what we were going to be doing that next year, partly because it felt like I've been doing sequels and things in the past. I just wanted to sort of break away from that. At the same time, you rarely get a chance to be involved in something that you would typically be an audience for. Katie, my wife, said, "If you want to do this and you don't, you're going to regret it." It was really about being willing to take that leap and jump into the possibilities of what these characters are doing and where they are.

KATHLEEN KENNEDY

We used [all those conversations I had with George] as a stepping-stone to move into what would become new—new characters, new stories, and new ideas. And the art department is very important alongside that, because our concept artists that work inside Lucasfilm work very closely with the Story Group, which is headed by Kiri Hart, our director of development. For instance, with *Episode VII*, Rick Carter was heading a group of concept artists that was creating artwork that we would put in the room while we discussed story. As they were developing things, they would come in with artwork that sometimes would correlate with what we were specifically discussing, or, in some cases, they might just "blue sky" something and bring in artwork that inspired an idea, and sometimes that would take us in different directions as we were talking about this story. It was incredibly helpful to the screenwriters and to J.J. This all developed because there's nothing better than being able to have images emerge from these ideas that we're putting up on a whiteboard. For the directors that we brought in, especially for the new *Star Wars* stories, this has become incredibly important to our process. And it's something the directors really love, because it's a great opportunity to be able to sit in a room with people who know this world and its history so well.

When the script for the film was first being developed, it was by Toy Story's *Michael Arndt, Simon Kinberg, and Lawrence Kasdan, the latter of whom, of course, famously cowrote the screenplays for* The Empire Strikes Back *and* Return of the Jedi *as well as* Raiders of the Lost Ark *for Lucas.*

SIMON KINBERG
(executive producer, *Star Wars: Rebels*, the X-Men film series)
We went up to Skywalker Ranch and started talking, really in the vaguest of terms, what *Episode VII* could be. We had a whiteboard and some pens and it was just three writers in a room, like a writing staff of a TV show, because the story we were telling was the continued story of *Star Wars*. And these were a lot of pinch-yourself moments where you were writing up on the board names like Han and Luke . . . and then the fact I was doing it with Lawrence Kasdan. We would work all day and then we would go back at night and all have dinner together where Larry would tell stories about working on *Empire* and *Jedi* and *Raiders of the Lost Ark* and *The Big Chill*.

RAY MORTON
The original idea was for the four of them—Arndt, Kinberg, Kasdan, and Abrams—to work out a revised story, after which Arndt would write the screenplay. However, the committee approach made for slow going—there was more discussing than writing and Arndt wasn't able to make much progress on the actual script. Disney had imposed a tight deadline on the project, insisting it be in theaters by December 2015, and the committee process was

going too slowly to make this date, so in October 2013, Arndt and Kinberg left the project, and Abrams and Kasdan took over. Preproduction and casting on the film also began at this time. Abrams and Kasdan wrote all through this period and finished up shortly before production began in May 2014.

J.J. ABRAMS

It became clear that given the time frame and given the process, and the way the thing was going, that working with Larry in this way and cowriting the script with him was going to get where we needed to be and when we needed to be. Working with Larry Kasdan, especially on a *Star Wars* movie, is kind of unbeatable. Working with Michael Arndt was a wonderful experience and I couldn't be a bigger fan of his or adore him more. He is a wonderful guy and was incredibly helpful in the process.

KATHLEEN KENNEDY

I was very excited about the story we had in place and thrilled to have Larry and J.J. working on the script. There are very few people who fundamentally understand the way a *Star Wars* story works like Larry, and it was nothing short of incredible to have him even more deeply involved in its return to the big screen. J.J., of course, is an incredible storyteller in his own right. Michael Arndt had done a terrific job bringing us to this point.

J.J. ABRAMS

There were times when certain images came in that we felt could be applicable to certain scenes. One of the great opportunities on this movie was working with Rick Carter and Darren Gilford, our production designers. I brought Rick into the story process at the very beginning, probably because I knew how inspiring Ralph McQuarrie's designs were to George Lucas when he was working on the original films. Rather than write the script and then hand it off to a designer and ask him to design everything that was written, it felt like we had such a brain trust—and I should also say a "soul trust"—in Rick and Darren. Rick is such a dreamer and such a glorious connection maker, with a capability to hear what we were talking about, and then go work on something and bring it in and show us; it might have been a detail we would have forgotten or overlooked, but Rick visualized it and brought it to life.

LAWRENCE KASDAN
(cowriter, producer, *The Force Awakens*)

I was pleased that there would be new films and that there was a chance to capture some of the spirit of the original trilogy that I'd worked on. I thought there was an audience out there—my grandchildren, lots of original *Star Wars* people—and there always will be. It's only good that we tried to do some more great ones.

J.J. ABRAMS

When Kathy Kennedy and Larry and I started talking about what this was, at the very beginning, the fundamental question was what do we want to feel, and what do we want people to feel when they come to this movie? That was really the beginning of the discussion. The answer was the kind of sense of discovery, exhilaration, surprise—the comedy that George Lucas put into *Star Wars* was the thing that made me love the movie. But when you look at all the things he got right, it's impossible and stunning.

LAWRENCE KASDAN

J.J. and I jumped into the thing under a lot of time pressure, and we had fun. In fact, the first day that we started real work on it, we said we must have fun with this every day. It's really a privilege, and you have to be very lucky to get to write the next *Star Wars*! So we didn't really have fear. I think we had trepidation about fulfilling people's expectations—that they'd be satisfied with what we came out with. But we didn't want them to know what we were going to come up with, and we wanted this . . . to be a fresh moment for as many people in the world who were interested in it. The only pressure is, can you do something that's worth that much anticipation?

SIMON KINBERG

I thought J.J. was the perfect fit for this film. He went on record when he was working on *Star Trek* saying he was a bigger *Star Wars* fan than *Star Trek* fan, and he really is as big a *Star Wars* fan as anyone I've ever met, which is saying a lot.

GEORGE LUCAS

I'd consistently been impressed with J.J. as a filmmaker and storyteller. He was an ideal choice to direct the new *Star Wars* film and the legacy couldn't have been in better hands.

MARK HAMILL

I have to admit I was a little suspicious when they said J.J. was directing. I was like, "Wait a minute, isn't that the *Star Trek* guy?" Listen, I like *Star Trek*. I'm friends with Brent Spiner, who played Data on *Star Trek: The Next Generation,* and there's no rivalry whatsoever, but I thought it just seemed odd. Not that I was predisposed to dislike him, I was just sort of cautious about it. But he's a really personable guy. He's really easy to talk to. He's very inclusive in terms of listening to your ideas instead of being adamant it's got to be his way. He's lovable.

ANDY SERKIS
(actor, "Supreme Commander Snoke")

J.J. was absolutely the right man for this, and bringing back *Star Wars* properly was, I'm sure, a huge objective. I know all this sensibility that I've witnessed was about doing exactly that. You know, I've grown up with *Star Wars*. I was a really big fan of the original films. A massive fan, and I never imagined in a million years that I'd be engaging with this. And it just came about so organically. J.J. and I met and there was just this real amazing vibe between us. He said, "I think you'd really fit well in this universe," and I was like, "Yeah, yeah, I think I probably could."

BEN BURTT
(sound designer, *The Force Awakens*)

J.J. represents the next generation of filmmakers from those that were making *Star Wars* when I started. When he was a teen, he was a fan of *Star Wars*, and a great deal of his love for movies came out of his reaction to that first *Star Wars* film. You feel that he's already invested so many years in it, and would propel it forward in a new way. In other words, you're having a fan who has grown up and developed tremendous directorial skills finding himself at the steering wheel to take the franchise into the next stage. I felt like I'm there watching history turn over from one era to another.

MATTHEW WOOD
(supervising sound editor, *The Force Awakens*)

Working with him, it was so obvious to me that J.J. and I have the same nostalgic love of that era. Now we have someone from that generation at the helm of the *Star Wars* franchise that I've known and worked on, so it's a great circle. Just seeing what he did with *Super 8* and capturing those moments, and knowing what was so special about that era, it speaks to a new generation of audience as well.

HARRISON FORD
(actor, "Han Solo")

It helps a lot to have somebody that gives as much as J.J. gives to the whole enterprise. And this is beside the direction of the movie and the engineering of this monster into something, to what it is today. The human kindness that J.J. brings to the set every day is part of what makes the movie what it is.

KATHLEEN KENNEDY

It was really interesting watching J.J. and Larry Kasdan when they started to really break down the storytelling [of] the first *Star Wars* and realized just how simple and great it was—and how difficult that is to do. I think people come at the franchise with lots of different points of view as to why it means something to them. It all usually has something to do with filmmaking, storytelling, and the fact that George always tried to push technology. A lot of things that we take for granted today were created over the years inside of *Star Wars*.

J.J. ABRAMS

Frankly, taking this on is vaguely terrifying, because you just don't know and you hope the fans will like what you're doing. They deserve something great, and we just worked really hard to give it to them. And this is very much a tightrope walk for the movie itself. This had to be new and it had to be a story that fans have not seen before. At the same time, it's *Star Wars* and you have to allow it to be inheriting what it's been. The trick is to be forward-thinking, but embrace everything that was built before us.

SIMON KINBERG

Nobody wants to do karaoke. Those movies exist. They're essentially perfect films. Nobody wants to repeat them, so I think—and this is true with adapting *X-Men* or *Sherlock Holmes* when I worked on that—you want to be true to the essence of the source material, but you also want to be original and give people something that they haven't experienced before and that they can't experience by just reading the comics or watching the original *Star Wars* films. That is absolutely the trickiest part of any of this: being reverent, but also giving yourself license to be a little irreverent sometimes, too.

MARK HAMILL

After I'd read the script, I saw some parallels between Luke's story and Rey's. I thought, "Well, she's been living in the desert sort of aimlessly," and I saw the parallels with my character and so forth. But heritage is so important in the *Star Wars* films. At the time we didn't realize how big Vader as the father was. When *Return of the Jedi* came along, because George had always made it seem like he had all these things mapped out in his head, when I read that Luke and Leia were long-separated twins, I said, "Wait a minute, is he trying to top Vader? If that's the case, then let's go for broke. Let's have them unmask Boba Fett and it's my long-lost mother!"

J.J. ABRAMS

While *The Force Awakens* features the return of Mark Hamill, Harrison Ford, and Carrie Fisher as, respectively, Luke, Han, and Leia, it also heralds the arrival into the franchise of Oscar Isaac as Poe Dameron, Daisy Ridley as Rey, and John Boyega as Finn, each of whom entered *Star Wars* fandom in their own way. Beyond them, there was Adam Driver as the villainous Kylo Ren and Andy Serkis (Gollum from the *Lord of the Rings* film series) as Supreme Commander Snoke.

MARK HAMILL

People wondered if we tried to offer any suggestions to the new cast, but there's no way you can really describe it to them. First of all, I went to the table read and was just knocked out at how good they are. They're just wonderful. If anything, I should be asking them for advice, but in terms of how your life is going to change, I'm sure they had an inkling, because there was something to base it on. We discovered it as it happened. At that table read, every person had a specific place to sit. It's not like we just wandered in and sat down. You sit here, you sit here, you sit here, and so forth. So I was across from Harrison and Carrie and Daisy Ridley was right between them. And I thought, "See, now people are going to start reading things into it," because when they saw the photograph, they said, "Well, she's got to be the daughter of Han and Leia, because look at where she's sitting."

KATHLEEN KENNEDY

That first reading was pretty amazing. We didn't quite realize until we all sat down to start the read-through that many of the legacy cast had not seen each other in years. There was that element, and there were all the new cast members. Then everybody got settled down, got their scripts out, and stopped taking pictures of one another. Mark Hamill had agreed to read the entire script out loud for everybody, and about five minutes into it, J.J. had to actually stop the read-through to say, "Does everybody realize what's happening here?" It was just kind of incredible. It was one of those moments where you realize it's a little slice of history happening in real-time.

OSCAR ISAAC
(actor, "Poe Dameron")

The first movie I saw in the theater was *Return of the Jedi*. For me, that moment when Darth Vader's helmet comes off and you see a fat, sad little man underneath, was incredibly traumatizing and you just never forget that moment. But it was interesting, because I was in my hotel room waiting to find out if I had been cast, and if I needed to stay for that reading—that iconic picture everyone saw. When I finally got the call that I was indeed officially going to play Poe Dameron, I was so excited/nervous. But I blasted the *Star Wars* theme as loud as I could, grabbed my shampoo bottle, and started swinging it around like a lightsaber and was like, "I can do this!" That's how I dealt with the nerves.

JOHN BOYEGA
(actor, "Finn")

I was actually exposed to the merchandise before the movie, so I had all the action figures, toys, and bedspread, and then I watched the prequels and then the originals after. I mean, with me the excitement just turns into absolute nerve, and I was scared to tell my parents that I got the part of Finn in *Star Wars* in case they didn't believe me. I waited until that cast photo was released before I told my parents. All that time my dad saw me leaving to go into this place, and I was reading all these red sides, and he's like, "What is going on." I just told him I was filming *24*.

DAISY RIDLEY
(actress, "Rey")

I actually did it that way as well. I did the prequels and then the original films; I was born in '92. I have no idea what I did [to get the role], I just tried very hard, and I hoped very much. There wasn't so much advice, there was a conversation with Harrison about anonymity and some things with Carrie, but it was more people leading by example. So, it was just amazing for me to see people so established with a huge career be kind and generous to everyone on set.

OSCAR ISAAC

Being cast in it, you kind of have to pretend almost that it's not a big deal. You almost diminish it a little bit for yourself, but then you just can't fake it anymore. You get out there in front of the fans and it becomes almost a religious experience.

ADAM DRIVER
(actor, "Kylo Ren")

I remember early on I did not think of Kylo being bad or evil or a villain, and tried to make something that was more three-dimensional, because that to me, when we were talking originally, seemed more dangerous and more unpredictable—someone who feels morally justified in doing whatever they need to, to publicly state that what they're doing is right. Seems kind of more active to play than just being evil for the sake of it. That's not really fun to play, I guess.

LAWRENCE KASDAN

That's why we were so excited about Adam playing this part, because there's never been a character like Kylo in *Star Wars*. He hasn't got his shit all together. And Adam acts it so beautifully, because what you're looking at is—you expect, "Oh, this is some evil genius," you know, but what you're getting is all the contradictions and the conflicts that people feel—any one of us can feel at any moment. That's what's so amazing, and I think that's what's unique about what Adam has done.

LUPITA NYONG'O
(actress, "Maz Kanata")

Fortunately for me, J.J. had me be a part of principal photography, so my very first experience with motion-capture was on the actual sets with the actual actors. So I'm eternally grateful to him for giving me that, because it was a great way to get into this wonderful, crazy thing called motion-capture. I got to be on those sets and see those things and feel them, and the art direction in this—there's so much detail! Even when you're standing on that set, it's mesmerizing. For me, playing a motion-capture character was something completely new to me. Walking into a room—I had to do this thing where they had to take my picture from all directions at one time, and I had to stand in the middle, and there were 360 cameras all around me, and that freaked me out.

J.J. ABRAMS

People have said to me, "I don't understand—you cast someone who is so beautiful as Lupita, and then you had her be a motion-capture character?" And I think, "Would it be okay if she were ugly?"

TODD FISHER

Carrie was basically going to come back to play Leia because it was like a reunion to her, and because Mark and Harrison were going to do it. In fact, when they were negotiating the deal, everybody got equal, because Harrison negotiated the financial deal first, so it allowed everybody to say, "I'll just take what he's getting." There weren't a whole lot of secondary negotiations going on. I was Carrie's date to the screening of *The Force Awakens* and people were just screaming. It was crazy. And this was right about when Carrie started to think, "Maybe there's something to this Princess Leia thing and me." Prior to that, she really hadn't embraced it throughout those years of the connection people had with the character. During the "quiet period," she still didn't really understand it for sure. It wasn't until the Disney era that she did and when we were watching the movie, each time she, Harrison, or Mark appeared, two thousand people just roared. I knew immediately that that's what they want from the franchise. It was like a soap opera where the characters come back from the dead. That was when we were like, "This is just never going to end."

One aspect of the original trilogy that Abrams wanted to get back to was to work in as much in the way of physical effects as would be possible without relying entirely on CGI. In many ways, it allowed for more of a connection between director and actors. The decision was also made that production would switch back to film rather than shooting digitally, which Lucas had heralded during the prequel trilogy.

KATHLEEN KENNEDY
Disney was always incredibly supportive of whatever format we chose, and shooting on film was something we decided right up front. It's something J.J. wanted to do; it's something director of photography Dan Mindel wanted to do; and we did the same thing, almost identically, on *Episode VIII*.

J.J. ABRAMS
Many of the innovations that we used were often steps backwards, using tangible tactile physical effects, where we could have used digital postproduction effects. What's incredible is that the technology that has progressed in physical effects is extraordinary.

KATHLEEN KENNEDY
One of the things that was so important to J.J. was that everything feel real. Part of that is having grown up with something that you felt was so real, and then when you get to 2015, you look at it and go, "Oh, you can kind of tell that's plywood." [laughs] So we have to step back and ask, What does "real" mean anymore? And how do you recapture a feeling when the execution has to be updated? That was a very interesting challenge. Even to the extent of looking at the actual plans of the Millennium Falcon . . . there were certain things we had to take inspiration from and then do differently, but anyone who knew the Millennium Falcon would not question that when Han Solo

walks back inside that ship, you are, in fact, in the Millennium Falcon. And when Harrison [Ford] walked into it, he looked around and said, "Oh, my God, it looks better than I remember!" That was an interesting, constant conversation with everybody in the art department, and it also affected the way everything was photographed and lit. [Employing] all of that new technology, and yet finding that familiarity and authenticity again, ended up to be more challenging than we thought.

MARK HAMILL

Here's the thing that I love: This is the first of the *Star Wars* films that's actually in the hands of someone who grew out of fandom, so he feels the way you feel in terms of wanting practical effects and real sets.

LAWRENCE KASDAN

I think the challenge had more to do with *Jedi* and the continuation of *IV, V,* and *VI.* This is *VII.* We were aware, we were respectful of the canon, but we really wanted to tell a story that interested us and delighted us, and we didn't really want any rules and parameters, particularly. We said we could do anything we want with this story—what would be the most fun thing to do on this page and the next page and the page after that? That was the guiding principle, more than the canon or anything that had come before.

J.J. ABRAMS

As this was developed, a lot of names came and went, and some names stuck. I remember when we wrote down "BB-8," it was the first and only name that droid ever had, but we called him BB-8 and still do. Rey and Finn and Poe went through many iterations. Kylo Ren was Kylo Ren fairly early on, and there was sort of backstory, and Maz Kanata I think was always Maz Kanata.

LAWRENCE KASDAN

As far as influences, all the movies of Akira Kurosawa have influenced me throughout my career. That's because he was sort of the Shakespeare of cinema. He did comedies, he did action films, he did Shakespearean drama, and all of life is contained in each one of his films. *Seven Samurai* may be the greatest film ever made. It's a personal drama, it's an action picture. So when J.J. and I were working, we kept referring to that.

And then we would talk about the great American movies that we loved, things that had influenced the first *Star Wars*: Howard Hawks, John Ford, all the Flash Gordons. When George made *A New Hope,* he was influenced very much by Kurosawa and by *Flash Gordon* and by *Wizard of Oz.* I think that all those movies, you can feel them in *A New Hope,* and everything that was in *A New Hope* has come down through the movies, to this day.

J.J. ABRAMS

What I really wanted to do was embrace a feeling more than a particular aesthetic. [It was] the feeling that I felt when I saw *Star Wars* for the first time; there was a scope and a scale and an authenticity to those early movies. When you looked at the gorgeous lighting in *Empire Strikes Back,* or the scenes in the ice fields of Hoth, or in the desert with the diffusion on Threepio when they shot in Tunisia for Tatooine; or if you looked at the forest of Endor, you knew you were in real places. And it gave you license, as a viewer, to let go and be in a real place, and it made all the other locations feel real.

JOHN BOYEGA

Every day you had a new set that's actually there. Obviously, we're using practical effects and it's insane to be in the *Star Wars* universe. This is the closest I'm ever going to be to being a real space traveler, and it's kind of insane to be a part of that.

J.J. ABRAMS

Part of it was location shooting, making sure that we were on actual sets and builds and locations wherever possible. The ability to shoot actual locations—in Abu Dhabi, or in the forests of Wales, or on [Skellig Michael] in Ireland, or getting plates in Iceland—was enormous. And part of it was embracing and encouraging the unexpected. Whether it's atmosphere or natural light, it's embracing the things that you sometimes desperately try to re-create in post, where you can spend a lot of time trying to make something that nature is often giving you for free.

DAISY RIDLEY

To be in Ireland was very exciting. The approach to Skellig was unlike anything I'd ever seen. First of all, I'd never been in a helicopter before, and it's just unbelievable. The pilot was like, "Someone's paid off the man upstairs," because the weather was stunning. It's just one of the most amazing places I've ever been. But it's tough—those steps were many. But it's weird, people are like, "Ooh, did you have to walk up those stairs a lot?" Colin, our incredible Steadicam operator, was walking backwards up the stairs with like, a hundred-pound camera. The whole thing was pretty awe-inspiring. And I was sick on the last day, so I was kind of feeling a bit awful. But it kind of helped with the emotion.

Back in April 2015, one of the true highlights of the Star Wars *Celebration held in Anaheim, California, was the unveiling of the second teaser trailer for* The Force Awakens. *Everyone involved with the film admits that they were nervous before it was screened, and that they were blown away by the response that it received, not only from the gathered fans, but from online viewers from around the world.*

KATHLEEN KENNEDY

The second teaser is probably one of the more nerve-wracking things we had to do, because we put something out that begins to represent the movie we're making and we don't know exactly what the reaction is going to be.

J.J. ABRAMS

Here's the thing: I was holding my breath for what felt like weeks leading up to our second teaser. When it was over, the sound that came from that space was almost a physical thing that I felt we were being pushed over with. It was incredible and I am so grateful that everyone was there.

KATHLEEN KENNEDY

We had reached a point where we could share something like this with twenty-three countries at the same time. You want to have them all in the room with you at once, but to be able to get a sense of how this is playing—and we looked at some of the fan reactions online—is really incredible. And it's incredible that we can connect people in that way, and *Star Wars* does that on a level that almost nothing else does. And then there was the escalation of screaming in that moment when Harrison says, "Chewie, we're home." The place just went absolutely insane.

OSCAR ISAAC

Everyone was breathing like one organism. We were all just on pins and needles. It was almost like a religious experience. It brought me to tears. My heart was just thumping, but not out of nervousness. Just out of the energy of the place.

SIMON KINBERG

There was an immense amount of relief and joy, because everything that Lucasfilm is doing, whether it's *Episode VII*, the animated show *Rebels*, or the stand-alone movie I was writing and producing, it's all made with a very genuine love for the material. Much more than anything else I've ever seen, and I've worked in lots of different universes. With the Lucasfilm group, called the Story Group, the people that work most closely on building the movies from the ground up, there is an immense amount of love and reverence for *Star Wars*. So unveiling the first real material to the most hardcore fans was nerve-wracking for everybody.

JOHN BOYEGA

As a group, with *Star Wars* fans there is always a feeling of hope and it's something that we saw there. Everyone just had a feeling of, "*Star Wars* is back."

OSCAR ISAAC

Mark Hamill said it best when he called it "family." It really does feel like we're part of a huge family. And it is about family, ultimately. The stories are about family. There's that Luke moment in *Return of the Jedi* where your father, who's this godlike thing and intimidating, is someone that you suddenly realize is just a vulnerable man. So I think the biggest thing about these movies is that it connects to the feeling of family.

DAISY RIDLEY

And finding your place within the world. When Luke starts out, he has no idea where he's going to end up, and because of what he does, he becomes this kind of reverential man in the universe. And it feels like that for us, I guess.

JOHN BOYEGA

The best sci-fi has a fantastic human story wrapped around in things like Force-sensitive Sith and Jedi, but it's something cool that everyone can relate to.

DAISY RIDLEY

The thing in life, which is sad, is that it's usually a bad thing that unites people. So to be part of something amazing that unites people of all ages, genders, races, all languages . . . it feels incredible to be a part of that.

As to the story of The Force Awakens *itself, Abrams's working method as a writer/director is to continue changing the story throughout filming and post, often radically reworking the original narrative in the process. In the case of Episode VII, the final narrative was not solidified until just before the film's release in December 2015. The end result was a story that was radically different than the one they started with.*

RAY MORTON

In the initial Abrams/Kasdan drafts, the story reportedly began with scavenger Rey discovering Luke Skywalker's old lightsaber—the one he lost when Vader chopped off his hand in the climax of *The Empire Strikes Back*. This blue-bladed lightsaber was last seen tumbling down into the airshaft beneath Cloud City, presumably to be ejected out of a vent and into the gas void of Bespin. The early scripts of *TFA* reveal that the saber has been floating around in space for the past three decades, still attached to Luke's severed hand (yes, you read that right), until it lands on Jakku, where it is found by Rey. After realizing what she has found, Rey and ex-stormtrooper Finn set out to return the saber to Luke. They start by seeking out Han Solo, who has returned to smuggling and has to be persuaded to accompany them on their quest to find Luke. Their search brings them into contact with Leia and the Resistance and brings them to the attention of Kylo Ren, who is determined to find Luke and kill him. In the end, after much *Star Wars*-ing, Rey finally meets Luke and returns his lightsaber to him, which will hopefully inspire him to return to save the galaxy in the next movie.

In the movie as finally released, it is not the discovery of Luke's lightsaber that sets the journey in motion, but Rey crossing paths with BB-8 that gets things rolling. She bumps into Han accidentally and comes across Luke's lightsaber in the middle of the movie, also accidentally. There is no active search for Luke, just a lot of running around trying to avoid being captured and killed by Ren. In the end, Rey finally finds Luke in a brief coda, after being given his location by a previously comatose R2, who just happens to wake up at the end of the movie and give Rey a map to Luke's location.

Abrams's habit of reworking-on-the-fly created a number of story-related problems: there's seemingly an entire trilogy missing between the original series and this one: at the end of Return of the Jedi, *the Emperor is dead and the Empire has been defeated; Han and Leia become a couple; and Luke becomes a Jedi. At the start of* The Force Awakens, *a new fascist entity called the First Order appears to be ruling the galaxy. There's a new evil ruler who calls himself Supreme Leader Snoke. Han and Leia have had a child and have broken up. Han and Leia's child has turned evil. Luke has failed as a Jedi and gone into hiding.*

RAY MORTON

Rey and Finn just happen to stumble across the *Falcon*, which just happens to be parked in a junkyard on Jakku. Despite being parked in the junkyard for what appears to be a very long time, the *Falcon* just happens to be in perfect working condition. Soon after fleeing Jakku in the *Falcon,* Rey and Finn just happen to bump into Han and Chewie almost immediately—once again, the *Star Wars* galaxy just seems to be getting smaller and smaller. Han takes Rey to Maz's bar, where Luke's lightsaber just happens to be stored (it is never explained how it got there). And, luckily, it just happens to have some sort of magic attraction to Rey that convinces Maz to turn it over to her. In the end, Rey does not find Luke as the result of any searching efforts on her part, but because R2, who knows where Luke is but has been inexplicably comatose throughout the film, just happens to wake up and provide Rey with Luke's location. R2 does not wake up as the result of any action or effort by the other characters in the movie, but simply—it seems—because it's the end of the movie.

The movie doesn't have much of a plot. Instead, the narrative is a collection of subplots (some of which pay off and some of which don't) and therefore never builds to a grand climax the way a more unified narrative would. *The Force Awakens* is a very energetic picture—there's a lot of action in the film and it's constant. However, most of the action is just the characters frantically running around. There's a distinct lack of memorable action set pieces (especially in comparison to the original trilogy, which is packed with them). All of the running around eventually becomes exhausting—*The Force Awakens* is a frenetic film, but it's never really an engaging one.

PETER HOLMSTROM

The film ends up being a sad remake of *A New Hope*. No character arcs in an emotional sense, and as such, the film feels like one long first act. I saw the film at a seven-movie marathon, following a showing of Lucas's original six films, and I was just floored by the utter lack of imagination by the part of Lucasfilm on *Episode VII*. The story was derivative, and without stakes or consequences. No one really explains why any of the characters stick around beyond the coincidences that lead them there. What is the Resistance and the First Order? Why do they want to kill each other? Rey begins the tale by wanting to go back to Jakku, and ends with wanting to go back to Jakku. Finn—who for some odd reason that's never explained, has an existential crisis in a battle—finds and obsesses over Rey at minute 15, and by the end of the film is still obsessing over Rey. Every planet in the film is a carbon-copy to the films from the original—so why even bother changing them? The cantina sequence from *Star Wars* spurred imaginations and spin-off stories for over thirty years, while the blobs of aliens from Maz's "castle" were quickly forgotten. Which can be said for the movie too.

RAY MORTON

The saga's original characters are not served well in this story. *The Force Awakens*'s primary new characters fare better: Rey has all the makings of a strong protagonist and hero—she's likable, resourceful, resilient, and talented. My only quibble is she's too talented in that she's good at everything: scavenging, flying, fighting, lightsabering, and so on. She's a Swiss Army knife of a character to the point where it starts to become a little unbelievable. Still, Daisy Ridley does an excellent job portraying a young woman coming face-to-face with the fact that there is much more to her than anyone—herself included—imagined. The mystery of her parentage is a good starting point for a potential trilogy-spanning arc.

Finn has the potential to be a great hero—a stormtrooper who quits the First Order's evil army and becomes a rebel is a terrific setup for a character. Unfortunately, once Finn is introduced, nothing is done with him. He follows Rey around like a puppy dog and that's about it. The writers have so little idea what to do with him that at the end they literally knock him unconscious to get him off-screen and then he stays that way for the rest of the picture. John Boyega is appealing in the role—one only wishes he had something to do.

One of the reasons Finn has so little to do is that much of his story function was given to Poe Dameron. As is well known, Dameron was supposed to die early on in *TFA*—the idea was to set him up as the film's apparent hero, then surprise the audience by killing him off, and then to eventually have Finn step up into the role of hero. But the casting of Oscar Isaac to play Poe changed all that. The actor has so much charisma and swagger in the role that the filmmakers quickly realized that it would be a big mistake to lose him. So, after his death had already been filmed, Poe was reintroduced later in the film and his disappearance in the middle papered over with some extremely clumsy exposition. Poe goes on to become the Resistance's lead pilot in the attack on Starkiller Base as a combination of Luke Skywalker and Han Solo.

However, not all of the new characters are successful: Maz Kanata is an annoying Yoda knock-off—an ancient, diminutive alien who is in touch with the Force and an unending font of wisdom and exposition. Supreme Leader Snoke is another knock-off—this one of the Emperor. He's big and mean and ugly, but we're never told who he is, where he comes from, what his connection to the Empire is, why he chose to resurrect it, and where he got the seemingly endless resources he has to do so. The movie wants us to be afraid of him, but it's hard when we have no idea who he is. General Hux is a standard-issue Imperial (excuse me, First Order) martinet. Unfortunately, Domhnall Gleeson plays him in such an exaggerated and campy fashion that Hux comes across as the SNL parody of himself.

On a conceptual level, Kylo Ren is by far the worst character in *TFA* and the entire sequel trilogy. It's bad enough that he is Ben Solo, the son of Leia and Han who has turned evil, which is the most boringly predictable bad fanfic notion ever. But the decision to make the character a literal Darth Vader wannabe (to the point where he even wears a completely unnecessary mask that causes him to breathe funny) is an even more ridiculous idea. The only thing that keeps the character from being laughed off the screen is the sincere and committed performance of Adam Driver as Kylo, which gives Ren way more credibility than such a ludicrous personage deserves. However, even Driver's solid acting cannot save the character when the writers have him kill Han Solo, his own father. This is such a miserable, unmotivated, pointless act and such an ignoble end for such a beloved character that from that moment on, it is impossible to give a fuck about Kylo Ren.

PETER HOLMSTROM

Han's death was sad, and not in a good way. There's a fundamental problem with the script in that Han's death matters to no one but Kylo Ren. Kylo's pretty much the only one with any emotional arc in the film, which is, "I'm bad, but conflicted," to "I'm bad, let me prove it, Daddy." Obi-Wan's death in the original *Star Wars* marks the low point for every single character in that film. The existential death for every single character we've known up until that point. Luke's mentor is killed, Leia's mission has failed, Han's source of income that's going to save his life is gone, R2's mission is ended, and Obi-Wan's obviously dead. Here—Han's death matters to exactly . . . one person. Kylo Ren. Finn called him "Solo" once or twice, Rey turned down Han's job offer, and Leia divorced his ass years before. While Chewie should've gone down in a hail of bullets—he instead gives a halfhearted cry and moves on.

Star Wars Episode VII: The Force Awakens *was in production between March and November 2014. Produced at a budget of $245 million, it grossed over $2 billion at the global box office. The reviews were extremely positive for the most part, and for many people, the film served as a palate cleanser for the prequel trilogy.*

RAY MORTON

In the end, Abrams gave Disney what it wanted—*The Force Awakens* definitely looks and feels like a *Star Wars* movie. Which is ultimately its biggest problem. The movie is frequently knocked for being a scene-by-scene remake of *Episode IV*, something I have never felt it was. However, it is undeniably a rehash: every element in the piece—every story element, every location, every bit of costuming and production design—is recycled from one of the films in the original trilogy. We have another empire, another rebellion, another lowly hero from another desert planet, another Sith, another Death Star (in the guise of Starkiller Base), another cute little robot carrying important info, and so on and so on. There is nothing fresh or original or new in the picture. When you make a movie that depends almost entirely on engaging the audience by recalling elements from earlier movies, you run the risk of reminding viewers of how much they liked those films and deciding they'd rather go back and watch them than sit through your film. I felt that way most of the time while I was watching *The Force Awakens*.

JONATHAN RINZLER

[*The Force Awakens* and *Rogue One*] are just not my cup of tea. They didn't strike me as being at all in the tradition of *Star Wars*, personally. But also, I was probably too close to the behind-the-scenes, and I had a bad taste in my mouth. I might feel differently if I saw them again. Like I say, many people liked *Rogue One* better than any of the other *Star Wars* films—and they have a right to their opinion. I don't want to say, "You can't have that opinion, what's wrong with you?" You have a right to your opinion and more power to you.

ALAN DEAN FOSTER
(author, *The Force Awakens* novelization)

It feels like *Star Wars*. You may disagree with this plot point or that plot point; "I'd do this instead of that" or "I don't like this as opposed to that." But the spirit is there and you walk out of the theater thinking, "That was *Star Wars*." I enjoyed it and can go pick it apart with my friends.

TODD FISHER

I remember Carrie and I sitting at the screening of *The Force Awakens* and it was déjà vu: she squeezed my hand just like she did during the first *Star Wars*. But in that film when the spaceship flew over, you felt like, "Okay, that's done." So then, when she goes back to make *The Force Awakens*, at that moment she knew that she and Princess Leia would go on forever. That was when she started to accept it; it didn't happen until *Star Wars: Episode VII*.

BRIAN JAY JONES

George Lucas cannot win for losing. He's done with the prequels and the day before *The Force Awakens* comes out, the fans are like, "George Lucas needs to keep his hands off of *Star Wars*. Look at Jar Jar Binks, look at everything that's happened. The prequels are just awful!" Then *The Force Awakens* comes out and the fans are like, "They need to bring George Lucas back." Then *Last Jedi* comes out and everyone's saying things like there's rumors Lucas is involved with the next movie. It's like everybody's desperately trying to fill this narrative out regarding Lucas's involvement. But I just love that so many people looked at him as the shittiest thing that happened to *Star Wars* until *The Force Awakens* came out.

PETER HOLMSTROM

The one silver lining of the sequel trilogy and the Disney acquisition is, it got people to revisit and reevaluate the career of George Lucas. The classic example of the artist who only became renowned after their death can be somewhat applied here. George was gone, and people suddenly realized, "Oh, *Willow* is fantastic! The prequels are great! *The Clone Wars* is epic!" I'm not sure we would've had this renewed appreciation for the man in his lifetime if not for this.

J.J. ABRAMS

I knew this movie needed to feel like it was part of a continuum, and part of it was a gut feeling of what makes a *Star Wars* movie a *Star Wars* movie. Films have been trying to do what George did since *Star Wars* came out, and this was an incredible opportunity because we were actually inheriting the legacy of *Star Wars*. The question became, What do we embrace and what do we let go of? And for certain elements—like the Millennium Falcon, an X-Wing, a TIE Fighter, or a Star Destroyer—that were so gloriously associated with this world, it felt criminal to not use them. And when you look at what Ralph McQuarrie did, and certainly Joe Johnston and others, there was a kind of unbelievable simplicity. When you look at a triangular Star Destroyer, or the sphere and two planes of a TIE Fighter, or the literal "X" of an X-Wing, there was such a "primary color" approach to some of these things, which were then rendered and executed in such incredible detail. The wear and tear and the sense of practicality to these fanciful designs were really inspiring.

So we knew that going forward we needed to embrace these iconic pieces of the puzzle, and yet we needed to adjust them in ways that made them new again. Sometimes the feeling you wanted to [evoke] wouldn't be effective if [you were] literally re-creating it as it was. Some things needed to be embellished; you want to see some adjustments, some changes, some advances for things to be believable in a story taking place nearly forty years after the first movie. With [costume designer] Michael Kaplan, there was an enormous amount of work to be done on costumes for characters that no one had ever seen before. And, of course, they all needed to be unique and stand out and be different from each other. The design of the movie—from locations to set design to props and wardrobe—all of it, even the casting of it, was about, What feels right? What feels like it is the *Star Wars* movie that's relevant for now?

14

REY OF HOPE: *THE LAST JEDI*

"This is not going to go the way you think."

Once Disney had acquired Lucasfilm, the engine that initially drove the *Star Wars* franchise was a new trilogy, episodes of which would be released two years apart from each other. But then, the idea was that a new stand-alone anthology film would be released in between new "episodes," meaning that every year a new *Star Wars* film would be released to theaters, redolent of the model that had been so successful for Marvel. The first of these—released between *Episode VII: The Force Awakens* and *Episode VIII: The Last Jedi*, was 2016's *Rogue One*, which many consider the best *Star Wars* film since *The Empire Strikes Back*. Despite a complicated production that resulted in director Gareth Edwards being sidelined by *The Bourne Identity*'s Tony Gilroy, who supervised extensive reshooting, it's arguably one of the best and most engaging films in the series.

The film is from a screenplay by Chris Weitz and Tony Gilroy, based on a story by John Knoll and Gary Whitta. Visual effects legend Knoll was the one who first conceived of the idea: Wouldn't it be interesting to know how the Rebels got their hands on the Death Star plans in the original film? *Rogue One* is an extension of that idea and would be the first feature film set in the *Star Wars* universe to not star a Jedi, or a member of the Skywalker lineage (or, regrettably, feature a title crawl, which is as jarring as the Bond movies not having a gun barrel sequence). Set just prior to the events of *Episode IV: A New Hope*, the focus is on a group of Rebels who are able to obtain the plans to the Death Star that would play so integral a role in that film. Produced at a cost of $200 million, it grossed a little over $1 billion. Surprisingly, despite a largely glowing critical and fan reception, Disney had expected more from its box-office receipts and was particularly disappointed at the performance of the film's toy line, which they felt underperformed at retail.

Rogue One was followed by *The Last Jedi*, the second film in the new *Star Wars* sequel series and the penultimate installment of the so-called Skywalker Saga. The film, directed by iconoclastic director Rian Johnson (*Looper*, *Brick*,

Knives Out), proved to be one of the most polarizing entries in the saga. Many fans lauded its risky, original take on a hermit Luke who has abandoned the Jedi ways along with its slick photography redolent of *The Empire Strikes Back*, including a tour de force sequence in which Luke confronts Kylo Ren in a holographic lightsaber fight. It also had surprising twists like the assassination of Supreme Leader Snoke and a revelation of Rey's true lineage (a reveal that would be revisited and retconned sadly in Abrams's follow-up). Detractors knocked the film's slow-speed space chase and lethargic Canto Bight diversion, which separated Finn from Rey for most of the film, and lambasted Luke's decision to abandon his friends and go into self-exile after almost killing Ben Solo, thus inadvertently creating Kylo Ren.

With *Episode VIII*, Lucasfilm's plan had always been to hire a different writer/director to create each episode of the new trilogy, especially after butting heads with Abrams on the first film. Before *The Force Awakens* had even finished shooting, Rian Johnson was brought on board to begin developing the new entry.

RIAN JOHNSON
(writer/director, *The Last Jedi*)

I had had a couple of general meetings with Kathy Kennedy after she stepped in and started running Lucasfilm. But they were very general meetings, and I didn't think that I was actually in the running for anything. And then at some point, I came in for what I thought was another just how-you-been, what-are-you-working-on meeting, and she felt out whether I would be interested in doing this. My jaw hit the floor. And I took some time to think about it. It was a big decision, actually. On one hand, it was something that I felt was a dream offer. On the other hand, it was a big life-changing deal. I wanted to make sure it was something that was going to be a good experience, and it really was. It's the second movie in the trilogy and I think we've been kind of trained to expect it'll be a little darker and obviously it looks a little darker. I loved the tone of the original films, which J.J. also captured in *The Force Awakens*. First and foremost, we were trying to make it feel like a *Star Wars* movie. That means you have the intensity and you've got the opera, but it also means that it makes you come out of the theater wanting to run in your backyard, grab your spaceship toys, and make them fly around. That's a key ingredient to it. So we go to some intense places in the movie, but I hope also it's fun.

LAURA DERN
(actress, "Vice Admiral Holdo")

And just to add to that, what Rian spoke to, that he does so beautifully, was describing the intimacy of discovering each character's conflict, which is just extraordinary. Given the enormity of the cast, that he gave us that in the experience of the workplace, and it was shocking, and Oscar and I always talked about just how stunned we were that we were in such a massive environment and did feel like we were making an indie movie. You were always encouraged to try things and explore character, and explore this duality of the light and the dark within characters, the movie speaks to so beautifully. Not just that there are alternative universes, but that that lies within, which seems to be the place where George Lucas first started the mythology. It's just so brilliant.

RIAN JOHNSON

One of the things I was the most afraid of coming into the writing process was that I'm a very slow writer. I will take years just thinking about something and working it out. And I knew I couldn't do that with this movie. I was afraid I would just go into a writer's hole and be on page three of the script with a month to go. So I moved up to San Francisco for a few months to write and come up with a story. A few times a week I would come in to Lucasfilm, sit down with the wonderful folks in the Story Group—Kiri Hart and her whole team—and I would just put everything up on the whiteboard that I was thinking of. And we would just talk through it. That wasn't the writing process as we weren't working out the story in the room, but just being able to come in and bounce stuff off of everyone and ask if it feels right to them was helpful. It made the whole writing process feel like collaborative play. That took a lot of pressure off. We would also watch dailies that were coming in from *Episode VII*. At that point, it was just the script and the dailies we were seeing. It was probably really healthy in terms of thinking about where the story goes next; it was entirely just based on our reactions to it, as opposed to based on the phenomenon that it would become or the cultural reaction to it. It was just a very personal idea of what do we connect with about these characters, where did they go next. And what would be the hardest thing for each of them to come up against? And once I got to a place where I had something for each one of them that made sense, I started drawing it out into a story. So, it's kind of like eating an elephant. You just do it one bite at a time.

After consulting with Abrams, Johnson began writing his screenplay. His primary mission was to pick up the many loose threads Abrams had left dangling in The Force Awakens *and weave them into an exciting continuation. What makes it especially interesting is that one of the first big creative choices Johnson made was to jettison most of those threads.*

RIAN JOHNSON

I knew that the bigness and the epic sense and all of that would sort itself out. I knew that would just naturally happen, because once we started playing with these toys, we came up with cool battles and cool stuff. What I needed to really work about it were the characters and the story. That was really the starting point of the whole thing. So I was never really worried about how we were going to make this big and cool. I was just worried about how are we going to develop these characters. Because it's the middle chapter of a trilogy, this is the one where we have to slow down a little and dig into everybody a little bit more. That's really where I put most of the focus. Then the rest of it was really like playing with a toy set.

RAY MORTON

(senior editor, *Script* magazine)

At the conclusion of *The Force Awakens,* Finn is placed into medical stasis after falling into a coma and we are left wondering if he will ever wake up and, if he does, how will he be changed or altered by his experience. Johnson develops none of this—at the start of his script, Finn just nonchalantly wakes up from his coma and carries on as if nothing happened. *TFA* ends with an earnest Rey dramatically holding Luke's lightsaber out to him as Luke contemplates whether or not to take it. We are left wondering if he will and, if he does, what will happen, with us fully expecting that if he does, it will signify his intention to return to fight the good fight. In Johnson's script, Luke accepts the saber and then—blithely tosses it away.

Much is made in *TFA* of Kylo Ren's desire to model himself after Darth Vader, to the point where he wears a Vader-like mask that he has no actual need for—a notion I thought was ridiculous, but that the film took very seriously. Apparently, Johnson felt as I do, because he has Supreme Leader Snoke ridicule Kylo for wearing such a silly thing and tells him to get rid of it, after which he has Kylo smash it to pieces. Also, *TFA* spends a great deal of time building Snoke up as the new trilogy's big bad. Johnson has Kylo kill him off in the middle of the movie. *TFA* makes much of the mystery of who Rey's parents are, leading us to expect that there will be a big revelation of some sort, with most betting that her great Force-sensitivity would mean she was the offspring of either Luke or Leia. In Johnson's script, Rey's parents are dismissed as nobodies.

The almost off-handed way in which Johnson disposes of these significant plot points—and how his doing so did not have a major impact on the overall narrative—makes it clear that there was no master plan for this new trilogy. No overall story that Disney or Lucasfilm or the films' creators were trying to tell. They were literally making it up as they went along. Which is rather extraordinary. When George Lucas decided to transform Star Wars *into a trilogy, he did not have all of the individual details for the two subsequent films worked out, but he knew basically where the story was headed and how it was going to end. The same was true when he made the prequel trilogy. This was not the case with the creators of the sequels. In making* The Force Awakens, *it seems that J.J. Abrams's goal was to craft a solid jumping-off point for a saga without knowing just what that saga was to be. This freed Johnson up to take the story off into new directions of his own, and that he did. In writing his screenplay, Johnson made a concerted effort to do something new and different with the material, rather than repeat the beats of the original trilogy's greatest hits as Abrams had done. The result was the smartest, most thoughtful, and most coherent narrative in the new trilogy.*

RAY MORTON

And the best movie. In addition to having the strongest story, *The Last Jedi* is the best designed, shot, and edited of the three *Star Wars* sequels. It's also the most entertaining—there's a lot of well-crafted action in the film, as well as a generous helping of good humor. Unlike *The Force Awakens*, which is mostly just a lot of frantic running around, *The Last Jedi* contains several truly memorable sequences, including Leia's Force-powered flight through space; the ramming of the Dreadnought starship; Rey and Kylo's battle with Snoke's guards in the Supreme Leader's throne room; and Luke's showdown with Ren in the finale on the salt planet Crait. However, just because *The Last Jedi* is the best of the sequels and contains so many strong elements, doesn't make it a satisfying film. The movie has a lot of problems—a lot of problems. And they begin with Luke Skywalker.

In *The Last Jedi*, Luke is depicted as an embittered exile who ran away to a remote island when one of his pupils went bad. Granted, it was Abrams who developed this backstory for Luke and put him on that island, but Johnson took these not-so-hot ideas and ran with them. In Johnson's script, we learn that the pupil who went bad was his own nephew, Ben Solo. Not only that, but one of the main reasons Ben turned evil was because Luke tried to kill him. The script explains that Luke became aware that Snoke was reaching out to Ben and attempting to corrupt him. (Again—who is Snoke? How is he aware of Ben? Explanations would have been so helpful.) Sensing Ben would go bad, Luke decided to kill him. Although Luke only entertained this murderous notion for a brief moment, it was long enough for Ben to discern his intention and strike back. Angry and hurt, Ben ran away, apprenticed himself to Snoke, and became Kylo Ren. All of this caused Luke to become so angry at himself and at the Jedi (I'm not sure how any of this is the Jedi's fault, but whatever) that he turned his back on the galaxy and went into hiding.

So, The Last Jedi tells us that the virtuous, idealistic farm boy, who became a Jedi and whose unwavering faith in his fallen father's innate goodness was so strong that it redeemed his dad from the dark side, has lost his faith, has become an attempted murderer, and created the third-worst villain ever in the history of the galaxy. Instead of sticking around to help save the galaxy from the monster he created, Luke abandoned his responsibilities and his civilization and ran away to become a bitter hermit who hates the tradition he once embraced and still refuses to help right his wrong even after millions have died and the galaxy is teetering on the edge of eternal darkness.

RAY MORTON

This is not the Luke we came to know in the original trilogy, nor is it a logical development of Luke's character. For some, including Mark Hamill, it was a betrayal of that character. Even if you don't feel that strongly about it, it is certainly a strangely sour and unpersuasive twist given to a character who neither needed it nor deserved it. And it only reinforces the deeply flawed core premise of the entire sequel trilogy—that the heroes of the original trilogy were all failures. Johnson does give Luke one gloriously heroic moment when he finally emerges from exile to face off against Kylo with an awesome display of Jedi power. This is the moment we've all been waiting for since Luke took his first step into a larger world way back in 1977—the moment when Luke Skywalker finally becomes the biggest, most incredible, most badass Jedi of all time. And it's a really great sequence until . . .

. . . Johnson pulls the rug out from Luke and all of us by revealing that it's all just a trick. Luke hasn't come out of exile—he's still hiding out on his craggy Irish island. And he isn't using his awesome Jedi powers, he's just using the Force to project an imaginary display of Jedi powers. So, it's all a joke—a joke that accomplishes nothing except to distract Ren for a few minutes. And then what does Luke do for a follow-up? He dies (I'm still not sure why projecting an image of himself takes so much out of Luke that it kills him, but apparently it does). It's not clear what dramatic point Luke's death is supposed to make or what dramatic purpose it is supposed to serve. But die Luke does—not as a hero, but hiding behind an imaginary image of one. Mark Hamill does a fine job of interpreting this material, but it was a depressing and wrong way to go with the character and it's a fatal flaw in the film.

MARK HAMILL

I don't think any line in the script epitomized my reaction more than "This is not going to go the way you think." And Rian pushed me out of my comfort zone, as if I weren't as intimidated and terrified to begin with, but I'm grateful, because you have to trust someone and he was the only Obi-Wan available to me, not only in my choices as an actor, but my choices in sock wear. Because—well, I was so embarrassed. I looked at my drab black socks and I said, "Curse you, Rian Johnson, I'll get my revenge!"

Rian came out to my house to discuss the script, and we spent several hours chatting, and I showed him TV shows . . . you know, important things. One reason I loved *Rogue One* and the prequels is because I wasn't in them. I told Rian we had a beginning, middle, and end in the original trilogy, and I don't want to tempt fate. Truth be known, Rian, I'm terrified. Know what he said? "I'm terrified, too." And that's a director I can love. A lot of times you can categorize director's films. But his films are all so original and ambitious. In this experience, he's rocketed to the top of my favorite directors of all time. He was my seeing-eye dog, and I knew if Rian was happy, I was happy. I turned my performance over to him. I know if he was satisfied, we got it right.

RAY MORTON

Johnson introduced a really interesting theme into *The Last Jedi*—the need for us to let go of the past so we can move forward into the future. It's an intriguing notion on its own, as well as an interesting meta-message (whether it was intended or not) for *Star Wars* fans and creators. Unfortunately, Johnson chose to dramatize this idea by continuing to dump on what has come before, especially the Jedi, by having Luke openly (and continuously) express his scorn of and disgust with the Order—essentially writing all the Jedi off as arrogant screw-ups and saying the Order must die.

The Force is given all sorts of new capabilities in the sequels (few of which are ever properly explained). Johnson gave it an interesting new wrinkle in his narrative's other major plotline—Kylo Ren's attempts to lure Rey to the dark side. In Johnson's script, Ren and Rey now have the ability to use the Force to create a psychic link with one another, which Johnson visualizes by having both of them appear to be in the same place, even though they are actually in vastly different locations. It's a logical extension of the Force and generates some striking staging and intercutting whenever the two attempt to communicate with one another.

Unfortunately, Johnson's invention does not extend to the core material of this plotline, which is just a retread of the Luke/Vader narrative from the original trilogy—there's a good Jedi and a bad Sith; the Sith seeks to convert the Jedi; will the Jedi turn?; the Jedi believe the Sith still has good in him; will the Sith be redeemed? Ridley and Driver play these scenes for all they are worth, but we've seen this all before and it's just not as interesting the second time around. (Also, it's understandable why Luke wants to redeem Vader—the dude is his father—but it's never clear why Rey cares so much about redeeming Ren, since they have no connection to one another, apart from the fact that Kylo has been trying to kill her from the moment they met.)

RIAN JOHNSON

Rey, at the end of *The Force Awakens,* has been thrown into this big adventure and been sent on a mission to find Luke. She has a desire for connection to her past and some notion that there are answers there that she can get. I think she probably expects there are some answers about who she is, and that's really what she is on a quest to find out. Not just meaning who her parents are or where she comes from, but meaning what's her place in all of this? When she shows up on that island, there's part of her, and there's a big part of us, that expects that she's going to get that information from Luke.

DAISY RIDLEY
(actress, "Rey")

I mean, the biggest thing for me when I read the script, because you know, even though you're trying to avoid what people are saying, it's hard to, and because people responded well to John and me as a team, I was a bit nervous about not being a team so much in this one. So I think for me personally it was a challenge. The film was a challenge and I don't know what it was like for anyone else, but to be in a different combination of people—we're in different situations, we're with different people that we are learning about, we're meeting for the first time. It felt pretty different to me.

RIAN JOHNSON

Kylo Ren was the character I was the most excited about getting into and writing. In the first *Star Wars* films, Darth Vader was a great villain, but he was never someone you identified with. You identified with Luke's relationship to him. So, Vader was the monster. He was the scary father, and then he was the father you had to reconcile with. He was an outside force, especially in the context of these stories being about the transition from adolescence into adulthood. You're identifying with Luke and he's the one going through that transition, and Vader is something he essentially has to navigate to get there. Whereas with Kylo, it's almost like Rey and Kylo are two halves of the protagonist. Rey is the light, and Kylo is the dark. And with Kylo, again, this is all about the transition from adolescence into adulthood. Kylo is that anger of adolescence, and wanting to reject your parents, and wanting to break away, which, to some extent, all of us can identify with as much as we can identify with the hopeful Rey looking up at the stars from her planet.

ADAM DRIVER
(actor, "Kylo Ren")

I think definitely there's a competition and it's maybe yet to be discovered where that comes from. If anything, I think that's more of a testament to kind of what everyone has been saying of Rian's inability to not mine a character in every moment, which seems like an obvious thing, but he doesn't, so he knows that spectacle, it won't mean anything if you don't care about anything that's going on, which again, seems very obvious. It's a really hard thing to balance with this many moving parts in the scale of something like this. So I love playing those scenes. Rian slows the pace and there's not a moment that's taken for granted. It's always broken up into little pieces and the story in our mind comes first before an explosion.

RIAN JOHNSON

For Kylo, Snoke is an important character. He's the leader of the First Order. In *The Force Awakens*, you get just little glimpses of him through a hologram. In *The Last Jedi*, we wanted to actually meet Snoke and have a little more face time with him. He is a very powerful villain. He's the source of evil behind Kylo Ren. Kylo is a more complicated villain, so you need that very strong malevolent being that is just a bad guy sitting there. Snoke looks like a bad guy, and he's got evil intentions. You need the monster back there, especially if you're going to have your villain be a little more complex. So, that's who Snoke is. Andy Serkis plays him. It was my first time working with Andy, and it was my first time really working with a motion-capture character. Snoke is entirely CG, and it's built from Andy's mo-cap performance. Andy's extraordinary. For the longest time in the cut, we just left Andy in the mo-cap suit in there, because just seeing him perform was mesmerizing.

DAISY RIDLEY

We had the most incredible time on the island. It was very nerve-wracking going back. The first time I was kind of bumbling around, but coming back the second time I felt so much responsibility, because I felt like I should already know what I was doing.

RIAN JOHNSON

Rey has her expectation of Luke when she shows up at the island. But, the first thing I had to really figure out was what Luke's deal is. Why is he on that island? Because I know he's not a coward and I know he's not hiding. I know if he's there, he's taken himself out of the fight, and he must have a reason for doing that. What is that reason? That was the puzzle that I felt like I had to solve before I could start anything. And I worked and worked and thought and thought until finally, I got to something where I could put myself in his shoes. Now, let's see what happens when Rey comes into his life and messes everything up basically by showing up on his doorstep with a lightsaber.

RAY MORTON

Finn didn't have much to do in *The Force Awakens*. He has much more to do in this movie. The trade-off is he becomes a coward. Finn enters *The Last Jedi* near the start by finally waking up from the coma he was put into at the end of *TFA*. Soon after, the Resistance fleet is attacked and decimated by the First Order. Realizing the Resistance is not likely to survive much longer, Finn decides to split. This is a very puzzling and weirdly disrespectful spin to give a character who was originally designed to be a hero.

RIAN JOHNSON

I gave a lot of thought to what Finn's deal would be after *The Force Awakens*. His big action was leaving the First Order, but he never joins the Resistance. Finn never joins a side; he never does anything for ideological reasons. He just does it for personal ones. He's just trying to help his friend. In this film, he's going to have to be pushed into figuring out what he believes in and what he's fighting for at the end of the day. That seemed interesting to me. The character of Rose, who is played by Kelly Marie Tran, is a true believer in the Resistance. She is kind of idealistic, but she is also very practical. She's the one who really believes in the cause, and she's going to be the angel on his shoulder for Finn.

RAY MORTON

Finn is talked out of running away by Rose Tico, a Resistance maintenance worker who catches him trying to steal an escape pod. The two are eventually sent on a mission to the casino planet of Canto Bight to find a master codebreaker who can help the Resistance disable the tracking device the First Order is using to hunt down the Rebels. They aren't able to wrangle the codebreaker they originally came for, but they do meet up with DJ—a criminal codebreaker played in supremely louche fashion by Benicio Del Toro—who persuades them he can do the job. The team sneaks onto the First Order command ship to disable to tracking device, but DJ betrays them to the enemy before the device can be taken out. Finn and Rose escape and eventually join in a ground battle against the First Order. At one crucial point during the battle, Finn decides to sacrifice himself to save his comrades, but Rose—who, it is suggested, has fallen in love with Finn—rams his ship with her own to prevent him from doing this.

PETER HOLMSTROM
(cohost, *The Rebel & the Rogue* podcast)
The film ends with Rey/Kylo/Snoke's confrontation—and then there's the battle on the surface which is . . . odd. Finn's arc is there, choosing to sacrifice himself for the larger good, as is Rose's, choosing to sacrifice the all for the one. Which, like the best of emotional arcs, is the opposite place from where Finn and Rose started from. However, Rey vanishes, which is a shame. Yes, I know she's flying the *Falcon* and "pew pewing" all over the place, but it's too bad she doesn't do more.

RAY MORTON
To sum up, nothing Finn does in the story has the slightest impact on the outcome. Finn and Rose do not find the master codebreaker, they do not disable the tracking device, and Finn does not save the day by sacrificing himself (which, had he done so, would have provided a solid arc—from selfish coward to self-sacrificing hero, for him). So, although he has much more to do in this movie than he did in *TFA*, Finn's role is still entirely superfluous. First a coward and then irrelevant. Poor John Boyega.

Out of the new main characters, Poe fares the best. He has a great introduction in the film—taunting Hux during the opening battle. From there, his character is given some genuine development as the hotshot pilot gradually learns patience and responsibility as Leia grooms him to eventually become the Resistance's new leader. There's a strange and unnecessary bit where the impatient Poe decides to lead a mutiny against Resistance commanders he feels aren't making the right decisions, but Poe is able to overcome this weird hiccup and, in the end, begins to display the mature leadership qualities Leia has been nurturing in him.

RIAN JOHNSON
The theme of mentors runs through this whole series, and to me, it made a lot of sense that Leia would be that to Poe. If Leia is the general in charge of the Resistance, her ace pilot is Poe. He's a great *Star Wars* character in *The Force*

Awakens, but there's not a ton of conflict for him. You know who he is because he's an awesome *Star Wars* pilot. And that's perfect. And you love him from the get-go. But with this I wanted to dig in and push him a little more and put him in a tough spot to test his mettle a little bit. Poe and Leia are kind of parallel and very different, but the same way that Luke and Rey play off each other, Leia and Poe play off each other during the course of the film.

RAY MORTON

For some reason, most of Leia's role in the story is given to Laura Dern's Vice Admiral Holdo. In the script, Leia is injured and becomes comatose after Ren attacks her command ship and wipes out most of the Resistance's command team, including poor Admiral Ackbar. With Leia out of commission, Holdo takes over the leadership of the Resistance for the middle section of the movie and thus it is she that Poe mutinies against rather than Leia.

RIAN JOHNSON

Holdo is the other part of the triangle with Poe and Leia. So it's Poe, Leia, and Holdo. It was like watching old war films like *Twelve O'Clock High* and seeing that dynamic inside a small group of soldiers put under high pressure. Since Leia and Poe have such a tight relationship, I thought we needed someone for Poe to have a little more abrasion with. And enter Admiral Holdo. So, she comes in and shakes up that dynamic a little bit. In casting the part, I wanted someone who was going to bring a really unexpected energy to Holdo. I didn't want to have just a hard-ass admiral; I wanted someone who was going to be not quite what you would expect. Laura has a real humanity to her; even when she's being tough, she has a softness to her.

RAY MORTON

Leia recovers in time to put down Poe's mutiny and teach her errant flyboy a few valuable lessons about leading wisely. Later, Holdo sacrifices herself to destroy the First Order's command ship in order to give the rest of the Resistance time to escape. It's not clear why Holdo is in the story—Leia could have done everything she did and made it all more meaningful, since she is someone we have known and loved for a long time, whereas Holdo is a character who comes out of nowhere and who we have no investment in. The only logical assumption is that the filmmakers didn't want Leia to sacrifice herself since she was intended to have a large role in the final sequel, and so they had to bring in a surrogate Leia to take her place. As good a job as the great Laura Dern does playing Holdo, it's a shame the filmmakers didn't allow Leia to sacrifice herself, because—apart from the sad irony that Carrie Fisher passed away after filming on *The Last Jedi* was completed so wasn't able to play that significant role in *Episode IX* after all—it would have been the perfect heroic ending for her noble, committed character.

ALAN DEAN FOSTER
(author, *The Force Awakens* novelization)

I felt really bad for Laura Dern in *Episode VIII,* because she's a wonderful actor, she seems like a really nice gal, but I felt that she was miscast in that role. You needed somebody badass to look the part. Not somebody soft. I love her, and I love her acting, but she was just wrong for that role. Of course, it wouldn't have hurt if the role had been written logically and realistically. This business that some people seem to like of Laura Dern's character redeeming herself—really hard to do—by suddenly blasting into the Imperial fleet at lightspeed and blowing them all up. Well, we don't need starships anymore. If you can do that, get an old freighter, with AI or at least some computer controls, set it for hyperdrive, and you throw it into any ships you want. Nobody gets killed on this side. People don't think about those things when you're doing these films.

KELLY MARIE TRAN
(actress, "Rose Tico")

I think that something about Carrie that I really look up to is, and something I didn't realize until recently, was just how much courage it takes to truly be yourself when you're on a public platform or when possibly a lot of people will be looking at you, and she was so unapologetic and so openly herself and that is something that I am really trying to do, and it's hard. She will always be an icon as Leia but also as Carrie. What an example, you know? And I am so fortunate to have met her and I think that she will really live on forever.

RAY MORTON

Rose Tico is an interesting new addition to the cast of characters and she is well-played by Kelly Marie Tran who, unfortunately, was subject to some extraordinarily cruel online harassment by internet trolls in the wake of the film's release. The problem with Rose is that she is Finn's partner in his subplot and since that is ultimately superfluous, sadly, so is Rose.

Like *The Force Awakens,* *The Last Jedi* doesn't tell a single, unified tale. Instead, it presents a collection of subplots, which is a very common thing in modern blockbuster filmmaking. The problem with this is that a collection of subplots just does not have the dramatic focus that a single story does and so it's never really clear what the overall story is that the movie is trying to tell. Also, a film made up of subplots rather than one that has a strong central narrative lacks the dramatic momentum and build that a single storyline can generate. Therefore, although the film is packed with action and incident, it doesn't always hold our attention the way it should. Also, the movie goes on forever. The narrative reaches its climax when Holdo rams her ship into the Dreadnought, but then the movie continues for forty or so more minutes until it reaches a second climax when Luke squares off against Ren.

Although Johnson was able to incorporate a good deal of new material into his story, the script still recycles a lot of elements from the original trilogy. Apart from the entire dramatic thrust of the Ren/Rey subplot, the final battle on Crait is far too reminiscent of the opening battle of *The Empire Strikes Back*—Rebel fighters battling Imperial Walkers in the snow (yeah, I know Crait is supposed to be a salt planet, but visually it looks like a snow planet). And many of the Luke/Rey scenes feel like repeats of the scenes in *Empire* in which Yoda trains Luke. Apparently, anyone who flies the Millennium Falcon instantly becomes a badass daredevil pilot. No one ever just flies that ship normally. It must come with Solo drive. And I can't be the only one who—when Finn and Rose were sent to Canto Bight to find a shady character to help the Rebellion—was really expecting Billy Dee Williams to turn up and was a bit disappointed when they ran into Benicio Del Toro instead.

The fact that the makers of the sequels did not know where their story was going leads to a feeling of ennui that sets in about halfway through watching *The Last Jedi*. At this point, we realize we've been following this narrative for a movie and a half now and we have no idea what the actual story we're watching is or is about or where this all might be heading. The problem of there being no overall master play for the sequel trilogy's narrative is compounded by the conclusion of Johnson's screenplay, which wraps up most of its loose ends and comes to a pretty definite conclusion. It doesn't feel like the second part of a three-part story in the way that *The Empire Strikes Back* or, to a lesser extent, *Attack of the Clones* did. There's no sense of a cliffhanger—no sense that there's more to come. So rather than leaving us eagerly anticipating what will come in the next movie, *The Last Jedi* leaves us wondering what could come in the next movie, which is a very different and not nearly as compelling of a feeling.

OSCAR ISAAC
(actor, "Poe Dameron")

I think the thing as well is that often with the second chapter in a story of three, because the first one kind of sets the tone and the world and the new characters, introduces them, in the second one you don't have to spend so much time doing that, you can really just delve into the story, into what's happening.

RAY MORTON

It's extraordinary to me that the production entities were willing to invest so much money in a new series of films without ever sorting out what those films were going to be about—what story they were going to tell and whether or not that story had enough material in it to stretch out over three movies. It seems more as if Disney had decided to do a new trilogy simply to do a new trilogy, because all of the previous *Star Wars* movies were grouped into trilogies and they figured that's what audiences were expecting—and that it didn't so much matter to them what that new trilogy was going to be about. Because maybe it really didn't; that as long as they could get their merchandising out of it, they'd be happy. From a corporate earnings perspective, this was probably the smart way to go. It's just not a very good way to make satisfying movies.

The Last Jedi was released in December 2017 and was a success at the global box office, costing $317 million and grossing $1.3 billion despite the polarizing nature of the film's reception by fans.

GLEN OLIVER
(pop culture commentator)

There's a narrow-minded, rigid toxicity rising within fan communities these days. *Star Wars* is confronting it, as are *Star Trek* and *Doctor Who*, as did *Game of Thrones*. It's a dogged sense of ownership—and coarse judgmentalism. An unyielding belief that simply because one invests time and affection into something, one's hopes for a show somehow gives one an inherent right to demand. Armchair quarterbacking and ill-informed deconstruction has risen to a bizarrely self-righteous fervor. I can't imagine this proclivity is making the already difficult job of creating these shows any easier for those making them. The expression of opinion should always be protected—I absolutely believe this. But the price for that freedom should be expectations of civility and it should be incumbent on those who are expressing opinions to do so in measured, informed, respectful ways. Sadly, this process seems to collapse frequently these days.

ANDY SERKIS
(actor, "Supreme Leader Snoke")

I was blown away when I saw the movie. I just was so caught up with it, because it was really intimate and very emotional and I wasn't expecting that at all. I knew obviously that it was going to go that way, but it was very, very powerful and it touches you and what Rian's done incredibly is make this dance between these great kind of epic moments and hilarious antics, literally flipping on a dime and then going right into the heart of these beautiful characters, and you really care.

PETER HOLMSTROM

Rian Johnson clearly knows how to make a movie, but he's stuck slightly in that he had to make basically part two of *The Force Awakens*. So it was limiting. There's a grandeur in scope to this film that was severely lacking in *The Force Awakens*. This feels like a motion picture. The characters have emotional arcs in this movie, which is nice to see. Rey, in particular, has a lot going for her here. I love how, at the beginning of *The Force Awakens,* she's "no one," and by the end of *The Last Jedi,* Poe says to her, "Oh, I know who you are." That's nice. Of course, it was meant to set up a Poe/Rey romance in *Episode IX* that never happened, but whatever. But, the problems are there. Finn and Rose's subplot means nothing to the movie; Captain Phasma is merely there for a five-second fight scene that Abrams didn't do in *TFA* and Twitter complained about; and plot holes abound in general. It's a bummer. But, I really hope Johnson does another *Star Wars* movie, because the man clearly loves the franchise and is a great filmmaker.

RIAN JOHNSON

My cinematographer, Steve Yedlin, who I've been best friends with since I was eighteen years old, we met in film school, and so to be standing next to each other on the *Star Wars* set was pretty surreal. I think *Empire* is the most gorgeous of the whole series. Steve and I looked at the lighting in that; it's pretty daring in terms of how dark they were willing to go with some of it—literally dark, and how gorgeous they went with some of the choices they made with the shaping of the lighting.

But then in terms of like an actual visual aesthetic, I made a choice very early where I could either try and copy my idea of what the original movies did, where the camera didn't move a ton and it was a much more formal-type visual aesthetic, or I realized we're going to take visual cues lighting-wise and design-wise from the previous movies, but I need to just shoot this movie the way that I would shoot a movie, because at the end of the day, if I'm not engaged with it, and I'm not trying to tell the story the way that really makes me excited, then it's not going to be up there on the screen. So I kind of cut myself loose camera-movement-wise and shot-wise from trying to imitate the past and just try to tell the story as excitingly as I could up on the screen.

RAY MORTON

The Last Jedi proved to be a very divisive film among fans. Many (mostly younger) fans loved the movie for its iconoclasm and its message that we must let go of the past if we are to move into the future. Many (mostly older) fans disliked the film for its negative reframe of the original trilogy and the original characters. Some (bigots, babies, and basement dwellers) objected to the film's lead and the prominent roles played by people of color. Excluding the last group (who are just deplorable), the passion both of the first two groups feel—which can unfortunately turn exhaustingly mean-spirited in some online discussions—proves that forty years after the release of the first film, George Lucas's modern myth still means a great deal to a great many people the world over. And nowhere is that meaning better captured than in the final scene in *The Last Jedi,* in which a young boy looks to the heavens and then—imagining his broomstick to be a lightsaber—raises it to the sky in an echo of the original poster for *Star Wars.* Because it symbolizes so perfectly the spirit of the dreams, the imagination, and the hope that movies in general and the *Star Wars* movies, in particular, engender in us, this is my favorite scene in the entire sequel trilogy.

15

THE SKYWALKER'S THE LIMIT:
THE RISE OF SKYWALKER

"I have died before. The dark side of the Force is a pathway to many abilities some consider to be . . . unnatural."

Only six months after *The Last Jedi* opened in theaters—evoking a largely positive reception from critics, but a more divisive one from fans—Disney released the second of the *Star Wars* anthology films, *Solo: A Star Wars Story*. (A third, *Rogue Squadron*, will be released in 2023, at the earliest.) A prequel which depicted a young Han Solo making his way in the universe, it was the first *Star Wars* film to be considered an outright failure at the theatrical box office (although characters, including a young Lando played brilliantly by Donald Glover, are still in play for television offshoots), albeit with grosses that would be enviable for many other franchises.

Despite early rumors that Alden Ehrenreich as the young rogue required an acting coach on set and was tanking in film dailies, the *Hail, Caesar* veteran acquitted himself admirably in the role. After all, who could live up to the swagger and devilish charm of a young Harrison Ford? Despite this, the film, like *Rogue One*, went through a number of production challenges, including the replacement of its madcap directors, iconoclastic filmmakers Chris Miller and Phil Lord (*21 Jump Street*, *The Lego Movie*), after a falling-out with producer Kathleen Kennedy, who reportedly felt they were taking the film in too comedic a direction. After their departure, reliable Lucasfilm vet and journeyman helmer *Willow* director Ron Howard was drafted to reshoot and complete the film. In the end, it was an unmitigated disaster, costing $275 million and grossing $393 million, the worst-performing entry (and worst-looking due to the muddy cinematography of Bradford Young) of all the *Star Wars* live-action features. The result? A complete rethinking of the *Star Wars* anthology films on the big screen concurrent with the release of the next installment of what was now dubbed the Skywalker Saga, which was set to conclude the nine-film series in 2019, and big-screen Obi-Wan and Boba Fett adventures both migrating to television instead. In addition, a little known anthology film spotlighting the Inquisitors, who had been introduced in the *Star Wars: Rebels* animated series as a band of ruthless assassins charged by the Emperor with hunting down the remaining Jedi and Force-sensitive children in the galaxy, was also abandoned.

When Rian Johnson was announced as the writer/director of *Episode VIII*, it was indicated he would also pen a treatment for *Episode IX*—presumably to ensure that the story he was telling in *Episode VIII* would be properly concluded. There were also hints that Johnson might direct the final sequel as well. However, in August 2015 Lucasfilm announced that Colin Trevorrow would direct *Episode IX* and that he would cowrite the screenplay with his regular writing partner, Derek Connolly. Trevorrow's first film was the well-regarded, low-budget indie sci-fi comedy *Safety Not Guaranteed*. That, and his subsequent success reviving the *Jurassic Park* franchise with *Jurassic World* for Steven Spielberg, made him a presumably smart choice to work on the finale of Disney's everything-old-is-new-again trilogy. Once Trevorrow came aboard, no more mention was made of Johnson writing a treatment—Trevorrow and Connolly would devise their own story.

Back when Trevorrow was announced as director, Kathleen Kennedy enthused, "Colin is someone I've been interested in working with ever since I saw *Safety Not Guaranteed*. The power of that film paired with the enormous success of *Jurassic World* speaks volumes about his abilities both as a storyteller and skilled filmmaker. We are thrilled to have such an incredible talent as Colin join our family and step into the *Star Wars* universe."

For his part, Trevorrow added, "This is not a job or an assignment. It is a seat at a campfire, surrounded by an extraordinary group of storytellers, filmmakers, artists, and craftspeople. We've been charged with telling new stories for a younger generation because they deserve what we all had—a mythology to call their own. We will do this by channeling something George Lucas instilled in all of us: boundless creativity, pure invention, and hope."

GLEN OLIVER
(pop culture commentator)

Rise of Skywalker was an enjoyable, unchallenging finale to the Disney-era sequel trilogy, but it was a relatively poor summation of, or celebration of, the history and nitty-gritty of *Star Wars*. It wasn't particularly concerned with addressing the core essence which *Star Wars* has explored, and been driven by, over the years. It's a very literal finale to a set of three sequel movies, with a few begrudging nods to the past thrown in for good measure. It doesn't truly service the heart and soul of its own mythology. Trevorrow and Connolly's work . . . was the opposite. Their approach was vastly more holistic and existential. They managed to juggle not only the narrative corners and requirements set forth by *Force Awakens* and *Last Jedi,* but also deep dove into the spirit and essence of what *Star Wars* is. And in doing so, seemed keenly interested in also illustrating what *Star Wars could be.* An example: for decades we've heard the term "balance to the Force" bandied about. What does that look like, literally and figuratively? What does that concept actually *mean* when all is said and done? What is the value, and the toll, of all that has happened leading up to this final tale?

Trevorrow and Connolly's notion seems to be that "balance" in the Force does not necessarily represent absolute purification of our innermost selves, or unequivocal altruism. They suggest that "balance" in the Force actually hinges on attaining our innermost, natural balance. There is good, and evil, in all of us. Dark and light. The friction between those two qualities creates unease and downfall. The reconciliation of these two concepts . . . coming to terms with them, and assuming command over both of them, is what leads to our most powerful, most capable selves. Empowering action and decision-making, which then radiates into the universe around us. This, coupled with the script's clearly stated "no one is no one" conceit, pulls messaging of *Star Wars* out of the established universe, and reflects it strongly back onto our real-world human condition as a whole. There's great power, and empowerment, in that approach.

Trevorrow and Connolly's story, Duel of the Fates, *finds now chancellor Hux, who has jammed communications between star systems to prevent insurrection, pursuing the Resistance, while Supreme Leader Kylo Ren travels to Mustafar and the remains of Darth Vader's castle in search of a clue to the whereabouts of Mortis and its purported wellspring of the Force. The latter point would have represented one of the first references in the films to something that was created for the animated series* The Clone Wars *(though a popular character from that show, Ahsoka Tano, shows up in both the animated* Rebels *and season two of the Disney+ series* The Mandalorian*). Force ghosts pay a visit to Kylo in the form of Luke Skywalker, trying to prevail on him to return to his mother; and of Rey, who is trying to lure him back to the light.*

PETER HOLMSTROM
(cohost, *The Rebel & the Rogue* podcast)

Unlike *Rise of Skywalker, Duel of the Fates* fully commits to a villainous Kylo Ren. While on Mustafar, Kylo finds an old communication in Vader's castle, a nice little nod to Ralph McQuarrie's early design and scenes from *Rogue One*, from Emperor Palpatine to Vader, telling Vader that if he should fall, to go to the Remnicore system and train with an ancient Force-wielder, Tor Valum, who instructed Darth Plagueis in the ways of overcoming death. In the process of accessing the message, Kylo is severely injured by an energy burst, and he must wear a new respirator mask even more fearsome than his grandfather's. This script is notable because it does not shy away from the darker, pseudo-horror/fantasy elements that made many genre films from the eighties so memorable, but have definitively fallen out of favor in recent years.

Unlike The Force Awakens *and* The Last Jedi, *which maintain a fairly limited scope in terms of characters and situations,* Duel of the Fates *expands the scope of the* Star Wars *universe.*

PETER HOLMSTROM

Trevorrow opens the film with a fun sequence of stealing a Star Destroyer, with Poe, Finn, Rose, Chewie, and a now fully trained Rey infiltrating a First Order repair facility and stealing it under their very noses. It's worth noting that *Rey kicks ass* in this proposed movie, leading the charge and in full possession of strength and power. She's a fully realized hero in this version, and I think it would've resonated with the fans. Rey and Poe have developed a romantic dynamic, but Rey resists, knowing her responsibilities are greater than any personal attachments. There's a heartbreaking moment where she uses a Force suggestion to get Poe to leave her behind, in the shape of a kiss— and it breaks your heart, because you know that she feels something for him, but can't risk putting him in harm's way.

Rey and Kylo have a shared vision of Mortis, revealing a pair of empty thrones designed for a Jedi and a Sith. Together, by drawing power from the wellspring, they are supposed to bring balance to the Force (of course, Anakin Skywalker was destined to do the same thing, but that prophecy didn't materialize given his turn to the dark side and transformation into the dreaded Dark Lord of the Sith, Darth Vader, in the prequel trilogy).
Training with Luke's Force ghost, Rey is told that Kylo must be killed before he can reach the wellspring. This infuriates her because of the continual battle between the light and the dark and the fact that nothing ever seems to change.

PETER HOLMSTROM

Kylo's storyline on Remnicore leans into the fantasy element of *Star Wars* in a great way. Tor Valum teaches Kylo how to siphon Force power off of other living things, in a decidedly vampiric way. Valum tells Kylo of the planet Mortis, and its connection to the wellspring of the Force. Kylo demands to know more of Mortis, but Valum deems Kylo not worthy of that knowledge, so Kylo kills Valum and extracts the knowledge from Valum's mind by force. The dangers of greed and selfishness are present throughout this film, and more than anything, you feel such pity as Kylo digs deeper into his suffering.

While a spiritual battle exists between Rey and Kylo, a more practical battle of good versus evil exists elsewhere.

PETER HOLMSTROM

Fans of Rose Tico from *The Last Jedi* would have much preferred this version of Rose over *The Rise of Skywalker*'s 1:14 minutes of the character. Here, Finn and Rose travel to the decaying Coruscant, which is the seat of the First Order, now under the control of "Chancellor" Hux. Their mission is to activate a long-dormant Jedi communication device to break the communication jam that's been set in place. Although their mission fails, they discover an underground city serving as home to thousands of the planet's downtrodden. Enough, per-haps, to serve as an army. Finn leads a rebellion against the First Order from the ground, while Rose attempts to activate the Jedi beacon in a last-ditch attempt to call for help. Poe, meanwhile, leads an aerial assault to keep the First Order fleet from firing on the Rebellion from above. Initially, they do well, but eventu-ally the First Order gains an advantage. The Resistance appears to be doomed.

The literal "Duel of the Fates," meanwhile, takes place on Mortis, where Rey and Kylo face off above the wellspring of the Force.

PETER HOLMSTROM

The crosscutting between the final battles on Mortis and Coruscant feels epic and large. Finn has managed to become a revolutionary leader on Corus-cant—a nice arc for a small stormtrooper with an existential crisis in *The Force Awakens*—while Rey faces off against the man who—she learns—killed her parents years before on Snoke's orders. Rey, though, continues to believe that only through forgiveness can balance in the Force be attained. Kylo manages to blind Rey with his lightsaber and enters the temple to reach the wellspring—which he discovers dried out long ago. Rey, near death, is given strength by the support of all of her friends via the Force and, while still blind, enters the temple in pursuit of Kylo, glowing. She nearly kills him, but offers her hand one more time, which he takes—only to drain her life force as Valum taught him, and using it to heal himself. Her screams of anguish reach

Leia across the galaxy. Sensing what's happening, Leia calls out to Kylo Ren and he—both healed and touched by goodness—becomes Ben Solo. He reverses the transference of energy back into Rey, saving her life and sacrificing his own. Before he dies, he tells Rey that her family name is Solano.

Back on Coruscant, the Resistance gets some last-minute support from Lando Calrissian and a team of mercenaries. The tide turns and the Resistance finally triumphs. Shamed by the First Order's defeat, Chancellor Hux uses a lightsaber to commit seppuku out of shame.

PETER HOLMSTROM

The film ends on a more spiritual/philosophical note, exactly as the saga should. Rey—teetering on the edge of death after her confrontation with Kylo—travels to the world between worlds, where she meets the Force ghosts of Luke, Yoda, and Obi-Wan. She tells them she has finally figured out that to balance the Force is to balance the good and evil within herself. This action firmly gives significance to each part of the Skywalker Saga, and also states Rey as the true living representation of a future era for the *Star Wars* universe. It ends with Rey being given the choice to remain as one with the Force, or to return to the land of the living and continue the struggle for peace. As someone who got a degree in philosophy largely because of *Star Wars*, I can say I and many others like me would've loved this ending.

Meanwhile, with the war finally over, Leia finds peace as she watches a star fall from the heavens. With the wellspring of the Force now full again, Finn and Rose start a school for Force-sensitive children, while Poe and Chewie prepare to set off in the Falcon *in search of Rey.*

As twin suns set, our heroes see someone walking toward them across the plain. As the person gets closer, they see that it is Rey.

GLEN OLIVER

Duel of the Fates asks a number of grander questions than *Rise* likely ever considered asking, and does so in provocative ways: Why does this ages-old conflict now appear to be coming to an end, once and for all? And the answer is decidedly *not* because the Emperor has yet another dastardly plan. He does have a plan here, but it's more of a will—an instruction—than a comeback. In Trevorrow and Connolly's work, it's time to end the war because war . . . exhausts. War . . . breaks. War . . . decays. Emotionally. Physically. Spiritually. *"We've been fighting this war for too long,"* says Finn. *Duel* shows us just this. *Rise of Skywalker* approached its resolution somewhat insularly—another plan by Palpatine, another crisis which compels our heroes towards battle. Its resolution was . . . amorphous . . . and seemed specific chiefly to the sequel trilogy, as opposed to embracing the whole of the thematics which drove the Skywalker Saga proper.

RAY MORTON
(senior editor, *Script* magazine)

It introduces a really smart and compelling solution to the eternal battle between good and evil by stating that the conflict cannot be won by facing outward, but only by turning inward and fighting the battle—and finding the balance—in our own hearts and souls. Heal yourself, heal the world. It's a lovely notion and the perfect way to resolve the balance issue introduced back in *The Phantom Menace*. It provides an excellent resolution to the question of Rey's heritage—her parents were nobodies and they are dead. Her old family is gone, but she has found a new one with Leia, Poe, Chewie, Rose, and Finn. It's simple and real and it works. Finally provides a plausible motivation for Kylo's murder of Han Solo—he is under the belief that the only way he can become a full Sith is to sever himself from all of his emotions, especially love. Killing Han was his way of demonstrating to Snoke that he has done so.

GLEN OLIVER

In *Rise,* and the sequel trilogy in general, there's a heavy focus on our core characters—who (I assume) are supposed to be representative of "resistance" across the galaxy. In *Duel* we *see* the faces of this resistance, via cutaways to the faces of everyday, ordinary folks looking up into the skies to see Leia's energy-carried call to unity and arms beam across the cosmos. We see them making a stand on Coruscant, and elsewhere. We feel that there's a galaxy full of people who are, quite simply, done with it all. Who are finally willing to, needing to, rise. This epic conflict, which had been somewhat microfocused, as well as immediately focused, throughout the Skywalker Saga is suddenly given a broader, vastly more connected, and meaningful scope in *Duel*. Rendering a baseline, pulp-serial setup—which might be fairly regarded as frivolous at face value—startlingly resonant, and easy to connect with.

PETER HOLMSTROM

Duel of the Fates is a proper culmination to the entire nine-film Skywalker Saga. Trevorrow honored each chapter of the series, and was clearly in tune with what George Lucas always set out to do with *Star Wars*. Anyone can throw up some X-Wings and TIE Fighters and go "pew-pew," but Trevorrow understood what the saga was "About." The conflict between good and evil isn't a conflict between blue lightsaber versus red lightsaber—it's a conflict within oneself between acting selfishly and selflessly. It's there from the earliest of scripts for *The Star Wars,* visualized in *Empire Strikes Back* and *Return of the Jedi,* and fully explored in the prequels. Again, Lucas was making Vietnam in space—the bad guys in the prequels were the Jedi, who had become so entrenched in their dogmatic, self-righteous heroism that they rejected their spirituality and emotions, and were too selfish to reexamine their own place in the galaxy. Luke chose to embrace love in his attempt to redeem his father, instead of doing what his masters told him was "right" in murdering his father—putting aside his own selfishness for justice and revenge against the Empire in favor of compassion and hope. J.J. abandoned that concept in favor of TIE Fighters and X-Wings and "pew-pew," but Trevorrow saw the value in the message.

RAY MORTON

As is the case with all first drafts, *Duel of the Fates* isn't very polished—there are a lot of rough edges and un/underdeveloped ideas. Still, it's a very decent start. To begin with, it picks up and carries forward the major themes and ideas of *The Last Jedi,* especially the notion that Rey's parents were nobodies unrelated to the Skywalker clan and therefore Rey must define herself unbound by lineage and/or expectations. And there's the notion that Rey has to decide if she will follow the Jedi path or go her own way as she continues to grow in her knowledge and use of the Force; Kylo Ren seeking to become the ultimate power in the galaxy; Leia grooming Poe to become a leader; Rose Tico is now a full-fledged member of the star warriors.

It finally gives Kylo a reason to run around wearing a Vader-ish mask; and Finn something neither the writers of *The Force Awakens* or *The Last Jedi* were able to give him—a significant role to play in the story. It introduces a wonderful bit of irony at the end when Kylo—after having gone to such lengths to reach the Force wellspring—finds it dry and empty. Provides a wonderful conclusion to Rey's story. She has the option to stay in Jedi heaven, but in the end, chooses to return to the physical world and continue to fight the good fight. This is the perfect conclusion for a hero.

GLEN OLIVER

But something about *Duel of the Fates* must not have worked. There's a moment in which C-3PO must basically wreak violence upon another droid, which sends him into existential angst. It's never clear if the tone of this is supposed to be dramatic, thoughtful, funny, or some combination—but it misses the mark. *"I've done horrible things. I may never be the same,"* he laments. An interesting flavor to bring to the character, and an interesting illustration of the weight of warfare. But also a precarious, slippery slope. On the other hand, a few wickedly funny moments throughout *Duel* are very successfully meta. This includes a line from Poe about needing to take out the First Order's signal jammer (so the Jedi Temple's signal can be sent). He references the jammer having no exhaust port, no oscillator, indicating the First Order has wised up to not engineering exploitable weaknesses into their technologies. *"They're onto us."* That's pretty funny.

RAY MORTON

There *are* some pretty big problems in the piece. The idea that just a few people can hijack an entire Star Destroyer and then get away quickly and that the First Order can't easily track it is far-fetched to the point of being unbelievable. The script's conception of the Force as some sort of natural resource that wells up from a spring in the ground (a spring that can eventually run dry) runs counter to the way the Force has always been described previously—as an energy field generated by all living things ("Life creates it . . . makes it grow . . ."). The notion that it can be drained from one being and absorbed by another doesn't square with this definition either. The script doesn't know quite what to do with Poe. Instead of continuing to focus on his ongoing development as a leader, it instead sidetracks him into a sort-of-a-romance with Rey and during the end battle keeps him as Leia's loyal second rather than finally allowing him to become the full leader she has been grooming him to be. Many of the action scenes in the piece feel rather generic. Kylo's change of heart at the end happens much, much too quickly and seemingly out of nowhere. Had the script continued to be developed, it is likely most of its problems could have been ironed out. And if they had been, *Duel of the Fates* would likely have served as a suitable continuation of the first two sequels and a reasonably satisfying finale to the sequel trilogy. But this was not to be.

Trevorrow and Connolly penned several revisions of their initial draft. Their efforts were complicated by the death of Carrie Fisher in December 2016—given the significant role Leia played in the story, the narrative needed to be reworked considerably to deal with her absence. However, Kathleen Kennedy was reportedly not satisfied with how the script was developing, so in August 2017, English playwright and screenwriter Jack Thorne (Harry Potter and the Cursed Child, Enola Holmes) *was hired to take over. A month later, Trevorrow left the project, and soon after, J.J. Abrams came aboard as the film's new director. At this point, Thorne departed and Abrams and Chris Terrio* (Argo, Zack Snyder's Justice League) *took over scripting duties.*

JASON WARD
(webmaster, makingstarwars.net)

I was told that basically Kathleen Kennedy and Trevorrow were getting along fine. It wasn't a bad relationship, but she just wasn't connecting with any of their drafts. Most of the people I've talked to at Lucasfilm who were privy to the information said it wasn't that bad, but it also wasn't that good. And that it was going to need much more work. Eventually they turn in their final draft and with all of the concessions they were forced to make, it was less than inspired by the end and they decided to part ways.

RAY MORTON

They kept some of Connolly and Trevorrow's ideas, although they reworked them considerably: Kylo searching for a mysterious planet—in this case, the mythical home of the Sith rather than the mythical wellspring of the Force. Kylo re-dons a mask, although in *Rise* he reassembles his stupid faux-Vader mask just because, rather than wearing a respirator mask because his injuries require it. Kylo learning from an ancient master—in this case, a resurrected Emperor Palpatine rather than Tor Valum. The return of Lando Calrissian. Finn running into another former stormtrooper—in this case, an entire tribe of them hiding out on an Endorian moon. Rey discovering she has the power to generate Force lightning and then using it in an ominous fashion. Kylo being redeemed by contact with a parent—although in *Rise* it is (the memory of) Han rather than Leia. Finn leading a ground assault, although in *Rise* he rides space horses across the hull of a Star Destroyer for a second, rather than leading a large ground assault on Coruscant.

GLEN OLIVER

If you squint really, really hard, you can sense fragments of *Duel*'s DNA in *Rise*. There are some broadly similar movements, and I suspect this is why Trevorrow shares "Story" credit on *Skywalker*. Texturally and substantively, however, they're night and day in terms of vision and execution. The most notable similarities include a search for a phantom power plant. In *Rise* it was Exegol, the world of the Sith. In *Duel* it was intended to be Mortis, previously established in *The Clone Wars* series and instrumental to Force mechanics in general. In both cases, there was stuff on these worlds which Kylo needs to deal with in order to do his thing. Also, Mustafar appears in both scripts, briefly in both, early on in both. In both instances, it's a waypoint to Kylo's broader journey towards badassification. Next, Han and Ben Solo reunite in both versions in sequences which are very similar.

A *Waterworld*-ish boat sequence appears in both. It's much more strongly emphasized in *Duel* (there is actually full-on boat action, poorly described and blocked in *Duel*—as opposed to merely using the boat as a means of transportation in *Rise*). Then, Palpatine appears in both. His role is much less meaty in *Duel* than the full-on resurrection we saw in *Rise*. In *Duel*, Palpatine's moment is very much akin to Obi-Wan's first appearance to Luke in *The Empire Strikes Back* ("*You will go to the Dagobah system . . .*"). In this case, he cameos as a recorded instruction left for Vader, which Kylo manages to activate. In the event of Palpatine's demise, Vader was to find Palpatine's former master and enhance his training. Kylo assumes this mantle.

RAY MORTON

There's also the arrival of a Rebel fleet led by Lando just in time to save the Resistance, although in the Abrams/Terrio script it is a massive fleet of independent ships from across the galaxy (a *Star Wars* version of Dunkirk) rather than a small armada of space pirates. Kylo bringing Rey back from the dead by passing his Force energy on to her, after which he dies. Rey communing with deceased Jedi—although in *Rise* it is by hearing voices from the past encouraging her rather than a meeting in an astral plane.

The use of these ideas earned Connolly and Trevorrow a co-"story by" credit, along with Abrams and Terrio. Abrams and Terrio also had to incorporate Leia into the story by utilizing some unused scenes from The Force Awakens *and the judicious use of doubles. Terrio and Abrams completed a script before the film went into production in August 2018, but following his usual process, Abrams continued to rework the narrative throughout production and then made many more changes during postproduction. He then made even more alterations after the film received a less than glowing response at several test screenings. As with* The Force Awakens, *the plot for what would eventually be titled* The Rise of Skywalker *was not finalized until shortly before the movie was released in December 2019.*

J.J. ABRAMS
(cowriter/director, *The Rise of Skywalker*)

Because we had worked on *Force Awakens*, Larry Kasdan and I and the producers talked about quite a few things. So *The Rise of Skywalker* was a bit of picking up where we had left off and the fact is what Rian Johnson had done in *Last Jedi* had set up some things that were sort of wonderful for the story. One of the things being that the cast was separated; the characters weren't together for the entire movie, essentially. So this was the first time the group got to be together. Chris and I got together and we knew immediately we wanted to tell a story of a group adventure. There were some very specific things that we were both drawn to immediately, and we just started doing that thing that you do, which is that you say, "What do you desperately want to see? What feels right?"

ANTHONY DANIELS
(actor, "C-3PO")

I just realized something in the last few months that I hadn't ever got before. Because I've been in all of them and all the spin-offs and stuff, I am so close to it . . . and I said it's rather like having your nose up against a planet—you can't see how big that planet is. And gradually now, I'm beginning to get a perspective on it, and that comes from talking to fans, to people who say what *Star Wars* has meant to them over the years. It's meant something completely different to me: it's a job, it's kind of fun, it's kind of awkward sometimes (as we all know), it's not a smooth ride . . . But finally, I'm getting to see it almost from the other perspective, and that's the perspective of the audience who've been there all this time. And I'm really glad to have survived all this long enough to get this perspective.

OSCAR ISAAC
(actor, "Poe Dameron")

[Poe's] always been a bit of a wild-card energy in figuring out where he fits in the story and what story is being told, and I think with this one . . . I remember J.J. being excited about kind of dirtying up the squeaky flyboy image that he's had for a bit and just revealing a bit more of his personality. And I think that really comes out because I've been taken away from my little box in space and I get to join my friends this time, and you really get to see the interaction with the three and the hope that he, in particular, brings to this one—there's a kind of relentless, almost aggressive optimism that he has—and how that is tested and how he tries to be there for his friends, tries to push them along even when it seems quite hopeless.

DAISY RIDLEY
(actress, "Rey Skywalker")

With the physical stuff, you train and train and train and then the adrenaline helps you on the day to like, do the thing (but obviously, the stamina needs to be there for you to continue to do the thing). But I would say I was more tired emotionally because there really wasn't a day where I was like "No, it's just a quick scene." Coming from the last one, which was quite heavy, even the joyous scenes I found quite strange to do, and obviously there's a lot of other stuff that's going on. There's more of a, I would say, *singular intention* that was tiring, because as well even in the emotional scenes there's a physical containment that is tiring. So really, I've not answered the question and both things were hard.

The Rise of Skywalker brings back all of the principal cast members from the previous two films, adding Keri Russell as Zorii Bliss, an old frenemy of Poe's; Billy Dee Williams as fan-favorite Lando Calrissian; Richard E. Grant as the creepy Allegiant General Pryde; as well as, and most improbably, Ian McDiarmid as the Emperor.

BILLY DEE WILLIAMS
(actor, "Lando Calrissian")

I didn't expect to be in this little adventure, but I got lucky. I ended up working with somebody I have a tremendous regard for, J.J. Abrams. I've been doing this for a long time—almost sixty years—and I've been fortunate enough to work with some pretty extraordinary people, but this I probably regard as a true, genuine highlight in my life. Lando's a shade older, but he's still hanging in there. When you're doing this kind of stuff, it's an opportunity to work with some really, really wonderful people and it's something I really enjoy more than just making money. Don't get me wrong, I love making money, but just to be able to hang out and play around with these ideas and with people like this.

J.J. ABRAMS

It was a big group scene, so there were a lot of extras. And Billy came onto the set and it just went silent and everyone's just watching. It was so sweet to see the reaction from the people who are working on the movie, but it was, you know, honestly an emotional thing. It really was.

BILLY DEE WILLIAMS

Lando has never left me. He's been in my life for like, forty years, so I had a lot of fun doing it and I was just trying to execute whatever J.J. had for me. It was relatively simple to get back into the role. I'm a very charming kind of person, so it was relatively easy for me. I love doing Lando. He's always a fun character and bigger than life.

IAN MCDIARMID
(actor, "Emperor Palpatine")

In *Star Wars* they've been very good at dealing with unexpected moments the whole time. Secrets are a big thing and nobody really ever knows what anybody else is doing. So it has been the story of the pictures to have different scripts, false scripts, sometimes no scripts at all, false lines. An aura of mystery is always a great thing to have when you're telling a great story, and that certainly continues apparently.

I do have to say that in some ways I find the popularity of myself and the character a little disquieting. In one sense I feel like I failed, because you're supposed to hate me. That is my function, to be really detestable when I say things like, "Execute Order 66." I mean, you can't get much worse than that, can you? But people tell me they love me, so all of the other lovable characters suddenly have a competition from the worst evil creature that cinema ever created.

Carrie Fisher was always supposed to play a major role as Leia Organa, but major changes had to be made after her unexpected passing. Through use of excised footage from the previous films, body doubles, and clever editing, she still has a fairly significant role in the finished film.

TODD FISHER
(brother of Carrie Fisher)

I don't want to toot my horn on this, but I put the screw to Disney regarding Carrie. And it was totally by accident. I was at a film festival and people asked me what was going on with Carrie and the next *Star Wars* film. And I said, "I can tell you from the family's perspective, from the brother's perspective, we would *love* to see Carrie's character go on. It should happen. The franchise deserves it, the fans deserve it." So I just made a casual comment like that. Well, that got back to Disney and someone from way up at the top said, "I have no idea what he's talking about. We have no intentions to bring her back." And in response somebody calls me up and says, "Are you aware that Disney has totally shot you down on the whole thing?" Again, I said, "From Carrie's brother's perspective, her character should come back. I don't care how we do it. We have the technology and it should happen." Over a period of months, I just kept saying that and it happened I was out on tour doing other things and was in the press a lot. Well, I got a cease-and-desist letter from Disney demanding I stop talking about this.

I had my lawyer write them a letter saying, "Unlike my sister, where you do have a nondisclosure agreement, you have nothing with me. So I'm just going to say whatever I feel and this is what I feel. If you don't like it, explain yourself." And I did. I never got into any great detail, but I knew there was unused footage of her. J.J. had told me there was footage. Then, of course, they embraced the obvious.

J.J. ABRAMS

We realized immediately that there was no way to conclude the Skywalker Saga without Leia. She's too important and we obviously didn't want to use a CG character—that never would have worked for us. And we didn't want to recast, of course. And then we went back and looked at the footage that we had cut, which I had bemoaned doing at the time on *Episode VII,* and we realized that we had the answer to our impossible question, weirdly, in this footage. And it's just her. I mean, she's in the movie. It's Carrie Fisher as Leia in a way that is still uncanny to me. Weirdly, it's even more impossible that she's not [actually here], because she was an actor in the film every day in the editing room, so it's very strange.

There were a bunch of challenges with this along the way, but the biggest was emotional. Everyone cared deeply and wanted to do the best that anyone in their positions could. It was incumbent upon me and Chris to make sure we were telling a story using the tools we had—and also the existing footage—to bring Leia to life. Carrie was a friend and I adored her and loved working with her; nothing was more important than doing right by her. The key was to understand the experience I wanted the audience to have, and the intention of that moment, and then make sure everything we were doing was saving that. In addition to the technical aspects of it, which were extensive, a lot of credit needs to go to the actors who performed in those scenes without Carrie.

Filming on The Rise of Skywalker *began on August 1, 2018, at England's Pinewood Studios, and concluded on February 15, 2019. It was produced for $275 million and had a worldwide gross of $1.1 billion. And the critical reaction was muted as well, with Rotten Tomatoes aggregating a rating of 51 percent based on 495 reviews, with an average rating of 6.1/10. It's considered the lowest-rated live-action film in the series' long history.*

RAY MORTON

The Rise of Skywalker is a terrible movie. It's the worst of the sequels and the worst film in the entire nine-movie series. The story in the finished film is chaotic, convoluted, and at times incomprehensible. As is the case in the other sequels, there's no overarching plot, just a collection of subplots scrambled together. There's a whole bunch of frenetic running around in search of clues and objects and people, none of which ultimately mean a damn thing. The storytelling is frantic and confused, full of plot holes, hard to follow, exhausting to sit through, and absolutely no fun at all. We're far, far away from the straightforward, compelling entertainment that was the original *Star*

Wars. The script and the film lack the references to myths and fairy tales, religion, cinema, and pop culture that gave texture and resonance to the original trilogy's narrative. In their place are nothing but references to other *Star Wars* movies. Most of the major elements in the script are recycled from the other films in the series in an endless stream of fan service, callbacks, and references. There's absolutely nothing original in the piece.

In crafting the narrative, Abrams appears to have been determined to undo just about every innovation Rian Johnson incorporated into The Last Jedi, *a charge he and cowriter Terrio deny. In the film, Kylo goes back to wearing his faux-Vader mask.* The Last Jedi *eliminated Snoke and made Kylo the trilogy's big bad.* Rise *replaces Snoke with the formerly late Emperor Palpatine (who is resurrected out of nowhere) and moves Kylo back to the subordinate position. Rey's parents are no longer nobodies. She is given the mysterious, connected-to-the-original-trilogy lineage that Johnson tried to get away from in* Last Jedi, *although the specific heritage she is given in* Rise *is the most ludicrous one imaginable—Rey is revealed to be Palpatine's granddaughter. And Rose's role in the story is reduced to little more than a glorified cameo.*

RAY MORTON

This might not have been so bad except that every new idea Abrams and Terrio came up with was really, really terrible: the aforementioned return of Palpatine, which goes completely unexplained. In the end of *Return of the Jedi,* we saw Vader hurl the Emperor down the reactor shaft and explode and yet here he is again, unexploded and still cackling, with no explanation given. Apart from being a bad idea all by itself, reviving Palpatine is yet another nail in the coffin of the original trilogy hammered in by the sequels—now not only are Luke, Han, and Leia failures, but so is Vader. We thought he helped save the galaxy by killing the Emperor, but—nope—that didn't happen either.

The aforementioned familial connection between Rey and the Emperor. Apart from being the most horrible, fan-fiction-ish plot twist conceivable, this plot twist forces us to ponder the notion that while Palpatine was plotting to subvert the Republic to become the Emperor, lure Anakin Skywalker to the dark side, murder all the Jedi, and conquer the galaxy by building a few Death Stars, he found the time to go on a few dates, get married, raise a few little Siths, and then become a grandpappy. W. T. F.? Palpatine is given a stadium full of acolytes down in his Sith hole. Since there is only supposed to be two Sith at any one time, who are these worshipful onlookers? It turns out Palpatine has been behind all the evil events in the sequels (including Snoke, who the Emperor apparently whipped up in a lab). Like Blofeld in *Spectre,* he is apparently the author of everybody's pain, even though he has been neither seen nor heard even once in this new trilogy up until now. It was a terrible idea in *Spectre*; it's a terrible idea here.

The movie does have a few good points: as always, the cast does its very best. Daisy Ridley continues to bring grace and dignity to Rey; Adam Driver continues to bring an impressive level of commitment to a difficult character; Ian McDiarmid is as good as always as Palpatine; Keri Russell is a lovely addition to the cast, even if we only get to see her eyes; it's good to see Billy Dee Williams again; and one longs for a new *Star Wars* movie that contains as much charm and energy and good-natured high spirits as Oscar Isaac brings to the role of Poe Dameron. Lando and Chewie flying in with the rescue fleet at the climax of the movie is a wonderfully thrilling *Star Wars* moment. The scene in which the spirits of all the Jedi speak to Rey and urge her to carry on is powerful and moving. The moment at the end in which Rey claims the Skywalker name for herself does pull at the heartstrings. It doesn't make much logical sense, but it does make emotional sense and it provides a lovely and poetic grace note to end the picture on. Unfortunately, these moments are diamonds in a field that otherwise consists of dross. If it wasn't already, one thing *The Rise of Skywalker* makes abundantly clear is that there was never a master narrative plan for these sequels.

PETER HOLMSTROM

Disney/Lucasfilm flip-flops again with the firing of Colin Trevorrow and the nixing of his *Duel of the Fates* script. But, because so much money had already been put into the production, the hastily put together *Rise of Skywalker* ends up looking like, frankly, a made-for-TV movie. More plot holes than connecting threads, and a solidification of the inactivity of each of the main characters. None of them did anything to solve the problems of the movie—it was all done by people off-screen. Poor Rose Tico too. They're pulling stuff from everywhere, and it ends up looking like a stringed-together Frankenstein's Monster of a movie. Again, Disney listened first and foremost to the angry fanboys on Twitter when making this movie. "Rey needs a lineage? She's a Palpatine! You hate Rose Tico? SHE'S GONE! You're shipping Rey and Kylo? HERE YOU GO!" I was at the *Rise of Skywalker* panel at *Star Wars* Celebration Chicago, and there was a five-minute standing ovation for Kelly Marie Tran. Longer than any other part of that panel. Toxic fandom is a very small percentage of the fanbase, and studios need to stop chasing their approval. *Rise of Skywalker* is a very good example of what happens when you do.

GLEN OLIVER

Lucas's genius is that he could see beyond the established conventions—and perceived limitations—of traditional filmmaking by taking a countertop of time-tested ingredients and convictions, and whipping up a new kind of cinematic soufflé on the spot. And when those conventions didn't exist, he invented his way to a solution. Which is the mark of a great chef and an extraordinary filmmaker. Lucas himself never bested the original *Star Wars*. I'm not sure anyone ever will. Is it the greatest movie of all time? It's really quite impossible to make that assertion, as time is still counting. Is it the most influential film of all time? There would be some very strong arguments for this. Which, at the end of the day, is a remarkable and admirable victory in itself.

PETER HOLMSTROM

Really think about character here. Who's leading the charge? Who's driving the action? No one. Lando "conveniently" convinces the galaxy to fight—in the most absurdly large fleet ever, I might add. Why now? First Order's been killing people left and right, and all the galaxy needed was Lando to come and say, "Hello, what have we here?" The fleet arrives just in time (at the same time), but the Emperor's fleet has difficulty leaving? Blah. Leia reaches out with the Force and brings Kylo back from darkness—again, no reason why she couldn't have done that before. Rey defeats the Emperor, but only after a bunch of Jedi possess her—again, what's so special about now? No structure, no emotional arcs—and I don't care what J.J. Abrams says—Finn, in the finished film, is not Force-sensitive. He's got the hots for Rey, wanted to tell her, but never did. That's his arc. That's what's on the screen. And that's (sadly) all he did.

RAY MORTON

From the release of *The Force Awakens,* Disney sold this new series of *Star Wars* movies as a trilogy—three films telling a single tale. But as the trio, and especially as *The Rise of Skywalker,* unfolds, it becomes increasingly obvious that the people responsible for making these new movies never bothered to sit down and work out exactly what the story was they wanted to tell. Instead, they just seemed to do the cinematic equivalent of throwing shit against the wall to see what sticks.

GLEN OLIVER

The sequel films don't carry the same quality of Lucas's. From the outset, and throughout the sequel trilogy, it was clear there wasn't a particularly strong rudder steering these films towards any kind of discernible endgame. Each installment felt as if it was trying to reconcile itself with, and make the best of, the picture which had come before it. Each installment felt compromised in some way by what had become before, instead of empowered and emboldened by the previous narrative. Each film felt reluctantly informed by its predecessors. *The Force Awakens* felt hamstrung by its devotion to the original trilogy. *The Last Jedi* felt unsatisfied with *The Force Awakens* and reactive against its content. *The Rise of Skywalker* felt like a pushback against *The Last Jedi,* and like a frenzied attempt to reconcile itself with the challengingly, dangerously amorphous vagaries introduced in *The Force Awakens* and *The Last Jedi.* The sequel trilogy was a scramble, a messy grab to try to compensate/cover up for the simple reality that there wasn't a cohesive vision in place for the films from the outset.

RAY MORTON

Whether intentionally or not, there's an arrogance in this—a sense that the companies felt that fans would buy any old junk that was thrown on them as long as the name *Star Wars* was slapped on it and that the companies were perfectly okay with this—that makes the whole thing feel like more than a bit of a cynical cash grab. This is something George Lucas would never have tolerated—even when the results weren't always as good as we would have liked them to be, there was never a sense that Lucas was trying to give the audience anything less than the very best movies and experiences he was capable of giving them.

JOHN KENNETH MUIR
(author, *Science Fiction and Fantasy Films of the 1970s*)

The Rise of Skywalker is the worst *Star Wars* movie ever made. In forty plus years, I have never felt so uninvolved in a *Star Wars* film; never felt that I was watching something utterly overproduced, but totally underplanned. Nothing in the movie matters, because as long as Disney strip-mines the property, there will never be a meaningful end to *Star Wars*. That knowledge robs the movie of any sense of importance or nostalgia. The plot is nonsensical, impossible to follow, and, most damningly, largely uninteresting. The promise of *The Force Awakens* is long since squandered. This is the worst film of the Disney trilogy, which is saying something. Watching it, I remember thinking how utterly mediocre the film is. It never creates any groundswell of emotion or nostalgia in the viewer. It's just . . . fast moving. It substitutes velocity for meaning; speed for intelligence.

Looking at the trilogy as a whole, it is apparent that Disney took arguably the most valuable IP in the world (and perhaps, in the history of the world) and utterly squandered its potential by failing to plan a three-movie arc that would complete the *Star Wars* saga in a meaningful and lasting way. That said, I love *Rogue One* and *Solo*. For me, Disney's only success with the property has been in the "side" movies or one-offs. The Disney trilogy is a mess.

GLEN OLIVER

The movies are playing it safe. The prevailing aesthetic is, largely, filled with aggravatingly neutral colors. How many sand/desert planets do we *really* need to see? The current films feel like they're set in a universe that is being controlled by a rigid, rigid, corporatized dogma of what *Star Wars* is, as opposed to imagining what *Star Wars* could be. I've seen it argued that fan investment in *Star Wars* is wobbling to some extent. I'd argue that, if this is true, it's likely due to the fact that the current iteration of *Star Wars* looks . . . literally . . . like the same old thing, over and over again. A phenomenon exacerbated considerably by Disney's proclivity to lean into nostalgia when cutting promos for the films, instead of exemplifying how each film feels distinctive from the last. It feels like protection and exploitation of investment over narrative sanctity.

RAY MORTON

And that brings us to the one thing that the sequel trilogy proves beyond the shadow of a doubt. Disney's goal with the sequels was to create a series of films that looked and felt like the films in the original trilogy. They managed to create three movies that reasonably approximated the imagery and the tone of those initial three pictures. However, they left out one crucial ingredient—the vision. What the sequel trilogy shows us is that while others may be capable of making movies that simulate the original three movies, in the end, *Star Wars* without George Lucas just ain't *Star Wars*.

GLEN OLIVER

Paradoxically, the current animated television product—which is as canonical as the films—feels much broader and less restrained in its interpretation of *Star Wars*. I'm guessing this is because they're cheaper to produce, have a smaller audience to upset, thus, exploring the potentials of the asset leads to less risk all around. It'll be interesting to see if, in the long run, in terms of texture and vibe and imagination, the new live-action shows feel more "familiar"—like the movies—or are wilder and more exploratory, like the cartoons. I'm betting they feel more familiar, because they will cost quite a bit more to make, and taking chances will seem less appealing in those instances. If I am wrong, I look forward to being wrong.

DALE POLLOCK

(author, *Skywalking: The Life and Films of George Lucas*)

I actually found the film very satisfying, kind of a suitable conclusion. Originally Lucas had this idea of three trilogies, so this really does tie into what he originally conceived of. To me, it was pretty satisfying emotionally. If you had told me in 1977 that this series would end on a female-centric note, where the real hero would be a woman, no one would have believed you. I think that says a lot about how the series reflects what's really going on in our world. I thought that by the end he really did reinforce the message that he wanted, which was compassion and love versus revenge and death, although there are a lot of deaths in that movie without a doubt. I don't know how much creative impact he had in these final films—very little, actually, I think—but the attitude towards him was take your money and go away. But I do think it ended up reinforcing the values he set out to instill in his audience.

DAN MADSEN

(owner, the Official Lucasfilm/Star Wars Fan Club, 1987–2001)

I don't want them to make mediocre *Star Wars*. That, in my opinion, is what really killed *Star Trek* for a while. They were just making mediocre *Star Trek*, and that's just not good enough to keep the audience coming back and keep them interested. I don't want to see *Star Wars* fall into that. That's why I was really concerned when they were doing one a year. I was saying, "No, that's just too much!" Part of the fun of the *Star Wars* films is getting to wait a couple of years and building up, waiting for the next movie to come out. But when it's like, "BAM, BAM, BAM"—one every year—you're not making it special anymore. Give people time to wait and build up that anticipation and make it really good.

GLEN OLIVER

The argument someone probably made, somewhere along the line, was that investors, or audiences or whomever, didn't want to do a *Star Wars* that was actually about much of anything. The safest, least challenging path equals asset protection. In all likelihood, *Duel* was probably scuttled because the Powers That Be made a safe choice. Economically, Disney and Lucasfilm probably feel it was the right choice. Artistically, and creatively, there's plenty of arguments to the contrary.

DAN MADSEN

Personally, I preferred the pre-Disney days. The sense that *Star Wars* was not likely to be oversaturated—the sense of wonder that was evoked every time a *Star Wars* movie comes about. The little franchise that *really* could. In the Disney era, we *know* there will be more *Star Wars*. It's a little less thrilling to have a movie drop onto screens, a little less unique to see a new series hitting the air. When it's predictable, it's . . . just not as special. And this may be one of the realities Disney should consider in the coming years. "The *Star Wars* Generation" was used to having to wait, and work for it, and wonder if more would come. All of which engaged passion and imagination far more fully than predictable patterns. The reality for fans has now been rewritten, and in doing so, a part of their very DNA as a fan has been indelibly impacted.

GLEN OLIVER

I preferred the more mercurial approach to *Star Wars* management, although I do think Lucas should've rallied his troops and beaten the canon situation far sooner than it actually happened. The situation felt a little scrappier, a little more home-grown, somehow a little truer and more genuine. *Star Wars* under Disney is just another cog in an incomprehensibly gargantuan corporate machine. Back in the day, by virtue of its very existence and its continued success, *Star Wars* was a reminder that *anything* can happen. We need more Little Engine stories these days; it saddens me that *Star Wars* has been diminished a bit.

One truth can't be denied: four decades on, George Lucas's Star Wars *remains a remarkable motion picture—as fun and as entertaining and inspiring today as the day it was released. The film is still a monumental technical achievement and its profound influence on the craft and the business of filmmaking is still being felt. The trilogy created by* Star Wars *and its first two sequels,* The Empire Strikes Back *and* Return of the Jedi, *remains a unique and landmark cinematic event. And everything else that original trilogy spawned—the prequels, sequels, TV series, books, comics, toys, games, and all the rest—constitute a unique and ongoing pop culture phenomenon that has brought joy and wonder to millions of people the world over. May the Force be with it—always.*

BRIAN JAY JONES
(author, *George Lucas: A Life*)

Overall, Lucasfilm is in fine hands. Disney is the biggest company in the world. They own *everything* now. They can market, they can merchandise, they can promote, they can distribute. It's your one-stop shop for everything you want to do. It's like James Bond or Woody Allen. Actors used to talk about how their agents would ask them if they wanted to do the next Woody Allen movie, and they would say *yes*. The agent would say, "Do you want to know what it's about?" and the actor would say, "I don't care . . ." *Star Wars* is that way. You know, it's like, "Do you want to be in the next *Star Wars?*" "Absolutely." Somebody like Laura Dern said about *The Last Jedi*, "I was so excited to be there." That's what's going to happen with stars. People *want* to be a part of that iconic galaxy. Again, I think *Star Wars* is in good hands and it's going to be around a long time.

LIAM NEESON
(actor, "Qui-Gon Jinn")

Star Wars provides escapism from newspaper headlines. During the Second World War, all these slushy old Hollywood films were made and people couldn't get enough of them as an escape. I'm not saying that *Star Wars* is slushy entertainment. People are, I think, all feeling like three-legged stools. They're totally confused and kind of don't know, subconsciously, which way to turn. So seeing something like *Star Wars* makes a world that size become comfortable and understandable. It's very appealing. It's like a giant kid's pacifier. They help to define a very confusing, complex world and made it palatable and understandable.

J.J. ABRAMS

The idea of good versus evil, light versus dark, is certainly the core of *Star Wars*. There's the temptation of power and greed—the dark side—and the sacrifice and nobility of fighting for justice, which is the light. These are the tenets of the *Star Wars* universe, and all the props and gizmos and spaceships are incredibly cool, but the core and heart of the story is family and which path you're going to take. The beauty of working on this movie was getting to play in this incredible sandbox that George Lucas created. Everyone who worked on *The Rise of Skywalker* approached it from a place of reverence, but everyone was also determined to do it proud and to tell that story of good versus evil. And, like the main characters of the film, we worked hard to make sure that the dark side gets its ass kicked!

JEANINE BASINGER
(film historian, founder and curator of the Cinema Archives
of Wesleyan University)

Star Wars shows the strength of visual storytelling. I think it shows how much these things matter to us. The people who saw *Casablanca*, the people who saw *Stagecoach*, the people who saw *Best Years of Our Lives*, *It's a Wonderful Life*, *Easy Rider*, *Mary Poppins*, *The Sound of Music*—you see a movie and it stays with you. The model of the new Hollywood was such that *Star Wars* could stay with us in a very strong moneymaking, product-driven way. It's also something that can regenerate itself by showing it to children over and over so that you create a whole new generation of people who will keep on with it. It's a testament to the power of the story to how much we love stories. Look, people are still reading the book *Little Women* written in the 1800s, and we're still making movies out of it, too. So, a great story with great characters in a setting that connects in any format will stay alive. Shakespeare's plays are still being put on. So, it's a testament to the power of the story that *Star Wars* told the tale of characters that we embraced and responded to and utilized incredibly intelligent technology that got that film up and moving and just sweeping viewers along.

ANTHONY DANIELS

Do I get sick of *Star Wars*? If I talk about it too much, I do. But generally, the fans and interviewers I talk to are so interested that they revive the interest in me. When people are intrigued, I should be glad of that and I *am* glad. And the fact that I wish I had gotten to play Hamlet, that's private. I should be immensely grateful. People always ask me, "What would you be doing now if it wasn't for *Star Wars*?" I generally reply that I would probably be working in a show shop. Who knows? But I've had this mighty piece of film in my life, this mighty character, and it's neat to be that person. I genuinely believe that it's in the eye of the beholder.

KATHLEEN KENNEDY
(president, Lucasfilm, Ltd.)

It is funny how you end up saying things and then think, "That kind of sounds like the Force." It continually reminds you that what George was creating was something that does have meaning. It comes back in different ways—in the way people establish their values and their idea of how to lead a good life. That's inherent in *Star Wars*. And that is, I think, what we always have in mind. Yes, we're exploring drama and telling a story about good and evil, and yes, it takes place in outer space, but it's grounded in human values and compassion and generosity, and those are the ideas that were so important to George. And I think that has a lot to do with why it's lasted.

J.J. ABRAMS

Since I was eleven years old, when I saw *Star Wars* for the first time, what it had at its core was a sense of possibility, optimism, and hope. It was the first movie that blew my mind. It didn't matter how they did any of it, because it was all so overwhelmingly and entirely great. It was funny and romantic and scary and compelling and the visual effects just served it, so the approach had to be in that spirit, in an authentic and not in a Pollyanna-ish way. From the very beginning, this was about embracing a spirit that we love so desperately.

KATHLEEN KENNEDY

We've always recognized that it's the Skywalkers, it's a family and it's a family drama. And the resolution around that is what was important in what we're doing with this episode. So that was certainly the focus. But it's also a huge opportunity for *Star Wars* now to take a pause and create the next saga, the next decade of movies, the next several generations of movies. That's what I'm incredibly excited about. I think at the same time that we find resolution in this, that the fans get to experience all these beloved characters and that story coming to an end, it's also launching a new beginning.

16

THIS IS THE WAY: *STAR WARS* ON TELEVISION

"I will help you. I have spoken."

For all its success on the big screen over the past forty-plus years, it took quite some time for *Star Wars* to have any modicum of success on the small screen. Even beyond the infamous 1978 *Star Wars Holiday Special,* in the mid-1980s there were the live-action TV movies *Caravan of Courage: An Ewok Adventure* and *Ewoks: Battle for Endor,* as well as the animated series *Ewoks* and *Star Wars: Droids.* However, none of those made any mark on popular culture with the exception of the *Holiday Special*'s dubious distinction of being one of the worst holiday specials cum variety shows of all time.

But *Star Wars*' fortunes on television began to change in 2003 with the arrival of the traditionally animated series *Star Wars: Clone Wars,* airing in the form of twenty "micro-episodes" on Cartoon Network over its three seasons, the first two running three to five minutes each, and the third, twelve minutes each. It was set between the events of *Episode II: Attack of the Clones* and *Episode III: Revenge of the Sith.* Developing the series was Russian-born Genndy Tartakovsky, creator of *Samurai Jack, The Powerpuff Girls,* and *Dexter's Laboratory.* The series immediately caught the interest of fans with its distinctive animation style and unique take on the *Star Wars* mythos.

GENNDY TARTAKOVSKY
(director/executive producer, *Star Wars: Clone Wars,*
2003 to 2005 series)

I was finishing up working on *Samurai Jack* and I was having dinner with two of my bosses. After dinner they were talking secretively and one of them said, "Let's go ahead and tell him. We might be able to do an animated *Star Wars,* but they would only be one-minute episodes." I said, "I don't really want to do that, because they're basically commercials if they're one minute long."

I didn't want to do it, but when they asked me if I had any interest at all, I said yes if there was more time for the episodes. They told George they had me and the team from *Samurai Jack*. George Lucas said, "Oh, I love *Samurai Jack*. They can have three minutes per episode." So we were three minutes' worth of *Star Wars* beyond what the initial idea was. I think they wanted to keep the episodes so short, because they were really afraid of somebody kind of ruining it, making it bad. I think the way George was thinking, if you do a minute, you really can't do anything that bad, you can't progress a story, you can't really set up any characters or anything. I think he kind of got burned on some other things before, so he went into it very skeptically.

It was a genuine challenge to create a series that could capture the essence of Star Wars *in what can best be described as bite-sized morsels, though each installment would have to have a beginning, a middle, and a cliffhanger.*

GENNDY TARTAKOVSKY

Besides working on *Star Wars*, which is a huge pressure to begin with, we also had to ask ourselves what we could do in three minutes. The first thing I did was cut together three-minute episodes of *Samurai Jack*, just to see how long three minutes really is. And I realized that you could put a lot of stuff in. Of course, the more dialogue you put in, the less stuff you can do, because dialogue just eats up time. So, we planned it that way and thought that if we were telling one story, it would seem longer, and eventually someone will cut it together and it will be a movie.

It *was* a challenge. The nice thing is that George very much became a fan of what we were doing. We had lunch once and he said, "It's great to be able to jump around the universe and have fun and not be tied down to such a hard story structure." That's exactly what we did: we had fun and let loose. And his son was a really big fan of it, too, so that helped a lot. Actually, as soon as they started seeing them, they started talking about different avenues and different things we could do.

Tartakovsky's short-form experiment didn't live long, but it did inspire Lucas to take a deeper dive into animated Star Wars *himself, but in a CG-animated format instead. The Clone Wars debuted as a 2008 theatrical film, which, like its predecessor, was set between* Clones *and* Sith, *and featured several already-produced segments for the weekly series and a new story as well. Ultimately, there would be a total of seven seasons and 133 episodes produced, and it would soon become one of the most acclaimed and beloved pieces of* Star Wars *storytelling, which in the mind of some fans even redeemed the prequels. The series would follow the adventures and evolution of Anakin Skywalker (voiced by Matt Lanter); Obi-Wan Kenobi (James Arnold Taylor); Anakin's Padawan, Ahsoka Tano (Ashley Eckstein); Yoda (Tom Kane); a resurrected Darth Maul (Sam Witwer); and various clone troopers (Dee Bradley Baker).*

JOHN KENNETH MUIR

(author, *Science Fiction and Fantasy Films of the 1970s*)

I think the series is incredibly significant in filling in the period between films. *The Clone Wars* makes *Attack of the Clones* and *Revenge of the Sith* actually play better. I am not a prequel hater, but the movies work even better if one has watched *Clone Wars,* which is quite an accomplishment.

Running the show was supervising director Dave Filoni, who had initially presumed that if he saw George Lucas once or twice a year during the process of making the series, that would be a lot. But as it turned out, Lucas began having a very active role in crafting the stories, guiding the visual direction, and honing the show into what it would become.

DAVE FILONI

(supervising director/executive producer, *Star Wars: The Clone Wars*)

When I was working early on with [writer/producer] Henry Gilroy, we were trying to figure out what the character makeup of the show would be, and how we could produce a TV series based on the time period of the Clone Wars. Because the Clone Wars is so vast, it would literally take thousands of clones battling thousands of battle droids—so we were bouncing around more of an original-trilogy idea of a crew. We were coming up with the character makeup. Frankly, that character makeup is close to what we ended up with in *Rebels.* So it just goes to show you that those ideas don't really die. When we took this idea in to George, he looked at it and went, "Hmmm. So, Anakin Skywalker is going to be doing this, and Obi-Wan is going to be doing this." We had never assumed that we'd be working with those characters. My opinion was, "Who am I to write Anakin Skywalker?" But George was like, "I'm going to teach you all about this," and he did. So we wound up with the show we did, under his direction.

GEORGE LUCAS

(creator/executive producer, *Star Wars: The Clone Wars*)

It was exciting. We were experimenting to try to move the medium forward, and we succeeded beyond our wildest imagination. As a result, I felt, "Wow, this is worth putting on the big screen, because I think the fans would like to see it in theaters rather than only on television." Animation and digital effects are quite different from each other. I'm not a big fan of realistic animation. I think that animation is an art form unto itself, and the whole artistic part of animation is the design graphics and style. To try to make something look like live-action is simply replication and it doesn't make *any* sense to me. Special effects, on the other hand, truly are photo-real, and the whole point is that you can put them into a live-action film and people won't know that they aren't real. So they're two different things.

JOEL ARON
(director of cinematography lighting, *Star Wars: The Clone Wars*)

We don't light it like ordinary animation. Dave said to me in the beginning, "We need to think Frank Miller, get it very graphic, make it look very different." And then one day George came in and had us push it even further, which was really good for the look. So because of that, we've tried to push it even more-so, cinematically. With influences from, obviously the feature films that are out there, but also the live-action movies that are out there. *Drive*, I'll see the movie *Drive* and instantly I have to have that look. That scene reminds me of this scene, and we try to push it further cinematically. It just helps with, especially with what [the actors] are doing. I can't just have them delivering lines to each other, you really have to feel it.

HENRY GILROY
(story editor, *Star Wars: The Clone Wars*)

Even the subtitles in animation are so much different than in live-action. If you're on a close-up of an actor's face, and he says a big block of dialogue, you'll be compelled to watch that dialogue, because the actor is putting so much really subtle bits of acting and emotions into that. You're never going to get that same connection with a CG puppet face. Or you can, but usually not on a television budget. It's a different kind of storytelling. You just have to be aware of it. I think the great thing about animation is you can do cinematic storytelling—larger scope—bigger things shooting at each other, whatever they are. Which brings more spectacle. But it takes extra work to bring those more intimate moments. We definitely tried to do that in *The Clone Wars*, by just trying to find the emotional reality of the scene. What's the better form for that than war? Telling war stories—and George had the guts to say, "Oh yeah, you want to take out that battalion of clones for the story, go for it." Nobody would want to do that in children's television before *Star Wars*.

DAVE FILONI

We would sit in a room for two weeks straight—me, George, and the writers—and we would hash out all the stories, all twenty-six episodes of a season, in two weeks. I think we had to do about three episodes a day. We had a whiteboard and wrote everything down on a whiteboard. Sometimes George would leave to go do something else, and the writers and I would keep writing on the whiteboard—and then George would come back in and read it and take his finger and erase. It was just really fun. We all stayed at the ranch during that time, so there would be some evenings where it would spill over. It was fun for him—I think it was fun for him to be basically teaching us *Star Wars* every day.

GEORGE LUCAS

My whole life I've heard, "Well, you can't do that." And, Dave had to put up with the same things that everybody at ILM had to put up with—you know, Dennis Muren and John Knoll and all them—they all had to put up with me. I would come in in the morning and say, "Well, we're going to do this, this, and this," and their jaws would drop and go, "He's not really serious . . ." And I'd say, "We'll do it!" I pushed them through it. And they came through. A lot of the things we did had never been done before and that scares everybody. They said, "We don't know how to do this." And I'd say, "Well, we'll figure it out!" With ILM we went from old-fashioned special effects to digital effects and created the digital cinema. It was the same thing with animation, especially with *The Clone Wars*. We set out to make a feature-quality TV show, and I think we succeeded. The lighting, the characters, the animation was all a feature-level quality, and we did it on a TV budget. We were able to tell stories and expand the universe, and bring in great characters like Ahsoka, that we would never have been able to have.

It really came out of the idea that there's a lot of stories there, and I'd like to tell those stories, but would never be able to put them in a theater because they are more interesting as a long form than as a short form. That's why I experimented in television. I wanted to be able to play with those stories and do things that nobody would ever do.

DAVE FILONI

The TV series let us do something unique which was, we were on all the time, week-to-week. We were able to give fans a *Star Wars* storytelling experience every week. There's stuff that we shot that never made it into the show at all. I try to never include stuff that you wouldn't see in the movies. I'm fully aware that there were kids who'd never seen *Revenge of the Sith*. Nor would you expect them to. It's a very intense movie. So that clearly expresses my problem—I've got *Attack of the Clones* on one side, and I've got *Revenge of the Sith,* which is a complete downfall of the good guys. So I can't go about this narrative like, "And everything was bunny rabbits until right up before then." So it's a hard place to be.

Making the films, George had so many ideas, and he knew that he was focused on the Anakin Skywalker story for the films—and he wanted to explore all these other characters and create new characters. And look at Anakin sometimes in more of a deft way than he had in the films—different personalities of him.

GEORGE LUCAS

The Clone Wars is like a footnote to the live-action features. The features are Anakin Skywalker's story. So, when you go between *Episode II* and *Episode III,* it's like there's a little asterisk that says, "More about the Clone Wars, the animated series." But it doesn't *really* have anything to do with Anakin's story, about his fall to the dark side. In the animated series, Anakin is simply a normal person. It's consistent with the live-action films, but in the movies, you never see Anakin as a normal person. He's always struggling. So this gives us a chance to broaden and show that, "Anakin was a regular guy," just like he was in *Episode I.*

DAVE FILONI

We had to stay true to the spirit of *Star Wars* and the look that had been established in the movies. There was fantastic work done by production designers like John Barry, Norman Reynolds, and Gavin Bocquet, and it was our job to reflect that, but through animation. But *The Clone Wars* shows us more of the galaxy than we ever saw in the live-action films, so we had to forge plenty of new ground, as well. We wanted to create something unique and fun. The movies are so recognizable, and we wanted to capture that flavor, but we also wanted our series characters to live on their own. With all those years of history, there were a lot of expectations that came with a new installment, and we wanted to be clear that this was going to be different from what had come before. Many of the backgrounds look painted, while the characters and physical objects look almost like they have been created by hand. Working in computer animation, it's easy to make everything look clean, but imperfection is far more interesting.

CATHERINE WINDER
(executive producer, *Star Wars: The Clone Wars*)
Since the earliest days, animation has been produced using two-dimensional storyboards to plan out the action. With *The Clone Wars,* George Lucas

wanted us to try something totally new, a process he had utilized extensively on the live-action movies.

DAVE FILONI

This is an enormously vast galaxy, and the Clone Wars affect almost every corner of it. We could finally show the adventure, heroism, treachery, and intrigue that was happening throughout the conflict. Now that *Star Wars* is no longer constrained by the Skywalker saga, the possibilities are as limitless as the universe itself. The Clone Wars are a time of enormous struggle and also great heroism. As a longtime *Star Wars* fan, it was exciting to be able to bring these stories to life, stories we've only wondered about. We learned just why the Clone Wars becomes the stuff of legend in the *Star Wars* galaxy.

ASHLEY ECKSTEIN
(voice actress, "Ahsoka Tano," *Star Wars: The Clone Wars*)

Dave is honestly the best director I've ever worked with, because he gets to know each of us individually. He doesn't have one directing style, he directs for the actor. So he knows exactly what to say to get us in the right emotion, to get us in the right headspace, to say the right things. Many directors have the one style, and it either works for you or it doesn't, but that's not Dave. Every actor is different, and there's a different approach to every actor. That's really hard. Literally, the best director I've ever worked with.

DAVE FILONI

It's easy to be a good director when you have great people. And I've been surrounded by great people. To me, it's a simple formula. I don't have to do many things or struggle, because I know what these guys are capable of. And that makes my life infinitely easier in all capacities. It's my responsibility to know the story, to know the characters, and communicate that to them—but as actors, they have to become that person and embody that role. I respect that. I see it as a shared collaboration to bring to the screen.

JAMES ARNOLD TAYLOR
(voice actor, "Obi-Wan Kenobi," *Star Wars: The Clone Wars*)

I have always wanted to be a voice actor, pretty much since I was four years old. I knew I wanted to do voices in cartoons, TV, and radio. I did little radio shows with my friends creating sound effects. When I was sixteen, I started as a stand-up comedian and I always did voices like Marty McFly and Doc Brown. Then I got into radio a year later and became a DJ. I taught myself how to work with all the equipment by staying over late at night and watching all the DJs working. I started to make my own shows and gave them to the program director. One day they asked me if I wanted to do my own show, because the overnight DJ didn't show up. So I ended up doing a show and from there on I went on and the rest is history, as they say. I actually did over eight thousand comedy bits that I wrote, voiced, produced, and directed for the Premiere Radio Network over the course of twelve years. From there on I moved into voice acting, getting an agent, and getting in cartoon work. I knew from a very young age that that's what I wanted to do. I loved watching all those greats like Mel Blanc, Don Messick, and Daws Butler, as well as the new breed like Jim Cummings, Jess Harnell, and Billy West. I've always been inspired by them and knew that this was what I wanted to do.

Taylor, as it turns out, was friends with Collette Sunderman, voice director of The Clone Wars, which got him the audition for the role of Obi-Wan Kenobi, in which he did his best to capture the essence of Ewan McGregor's take on the role in live-action.

JAMES ARNOLD TAYLOR

Collette thought it was a perfect match. Her words, not mine! I always study the actor's voice for voice matching. I've studied Ewan's voice more than anybody but I also studied Alec Guinness. I wanted my Obi-Wan to be a combination of both. I feel I have the ability to do that since I don't have to look like them, but just to sound like them. I try [with Alec Guinness's voice] "These aren't the droids you're looking for" and [with Ewan McGregor's voice] "May the Force be with you," and combine them both so you get [with his own Obi-Wan voice] "My Obi-Wan Kenobi." The trick is not to do a voice characterization, but to be able to step in seamlessly and be the person when they are not available. I've had the honor to be Obi-Wan for so many years and have voiced him more than anybody else. Both George Lucas and Dave Filoni said, "This is your role now, so take it and do with it as you would." So I don't have to worry about sounding exactly like Ewan or Alec.

MATT LANTER
(voice actor, "Anakin Skywalker," *Star Wars: The Clone Wars*)
I did some background extra work for a film called *Bobby Jones* that shot in Atlanta. After falling in love with the magic of it, I decided to finish out my semester at UGA, save up some money, then packed up my car with what I had and drove out to L.A. to make a career. It was a standard voice audition

for a project that I knew nothing about, just that it was *Star Wars* something. Dave Filoni was there, as well as Catherine Winder, and they asked me to read the copy as a combination of Han Solo and Luke Skywalker.

Of course, I watched all the prequel films to gather what I could about Anakin, but I'm not trying to copy a voice performance in any way. George and Dave and I have all chatted about how this Anakin is a bit different than what we have seen in the films and I feel I have the liberty to extend that into voice quality as well. I was cast with my own spin on the character, not as a voice double, so it's actually really nice not having that pressure like a few of my other castmates.

DAVE FILONI

All the kids who have watched *The Clone Wars* have a really good sense of who Anakin Skywalker is. When I was a kid, and watching *A New Hope*, I had no clue. When Obi-Wan says, "Vader betrayed and murdered your father," I was like, "Wow, that sucks for Luke." But these kids now, if you play *A New Hope*, that's how they find out their hero dies and Vader killed him? It's totally different for them.

I love Matt. Matt came in and looped the first several episodes that we did. We had a different actor as Anakin, and we changed out and brought Matt in. So I had to do actual auditioning for Anakin, and Matt came in. I had Matt come in with Ashley and Cat, and I was really paying attention to what Matt was doing when he walked into the room. I don't know why this was important, but I felt very strongly that whoever was playing Anakin Skywalker, it wasn't just the voice—they had to embody what I always thought Anakin Skywalker was when I was growing up. This guy that everybody liked. You have to have a likability to Anakin to understand when he falls apart, and he thinks it's doing the right thing, it's that much more devastating, because he's trying to hold on to everything so tightly, and thinks he's doing good—except he's doing evil. And Matt, when he walked in, he's just that likable person. He is.

MATT LANTER

It's fun for me to be able to perform the whole spectrum of Anakin over the course of *The Clone Wars*. I love when *The Clone Wars* started, he was a little more swashbuckling and innocent and everybody's hero. I love that part of him, but it doesn't have a lot of give and take. It's a fun challenge to smoothly take him in that direction. It's fun for us as fans to see those times where he dips. And that's great, because we know it's coming.

DAVE FILONI

The point of Anakin Skywalker's story is that we are all making tough decisions every day—as Anakin Skywalker does. We start out our day, we don't intend to turn to the dark side, but we so quickly make choices that tunnel us down into the darkness. Now I've had a bad day, now I've had a good day. When do you feel bad? When you make choices and you feel angry, maybe have road rage—and when you feel anger, hate, you feel bad. When you feel good, you do something selfless, give someone something that's meaningful to them, don't you feel better? That's kind of the whole point of *Star Wars*. Either be selfless or selfish. This is what George spoke about the most—selfish/selfless. This will lift you up, this will bring you down. And that's the Force in a nutshell.

TOM KANE
(voice actor, "Yoda," *Star Wars: The Clone Wars*)

I got started at Lucasfilm just doing miscellaneous small parts for their video games. I guess I was actually on the very first they ever did, it was called *The Dig*, I think. Just goofing around I would read other parts to show off. One day they were doing some TIE Fighter game. There were the voices of Yoda and C-3PO, I read them and they hired me to do them. As far as Yoda is concerned, I didn't work on being Yoda. I saw the movies fifty-three times so the voice was very much in my head. Everybody tries to do Yoda, not just voice-overs, but everybody. I was doing stuff for LucasArts and I was going around reading Yoda lines and what I didn't know was that Frank Oz was directing a movie. They recorded it and played it for George and I've been Yoda ever since. I have never met Frank Oz. I once saw him at a recording studio, but didn't have the guts to come up and say anything.

CATHERINE TABER
(voice actor, "Padmé Amidala," *Star Wars: The Clone Wars*)

I naturally have a voice similar in tone to Natalie's, and I certainly have watched her performance from the films many times. I also studied the wealth of data on Padmé and her history at the *Star Wars* online database, but, after that, Dave was really great about letting me just play Padmé as I see her. Whether you are doing theater, such as a Shakespearean piece, or film or television, I believe when you take on a character it's important to make it your own, and not just try and copy another actor's performance. I feel honored to be the one bringing Padmé to life in all her new trials and adventures.

DEE BRADLEY BAKER
(voice actor, "Captain Rex," "Fives," "Commander Cody,"
and others, *Star Wars: The Clone Wars*)

I was called to audition for this "unnamed" project. Had to voice match the clones, they liked me, I booked it. I'd already worked with director Dave Filoni on Nickelodeon's *Avatar: The Last Airbender* television series—really proud of that show—as well as with the incomparable voice director Andrea Romano, who was helping cast *Clone Wars* at the time. They knew and trusted my acting ability and I gave them what they needed, I guess. Couldn't believe it. I'd never done anything so "normal." Most of my roles were either cartoony or creature-oriented up to that point. This was a whole new thing, plus it was dear to me, as I really loved *Star Wars* as a kid.

I got specifics from Dave Filoni, plus the scripts were well written and show the way. It's specific, but I wouldn't call it "strict." Also, we get a drawing of the character to get a sense of the size, attitude, etc. Dave is supportive and trusts us, yet has a specific idea of the feel of what the character needs to be. From that, we are free to find it with imagination.

If The Clone Wars *is to be remembered for one thing, it's the introduction of the character of Ahsoka Tano to the* Star Wars *canon. Although fans didn't embrace the character initially, Anakin Skywalker's Padawan has gone on to be considered a fan favorite. Initially portrayed by Ashley Eckstein in the animated* Clone Wars, Rebels, *and* Forces of Destiny, *with Rosario Dawson carrying on the role in live-action with appearances in* The Mandalorian *and its subsequent spin-off,* Ahsoka. *With Ahsoka's popularity, Ashley Eckstein founded the Her Universe clothing line, and became a major ambassador to promote female voices and representation in geek culture.*

ASHLEY ECKSTEIN
Matt Lanter and I were so lucky, because we had both come from the live-action world and were fairly new to voice-over. This was my first big job. I walked into the studio and it's Dee Bradley Baker, Tom Kane, James Arnold Taylor, and I very much felt like a Padawan. Life imitates art.

HENRY GILROY
A lot of times actors come in and they're not really familiar with all of what preceded before. So I think for Ashley, she came in and had seen the movies, but didn't know *all* of it. So we did one of these things where we used fake names when we were casting it, "You're going to do duh-duh-duh to

Starkiller," or whatever. We definitely played that. So when we told her she got the part and was going to kind of be the star of the show, she was like, "Oh, cool!" She didn't really realize that part of that was kind of awesome—she could grow into the role.

ASHLEY ECKSTEIN

I was born in 1981, so obviously I missed *A New Hope*, but what I do remember specifically, and I was so young, was the scene with R2-D2 and C-3PO on Tatooine in the desert. I loved Princess Leia, but I loved R2-D2 so much, I wanted to be R2-D2. My memories are watching it on VHS at home, and obviously, we had all the movies, so it was just something that was just there. It was a part of our childhood.

HENRY GILROY

Here's this young person, she's thirteen years old, she's grown up on a temple on Coruscant, she's never really seen the worlds—and suddenly she's thrust onto the front lines of a war, going from planet to planet. And that's something we wanted to do for our audience, was to introduce them to the galaxy through Ahsoka Tano. And with every episode, the more that Ashley brought life to this character, we started to feel the experience she was getting.

ASHLEY ECKSTEIN

Dave very much worked on a need-to-know basis. But he did let me know that Ahsoka was walking away [from the Jedi Order at the end of season five], and that I wouldn't be back for a while. I knew that I would be back, but it would be a while. So for me, it was goodbye. I recorded these episodes, and literally, it felt like my heart was beating outside my chest, because I was essentially saying goodbye to these guys for a while, and I didn't know when I'd be coming back.

On the show, Yoda obviously recognized something in Ahsoka, where he saw that Ahsoka was the perfect Padawan for Anakin. To me, she's a mix of both Anakin and Obi-Wan. She obviously is very smart and she's very by the book. And she really takes pride in the Jedi way, which I think is why she took the ending—the season five finale—so hard, because she literally put her heart and soul into the Jedi and when they betrayed her so badly, it just broke her. But she grew up a lot.

DAVE FILONI

When we started with Ahsoka, George and I had a moment looking at the early days and such, and he and I were like, "Well, this is either going to work, or people are going to hate it." But there's not much in-between when you give Anakin a Padawan. And you dare, back then in 2005, to make it a little girl. But George always had a great mind for a bigger picture. And we evolved the character as we went, and she grew into someone obviously a lot of fans have grown to love and respect. That's why the character continues to persist, because they show such tremendous support for her. We all feel we earned that, because she wasn't universally liked at the beginning.

HENRY GILROY

It's extremely satisfying to see her popularity. And also, for the generation of young women who were inspired by her. Before I talk about the good stuff, let me talk about the bad stuff. I don't know who the A-hole is who wrote the August 2008 version of *Entertainment Weekly*—he wrote an article, "The worst characters of *Star Wars*," but I never forgot that, because I was saying, "You have to give her a chance, and let her grow into the character we know she's going to grow into." So, yeah, it's extremely satisfying. I don't think I really realized it until the final episode of season one of *Rebels*, when Ahsoka returns, and somebody sent me a reaction video of all of these kids screaming and running around and jumping up and down. And I was like, "Oh yeah, she's an extremely important character to this second generation of *Star Wars* fans." So, yes, I'm extremely grateful and satisfied.

In addition to the introduction of Ahsoka Tano, The Clone Wars *did the one thing George Lucas specifically set out to avoid while making* The Phantom Menace: *they brought back villainous Sith Lord Darth Maul, who was previously sliced in half on camera at the culmination of the epic lightsaber duel on Naboo. George Lucas refused to hear demands for his return in future movies. Of course, ultimately, his return was Lucas's idea.*

SAM WITWER
(voice actor, "Darth Maul," *Star Wars: The Clone Wars*)
In terms of Darth Maul, the guy's got the Boba Fett factor going for him, you know? He looks cool, and there's an attitude that was established in *The Phantom Menace*. I mean, you can't do the same thing. You can't bring the character back and have it be exactly what it was. So we actually had to sit around and talk about if there can only be two Sith, he can't just be good at sword fighting, he has to be good at everything. If you're going to pick an apprentice and spend years training him, he's got to be *really* smart. He's got to be someone who could eventually take over the role of master. It was always our aspiration to go there, but the big thing for early on was to describe the

cost of what had happened to him—not just physically, but mentally—and to show you the unadulterated dark side of the Force. This is what it is. It's not just cool leather suits and red lightsabers—it's madness and despair and pain.

Despite Disney canceling the show not once, but twice, public outcry for the series' continuation prompted its return first for a truncated sixth season on Netflix in 2014, and then a "Final Season," perhaps its best and most powerful, on Disney+ in 2020. The final episode of Star Wars: The Clone Wars *aired on that streaming service, the show having proved itself to be one of the most popular and critically acclaimed entries in the history of the franchise. And fans are still clamoring for more: they continue to be enchanted by the possibilities of more adventures with Anakin, Obi-Wan, Ahsoka, and the Clones.*

GLEN OLIVER
(pop culture commentator)

The initial impulse to mirror *Star Wars* onto television was absolutely a correct one, although they didn't go about doing so the right way—at first. Sure, there are considerations of "cinematic" scale and so forth, but whatever scope *Star Wars* might lose on the small screen can be (and, in some cases, has already been) more than compensated for through television's ability to explore stories in more depth, by exploring a far wider variety of stories than films are, quite frankly, allowed to explore. Which, at the end of the day, are key elements any franchise needs to better thrive and survive.

JOHN KENNETH MUIR

The Clone Wars is a remarkable series, and adds to the luster of the prequel film series. The stories go deep and develop characters like Obi-Wan and Anakin in ways unexpected and welcome. Ahsoka is a remarkable creation, and now one of the most beloved characters in the franchise. The series demonstrates that *Star Wars* can stand up to long-term, serial storytelling, rather than just rinsing and repeating old formulas (like the sequel trilogy). By revisiting the Gungans (in stories such as "Gungan Attack") or Watto's people, the Toydarians (in stories such as "Ambush"), the aliens take on new substance, and the universe seems, oddly enough, less like a cartoon designed to sell toys.

GLEN OLIVER

Unfortunately, the animated—and canonical—animated *Star Wars* offerings have been short-shrifted by many fans. There often doesn't seem to be an understanding, either tacit or otherwise, that animated material like

The Clone Wars, *Rebels*, and *Resistance* are sanctioned, canonical, and even referenced at times by their live-action counterparts. There's a lot of remarkable *Star Wars* being missed and misunderstood, largely because I don't think the animated series have been properly framed by the Powers That Be. I also think animation still, to a large degree, carries with it an unjust stigma of frivolity and an assumption of childishness. Which should be factored in when positioning the importance of their storytelling to the overall franchise. I could certainly be wrong about this, but their being "cartoons" may well have, to some degree at least, marginalized them in the eyes of fans and the Powers That Be. The movies have always felt like "bread and butter"—which is absolutely the way it *should* be in the grand scheme of things. But it feels like the shows have sometimes been undersold, or mispositioned, to preserve this focus. And I don't think that's fair to fans, to storytellers, or the franchise in general.

JAMES ARNOLD TAYLOR

I'm in love with the show. I think it was one of the best shows on television and I'd also say that if I wasn't in it. There are several actors, friends of mine, seasoned actors, that watched the show religiously with their kids. I think it is due to the storytelling, the art, and the love of filmmaking.

SAM WITWER

The great thing with the show is the patience of the storytelling. How it started as a brighter, simpler series, and as it's gone on, things got more complicated. And more adult. What's cool is, as those stories got more complicated, the show became more visually stunning and complex. They all could've been more impatient. They could've gone straight for these things right away. "Let's do a Mortis thing in the first season." But it wouldn't have been the right call. You want to know what you're doing by the time you get to those heavy-hitting things. And you want to have the characters established so the audience feels something huge when something happens to any one of them. That patience of storytelling is something I admire.

CATHERINE TABER

Things get darker as the series goes along. I think they kind of had to in order to be true to the overall *Star Wars* "legend." Ashley and Dave took Ahsoka in a very cool direction as she matured and came into her own. We know the path Anakin is headed down, and we started to see that transition. Everyone is affected, not only by the war itself, but also the hidden politics that are below the surface. There was still the classic *Star Wars* humor and light-hearted fun moments, but the darker, more mature tone continued.

The first Star Wars *CG-animated series created after Disney's acquisition of Lucasfilm was* Rebels, *set five years before the events of* A New Hope *and running from 2014 to 2018. The show, created by Dave Filoni, Simon Kinberg, and Carrie Beck, serves as a bridge in the same way that* Clone Wars *bridged* Attack of the Clones *and* Revenge of the Sith.

In the beginning, the show's core group of characters consisted of Ezra Bridger (voiced by Taylor Gray), a fifteen-year-old human con artist on the planet Lothal who discovers he has Force abilities and finds himself a crew member of the ship the Ghost; *Kanan Jarrus (voiced by Freddie Prinze, Jr.), a Jedi survivor of* Revenge of the Sith's *Order 66, which saw the near extermination of his kind; Hera Syndulla (voiced by Vanessa Marshall, the Twi'lek owner and pilot of the* Ghost; *Sabine Wren (voiced by Tiya Sircar), a sixteen-year-old Mandalorian who is a graffiti artist, as well as an expert in weapons and explosions; Zeb Orrelios (Steven Blum), a Lasat honor guard whose people were one of the first species to rise up against the Empire and, as a result, were all but exterminated; and C1–10P (also known as "Chopper"), an astromech droid built and owned by Hera.*

Star Wars: Rebels began with a one-hour film in October 2014 and that same month launched as a weekly series on Disney XD, running four seasons and seventy-five episodes by its conclusion in March 2018.

DAVE FILONI
(executive producer/director, *Star Wars: Rebels*)

One of the crazy things about *Rebels* is that when I sat down at the table, we pitched around really quickly what kind of show we were going to make. We had a matter of, honestly, weeks as opposed to where you would normally have months. Carrie Beck said, "What about something that kind of feels like *The A-Team*, with a small group of people in a van? They're rebels fighting for a cause and will fight small fights." I liked that. If you look at the *Art of Clone Wars* book, one of my original pitches for that show was exactly the show that *Rebels* turned out to be. Which is a group of people living on one ship travel around trying to do some good underneath the bigger war. Then we added Simon Kinberg.

SIMON KINBERG
(cocreator/executive producer, *Star Wars: Rebels*)

I was already working in some capacity on the *Star Wars* features when Kiri Hart, who's the head of the Lucasfilm Story Group, reached out to me and asked, "Do you want to do an animated show for Disney Networks?" I was obviously very interested. They had an idea for an *A-Team* style show. It was about the birth of the early days of the Rebel Alliance and it was an ensemble show. The thing that I brought to it was to try and turn that group into a proto-family unit. None of them are actually blood-related, but they operate like a little family. I had a perspective about who the main characters should be as a way into the show. Everybody had different parts of the concept and we all just combined and worked hard together.

HENRY GILROY
(executive producer, screenwriter, *Star Wars: Rebels*)

The family component is what brought people back week to week, because you're watching this family go through this struggle, but you're also seeing them grow together. You're seeing the various personalities merge and the conflict that's there. That's something that everybody can relate to. *Clone Wars* was almost more esoteric, because you would spend four hours with these characters over here, then you would spend four hours with these clones over there; and then you'd spend four hours with the bad guys, like the Sith. It was awesome, because you're telling this epic expanding storyline. It basically gave you a taste that the galaxy really is at war, whereas *Rebels* really allows you to get into the interpersonal dynamics of the family structure, even though it's sort of a dysfunctional family. You're attracted to the characters and the show just because of that. All the space battles and lightsaber stuff kind of goes on top of it, and it's awesome, but underneath it all I get more worried if Kanan and Ezra are fighting.

SIMON KINBERG

There are missions and plots in every episode, and pretty intricate ones—especially for a half-hour show—but it is *so* focused on the characters. We talk in arcs of seasons about them. What their story is, what their emotional arc is. All of that is discussed preseason. The first season for us was very much a family coming together and starting to fuse that family. In the second season, it was very much about the family getting challenged, fractured, and having to expand and create upon itself with new members.

HENRY GILROY

In the beginning, the characters were a small group performing hit-and-run tactics, but by the end, they were basically challenging the Empire. When you blow up Grand Moff Tarkin's Star Destroyer, you're in trouble. [laughs] And once you get the attention of the Empire, you're going to have to deal with the consequences of that.

A guest star on the show was Ahsoka Tano, Anakin's former apprentice from The Clone Wars, *an addition that helped further deepen the existing characters and relationships on the show and was welcomed by fans.*

DAVE FILONI

Bringing Ahsoka in was always the plan. I didn't want to be selfish, but I really like that character. I did feel she could have a role to play, but none of us were prepared for the reaction. The fans have been very vocal about their excitement and that was surprising. *Star Wars* is changing a bit. Where it's always been about the original trilogy fans—they've been the ones that have ruled and run things from the beginning—I've found that over the last several years the prequel generation has become very vocal as they've grown up. Now the—you can almost call it—animated generation of *Clone Wars* is vocal in their own right. I imagine in the future the *Force Awakens* generation is going to say, "*Ours* is the best."

But perhaps the most satisfying reprise of all in Rebels *was the unexpected return of James Earl Jones as Darth Vader in a recurring role on the series.*

DAVE FILONI

We never wanted fans to think *Rebels* was going to change into some kind of Vader show. I've just always felt that our characters, in the great scheme of things, are small potatoes for Darth Vader. If Vader is going to come in, he's going to deal with things and deal with them simply. A bit of a game-changer for Vader was his realization that Ahsoka is still alive, and not only is she still alive, but early on he thinks he knows where she might be and she might be able to lead him to other surviving Jedi. And like any really smart villain, Vader will withdraw from the story and send out his attack dogs, which are the Inquisitors. They're the ones that really sniff things out and figure out what's going on. To say the Emperor is a genius is an understatement.

HENRY GILROY

Vader as a regular character wouldn't happen, because it would be a situation of diminishing returns for the character. One of the things that George Lucas asked Dave, when he was basically passing on the baton to him to continue on making *Star Wars,* was not to diminish Vader. To not ever make him lighter.

That whenever we are going to have James Earl Jones doing the voice of Vader, he will always be a formidable character.

DAVE FILONI

What's great about Vader and the Emperor is that they're willing to play a very long game for victory. Vader appeared a few times in season two, but Ahsoka actually had a larger role than he did. It's more interesting to see this all from her side, a lot of that having to do with maintaining the mystery of Darth Vader. We know so much about Anakin, but as Vader, his story is really about him and his son, Luke Skywalker. That's the story that George chose to tell, because it's so important.

SIMON KINBERG

The thing that drove everyone working on the show is that we all love and take *Star Wars* so seriously. We didn't want to do a show that was a mission of the week. It was so important to us for the characters to live and breathe as much as the characters in the movies do. The approach for everyone is not that it's a cartoon, or it's an animated show. It's an adventure show about these characters that are going to live alongside the greatest characters of all time. They occupy the same universe as Luke, Leia, Han, and Darth Vader. We need characters that you could put in a scene with Darth Vader and not get eaten alive.

The next animated series, and least popular of the animated Star Wars *series, was* Star Wars: Resistance, *set before and during the events of the sequel trilogy and focusing on New Republic pilot Kazuda Xiono, recruited by the Resistance to spy on the growing First Order. That show ran for just two seasons and forty episodes from 2018 to 2020.*

JUSTIN RIDGE
(co-executive producer, *Star Wars: Resistance*)

This was actually an idea that Dave Filoni had awhile back. He had this idea percolating about what was happening before the events of *The Force Awakens*. One day in his office, he called me in. He's like, "Padawan, come over here." He's called me *Padawan* awhile. So I go into his office and he shows me this early concept art for *Resistance* and I leave. Later on, he calls me in and he's like, "How would you like to show-run this show?" I was beyond honored that he was trusting me basically with the keys to this new car. "Okay, here you go. Crash it. Have fun." I was just beyond honored.

BRANDON AUMAN

(head writer, *Star Wars: Resistance*)

It was very intimidating. We broke the first set of stories at Skywalker Ranch, we got together with a bunch of writers. We just started talking about what would it be like six months to a year before *The Force Awakens*? What would happen? What is the state of the galaxy? What's going on? It's kind of a time of peace but it's also—there's some things boiling under the surface. The First Order is starting to rise, so we talked about Poe and the different characters that we want to bring in. Leia, obviously. We really just kind of spun it from there.

Although Resistance, *which featured voice cameos from Oscar Isaac as Poe and Gwendoline Christie as Captain Phasma, helped tie the series into the sequels and improved substantially in its second year, it didn't receive a third season with the studio migrating its* Star Wars *properties to its new streaming platform, Disney+.*

Launching in 2021 was The Bad Batch, *told from the point of view of the title characters, a group of Dirty Dozen–like mercenaries having adventures in the early days of the Empire. The concept of* The Bad Batch *was introduced on* Star Wars: The Clone Wars *and revisited in a beloved arc of the final season.*

DAVE FILONI

(executive producer, *The Bad Batch*)

George wanted to explore the idea that there were clones that had, at birth, had specialized traits—and after the Clone 99 incident at the beginning of [*The Clone Wars*], the Kaminoans and the Republic have decided not to dispose of them, but to actually impose further mutation on them to create genetic supersoldiers. So the Bad Batch were the expression of this elite squad of supersoldiers. The writer, Matt Michnovetz, got really into *The Bad Batch*, which was very gratifying. Though I keep forgetting, he didn't write the first arc, that was Brent Friedman. Matt talks about *Bad Batch* all the time—we were in *Rebels* and he'd be talking about the Bad Batch. It's very different to have clones that aren't quite clones. It works more in the original super-commando idea that you see Boba Fett being thought of in *Empire*, or along those lines.

So, this was a funny joke, because I realized at one point that none of the clones outside of maybe Rex knew that Anakin was seeing Padmé, let alone married to her. So when you see the Bad Batch's gunship on *The Clone Wars*, they actually have a [Padmé pinup design] on the nose. Anakin sees this and looks at Rex and is like, "What is *that*?" And the Bad Batch is like, "Oh yeah, that's that senator from Naboo. She can negotiate with me any day." They get on the shuttle and Anakin looks at Rex and is like, "That is *not* staying there." I thought it was a funny look at the world. A bit of a World War II nod.

But Star Wars *hasn't always been so lucky on the small screen. Two highly anticipated projects George Lucas had personally shepherded before selling his studio to Disney both failed to materialize despite seemingly having vast potential. In the years prior to the Disney acquisition of Lucasfilm, the animation arm was working on several projects that Disney, after the acquisition, decided not to go forward with. The most infamous of these was the ill-fated* Star Wars: Detours, *a half-hour animated comedy series headed up by* Robot Chicken *cocreators Seth Green and Matthew Senreich. In the classic Lucasfilm tradition, nearly forty episodes of the show were completed before Disney made the decision not to air it. Rumors abound that it may still stream on Disney+ eventually.*

BRENDAN HAY
(head writer, *Star Wars: Detours*)

It was a totally unique process. George really had the vision. He figured everybody else had gotten to do *Star Wars* comedy except him, so, why not him, too? So he reached out to Matt and Seth and became friends with them, and liked their *Robot Chicken* stuff. The goal going in was, the point of view of the *Robot Chicken Star Wars*, but for all ages. So that was one of the guidelines for the show—to make it all ages.

George had a very specific format, that, in 2010, seemed a little restrictive—but man, as always, he could see where things were headed. He wanted it to be a show that could be broken down into small sections, so it could be streamed and basically watched anywhere. So it was three six- to six-and-a-half-minute segments, and then two one-minute segments. That was the structure of the show. He had a lot of ideas about design, but otherwise it was just sort of, "Have fun. Set it in between the prequel trilogy and the original trilogy and do what you want. Pull the parts you want. Tell the stories you want." He said early on, "Maybe it's like, you do one thing on the Death Star, one thing on Tatooine, and one thing in Dex's Diner. So you're always varying up the worlds." But other than that, we were given really free rein. We created some original characters—like specific stormtroopers or specific characters who worked in Jabba's palace. But also giving more to characters like Dexter Jettster, who only had like one scene [in *Attack of the Clones*], and going, "Oh, is he the Sam Malone of Coruscant?" And our biggest fun was going with characters like Admiral Ackbar and the bounty hunters—who are iconic enough that everybody knows, but still have some real freedom to explore what the rest of their lives are like. Tarkin was another big one like that.

GEORGE LUCAS
(executive producer, *Star Wars: Detours*)

This one is definitely off the charts, it's purely to have fun. We've always been working outside the box, but this is so far outside the box it's . . . a space shopping mall.

SETH GREEN
(cocreator, *Star Wars: Detours*)

That's been the mandate at every turn, is make it more fun, make it more silly. Never in a way that's disrespectful to the lore, but always in a way that gets you into the stuff that you know. But I think it's accessible to people who have never seen it, too.

Another series that never came to fruition was the Lucas-created Star Wars: Underworld, *announced at the same time as* The Clone Wars. *Art and concept designs were created and Ronald D. Moore, Chris Chibnall, Fiona Seres, Stephen Scaia, and many other top sci-fi writers from around the world were brought on to write the first fifty scripts for the series. While that was being done, Lucas attempted to develop the technology to produce a high-end series at television budgets. After exploring production of the show with several networks, including Syfy, no one in the prestreaming era was willing to foot the bill for the series, feeling* Star Wars *was a property on the wane. Expectations that the show would commence continued, though, until the Disney acquisition put the final nail in the coffin.*

Star Trek: The Next Generation *and* Battlestar Galactica *writer Ronald D. Moore told* Collider *of the project, "I was one of several writers they assembled . . . We would gather up at Skywalker Ranch once every six to eight weeks and we would break stories together, and right after we'd go off and write some drafts and bring 'em back, and George and we would sit down and critique them, and then do another draft and break more stories. It was great! We wrote somewhere in the forty-something, forty-eight scripts, something like that . . . The theory was George wanted to write all the scripts and get 'em all done and then he was gonna go off and figure out how to produce them, because he wanted to do a lot of cutting-edge technological stuff with CG and virtual sets and so on. And what happened was we wrote the scripts and then George said, 'Okay, this is enough for now, and then I'll get back to you.' And then like a year or something after that is when he sold Lucasfilm to Disney."*

PETER HOLMSTROM
(co-host, *The Rebel & the Rogue* podcast)

Underworld was meant to be George's final "Fuck you, Hollywood" statement. He had bought land with the plans to build a large live-action studio and soundstages there—he was going to build his own Pinewood—so he'd never have to negotiate with corporations again. The plan was to film *Underworld* and the *Star Wars* sequels there, but those plans fell through.

Despite the setbacks, Star Wars *would still have a bright future on television. Representing what would be the next quantum evolution in the* Star Wars *franchise was the arrival on Disney+ of the* Mandalorian *TV series, which helped launch the new streaming platform. That show, an immediate hit among the critics and the fans, will eventually be joined by* Andor, *focusing on* Rogue One's *Cassian Andor, a third that will see Ewan McGregor reprising his role of Obi-Wan Kenobi, and a litany of additional series including shows devoted to Ahsoka Tano, Boba Fett, and the rangers of the New Republic.*

The Mandalorian, *a space Western series in the tradition of* Lone Wolf and Cub, *was created by Jon Favreau and set five years following the events of* Return of the Jedi. *The title character is bounty hunter Din Djarin (Pedro Pascal), who has acquired the nickname "Mando" through his various successful missions in the outer rim. Often focused on the seedier underpinnings of the* Star Wars *universe,* The Mandalorian *is noted for its strong writing, lavish visuals, and arguably the cutest addition to the* Star Wars *canon since the Ewoks, in the form of "The Child" (aka Grogu), dubbed by pop culture as "Baby Yoda."*

DAVE FILONI
(executive producer, screenwriter/director, *The Mandalorian*)

The important thing about the Mandalorians is to realize that they are a culture, and like any culture in our world, they change and evolve. They have highs and lows. They adapt. If you're a warrior race for thousands of years, at some point you probably almost got yourself destroyed or destroyed yourselves, which would have a pretty devastating effect on your people. But the big question is, if that is truly who you are in your soul and in your heart, how long and how successfully can you deny that? I think that makes it a lot more interesting to them as a civilization. We really knew from the get-go that we wanted the Mandalorians to be a very high-tech, sophisticated military society. They can resort to barbarism when they're on the run and when they're weak and they don't have a lot of resources—but like any military, they need resources, they need backup, they need fuel. So many tank battles simply die out because they ran out of fuel—as you discover if you study military history.

The *Mandalorian* series idea really starts with Jon Favreau coming forward saying he'd like to develop a concept and talking with Kathleen Kennedy about it. She knew I had done a lot with Mandalorian people and culture on *Clone Wars* with George Lucas over the years. She also knew that I knew Jon Favreau. She called me in when Jon pitched this idea, and he really loved the imagery of a lone gunman and Western. When we were kids, Boba Fett was a "Man with No Name." Even his publicity stills were evocative of the Sergio Leone *Dollar* trilogy. Jon's idea was to reimagine that character as a straight-on bounty hunter and take that imagery of the lone gunfighter. The revelation was this idea of this child in a *Lone Wolf and Cub* sensibility.

JON FAVREAU
(creator, screenwriter, *The Mandalorian*)

A Mandalorian is alluded to in the original films that I grew up with. Boba Fett was a bounty hunter and he wore Mandalorian armor. There was such a fascination with that character even though he didn't do much in the films. And I like the image of the Mandalorian, because it really does hearken back to the Westerns and samurai films that had originally influenced Lucas. That's a great, mysterious, fun character to see the world through.

As somebody who grew up with *Star Wars,* and really having been formed around what I experienced when I was little with the first film, there was some aesthetic to it that I think that I really loved, that I really gravitated to, and my whole taste in movies was probably formed in a big way from seeing George Lucas's original film. I learned about cinema through the lens of that film, because my father would explain to me, "This is a lot like a samurai movie, this is a lot like Westerns, or World War II films." So that became my inroad. Then there was the whole *Power of Myth* with Joseph Campbell and the special that was filmed up at the ranch and that opened me up to the mythic structure and the mono-myth and my understanding of mythology and storytelling. So to return to this with the freedom that this new platform affords, because there's nothing to compare it to. Nothing has been on TV other than the *Holiday Special* and the idea of telling us the story in just a few hours over several years opens us up to this novelization of story and a return back to the roots in many ways of the Saturday afternoon serial films. My parents' generation grew up with cliffhanger adventures, and drawing from that type of stylish storytelling lends itself really well to what we're tackling here.

It's fun not to have a preciousness to the way we're telling stories, because we're coming back to you next week with another one. To engage the audience in the way that I enjoy being engaged with, with the shows, specifically what the BBC has done with the streaming services, where it's bigger-budget and has the qualities of a film, but with serialized storytelling. To me, that's where it really opened up a lot of freedom and opportunity, where we don't feel that we're repeating or copying anything else that people have experienced from *Star Wars*.

DAVE FILONI

I think as a kid growing up, you watch *Star Wars* and you think, "I would watch this every week." I remember when *Star Trek: The Next Generation* came out with the promise of better visual effects on television and it took big leaps. As somebody that's always been into fantasy science fiction, you were always waiting for a moment where you thought the images on television were as good as what we were seeing in the theater. But there was a *big* separation when I was a kid. Now I think it's gotten so close and one of the thrilling things is we can make something like *Star Wars*. Technology has advanced to the point where we can do this and that's one of the dreams George had. When I worked with him on *Clone Wars*, he would talk about the future being streaming episodic serialized *Star Wars*. It's cool to get to help make it happen.

To make that work, The Mandalorian *has also been a pioneer in visual effects, not unlike the* Star Wars *films that preceded it. In this case, it has been the use of state-of-the-art visual effects in which the episodes are largely shot in a studio in front of a series of large LED screens and the backgrounds are programmed using an Unreal game engine, allowing the images to move with the camera and rendering the need for a green screen on these shots obsolete. It is one of the most significant advances in visual effects since the groundbreaking work of Lucas in digital effects on the prequel trilogy in the early 1990s. The series' special effects supervisor, Richard Bluff; the chief technology officer of Epic Games, Kim Lebreri; and showrunner Jon Favreau did four months of R&D with production beginning in October 2018.*

PHIL GALLER
(co-CEO, Lux Machina)

I was involved very early on, because we had been doing *Solo* and *Rogue One*, and all these things are really leading up to this moment. At Lux we had actually deployed a real time system of camera tracking in February of 2018 and I don't think anyone except maybe David Morin, the head of the Epic Games Los Angeles Lab, had put the pieces together yet. David saw me do a presentation in March about the technology and the workflow using camera tracking in a game engine and it was about March or April when Lucasfilm reached back out and asked if we would be willing to come back onboard and help with this from the point of view of display and engineering and camera sync. And at that point, I think that everyone realized that we all had been independently working on something and it had all come to a head. Lucasfilm and Jon and Epic had some really awesome stuff. The stuff they did looked amazing, so it was an opportunity to go into this new world. The technology matured very quickly and we all got to the same spot. I think it was something we had all been chasing for a decade.

This isn't just about let's put some content on an LED wall. It's about making sure that the content on the LED wall blends and bleeds into the physical and vice versa. That's the biggest challenge for anyone doing this. I could put anyone in front of our projection screens, shoot them from the waist up, and make them look like they are in an environment. That's easy. We've been doing that for a decade. That's not a problem. It's this concept of, I am going to see someone walking down a street and I want to really believe that they are walking down a street and that they can walk into this expansive, immersive environment that actually isn't there. *That* is the thing that is so challenging and that is the challenge that everyone will have with this. The reality is that when you are building out a set that is fifty feet wide and you need to have a battle scene in there, it's a far more complex problem than just trying to deploy a small studio or shooting from the waist up.

In addition to the top-tier talent behind-the-camera, there is a first-rate cast in front of it as well, including Game of Thrones' *Pedro Pascal and ultimate fighter turned actress Gina Carano.*

PEDRO PASCAL
(actor, "Din Djarin," *The Mandalorian*)

Putting the helmet on—they had handed it to me in our first meeting to see if it would fit perfectly. Putting the costume on for the first time, and looking in the mirror . . . you can't see very well through the helmet, but I got a pretty clear impression. If you grow up playing with *Star Wars* toys, and obviously seeing the movies, and then you're staring at yourself and you are the image of that kind of childhood imagination, it's a super pinch-worthy moment.

JON FAVREAU

We roped Carl [Weathers] for more than he signed up for. It started off as, "Hey, maybe you'll do one or two . . ." and then it turned into, "Well, now we really like your character . . ." We worked him in a lot. More than he agreed to. And with season two, he was part of our directors' brigade. I know him through the Directors Guild. We met and I was a fan of his acting, but he's been directing more lately. So, this whole high-tech, innovative set that we've developed for these specific stories, by Carl being there and being a part of it, and seeing how we were putting this together and experimenting with it, and seeing it all come together, he was perfectly qualified. He understood the story, the characters, the cast, and the technology, so it's really fun to be working with Carl now.

CARL WEATHERS
(actor, "Greef Karga")

Jon knew that I want to direct more and more. He promised, when I agreed to do this, that if it got a second season, he'd give me a shot. And I've got to tell you, I've been around enough to know that people don't always keep their word. Being a part of this is one of the greatest things that's happened in all of the years that I've been in entertainment.

PEDRO PASCAL

I was a little more generous. Stunt doubles are essential to every large production, just so you know, even for the strongest and most agile people. None of it can get down without the incredible stunt work. You have no idea, the amount of star power, from every department that goes into making something like this. There's a person working on the shine of my shoulder, and a person who built the entire ship that we're shooting on, or the whole set. I've seen some pretty big shit, and I haven't seen anything like this.

JON FAVREAU

You're gonna see a lot of people that are working in this incubator of story and technology come together because they love *Star Wars* with an enthusiasm that seems to be very contagious. There's a real enthusiasm that's very organic, as we're telling the stories. It's a very collaborative environment. We talk a lot about story, and I write most of it, but that's just the jumping-off point for the directors to be very involved and very collaborative.

When you bring in a director like Taika Waititi, he's clearly doing it because he wants to. The guy is just such a powerhouse right now, creatively. Everybody's really discovering what a talent he is. People who follow comedy or independent film knew about him long ago, and now, he's really enjoying a wonderful run. So, when he shows up, it gets everybody excited, because it's a fresh energy on the set. He finds opportunities for humor. He brings his style of humor to it, but he's also a fan. To me, that was the bottom line and the prerequisite. You didn't have to be the most experienced. You didn't have to have worked on *Star Wars* before. You didn't even have to have ever directed live-action before. We had a few people that hadn't done that. The thing was that you had to be willing to collaborate, you had to love *Star Wars*, and you had to want to do something great and help invent this new thing.

DAVE FILONI

The Mandalorian has become a really special thing for me. I became interested in doing live-action from working with George, and the way he talked about how we should shoot *The Clone Wars*. He always spoke in live-action terms. George was so steeped in technology and pushing technology forward, with pre-viz and stuff like that, on *Clone Wars*, that it just became the language of filmmaking for me as well. Working with Jon is really natural, because he's really forward-thinking with technology as well, and using technology to enable greater storytelling. So for me, it was a great opportunity to work with someone who works in a similar vein [to George], but I could be challenged. And Jon has challenged me—I will say that—creatively and storytelling-wise. And you need that; you need that sharpening to improve and continue. It's very *Star Wars*. I've had a couple of mentors now, and I'm very privileged to have the ones that I've had. I'm definitely the better for Jon taking me in and showing me the ropes of live-action. It's improved my writing. I learned a tremendous amount every day. I was on set every day the whole season, so I learned from all our directors, all of the cast, and everyone behind the scenes. I treated it as boot camp for me to learn this type of filmmaking. But I also tried to offer the knowledge passed on to me by George about *Star Wars* and the way he liked to shoot things. But it definitely has affected the way I look at a day—what can I accomplish in a day?— that's a big difference for me filmmaking-wise. We arrived on the backlot and the [director of photography] is like, "Well, the sun's up. We got to get going." And I'm like, "Oh right, because it's going to go down." In animation, we don't really have that problem. So, you know, you're getting on six o'clock, and everyone's getting squirrely, like "The sun's going down; the sun's going down!" And I'm like, "Right. Then we're screwed, because the whole set is going down."

There are advantages and disadvantages to both live-action and animation. At this point, I don't prefer one or the other. I like both experiences, and they're both unique. There's something about the concrete nature of live-action. It's incredibly spontaneous. It's gonna happen right there, in the moment, and then, that's it. Whereas in animation, I can tweak a tiny eyebrow or a tiny smirk, or give a little bit of a push in a direction that will dramatically change the character. You have to get all of these variables to come together and be aware of it. It's not like you're controlling any of it, as much as you're guiding it. You're looking at everything, all at once. Whereas, in animation, it's like a recipe that I can keep adding ingredients to. You have a lot of flexibility in digital, thank God, and in post, you can do a lot. But capturing that moment, right in front of you, is the real magic of it all, and is something that I'd been craving to try. Luckily, we have an incredible crew and cast that can capture those moments.

JON FAVREAU

I met Dave because I was up at the ranch mixing *Iron Man,* and he was secretly working with George on *Clone Wars* before anyone had ever heard of it. I showed him *Iron Man,* he showed me *Clone Wars,* and I was like, "If you ever need a voice on this, I'd love to do it." And sure enough, I played a Mandalorian, named Pre Vizsla, on his show. But what's so nice is, George had worked with him for ten years on his show, and so they had worked together. So a lot of what's wonderful about working with Dave is the continuity of vision. I know George came with Kathy [Kennedy], because they have a long-standing relationship, but the thing that really stood out was, you could tell he was very proud that Dave was taking this next step. When George discovered Dave, he was just an animator he brought in. I'm sure you've heard the story, Dave thought it was a joke—that someone was playing a prank on him. But after meeting with George, he asked Dave, "Do you want to run this show?" It's been a long relationship, understanding filmmaking, understanding *Star Wars*—and now, as we get into live-action, to take the next step. So a big reason that he was there was because he wanted to make sure that I was continuing Dave's journey with him. I thought it felt very special. It was a very special day.

EMILY SWALLOW
(actress, "The Armorer," *The Mandalorian*)

The original trilogy has always been the favorite, so he [Favreau] was smart to replicate the feel of those worlds. That immediately appeals to fans of those movies, and there are lots of nods to things we've already seen in those films. But the show is also incredibly appealing to folks who know nothing about *Star Wars,* because it has the feel of a Western and has, at its core, a hero on his formative journey. I also attribute the success to the caliber and styles of the different directors, and the way Jon encouraged them to work together to create a cohesive story arc *and* pushed them to draw from their unique styles of storytelling.

DALE POLLOCK
(author, *Skywalking: The Life and Films of George Lucas*)

The Mandalorian clearly shows that there's a whole generation of creative people who were raised on these films, and they're now going to represent the new wave of *Star Wars*. And I don't think in ways that Lucas and Kathy Kennedy and other people who've been with the series since the beginning could have anticipated. I mean, Baby Yoda? Who would have thought of Baby Yoda? It just shows you the unanticipated ways all of this could go on forever.

KYLE NEWMAN
(director, *Fanboys*)

You know what got me so excited this morning? I woke up and the first email I saw was from a longtime friend back in New York who's now living in Singapore. They sent me a picture of their daughter all excited, dressed like Princess Leia. She hasn't even seen the movies, and now they're throwing her a *Star Wars* birthday party . . . in Singapore. She doesn't even know the movies, but something about the character pulled her in. She was hooked before she'd even seen the movies. It was just like, "There's the next generation already."

ACKNOWLEDGMENTS

The authors would like to profusely thank the following people for their help in making this book possible. First and foremost, the authors owe a tremendous debt of gratitude to Steven A. Simak for his extensive contributions to this volume. Steven, whose immense knowledge of visual effects along with the numerous interviews he conducted, proved invaluable. Also a very special thanks to our superb research consultant, Peter Holmstrom, who also provided incalculable help in scheduling interviews, contributing, transcribing, advising, and conducting research for this project, and whose love for the material is boundless. He is one with the Force and the Force is with him.

We are also deeply grateful to our partners at the Electric Surge Network, including Dean Devlin, who allowed us to excerpt interviews and material from their popular podcasts *Inglorious Treksperts, Best Movies Never Made,* and *The Rebel & the Rogue,* including their respective hosts Daren Dochterman, Stephen Scarlata, Josh Miller, Jason Tobias, and Victoria Cheri. You can enjoy these podcasts on the Electric Now video streaming app, available free on your favorite app store.

In addition, we once again would like to share our deep appreciation to Dan Madsen, founder of the Official Lucasfilm Fan Club; Stephen Pizzello and David E. Williams of *American Cinematographer* for their support, research materials, and interview excerpts; as well as current *Cinefantastique* publisher and owner Steve Harris for allowing us to dip into their archives for material to supplement this volume in order to assure a complete and accurate overview of this dense subject matter. Also, our gratitude to Ian Spelling, Randy Lofficier, Lee Goldberg, Jonathan Wilkins, Nick Jamilla, Corey Van Dyke, and Dennis Pellegrom (author of the multivolume Star Wars Interviews books, available from Amazon, among others) for sharing additional interview material with us; and Eric Townsend of the Making of Star Wars Timeline.

Genuine thanks are also offered to Ray Morton, Glen Oliver, and Ric Meyers for going above and beyond in offering up their views of the entire franchise.

In addition to the majority of interviews that were conducted by the authors, some additional quotes come from press conferences, promotional appearances, as well as film festival tributes and conventions. As George Lucas did not make himself available to the authors for this volume, all quotes from him are taken from public and promotional appearances by the filmmaker.

Finally, a very special thanks to our previous editor Stephen Power for proposing this book to us in the first place, as well as our terrific, diligent and enthusiastic new editor, Michael Homler, as well as our original, wildly supportive editor at St. Martin's, who got the boulder rolling (oops, wrong Lucasfilm franchise) in the first place, Brendan Deneen; and our erstwhile agent Laurie Fox at the Linda Chester Agency for making it all possible.

ABOUT THE AUTHORS

EDWARD GROSS is a veteran entertainment journalist who has built his career serving on the staff of a variety of publications, most notably *Cinescape, Starlog, New York Nightlife, Cinefantastique, Fangoria, Femme Fatales, SFX, Sci-Fi Now, Life Story,* and *Movie Magic.* Online he has served as executive editor, U.S., for Empireonline, film/TV editor at CloserWeekly.com, and nostalgia editor at DoYouRemember.com. He is currently senior editor of *Geek* magazine.

Additionally, he has authored or coauthored numerous nonfiction books, among them the two-volume *The Fifty-Year Mission,* which covers the history of the *Star Trek* franchise; *Rocky: The Ultimate Guide;* the *Buffy the Vampire Slayer* and *Angel* oral history, *Slayers & Vampires; Planet of the Apes Revisited; So Say We All,* the oral history going behind the scenes of *Battlestar Galactica; Spider-Man: Confidential;* and *Nobody Does It Better,* an oral history celebrating all things James Bond.

MARK A. ALTMAN is a television and motion picture writer/producer who is the showrunner, creator, and executive producer of *Pandora,* the hit sci-fi action-adventure series for Sony Pictures Television that *Programming Insider* lauded as "*Stranger Things* meets *Riverdale.*" He most recently served as co-executive producer of TNT's hit series *The Librarians,* as well as such shows as *Agent X* (TNT), *Castle* (ABC), *Necessary Roughness* (USA), and numerous television pilots.

In addition to directing the comedy special *Aries Spears: Comedy Blueprint* for NBC/Universal, Altman produced the $30 million film adaptation of the bestselling video game *DOA: Dead or Alive,* which was released by Dimension Films. His first film was the award-winning *Free Enterprise,* starring William Shatner and Eric McCormack, which he wrote and produced and for which he won the Writers Guild of America Award for Best New Writer at the AFI Los Angeles Film Festival prior to its theatrical release. He was also a producer of the *House of the Dead* series, based on the video game from Sega, released by Lionsgate. In addition, he produced the Craig Mazin (*Chernobyl*) and James Gunn (*Guardians of the Galaxy*) superhero satire *The Specials*.

His bestselling two-volume book written with Edward Gross, *The Fifty-Year Mission: The Complete, Uncensored, Unauthorized Oral History of* Star Trek, was released by St. Martin's Press in 2016 in hardcover to unanimous critical acclaim, including raves in *The Wall Street Journal, Booklist,* and *Publishers Weekly*. His follow-up with Edward Gross on *Battlestar Galactica, So Say We All,* was released in August 2018, and his latest oral history, *Nobody Does It Better,* chronicling the history of the James Bond franchise, was released in hardcover in February 2020.

Altman is a former journalist and has contributed to such newspapers and magazines as *The Boston Globe, Written By, L'Cinefage, Geek, The Guardian,* and many others, including *Cinefantastique,* for which he launched their independent film division, CFQ Films. He has also written numerous comic books for DC and Malibu Comics.

In 2018, Altman launched the Electric Surge Video Podcast Network with producer Dean Devlin (*Independence Day, Stargate*), and in addition to producing numerous weekly podcasts for the network, they recently debuted video versions of their popular series on the Electric Now streaming channel. In addition to producing, Altman also cohosts *The 4:30 Movie,* in which a band of experts curate dream movie theme weeks, as well as the immensely popular *Inglorious Treksperts,* the only podcast for *Star Trek* fans with a life, featuring high-profile guests from across the *Star Trek* universe.

Altman has spoken at numerous industry events and conventions, including ShowBiz Expo as well as the Variety/Final Draft Screenwriters Panel at the Cannes Film Festival. He was a juror at the prestigious Sitges Film Festival in Barcelona, Spain. He has been a frequent guest and panelist at Comic-Con held annually in San Diego, California, and a two-time juror for the Comic-Con Film Festival. He is also a graduate of the Writers Guild of America Showrunners Training Program and a member of the Television Academy.